# The Girl from Borgo

## a memoir

## Sybil Fix

Print ISBN: 978-1-54393-226-3
eBook ISBN: 978-1-54393-227-0

BookBaby
Pennsauken, NJ, USA

*For my parents*

*For Sabrina and all others in the book*
*who left us during its writing*

*And finally, for all those who have suffered the loss of home*
*May we find peace, someday, somewhere, somehow*

# The Girl from Borgo

**A**ndrea looks at me and smiles. I see reverie in his dark eyes, and tenderness, too, like he's traveling back to a memory held dear.

Yet, there is a place, recessed and obscure, that stows the soft scarred shadow of an old grief. I still recognize it, under the layers of more recent losses and disappointments, after all these years.

What happened then, I ask.

— *E poi?*

We are standing in the Bar Sport, our old bar, next to the big windows looking out onto Cetona's piazza, and the fountain, trickling on as always. Andrea's hair is graying and he has put on a slight belly. He just quit work for the day, a successful woodworking business, and he's dusty. His hands rest in the pockets of his gray cargo work pants and he stands the way I have always known him to stand, feet wide apart like he is bracing for a soccer ball coming at him fast. It's the goalie in him, the goalie he was.

Through his pants I make out the muscles of his thighs, still lean and strong. In my memory I retrace his angular jaw line, his playful smile, and the taut stomach. I see a tangle of gold chains just below his collar bone and I imagine a blue T-shirt like an August sky above our mountain. Three buttons away from bliss.

The way we were.

He looks off somewhere in the piazza, in the stillness, then returns to me and focuses.

— *Mi ricordo tutto, fino all'ultimo dettaglio.* I remember everything, to the last detail.

That late August at dawn, Andrea and our friend Tullia came to pick me up. The sky was turning a tender pale blue and the slightest of pinks streaked from the east like threads of cotton candy pulled by the fingers of a child, fuzzy and warm.

Across the way, in Città della Pieve, the sun crested barely above the cobblestone streets, but the air was motionless, suspended as if the day were holding its breath for me to walk out.

Standing outside my house we whispered, I remember. It was like we didn't want to wake the neighbors, but, really, we didn't want to wake ourselves either, to the morning and the shock, awaiting.

Andrea had on pilot's Ray-Bans and a lit cigarette in his hand. His thick black hair was slicked back, grazing his shoulders, and he was clean-shaven. The muscles of his back and shoulders stretched his blue cotton T-shirt opening at the collar. He looked neat and decent and heavyhearted.

Smiling slightly, my father shook Andrea's hand and quietly thanked him for driving me to the airport. Andrea nodded politely but with reserve—*di niente*, he said.

Dad had on that mask that grown men pull on when they are splintered by emotions but they just can't let them burst through: a mix of apprehension, love, and denial of it all.

And pride, too: I was off to college, in America, where he wanted me to go.

— Goodbye, Birdie, he said, hugging me.

My childhood nickname, Birdie—because I fluttered.

Andrea loaded my two suitcases and we got in his car, a white VW Golf whose soft rumble I could identify from miles away and that through my teenage ecstasy I tracked through the years with the tremulous heartbeat of a bird. The car whose sight in the piazza signaled the unmistakable presence of him. It was the keeper of our secrets, at night, in the countryside, with the crickets pulsing along with us.

We roll down the hill soundlessly under the rising sun, a loaded ball of tangerine in the hazy hot sky above Città della Pieve's sage-green hills, soft in the early morning light.

As the car descends Via Sobborgo, out of Cetona and onto the road of Il Piano, I turn to look at my house, up on the hill, the house where I grew up. In mere seconds the stone tower becomes vaguer and vaguer, and, with it, my bedroom window, smaller and smaller. I can no longer make out the green of the shutters, and then the house itself, and sadness brings a flood of tears to my eyes.

I wipe them away so I can see this place I am leaving and witness my own receding into space, but they flow too fast, and meanwhile we thread under the bridge of the *autostrada* and turn onto the road towards Ponticelli, moving farther away. Andrea shifts gears, third, fourth, fifth, and in the leaden silence he takes me away.

Then, in a flash of a turn Cetona itself disappears, and the Rocca, too, and the people I imagine waking up now to this pink day, Costanza to feed the pigs, and Unico to sell papers in the piazza. Monte Cetona is now the only thing left in my view, the big mountain I would like to pack in my bag and take with me.

Distance gobbles the details ferociously. I want to scream, please, wait, please stop. Stop everything. Maybe I can still see it, this mountain, this house, this place. Maybe I can grasp it and hold onto it, for one moment longer, this present that is slipping through my fingers and becoming past and future all in the same moment. I look back to search the landscape again, but everything has changed and it's all gone.

My hill, my house, my town. It is all gone.

You could stop it. You could ask Andrea to stop and turn back. Like a cartoon moving backwards, you could go back through the fields and up the hill and knock on the door and say, Dad, I don't want to go. I want to stay here, where I belong. I want to stay here in this place whose winds have forged me, whose smells have fed me.

But you don't, you don't. So much has already been done and you don't have the courage to take it back. To face the disappointment, and the immovable walls of the town.

Besides, you can't foresee how much is going to be lost, and how much it's going to hurt, and for how long. You don't understand how immutable this is going to be. You can't know how much life will throw onto your path to keep you away, and how, in the passage of it all, home will be lost, perhaps forever.

You are too young to know, and no one tells you. No one understands what it will be like for you.

And so you stick to it, and in a sudden slide of reality you are in a crowded airport, and then a plane, and, hours later, an unknown country a world away, so far away it might as well be on another planet.

Like a fancy red dress put in with a batch of bleach, your life is transformed. A path chosen, another shut.

That was thirty years ago—pages and pages of life ago.

And yet, the tremor of that August morning still churns my soul to the core.

Because since that day, my every day has been a goodbye renewed.

And since that day, every day I have dreamed of return.

# Fall

One spring night last year in my bed on Edgewater Park, a teardrop of land on the marshy shores of South Carolina, I dreamt of a beautiful festival taking place in the piazza.

Crowds of people strolled and talked, and stalls and flowers extended from edge to edge. Maybe it was market day on Saturdays as I remember it growing up. In the dream I was walking along with Maria, Ottavia, and Tullia, three of my four or five uninterrupted friendships in Cetona over forty-some years, and as we passed the street leading back toward Piazza Parè, right next to the church of San Michele, I saw a cluster of mesmerizing orange trees in full bloom.

— *Guarda l'aranceto, che bello!* I said pointing at the trees. Look at the orange trees, how beautiful!

Ottavia turned to me with a mocking tone.

— *Macché aranceto! Vedi che tra un po' non riconosci nemmeno più gli alberi qui!*

Those are not orange trees, she said using the word *macché*, which summarily captures disdain and dismissal. See, she said putting her hands together in prayer as she does with her long fingers, rolling her eyes, soon you won't even recognize the trees here anymore.

I awoke aware that my dream had voiced my own fears, a warning of sorts. Tears pooled in my eyes. I looked around at my room I so loved—my orange tabby, Joe, sprawled on my bed with his belly up in the air, and next to me my lover, Aram, dark-skinned, kind, and tender to me. My life of more than twenty years in Charleston. My paintings, my chickens roaming outside.

My life, here.

It is my half.

But the other half calls. For me, there has always been another half, and it has always called. It is constantly calling.

Like a bird drawn by memory of landscape or an animal by scent, I must go back. I must go now.

I laid back in my pillow and thought of the past thirty years. On a life-like reel I watched myself barter and bend, live and pretend and make do, determined to survive in a reality other than Cetona. Indeed, I made the best of wherever I have been. I have tried with all my might to overcome the heartbreak.

Yet, all these years I have dreamed of my little town on the hill catching the sun of the fields I have not seen in spring or fall for decades. I have cried at night, missing, always missing the fulcrum of my being—the countryside, my friends, the air, whatever summed up makes up that special thing that is home.

I laugh at myself pointing up at the sky like E.T., but it's been no laughing matter. My incompleteness has stilted my life, eaten at me, defined me, my heart always looking back or forward to the time past or the next time for an insufficient, miserly visit couched in a glorious return. It has undermined my commitments and stolen any promise of making promises.

Meanwhile, the years have gone by. I likely have fewer years ahead than I have behind; memory is fading, and people are changing and dying. We are dying.

After the dream woke me, I floated in my head the concept of returning to Cetona for a year. A *whole year.* I dared only think of a year; surely, I could not return, not to stay. Forever.

How, with this lover, and this cat? So much would be lost.

When I started thinking about it, it was almost like I was kidding myself. A year, I mused in my head, smiling. I tried to imagine what that might be like: Time enough to sit with my friends, to relearn their presence, and our code, perhaps. To take back into me the rhythms of the town.

A year to see the seasons unfurl, calmly, unrushed, all four of them, from the emerald green of winter to the golden hues of summer, and the lush purples and ripe reds in fall. A year to see the piazza in the rain and fog; to walk the streets when the humidity clings to the stone houses like a chilly cape. To hear and smell the silence of summer nights, punctuated by the rhythmic pulse of the crickets that stop only in alarm.

A year to see the children coming and going to school; to witness the burials and the wailing of the deaths and the births; to watch the piazza in the morning light. A year to relearn the impulses of the native plants, of the sweet broom and the tender violets.

A year to dance on the backdrop of the past as I am today and to see what it's like *now*. A year to understand the chasm I have felt since I left and to let it go.

I am not sure if letting go means staying there forever or accepting that it's no longer where I live. Or simply verifying that I will never be whole.

A year to just be there. I don't know what it will be or how it will be, but I need to know.

I need to know my truth.

I considered how to do this, to sell my belongings. Rugs, pictures, furniture, clothes, trinkets, everything. The idea seemed drastic, and even as I think of it, it makes me want to cry. What if I go home to Cetona and there is nothing left there for me anymore?

— *Impossibile,* says Maria, after listening intently on the phone. Impossible! Of course, you can come back! We will always be us. *Noi.*

— *Sono contenta se vieni,* she says. I am happy if you come. You will figure something out. You can make it work.

My lifelong friend Fabrizio, on the other hand, says ... *No*. That Italian smoke-filled *No* that I know so well.

— *Guarda, Sibilla, c'è la crisi,* he says calling me, as everyone does there, by my Italian name, and mentioning the recession that continues to strangle Italy.

He sounds genuinely concerned. People are selling their homes, moving into the streets, he says. There are immigrants everywhere and no jobs. *La crisi. La crisi.*

I shrug it off. I have been hearing about the recession in Italy for ten years. The polar cap is going to melt before the Italians figure how to restore their economy, and I cannot wait for that kind of change.

Life is finite, I tell him.

Fabrizio starts laughing and adds another note of caution— against going to Cetona in winter.

— *Ti sarai dimenticata, ma a Cetona d'inverno* ... he starts, and I know from his voice that he will deliver something funny that only a Cetonese can.

— ... *A Cetona d'inverno ti devi da' le martellate nell'ugni per sape' se se' viva.* You might have forgotten, but in Cetona in winter you have to hit yourself on your fingernails with a hammer to check if you're alive.

Born and bred in Cetona, Fabrizio articulates its vernacular better than almost anyone I know, both in tone and words, with the added distinction of having escaped Cetona—he splits his life between Provence and Florence with his American wife—and being able to observe the town with a bit of mockery, or self-mockery, enlightened yet affectionate.

— *Ma davvero, Sibilla, ma che fai lì d'inverno? Ma perché n'aspetti l'estate?* he asks, wanting to protect me. Really, what are you going to do there? Why don't you wait for summer?

I know. Winter in Cetona can be dismal. I lived there many winters. But I am going there with a task of discovery. Plus, however you look at it, if I can do a full year it will encompass a winter, regardless, and I can't avoid it. I might love it!

I dismiss it all and write a letter to Peter Matthiessen, the distinguished writer, my former professor and mentor, and my admired naturalist and bird watcher. At Yale he edited my first confused short stories about Cetona and my sense of loss, and he did so with a kindness and a humility that I still hold as the golden standards for those particularly beautiful human traits. I still have those edited pages and have held them in my hands many times wondering when I am going to resume that thread.

I have wanted to write about Cetona and my love story ever since.

Would my return home make a good story? Of course it could make a good story, he wrote back, but you need to give it everything you have. You should go.

I meet with Charleston writer Josephine Humphreys to ask for her advice. She is a good storyteller; we have known each other through the years through various channels, including my journalism in Charleston for ten years. I tell her of my idea, and we talk about the concepts of home and return.

— You are lucky, she says. Most people don't even have a *there* to return to. Who would want to go back to Ohio and write about it? There is no *there* there.

A few days later I have lunch with my mentor and friend Andy Anderson. He was the publisher of the *Post and Courier* when I began as a reporter in Charleston twenty or some years ago, and he was my boss for ten years. I like to get his advice every now and then, and I want to ask him for work suggestions. I am nearly destitute and I need work. I am painting a lot, and, since I began freelancing I continue to find small writing jobs to pay the bills, but I am biding time. I feel under-utilized and I lack purpose and inspiration.

Andy, a conservative man, a banker in spirit and trade, is not known for being empathetic or intimate, or even personable for that matter, though my experience of him is that he is all of that in his own way and I am fond of him. He looks up at me from his sandwich.

— If you could write your own ticket right now, what would it be? he asks.

I have been shy about speaking up about this idea, questioning if it is really a legitimate proposition. I tell him: I would go back to Cetona for a year, to heal this ever-oozing wound, to see what it feels like to be there, and to write. It's not a writer's ambition, though it is also that: It is a personal quest, a quest of the heart,

I dream about Cetona almost every night, I say.

— Most people never even know what their ticket is, he says.

He peers at me over his glasses.

— Time is wasting away, he says. Go.

After reaffirming my idea to myself and embracing this as something I should allow myself to do, I set out to talk with Aram.

My love.

Aram and I met through mutual friends. He is a musician, a guitar player, and an avid and talented surfer, a proclivity that has come to define his being. He has long wavy brown hair, now graying, which he pulls back in a ponytail, and a strikingly handsome face of elegant, strong features that he can trace to his Armenian descent. His great-grandfather was killed in the Armenian genocide, an event he carries in his heart with solitary outrage like a badge of distinction, but from that ancestor he drew his olive skin and full lips and penetrating brown eyes that can pull me in all sorts of unexpected directions, sometimes leaving me bottomless and confused. He has been the fullest love of my life, pushing me with his kindness and insight to discover myself and be more of who I want to be. He is tall and skinny and I call him Slim.

The first time he called me he said, Sybil, hi, this is Aram (pronounced with an A like America). He told me he was skateboarding. He was short of thirty-seven. After we got together I learned about his passion for surfing, which is different when you live it than when you listen to stories about it, uninvolved. It requires more discipline and stamina and intelligence than I had thought. And, he had a black wetsuit that made him look sexy and elegant riding a wave, and he was good at it.

— Don't go watch him surf, in his wetsuit and all ... You will fall madly in love, my friend Bobbie said at the beginning of our relationship.

And so it was. I would wait for him to return and get back into our warm bed to make love and smell the ocean in his hair and taste the salt on his skin, our skins sharing heat and cold until everything was mixed and we were spent and briefly back asleep. Every day was like that, a feast of having, of holding, of merging with the smell of ocean and salt.

— I would like to go to Italy for a while, I said, crying.

It was hard to say, to pronounce.

— I need to go home.

I'm not leaving him, I explain. It's just something I think I should do.

As Aram does, he sat quietly for a moment and took it in, his handsome face intent, his eyes focused. He swallowed some emotion that stirred up in him. He quieted it, and I guess thought of me, being in my shoes. He is so compassionate. How many times had I cried on his chest in bed over the years because I missed Cetona? How many times had I cried because I missed Maria, and Ottavia, and the countryside, and my sense of belonging there?

It was not hard for him to understand, with the open heart he has.

— I think you should go, baby, he said. I will help you however I can.

And he did, selflessly, and from that moment on it was a reality.

I set out to find a new home for the chickens, the last remaining eight of the flock of twenty-seven I had gotten five years earlier. I was not willing to schedule my trip or buy a ticket until I knew the chicks were settled. Bella, Cara, Wings, Victoria, Rays, Ellie, Bianca, and Queenie. After a couple of false starts and bad calls, Willis, a beloved teacher at the yoga studio where I practiced, offered to take them in. A couple of weeks before my departure I drove the chicks to Wadmalaw and left them on Willis' beautiful property, in her generous and wide-hearted care, with her little girl, Talula, running around and playing with them.

Then I drove my orange tabby Joe to Miami to be adopted by my father and his family, a task I was dreading most of all. I spent a couple of days with them so I could escort Joe through the transition, and then I hugged him hard and drove off, back to Charleston, sobbing along the way. Leaving Joe brought me childlike grief and was perhaps the hardest thing of all, leaving this orange cat with green eyes that blinked when I said hello or goodbye, who had been my buddy since I found him ten years earlier.

He came to my door as a tiny kitten, so small he fit in the palm of my hand, his limbs dangling over. He was abandoned and sick—thrown from a car, perhaps—and I took him in and nursed him back to health. We became one, if that is possible with a cat. He waited for me while I showered, hung out on my desk while I wrote, sat on my lap for TV, sat at our feet while we cooked, and slept with me every night, tenderly and peacefully. I made sure he was safe, I chose places to live that would afford him outdoor space away from traffic, he had a cat door so he could be free, and he was loved, deeply, all his life. He is my animal, and leaving him was searing.

I had a large sale of painting and belongings, but hardly enough to hold me for long. After that, I finished packing and Aram and I moved my stuff to a storage unit, a tin box fifteen by twelve, everything I own, my books, furniture, clothes, and art heaped up to the ceiling and right up to the pull-down door. I tried to sell my wedding dress, but I couldn't, so I hauled it back to the storage unit with the last batch of miscellaneous stuff. When you open the door it's the first thing hanging there.

I mailed a few boxes ahead to Ottavia, with clothes and painting supplies, and on a sunny morning in late October Aram drove me to the airport and said goodbye. We stood in the line together until he could come no further, and in the hushed hum of the airport he kissed me and walked away, with his dark arms hanging at his side. I watched him go, crying quietly, but it didn't feel like a farewell. It felt like a separation that would lead back to a reunion.

You don't walk away from a love like that. We would be together again.

The immensity of my decision struck me when I reached over the passenger asleep next to me and I slid open the window shade to see the lights of the Alpine towns dotting the dark land below, readying to wake.

I thought of my things in storage. Joe, at my dad's house. My chickens, in their new home, and a relationship of nearly ten years put on hold and imperiled. Aram, asleep in his apartment, in grief, perhaps, his chest, kind and so comforting to me, rising slightly at his every breath.

As I looked at the pink glazing the Alps, I searched for the happiness that that very same sight has given me at my every return, and it struck me that I had left home behind—the other home—perhaps never to find it the same again. Meanwhile, the memory of Cetona wavered like a mirage at sea.

Home. Where is it, for me?

With a heart half-here and half-there I landed and began my adventure of return. These are my stories. They are stories of beginning and of ending. Stories of heartrending grief and exhilarating happiness. Of loss and reunion. Of getting to know, and of revisiting. Of shedding and rebuilding.

They are stories of making—who I became—and the undoing of that.

Mostly or equally, they are stories about Cetona and its inhabitants, the Cetonesi, an ancient and recalcitrant mountain people, funny and endearing, with a tried history and a loving, ornery heart.

My story would be nothing without them.

I awake to the sound of voices outside and I run to my window. It takes me a second to take in the fact that I am really here, in Cetona—that I actually did this—and I am stunned that I am living on the piazza.

— *Penso t'andrebbe bene!* Ottavia had said on the phone months earlier. I think it would be a good place for you.

When I began considering this return, I asked my friends for suggestions. How could I do this, and where could I stay?

I wanted a place in the countryside, with views that would mimic those I grew up with, but Ottavia recommended I talk with Anna, a friend of ours who owns an apartment in a palazzo in town, on the piazza. It has a good heating system, she said, and you can walk out and be in piazza. I'd have no need for a vehicle.

Besides, she said, Anna is flexible; if you stay for three months, fine; if you stay for a year, fine. If you never leave, that would probably be fine, too.

*Never.* I smiled. The mere idea catapults me into another world.

Anna, a bright red-head, an accountant, is the daughter of the man who for many years ran the post office here, Signor Bernini. Anna and I grew up together, and though we have not been in touch in several years, we have always been more or less informed of each other's news through mutual friends. In the past few years Anna lost her husband, Francesco, to cancer, and she inherited the palazzo on the piazza that his family had owned for decades. The building, one of the prettiest on the piazza, is earth-toned, three stories, with an entrance up an alley that skirts secretively behind the piazza. Francesco's parents' apartment is on the second floor and had been shuttered for some years.

— *Magari a te te l'affitta, perché sei te,* Ottavia said on the phone. Perhaps she would consider renting it to you, since it's you.

Ottavia is one of my three closest girlfriends in Cetona, what I consider my circle of sisters. Four years older than me, she is tall, with generous bones and breasts and hips. She has smooth olive skin, straight dark brown hair cut fashionably at her jawline, brown eyes that flash about in rhythm with her feelings, a lovely open smile with tight, well-shaped teeth, and long, linear hands with which she gesticulates constantly.

Ottavia owns a clothing store in Chiusi, whose sluggish business she laments daily, and perhaps not coincidentally she is a clothes horse with an obsession for fashion and looking good, the so-called *bella figura.* She follows strictly whatever the Italian fashion trend-setters—I call them the Italian fashion police—dictate through fashion shows and magazines, though her style runs simple and boylike. She wears no makeup and tends towards natural colors and she would not be caught dead in a skirt or dress.

Ottavia grew up a single child in a tight-knit household of humble, hard-working origins, like most people in Cetona. Her father was a gardener, and her mother worked around town ironing and taking care of people's homes. Her father was strict, intransigent, really; yet, or perhaps because of that, Ottavia turned out independent and strong-willed, with a big tenderness that took her some years to unpack.

Now, she lives alone in a lovely little stone house off a narrow alley into town. She spends her free time traveling with her boyfriend, Giacomo—Cetona's handsome former mayor—and while she has never married or cared about having children, she has taken in eight oddly similar long-haired cats with big green eyes who rule her world, enslaving her to a cleaning routine that she claims massacres her. She is, truly, her cats' maid, always dusting and beating pillows and taking coverlets and blankets off to be cleaned.

— *Ma guarda 'sti gatti, i peli dappertutto!* she says walking about her house, her long fingers joined in prayer. Look at the hair everywhere!!

Ottavia and I have known each other since childhood, but we have not always been friends. We travelled in different circles for many years—I don't really remember Ottavia being out and about much when I was little. Then we became rather unfriendly when I stole her boyfriend, a fact that we pass over now and for which she has forgiven me. We began to be very good friends after I left for the States for college, and in the past twenty or so years our bond has expanded with love and understanding. One could argue it's the absence that keeps us together, but I really like to be in her presence. I love Ottavia. With me she is kind and reasonable, even-tempered, and tolerant. We get along easily, with affection and openness, and we comfort each other somehow. I can ask her for any favor, even after all these years, though I discovered that that is true for all of my old friends in Cetona, and some new ones too.

So, back to my apartment, Ottavia brought up Anna's place. I think you would be happy there, she said. You'll see when you get here.

And so, it was arranged.

Almost every year since I left I have returned to Cetona for a summer visit, and nearly always the trips have been marked by an intense, nearly uncontrollable state of anticipation and excitement. Irrepressible joy triggered a mad rush from baggage claim to the door of the piazza. From the *Raccordo Anulare* to the *autostrada,* I'd drive like an Italian for two hundred kilometers till I sighted Monte Cetona on the horizon, its deep, lush curves sideways to the highway, and then to the Chiusi-Chianciano exit where the same man who worked the *autostrada* booth for years said *buon giorno* and took my money with a look of vague recognition. The adrenaline made it impossible for me to focus on any one thing or breathe or relax until my car was parked in the piazza, under the glaring sun—it was always sunny when I got there, every single time—and Maria had hugged me, looked me in the eye, and smiled. The joy enveloped me, and from there it was a mad feast of numbered days rushing at me inexorably until I had to leave again.

This time, for the first time it was different. This time, I could stay.

When I arrived at the airport I did not rush or fret. I relished the ecstasy that comes with having made a decision that gladdens you even if it's terrifying. I got my luggage calmly and I waited in line patiently for my rental car. I left the familiar hazy sky behind in Rome and drove slowly on the *autostrada*, looking about, not letting anyone rush me. I noticed the temperature and the colors, more fall-like and damper than when I usually arrive. I have not been here in fall in nearly thirty years, since I left for college that fateful August dawn.

I stopped for water at the Autogrill and used the restroom. I talked with the barman for a minute and asked about business. I got back on the road mindfully, and I smiled when I saw Monte Cetona on the horizon wearing a different dress, yellow-green with a bit of red.

I got off the *autostrada* slowly and I talked with the attendant, someone, again, who I vaguely recognized. I drove the road to Cetona calmly, noticing the landscape, and my heartbeat, and the gladness. A relief unimaginable.

The dream, long-awaited.

With disbelief, I considered the time ahead of me. A year. Could that be? Might that be possible for me?

When I came to the piazza it was shortly after lunchtime. The sky was a dull white and the town looked vacant like I had never seen it. There was no one. I felt none of the butterflies, no concern for my hair, no vanity. No lifeline, and suddenly not even any happiness.

I took in the deserted piazza, larger and plainer than I had remembered, and a swell of terror ambushed me, a sense of having transferred myself from one place and time to another at great risk of loss, all for something evanescent living somewhere in my heart.

Reality and nostalgia collided, leaving me suddenly stranded and profoundly alone. Alone with my choice.

What have I done?

Sitting on the wall by the bank I took my face in my hands. I closed my eyes and nausea washed over me. I took measure of the great distance I had just placed between me and my most recent life.

I raised my face and I looked out. I felt the light on me and I paused to listen to the sounds of the piazza, searching for something comforting to remind me why I had come all this way.

Then, the school bells rang out, ancient and familiar, and I saw myself running out with my little white uniform and my olive-colored satchel. My childhood, here, right here.

I inhaled and thought of how much I had wanted this, for so very long. I let the love fill me and the fear recede.

This is where you wanted to be, you fool, I heard a voice say, and, finally, here you are.

A few minutes later, Anna met me with a big hug and keys to my new apartment, and it is beautiful, better than anything I even imagined in these old buildings on the piazza. It is cozy and comfortable, nicely furnished, with smooth, shiny mahogany floors—leftover from when it was ok to harvest mahogany—and a lot of good art, left by Anna's sophisticated mother-in-law, which comforts me.

I have a spacious bedroom with a wall lined by modern, floor-to-ceiling closets—unheard of here in old houses—with elegant polished furniture, quality sheets and towels, tons of them, and windows onto the piazza.

There is also a simple but functional kitchen, stocked with old pans and dishes, and a dining room, a spacious, warm central room that connects all the others like the spokes of a wheel. That is where I write. My favorite room, intended perhaps to be a sitting room, I have transformed into my studio to take advantage of the bright light from the other window onto the piazza.

I have no belongings here except for my clothes, some books and papers, a few photos I have placed here and there, and my painting supplies, which I shipped to Ottavia ahead of my departure. I got the boxes the other day, and for a day I watched them suspiciously thinking of sending them back and following right behind on a plane. Finally, I unpacked them, the boxes, and I arranged my painting supplies on antique tables in front of the window of the studio. I placed the furniture to maximize light for painting while leaving enough space in the middle of the room to practice yoga.

As I look around, those certainties stabilize me for a moment, as do the views from my windows of what was once my daily scenery: a close-up of San Michele, Cetona's prominent ochre-colored Romanesque church, a view of Le ACLI, one of Cetona's bars, and of a slice of the piazza, which, when I lean out, becomes a full-length view with everyone and everything in it, including Via Roma, which heads up to the old part of town, and Cetona's Rocca, its castle.

I awoke the first few days startled to find myself living on the piazza. I opened the windows of my bedroom and staring in my direction were all the guys sitting outside Le ACLI. In opening, the window panes clanged, and everyone's head shot up simultaneously. Several other people looked up, too, and I felt conspicuous and out of place.

Transposed, somehow, and on view.

I admit, I am terrified, here, in the most familiar of places.

I tell Ottavia this, and, as I do, I want to cry—cry in English. Tears streak my face.

— *Lo sai com'è qui,* she said, scolding and comforting at the same time. You know how it is here.

Yes, I do. But there is knowing, and then there is knowing. It hurts me to admit it, like I am saying I am not used to my own skin anymore.

— *Dai,* she said, hugging me. C'mon. It's beautiful to be on the piazza. You'll get used to it again.

19

Cetona sits nestled halfway down the gentle terraced slopes of the eponymous mountain—*la montagna di Cetona*, or *il Monte Cetona*—whose harmonious profile and expansive footing rise clear and unmistakable a few minutes north of Orvieto as you drive on the autostrada toward Florence.

It, *la montagna*, is a milestone on the highway, the highest peak in many kilometers, and a memorably beautiful one with a series of rounded curves and, on its summit, a 50-foot steel cross, visible for miles and miles. When I first got to college, at night I would fall asleep tracing the slopes of Monte Cetona in my mind, air-drawing, and I would finish by planting the cross on top of it as one would dot an i and cross a t. Only then could I sleep.

At the height of Cetona the autostrada jogs some kilometers towards the mountain's foot and then curves away from it quickly, so while you are driving you have to look hard to catch a glimpse of my town hidden in the landscape, which, at that point, is particularly lush and forested. While the rest of the world seems to be increasingly deforested, Monte Cetona seems to have become more heavily wooded, and from that angle, the town, with its muted stone colors, is almost camouflaged, like it does not want to be found.

And indeed, to some degree Cetona has remained a bit of an undiscovered jewel.

Unlike many Tuscan towns like Pienza with its cheese, and Montalcino with its wine, or Cortona with its churches, Cetona lives still in relative anonymity, in spite of its VIPs and bouts of fame. A wave of famous Italian movie producers and actors descended here in the late sixties and seventies, together with a few important industrialists, shipping magnates and interior designers, who bought secluded houses in the countryside and spread the word. Another wave of people followed, mostly Italian politicians and self-important Italian journalists and intellectuals, but also fashion designer Valentino. And a more recent sprinkling, over the past two decades or so, brought more pedestrian nouveau riche foreigners and Italians, also here to buy houses, and sprinklings continue to this day, bringing more foreigners and the occasional rich or famous important person to visit, eat at a restaurant, or buy a house. The Agnelli family has a house here, and the former Queen of Belgium is a regular.

Through these bouts of fame—some of which have left behind an afterglow of flair and sophistication, some of which brought a substantial jump in home sales, and some of which brought simply an increase in the number of people sitting about the bars speaking different languages—the Cetonesi have lived with a mix of curiosity, apathy, and disdain, the latter of which may account for why Cetona has not capitalized more on the developments. This has made for a less eventful and less economically fruitful life there, but also perhaps a greater preservation of the town's rhythm of life and the people's character.

Now, mostly, Cetona has its moderate, regular share of visitors and out-of-town homeowners whom the Cetonesi look upon mostly with indifference—or lack of interest—except for Nilo, the owner of the eponymous restaurant and of the Bar Sport, a staple figure in town whose business depends on the traffic and who keeps a vigilant eye on the piazza day and night, asking, *Ma dov'è la gente?* Where are the people?

Dating back as early as the year 900, but built mostly between 1100 and 1500, Cetona has a distinctive medieval profile and a quintessential medieval story. It was fought over, traded, bought and sold by neighboring cities, mostly Orvieto and Siena, as towns once were.

Atop the town sits the *Rocca*, the castle, with its square tower peeking out from a thick of pine trees and cypresses. The bastion of the rich lord, it was the town's beginning, built on a rock formation that towers above all else. Next came the town's first church and small groups of houses immediately cascading down from there, inside the first walls and fortifications, including Borgo, the street where I grew up.

The rest of the town, including several more sets of ancient walls and fortification, were built over the ensuing three centuries, and they descend in almond-shaped tiers like layers of frosting arranged atop each other, down to the piazza, which was built last, in the late 1500s and early 1600s. And, finally, the bottom layers of town, the newer parts, scatter down unevenly until the final few houses peter out on the edge of town and out toward the countryside. All said, Cetona has medieval, Romanesque, and gothic flavors, down to the piazza, Piazza Garibaldi, with its large majestic buildings carrying a flair of the Renaissance.

Piazza Garibaldi, vast and nearly rectangular, with a big hexagonal white stone fountain at one end, is the heart of Cetona. There, all of the town's streets converge, and, starting when the day's first light peeks over the rooftops, here the life of the town unfolds, like the stage of a small theater, with its quirky characters, its prima donnas, its stars, and its extras, more muted but no less savory. Here people convene for company and commerce, and, really, one cannot live in Cetona without the piazza.

Most of the Cetonesi are a distinctly proud people with humble yet rebellious blood rooted in a long agrarian tradition that is the very bedrock of the town's character and life. Known to each other by family nicknames dating back centuries—names like Sbragia, Capoccia, Calano, Dondo and Lombrico—they make a living partaking in the necessary economies of a small hill town. They are shopkeepers, merchants, artisans, laborers, teachers, bureaucrats, bankers, and many farmers. They live uncluttered, modest lives, mostly, in small houses, driving small cars.

And here, on this land of rare, ancient beauty where the Cetonesi are born and die, here I was lucky to grow up.

But let me start at the beginning.

We moved to Italy when I was a little girl. My father, thin, handsome, with thick dark hair and smart brown eyes, had been a young architect in the offices of Mies van der Rohe, in Chicago. He was an exceptional drawer—he had been accepted to Yale Architecture School by Paul Rudolph on the basis of his drawings alone—and he was on a fast track to success, I imagine. But after the icon died, my father, an uncompromising idealist and perfectionist, reimagined his life. The practice was taking a different path, and Dad, driven partly by professional and intellectual disenchantment and partly by political and social dis-ease, sought a new start. Freedom, perhaps, to be new. Surely it helped that Chicago was torched by the flames of civil rights and racial riots. The world was, indeed, a flaming cauldron.

But, at the core, Dad had decided to learn something new, violinmaking, an art that harkened back to the very start of him, when four events happened to miraculously direct his life away from the place of his upbringing, Lynchburg, Virginia, and, perhaps already onto the path to Italy.

The first happened when my grandmother, the educated daughter of a respected obstetrician, woke him one morning to announce that that evening they would be going to the symphony. My father pleaded against this and argued valiantly why he should not have to do this, but ultimately my grandmother prevailed and off they went to hear Hans Kindler conduct the National Symphony Orchestra performing Smetana's Die Moldau.

They were seated in the fourth row, my father in his little Sunday suit, and the music, otherworldly, swept him away. In his childlike fantasy he imagined becoming one day like those cats up there playing their violins, their bows breezily tracing arches through the air and making this heavenly music.

The second happened at the house of his friend Joe Cunningham, whose father was a successful, well-traveled geologist. When they played there—a house full of books and wonderful treasures—Dad took books off the shelves and splayed them on the ground to look at the pictures. One he favored was about art and architecture of Rome, and one of Greece, he remembers, and while he turned the pages he thought they were the most beautiful pictures he had ever seen.

— Mrs. Cunningham, are these places real? he asked Joe's mom when she came upstairs to check on them. Do these places really exist?

— Yes, David, they do, and one day, I am sure, you will see them.

The third event that chartered Dad's course happened when he took music lessons with Mrs. Graves. While waiting for the student ahead of him to finish, he sat looking at a wall full of art that entranced him. Among the small paintings and prints he saw an etching of a dancing character that he particularly liked. When Mrs. Graves came out of her lesson Dad asked her about it.

— Mrs. Graves, this is the most beautiful drawing I have ever seen. What is it?

— It is a drawing by Albrecht Dürer. Do you like it?

— I love it, Mrs. Graves, Dad said. Can I have it?

Mrs. Graves, moved by his precocious fondness for the drawing, promised he could have it when he finished his piano lesson book, and so it was. She gave it to him and he took it home like a most precious treasure.

The fourth transpired on the bus to school. My father, by then twelve or thirteen, was riding at the back of the bus when Pierre Daura, a Spanish painter who had reached America during the Spanish Civil War and found a faculty position at Randolph Macon College, got on. In little Lynchburg everyone knew about Daura and talked about him; he was a man so interesting that all wanted to meet him. Yet, he was so foreign to the landscape, my father said, that even a child like himself noticed and knew.

But Dad was immediately attracted to him and he approached him, introducing himself.

— Mr. Daura, he said after a few minutes, I have a Dürer drawing. My teacher gave it to me. Would you like to see it?

— Do you, now? Daura asked him, his eyes widening in disbelief.

Yes, my father said proudly. Daura gave him an appointment at his studio and Dad put his little Dürer drawing into his knapsack and took it to him, and from there a lifelong friendship began. Daura taught my father to paint, the art that ultimately ended up being my father's greatest love.

Ultimately, during the course of his life my father studied music and art, painted and played the violin, and then, by a series of forces some of which beyond his control, decided to become an architect— architecture being a practical art my grandfather endorsed. But each of those moments threaded everlasting into who my father became, and, eventually led to violinmaking, like a grafting of new branches, and took him onto the road to Italy to seek further development and understanding of his original passions. And, as I said, he was enormously talented and a capable craftsman.

Cremona, the land of Stradivari, was the place to do this, and my parents decided to go. My mother, a talented, dark-haired pianist born a prodigy in an immigrant German family in Philadelphia, supported my father's dream. Is that simplistic? Probably. I was too little to know. But, they had been married fifteen years, then; they had bought and restored a solid-boned brownstone in Chicago, and they had a vibrant social life and steady, successful jobs. They had many friends and kept interesting company, but it was an adventure and they took the chance, with my brother and me in tow.

I was skinny, with a trusting, radiant face and light brown hair. I was attending a kindergarten at a private school in Chicago then. I wore glamorous leather outfits given to me by my Auntie Phil, a friend of the family who doted on me. I played the piano in our sunny living room, and I had a cozy bedroom full of dolls and stuffed animals. A series of pictures from that time on the beach at Lake Michigan show me in a white and orange bathing suit, happy, jumping ecstatically and making a peace sign with my fingers. In another I am standing with unbridled energy bursting forth, looking like I just threw a handful of sand in the air, and perhaps I had. I have strong pectoral muscles, froglike slender thighs, and I am laughing. I am bursting with joy, actually, like I have a special magic stone in my pocket.

I don't remember much of my childhood till then, just little threads of something. A smell, a shot of Christmas, some visits with my grandparents. The next picture shows me bundled up with a big brown hat, huddled next to my parents and my brother getting ready to board the ship to Italy. We had said goodbye to my grandparents and we were headed to Boston to depart. For months my parents readied to make this great escape. I cannot imagine it, really, though I guess it's a bit like mine in reverse. We found a new home for our German Shepard, Frida, and drove her out to the country somewhere, my mother sobbing on the drive back. We sold our house, our furniture—everything except our car.

Each of us was allowed to pack one single trunk of our most precious or necessary belongings, including clothes. With horror I confronted the task of sorting through my bunk-bed, home to layers and rows of dolls and stuffed animals, and in a state of inconsolable sadness I chose the few characters that would escort me through this unimaginable move: Raggedy Anne, Winnie the Pooh, and my cousin Rob's Tigger, which he gifted me for the voyage. I cried for those who stayed behind.

I also took a special doll, a going-away present that a friend of my parents had bought for me at Marshall Fields, chosen from the store's mile-long wrap-around doll display with warm lights and vel-vet-draped shelving from which stared the marble-like faces of every type of doll one could possibly dream of. There were blond princesses and dolls drinking from bottles and Barbies with manes of coiffed black hair longer than their bodies. Each held her own imaginary world of possibilities and choosing among them was nearly impos-sible. I crawled around the display on my hands and knees, studying every doll in the case. It must have taken all afternoon. I finally chose the one single black doll in the whole case. She had dark mahogany skin and amber eyes and she was dressed in a white baptism dress with a white bonnet. I thought she was the most beautiful doll I had ever seen. I took her home carefully and placed her in my trunk with everything else—books and favorite clothes—that I thought precious to me.

We sailed out of Boston on the *Cristoforo Colombo* on a cold and foggy day. I don't remember any fanfare about our departure, or any sense of loss except for parting with my stuffed animals. I stood next to my parents looking out over the railing and the vanishing land. I was bundled up, perhaps holding my Raggedy Anne, or maybe Tigger, who at some point became lost at sea.

We spent ten days surrounded by the frigid gray ocean, and except for a day stop in Malaga and one in Lisbon, to refuel, we saw nothing but water. One night, about halfway through the trip, in the middle of the dark ocean we crossed the transatlantic *Michelangelo*, headed to New York. Sky and water melded in a vastness of black, the stars lone witnesses to this crossing. All lights were lit festively on both ships and the passengers, quickly torn from sleep, climbed on deck to watch. I stood at the railing waving at the strangers across the water as we passed each other like giant moving skyscrapers.

When we docked in Naples a fierce winter storm churned the gray waters of the port and the luggage slid down the corridors of the ship banging against the walls. Red, orange, and yellow fruits bobbed in the water, thrown aboard by angry farmers in the throes of a riot to protest escalating food prices.

Amidst the clamoring chaos of screaming workers, moving ships and equipment, and people hugging goodbye, a crane lowered our four trunks and our Volkswagen station wagon and set them on the dock. To dissuade the customs agents from tearing our trunks apart, my parents gifted them cartons of American cigarettes brought specifically for that purpose, and after signing some papers we drove out of the port of Naples and toward our new life.

We drove north heading toward Cremona. Christmas was fast approaching and we stopped to spend the holidays in Rome.

And there, it seems, the memories of what I call my life begin.

On the steps of Piazza di Spagna was a nativity scene in a manger with live animals, the sight of which transfixed me. The characters stood still as statues, and people dressed in heavy coats and elegant furs and hats gathered in wonder to watch. The steps were lit with thousand tiny lights, and it was the most enchanting sight my childhood thus far had gifted me.

The streets of Rome, narrow and meandering, were decorated with festive lights, as were the storefronts and restaurants. We stayed in a *pensione*, the Hotel Artis, in the city's red-light district, which, unbeknownst to my young parents, was a *casa di tolleranza*, or a bordello—called *case di tolleranza* because prostitution was tolerated there. Prostitutes and their clients were numerous among its customers, but it must have been discreet enough for my parents not to notice. Nothing bad ever happened to us there. The funniest thing was that while we were in Rome we attained our *permesso di soggiorno* to live in Italy—things must have been very different then—and for the following two decades our residency documents bore the address of the brothel, a fact that, each year at renewal time, immigration officials looked upon with great humor.

Rome, and Italy in general, were much less populated then than they are now and more Spartan. In some ways the fifties and sixties had not sufficed to put the war behind, and this was true particularly in the countryside. Everywhere were fewer stores, fewer lights, less noise, and many fewer tourists; cars were small, and life was simpler. We spent leisurely days walking around Rome. For the first time, I ate roasted chestnuts wrapped in butcher paper, hot from the little street grills of old Roman men, and pizza whose taste must have immediately replaced anything I had known before. For Christmas my parents bought me a pair of tall, brown boots that laced up the front and made me feel like a child out of a romantic Victorian novel. They were the most beautiful shoes I had ever owned, and I remember them with tenderness, perhaps because they were my first Italian belonging, but perhaps because my parents had no money to waste. It was the beginning of a long frugal life.

After our few special days in Rome we traveled north to Orvieto, a town perched on a steep mount of volcanic rock and dominated by a splendid cathedral in alternating layers of alabaster and travertine positioned at a great height above the surrounding valley. My parents had intended for us to stay only briefly, but we stayed on for New Year's Eve and through the wet and dreary first days of the New Year. While it rained outside, we sat in our warm hotel room playing cards and eating brown pears and cheese, gorgonzola for Dad, Swiss for me. Using his sharpest knife and the masterful gift of his hands, Dad cut the pears in quarters and carved them into mice, complete with eyes, ears, and whiskers. Those were our little brown mice, as Dad called them, and my fondest memory of our time as a family in Orvieto.

Finally, on the eve of the Epiphany we arrived in Cremona, on the shores of the river Po, the city of the violin, with its warm Romanesque cathedral and its generous, rose-tinted piazza full of cooing pigeons.

Cremona is not well known to people outside the violinmaking industry, which is largely responsible for the city's fame since the 1600s, when Stradivari, Amati, and the Guarneri del Gesù families lived and made their prized instruments there. The legacy of their work passed on through the generations through a lineage of *maestri*, and then through Cremona's Scuola di Liuteria, to which appassionati of string instruments have flocked through the years from all over the world. Once secluded behind the doors of quiet workshops, the violinmaking industry has become increasingly conspicuous through time, and in recent years shops of *liutai,* or luthiers, have popped up on nearly every street corner.

But equally present in the life of the city is its venerable and lucrative agricultural and food industry, to which the town has owed its financial solidity through the centuries. Cradled as it is in the Po Valley, Italy's flattest, most verdant and fertile land, and home to a pervasive dairy and meat industry, Cremona is known for its provolone and salted meats, Sperlari candy, *gianduia*, and *torrone.* Abundant throughout the city are stores with the most sumptuous displays of artfully crafted, luxurious candies and intricately decorated cakes and pastries, surrounded by piles of *gianduia* and *torrone* and jars of *mostarda.* As a child, when I walked anywhere from our home on

Vicolo Pertusio onto Via Solferino or Corso Mazzini, I was lured to the warmly lit storefronts laden with trays of delicacies and piles of candy of every color and shape.

Cremona's streets color my earliest memories, and the Duomo too, a structure of pink and white marble and dark red brick that dominates the surrounding piazza regally. It has the tallest brickwork bell tower in the country, the Torrazzo, and the third tallest in the world; the oldest astronomical clock in the world; one of the most remarkable *battisteri* in the country; and one of the most stunning rose windows you will ever see.

After a short stay in a *pensione*, with the help of a violinmaking apprentice named David—now a famous restorer and trader of instruments in New York—we found our first apartment. David, bearded, with olive skin, a luscious smile and deep green eyes, was one of the dreamers who flocked to Cremona to make instruments, an Israeli son of Latvian immigrants. He had been in Cremona studying and working for some time before we arrived, and he helped us set up our new life and find a place to live and schools for my brother and me.

Our apartment was in Vicolo Pertusio, a bustling alley in the heart of town, a short walk from the Duomo. It was spacious and sunny, with large rooms, high ceilings, huge windows with shutters, and a balcony that ran the length of the kitchen and dining room and that overlooked the building's central courtyard. The kitchen was airy and full of light, and we had a generous living room, dining room, separate bedrooms for Paul and me, and two bathrooms, all for a paltry sum. A double French door with panes of frosted glass led into my room, and my window, though I could not quite see over the sill, looked out over Corso Mazzini, with its well-dressed shoppers and strollers.

On Vicolo Pertusio were a shoemaker, a butcher, a fish monger, a fur shop, an electrician's store, and a beautiful *negozio di alimentari*, a grocery store, that sold the most perfect pope-nose rolls—*rosette*, they are called—for *prosciutto cotto*, one of Cremona's specialties, or Nutella, for many years my favorite snack.

Every morning at sunrise, Dad walked us to our respective schools on the way to his. Mine, the elementary school where I was enrolling in first grade, was located in a building that had been a convent, with an imposing wooden front door that opened to a courtyard and tall arched doorways leading this way and that. My parents must have visited the school and arranged for my enrollment before they dropped me off that first day. The principal met us in the courtyard and escorted us to what was going to be my classroom to introduce me to my teacher and my classmates.

When the door opened and we walked in, my assigned teacher, Maestro Fazzi, came to greet us.

In his mid-fifties or so, he wore a gray suit and glasses and his thinning hair was combed neatly straight back. He looked reserved and a bit concerned. Fifteen or so children in black smocks gathered around to examine my parents and, mostly, me. Some niceties and reassurances were exchanged among the adults, mostly gestures and looks I did not understand, and finally words ran out. There was nothing left to say. My parents spoke barely a few words of stilted Italian, and no one at the school spoke English.

Quickly it became apparent to me that my parents were going to leave me there. My mother was crying, I started crying, and Maestro Fazzi was wringing his hands, looking a lot like he was about to start crying, too. My parents were ushered out and Maestro Fazzi showed me to my desk, which awaited me somewhere in the middle of the classroom surrounded by the desks of other children. Perhaps my difference became apparent to me then, as well as my efforts, deep within my heart, to build tribe. To be one with others.

With a hand on my shoulder Maestro Fazzi introduced me to the class. *Sibilla*, he called me, which forever became my name. The children looked at me; some stared, some giggled, and one, Michele Barbieri, a tender brown-haired boy, smiled at me sweetly.

The following day, and every day after that for the following several weeks, Maestro Fazzi brought to school word cards he made especially for me, each with a handmade drawing and, underneath, the corresponding word written in impeccable calligraphy. While the other children worked quietly on their own, he pulled a chair up to my desk and helped me sound the words.

*Casa, mucca, gelato, penna, matita, mamma.*

When we came to the first words with r's in them—*carro, porta, finestra, prato*—Maestro Fazzi rolled his *erre* for me, vocalizing the rolling sound so singular to the Italian language. In the first few days of that exercise I went home after school and ran around the apartment at full speed through the rooms rolling my r's like a cartoon motorcycle. *Rrrrrrrrrrrrrrrrrrrrrrr.* Slowly, Maestro Fazzi increased the complexity of the words, masterfully engineering and tweaking the steps of this magical ladder that allowed me to conquer the Italian language and make it my own.

I was fluent in less than two months, and that was my ticket to bonding.

While I was learning Italian, I was also learning the ways of the school, my new country and people. I remember discovering with horror that the bathrooms in our school had no toilets but rather large gaping holes in the floor with places to put your feet and squat. Turkish bathrooms, they are called, and in fact I found them again throughout Turkey many years later. Water gushed everywhere and flooded your shoes if you didn't move quickly enough after flushing. I was horrified when I had to pee there and it sprinkled around my shoes; it was worse when some time later, but not long after I had first arrived, I had a bout of stomach flu.

It was an awkward time for me. It did not help that my parents decided simultaneously to cut my hair boylike and to get me glasses, which I needed but hated. At one point, with glee I bribed Michele Barbieri, with whom I often exchanged lunches, to step on my book-bag and break my glasses, which he did, though he now denies it.

Maestro Fazzi was my teacher through second grade, when we moved to Cetona. But I remained his grateful student for a lifetime. Many years later, when I was in my early thirties and working as a journalist in America, I wrote Maestro Fazzi a letter thanking him for all that he had done for me—for easing my life by teaching me his language so proficiently. He answered back, in his still perfect calligraphy, saying he remembered me well and always dearly. My letter had moved him, he wrote. Alas, I never saw him again.

During those first days in Cremona I remember the comforting presence of my dad as he walked me to school every morning, my gloved hand in his, reassuring me against the unknown. He, meanwhile, was finding his own way. He had begun his apprenticeship with one of Cremona's most celebrated violinmakers, Maestro Bissolotti, revered in Cremona for making some of the best contemporary instruments and for teaching dozens, if not hundreds, of the finest violinmakers the city produced. They worked in Bisso's studio, in a big *palazzo* where the Bissolotti family also lived and two of his sons also made instruments. The bottom floor housed Bisso's labs, full of wood and tools and work benches, cuttings, wood shavings, pots of glue boiling and students working, and on the top floors were cavernous, temperature-controlled spaces used for drying and storing instruments.

While my father went to the Scuola di Liuteria and immersed himself in his new art—he recently showed me carefully conserved books containing his painstaking notes and drawings from that time—my mom worked at adapting and learning her new life in happy and less happy ways. One day we came back from school and poor Mom answered the door sobbing; she had just washed all of her new dishes and the entire dish drain had toppled over. Every single new dish sat on the floor in chips and pieces and Mom was a wreck.

She trudged on, though, as my mom always did. She learned Italian, swallowing the humiliating experiences that come with that—ordering a *torta di pesce* instead of a *torta di pesche* (a fish pie instead of a peach pie), and such. She cried a lot, and later confided that times had been a bit harder for her than I perceived at the time.

Sometimes my parents had new friends over, people I remember vaguely, and things were happy. My parents played for weddings then, Mom on the piano and Dad on the violin, and I remember them rehearsing in the living room and dressing up to go.

On our way north to Cremona the first time, just before the Epiphany, we had stopped in Florence to see Orazio and Giannina.

Orazio, a famous Italian pianist, was for many years a beloved and renowned teacher at the Eastman School of Music, where my parents had met as students and married. At the time, my mother was the school's star student pianist. She had been a prodigy, schooled by her father to practice the piano many hours a day by the time she was six or seven. By the time she was seventeen she was rumored to have sight-read the piano score of Beethoven's Kreutzer violin sonata, and by the time she finished Eastman she had performed concerts and recitals on the radio and she had to her name solo performances and recordings. Her intimidated classmates called her "Rene the Mean Queen." This is not surprising knowing my mother, though still awe-inspiring for me.

Mom had not been a student of Orazio's, but when they learned of our move they invited us to call on them, in Florence, where Orazio had been teaching for some time.

Orazio was tall and handsome, with a voracious personality and appetite, huge hands, and a prominent aquiline nose. His jet-black hair—later, snow-white—was combed back to leave his lively eyebrows free to move on his broad, open forehead, always an accompaniment to his stories. Born into an educated, refined family in Lugano, on the northern lakes, Zio had left home in his twenties to study the piano. He had escaped to the States during the war, though not before eating his fair share of mice and cats, which he told about with sadness and laughter.

Giannina was from a wealthy Boston family of some prominence. Her parents had had lofty expectations of her, which, however, she had thwarted by taking off for France when she was barely eighteen to sing opera. There, while she worked in a music store, story goes, the young American sophisticate met Orazio and they fell madly in love.

During our visit, Orazio and Giannina told my parents about the house they had recently bought in a tiny medieval town in Tuscany, on the Umbrian border. They invited us to visit in spring or summer, when the weather warmed. We did, on a beautiful weekend when school was out, perhaps in early June.

We drove the six hours or so of *autostrada* from Cremona and arrived in Cetona around lunchtime. We checked in at the Pietreto, the only hotel in Cetona, a clean, modern-looking place on the outskirts of town that became a temporary home to the handful of foreigners who happened, around that time, to have bought a house in Cetona to restore.

At the Pietreto we asked for directions.

— *Il Professore! Si, si, glielo spiego subito!!* Franco, the young hotel owner said immediately. The professor's house? Yes, I will tell you immediately how to get there!

Leaving the hotel, we walked down the road toward town, and, as directed, we cut through the piazza, which stood quiet and deserted under the midday sun. We found Via Sobborgo and followed it downhill as it meandered around the southern edge of the town and out to the country.

About halfway down Via Sobborgo was a hamlet of houses where one could picture guards living with their families in dark medieval times. Simple stone houses bunched along the narrow gravel road, no more than ten feet wide. Among them, the last one in the row, was a decrepit three-story tower and, at its base, a long row of stalls that had recently been vacated. In those days, the big white oxen, le Chianine— those massive animals peculiar to the Tuscan countryside at the time, and now making a resurgence—were still pulling wooden carts up the steep street, laden with straw and sacks of wheat. I could picture them sleeping there.

Dad peered in through the stalls and through the crumbling walls that opened in the rear to an immediate and sweeping view of Monte Cetona. The roof was caved in and, in the rear, it looked like the structure, or what was left of it, was about to slide down a steep hill. The upper stories of the tower opened onto an unbroken view of land and neighboring Città della Pieve, directly across by sight.

After Dad peeked in and walked around, we continued on down the gravel road away from town and toward the countryside. Via Sobborgo merged with a larger paved road, flanked by fields of young wheat and corn. We passed emerald green fields with shacks where farmers kept their tools. Every now and then a road led off the main road and at its end you could see an old stone farmhouse, quiet and peaceful, an old cart parked outside, a dusty car, a dog lying in the sun, chickens strutting in the gravel.

Once or twice during our walk the odd car came along; as it approached us it slowed down and its passengers strained curiously, suspiciously, to look at the strangers walking along the road. My father, in his typical and friendly American way, waved at everyone, a gesture that in my teenage years caused me endless and silly embarrassment and that now makes me proud.

We found Orazio and Giannina's house nobly positioned atop a hill looking toward the countryside leading to the town of Piazze, a patchwork of fields full of spring flowers. Zio and Zia, as I soon began to call them, greeted us warmly and introduced us to Bruno and Adelina, the farmers who worked for them. They literally were called *their contadini*, their farmers, and they came with the house, like fixtures, when it was purchased. At the time in Cetona that is how many farmers lived, their incomes and home tethered to the property in their care as sharecroppers. The *contadini* were spoken to informally, by their first names, but Bruno and Adelina called Zio *professore* and Zia *signora*. It would have embarrassed everyone otherwise.

Zio and Zia's house was in disrepair, some parts of it nearly in ruin, except for the portion where Bruno and Adelina lived and parts of the first floor, included an old kitchen where Adelina and Zia were preparing a festive lunch. A fire burned in the old kitchen fireplace and Zio made bruschetta, or as it is called in the north, *fettunta:* hard Tuscan bread, thick and unsalted, grilled on the fire, rubbed with garlic and generously doused with salt and new olive oil. Zio was a master of fettunta, an expertise honed in wartime, when there was little else to eat.

Adelina, her coarse curly hair covered by a flowered kerchief, was busy making tagliatelle on an old floured table; *sugo* and water were boiling on the stove, and a chicken and a rabbit were roasting in the oven. Rosemary and the smells of straw, firewood, and fields—the smells I later always associated with Adelina and Cetona—mixed in the warm air, and for the first time of many in my lifetime we ate in Zio and Zia's simple stone-and-stucco courtyard, surrounded by a half ruin of a house, on a large wooden table covered by a plastic flowered table cloth: Zio and Zia, my parents, Paul and I, and Bruno and Adelina. Platters of simple delicious food were laid out plainly, with no attempts to romanticize or stylize: loaves of bread, water, wine, and oil.

We have pictures of that day, Mom in stylish bell bottoms and sunglasses, and Dad with black pants and a sophisticated black turtleneck, both young and thin, and Zio and Zia handsome and happy. Paul and I looked a bit like hippie American kids.

At that first lunch, on that first visit to Cetona, over copious amounts of food and bottles of homemade wine—truly stomped by foot—Zio and Dad started talking about houses and their prices. Dad mentioned the tower he had noticed while walking down Via Sobborgo, the one with the stalls.

— What would something like that cost? Dad asked.

Zio turned to Bruno and asked him in Italian if he knew the house in question.

Bruno was dark-skinned with chestnut brown hair and light blue eyes set in a rugged face with a narrow bristly moustache. His hands were thick and rough and he always wore a dark beret that sat a bit sideways. His clothes were a uniform of sorts—a plaid flannel shirt under a simple sweater, green or brown, heavy work pants, work boots, heavy socks, and a plain jacket.

There was nothing frivolous or unnecessary about Bruno. He had a serious, proud countenance. He spoke little and simply, with a tight Cetonese accent. *Di campagna*—from the country. He smiled genuinely but he laughed with restraint. In his manners were the plainness and savvy that through the years I came to associate with Cetonesi of his generation.

— *A Borgo? Si, si, è di Arduino Del Cascio. La conosco,* Bruno said, nodding knowingly and mentioning the name of the owner. Arduino Del Cascio, so-called Dolco.

Referring to the street as Borgo, he said he knew the house and that it belonged to a good friend of his; as a matter of fact, he thought it was for sale. If Dad was interested, he said, he would inquire.

After lunch Zio and Zia showed us around the property—the old hay house, the stalls, and the house itself, where so much work was to be done in the years to come—and late in the afternoon, near sundown, we embraced and parted. Zio gave us a ride back into town, dropping us off at the Pietreto, and the following day we traveled back to our lives in Cremona.

A couple of weeks later the postman brought a telegram from Zia asking that my parents call as soon as possible. At the time, and for the following many years, we didn't have a phone; calls were made at a central phone bank called SIP, or later, in Cetona, at the Bar Sport. The following day, on the way to school, Dad stopped at the SIP and called Zia.

— If you are interested in Del Cascio's house on Borgo, you need to come back as soon as possible, Zia said.

Bruno had reported back to Zio that Arduino was eager to sell, and, as it happened, just days earlier someone else had expressed some interest. Citing their lifelong friendship, Bruno had asked Arduino to wait for the friends of the *professore*, the Americans, to return. Arduino promised he would, but not for long; he was a shrewd negotiator, and there was no time to waste.

That weekend or the following we drove back to Cetona, Paul and I asleep on blankets on the back seat of the car. We checked back into the Pietreto and Bruno and Zio hastily arranged a meeting with Arduino and the Del Cascio family, about a dozen people in all.

Arduino was a slender older man with sly, crisp blue eyes and a sharp business acumen. He had owned a butchery in town for many years, on Piazza Parè. The whole family lived above the store—his wife, Albertina, his son Benigno, a school teacher; Benigno's wife, Fortunata, and their daughter, Romina. He was a big property owner in town and he was known for being tight with money and tough to negotiate with. *Tosto*—tough.

At the meeting, sitting around a table in an office on Via Risorgimento, negotiations began, starting from a figure put forth by Arduino. Zio and Dad went back and forth on the figure, consulting with Bruno; then Zio translated a counteroffer, negotiating on Dad's behalf. It was the first house the Del Cascios had sold off, and there was apprehension in the family. The first American family in town. What would the Americans bring? Where would this lead them?

Dad, meanwhile, wondered what a house like this could be worth. How could he know? He listened to Zio whose ears were tuned to the snippets of conversation coming from the other side.

Finally, after hours of hard negotiations, stories, explanation and meandering conversations, Arduino and Dad reached a deal. In earnest they rose from their chairs, shook hands, and signed a contract. I imagine they had some vinsanto, and I imagine, through tears, what my father's smile looked like at the moment.

And so it was that on that bright summer day, almost by fluke, the little house on the hill became ours. And with that my parents chose my beloved home, on a narrow street in a solitary medieval town at the foot of Monte Cetona, population 2,800.

A few days after being back, while still exploring and reacquainting myself, I went to buy some wine in Piazze, here also commonly called Le Piazze, a sub-municipality (called a *frazione*) of Cetona about ten minutes away that you will often hear about. The name Piazze has nothing to do with a *piazza* as we traditionally know it, and in fact Piazze doesn't even have a piazza, which will explain what follows.

Luca, whose family of winemakers owns the Cantine Gentili, greeted me in their store and we chatted for a minute about this and that. Then I asked him what, if anything, in his opinion, makes the people from Cetona and the people from Piazze different.

— *La piazza. Ai Cetonesi piace la vita di piazza.* The piazza, he said, without hesitation. People in Cetona like life in the square.

The term *vita di piazza* captures not only a somewhat leisurely lifestyle, but a habit of the mind—the meeting, looking, and gossiping that comes with life in a village with a big space right in the middle of it.

What wisdom.

Americans think of the piazza as an interesting and quaint architectural phenomenon, and it is. As visitors, they like to sit out at a bar and drink cappuccino and savor this quintessentially European civic and architectural marvel. But most Americans don't understand how vital the piazza is to the urban dynamic of a town like Cetona and, indeed, how much it and its bars and stores sustain the social fabric and the very survival of the town. It is fair to say that without the piazza Cetona would no longer exist—or its residents would die of loneliness. Or, as Luca might say, they would work harder.

Cetona's piazza, large and nearly rectangular, is flanked on its two longest sides by imposing three-story *palazzi* of muted natural colors standing flank to flank. Those buildings house, on the ground floor, most of Cetona's stores, and, on the floors above, some of Cetona's largest and loveliest apartments, with huge rooms and expansive frescoed ceilings, mostly owned, these days, by foreigners.

When we moved to Cetona the piazza had a sleepy feel to it, like a Tuscan Wild West of sorts. It was dusty, plain, and smaller-feeling. In some ways, it was nicer. It was paved in worn gray asphalt and there was herringbone parking on the sides, in front of the stores, and in the middle. It felt old and rustic and in tune with the surrounding buildings. The cars were tiny, and if someone came into the piazza driving an odd- or new-looking car, people took notice and stared, unabashedly.

Back then, much as now, the piazza was ringed by stores—the staples of town, the essential locales where everyone shopped for everything that was needed, and, plus, communed, gossiped, and checked in with one another. Clock-wise from the south was Pippo, Cetona's legendary ceramist, white-haired and rambunctious, with his hand-painted plates and bowls hanging from his open wooden doors; Pino the electrician, tall and broody, with an old fridge in the window; Ottorino the *giornalaio*, jovial and funny, who sold everything from bras to newspapers to school supplies; and the *lattaia*, the milk lady, red-headed and quiet, who transported the milk from her farm on the mountain in her ancient red Fiat 500. The smell of the milk oozed from the store and always made me mildly nauseous.

Then there was Alvaro and Franca's *ferramenta*, the hardware store, which sold everything from nails to agricultural implements and solvents, paints, pots and pans; the pharmacy, then run by a stern, chain-smoking but knowledgeable *farmacista*, Anna Maria, who gave me penicillin shots when I once got shingles; and Valfrido, grumpy and bald, who owned the shoe store.

Following along the other side of the piazza was Lavinia's *alimentari*; the butchery owned by Andrea's in-laws; the immutable Bar Cavour, sitting right in the middle of that side of the square, with just a few chairs lined up against the wall for the old men to sit in the sun; a cooperative food store; a hairdresser, the vegetable store owned by Crema, the Monte dei Paschi di Siena, which is still there, and Lelia, the mother of my soon-to-be friend Ida, who sold clothes.

Framing the piazza at the north end was Wando's bar, which has since closed; a *tabaccheria*, owned by my friend Pierpaolo's father, a crotchety old man; and the Bennati car mechanic shop. The family lived above the shop, and the son, Marcello, a leftist rebel with a histrionic personality, spent his spare and more benevolent time putting walnut shell halves on the bottoms of the paws of his cat and sliding him on a wooden board down to the pavement of the piazza below.

At that end were and still are San Michele's, the most prominent of the churches, home to most funerals and weddings; Le ACLI, which is known as the priest's bar; the imposing red building of my elementary school; and the main roads out of town: Via Remo Cacioli, towards Chiusi, our Etruscan southern neighbor, along which is located much of the town's newer housing, and the other, Via San Sebastiano, towards Sarteano, up through the hills to the north. Heading out of town up that way was and still is Cetona's retirement home, *casa famiglia*. Back then it was a dreary old place, but it's since been renovated and on sunny days the elderly sit outside basking in the warmth, watching the town go by.

At the southern end of the piazza were Via Roma, which leads steeply up into the oldest, highest part of town, to the church of the Collegiata; another *tabaccheria;* the butchery that belonged to my boyfriend Lucio's father; and finally, the Bar Sport, our favorite hangout in youth, with a restaurant underneath, and the florist, Savina, next to it.

Also at that end of the piazza, of great note but often unsung, was Cetona's loveliest tree, *il tiglio*, a linden tree tall fifty meters or more. Il *tiglio* was one of three trees planted after World War I to bring beauty and shade to that end of the piazza. As the story goes, bombings during World War II took out two of the three, leaving what became the piazza's single most regal tree. Its branches provided secret cover for play, and when it flowered in spring the whole end of the piazza was covered in tiny white flowers sweet like heaven. Unfortunately, some years back a tornado yanked it up by the roots and rested it against the buildings like a majestic and dead friend. A smaller one planted in its place is slowly trying to catch up.

And finally, at that end of the piazza, right next to the Bar Sport, is Via Sobborgo, the street where I grew up.

After a dramatic descent out of the piazza, the narrow roadway evens out and curves gently around the base of Cetona, tightly hugging its southern walls on one side, and opening, on the other, to the well-tended vegetable gardens and fields that cascade all the way down to the rock bed from which Cetona's foundation emerged millions of years ago. Just beyond rises immediate and lush Monte Cetona, Cetona's mountain. Its bottom tiers, a patchwork of olive groves and cypress-lined gardens and villas, give way to thick woods as its soft terraced flanks move upward gradually toward the sky, capped by the monte's famous 50-foot steel cross.

As one leaves the piazza behind, heading down Via Sobborgo, the temperature drops and the crisp mountain air rises from the fields. After about five hundred meters one comes to the heart of Via Sobborgo, a hamlet of a dozen or so houses that constitute Cetona's southern outpost. I suspect that is how Via Sobborgo got its name—via of the *sub borgo*, or *borgo di sotto* (burgh below). It was Cetona's first neighborhood, and in medieval times this is where visitors might have passed and perhaps stopped to show their papers or feed their horses, before gaining access to the town and making the final uphill trek. The street runs narrowly between the houses and at its narrowest Borgo accommodates only one car at a time.

Our house needed nearly complete rebuilding, which led us up and down the *autostrada* between Cremona and Cetona for months. The project involved the usual bureaucratic maneuverings, intricate permits, meetings with all sorts of authorities, the involvement of the appropriate people, and finally the hiring of the artisans and workers who would do the work. We were escorted through this by a man by the name of Fabio Angiolini, a handsome and colorful *geometra* from Siena who had served as Cetona's town *geometra* and had connections everywhere.

A *geometra* is a cross between a surveyor and an architect of record, which requires understanding building and drawing, but, equally important, an ability to politick and negotiate. Smart, persuasive, and a generational Senese, capable of gauging when it's time for a joke or, conversely, a veiled threat, Fabio had the abilities for the job.

I am not sure what lucky encounter brought us Fabio, but, in our case, he did whatever was necessary to get the drawings for the house approved, secure the permits, and choose the people who would do good work without gouging us. It's important to say that Dad had a distinct appreciation for Cetona's place and history, and hence his ambitions for the house were respectful of its origins and context. He did not aspire to undo or updo, but rather to reproduce a house as might have been in 1365, when it was first thought to have been built. That required, nonetheless, a bit of ingenuity here and there, and Fabio was endlessly resourceful. It was a combination of my father's architectural integrity and Fabio's savoir-faire that led to the house that it became.

The contractor Fabio preferred and recommended was Ugo Rossi, a decent man from Piazze with crystal blue eyes and jovial, humble ways. Every time we went to Cetona to check on the work we visited with Ugo on the site and spent time with his family at their home, his wife always offering coffee or vinsanto or cookies or something.

— *Per Natale, per Natale si finisce!* Ugo promised my parents. For Christmas we will finish! For Christmas!

Since Paul and I were still in school in Cremona, sometimes Dad traveled to Cetona by himself, on the train, to meet with workers and oversee matters. When he returned he brought with him baskets full of cherries and pears and vegetables, some gifted and some our own. On the property were beautiful cherry trees, a lush pear tree, peaches, walnuts, chestnuts, and, naturally, olive trees. But most often we went along, and we stayed at the Pietreto or at the Pensione Alma, a little inn in town. On Sundays we had breakfast at the Bar Cavour, sitting inside on the worn plastic chairs surrounded by workers talking and reading the paper and smoking. We had cappuccino and pastries and the Italian *succhi di frutta*, the fruit juices in tiny bottles. Apricot was always my favorite. At the time, the Bar Cavour was owned by Giulio Bussolotti, a tall, balding, friendly man who was involved in the Communist politics of the town, and the bar attracted the men and the workers of the town whose faces and hellos escorted me through my upbringing and youth—the likes of the mayor, Aldo Giuliacci, a short but charismatic man who often rode through town on horseback who'd hang out there, too, and talk politics.

Just steps away, tucked in an alley off the piazza, was our favorite place to eat, the Osteria Vecchia, run by Graziella and Dino. It was the only restaurant in town, except for the Pietreto, and from its tiny smoke-filled kitchen with blackened walls, Graziella, dark-haired and resilient, with a kind smile, delivered the fare of kings. Graziella and Dino had acquired the restaurant to escape the suffering of the land, a recurrent theme we came to discover in Cetona's history, and they had made it their survival and a source of joy and pride, too. Graziella's specialty was old-country Tuscan food—*tagliatelle al sugo di fegato, panzanella, coniglia alla bracia, crostini coi fegatini, la bieta, crostata di melecotogne*—food that, for the most part, has been since supplanted by more refined, fastidious versions.

And there we sat, at the long, rustic tables in the shady and fragrant cobblestone courtyard, lingering well into the afternoon over the many abundant courses, listening to Zio tell memorable stories about the war and his lovers and his concerts. Dino patiently brought more wine and their son, Stefano, ran about. Finally, with the shadows lengthening, Graziella would come outside to say thank you and bid us goodbye.

I have been here a few weeks now and I am working through a humbling process of rediscovery, full of unsettling trepidation in some ways and comforting reassurance in others.

Growing up in a town like Cetona means you know almost everyone, and those you do not know personally, you know *of,* and most everyone knows *of* you—and certainly that is the case for me. It's always been so, perhaps because of my parents being American, and perhaps because of the love and attachment I have felt since I was brought here and that has always caused me to return.

Yet, after many years of being away the confidence I might have had in memory has slackened. Fear has settled in, and a bit of tentativeness and shyness. Will they know me, I wonder sometimes, and does it matter?

Of course, they will, and of course, it does; I just need to trust in it again.

At this point, in addition to my closest friends, I have greeted most everyone in town who I have known all my life—the people you will meet and read about in the coming pages. Those are the people I have seen on every visit home, whose news I have known and who have kept up with me to some degree either directly or through the grapevine. We have talked on the phone and written. There is no awkwardness there; just normal affection. I celebrate them and feel celebrated and welcomed.

— *Bentornata!* they say, hugging me. Welcome home! How long are you staying?

I have also begun to say hello to people who over the years have become vague simply by lack of contact or knowledge—a form of fuzziness due to time and space. Some are my age, and we grew up together, but I have lost track of them; some are older—people who over the years have become elderly, with a past now indistinct, in some cases nearly forgotten. *Was that the little lady who owned the vegetable garden above our house,* I think to myself. *Wasn't she the one who lost a son in a car wreck?* Slowly, as I stay longer and see them more often, we rekindle the knowledge of one another. We look at each other in a store, then we break the ice and chat for a minute waiting in line. We ask each other about our work or families, and slowly the hesitation falls away, leaving space for familiarity to grow back like new skin.

And then in Cetona there are those people whose faces are familiar but whose story or even whose name I have never known. That is common even to the most ingrained of Cetonesi—to know someone *di vista*, by sight, but to know nothing of them other than passing gossip. To not really *know* them. I have committed to change that and to use my time here to get to know people again. It is unusual in Cetona to introduce oneself—or to introduce others, for that matter—yet I have started doing that, reminding people of my name and asking them theirs. I am surprised, and happy, that people remember me and my name, though chagrinned when I have forgotten theirs.

Some people come up to me tentatively, not sure if I remember them, or if it's even me.

— *Ma te sei la Sibilla?* Are you Sibilla?

This gladdens me and reassures me, which I need.

Yet, at moments I feel deeply skittish and I walk around guardedly like a spooked cat. The intimacy requires a new kind of shedding, of baring, of letting go. Besides, partly I don't know how to relate even to myself here. The sureties that across the ocean make me confident are shaky now.

Ottavia, together with Maria and Tullia—my longest-standing and evenly cultivated girlfriend relationships through time and distance—check up on me. They meet me in the piazza for an *aperitivo,* they call me, or they call up at me from under my windows, which brings me running, and smiling.

— *Com'è?* Maria asks, assessing my eyes. How is it?

I don't need to say anything at all. Tears pool, sometimes in joy, sometimes in anguish. What will happen, I ask?

— *Datti un attimo di tempo, Sibilla,* she says, hugging me. Give yourself time.

Maria is, still, my lifeline here, the intuitive reader of my moods and unspoken emotions. I have called Maria "Topo," an abbreviation of Topolino, or Mickey Mouse, since childhood, when her round face, soft, rounded features, and innate *simpatia* earned her likeness with the cartoon character.

Maria is lovely, of medium-height and lean build, with warm brown eyes and full lips that open into a sexy, generous smile. Her signature feature is a mane of wildly curly brown hair that lends flair and conspicuousness to her look and that in our youth lent her an aura of specialness and high maintenance. When we were teenagers our group spent afternoons waiting for Maria to wash and dry her hair so we could go dancing or riding around, a fact that reinforced Maria's already claimed position as princess of our tribe and of her family. She liked to sleep late and take her time, and all of us growing up knew and respected (or resented) this. We waited for her always, nonetheless, because she was very cute.

Partly because she was somewhat nihilistic and uncommitted well into her twenties, which she openly admits, and partly because she could—she was born into an indulgent and kind family of prudent landowners—Maria lived a life of mostly leisure at home with her parents, babysitting part of her time and devoting the rest to a series of boyfriends, including some dear friends of ours. Finally, though, in her late thirties she bought a *profumeria*, a cosmetic store, on the piazza, learned how to run a business, and kept it successfully for ten years.

Unfortunately, the recession forced her to close the store, and finally, in her late forties, she married Lauro, a strong-willed, ropy electrician we have all known a lifetime, a mercurial, smart guy who calls it as he sees it and who challenges her and complements her. They moved in together and finally bought a house, fulfilling at least in part her longstanding dream of marrying and having a family of her own. Maria's father has since died, and Maria spends much of her time taking care of her mother, who in recent years has begun to lose her memory. Maria has met this demand with endurance, even-handedness, and patience that might not have been portended years ago and that I admire.

Maria is sweet, a bit temperamental, loyal, stubborn, and deeply protective of her feelings—a lovely mess of closure and openness who through the years has given me the comfort of armies. We are bonded inexorably, though our temperaments and approaches to the world are different and our intersecting love lives have, occasionally in the past, threatened our friendship. Its survival enriched us with humor and resilience, and a badge of sisterhood. We love each other, really, unconditionally at this point. With me she listens and she stands by me, and most often makes me laugh with her vernacular, bottom-line take on things, accompanied by unvarnished facial expressions. She is the only girlfriend who has come to see me in America, not once but four times. She has seen my homes there, eaten the food I cook, and seen me dress and go to work.

— *Come ti senti?* she asks, seeking the truth, not a simple answer. She makes herself available for a long answer if needed, even if her car is parked on the side of the road or in a tow zone in the piazza. She knows this is not easy.

I don't know how I feel here, and I miss ... I miss what I left behind.

Tears stream down my face. I wouldn't cry with anyone else now, but there is no one in the world it feels better to cry with.

And then there is Tullia, my most free-spirited friend.

Tullia is a school teacher, smart and competent. She has thick, glossy black hair cut at her shoulders that curls around her face softly. She has a friendly round face with a small baby-doll mouth and round green eyes most often hidden behind matter-of-fact glasses but every now and then showcased fashionably with black eyeliner.

A native Roman, vivacious and gregarious, Tullia is my live-and-let-live friend in the truest sense. Five years older than me, she moved here as a teenager with her family when her parents decided to leave Rome and buy the Bar Sport. Another notorious late-sleeper (until she became a school teacher), Tullia had to work the morning shift at the bar, a fact that she hated and caused her to hate life itself for several years. She used to ride a motorcycle—the only girl I had ever known to do that, which impressed me—and she didn't like Cetona at all. That is when we became friends.

Tullia speaks in streams of words that rush and surge, particularly when something captures her passion or about which she has developed a strong opinion, and at those times it is nearly impossible to get a word in edgewise. She is a quick read of situations and non-judgmental—at least with me. She likes to see light in things, and is funny, with a flowing low laugh, a strong Roman accent, and a gravelly voice from unrepentant smoking.

Tullia is married to Duccio, a good-looking guy with long dark hair and bronze skin, a gaming parlor attendant now—he lost a long-standing job in a shoe factory in the recession—and he and Tullia have a daughter, Sofia, who is in her teens. Tullia is immersed in Cetona's politics—on the left, obviously—as is her brother, a former mayor, and once she starts talking politics she will never stop, though in conversation with me these days she eases quickly into Cetona and how I am adjusting.

— *Non mi di' che ti sei già annoiata!* she asks, hugging me and kissing me. Are you already bored?

Tullia, Ottavia, and Maria watch over me tenderly, a bit concerned. Will I make it, and for how long? Will I crumble and go back? How will I fit? Will my heart be broken?

For now it's unclear. Meanwhile, I look out, studying this little town whose rhythms and faces, streets and colors, I have missed so deeply and I hunger to know anew.

Having windows on the piazza has stopped bothering me, and, in fact, it comforts me. I have begun to find company in the faces and the movements I see each time I look out. The guys at Le ACLI, and others, have started waving at me every time they see me in the window, and I enjoy waving back. It is a privilege I had forgotten, this love.

Looking out and exploring, I realize that many things have eluded me in my visits back over the decades, my attention scattered among so many things, my emotions torn with barely enough time to recover between arrival and departure. Now I am noticing everything—starting right here in the piazza, which, I regret, has so changed.

Some years ago, the town administration decided to pave the piazza in white stone and close it to vehicular traffic to preserve the historic character of the town. As a result, there is no driving in the piazza, and, with the exception of a handful of short-term parking spaces scattered here and there and allotted for a quick coffee or an errand, parking has been moved to lots around the edges of town. In addition, only people who live in the historic section can drive there by circling in a treacherous circuit behind the piazza.

The decision to close the piazza sparked acrimonious controversy at the time, and it still has not subsided—and in fact, the town may be about to revisit the whole matter in what promises to be a historic showdown. Opinions are split mostly along party lines: People on the left, loyal to the administration, favor the closing, which, they argue, allows unimpeded pedestrian ease and preserves the town's quality of life. Opponents on the other side argue it makes access more difficult for the elderly, and, generally speaking, it discourages people from coming into the piazza, thus cutting off bustle and commerce. Or maybe it just makes access more difficult for their own purposes.

From my perspective, the immense unadorned whiteness of the stone, desert-like without a tree or a flower pot, makes the piazza look empty, huge, and incongruous, particularly in fall and winter. The traffic route behind the piazza is chaotic and dangerous, and making matters worse, the few parking spaces at the ends of the piazza are poorly placed and unsightly, and all this gets people riled up one way or the other.

— *Ci hanno fatto un museo di 'sta piazza, ma non è un museo! Ci si vive qui noi!* says a friend irately, joining his hands in exasperated prayer. They made a museum out of the piazza, but it is not a museum! We live here!

Aside from the paving—which is the single greatest change the piazza has seen since the end of the war other than the death of the *tiglio*—a few new stores have popped up over the years and some have changed hands. There is a bakery, under new ownership. I don't know them yet, but the bread is good. A realtor has opened shop in the old *cartoleria*. Of course, the *lattaia* closed many years ago, when fresh milk went out of style, and that store has long been shuttered. The beauty shop has changed ownership, as has the butchery. The shoe store is still a shoe store but under new ownership; Maria Letizia's clothing store has moved into Lavinia's old grocery store; our friend Sabina opened her clothing store in the old tobacco shop, then moved it again, to Pino's; a jewelry store opened, as did, incredibly, a tiny book store which, not surprisingly, struggles to survive. Maria's *profumeria* has been replaced by the new florist, Vasilika, and, all said, a few storefronts sit empty.

Up Via Roma, Gustavo's butchery has become a fur and accessory store, and next to it are another clothing store, a hairdresser, and the Della Vignas' *cantina*, which sells and serves wine, cheeses, and prosciutto. What used to be Lelia's clothing shop, and then became my friend Allegra's, has long been a vegetable store, run by Mercede and her daughter. Above their shop is an apartment where Garibaldi himself, during his cross-country crusade to unify Italy, spent one night, a historic event that gave Cetona's piazza—and, similarly, that of many other towns—its name.

Somewhat changed from when I was growing up are the handful of commercial activities that sit sprinkled on the roads heading out of town. The town's largest supermarket, called the Simply, sits a few steps outside of the piazza, toward Sarteano, which forced the closure of all but one little grocery in the piazza, and a few stores have sprouted down Via Remo Cacioli, in the opposite direction: Federica the hairdresser; the *merceria*, which sells bras, ribbons, stockings and baby clothes, owned by my childhood friend Ausilia; the bustling bakery of my childhood friend Leonardo; and Antonello's take-out store, where people stop to buy take-out food if they are too late to cook lunch, which in itself is a curious development.

Lastly, heading out of town one finds Signor Bozzini's antique shop, where, lacking business, Bozzini can be seen from the window, glasses perched atop his head, accounting book open before him, napping soundly at his desk.

My senses can barely make up for the hunger of all I have missed—the sight of Cetona and the rhythms of a day that make up the tender heartbeat of this town.

Today I opened my shutters to a stunning dawn. I wished I were in the country, with the view of the mountain, but the sky is extraordinary nonetheless. It is already late fall and morning is getting sleepier. It is crisp and a bit chilly, and the piazza is hushed.

Yet, a few of the retirees who make up the piazza's most assiduous residents are already out, standing under my windows, talking. As my window clangs they look up with mild interest. Someone waves, then quickly they resume their conversation. I have become old hat already, for which I am exhilarated, and they move their gaze toward the end of the piazza to see who might be coming.

I make tea and lean out to take in the sun rising behind the church. The light is soft like the petals of a First Lady rose. The bells chime seven and the first workers approach the bars. I watch as a few of the town's most active elderly come for their first walk around the piazza, which marks the beginning of their day. Not long after, the piazza's storekeepers roll up their portcullises and unlock their doors, straightening the storefronts and readying for the day.

Before nine, our friend Sabina opens her clothing store, across from my windows, and lets out Mixo, a spunky, sweet gray-and-white cat that she adopted after Maria closed her store and Mixo was left homeless. He is now the piazza's cat, a nomad. He jumps on the bench and Sabina pets him. The light of the early sun dusts her blond curls, and she is smiling. Then she shoos Mixo away and goes into the store; she comes back out with bucket and cleaning supplies and begins to wash her store windows.

Stefano, who owns the tobacco and newspaper store at the end of the piazza, walks through on his way to get coffee and stops to talk with Sabina. As I wave at them, the town workers arrive in their Ape—the ubiquitous Italian three-wheeled vehicle—and fluorescent uniforms and start sweeping the piazza with the long-handled brooms. I am relieved they don't have leaf blowers. A few minutes later they will fan out through town and its countryside, some to patch potholes or cut grass, some to steer the town's garbage trucks awkwardly through the narrow streets.

Amato pulls up with his green-and-silver pickup and parks illegally, straddling the sidewalk, something I am learning he does every day. Amato, in his late sixties, I would guess, is the middle brother of Alano and Adelfo, a flirtatious duo I have known all my life—Alano a woodworker and Adelfo our old plumber. Amato is the lesser known of the brothers to me, but he has a playful smile, lingering good looks, and a respectful manner, and since my arrival he has greeted me and spoken to me kindly.

Today he is wearing his olive green jacket over a white button-down shirt and jeans. He pulls up on his pants as he walks toward the other men and he joins them, leaning against a truck. His white hair sparkles in the morning sun and he looks handsome. Judging from the time he spends in the piazza—he is a widower and his children are grown—we will become good friends: I could tell time by the presence of his pickup if we didn't have the bells of the school marking every half hour.

Vasilika, the florist, arrives. Blonde, with a pale, pretty face, she is a young woman from Romania who came here to follow an Italian man she met in her country. I had never met her before, but I like her already; I introduced myself and she is gregarious and friendly. Twice a week now I watch her unload bunches of fresh flowers into her store, under my window.

Children heading to our old elementary school at the end of the piazza trickle through the streets with their book bags bouncing on their backs and their blue uniforms—no longer black and white now, an Italian nod to gender equality. Dino, of the old Osteria, walks Giuseppe and Filippo, his grandchildren. I watch them intently—I am glad to see my friends' children, to have this time to get to know them—and Giuseppe looks up and yells, *Ciao Sibilla!!* They are getting to know me for the first time and I wave, smiling.

I like to paint or write early in the morning, in the soft light near the window. I have placed my new easel there, which came to me courtesy of Anna Maria Costantini, an eccentric, friendly painter with a bushy head of curly hair who has a studio at the entrance to the piazza. I have known her, her husband, and her parents as background characters all of my life, but with no more than a passing acquaintance.

Recently, though, Anna Maria and I had a meaningful encounter: I was standing at the end of piazza talking with an elderly man in town, leaning against his Ape in the sunshine, when Anna Maria, in her white smock, walked over to ask if he could move an old TV for her.

The man said he couldn't lift anything due to a back injury, so I volunteered. Anna Maria looked at me without recognition, then we shook hands and I told her my name.

— *Certo che ti ricordo! E tuo fratello?* she said. Of course, I remember you! And how is your brother?

She led me upstairs and I picked up the TV and took it downstairs to her studio. She was going to take it apart to use it as a box, or something or the other. After I moved the television I asked Anna Maria if she knew where I might find an easel to borrow or rent. I need an easel, I recognize, like I need a computer.

I started painting about ten years ago, during my relationship with Aram. I had decided to give away my wedding shoes—which I wore years ago on a beautiful July day here in Cetona—and I had put them by the front door of my house in Charleston to take them to a friend's store, Lee Magar, a famous hat maker who sews beautiful things. She would sell them, she said.

But the shoes, pearl patent leather by Bruno Magli, sat there for weeks, in silent protest. I couldn't bring myself to give them away until I had somehow celebrated them and commemorated the occasion for which they had come into my life. On a whim, I bought a pad of drawing paper, an ink pen and a box of colored pencils, and one evening I put the shoes on the kitchen counter and drew them and colored them with pale yellow pencil. This launched me into painting and a new world opened for me. I have since moved from shoes to portraits of chickens and roosters—mostly my own birds, which I also started raising shortly thereafter—and now, in Cetona, I hope to move to the exploration of new things, other birds, townscapes, and people. Paintings of my place.

When I voiced the question about the easel, Anna Maria smiled mischievously and disappeared down a set of stairs. She reemerged a few minutes later carrying an old country easel, rickety but standing.

— *Tieni, questo è un cavalletto di campagna! Ne ha viste tante! Te lo presto volentieri!* she said, handing it to me. This is an old country easel. It's seen a lot, but I'll loan it to you happily!

I thanked her gratefully and promised to bring it back sometime.

— *Non ti preoccupare, tienilo quanto ti pare!* she said, and she gave me a hug. Don't worry, keep it as long as you want!

I like being near the window to paint, for light, though it causes me a good amount of distraction as I hear all the cars and people come and go out of the corner of my eye. I turn every few seconds, curious. There is a constant and joyous sound as people cross under my window saluting each other.

— *Ciaooooooooo, ciaoooooooooo!!! Buon giornooooooo! Come vaaaaaa? Bellllllaaaaaaaaaaaa!*

I hear Tatiana, a Romanian immigrant who takes care of an elderly woman my memory struggles to place. She is one of the new caretakers—*badanti*, as they are called— who have come from foreign countries to watch over the elderly of the town, a job nobody else wants. Tall, with short, straight black hair, Tatiana has rosy cheeks and a shrill voice that wakes the dead.

— *L'ha' preso il caffèeeeeeee?* she yells at someone while walking. Have you had coffee yet?

Through the early hours of the morning the piazza is at its busiest: trucks delivering goods, salespeople bustling about, construction workers going for a *caffè corretto*, the president of the bank rushing somewhere, ladies shopping for lunch, new mothers pushing their babies in strollers.

When not busy, the merchants of the piazza linger in the doorways chatting with passers-by or they sit on benches outside their stores. The butcher, Osvaldo, leans against his storefront watching the cars, waiting for customers, as does Franco, a friendly white-haired man who since my last return has come to own the hardware store, now fully stocked with expensive furniture and lighting fit for the foreigners furnishing their new houses and apartments in town.

With a final sweep of the piazza, of which I cannot get enough—I could sit here all day and watch and wave!—it's time to retreat to my work. I approach my computer, sitting on a table in the dining room-now-office, and I look out my side window, which opens onto the alley behind my house, leading from the piazza to my door.

There, barely ten feet from me I see the face of an elderly woman, her hair as white as snow, set against the backdrop of her dark kitchen. Her face lit as a Madonna is nearly stuck to the panes of her window.

I learn, over the ensuing days, that she is the mother of our old middle-school secretary, Enzo. She is elderly now—imagine, she was in her twenties when the Allies arrived in Cetona—and her window is her lookout on life. Every time I come out of the house and into the alley she waves at me and smiles, kindly and near toothlessly, and I look up and wave back.

It is our daily routine now.

In cold and damp weather, when the piazza is dreary and there is no place to go, a number of Cetona's older men find shelter in Armando's vegetable store, next to the Bar Cavour.

Most regular among them are Amato, the gentlemanly retired construction worker with sparkling silver hair and handsome features; Amedeo, a chatty retired agricultural machine salesman, balding and friendly; Adelio, short and courteous, a retired game warden who I have known since I was a kid; and Renato, a white-haired lifelong bachelor who walks with a cane and wears ascots, and who I also have known for a long time.

In Armando's store, dank and smelling of vegetable cuttings and fruit, bonded by the shared space and rhythm of this tiny town, these men gather to gossip, laugh, and banter, or, lacking in subjects, which is rather rare, to sit in silence and watch people come in and out, which usually also provides them with something to say. When the weather is nice, the group moves to the bench outside the store, which affords a more interesting view of people crossing the piazza and fresher news to talk about.

Armando had not owned his store here on my most recent visits, but it's not taken much to make up for the lost time. The others have told him all they know of my life here, and now that I have been back awhile, when I walk into the store, whether they are inside or out, the men pause to greet me more or less gregariously, a combination of shyness and affection, familiarity and reserve. They look me over, ask how I'm doing—if I've been running, if I've settled in—and sometimes they answer the random question I have, which generally leads to some kind of conversation.

Armando himself is a bearded, strongly built man from outside Rome with darting black eyes, a theatrical personality and a penchant for proverbs, funny sayings and stories. In his mid-fifties, he is fit, with dark skin and strong hands, and he fashions himself as a bit of a Lothario. When he was young he enlisted in the seminary, but they expelled him because he was pursuing the priest's niece, a story he likes to tell. Whenever you go in the store, unless he's in the doorway chatting Armando is busy cleaning, trimming, and culling his fruits and vegetables, separating the good from the bad and peeling things like *puntarelle*, tedious chicory tips that are popular around Rome. He seems rather meticulous about his produce, yet—and he would be offended to even consider this—he doesn't quite meet muster with the more finicky housekeepers and cooks in town, who, it seems, bypass his store and head to Mercede's, at the end of the piazza.

Mercede, blonde and persnickety, has been in business for forty years and is the recognized produce master of Cetona, though for many years I avoided her store because of her gossip and malice, traits I tested on my own skin quite a few times in my youth. I don't like the idea of people talking about others the minute they step out the door, though the men at Armando's do a fine job of that themselves, I am sure.

On this stay, however, I have decided to let bygones be bygones—Mercede and I have since greeted each other more or less warmly—and to patronize all stores equally, which gives me freer rein when I go perusing for vegetables in what is an already scantier market: Here there are no tomatoes in December, no oranges or broccoli in summer, no kiwi in fall—neither at Mercede's nor at Armando's. So, I go wherever my mood takes me, to check out who has what.

Sometimes Armando amuses me. He is averse to organic—he says it's propaganda designed to ruin small farmers—and he pouts if you tell him that he sold you a mealy apple. His service is slow, too, particularly if he is busy joking around and particularly with female customers he likes. You have to listen to a story every time you go in there, another habit I have lost—stories. Yet, Armando's are often good; besides, he is closest to my house, I like the guys who hang out there, he sells an odd mix of things I like, including good fresh ginger, avocados, dried figs and apricots, and he flirts with me and says all sorts of slightly inappropriate and generally hilarious things that always give me a good laugh. He is truly *simpatico*.

The other day I was sitting outside the Bar Cavour when Armando, standing in his doorstep, yelled after Tatiana, the *badante*.

*— Ti sei dimenticata le zucchine!* he said. You left your zucchini here!

I can tell he already knows the answer.

*— Perché erano moscie!* she answered shrilly, turning back with a flirtatious smile. Because they were limp!

*Moscio* is also the term used for a limp penis, and the double-entendre was not lost on the card players at the tables at Bar Cavour or the men sitting on the bench outside Armando's store whose ears perked up on cue. They laughed.

Amato smirked quietly—too reserved to comment on such a topic, I am learning—and Giovanni, known as Nanni, laughed heartily.

Among the men who hang out at Armando's most regularly, Nanni is the man I have known the longest, dating back to our first days here, when our house was not yet finished. The contractor promised to be done by Christmas, and since Dad was still completing his apprenticeship in Cremona, Paul, Mom, and I moved to Cetona in fall for the start of school.

Donna, an organist and a beloved friend of my parents who also had gone to school at Eastman and who had studied with Zio, offered us the tiny vacation house she had recently bought in Patarnione, a hamlet about five kilometers from town, little more than a cluster of houses and, up the hill, a small piazza nestled around a tree and a drinking fountain. Donna's was a lovely little stone house with a cozy kitchen, a living room flooded with sunlight, a terrace, and a secluded garden. In the warmth and comfort of summer and spring, it was a beautiful place to be, but in winter, like many houses in Cetona, it was brutally cold and damp, especially back when plumbing and heating systems were rudimentary, which they were for decades. Upstairs there was no heat other than the fireplace, and downstairs, where we slept, was a kerosene furnace that spewed lethal fumes and barely heated.

That late fall in Cetona the weather was dreary and rainy and the house was numbingly cold. Hot water was in short supply, and when Mom did the laundry and hung it out to dry it froze on the line, my skinny little jeans and shirts looking like stick people swaying in the wind. In the early mornings Mom got us up and took us to school, shouldering the cold and the rain up and down the muddy road leading into town.

Once, in November or early December, it snowed heavily. Mom, in good American can-do spirit, got us up and into the car and braved the storm to make sure we got to school. She didn't want us to be the foreigners who missed. We got to town and school had been cancelled, and on our way back we got stuck halfway up the hill, unable to get traction in the sleet and mud. Finally, a farmer who lived in a nearby house came outside and helped us push the car back up the hill and home safely. He waved as he walked back down the hill, and I imagine tears welling in my mom's eyes, as they often did in those days out of gratitude for people's small acts of kindness.

I think back with great empathy and love for my mother, who, in her late thirties, had transitioned from Chicago to Cetona. She was alone with us, barely speaking the language, knowing nearly nobody, making her way into a new life in this foreign village with little to do, sliding up and down unfamiliar muddy roads, with no phone, no television, no heat, and Dad off learning a new art and a new career. A lot to manage.

The people of Patarnione—about a dozen in all—took a curious but kind interest in our lives and a particular liking to my brother and me. In the afternoons after school I sat outside to warm myself in the sun with Argilia, a kind-hearted elderly lady with twinkly periwinkle eyes who lived with her husband in a house across from ours. She'd sit knitting or simply looking out, with me reading beside her. If I was hungry Argilia kindly retrieved from her kitchen a slice of bread with the sticky-thick, brown plum marmalade she had made the previous summer. She gave Mom eggs from their chickens, their olive oil, garlic, and vegetables from their garden.

But back to Giovanni, the neighbor who lived adjacent to Donna's house was Clemenzia, a hefty woman with fat rosy cheeks, a broad forehead, and stubbly whiskers. She wore big layered house dresses for her work out in the field and always a kerchief over her hair. She walked with a heavy foot and talked with a booming voice that would wake up the dead and that preannounced her arrival long before she appeared coming up the street, talking loudly with this neighbor or that.

Clemenzia adored Donna, and, by extension, our family, and this manifested every time she saw me and she grabbed ahold of me with her big arms and covered my face with wet kisses. Then she buried my head in her huge breasts that smelled like country and held me tight, nearly lifting me off my feet. Though I knew she was being loving, I squeamishly ran from her clasp, though not nearly as much as I did from the sight of her son, Giovanni.

Poor Nanni—none of it was his fault! Ironically called *Giovannino* at the time, Nanni was a hulking man, with broad shoulders and massive arms that, as a young girl, seemed to tower above me. He had (and still has) huge hands, which he interlaces behind his back when he walks, his gait slow and deliberate, a bit bow-legged and now labored by time and age.

But Nanni's most prominent feature was and remains a big, red, watery eye, a remnant of an old injury, which, when I was a child, reminded me of legends of Polyphemus. When I saw this giant emerging slowly from his tiny car or making his way up the road with his slow, arduous steps, I ran inside or tried to make myself as small as possible. No matter how kind-natured he was, he terrified me, and this childish fear lingered years later, as a teenager and, even, I am ashamed to say, into adulthood.

Until now. On this stay I decided to change that and, luckily for me, he seems amenable.

— *Buon giorno, Giovanni,* I say walking into Armando's store on a recent morning. I like to look at him directly now, in the eyes.

— *Buon giorno, Sibilla!* he says emphatically and smiles.

*— Giovanni, ma lei vive ancora nella vecchia casa a Patarnione?* I ask, addressing him formally. Do you still live in the old house at Patarnione?

*— Eh, certo che sì!!* Most surely, he says, asking me then to address him informally.

I smile and he smiles back.

There are a million reasons for me to be here, and I confirm a good one almost every day.

Today from my windows I saw Bruno, who, with his wife, Adelina, worked for Zio and Zia many years ago.

He walks in short tentative steps now, and he looks old and a bit lost. He was getting in his car, an old blue Fiat, which made me do some quick math and wonder if he should still be driving. As he left the piazza, the car mooed under the straining gears and everyone at that end made room and stopped to watch.

I felt sad watching him go. Years flashed before me—the years since I ran with Adelina.

In a way, Bruno and Adelina *are* Cetona and my childhood here, of the purest, most foundational kind. They are everything about a time and a place that no longer exist.

Bruno and Adelina lived in a house adjacent to Zio and Zia's, and perhaps they had lived on the property before Zio and Zia bought it and merely agreed to stay on. Their house was small—a plain bathroom, two small rudimentary rooms in the back, and the kitchen, onto which the front door opened. The floor was tiled in gray, with an occasional flower here and there.

When we first came to Cetona to visit Zio and Zia on weekends, and later, when we already lived there and visited with them, I would quickly say hello, then round the house to knock on Bruno and Adelina's door.

— *Permesso?* I'd say, knocking then turning the key that never left the door. *La chiave sulla porta,* they say here—the key in the door—an image that conveys a trust and a time now gone.

— *Vieni!!! Vieeeeeniii!!* Adelina yelled when she heard me. Come in, come in!

Their house was plainly furnished. In the middle of the kitchen simple wood-and-straw chairs—made by hand in the old tradition—surrounded a small table covered by a worn plasticized tablecloth. On top of it was a small bowl of salt. There was a sink, a *madia*—a common piece of furniture where farmers keep their dishes, baked goods, and other food items—and a small TV atop a table off in a corner. A Madonna and a cross hung on the wall, each with a red votive, and a picture of the pope.

A window almost too small to look out of was shaded by a white lace curtain hanging from a simple iron rod, and in a dark corner hung a prosciutto and sometimes a string of sausages.

Dominating the kitchen was the *stufa*, an ingenious and heavy wood-burning cast iron stove that was—and remains, in many old country houses in Cetona—the main source of heat in winter as well as the main appliance for cooking. A *stufa* has multiple and sometimes mysterious compartments and drawers for gathering coals, heating water, and for baking. Atop it are a series of concentric rings that can be removed to feed the fire and accommodate various sizes of pots and pans. With a constantly running *stufa* you can bake, cook, boil water, have a full heating fire, and nurture coals all at the same time, and this acquires urgency in houses where there is no other source of heat or energy for cooking,

In winter Adelina fed the *stufa* all day at regular intervals so it would never go out, and at night before bedtime she drew from it the coals to heat the bed. Opening a small drawer into the bowels of the *stufa*, she shoveled red coals into small metal buckets; then, carrying them carefully into the bedroom, she hung them on hooks from something called *il prete* (the priest), a wooden contraption shaped like a 3D ellipse that, carefully positioned under the bedcovers, allows for the bed to be warmed without catching the sheets on fire. In winter in old houses in Cetona the *prete* was the salvation, and perhaps that is how it got its name—or because priests were in everybody's beds!

Adelina also cooked dinner on the *stufa*, juggling the constantly changing temperatures, every now and then opening a drawer or removing some rings to throw in a piece of wood. If the stovetop got too hot she shifted her small enamel pans and pots to the side, moving them back to the middle minutes later. The house always smelled like burning wood and cured meats, even in summer when the front door was left open to the breeze drifting from the fields in bloom.

Adelina was thin with bushy curly hair that sprung out in rebellious snippets from the flowered handkerchief she always wore on her head. Through the years I saw her hair go from dark brown to salt and pepper—when we met her she was in her early forties, I think—but, for as long as I can remember, it was dusty and full of twigs and leaves, much like the skirt, her sweaters, and the gray opaque stockings she wore to the fields, bundled up against the winter wind.

Adelina had the reserve and humility of country people who are bred to know their place—the unhappy world of rank that colored the Italian countryside. But once you broke through that perceived boundary, and as a child I did not know it or acknowledge it, Adelina shared herself, trusting and funny. She had a ready, clean smile and a throaty mischievous laugh. She liked to get right in your face, to look at you closely as if she were inspecting you. When she was happy her smile rose from deep within her. Her green eyes sparkled like emeralds against her dark skin, worn rugged by her man-like work and the constant wear of the sun.

Whether in the pastures, the stalls or the barn, the vineyard, the olive grove, the fields of wheat or Zio's vegetable garden, Adelina was out there from sunrise to sundown, seven days a week, year-round. If she was working somewhere within reach of the house, when she saw us coming in our car she'd look up, slowly put us in focus, and walk quickly toward us, smiling. Always, she hugged us and greeted us like we had gifted her a welcome surprise. Adelina smelled like a poem of animals and fields, dirt and flowers, mixed with the wind.

— *Sibu! Venghi, pichina!* she'd say as I got out of the car, leading me off by the shoulder. Come along, little one, come along.

Sibu was Adelina's version of my name, an affectionate abbreviation of Sibilla tempered by what she heard my parents call me, Sybil, and Zia, Sybbi. Adelina spoke a language that to me, in the process of minting a new Italian, was mysterious and foreign. It was unadulterated Cetonese, a mix between Latin, a Tuscan vernacular with a lot of abbreviations and dropped endings, and a lot of strange guttural sounds. Yet, through time I listened so that when I was with her I could speak like her. It didn't take long for Zia to say that I was speaking Cetonese *alla contadina* like Adelina—like a farmer—and for many years I considered that a badge of honor.

When I was with her, Adelina went about her work as usual, making the rounds of the property to check on what needed to be done and who needed to be fed. She talked the whole time, a bit to me and a bit to herself, me following along like a loyal stray dog in tennis shoes and pants. I helped her feed the chickens and went with her *a fare l'erba*—to cut the grass—by hand, with sickles, for the rabbits and the horses that Zia kept. We spent a lot of time cutting grass, Adelina teaching me to hold the sickle properly so as to not cut my legs off.

Work around the farm, of course, changed all the time. In summer, the vegetable garden—the *orto*—was a priority: it needed to be watered and weeded, and the vegetables needed to be picked, hauled back to the house, and preserved. The fruit needed to be picked and made into jams and, a bit later, the corn and garlic needed to be braided and hung to dry. In September, the grapes needed to be picked, and in November the olives. In December, after Bruno had tilled the fields with the tractor—when we first moved there they tilled by oxen still— they had to be seeded, and I helped Adelina do this by hand. In summer, the wheat had to be harvested—by hand, with scythes—and then the corn.

It was an endless job. Then, all of a sudden she'd remember the *stufa*.

— *Uhhhhh, la stufa!! Mi si spegne la stufa! Bisogna anda' a governa' la stufa! Sibu, corri! Corriiiii!* she'd yell from the middle of a field. We have to go feed the *stufa*!! Run, run, Sibu, run!

And through the fields she ran, me in tow, up to the house to feed the *stufa*.

My favorite part of the day with Adelina was *merenda*, or snack, in the late afternoon, in her kitchen. In winter when it was cold Adelina made me tea and gave me leftover bread with sugar—sugar drizzled with hot water, sometimes with a tiny and precious piece of butter thrown on top. I huddled by the *stufa* to eat while Adelina went about the kitchen warming her hands, chapped red from the cold.

— *Magna, magna,* she'd say, in Cetonese, softly with a smile. Eat, eat.

In fall Adelina fed me bread with *marmellata* she made, most often from *melecotogne*, quinces, thick, brown and sweet, and in summer the best treat was bread with tomato. She'd pick up the big loaf of bread, hold it between her arm and her chest, and slice it toward her, upright, with a big serrated knife. Then she cut a fresh ripe tomato in half and, holding it by the skin with her fingers she rubbed it onto my slice of bread until all the red pulp and juices were out. Then she drizzled it with olive oil and a pinch of salt. It was plain and delicious, and I'd eat outside on her front step, while inside she got things ready for dinner and for Bruno's return.

Often Bruno stayed out all day, working on the tractor, in the fields, or doing things for Zio, or in Chiusi buying seed or getting a part for the tractor. Bruno was a quiet man. He walked with his head down, slowly, like an ox, enduring. Every now and then he adjusted his beret with his hand, scratching his short bristly brown hair at the same time. He drove a red Fiat 126, slowly and carefully.

In the evening when he came in the house after a day in the fields, Bruno washed up quietly, soaping his arms and his sunburnt face at the kitchen sink, and after toweling off he sat down heavily at the table, looking wearily at Adelina and rubbing his face silently. Another day toiling for others—*a tribbola'*, they say in Cetona.

While he sat, Adelina took the pots and pans from the *stufa* and served his food, then hers, quietly, on simple plates. Sometimes while they ate I sat there with them, waiting for my mom, in silence, with the fluorescent light humming above.

Finally, shortly before Christmas our house was finished.

Back in Cremona, Dad hired a small truck and David and some other friends helped load up our apartment and move south. Like a teetering moving pile of stuff, the truck lurched southward slowly on the *autostrada*, belts and tarpaulins holding it together precariously. Paul, Mom, and I, meanwhile, moved out of Donna's, and on Christmas Day we had our first meal in our house.

In the days preceding Christmas there had been a severe oil shortage in Italy, but our plumber, a wiry guy from Piazze, promised to find us enough to heat the house and cook. And he did.

Zio and Zia came with Bruno and Adelina, incredibly, and the house was warm and festive. Mom made her first homemade *fettucine*, laying them out carefully on her grand Steinway to dry, and Zio, with his usual flair and exuberance, made a delicious *zabaglione*, spiked with an extra bit of cognac for celebration.

Our house was simple but warm and inviting. The front door opened onto an oblong first floor, one large space comprised of a rather square dining room with a fireplace, and to the left, through a wide-open brick arch, a large, rectangular and sunny living room running the length of the house. Behind that lay my father's workshop, hidden by a three-quarter wall. To the sides of the fireplace and moving toward the back of the house opened a small but sunny kitchen and bathroom.

Upstairs, up flights of a wrought-iron spiral staircase made by Cetona's *fabbro*, were my parents' bedroom, with a dressing nook that had been a marble sink, then mine and my brother's, and a third floor that ultimately became another bedroom. I loved my room, separate, as it was, on its own floor, with windows facing town and Borgo, on one side, and, on the other, the vast terraced countryside and its ever-changing beauty. It was cold in winter but reassuring at every other time of the year.

But the most memorable trait of our house was its position, opening on one side to the street and the urban fabric of the town, and, on the other side, to what I have always thought was the most beautiful countryside in the world. Our large terracotta terrace, running the length of the house and onto which opened French doors from every room, gave way, on the right, to a full view of Monte Cetona, with its terraced layers cascading down from the west like hoops of a skirt, and, to the left, to the landscape running all the way to Città della Pieve and to the horizon. In totality we enjoyed one hundred and eighty degrees of singular beauty, encompassing a direct view of the sun rising over Città della Pieve and dipping behind Monte Cetona.

In the evening, from the terrace and our rooms upstairs we watched as Città della Pieve picked up the sparkle of the sun setting across the way. Rays shone in every window, ablaze—the houses, and steeples, and even the minuscule cars traveling along the cypress-lined road below the city's walls—each catching the sun and carrying it with them. For a moment the light climaxed as if the whole town were set on fire, reflecting the sun in salute.

A deeply wooded hill faced our house, kissing our property at the bottom of a series of terraced fields. At the very bottom was a tiny creek that in summer turned into a trickle and hosted suspicious tiny red worms that pooled in great numbers around the rocks. In spring, though, when the snows to the north melted, the stream swelled with gushing water, sparkling and cool, and the earth around it sprouted fresh ferns and moss and sweet, fragrant flowers. Its smell, carried by the rush of the water, was inebriating, alive and sweet to me.

I have always liked that our house was not a secluded villa outside of town but rather a living part of a street, with a personality all of its own, and it was on this street that the first roots of my love for Cetona and its people dug in.

In my youth Via Sobborgo was unpaved and heavily travelled at high speeds in spite of its narrow width and blind curves, and it was by mere dint of the peculiarly astute local driving gene that every day accidents were averted, cars coming from opposite directions skidding to a halt just inches from each other. My mother was always frazzled when this happened to her in her white Renault 4; others just told each other off with a wave of the hand and took off again at great speed.

The traffic on Borgo irked Bastiano, who lived with his wife, Costanza, and their young son, Bennato, in the first house on Borgo, coming from the piazza. Sitting at the kitchen table eating his dinner in his white undershirt, back from his day as a construction worker, beret tipped back on his balding head and, front door propped open to the fresh air, he would launch into loud tirades against the church, the pope, and modern drivers every time a car raced up Borgo, tires skidding and gravel and dust flying. His first moment of peace all day, shattered.

— *Ehhh, Madonna cagna,* he cursed loudly (untranslatable curses against the Virgin Mary), sometimes getting up from his chair and hurrying onto the porch, shaking his arm at the drivers. — *Che ti venga un colpo a te e a alla tu' mamma, Madonna avvelenita!* he'd say, wishing them a heart attack.

After adjusting his cap and yanking up on his tan work pants cinched around his slender waist by a worn leather belt, Bastiano would sit back down at the table mumbling under his breath about the changing times and the new ways of the world. He was like an adult rascal, gangly, mischievous, and fun, and always looking for the turn of the word or the hidden irony. He was a master of vernacular sayings and of *bestemmie*, typically Tuscan religious curses such as the ones above, which the Cetonesi excel in stringing together artfully and to which they contribute all their zest and imagination. I heard a particularly sweet one the other day—*Dio orso col pelo ritto sulla schiena.* Bear God with fur standing straight up on his back.

Bastiano's wife, Costanza, spent hours sweeping the dust off their front porch and trying to quiet Bastiano after his tirades about traffic on Borgo. Finally, after years of complaints, following a gathering of signatures the town paved the road and made it one way into town. My father viewed the development as misplaced progress—he wanted everything to be as unlike as possible what he left behind—but it improved the quality of life on Borgo and calmed Bastiano significantly.

Rhythm and routine marked the sounds of life on Borgo through the hours of the day, through the days of the week, and through the seasons of the year—and the years of my life. They were consistent and reliable, involving the same people and their lives, and if any of it suddenly changed it meant something had happened: someone was ill, had died, or someone was having an affair, or someone had left. Gone. And one just knows.

Even before my alarm rang for school at 6 a.m. Costanza walked past our house to feed the pigs, which they kept in sties just a short way down the hill as Via Sobborgo curves along the eastern edge of town and strikes out into the fields and toward Piazze. The heftiness of her steps, the way they reverberated against the walls, indicated she was carrying a heavy load—two huge buckets of slop and sometimes some plastic bags of trimmings, too. Medium-sized, Costanza was a bundle of muscle. She had sculpted arms and shoulders that she wore proudly with sleeveless tops; her shapely calves protruded at the hem of her housedress, nearly always in a pattern of flowers, followed by heavy work boots, and in summer, sensible flat sandals. She had a high-pitched voice and wore small rectangular glasses; her high rosy cheeks were framed by the flowered head scarf holding back her hair.

A few minutes after the sound of Costanza's downhill footsteps receded, the steel doors of the sty banged open and the screech of pigs feeding filled the dawn with their *weee weeee weeeeeeeeeeeeeeeeee.* A few minutes later Costanza came back uphill treading lighter, her breath a bit labored. By then Bastiano was up and ready to go to work, and he and his father, Tatta, a cranky man who lived a string of houses up into town, commenced their morning conversation—not by phone.

— *Bastianooooooooooooooooo!* his father called from above at the top of his voice.

— *Babbbboooooooooooooo! Venghi giuuuuuuuuuuuu?* Bastiano called back.

And so it went for several minutes back and forth until they exchanged the information they needed about the day and its doings, then Bastiano started his Ape and left for work while Costanza shook out the bedlinens and tidied the house.

Three steps lead to the door into Costanza and Bastiano's small kitchen, the main room of the house; the rest consists of Costanza and Bastiano's bedroom, a single bathroom, and the bedroom of their son, Bennato, who is three years older than me. Bennato has since married and moved to a house they bought across the street, so his bedroom has been transformed, but otherwise Costanza and Bastiano's house has stayed the same.

Every time we see each other now—Costanza is like a favorite painting from the living room of my childhood and I visit her often— she pulls me into her kitchen to have some vinsanto and she pinches my cheeks and grabs my breasts and hugs me till she takes the breath from me. We reminisce about the past, when I was *pichina*, or small, and with a big smile she proudly retrieves from a cupboard a faded picture of me and Bennato as kids.

— *Ehhh, Sibilla, quelli erano bei tempi, ehhhh!!* Those were good times, Sibilla.

You remember, yes, she asks, using that Cetonese *ehhhhh*, which means something specific and different—good or bad—depending on the tone of the voice and the length of the syllables. A smile blossoms on her face, sometimes a tear, while she shows me the picture of these two smiling kids, innocent, haphazardly dressed, standing side by side in the middle of the dusty street.

Back then, by the time Bastiano headed out to work and the ladies of Borgo to their chores or shopping in the piazza, our neighbor Aldo, meanwhile, left for his job in construction, stopping to get his Ape, dark green, in his shed next to our house.

Aldo was a part-time farmer and part-time construction worker. He and his wife, Beppa, lived with Aldo's mother, Assunta, in a house nestled in the middle of Borgo. Their house didn't have any land, however, so Aldo and Beppa owned property adjacent to ours, with a shed, their vegetable gardens, and the shelter for their animals, chickens and rabbits mostly.

Beppa and Aldo came down to their *orto* in the morning and the afternoon, after Aldo got off work, Aldo in his dusty work clothes and light-colored cap on his balding head. He had beautiful blue eyes and a boyishness that shaved thirty years off his life every time he smiled. Beppa had black wavy hair cut short but stylishly parted on the side. She had rosy cheeks and a mole on her nose, and she wore colorful kerchiefs and tiny gold earrings.

Nothing but a decaying fence separated our properties, so Beppa and Aldo were part of our lives from the start. Well into my teens, and even later, in college, I visited with them in the afternoons, keeping Beppa company while she cared for the chickens and waited for Aldo to finish his work. She piddled about picking vegetables, planting seeds, watering and talking with her chickens, our cats, and any neighbor who stopped by to sit with her *a veglia,* a term that means to watch over but mostly, in Cetona, to hang out, to sit and talk in quiet intimacy. Once while we sat together a wasp stung my nose. Quickly she ran about her garden gathering garlic, parsley, and onion grass, and with her *mezzaluna* she made a paste that she rubbed on my nose until the swelling vanished. I still have a tiny hole on my nose from the puncture, and now the scar is dear.

Assunta, Aldo's mother, by then elderly, also came in the late afternoon, weather permitting, and sat *a veglia,* in the traditional black of mourning, though her husband had been dead many years. She wore her black head scarf loosely around her face, errant puffs of snow white hair poking out here and there. In the sea of black Assunta's eyes shone like aquamarines and made her whole face glow; when she smiled, her wrinkles gathered like delicate threads pulled by the magnetic strength of her eyes, and everything in the world seemed to smile at the same time.

While the chickens scratched about, Beppa fed the cats and rabbits and Aldo worked the land; he weeded around the garden, hoed, tilled, trimmed the grape vines and the olive trees, watered, picked fruit, and fixed this and that. If it was that time of year, Aldo sprayed the grapevines with copper sulphate with a machine with a handle that he carried on his back and that made a distinct *eeh-aww eeh-aww* sound as he went. Aldo knew how to do everything on the land—how to build everything and fix everything—and through the years, and particularly at the beginning, he and Beppa helped my parents learn to pick olives, figure out what grew best where, why the pear tree was not producing, or where to take the grapes after harvest. His work was an act of daily commitment that contributed pace and reassurance to life on Borgo.

Meanwhile, with Aldo and Bastiano off to work and Costanza and Beppa feeding the animals, the children on Borgo—my brother and I, Bennato, Claudio, and Mario and Elio, the Tassi boys, who lived two houses up—were off to school, on foot, rain or sunny dawn. The boys, all at the *scuola media* by then, the middle school, left a little earlier and took a steep shortcut uphill through the heart of town, ending up at the Collegiata.

I, on the other hand, walked up Borgo to the elementary school in the piazza. By then some friends had come to visit from the States, and for a birthday they had bought me a leather schoolbag, a rectangular satchel called a *cartella*. It was olive green, with shoulder straps and a big yellow smiley face on the front flap. With its happy face and its clean smell of leather, that *cartella* escorted me every day of elementary school, and to this writing it stays in my memory as one of my dearest possessions, now lost.

When I first conceived of this return home, I wrote a letter to the Questura of Siena, the office in charge of immigration in the province, to inquire about procedures for my stay. A tourist visa grants three months' time—not enough for me. Without a *permesso di soggiorno* my dream was dead on conception.

In the letter I explained who I was; I wrote that my family had lived in Italy for some twenty years, that I had grown up there, gone to school there, that it was my home. I just wanted to come home for a year, possibly to write.

I know you have a lot of immigrants, I said, but might I be different? Could you simply renew my *permesso di soggiorno?* I kindly asked.

And off the letter went.

— *No,* said a voice on the phone about a month later.

His name was Benvenuto Petrini and he was calling from the Questura.

Signora Fix, he said in Italian, the laws have changed. Everything is different now.

— *Io mi sono interessato del suo caso,* he said, addressing me formally. I have taken an interest in your case. I have looked up your family and I know your history. While I understand your situation and I feel for you, he said, this is the process you have to follow: You have to apply for a visa to stay for more than three months; if the visa is granted, you come and you apply for a *permesso di soggiorno.* Then, we see.

Benvenuto and I exchanged emails in case I had questions, which I did, and by the time we had talked three times we had become friends on Facebook, we had learned we are the same age, we had switched from formal to informal, and we were exchanging hugs and kisses.

He never told me that he was the head of immigration for the Questura.

— *Dai, vieni qui che ti aiuto io,* he said. Come over here and I will help you.

The biggest hurdle was getting my visa, without which I couldn't stay in Italy beyond the time allotted tourists. To get one as a self-employed American citizen, I had to prove that I had at my disposal 5,000 euros with which to live each month, or about $70,000 a year, about two and a half times more than most Italians live on these days.

After considering various fraudulent ways of proving this, and after sending in all the documentation and meeting all other requirements, this was a stumbling block I could not overcome. At that point Benvenuto offered to help by writing a letter to the Italian General Counsel asking him to consider my case in a special light.

— *Gli scrivo io, non ti preoccupare, gli dico come stanno le cose. Mi prendo responsabilità personale!* Benvenuto reassured me on the phone in a buoyant voice. I will write them and tell them the way things stand. I will take personal responsibility for you!

And he did. He explained my situation, asked that reason be applied to my request, and the following day he got a call saying that my visa would be granted.

After arriving in Cetona I filled out a few more pounds of paperwork, sent in more *bolli* worth several hundred more Euros, and little more than a month later I was given an appointment to apply for my *permesso di soggiorno.*

— *Quando vieni ti porto a pranzo e ti fo ubriaca'!* Benvenuto said in his mixed Senese-Foligno accent. When you come I will take you to lunch and get you drunk!

I went to Siena by train and I enjoyed the stops along the way, which in the case of the Chiusi-Siena train are many (here they say *il treno si ferma anche per pisciare*; the train even stops to piss). I loved the unfettered view of the small household farms and the backyards of the modest houses along the tracks, and the *crete senesi*, with their splendid unfolding of color.

In Siena I walked the old streets I had not walked in many years. The sunlight was coming down the street from the top of Via di Città, straight ahead of me, this beautiful Tuscan light nearly blinding me. It was freezing cold and windy and I had to stop and sit in the sun for a while to warm up. Most people were still at lunch, and the street was nearly empty. When I started walking again I crossed a young guy, Middle Eastern or North African. He bumped into me just slightly and proffered a box of Kleenex and asked me for money.

— *Signora*, he pleaded.

They are everywhere here, poor people from all over, always stopping you and trying to sell you something, Kleenex or whatever, and I just passed him like I was sleepwalking, acknowledged at the mere periphery of my being. But then I stopped, with my back to him, and I stood there for a moment in this bath of sunlight, right in front of La Chigiana, where my mom used to work in summers playing the piano, this beautiful Renaissance building whose walls curve along Via di Città like someone took them magically between their palms and curved them like pieces of marzipan in this medieval landscape.

It stunned me that for a second I had considered not giving this guy money; that I had come here to this land and he from his, and I was just going to walk by him like this, with no human acknowledgment or consideration.

I turned slowly to look for him and somehow I knew that he would be there, showered in sunlight, waiting for me just a few steps away, perceiving my soul. And there he was, still holding the Kleenex, looking at me like, 'what's it going to be, lady,' but not impatiently. Kindly, in fact.

I put my bag down—I had bought a palette and a sketching pad—and searched in my purse for some change. I count out some coins in his palm, looking them over carefully to make sure I have given him enough for something. I feel stupid. I look him in the eye drearily, and I want to apologize, and he smiles. He is young. What is he doing here, and what am I doing here, and how did we come to meet on this street so randomly?

He says *Grazie* and asks if I want the Kleenex and I shake my head, though I could have used them. He says *Dio ti benedica, buona fortuna,* God bless you, good luck, in a language that is not his, and I want to hug him. I would have wept on this stranger's shoulder, right there on the street, like a child. But that would have been too weird, even for me.

First thing the following morning I went to the Questura to meet Benvenuto.

— *Lei ha un appuntamento con il Dottor Petrini?* the officer at the door asked. Do you have an appointment with Dr. Petrini?

I was surprised by the formality, but, then again, I had no idea of his position.

After going through the many layers of equally and uncannily good-looking uniformed members of the *polizia di stato*, with their crisp blue uniforms, I was escorted to his office. He stood talking on the phone, in plainclothes, tall and athletic, with salt and pepper curly hair and kind blue eyes. After hugging warmly like we had known each other forever, he escorted me to a building down the street, with the Italian and European Union flags flying side by side.

Professional and courteous, he directed me towards a nondescript door and reassured me that my name would soon be called. I walked in and found a room large, bare and bureaucratic, with legal notices and posters hanging here and there, and brimming with immigrants. There was a row of chairs and seats along the wall, and people working behind a glass partition. A nice-looking gray-haired man in uniform, older and matter-of-fact, was taking someone's fingerprints.

All the seats along the wall were taken except for one, and several people were standing. There were a lot of people, maybe thirty or more, waiting, and I wondered where they were from, what they had gone through to be here, and why. A woman who looked Middle Eastern, with a head scarf and eyes like dark pools, was seated in a chair behind me, by the door. Seated beside her were several men who also looked Middle Eastern. Two tall bearded men with turbans, maybe Pakistanis or Afghans, stood against the wall as did two other men with dark olive skin, wire–rimmed glasses, and short haircuts, professional-looking. They were all waiting for their turns. One was holding a document, a piece of paper, and he had a question, it seemed. He looked through the glass, trying to get someone's attention, but no one looked his way. I sat in the only empty seat for a moment and looked around.

I don't know how long anyone had been sitting there, but barely ten minutes passed before the nice-looking policeman called my name. I got up self-consciously and walked over.

— *Buon giorno,* he said when I approached.

He looked me in the eye and smiled almost imperceptibly. Next to him was a thick file with my name written on it, many scribbles on the front. Codes. I handed him the pictures Benvenuto had asked me to take on my way in, which he cut and stapled to various forms, then slid them toward me to sign. He then directed me to rest one finger at a time in a small fingerprint machine on the counter.

When we finished he gave me a piece of paper and said I would get a call when my *permesso* was ready. I asked if I could send a friend to pick it up for me. He smiled.

— *Se manda anche la mano però!* he said. If you send your hand along too, implying that they confirm your identity with your fingerprints.

Then he moved to his left and opened a glass door and invited me in, behind the glass partition, quickly shutting the door behind me. Benvenuto greeted me and introduced me to his colleagues, then he escorted me back to the Questura for the forensic part of the process— the documentation that makes you part of European intelligence and Interpol, he explained in a kind but official tone, trying to be clear with the American citizen in me.

— *Se ammazzi qualcuno ora, qui ti si trova!* he said. If you kill someone here we will find you, he said, half-jokingly. I thought of Amanda Knox and shivered.

He handed me off to a handsome man in a white lab coat, in his late forties, with a goatee and salt-and-pepper hair cut close to the scalp. I put my stuff down and I watched as he entered my name, personal information, and physical description in a digital form in a computer. Every few seconds he glanced at me and swiftly picked adjectives out of a long list to describe me down to the most minute detail. Face, oval. Chair, chestnut. Eyes, brown. Scars, none. Eyebrows, wide. Then he moved to the other side of the computer, toward me, and invited me to give him my right hand.

He fingerprinted each of my fingers, on the left hand and the right, twice each, then took prints of my full palms and my fingers together. I left like a kid in elementary school submitting to vaccines, and I smiled thinking of this, and of the fact that I had to do this to be back here, after living here for so long. A part of me felt outrage, but I felt lucky, too, blessed, so privileged to be here, and I smiled. When we finished, the officer shook my hand and gave me directions back to Benvenuto's office downstairs. I saw no other immigrants.

— *Praticamente ti ho adottato!! Ti ho adottato!!* Benvenuto yelled afterwards over a bottle of red wine in a trattoria not far from the Questura. I adopted you!! Practically I adopted you!!

I smiled, tears welling in my eyes for his kindness and his affection—toward a total stranger.

— *Te sei una di noi ... e io me ne sono occupato personalmente. Non è possibile che facciamo entrare tutta sta gente qui in Italia e non ti danno il visto a te. No!* You're one of us, Benvenuto said, and I wanted to take care of it personally. It is not possible that we let all these people into Italy, but they won't give you a visa. No!

Between stories and jokes I learned a little about this smart cop with two master's degrees, including a law degree; a marathoner and a family man, a reveler fanatically devoted to the Palio, and a joker, too, but also deeply conscious of the importance of his job. He is in charge of the entrance and exit and stay of all immigrants in the small but traveled province of Siena. It is a world laden with grief and shadiness—people who will do anything to be free, to have an inkling of possibility—and Benvenuto knows its subtleties, folds, and darkness like the meandering alleyways of this town he has called home for decades.

After lunch we walked arm in arm to get a *caffè*, and then an *ammazzacaffè* (a drink that kills the coffee), then to meet his family at their home on the top floor of an impossibly tall building not far from the Questura. And finally, to drink a glass of wine in Piazza del Campo, as promised.

Sitting at on outdoor table with our legs covered by blankets, we braved the freezing weather to watch the sun set behind the tower of the Duomo. In twenty years of living here, and many of visiting, I had never seen the sun set in Siena. I had always gone back to Cetona with the train before dark. This time I watched as the light on the piazza moved from apricot to a soft rose, then to the most translucent and lightest of blues. Finally, the light gathered softly at the top of the buildings and disappeared.

Benvenuto and I took pictures with Piazza del Campo as backdrop and parted with a hug.

— *È stata una bellissima giornata. Bellissima,* he said on the phone the following day when I called to thank him. It was a beautiful day, absolutely beautiful.

I should have my *permesso di soggiorno* any day now. I won't be able to work here, and it won't give me the answers I am seeking, but at least I can stay for a while—perhaps even the year that I dream of.

Certainly, the most curious of our neighbors was Caio, a gruff man as wide as a barrel whose walk up Borgo eclipsed the sun itself.

Caio and his wife, Arzelia, lived in a dirty-white house that was attached to ours at a ninety-degree angle so that if you were facing our front door and you extended your right arm, his house was a foot or two from your fingers. Their front door was up the street, and up a few steep steps, but his *cantina*, his cellar, was beside our front door and that's where Caio spent most of his time, standing silently in his beret, vest, and rough suspenders, elbows leaning firmly onto a worn piece of furniture, smoking and drinking. At frequent intervals he loudly coughed up phlegm that he spat into a spittoon located somewhere at his feet—not that I ever saw it. From the street one only saw of Caio's cantina what was in the immediate shaft of light let in by the open door. The rest was cavernous and dark and ominous, and in twenty years I rarely stopped in front of his door long enough to cast anything but a stolen glance inside—unless I was feeling particularly courageous.

From the room emanated a peculiar smell of cigarette smoke mixed with must and sour wine, even when the door was closed. If the door was ajar you knew Caio was in there, facing the door and the street, his elbows planted, his yellowed fingers, large and thick as steaks, up in the air, holding a burning cigarette, a Nazionale unfiltered. Sometimes he stood there for hours, making no noise except for clearing his throat every now and then and saying, *Ehhhhhhhhhhhhhhhhh*—something that in Cetona can mean knowing, warning, or foreboding—sometimes followed by a string of curses, usually against the Madonna.

Caio had few or no teeth, and he spoke in gnashed words strung together in a heavy country dialect. He was gruff and hard to understand, and as a little girl, and even later as a teenager, I kept a wide berth around his cantina. Most of our interactions happened through the opening of his cantina door.

— *Sibilla, piove?* Is it raining? he'd say from the darkness, startling me as I put the key in our front door.

Sometimes I found him on the threshold and he seemed in a good mood.

— *'na sera, 'na sera, Sibilla, buona sera. 'n do' va', a spasso? A ballo?* he'd say. Good evening, Sibilla, are you going to take a walk? Or dancing?

Through the years I had always wondered about Caio, my memories of him threadbare, like a child's drawing later filtered through the incomplete perceptions of a teenager, so I decided to go visit with

Caio and Arzelia's daughter, Rosalia, who is the mother of my childhood friends Lapo and Amerigo.

I called her and introduced myself.

— *Certo che ti ricordo. Vieni, vieni,* she said kindly. Of course, I remember you. Come, come, I'll expect you.

We visited around the table in the kitchen of their house, on the way to Chiusi, and the story she told me, Caio's story, is the story of the many people who made a meager living from the land here. It's a universal story of loss, of *disgrazia,* as people say here—disgrace, poverty—starting right before World War I, in the countryside. *In campagna.* The word carries a layer of implied meanings: earth, isolation, poverty. History, pride, and beauty, too—suffered beauty.

Like most farming families at the time, Caio's family, and later Caio and Arzelia themselves—Arzelia was from Piazze and they had met there in their youth—were sharecroppers under the system called *mezzadria,* the owner-farmer arrangement that shackled (or built?) Italian agriculture from Roman times through the twentieth century: Land owners, mostly wealthy people who lived in Rome or Milan and bought country properties as an investment, provided farmers a house to live in, a *podere,* in exchange for their work on the land and half the crop.

Half and half, they say, with a wink.

This was the system that governed the lives of most Cetonesi: They all toiled for a handful of landowners, men by the names of Terrosi, who owned the Parco Terrosi and more than thirty farmhouses; Grottanelli, who owned the Rocca and other properties in town, in addition to dozens of farms; and Erasmo Sgarroni, a businessman from Orvieto who had come to Cetona in the twenties seeking to invest money from his construction company. He built sections of the *autostrada,* electrical plants, dams, road and factories; he also owned more than a dozen farmhouses around Cetona, in addition to a big building on Via Roma where he had his offices and where his overseer lived with his family. These are the names of those who ruled the working people of Cetona for a century or better.

Many will tell you that farmers agreed to *mezzadria* and that the system was good for all. The land got worked cheaply, and farmers got work, food, and a place to live. Some, it's touted, even managed to get work in the city as a manager or a doorman—anything that would get you away from *la campagna*. Sometimes that happened—if they worked for nice landowners, and some were nice, occasionally.

Sgarroni was one of them, his daughter, Franca, told me. I called her in Rome to ask about her family, whose name I have heard all my life. She inquired about the nature of my interest and she was proud to talk about her father, a proud man who, she said, connected running water and electricity to the farmhouses he bought. She said he bettered the *poderi* he owned as well as the quality of life of his farmers. He gave work to many, not only on the land, but in his companies, which, in addition to the construction company, encompassed a brickyard in Chiusi that supplied bricks for reconstruction after the war. When he died, the funeral procession snaked through Cetona and throngs of people lined up to see his casket go by. Many of them had worked for him; they were grateful for what he had done for them, or what they thought he had given them. I can imagine that.

But history is always two-sided, and gratitude can be a searing knife.

Many farms under *mezzadria* were poorly managed and barely produced enough for one family, let alone enough to split. The farmers were indentured, with no home of their own, with no power to leave and nowhere to go, at the mercy of what the owner gave them, unable to ever accumulate wealth and forever competing among themselves for bigger farms that could better support their families. Meanwhile, because landowners let their properties to farmers with the greatest ability to work them profitably—with more boys to help—farmers often had more children than they could afford and suffered great financial duress as a result. Yet, when hard times came and debts or taxes could not be paid, or food was not enough, the landowners were often intolerant and cruel, even in the face of the greatest of needs. People of Cetona still tell stories of humiliation and rejection, laden with anger.

Alongside this chafing standoff of opposing interests were two groups of people who stocked the fire: On one side were the malcontents of the town, who liked to incite the farmers to rebellion and hatred, much to their own disservice, and on the other were the overseers, the *fattori*, whose power resided in manipulating this uncomfortable owner-farmer relationship to their own advantage. To the owners who employed them they painted the farmers as lazy thieves, yet, behind their backs, they finagled with the farmers, promising them better contracts in exchange for more chickens or bigger cuts of their crops. As they say here in Cetona, the *fattori* were the ones who got fat, and their names and reputations are reviled to this day.

In the middle of this were the good people who just wanted to survive fairly. Those people got angrier and angrier as *mezzadria* went on, and among those are many Cetonesi and their families. Even before World War I farmers had begun to revolt to *mezzadria*, demanding better working conditions, larger percentages of the crops, and more freedom (imagine that at the time there were laws prohibiting farmers from coming into the piazza during the work week, lest they be slacking off). The system limped through Fascism, but after World War II there was no turning back: The farmers had had enough. They wanted bigger percentages of the crops and exemptions from paying taxes on land they didn't own.

As the left gained strength all over Tuscany, they finally got their wish and, eventually, this perfect storm of events brought a collapse in the system: Land lost value, landowners lost money and could no longer pay their taxes, and finally they began to sell off their properties.

*Lo sgretolamento delle proprietà,* Signora Sgarroni said, her voice tinged with sadness. The collapse of the properties. An inevitable dissolution.

I understand her pain in seeing everything that her father built fall away. Yet, there was some poetic justice in it too, finally. Facilitated by new no-interest loans and laws encouraging landowners to sell to their own farmers, some *contadini* managed to buy the farmhouses they had lived in and the land they had toiled. Many took advantage of this, including Rosalia's husband's family, which managed to buy a beautiful farm where the extended family, five cousins and their children, still live in harmony. It is a badge of honor and distinction to finally own the land you worked for so long for somebody else.

Many others, though, didn't want to buy their owners' land. They didn't want to get into debt, and many simply didn't want to live on the land anymore, with or without water or electricity. They were tired of being poor, and tired of the dirt. Populations in towns like Cetona fell by half over the course of thirty years.

Some farmers, though, had the wherewithal to do neither—to move to a city or to buy a farm. They continued, semi-indentured, to work for others, as did Bruno and Adelina, barely surviving.

Caio was among them. He worked in poverty, growing vegetables and raising animals, lambs and calves, for sale. They moved from one farm to another, in Celle. Eventually, after their children had married and gone, Caio and Arzelia managed to retire, with a meager pension, and moved to Borgo, just a couple of years before us.

Sitting in her kitchen, Rosalia showed me some pictures of her parents standing on the steps of their newly bought house. In one of them Arzelia was caressing Caio's face, affectionately, and Caio was smiling. It brought tears to Rosalia's eyes and it gave me a glimpse into a life I had never witnessed. When I was little, Arzelia, white hair pulled back in a kerchief, seemed ever-dour, though now I understand better why. She spent most of her time serving Caio and sitting on her steps knitting sweaters for various customers in town. She was also some kind of healer or witch. Women brought sick infants to her to remove the *malocchio*, the evil eye. It was rumored that Arzelia immersed them in tubs of hot water and poured olive oil over their heads, and from the way the oil behaved she could tell something or the other—if the devil had got them. Then she would say some magic words or curses and the *malocchio* was supposed to recede. When I was little I sometimes crossed these women carrying the children away in bundles, back up the dark road, with a new spark of hope in their eyes. It was all a bit spooky.

Even after he retired, Caio kept a small field—a *campo*—at Il Piano, not far from Costanza and Bastiano's fields, and he went there in the afternoons to tend to his *orto* and harvest his vegetables. He drove a baby-blue Ape that he parked in front of his cantina, and when he left he revved the motor till it made a high-pitched screeching noise, then took off uphill in a cloud of exhaust and dust, right in front of our door, which always caused my mom to groan and fan the kitchen table with a towel.

Sometimes Arzelia went with him, sitting in the back of the Ape, and when Caio returned home he carried cases of beautiful vegetables that he unloaded preciously and took inside. In the evenings, just before the sun dipped behind Monte Cetona, Caio would emerge from his cavern and pull his little green door closed and make his way up to his kitchen for dinner. He locked the cantina, then slipped the key in its hiding place above the door, and after clearing his throat and saying *Ehhhhhhhhhhhh*, he walked slowly up the street, a bit unsteady. As he walked uphill, the setting sun at the cusp of the mountain's edge cast behind him a shadow twice his size, as if he were pulling a large monster behind him on the ground.

After he walked inside, sometimes he and Arzelia would quickly start fighting, and their bickering flowed from the open windows onto the street. Most times, though, the only noise was the clinking of silverware and the theme music of the *telegiornale*. The same sounds came from all kitchens on Borgo as families, tired from a long work day, sat down to do the same.

One such evening during the first or perhaps second summer we lived there, when Mario Tassi and Bennato and Silvio Della Vigna and I were playing outside—Silvio's grandmother Annita lived on Borgo and he would come spend the night—I decided to play a joke on Caio: After he walked upstairs for dinner, I ran down the street and, unbeknownst to the others, I reached into his hiding place, took out the key to the cantina, and slipped it in my pocket. I can still feel it in my hand, light as a feather, heavy as a rock.

We were all playing outside when Caio came back down to his cantina after having dinner and reached in the cubby for his key. The key was not there, and Caio became immediately and explosively irate. He did not laugh and say, c'mon kids, give me the key. He was violently angry, and I was flustered.

He made his way up the street yelling and cursing and started arguing with young Mario, possibly the first person he ran into since they were immediate neighbors.

In a moment of panic, and my first memorable instance of cowardliness, I shrunk from presenting the key, and while the seconds passed, Caio's anger escalated, perhaps prompted by Mario's fiery temper, already pronounced, and suddenly he slapped Mario across the face with his big thick hand, leaving his cheek hot and red.

Mario, with tears streaming down his cheek, flushed and angry, this tall, strong boy, walked inside his house, whose front door stood not two feet from Caio's, grabbed his father's shotgun, loaded it, walked back outside, removed the safe and pointed it at Caio's chest. He nearly rested it there.

Time stood frozen for a single second whose crystal clarity I have never forgotten.

Rita, Mario's mom, came out yelling, and Arzelia was yelling, and in seconds my mother came to our front door and called me for dinner, likely unaware of what was going on. She could not see this from our house, which was slightly further down the street, and likely would not have understood it anyway, though if she had she certainly would have sent me up the street to tell the truth. Detaching myself from this terrifying situation, I ran down the street, and as I passed Caio's cantina I slipped the key back into its place, shaking.

Innocent to all but myself, I sowed a bad seed and I carried it for years.

Just days ago, I finally apologized to Mario for the slap he caught and for the humiliation and terror of that moment. I ran into him on the road to his house, where he lives with his wife, my child-hood friend Giulia, and their son.

I am so sorry, I said. I have regretted this all my life.

Tall, dark, and kind, Mario put his arm around my shoulder and smiled at me, as old childhood friends. Perhaps he always knew.

— *Sibilla, so' passati anni. Lascia anda'*. Years have passed, he said, laughing. Let it go.

Nonetheless.

Eventually, in the late nineties Caio got sick and he was con-fined to his bed. The *casa famiglia*, in an unprecedented decision, refused to take him. He died in his bed, at Borgo, but before he got to that, story goes that Arzelia, in her farmer's clothes and her kerchief on her head, walked around the bed and taunted him.

— *Vecchio, dammi ora se ce la fai!* Hit me now if you can, old man.

And she laughed, as did Rosalia.

— *Se guarisco t'ammazzo,* Caio replied as Arzelia ran around his bed. If I get better I will kill you.

But he didn't, and not long after they carried Caio's frame down the steep stairs of the house and buried him at the cemetery. Arzelia died a few years later, at the *casa famiglia*, and now they are gone, all of them, gaping holes in the windows and doorways of my street, peo-ple who wove the safety of my youth and the comfort of love and habit. They were not neighbors; they were part of my family.

I hold onto the memory of a day I came home during college and Caio came out of his cantina and shook my hand and smiled, with-out a single tooth. It was the first time he had ever done that, in all those years we lived side by side, that he had looked me in the eye and smiled, fully, frankly. I wish I had given him flowers, or something.

Back on Borgo, on summer nights, Bennato, Mario and his brother, and I played soccer on the street. Later, when I was in high school and I was allowed to go to the piazza at night, I'd stop by

Bastiano and Costanza's to get Bennato so we could share the walk in the dark. Sometimes when it was cold outside I went to Costanza and Bastiano's to play cards with Bennato, or to watch TV at Beppa and Aldo's, a rare treat since my family did not have one. I particularly liked watching the popular show "Sandokan," broadcast weekly, about a handsome Malaysian pirate and his battles against the British and the French. The show starred French actor Philippe Leroy, who owned a house in Cetona and who we thought of as our resident star. I could not bear to miss a show.

After dinner, I let myself into the house and sat with Beppa and Aldo in their tiny kitchen as they finished dinner in the heat of the *stufa*. Then Beppa would turn on the TV and watch a bit of the show with me, but by the time it was over both of them had fallen asleep, arms crossed on their chests, heads down. When the show ended, I'd say *buona notte* and let myself out quietly into the cold air and down the street.

In winter, at night all life at Borgo, and all over Cetona, withdrew onto itself, then as now. A few lights shone from windows here and there, and one street light hung in the middle of the cluster of houses, dim and alone. Smoke billowed from every chimney, but the street was otherwise still, save for the occasional cat moving quickly in the cold, or me as a teenager coming home late, tiptoeing.

But in late spring and on summer evenings the ladies of Borgo came out to sit in a cluster on chairs or stoops and walls here and there to knit and gossip. The chorus of their voices hummed through the quiet street, broken every now and then by the screech of an animal from the fields below or a loud burst of laughter from someone's house up in town.

Finally, Costanza or Beppa put the needles away and got up to go.

— 'Notte ... they'd say as they walked the few steps home in the shadows.

— 'Notte ...

Doors closed, keys still in them, as Borgo's fountain trickled into the night.

Almost from the day of my arrival, like a man thirsting for water I have returned to run the roads of my landscape, and it is this, as much as the people here, the true hand that holds my heart. I don't run anywhere else in the world anymore, that old sport having been replaced by my yoga practice and walking. But here, here my legs carry me like the wind, for miles and miles, buoyed by the sight of the countryside over which my spirit flies and lingers in absolute and tender bliss, taking me home to my truest being, my purest happiness.

It is here in these fields that I rekindle the ancient relationship between landscape and soul—the senses and affinities one develops, symbiotically, growing up in a place where landscape is integral to every daily activity, to what people eat, what they talk about, the time at which they do what they do.

Somehow it has nourished me simply, and always.

As a kid, I spent my hours reading in trees, playing in the woods, or walking miles through fields searching for flowers and bugs. Eventually, with the money I saved from my summer babysitting jobs, I was able to buy my Bravo motorbike. I loved my *motorino*, a coveted source of joy and independence, the rubber tires flying me over the hilly countryside to freedom from all others. Thereafter, the radius of my meanderings grew exponentially, deepening my love for exploring the back roads through the country, up into the *montagna*, through fields in bloom.

There was not much else to do in Cetona at that age, but it was never a question for me, at least for some years. Cetona had everything one could need, right there, in its fields and woods where I sought secret places and hidden paths and I walked and walked. In all shades of light and forms of weather, I walked to the piazza, to school, to friends' houses. During it all, sight and hearing and smell were at work, finely tuned to the surrounding world, forever molding my senses, and every time I walk this landscape I revisit the landmarks that developed those senses and sensibilities and made them mine, indivisibly and immediately linked to memory and my perception of the world.

The countryside here is as terraced horizontally as it is vertically, with handkerchiefs of disparate fields patched together like an enormous intricate quilt of a thousand shades of green stretching all the way to the horizon. The quilt rolls as if on the surface of an ocean, hills cresting so very softly then falling again, fields rounding upward and kissing seamlessly like a succession of small waves in a harmonious act of supreme perfection, all the way to the sky beyond and above.

My eye dances on the fields like a surfer on water, and here, like my lover on the ocean, here I find my joy, delighting in rediscovering the routes in the countryside that I love most, and, too, developing a few new ones, a repertoire I will spend the next several months exploring and enjoying. They thread through places by the names of Patarnione, Poggio alla Vecchia, Le Gore, and Piandisette, Belverde and I Frati, and Il Piano, where Andrea and I drove that dewy morning long ago. Or the Strada dei Poggi through the fields, and La Paolina. Each route is between ten and fifteen kilometers, full of stiff hills and rocky descents, but the exhilaration of seeing, of being here, takes my mind off the distance and the exhaustion.

Today I ran the road toward Piazze to the turnoff to Patarnione, up Donna Morta all the way to the paved road to Belverde and back. Donna Morta—the road of the *dead lady*, a name of mysterious origins, though after I run it I always feel like a dead lady—is my favorite uphill stretch. It includes two miles or more at a preposterous incline that strips my lungs and thigh muscles but feeds me with a countryside divine, lush, full, and varied, heading up toward Monte Cetona, with the cross in my face.

I pass through the eponymous *podere* of Donna Morta, a farm whose property straddles a meandering road with barns and huge piles of rolled straw and farming machinery, and then through tilled fields lined by cypresses. Those fields right now are freshly turned and

dark brown—the wheat, sunflowers and corn all harvested and gone—
and ready for reseeding.

I have not seen this exact landscape in years, and it penetrates
me and breaks me. So much has happened since. The smell of the earth
carries in the breeze and I stop to inhale, to breathe in the scent—of
warmth, rain, minerals, animals, sun, sweat, brown, unadulterated
earth. It makes me cry that I have not seen these fields in this season for so long, that dense, rich brown that colored my every fall and
winter. I stop to pick up a clump of earth and I bring it to my nose. I
wish I could carry it with me in my pocket, and I smell it again before
I release it reluctantly through my fingers.

When I left early this morning there was a heavy cover of fog,
dewy and cool. Through passages in the woods all the vegetation
seemed covered by mysterious threads of gossamer so fine that from a
few feet one struggles to make out what they are. But I near and I see
they are spider webs dotted by the finest of droplets of water, making
them look like strings of the most delicate miniature pearls. There are
myriads of them, like thousands of tiny spiders fell suddenly from the
sky and got busy with their work, on a pressing and exhilarating mis-
sion to embroider my memory.

Roads are lined by piles of firewood, fields and fields of piled
cut wood, this season's harvest, and I quickly think back to the sound
of saws I have been hearing for the past few weeks. I feel for Monte
Cetona, but then I remember a conversation with my longtime friend
Aldo Della Vigna, during which he reassured me that all trees on
Monte Cetona, oaks and maples, reseed. I breathe. Olives are on the
trees, and pomegranates, with their pink skins taut and bright green
leaves, and all of it, the olives and the pomegranates, fill me with
extraordinary joy.

People here are not used to many runners, and you have to
be aware of drivers who, in truth, could care less if you live or not
as long as you don't get in their way as they go about their business
at great speed. Seeing a runner causes no let-up on the accelerator,
and indeed, sometimes, quite to the contrary, you perceive a bit of an

acceleration. I am vigilant of this, but mostly people wave and honk at me when they go by, and I feel remembered and cherished, more than I have in many years. Perhaps since I first left.

Nothing, while I am running on these roads, nothing wipes the smile from my face.

The threads of Cetona's social life are forever strung like constellations between the doors of the town's bars, four in past years, three now. These locales, each with its peculiar identity and clientele, are—in addition to the piazza—the places where people congregate, exchange information, and otherwise make their social life, or at least a great part of, starting at the northern entrance to the piazza, with Le ACLI.

Nestled in a corner off the piazza proper, Le ACLI has historically been the bar associated with the Christian Democrats, perhaps not surprisingly given its proximity to the church of San Michele Arcangelo. My windows, as I have noted before, give me an unfettered view into the Le ACLI's world, populated by distinct groups of people at different hours of the day, though some commingling happens occasionally:

During the early morning hours Le ACLI is visited by a loyal group of citizens who prefer to have their coffee there, or their first glass of wine, perhaps less because they like the coffee or the wine there than because it is close to the few parking spaces at the end of the piazza and easy to get in and out of. In fact, the bar is quite squalid though clean, and offers nearly nothing in matters of pastries or, for that matter, choices of good wine.

During the late morning hours a few people—retirees, unemployed—sit outside the bar reading the paper, weather permitting. Then, after lunch a large group of workers, young and old, and a small group of female followers, go there for coffee and a moment of relaxation before returning to work. I see that the housepainter Ugo hangs out there after lunch with his crew—and Ugo is still nice-looking—and Silvanino and Lapo too.

Le ACLI is also frequented by an assiduous crowd of card players, especially after lunch and late after dinner, when they gather at tables in a side room, the largest of the spaces, and play long and often contentious, loud games whose outcome dictates the players' moods for the rest of the day or night. While a large window opens from the street into the room, the players are shrouded by a thick crimson curtain that gives them privacy to gamble and smoke, abetted by the acquiescence of the people who run the bar and who want to make sure their customers consume their fair share of beverages while visiting. All of this is all the more ironic since the building that houses Le ACLI, as well as the bar itself—which is technically supposed to be a social club—are owned by the Catholic Church, and in fact, Cetona's priest, Don Prospero, who you will learn much more about, lives above the bar and is often seen hanging out in front of it, and, I am told, he often partakes in its social life, drinking and hanging with the crowd.

Of course, this may very well be rumor.

A large crowd—the most vociferous—also visits le ACLI late night in summer and on winter weekends, when throngs of twenty- and thirty-something-year-olds gather under the yellow glow of the lamps outside to drink, smoke, laugh, and talk into the late hours of the night, and, indeed, long after the rest of the town has gone to sleep.

While the bar is owned by the church, it is run by a couple—lay and apparently not church-going—who I have crossed paths with all my life, though, in that odd and common Cetonese way, I have never really known them. In the evenings, the wife, Serafina, petite, short, with fleeting black eyes full of judgment (or perhaps shyness?), sits behind the bar—a counter no longer that an average dining room table—and reads quietly. One knows, however, and jokes are made of this, that she listens to every word spoken around her and sometimes you can imagine her ears growing like Pinocchio's nose. If the conversation gets provocative or the gossip particularly juicy, she turns to hide the smile creeping up on her face. Discretion is not a trait of Cetona's bartenders. Quite to the contrary.

But the interesting thing to me is that when I was little, Serafina and her sister, Giuditta, a few years apart but visibly related, owned a field somewhere near my house. All these years, and still today, they have kept chickens and rabbits in a tiny coop up from Borgo. Every day rain or shine I would see them walk together to cut grass and feed their animals. And yet, barely ever have they said hello to me, well, until now. Giuditta, still single and no-nonsense, lives up the alley from me, and every day I see her in her plain skirt with a large, plain coat on top, or a simple summer dress with tiny flowers, going about her errands and jobs, among them, feeding the animals they still keep in that hole in the wall above Borgo. Her hair is short and she wears no makeup, and her only concession to femininity is a long thick gold chain on which hang a large cross and a religious medal of some kind.

Among other jobs, Giuditta is a caretaker for several elderly people in town. I see her walking to and from somewhere up and down the alley with her soldierlike step, often carrying heavy loads of bags and packages. We have warmed to each other a bit, recently, and we always stop to chat. She looks directly at me now, with her kind brown eyes, and she smiles, and I feel like we are making up for years of past foreignness that I could never explain.

— *Buon giorno, Giuditta, come va?* I ask.

— *Eh, Sibilla, buon giorno! Si va avanti, si va avanti!* she answers smiling, using an expression that means we go forward, or we live.

Then off she goes with her bundles.

Back to our bars, the second bar in town—one of the two most prominent—is the Bar Cavour. Positioned in the middle of one length of the piazza, the Bar Cavour occupies the sweetest and sunniest spot, which has forever made it a preferred choice for winter Sunday morning drinks and a good place for the elderly to sit in the early afternoon, even back when it was simple and dusty and without tables outside.

Owned for nearly two decades by the brothers Felice and Giotto Rossi, the Bar Cavour has had, for most of its life, a spacious front room with a long counter, a gelato display, a pool table, a large TV, which reigns above the front room from a corner high up on the wall, and a handful of tables and chairs surrounded by candy displays and racks of potato chips (a recent renovation and unfortunate change of ownership changed some of this but it did not last long). Card tables occupy the bulk of the back room, together with pinball and slot machines.

The Bar Cavour is considered Cetona's leftist bar, and as such it attracts the bulk of the working-class folk in town—though Le ACLI takes its share—in part because it serves sandwiches and homemade gelato and is, plainly, a tad more sophisticated than Le ACLI. It is here that most of the workers and regular folk as well as kids and the elderly come for coffee and pastries in the morning, coffee and cognac after lunch, cognac, gelato, beer, and card games after work, and soccer matches on TV in the evening.

Though the Bar Cavour is not famous for elegance, and perhaps exactly because of that, it attracts a large crowd of people who, mostly men, of all ages, have no expectation of sophistication, nuance, or elegance. They just want to talk and drink inexpensively, and it is much cheaper to drink there than anywhere else in town. They come in the morning and early afternoon to read the paper, and in the late afternoon to play cards. In the evenings they gather in front of the bar counter, under the industrial white light, drink wine, watch soccer, play cards, talk politics loudly, yell and tell good stories.

Through the years, because of its position on the piazza and the large number of tables it has acquired outside, extending out nearly to mid-piazza now, the Bar Cavour has also come to attract a significant share of tourists and visitors with more discriminatory tastes who sit drinking white wine and eating nuts and whose patronage has forced the bar to spruce up a bit, both in looks and selection of victuals.

Much to my pleasure, this has improved the selection of wine glasses, which Giotto and Felice allocate to their more important customers (and I fall among them, for longtime friendship).

Except for August and Easter, when all hands are on deck, Giotto and Felice take turns running the bar. Giotto, the older of the brothers, is in charge in the early mornings while Felice sleeps off his late-night shift—entirely a matter of tiredness and not drunkenness. In the early afternoon, Felice takes his place, then Giotto returns in the early evening for the *aperitivo*. Giotto's wife is in charge in the late mornings.

Felice, who was my classmate in elementary school, tends bar after dinner and into the late night, when I see him the most.

— *So' diciassette anni che so'qui, diciassett'anni!!! So' tanti!* Felice laments to me one night. I have been here seventeen years!!! That's a long time!

Felice talks fast, with a slight lisp, and his voice is higher-pitched and more melodious than one would expect, perhaps because of his height and strength, or his pronounced Cetonese accent. He loves to tell stories and he punctuates them knowingly with sayings, adages and aphorisms that speak to his upbringing and long roots in Cetona. Though some people like to treat him like a country bumpkin of sorts, Felice is smart and observant; he remembers everything about everyone, and to those memories he adds the color of witty insight and a keen Cetonese inventiveness.

Yet Felice has a childlike naiveté and happiness, which, coupled with his large, cornflower blue eyes, charm me and remind of goodness. Indeed, of Felice one could say *è boncitto come il pane*, a Cetonese saying that means he's good like bread. I love that since our childhood together Felice has grown into a respectable business owner: He is a genuinely kind person, friendly, well-mannered, and respectful. When he laughs, his nose, which is pronounced and strong, crinkles and his blue eyes take center stage in his long, oval face. Felice and his brother both have that Cetonese savvy, a deductive, humorous way of making sense of the world and stating one's observations of it.

— *Bondi! O se' venuto con la moto o c'è il vento!* Bondi, either you came on a motorcycle or it's windy out! Felice said one recent evening greeting a customer who walked in with particularly tousled hair.

A couple, English, came into the bar recently and wanted to buy some cigarettes. They were trying to explain that they wanted a brand of light cigarettes, but they were having difficulty making themselves understood. Felice enlisted our friend Fabrizio, who was there on a visit home to see his family.

Fabrizio is one of a handful of true generational Cetonesi who have left the nest. He is married to an American woman he met in Kentucky, where he ventured quite courageously to learn to be a horse dentist. Married some twenty years now, they split their lives between Provence, the Tuscan countryside, and a house in Florence, and he stumbles through decent though heavily accented English.

When Felice proffered the couple a pack of Marlboro Lights, they said through Fabrizio that they wanted even lighter cigarettes, something like ultralights or even lighter.

Felice looked at him with a smirk and shrugged.

— *Ma che le vogliono, vuote? Eh, io gliele posso da' vuote!* Do they want empty cigarettes? I can give them some empty cigarettes! Felice quipped, causing Fabrizio to kneel down laughing.

The company at the Bar Cavour makes for steady laughs and good learning about the many characters of the town, most of whom spent many hours making history here between those same walls. Eager to get out of the house for a few hours before bedtime, they gather there to read the paper, or watch a soccer game—people like Amato and Amedeo, and Marcello, a boisterous construction worker. And Brunino, a retired military nurse, now ninety, who drives around in a little red Ape, gratingly loud. During the day he can be seen tending to his field and vines and those of others, too, or sunning himself on the benches of the piazza. In the evenings, he comes to the Bar Cavour to watch TV. He sits there and stares up at the TV and talks to it, partially incoherently because he cannot hear what the TV is saying.

When I first arrived, he came up to me one evening after watching me for a while.

— *Ma te di chi sei?* he asked, using an old Cetonese expression that means, who do you belong to?

— *Ma te sei la figlia del liutaio di Borgo?* Are you the daughter of the violinmaker from Borgo?

I nodded and smiled, moved that at his age he would remember my father or what he did, or me, for that matter.

Around us, Felice is telling a funny story, then suddenly he curses about something behind the bar.

— *Budella impestata* ... he says loudly, just short of a true *bestemmia*, cursing someone.

Evenings at Bar Cavour can be filled with random entertaining episodes—turns of phrase, non-sequiturs, entirely personal interpretations of the world that one simply cannot and should not argue with.

Felice looks on it all with a smile, like he is in the company of spoiled and eccentric children whom he loves in spite of their oddities. He wipes his large hands on his spotted red apron, tied atop his all-black bartending outfit, and pulls on his black Clic magnetic eyeglasses, his only nod to modernity or sophistication and one that suits him—strangely. He works eagerly behind the bar and tries to deal fairly with the regular drunk of the night, or the person who never wants to leave—the person who wants to lose everything in the slot machine while drinking endless cheap beer like there will be no tomorrow.

While he waits and talks with us, he cleans the long-forgotten candy display cases full of dust.

— *La mi' cognata lei mica le vede 'ste cose.* My sister-in-law doesn't see the dust, he says, lamenting that Giotto's wife doesn't clean.

Giotto, a handful of years older than Felice, is tall and balding, with a round face and large round eyes and large square dark-rimmed glasses that make him look like an old owl. He walks slowly, belly forward and like a duck, feet askew, shuffling almost, and he drags one leg slightly. His apron is always spotted, and most often he has crumbs on his thin lips from nibbling on the potato chips and nuts that he replenishes in the chipped bowls on the bar or that he eats after the customers have vacated a table. He spittles a bit when he talks, which spawns some funny commentary about bits of chewed peanuts in the glasses of wine.

But, since my arrival Giotto and Felice have always treated me with affection and courtesy and I am glad for their conversation and kindness, which I need. I am fond of them, without judgement, perhaps having maintained a childhood vision of them to which I would like to return. They are comical and intrinsic parts of Cetona in every way.

Indeed, spittle notwithstanding, Giotto is smart and agile with words, well-informed, and sharp-tongued in conversation with patrons, most of whom he has known his entire life and, perhaps most importantly, he knows through daily and sharp observation. While he seems quietly busy behind the bar, polishing glasses or piddling in his slow, deliberate manner, he pays attention to everything in his place— the news on TV and, simultaneously, every word said at the bar.

In the evenings, after his *aperitivo* shift, when he trades off with Felice for the night, I see him walking under my window on his way home, quietly, to the house on the edge of town where their whole family has always lived since we were little.

With affection I watch him go, limping a bit, and I remind myself to ask him if he has a bit of sciatica, like me.

And then there is the Bar Sport, the sanctuary of our youth.

Perhaps because it's the nicest and best-appointed, or perhaps because it's located in an important building capping the piazza toward Monte Cetona, the Bar Sport has always held the position of best and most popular bar in Cetona. This status dates back through the decades to when it was purchased and run by Elide, a woman who ranks among Cetona's most formidable characters, in part because she was a woman, but that may not be the most salient trait of hers.

I was a girl when I met Elide, and I remember her as tall and heftily built, with mercurial eyes the color of tropical waters and a wide square jaw that meant business. She was always meticulously dressed and made up to the last hair and touch of bright pink lipstick. She wore high-heels and tight skirts no matter the occasion, and she was the first woman in Cetona to get a driver's license. When I was little, she and her husband, Remo, drove a big cream-colored Mercedes that she directed into the piazza with the majesty of a queen, and I will never quite forget that image.

But perhaps the reason I remember her so well is that Elide was a tough, self-made woman, and in dusty little Cetona she stuck out for her elegance, presence, and visible determination. She was someone to reckon with, and I knew that just by looking at her. She embodied a powerful mix of humility learned from past hardship and pride in having overcome it, both honed at the town slaughterhouse, the *macelli*, where she grew up.

Elide deserves a page of history for having given us the Bar Sport, but also for embodying a quintessentially Cetonese story. Her grandfather was the town traffic officer, the gravedigger, and the keeper of the slaughterhouse, a professional combination long popular in Cetona, and as a result of this role, the family was given lodging in an apartment above the slaughterhouse and the stalls. Elide's mother was born there, followed by Elide and her sisters, and then, in 1949, Elide's daughter. After that, the grandfather of my friend Daniele, owner of the Merlo restaurant, took on the role of guardian of the slaughterhouse. Daniele, too, was born there, and as a kid he watched mesmerized as the steam from the boiling water used to skin the animals rose through the floor and into the house.

Cetona in the twenties was rural and poor, unsurvivably poor: Either you knew and practiced a trade, or you could not survive. Hence, Elide learned to be an entrepreneur early on. She cut grass for people and cleaned; she did chores for women around town and made *ciacce di Pasqua*—a prized Easter bread—and whatever else she could, even in the morning before going to school.

And then she learned to work the slaughterhouse. At that time, animals for food were bought by the butchers from the farmers in town. They were transported to the slaughterhouse, where the butcher arranged their slaughter and butchering, followed by their certification by the health inspector or vet, and their transport to the butcher, where they were hung by cold metal hooks and sold off by the slab and slice.

Growing up on the grounds of the slaughterhouse Elide identified her work there quickly and early. Even as a kid she refused to kill the animals, but, once they were dead, she readily cleaned them, skinned them, and butchered them. She was smart and curious, her fervor fed by poverty and hunger, and soon she learned discernment in judging the health and quality of the animals. She became invaluable to the butchers—of which there were a surprising number in Cetona—and in exchange for her work she and her family got free meat. They never had to starve again.

After her mother died in childbirth when she was in her late teens, and her father remarried and left, Elide and her sisters pulled through the war, aided in great part by Elide's resourcefulness, until she met and married Remo, a handsome, tall laborer who worked for Sgarroni. Elide was crazy about Remo, but he made pennies per hour and Elide was not satisfied. She wanted out of poverty—however she could get there. At one point, she began to ferry meat to friends of friends in Rome, for a good profit, going back and forth on the train in her high heels and the clothes that flattered her. She began to make a little money, and around that time she and Remo could be seen driving around town on twin red-on-black Gilera 150s.

In 1958, when Elide was thirty-three, she and Remo had the vision to borrow money to buy the license to run our bar. At the time, the building in which the bar was located housed an olive mill downstairs, a carpentry shop next door, and storage rooms for local businesses upstairs. The bar itself consisted of one rather dark room outfitted with a counter—made of wooden boards from an old armoire—and a few chairs. It was a simple place where people had coffee and placed and received phone calls (and that continued for many years afterwards as even my parents received calls there before we got a phone).

Elide was determined to improve it and take it into the next decade. She replaced the long counter, got one of the first televisions, then she expanded the bar into a room next door, adding a pool table and pinball machines, and by the early seventies, when prominent writers and people in the film industry started dropping by Cetona and buying property, the Bar Sport became the place to socialize.

Elide looked everywhere for novel ideas. She added *granite* and milkshakes, and cups full of salty sunflower seeds to encourage people to drink more. When the government built the portion of the *auto-strada* between Val di Chiana and Fabro, she and Remo began delivering cold drinks and treats to the construction crews, and the good news of the bar spread. It didn't take long for Elide to have a long list of famous guests, from Vittorio Gassman with his low-to-the-ground green Porsche, to Nino Manfredi, the famous comedic actor. The bar drew people and helped make friends. Many of them bought houses in Cetona, and Elide played intermediary, earning herself a buck on the side.

Even when she had the bar, and for many years afterwards, Elide continued to help at the slaughterhouse, out of a call for service, to help others. Covered in blood and guts at dawn, town people remember her cleaned up and coiffed for business by the time they came into the bar for their morning coffee. Sometimes she worked way into the night, entrepreneurial in more than one way, and more than once, rumor has it, she was found sound asleep in the most comfortable of places, the pool table, in the middle of our dearest bar.

Finally, Elide and Remo made enough money to buy the bar and the building around it, and after their retirement they restored it, making the floors above the bar into apartments and the floor below into a restaurant. Eventually, they sold it all, but, of course, by then they had given generations of Cetona's youth the makings of shelter, comfort, and indelible memories. Among them were our jukebox, and right behind it, a secluded place to hang out. There, sooner or later, nearly all of us made out, heard a song we considered our own, and, eventually, suffered an unforgettable heartbreak.

I don't have money to buy or rent a car, so for the first time since my twenties I am on foot, which is fine for the most part. It's liberating to not drive and, mostly, to not need to. Yet, every now and then I yearn to meander the country roads farther than my feet can take me, so I call Mauro, our longtime mechanic, to borrow a car for a few hours.

Mauro has known me a lifetime, since we moved here. His son, Simone, and I were in class together at the elementary school, and for as long as my parents lived here Mauro was our beloved, loyal, and honest mechanic (and patient with outstanding debts, too). He would come to your need in any way possible. On one occasion, I borrowed my mother's car and dragged the side of it alongside a stone wall. Sobbing, I took it to Mauro and asked if he could fix it so my mother would not notice, and he did. He is a good soul.

Every time I return I go say hello and he is unfailingly affectionate and kind, and he still extends me the courtesy of loaning me the random car he has sitting about his shop as loaners for clients.

— *Certo! Vieni! Vieni!* he says on the phone. Sure! C'mon down! I'll get it ready.

I walked down to his shop and he awaited me with a dusty, cherry-red Twingo. While he ordered Luca, his grandson, one of Simone's children, to put air in the tires, I walked around his shop checking out the vast collection of posters of naked women and smiling at the particular smell of oil and tires, unchanged over all these years.

Luca, a punk-rocker with a spiky haircut and ear piercings who seems too old to be Simone's son, mumbled at his grandfather's orders.

— *Ma 'n'avevi visto che le gomme erano basse?* he asks Luca. Didn't you notice the tires were low?

Luca works quietly. When they finish, Mauro turns to me.

— *Non è una Ferrari, ma va!* he says, opening the door for me and smiling with his ever-handsome blue eyes. It's not a Ferrari, but it runs.

I thank Mauro for this gift and head out into the countryside that today was beyond sublime. The sky was crystalline blue all the way to infinity, making for an unhindered view of the undulations and slopes of the land. Every tree, every slice of a hill, field, patch of grass, branch of olive tree, shone distinctly. The palette of colors was dazzling, moving now more toward the dark yellows; the grapevines are turning dark cadmium, alizarin even. Every nuance was ethereal and magnificent.

From Piazze I drove to Fighine, a hamlet surrounding a castle high up on the side of Monte Cetona facing San Casciano. I had not been there in decades, and never in weather like today. At every turn as I rose up the mountain on the curvy road, another distant set of scenery opened before me, another town on the horizon, another set of hills, farther and farther away, until I could see mountains I had never seen from here. Their highest peaks were pink and topped by snow. The Appennino Toscano, perhaps.

To my side, Monte Cetona sat like a big giant, its shoulders and back rolling in sliding slopes densely vegetated, thick with dark trees and bathed in sunlight, opening, as you descend, to fields of olive trees and rows and rows of grapevines. At the height of Fighine, the top of the mountain, *la cima,* bristly with pines and other mountain-ous trees, stands almost to your side, like you could wave open your left arm and hit the cross with the back of your hand. It is immediate and magnificent.

I was disappointed that Fighine is privately owned now and there is no access to the castle, or, for that matter, any lookout. Workers were there restoring another portion of the town, and I briefly hoped they could show me.

— *No, signora*, they said, there is no place to look out. No, ma'am.

I noticed the *signora*, a new development since I was last here.

On my way back down I relished the view, and I headed to another hamlet nearby, Camporsevoli, on an adjacent slope of Monte Cetona, a tiny group of houses surrounding a church and another small castle or fort of some kind, another place I had not visited in decades. The town was deserted—I saw not a person or a cat—but recently and immaculately restored.

On the outskirts of the village I stopped to take a picture. A man was picking olives in a field below me, the first harvest I am witnessing here on this stay. He stopped his work and came towards me, stopping to chat. I asked him about the town and he tells me that one family owns the whole of it; that when they bought it, it was all falling apart. They do good work, generous; they keep it in good shape and clean, and they pay for it all, too.

Without them, he said, it would be a ruin. It *was* a ruin.

I think back to when Aldo and Anna, friends of my parents, owned the Rocca, Cetona's castle. They had just bought it and, high-mindedly, they decided that they wanted to give the Cetonesi a chance to celebrate the property and see it. They opened it for a day: They put out beautiful food and generous drink and let people roam through the carefully manicured hedges and the rose gardens and take in the spectacular view of the countryside and the town below. Town folk came, hoarded the food like they had not eaten for a month, drank all the wine, threw garbage on the paths, and talked trash behind Anna and Aldo's back for trying to do something nice.

Never again, said Anna, seething, and rightfully. Never again. I guess I can see why castles are private.

While I was talking with the man I noticed a tiny chapel set off the road, a matchbox of a building, stone, surrounded by a simple wooden fence and a metal gate in a patch of brilliant green grass. There was a plaque, dated 1916, and I asked him what it was.

He said it was a votive chapel. They built it during World War I so people could go there and pray for the lost and the wounded.

— *Quando ancora la gente ci credeva. Adesso non tanto,* he said. When people still prayed. When people still believed. Now, he says shrugging, not so much.

The man offered to get the key from his mother, who is the caretaker, and he let me inside. It was lovely, plain but with dozens of tiny lights, pictures of the Virgin Mary, and plastic flowers. I think of what it must have been like there during World War I, in the middle of nowhere, high up on the mountain, with no news, no information, no phones, praying for a son who had gone, a husband. 1916.

— *L'anziani, i giovani l'avranno costruita,* the man said. Old people and children must have built it—people who had not gone to war.

— *Chissà,* he said, looking out onto the landscape. Who knows.

Our wondering hangs in the air.

I commented on the weather, the beauty of the day, and the peace I am retrieving, slowly, here.

I have missed it so.

He smiled.

— *Eh si, qui è diverso. Qui, se senti passare una macchina è strano,* he said. Yes, here it's different, not like other places. Here, it's strange to hear a car.

On a recent evening at the Bar Cavour Felice and I started reminiscing about elementary school. We made most of the list of our classmates, easily retrieving the little faces from our shared memories. Life never seemed to move far away from the crimson school at the end of the piazza where everyone has gone to school for the past hundred or more years, and, in fact, as I sit writing now, I hear the children at play in that same old garden. I recall the rooms where we spent most of our time, most vividly the one in fifth grade, so spacious and sunny, with the birds outside distracting me in spring through the open windows.

— *Purtroppo poi vi ho lasciato perché la Marga mi bocciò.*
Unfortunately, then I left the class because Marga flunked me, says
Felice, a bit of sadness tinging his smile.

He shakes his head. Marga.

On one of our visits to Cetona while our house was being
restored, Zio and Zia invited Signora Marga and her husband, an
engineer, to dinner. Ingegnere De Rosa, as he was known to most,
was a short, polite, balding man with a distinguished moustache.
He spent much of his time traveling for work, mostly in the south,
*il Mezzogiorno,* where he supervised the construction of bridges and
other large civil engineering projects. But the reason we were introduced was for my parents to meet Marga, the most feared and beloved
teacher at Cetona's elementary school. We would be moving to Cetona
soon, and, Zia insisted, Marga had to be my teacher.

To this day adults in Cetona can be sorted based on whether
they were taught by Marga or someone else. The alternatives to Marga
ran from the bland to the preposterous: I don't remember all of them,
but there was Maestro Ciacci, an old man who used to send my friend
Fabrizio, then nine or ten, to Vando's bar to buy him mini bottles of
Vecchia Romagna during class; Signora Bencini, a nice older woman,
a widow, kind and even-tempered but academically undistinguished;
Fosca, a crusty, gossipy woman of mediocre teaching ability; Signora
Sacuto, mean as the devil; and, finally, we had Benigno, the son of
Arduino, a well-educated if persnickety man who had eschewed the
priesthood at the last minute and who liked to keep an eye on the busi-
ness of the town during lengthy sweepings in front of his house in a
perfectly white undershirt.

And then there was Marga.

Marga was a petite woman with beautiful dark skin and swift jet-
black eyes. Her hair was dark, just above her shoulders, pushed back
from her face, wavy and natural. She wore glasses, most often perched
on the top of her head or, menacingly, on the bridge of her nose.
From the way she spoke to the way she dressed, Marga was no-nonsense: She walked head down, absorbed in thought, quickly and with

focus, her arms straight along her body, a cigarette in one hand and a short-handled and elegant purse in the other. She wore smart sensible skirts—never pants—and elegant blouses, or sometimes a simple button-down dress that showed off her slender figure, and shoes with a sensible heel. She wore no makeup and always specific pieces of gold jewelry, always the same—a tasteful gold wristwatch, a sizeable gold necklace with some kind of medallion, her thick gold wedding band, and another gold ring on the same finger, heavy, with a stone. When we met her, she was in her early fifties and her sober beauty lived solidly in her pronounced cheekbones and high eyebrows.

Marga was from Piazze; her father's family owned the olive mill and the combines there. Her mother and her sisters ran a *pensione*, an inn, and people from all over Italy, including conductor Arturo Toscanini and some royalty, stayed there when they came to be treated by the famous Dottor Rinaldi, whose care miraculously banished rheumatisms and arthritis. In any case, Marga grew up in the light of a certain sophistication, and perhaps because of her family's stature, Marga was volcanic, mercurial and independent. In her twenties she had owned a red Moto Guzzi, which she drove every day to a country school in San Casciano where she first taught, after the war, and she carried a pistol—against the times and the solitary stretches of country road.

Marga chain-smoked and she had a deep throaty voice that carried loudly. Whether in a classroom, the bar, or the middle of the piazza, you always knew where Marga was. When she laughed, which was often and with exuberance, she did so till she exhausted the air in her, then she put her hand theatrtically to her chest, most often holding a cigarette, and gasped for breath, inhaling dramatically like she was about to die. Like many Cetonesi, Marga said exactly what she thought and tolerated no challenge to her authority or her way of seeing the world.

On one occasion, the *guardie di finanza*, the much-loathed financial police, always chasing after tax evaders with the myriad of absurd Italian laws, stopped Marga while she was going home with a plant she had purchased. She did not have the required receipt for the plant and the police hassled her. Had she paid for the plant? Where did she buy it?

— *È la mia pianta! La sto portando a prendere un pò d'aria! È contro la legge?* It is my plant and I am taking it for a ride to get some fresh air, she answered them with a mix of outrage, charm, and simple logic. Is that against the law?

And so, she argued with all. Nearly every afternoon, weather permitting, Marga stopped at the Bar Sport for an espresso and a moment *a veglia* at her favorite table, to the left of the door. She lit a cigarette, and while picking her teeth with the unburnt end of a wooden match, she held court, pontificating with anyone who came along, or with no one in particular, about the issue of the day, be it a national event or a matter of the town—maybe a death or a divorce or the affairs of someone's personal life, which caused her to speak no less loudly.

Then, all of a sudden she'd look at her watch, gather up her purse and cigarettes, and drive off in her dark blue Fiat 500, which she parked in front of her house, one of the most beautiful *palazzi* on the piazza, where she lived with her husband and their son, Taddeo, thin and beautiful.

But aside from her colorful personality, through the decades, in this sleepy town where few people had a formal education, by dint of being cultured and ironfisted Marga had acquired the reputation as best teacher in town. So, when September rolled around I entered Signora Marga's class with fifteen or so other children, all of us in our smocks, white for the girls, black for the boys.

Our school was—and remains—lovely. Located at the main entrance to the piazza, and surrounded by tall pine trees and a garden, it has large spacious classrooms, high ceilings, and huge windows, many of them looking out toward the piazza. Back then, elementary school started at 9 a.m. and ended at 1 p.m. A different subject was taught each hour, with short breaks in between, during which Marga left the room and went outside to smoke. At 11 a.m. we had *ricreazione*, a half-hour break, and all the children spilled out of the classrooms in their smocks and down the steps to the graveled and sunny garden. There were trees and sun and shade, and there we played and screamed, skipping rope, running, chasing each other, and eating our snack, if we had one. Teachers stood by, smoking and talking, taking turns supervising. Every now and then a fight broke out or someone started crying.

My classmates were children of Cetona: Matteo, son of a contractor; Simone, son of Mauro the mechanic, sweet, blond with sky-blue eyes; children of farmers who lived out in the country, like Ausilia, Cristina, and Felice; Ilia from Patarnione; Agata, whose father was a construction worker; Donatella Scarpi; Ida, the dentist's daughter; Carla Mugnai, and Claudio, a boy with coal hair and azure eyes who I was distraught to learn killed himself some years ago. As the system dictated, Marga would remain our teacher for the length of elementary school.

On our first day, she hugged her returning students, most of whom she had seen throughout the summer in the piazza or at the bar. She pulled their ears and pinched their cheeks, and gave them *gnocchetti*, rubbing their hair with her knuckles. Then she introduced me as the new student. She had a special place for me at the front of the classroom, perhaps because of Zio and Zia's friendship, or perhaps because I was new. She lauded my Italian, learned from Fazzi in Cremona, which resembled more closely the Italian she spoke than the mountainous and rough Cetonese, particularly out in the country, bent in every which way ingenious and comedic.

Anyway, Marga's ways and routines made themselves plain quickly, a maddening mix of unbridled affection and competence and off-the-wall cruelty. She taught a lot of material every day—geography, history, science, math, Italian poems, art, and art history—and she expected us to learn it quickly. Her preferred method for verifying that we had learned were regular oral examinations, or *interrogazioni*, several times a semester, at the blackboard. She kept records of our turns and performance in a big gray book prominently positioned on her desk.

When Marga opened her big book and with her glasses began trawling for a name, we collectively looked down and willed ourselves invisible. Finally, she called on someone and the unfortunate child shuffled slowly to the front of the class. We could predict from Marga's face how it was going to go—whether she was in the mood to be satisfied or not, or whether she was kindly inclined toward the child. If she was feeling impatient and the child was not one she liked, it was doomed from the start; if the child was prepared it helped, but mood and temperament added an element of unpredictability that made everyone edgy.

Often the interrogation simply came to a standstill after a few laborious minutes during which the child began to stare into the floor and eventually to cry. This happened particularly when she asked us to recite poems by heart.

— *La nebbia agl'irti colli...* the child would begin to say, reciting "San Martino," Giosuè Carducci's famous poem, which all Italian children must learn.

Then, he or she would get flustered.

— *Non mi ricordo più, Signora...* I don't remember anymore ...

Marga would frown and drag deeply from her cigarette.

— *Via, su... La nebbia agl'irti colli ... Piovv...* C'mon, c'mon, Marga would say, dropping a hint.

— *... igginando sale ...*

Another drag of the cigarette.

— *E sotto il ...*

Silence again. Then Marga would start screaming, bringing to a crescendo a familiar pattern.

Besides, there were the rings: If Marga walked into the classroom and took off her rings, placing them on her desk with a loud clink, we knew it was bad news. That foreshadowed that she'd call someone to the blackboard, and if she found us unprepared or flustered, she'd light a cigarette, rise from her chair, walk straight up to you and hit you about the head, sometimes flat-handed, sometimes with her knuckles.

The first time, or the first slap, was funny; the rest was not. If it was Felice, or Matteo—those were her favorite targets—she would hit them upside the head until they were red in the face and sometimes sobbing on the floor. The rest of the children in the class, used to it, I guess, kept their heads down until it was over and Marga walked back to her desk and Matteo got back on his chair and straightened out his straight brown hair and dried his tears.

I, however, had never experienced anything like that and I was horrified and terrified. Sometimes on the drive back to Patarnione Ilia would cry in the back seat of the car. I was unsure if she was crying for what Marga had done or for what awaited her when her father found out and blamed her. Poor Felice, meanwhile, got horribly flustered in class and Marga gravitated to him like vulture on carcass. He'd cry and flail his hands about, aggravating the ridicule and shame that our merciless classmates piled on him day in and day out. He survived all this valiantly.

Once, but only once, Marga hit me—upside the head with a wooden measuring stick that she had ordered us to buy from the local carpenter to study the metric system. That day she called me to the blackboard with my measuring stick, and during the ensuing math interrogation I got nervous and froze up. She walked over to me, took my stick from my hand, and striking me firmly, she broke it across my head (she did that to many others, as well). When I went home I had a bulging egg-sized swelling on my head, and the following day my mom came to talk with the principal.

Marga never hit me again.

The same happened with Donatella Scarpi, though her father, Franco, a gardener from Cetona, reacted more assertively: When he came to school to confront Marga—an episode he still remembers distinctly—he grabbed her by the shoulders, lifted her up, and dangled her outside the window by the arms.

— *A me me le dava così tante che camminavo all'indietro dalla vergogna di fa' vede' le gambe!* I got whipped so much by her that I walked backward from the shame of showing my legs, a man in town told me. Marga had taught him some ten years before my class.

Yet, through the years Marga kept the loyalty and love of many in town. She was not all bad, and, indeed, I suspect that under all that disciplinarian rage was a tenderness she couldn't manage, fed in part by the loss of a child some years earlier. This bled through every now and then, when she stuck up for a shamed child, for example, or when she ordered her colleagues to stop gossiping about this or that.

One day shortly after our arrival in Cetona, during *ricreazione* I told some of my classmates about the skyscrapers in America and how they reached into the sky with hundreds of floors. Children in Cetona had never heard of such things and they didn't believe me. They said I had made it up, that I was just showing off. Matteo, Donatella, and a few others circled me and chanted *bugiarda, bugiarda*—liar! liar!—until I cried. I felt humiliated and wronged, and I recall it as a defining moment in my awareness of meanness and dissimilarity. I vaguely remember Marga reproaching the class afterward—in spite of her gusts of temper, she had little tolerance for bullying or meanness, or perhaps it depended on who was meting it out—but the wound of that experience stuck with me nonetheless. I wasn't Cetonese, nor, perhaps, would I ever be.

Every now and then Marga would pontificate in class and go on tirades about current affairs and culture. Once, during a lesson about art history, she said that contemporary art was rubbish—a waste of time, a fraud. Though I was only nine or ten, this incensed me: My father was a big fan of Rothko, Picasso, Mondrian, Pollack, de Kooning, already household names to me though I understood nothing of their work, of course.

But perhaps most visceral to me was the fact that one of my parents' best friends was Gert, a bearded abstract painter and photographer who owned a house up in town, up the street from us. He was a German-born Jew from Berlin whose family had been killed in the concentration camps—he had escaped as a child, through Sweden—leaving him an orphan and a man alone in the world, though later he married and had a son.

Gert spent the rest of his life in New York painting and taking pictures and battling the horror of his grief. My father loved his work, which hung in our house, and he was teaching my brother to paint.

I raised my hand, my heart beating in my throat.

— *Signora Marga, non è giusto che dica così! Il nostro amico Gert è un eccellente pittore!* I said. It is not right for you to say that! Our friend Gert is an excellent painter!

I sat down and Marga went out to smoke without saying a word.

But Marga did not like to be contradicted and she took notes in her big book. One day I decided I wanted to see what she had written about me. When she went out for her hourly break, I walked over to her desk and I opened her big book, turning the pages to read her notes.

A little girl in my class, my friend Agata, shot up and threatened to tell on me.

— *Lo dico alla signora Marga, glielo dico!* she said. I'm going to tell Signora Marga, I will tell!!!!

As a child, Agata was bone-skinny and mildly strabismic. She wore huge glasses that constantly slid down her narrow nose, and she pushed them back compulsively with nervous long fingers. She had pale skin and soft black hair to her shoulders, with bangs, and she spoke in a birdlike voice, thin and nervous, like everything else about her. She had a big, sweet smile, though, full of teeth, and she laughed joyfully and fully, her laugh shaking her narrow shoulders, her mouth wide open to the sky. When she cried, she cried equally without restraint, sobbing and sniffling and drying her tears with her long fingers as they pooled under her glasses, her eyes red and sad.

I remember seeing Agata cry often, and I have a bad feeling that at least on one occasion it was my fault. She was a loyal friend, though, and she was happy and nervously excited when I went to her house to play.

That day I begged Agata, then threatened her. We got into an argument and, finally, as she repeated that she was going to tell, I slapped her face, catapulting her glasses into the middle of the floor just as Marga opened the door and walked in.

The class paused quickly in terror, but Agata ran to retrieve her glasses and sat back down. No one said a word, and the incident was forgotten.

One the last day of fifth grade we gathered in our classroom to get our final report card. We would be attending a different school the following fall, the *scuola media*. Marga gave me my report card—a list of straight tens, the highest of grades—and pulled me to her with tears in her eyes.

— *Sii brava, Sibilla. Stai sempre brava come sei,* she said. Be good, Sibilla, be good always as you are.

She said the same thing to me often when she saw me during the *liceo*, and when I left for college. She was proud of me, and, in some way, I was grateful to her.

One day recently, while I was walking around the piazza I noticed that the big door to the elementary school was open. I walked to the end of the piazza, and when I got to the top of the front steps I saw the school's custodian, Giulio, who I had not seen in many years.

He greeted me and asked me about my life in America.

— *Ma Cetona te la ricordi sempre, eh?* he said, rhetorically. You still remember Cetona ...

He asked me if I wanted to walk around the school. It was afternoon, and our voices reverberated in the empty hallways and classrooms, with their high ceilings and immense windows. We found the rooms that had been my classroom in third grade, then fourth, and finally in fifth, my favorite. I wiggled myself into one of the little chairs and, facing the big windows open to the piazza, I closed my eyes. Our crazy screams played back in my ears, and the birds chirping outside, and I saw myself in my little white smock, running.

I miss NPR and *60 Minutes*, and the bustle and anonymity of a larger city where something is happening. I don't have TV and I feel a bit cut out of the world. My most recent habits, none developed here, pull at me.

Then, I remember that that's not why I am here. I need to let go of the other side, in reverse, and when I manage to do that I am deeply happy, fed by the comfort of revisitation.

In my travels to reknow and rekindle, I seek out the mothers of childhood friends, who, to this day, feel much like mothers to me. I love meeting them again as a grown woman, in a town where, as a grown woman, I have been much of a visitor.

When we first moved to Cetona and I was the new kid in town, going home from school to my friends' houses for lunch or being invited for a Sunday *pranzo* was the pinnacle of acceptance and belonging. Whether it was a *panino*, or *merenda*, tea and cookies during home-work or afternoon play, or a *crostata*, or a piece of Tuscan bread with tomato, and whether their households were wealthy or poor, whether they were the homes of the dentist or the farmer, for me it was special. Their kitchens were places of refuge and company, warm and gener-ous, enveloping like a blanket.

— *Vieni!!!!!* they would yell from inside when you knocked on the door. Come in, come in!!

I still feel that same way when I visit Ave. I seek out her kitchen, and her smile, and today we decide to make gnocchi together.

Ave is the mother of my friends Silvio and Aldo Della Vigna, the former three years older than me and the latter ten or so. For years I viewed Ave through the lens of my friendship with Silvio and Aldo and my affection for the family as a whole, but in recent years I have begun to regard Ave as my own freestanding friend and to cultivate our relationship independently. I like to drop by her house, in an imposing building at the entrance of town, and chat, to give her a hug and say hi, and I like to visit in the piazza with her, when I see her in the afternoons, always purposefully dressed, sensible, with care yet modesty.

Mostly, I love to explore her inner being at the confines of the roles she has lived as a wife and a mother, which, for many women in Cetona, have come with enormous expectations of acquiescence and competence from the men in her life. Ave is not used to the spotlight, and at first approach she shies away from it; but her timidity, learned rather than natural, eventually falls away, and a feisty and adventurous personality comes out sparkling.

Ironically, perhaps, my explorations of Ave come from cooking with her, a talent for which she is known and which happens to bring out something fluid and natural in her. She pours and folds and stirs and chats and cuts and laughs breezily, and taking it all in requires some concentration. Everything is so simple to her, so known: If you miss a step or a measurement, she shrugs and looks at you with her dark eyes as if to say, how much simpler can that be? Are you dumb?

On this day she pulls out what she needs to make gnocchi, something she has known to make almost since her birth in 1933 on a farm in San Casciano dei Bagni, about forty minutes from Cetona.

— *Vengo dalla campagna io, eh!* she says, proud. I come from the country. That word, *la campagna,* proud and laden.

Starting as far back as her great-grandfather in the mid-1800s, possibly a bit earlier, when Italy was still divided between the Vatican, the Grand Duchy of Tuscany, and various kingdoms, her family worked for a wealthy landowning family as sharecroppers, the same as Caio and many others. Her parents, the fourth generation to work the property, shared the farmhouse with her paternal grandparents, two brothers of her father, the wife and children of one of the brothers, and the animals downstairs.

— *Era un podere bellissimo,* Ave says, smiling dreamily. It was a beautiful farm.

In a place where land brought much subjugation, Ave's feelings are endearing, though likely, like my own, colored by the romance of childhood.

She pulls out a box of pictures. There is one of her in a Holy Communion dress, a petite, dark girl with a round face, flawless skin, wearing a tall hat of sorts, something from another era. Other tiny black and white pictures show her and her family in front of the farmhouse, and then the family in the grass, smiling, perhaps for a rare party or a picnic.

As a young girl Ave shared the family chores, mostly tending the pigs, cutting the grass for the animals, ironing, and sewing. She went to school through fifth grade and dreamed of being a teacher, but continuing school was impossible—too far and expensive. Fascism and soon a war convulsed the country, and she was needed on the farm.

Ave learned how to make bread and pasta before she was tall enough to reach the cupboards, she said. She'd stand on a chair and knead the dough on the *madia*.

— *Facevo la pasta ch'avevo nove anni!* she says, laughing and cupping her face in her hands. I wasn't even nine!

In her late teens she met Onorato Della Vigna, a handsome young man from Cetona. He worked with his father cutting wood for firewood in winter and harvesting wheat and corn in summer. The Della Vignas owned some of the earliest combines in the area—stationery at the time—and they worked for hire, here and there. On one occasion Onorato went to Ave's house to chop and haul off wood, and he spent several days and nights there, sleeping in Ave's house. A courtship ensued and they fell in love. While she tells this Ave smiles shyly and I see the memory of a spark flashing in her eyes.

They married in 1955, on a sunny day. Ave shows me pictures of their wedding, she petite, dark, dressed in a white suit, and Onorato in a handsome dark suit with a flower in his lapel, swarthy and flirtatious. He has short tight curly hair and a winsome smile, and he exudes the strength and character I came to know in him. On my returns home, he always greeted me with a strong handshake and a hug, and a smile full of welcome and affection. In the pictures I see hope in Ave, and happiness.

As was customary at the time, Ave moved in with her in-laws, and from her mother-in-law she learned what she didn't already know: how to make *sugo*, how to cook meat, and how to sauce and dress everything else. How to please everyone.

— She would say, add salt there, put this there, and I learned, Ave recalls.

Over the ensuing decades the Della Vignas went on to become large landowners themselves, buying land, restoring old farmhouses in Val D'Orcia, and acquiring the biggest combines and most sophisticated farming machinery in the area. And as they went, so did Ave, with her growing responsibility to support the business. Ave's culinary prowess blossomed and; she followed the men, food in hand.

— Back in the old days I'd go up to the farmhouses and there was nothing, no water, nothing. I would cook for them, take the food out to the fields, bring the baskets back into town, she says.

She takes her face in her hands, assessing the toll it took on her family.

— *I sacrifici che abbiamo fatto per la terra,* she says. The sacrifices we made for the land.

I met the Della Vignas harvesting wheat for Zio and Zia when we first came to Cetona to visit. Aldo, and some years later Silvio, had started working with Onorato and their grandfather. I remember watching this kid covered in thick dust, helping load freshly harvested wheat into an old smoky, sputtering red stationary combine parked in the middle of the *aia*, the gravel courtyard that is in front of traditional Tuscan farmhouses.

At that time, wheat was cut by hand, with scythes and sickles, and gathered by tractor through the fields. Now, in the heat of summer you can drive to Val d'Orcia and, if you scan the expansive landscape of golden wheat from the top of a hill, you will spot a cloud of dust. Below are the Della Vigna brothers, coursing up and down the hills in their barreling air-conditioned combines, Silvio, temperamental, with prominent eyes and a boisterous manner, and Aldo, older, short, calmer (for the most part), a carbon copy of his father, with a streak of Onorato's old stubborn tenaciousness and gentility. In Aldo I see Onorato's steadfastness and moral stature.

In fall the Della Vigna brothers harvest grapes and olives, their own and for others; they cut and deliver timber, and they prepare the land anew, theirs and for others, and seed it for wheat and corn, hundreds and hundreds of hectares all over the countryside, from Cetona west to the Val D'Orcia and south to San Casciano and all over the Val di Chiana. In spring the seed sprouts in endless and glorious stretches of sprawling gem green, and in summer it all starts anew, with the dusty golden wheat—if one can trace a beginning or an end to that kind of work.

Ave shows me some pictures of the old *poderi* in Val D'Orcia, these old poetic farmhouses with their stalls and old porches and ancient staircases outside, abandoned by families and history. Now that their *poderi* are restored and rented to foreigners for the summers, Ave runs back and forth making sure everything is perfect for the guests—the linens, the swimming pools and towels, the food, and the houses.

— *Il lavoro non finisce mai, e non si fa pari,* Ave says, looking at me.

I see worry in her eyes. The work is never done. There is a new combine to be paid for, and more land to work, and only so many days to the year, all dictated by nature.

We finish making gnocchi and they are spread all over the table, plump and beautiful. It seems like they happened by magic, though we know that nothing does.

Silvio comes in with Emanuele, his youngest—they live next door—and Emanuele demands lunch.

He gobbles a few raw gnocchi and asks when he will be able to go swimming up at the *poderi*. He complains that they will be occupied all summer.

— *Emanuele, non ti lamenta' che un giorno saranno tuoi,* I say to him. Don't complain so much! One day they will be yours.

I struggle to imagine what that would be like, to inherit this land.

Silvio bursts out laughing. I hear wheezing and I think to myself that he needs to stop smoking.

— *Beato lui, dopo che ho lavorato e pagato io,* Silvio says, nodding toward his son, sarcasm brimming on his face. Lucky him, after I will have done all the work and paying.

Ave raises her eyebrows. It's the cycle, and all for the children— as she and Onorato gave to Silvio and Aldo.

Onorato died last year after a long battle with cancer, through which Ave escorted him day and night for many months. Yet, now Ave feels guilty to draw even a breath of relief and enjoy some peace. I suggest she rent a house at the beach and get away from the needs of children, the work of cooking, the obligations of fields and houses. I wish I could take her.

She looks at me and shrugs. It may be a hard concept to tackle.

# Gnocchi

Ingredients

    1 large potato per person

    1 egg every four people

    3 cups of flour

    Salt

Directions

    Boil the potatoes until soft, peel them, and put them through a food mill using the disk with the smallest holes. Using a fork, mix the milled potatoes with the eggs, and turn them out onto a floured wooden board (for pasta-making). Add the flour to the potato/egg combination, flouring the board as well, and begin working the dough with your hands like you would bread. The dough should have a firm, bread-like consistency. When all the flour is incorporated, shape it into a loaf and cut it in thick slices, like bread. Using your hands, roll the slices into snakes about an inch in diameter, then with a knife cut them into chunks, about the size of a hard candy. Make sure the gnocchi are floured as you go so they don't stick to each other. Gnocchi do not need to sit; in fact, Ave recommends cooking them as soon as possible. Cook in boiling water for a few short minutes, then mix with sauce.

On a recent day Maria showed up holding a number of bags each containing a package of letters—our letters—neatly tied with twine and dated with little labels: 1974 to 1986, 1987 to 1992, and so on.

— *Le ho rilette tutte!* she announced proudly, smiling. I re-read all of them!

— *È stato molto commovente,* she added softly, looking away. It was very moving.

I hugged her and took the bags from her, staring down at this vast and carefully packaged lens into our lives, beginning in childhood. It is an unimaginable gift of memory and magic, a bit like our childhood itself, a time I recall as safe, warm, and full of little girls. The princesses of my girlhood.

Agata, the girl whose glasses I knocked off in my class with Marga in third grade, was my first. She rescued me from many dreary days in fall and winter, when Cetona can yield seemingly interminable spans of rainy, cold weather and playing outside is impossible. Fog descends on the town and the surrounding hills like an impenetrable curtain of white mist, impossible to see through, and it rains, steadily, stubbornly, for days.

On days like that, Agata and I would schedule a play date, and before school let out at 1 p.m. we had settled if she was coming to my house or I was going to hers. We were eight years old, yet there were no phone calls to parents for approval, or driving here or there to accompany us. There were no phones then. Besides, Cetona was so small that everyone knew everyone else, at least by sight. What could possibly happen? Where could we possibly go?

Of course, my dad didn't know Agata's parents, and probably couldn't have picked them out of a crowd if he needed to, but with rare exceptions everyone knew who my parents were—the *americani di Borgo*—and all the moms knew who my mom was, if nothing else from seeing her shop around town.

Could we play together was not something that needed asking.

Agata's family lived—still lives—on the top floor of a tall building just off the piazza, above the *tabaccheria* and in front of the *torre* of the Carabinieri, the police. To get to her apartment I walked up several narrow flights of steep steps leading to a small brown door.

— *Vieni, Sibi, vieni,* Agata's mother, Bruna, would call out from inside.

Agata's mom, plump and short and with curious brown eyes, was a homemaker, and her husband, Lidiano, was a construction worker who came home every night covered in a thin layer of white dust. He put his work things down while Bruna served us tea in china cups with generous piles of buttery cookies. Sometimes we covered the whole plastic table cloth with tiny mini cups and saucers for our dolls, and Bruna indulged us patiently as we poured tea everywhere. I never saw Bruna mad.

Sometimes in the afternoons during play we bathed Agata's cat in the bath tub, and the cat ran down the stairs soaking wet and howling.

— What did you do at Agata's? Dad would ask at my return home.

— We bathed the cat, I would reply, giggling.

My father was always incredulous when I told him this, which apparently was pretty often. He always laughed about it.

Agata came to my house, too, even when it was raining. Daintily, as Agata did, she'd walk under the shelter of her little umbrella, skipping over the puddles and the rivulets that coursed down Borgo, and she'd knock shyly on our front door with her nervous, thin fingers. At that time my mom had started teaching piano, and she had built a solid stable of students, some in Cetona but most in the neighboring towns of Chianciano and Montepulciano. Nearly every weekday, inclement weather notwithstanding, she left the house after lunch and came home around 8 p.m., except for days when she had her Cetona students and she taught at home. On those days I always scheduled play and homework at someone else's house. Otherwise, I was happy to stay home with Dad, who worked quietly in his lab, making violins in his white lab coat, the stereo in the living room playing Dvorak, Beethoven, Bach, and Chopin... and so much more. That was the music of my home.

During our time alone together, Dad took care of my earaches when I was sick, and taught me how to make miniature pizzas, and Christmas ornaments out of clay. His work required a lot of concentration and presence, so he was not big on having lots of kids at the house, but he liked having Agata around. We'd sit on the big rug in the living room and play quietly, except for our giggling, and Dad would make us tea. We'd make paper dolls and clothes for them, covering the floor with sheets and scraps of paper and fancy dresses and fashionable pant suits colored with magic markers and crayons. Agata and I spent hours drifting in a luxurious world of make-believe fashion and lifestyles that transported us out of our rainy landscape, trading dolls and bartering clothes until darkness fell and we had to part.

In spring, we dressed my cat Amonasro in doll clothes, particularly the baptism dress from my doll, and took him for rides down Borgo in my doll carriage, strapped in like a child. Amonasro was a patient cat.

*— Ci siamo inventate tutto quello che non c'era, di sana pianta.* We came up with everything we didn't have, from the ground up, Agata said when I went to visit her a few days ago.

And it's true. There was no theater, no movies, nothing. We had to entertain ourselves, and perhaps because of that, our childhood still seems simply and richly magical. We lacked for nothing.

Agata and I are visiting in the kitchen of her home, in Chiusi, which sits next to a big store that sells Chinese products—everything in the store is Chinese, without exception. *Il Cinese*, they call the store, the Chinaman, and it's an ugly reminder of what is happening to all of Italy. In any case, Agata and I have not seen each other in a decade or more, and then only briefly, so she invited me to come and catch up.

Over the course of an hour we hit the highpoints of a new lifetime. She is married now, which I knew, to a nice man who works in a chemical plant, and she has a daughter who recently had a baby. Recently she had a bout with cancer that she ignored for months, out of fear, and that could have killed her. She is lucky to be alive, I tell her, and we take stock in that for a moment, that it all could have gone differently. I think of our paper dolls strewn on the floor, and she reminds me of postcards I sent her of skyscrapers, the Twin Towers, maybe in college. I am happy to see her and her warm and affectionate smile and now-healthy, strong body. We look at old pictures together; she shows me her two pet turtles and tells me some stories. She is still funny and girly as she was, yet she has acquired an unexpected wisdom and surety, which mixed with her old Cetonese piazza-savvy banter, leaves me little to add. I have never done well with small talk, and the larger questions are just too big for me right now.

What about your life, she asks. Are you happy? She mentions my divorce. How to explain to others what is unexplainable even to oneself? I struggle awkwardly in these few minutes to identify words to embody the complexity of my thoughts and feelings and capture the chapters of my life far away in places that she cannot imagine. Everything sounds overly simplistic, reductive and unexpressed.

I shrug. I let the familiarity and the memories, warm and cradling, suffice.

I want to leave things simple, the way they look.

— *E Ida l'hai vista?? Com'era drammatica, ti ricordi?!* Agata says, laughing. Have you seen Ida? She was so dramatic, do you remember?! She still is!

Ida was my other early childhood princess.

Skinny, she had a thin heart-shaped face, serious and even a bit pinched, until she laughed and it opened like the sun. Ida's father, Giampiero, was the town's dentist, a self-assured man who did a lot of unpaid work for people who could not afford it, including my parents at one point. He would turn down money, or completely forgive debt, if someone could not pay, and he did it with true generosity.

Giampiero drove a Citroen DS, a car whose rear end lifted upon ignition like magic, something having to do with pneumatics. It was a bad-ass car—in fact, it came to be recognized later as one of the most beautiful cars of the century—and by dint of this car Giampiero might have just been Batman, as far as I was concerned. His dentistry studio was in the upper part of town, and to get there every day he had to navigate his luxury car through one of Cetona's narrowest streets, Via Roma, which had been designed in the 1400s for the passage of mules and carts. The fact that the street accommodated the Citroen with less than an inch to spare on each side did not tame Giampiero's lust for speed, and he blew through the passage daily, going thirty or so kilometers an hour, with seeming mathematical precision, car unscathed. This fact filled me with awe and added to Giampiero's aura as the coolest dad in town.

Ida's mom was Lelia, a tall—a foot taller than Giampiero—beautiful blond woman with a sinuous figure and sea foam green eyes that juggled kindness and play and patience, eternal patience. She had had Rossana, her first child, Ida's sister, when she was barely eighteen, and by the time I met the family, Rossana was married to a man by the name of Diego and she was getting ready to have a child of her own. Ida's older brother was Teodoro, affectionately called Teo, a skinny, charming and already beautiful kid who became one of my brother's best friends, and eventually one of mine.

Lelia managed home, children, and being Giampiero's wife all with great charm and poise. She wore elegant long leather coats with fur collars and had beautiful clothes and gold rings on her fingers. Their apartment, on the third floor of a post-war apartment building at the edge of town, had psychedelic seventies lamps and leather furniture, and, I regretfully say, a big leopard skin rug on the floor of their bedroom, where often we played except when Lelia suffered from sciatica, and then the room was shuttered and darkened and we made not a peep.

I loved going to Ida's house for lunch or dinner; the whole family was there, and it was noisy and festive. Giampiero would bicker with Teo, who was on the threshold of high school but whose interests were murky and shiftless—aside from soccer. While the family ate and carried on, from the little kitchen with a balcony overlooking Via Risorgimento Lelia brought out course after course of delicious food, and she'd say, *mangia, Sibilla, mangia!!* I was always thrilled to be included. The whole family felt particularly special to me, and to this day I have for them an affection that exceeds reason, perhaps because of their togetherness and the fact that their front door was always open.

Quickly Ida and I became nearly inseparable, for many years. We looked alike in the way we were built, slender, with light brown hair, and we had similar mannerisms as girls, vivacious, funny, irreverent, a little bossy and argumentative. We took to each other easily.

We met for play at her house or mine nearly every day after school. The week Rossana was due to have her baby—*in casa*, a home birth—everyone was on edge and I stayed away. But a few days after Rossana gave birth, to a healthy baby boy named Adriano, and I went to visit. Ida led me to the bedroom where her sister had given birth and she showed me the railings of the bed.

— *Guarda*, she said. Look.

We stared at the bed. Its metal headboard had been pulled forward dramatically in the throes of childbirth. It was like an extra-terrestrial phenomenon had manifested in their house—perhaps an alien. I had never heard of such a thing, and it was nothing less than awesome.

At my house, we played teacher in my room, bossing each other around loudly and quizzing each other at my blackboard, the windows open to the sunny landscape around us. We played kitchen, with little pots and pans, using leaves and rocks as food, and we played down at the creek, moving rocks around and changing the course of the stream, which made Beppa shake her head. And gathered in the fronds of the tree house, we played secret club. We wrote mysterious notes in lemon juice and signed them in blood, pricked from our veins, and delivered them to secret places for our rival club, which by then included Agata.

In our most memorable phase, we played pranks on people, the ladies of Borgo being prime victims: We'd gather around a curve right before reaching Borgo and switch clothes. I would pull my hair up like Ida, then walk down the street where Beppa and Arzelia and the other ladies were sitting chatting and knitting, and I'd ask, *Buona sera, avete visto passa' la Sibilla?* Buona sera, have you seen Sybil go by?

—No! they'd say back, we have not.

Then I would run back up the street, Ida would put on my clothes, run down the street and ask if they had seen her, Ida.

—You just missed each other! the ladies would say, telling us which way the other went.

Ida liked to poison the waters and start chatting longer to test the ladies, then finally she would run back and we would nearly die in peals of laughter. And so it went, a dozen or so times until one of them got exasperated or started laughing and chased us off affectionately. I don't know if they played along with us or not, but it made for long funny afternoons.

One winter we embarked on a series of prank phone calls from the telephone booth at the end of the piazza, in front of Vando's bar.

We snuggled in the booth in the late afternoon—it must have been winter because I remember it being dark early—and did the usual hanging up on people, or sometimes called restaurants in the area to order meals and organize fictitious events such as birthday parties and weddings.

Then, sometimes we chose a specific phone number and called it back repeatedly over weeks.

— *Pronto?* someone at the other end of the line would say, and we would stand there quietly until we could hold our laugher no longer and we'd crack up laughing. This went on and on.

Once we chose a particular number and called it various times until the woman who answered started crying.

— *Per favore la smetta, la prego*, she begged. Please stop, please.

We hung up and ran out of the phone booth laughing but perplexed. We didn't understand the severity of the matter until we called the same number several more times and, finally, one evening, a different woman came to the phone.

She sounded younger.

— *La smetta, per favore. Lasci mio padre in pace!* Please stop, she said. You are ruining our family. Leave my father alone. Please!

Rather innocently we had tapped into some kind of ongoing and quite real family drama, a betrayal, it seems, which we could not have possibly imagined or understood, but the perceived seriousness of the matter caused us to finally abandon our phone tricks. Off we ran through the piazza and the roads that carried us home, and forgot all about it, for the moment, at least.

Childhood was simple then, though not without drama, to which my letters to Maria attest.

I don't remember exactly how I met Maria, though she likes to say that she chose me. She came up to me in a shaft of sunlight in the schoolyard while the other children ran around us.

— *Come ti chiami?* she asked.

I certainly don't remember a life *without* Maria. She was a tree in my childhood garden, always.

Once, she told me recently, when we were little we kissed on the lips on a park bench at the *campo sportivo* and we giggled for hours afterwards. Later, when we were adolescents, she was a somewhat indifferent, aloof girl, with this unmanageable head of curly hair and a slight attitude of disdain. She wore jeans overalls and a T-shirt, the only thing she wanted to wear at the time, though her mother begged her to go shopping. I have a clear image of us walking hand in hand as little girls, nine or ten, her curls and lovely round features etched in my memory.

At her house for Sunday lunches I basked in the kitchen where her mother, Elia, set everything so nice for me. Upstairs in her room she'd show me her things, her soaps and Spuma di Sciampagna bath gel, which seemed particularly special and which I admired with trembling delight and a bit of sorrow, I don't know why. I loved everything about Maria with childlike adoration.

Maria didn't play at my house like Ida or Agata, perhaps because our friendship really blossomed in our tweens, just as life shifted from play to existential becoming. That shift unfolded in an epistolary relationship that to this day astonishes me and moves me. Even though we lived just minutes away from each other and saw each other every single day—except for the month her family spent at the sea each year and, later, the time I spent at the sea babysitting—Maria and I wrote each other daily. We hand-delivered the letters to secret places before going to school or to bed. My letters are written on stationery filled with trees and rainbows and bucolic scenes, and some on paper with pink roses surrounding a house, given to me by my mom as a birthday present, a beloved token of my girlishness and my love for writing.

In our letters Maria and I fervently dissected our love for one another, swearing, off and on, eternal friendship and loyalty, as girls feel the need to do, or I did at least, and, over the years she became my dearest confidante in all matters related to angst about boys, love, and family. And there was always much of that, beginning with our older siblings, who were regular causes of strife in each of our families.

Maria's sister, Emma, five years older than Maria, had the face of a movie star and the theatrical flair to go with it. Everyone doted on her and followed her every move, it seemed. She was in an explosive relationship with Pierpaolo, a bearded rabble-rouser ten or so years older than us whose family, like most, had lived in Cetona forever. They were activists in Lotta Continua, at a moment of particular violence and conflict in the Italian political scene, both overt and covert.

Emma and Pierpaolo's relationship existed in an aura of melodrama and romance mixed with political rebelliousness, which, together with Emma's way of being, brought a fair amount of drama to Maria's family. Maria, a calmer, more reserved type, absorbed this, finding her place in the penumbra, though she adored her older sister.

The same went for my brother, five years older than me, who by then, though still at an early age, was becoming an artist and a musician and overthrowing the rules of school and family, as well as parental expectations, and getting in a fair amount of juvenile trouble. This pitted our parents against each other and caused regular and often explosive friction. My parents argued over my brother all the time.

As Maria and I each weathered the ever-growing circle of waves that came from having older siblings thrashing about in life's pond, we became bonded by the impact and a mutual empathy we retain to this day.

At some point, angst about boys set in, too, beginning with Fabrizio, the friend I have mentioned before. Tall and gangly, back then he was an irascible boy with bushy black hair and a prominent nose whose love we ended up sharing—the first of several we shared. I had a heart-rending, awkward crush on him—though in reality it probably lasted a month—and he went on, some years later, to be one of Maria's greatest loves. As for me, he remains one of my dearest friends.

In a letter to me around that time, in one of her bouts of cynicism, Maria must have said I was too young to love, anyway. I was fourteen. Setting out a somewhat persuasive if indignant argument, I replied that the ability to feel love was parallel to one's moral growth—a topic that engrossed me—and that I had asked my parents if I had the ability to love. They must have said yes, and I felt ennobled.

Yet, with the new ability to love came also a new and morbid sense of abandonment and sickly dependence, feelings that over the ensuing few years we righteously expressed together in the loud singing of songs whose lyrics reflected our lovesickness, such as Gloria Gaynor's "I Will Survive" and Donna Summer's "Enough Is Enough" (which is still our banner friendship song).

In any case, it was through these simple shared facts of life and spasms of growth that we became sisters of sorts, and one day, a sunny day at the fountain, Maria and I broke in half an alabaster medallion painted with the face of a dark-haired woman. We each took a half and promised to be forever joined.

I still have my half, somewhere.

Being here stirs the most tender corners of my being, the child within me, and I feel exhilarated and giddy.

Yet, I also feel raw, lonely, and vulnerable. All my parameters feel shifted. I am comforted as I have never been by the act of revisiting that which I know, yet also hollowed by the knowledge that time can harm even the most precious of things. One moment the recognition of faces and the ancient ring of my steps on the pavement root me like anchors, yet moments later I feel deeply estranged, retreating in an interior world quashed inside that I cannot vocalize.

I need faith and time to know again, and to be known, yet a fearless willingness to recognize that some things may have changed forever. I am discovering within me responses that were not there before, protests of time and distance.

*Non ci sono più abituata*—I am not used to it anymore.

At moments the piazza strikes me as stark and desolate, lacking in life and vegetation, maybe lacking in texture, music and dance, things that in my adult life I have come to love and place deep meaning into. I love music and dinner parties and congregations of people that allow for meaningful exchanges. This quiet and lack of people feels foreign and odd. The buildings are beautiful, but now they glare at me like big empty screens. I don't know who lives there anymore, or does anyone even really live there anymore?

Soon is a holiday weekend and everyone hopes it will bring people, that it will usher in some kind of temporary respite from themselves, from the inexorable fate of the lost town in the hills sitting quietly, waiting for something. The dialogue is constant: How many people will come? How long will they stay? Please, let them come!

— *Madonna, non c'è nessuno. È un paese morto.* It's a dead town, there's no one here.

It is quiet indeed, perhaps quieter than I have ever seen it—disquietingly quiet, I think—but the talk about it makes for a constant lament that I suddenly find futile and grating. People can talk for hours about absolutely nothing, and I realize that perhaps I have become (or was I already?) introverted and quiet. This is the Cetona I know and love, yet I had forgotten the details that suddenly find me unaccepting.

I am suddenly irritated by how people drive, how they hug the curves going too fast, how they don't care about what is around the curve. They have always driven like this, and yet ... I am irritated by how loud everyone is, by the lack of privacy, by the fact that you walk through the piazza and you feel naked and observed. It makes focusing on my interior world and on my thoughts difficult, almost impossible. I am irritated by how the children scream and their parents let them scream. I feel out of place, and judgmental, and irritated by my own judgment and discomfort. I am missing anonymity.

I remind myself to remember why I came. I came because I missed it so bitterly and for so long. I came to visit, to find the bond that has kept me all these years, and to see how it fits me. I came because I have always wanted to be me here again, to merge my heart and creativity here as an adult; to see what the adult me does here—can do, here—in the place I love. It's the impetus of moving backward to go forward, tapping into what was, what made me, to find what I will be. The idea of rediscovery to remake, to recreate, to find and redo: to find a purpose from something old deep within me.

And here I am. I acted on it, I did, but I can't deny that it's unsettling. Exhilarating and unsettling.

I like that my life has become simpler, and I am doing without many things. I like my new (old) routine of buying a few things here and there, just what I need for tonight and tomorrow morning, then tomorrow I worry about another day. It gives me chances to walk through the piazza and see people and hug them. It puts me in a better mood and gifts me the joy of company that in the States is no longer a daily part of life.

And I like the quiet routine. Like most nights, unless I want to go out, which I can't afford to do, I eat dinner by myself, at my computer. Sometimes I write while I eat; sometimes I watch a movie. I like cooking in my kitchen, but it is a utilitarian pursuit devoid of extravagance or great expectations. I enjoy the ritual of shopping and making my dinner, a simple routine without frills or even searches for beauty or perfection. Sometimes I think I would like to invite some friends over for dinner; I imagine them at my table in Charleston, the way I used to entertain. But suddenly I feel incompetent, oddly, in one of the areas of greatest competence I have, that as a cook and a hostess. It's not my kitchen; it's not my house, I say to myself. But when I'm honest about it I realize I feel shy and afraid. People here can be disconcerting in their judgment and outspokenness. They would laugh at me, I think to myself, or talk about me afterwards. Then I realize that I have never thought that before—perhaps never before in my entire life.

The reality is that I have never lived here independently or owned a home here as an adult. I have never established my skills here, and my identity and competence feel flimsy and rootless now.

Perhaps I will be able to fix that or adjust to it. Perhaps not. We will have to see.

I lean out and look up at the sky. I inhale and I struggle for a sense of bearing. With solace I think that the Rome airport is only an hour and a half away, though right now it feels like it might as well be on the moon.

I miss Aram, and Joe, too. I miss the other side, a dark ocean away.

Today on my run I left the road and cut through a field of perfectly ordered rows of bud-green wheat to reach a house on a hill that I had never visited.

At the end of the field was a wide culvert I had not foreseen—eight-feet-wide or so. I backed up a few steps to give myself momentum and I jumped, screaming giddily. I made it over and I climbed up a grassy embankment leading to a road. I passed a secluded patch of woods dotted by clusters of yellow primroses and dainty pink cyclamens, which made me inordinately happy.

I stopped to look at some rocks that reminded me of fossils I once found down in our fields, and I put one in my pocket for safekeeping, feeling free and whole like a kid again, the way I did always in this countryside before discovering the addictive art of hanging out in the piazza, or before we began losing ourselves to boys.

Indeed, looking out on this land long known it takes a mere breath to return me to the state of adventure I relished as a child here. Back then, the time that most pleased me—it might have pleased me more than anything before or since—was spent in the exploration of the world around me in its simplest form. Being in a field or crawling through the woods gave me peace that human interaction already denied me, and would continue to deny me. It gifted me magic and wonder that needed nothing else, precluding the very meanness and feelings of inadequacy that relationships with girls, and then boys, always somehow included: the feeling that I was not whole, either because I was not pretty enough or because I was somehow different, or because the spoken word never sufficed to explain the greatness my heart held.

In nature none of those problems existed. In nature I was perfect, and nature was perfect to me, and it was always easier to be alone there, with the birds and the wonderment and exhilaration, beginning in my own backyard.

At any time of the year I'd walk down our terraced fields, fallow in winter and planted in summer with vegetable gardens and sweet corn, then hop across the stream's slick rocks, and venture up the hill into the woods across from our house. There I paced around slowly listening to the silence, watching, entranced by the smell of the ground, the green of the damp moss, the variety of birds and bugs and flowers.

In fall I collected dead bugs and pretty leaves of dramatic colors that I took home and placed in books or assembled into paintings. The rest of the year I loved looking for flowers for my mom—in spring the first delicate early violets and tremulous cyclamens, and in summer the wild daffodils, with their intoxicating, joyous perfume. I held my bouquet tightly in my hand for hours as I gathered more and more flowers, and finally I took it home, slightly wilted and mangled, and delivered it to my mom with the pride of a true collector.

Sometimes on my walks I stared through the woods—particularly at winter's peak, when it was all uniformly brown or gray and the tree trunks looked like stick figures—and imagined seeing a mysterious and scary man camouflaged among the trees. I would try to talk myself out of my visions, but finally, spooked to terror, I let out a scream, threw down my treasures, and ran down the hill breathlessly to the safety of home. There, Dad would make tea for my dolls and me and I slowly forgot the man in the woods.

Not far from our house were—and still are—the abandoned *lavatoi*, the public washhouse, whose source of water was the same stream that came through the bottom of our field. The washhouse was choked by vines and thorns and had crumbling walls, and, positioned as it was in a shady damp ravine that never caught sunlight, it was forbidding and mysterious. Though there were no vagabonds or homeless people whatsoever in Cetona, I imagined that mysterious goblins lived there at night, and that drew me there. I reached the *lavatoi* by walking along the stream through our fields and the neighboring vegetable gardens, then leaping across waterholes and rocks and venturing across scary patches of tall grass, all the while breathing in the sweet fragrant smell of flowers, fields, grass, and water. When I got there, I'd stand in the ominous shade listening and watching until fear overpowered me and with a scream I'd run up the path to Borgo as fast as I could, my legs powered by the mere force of my imagination.

Of course, those flights were never as bad as running from Il Cane, Cetona's known werewolf.

Tall and skinny, Il Cane had all the characteristic features one would imagine in a werewolf, well, minus the fur. He was anti-social and gaunt and dark, with broody dark eyes. When it was full moon he could be seen drinking at a fountain up the hill from Borgo and howling at the moon. Well, to be honest, I never saw him howl at the moon, really. That was more hearsay—*per sentito di'*, as they say, meaning, for having heard about it. But, I did see him creep through the alleyways and drink at the fountain. There was a street light right above it, so if you walked by, or spied on him, which we were wont to do as kids, our hearts pumping in our throats, you could catch a glimpse of him bending over to drink. And then he would howl and lurk through the dark alleyways through the night, meandering all the way up to Le Monache and under the Rocca.

Il Cane lived down an alley off a street I had to pass to get to and from the piazza via the upper part of town, by the Collegiata, a steep and meandering route I chose at night because Borgo was so dark you couldn't see a hand in front of your face. It was so dark you could actually run smack into someone had there been anyone else on the street and had you not heard their footsteps. Anyway, as a teenager, when I went that route on my way home, out of fear of running into Il Cane, and to make sure that, if I did, he couldn't possibly catch me, I'd start running right at the top of the hill, by the Collegiata, and by the time I got to Il Cane's turnoff, my legs would be moving so fast that I could barely control them, cartoon-like. By the time I reached home, at the bottom of the hill, my heartbeat was wild and my legs were twitching, but I had eluded a potentially deadly encounter with Il Cane.

The poor Cane is now dead, rest his soul, and I don't even know what his real name was.

By my early teenage years my brother was in and out of the house and of my life. He moved out of the house when was I was twelve or so, first for art school, then for a series of apprenticeships—learning the restoration of paintings, and later furniture—so we didn't share much daily life anymore.

In summers, though, he came to Cetona more often, particularly when Mom was away in Siena at the Accademia Chigiana, where she was an accompanist to the master classes of important musicians, people like cellist Francesco Navarra and violinist Salvatore Accardo. During those months Mom stayed in Siena for weeks, from June to September, so she could be there for practices as well as student performances on weekends.

Paul and I were charged with watering Mom's vegetable garden, which she had lovingly seeded and planted before her departure. Laid out in terraced fields below our house, the garden unfurled through the summer with an abundance of tomatoes, peppers, green beans, zucchini, and everything else one could imagine, including sweet corn and yellow squash.

— Remember to water! she'd caution before going. Don't let the green beans get too big! Don't let the tomatoes rot!

— Yes, Mom! we'd say.

Most times we did it, and I remember feeling responsible for this. Aldo would check on it, too, with care. He knew what it meant to work for food, and the bounty was precious. Our tomatoes, laid out, with Aldo's help, in meticulous rows at the bottom of the field with the sweet corn, were plentiful and delicious, and Dad awaited us at the top of the steps as we hauled them up by the basketful.

But sometimes we checked the garden, and in spite of the vegetables' advanced ripeness, we didn't feel like picking. We were teenagers. Paul and I would look around and ignore them, the green beans—he reminds me now—fat enough to braid into ropes and the zucchini large enough to be carved into boats for my Barbies. And not to mention the tomatoes, which were out of control both in size and number.

— They're not ready yet, Dad! we'd say, returning to the top of the hill empty-handed.

A day or so later we'd head back to the field and face the over-ripe fruit.

Rotten tomatoes seemed like something fun to throw, and during the course of the summer we embarked on several prolonged and messy tomato fights. There is not much that smells as bad as a rotten tomato, yet that seemed only to magnify the grossness and fun. Dad got furious at us, though a few times he could not keep himself from laughing, and at least once he participated. He came down to the field—he should have known it was bound to happen—and Paul hit him in the back of the head with a huge rotten tomato.

Dad gritted his teeth and chased Paul around the garden for several minutes until I came to my brother's aid. We bombarded Dad with rotten tomatoes until he was covered with seeds and skins, which we rinsed off with the foul, smelly water of the stream.

My mother, meanwhile, came back to find her garden half dead, and she sat down and cried, her face in her hands, an image that haunts me to this day. Aldo must have shaken his head, too, about the waste, though he was not one to judge—and certainly not my mother, of whom he was fond. He taught her to pick olives, and he and Beppa would kill the occasional chicken my parents raised, mostly unsuc-cessfully, snapping its neck stoically. My parents preferred to stand on the sidelines when it came to raising and killing animals, though in winter, of course, the slaughter of the pigs, one of the notable yearly events throughout the *campagna*, and on Borgo too, pulled everyone in the fray. Pigs everywhere reached that inevitable cold, foggy day, and several times when I was little I crowded in the sty with others to watch as the terrified squealing animal, this intelligent, peaceful being, sensing a terrible event ahead, was chased in circles and finally shot and killed.

They slaughtered him and hung him, then, by big metal hooks. With the vast vats of scalding water, men and women boiled and washed and skinned and sliced and prepped and ground, right before our eyes, the eyes of children. Gathered around long wooden tables, dozens of people worked together to make *salsiccia, prosciutto, ventresca, guanciale,* and *bistecca* until there was nothing left of the animal at all.

Then, everyone sat down to enjoy a massive feast in the cold, damp winter air filled with the smell of firewood and blood and flesh. Of course, animal flesh was a normal sight. Once a week or so, Gustavo the butcher, the father of my future boyfriend Lucio, could be seen coming from the slaughterhouse pulling a butchered cow stretched out on planks of wood behind his blue Fiat 500 station wagon. And every day the *lattaia,* the milk lady, hauled huge metal jugs of fresh warm milk from her farm to her odd-smelling shop, no bigger than four feet by six, and there she sold it, still warm, in bottles brought from home.

There was no doubt, back then, where food came from.

Mercede, meanwhile, the vegetable lady, received truckloads of fresh vegetables every day, brought by farmers in the country, and at Easter the women of Cetona baked their rounds of *ciaccia di Pasqua,* the Easter bread, at the public ovens. They'd cross the piazza with their loaves of *ciaccia* expertly balanced on wooden boards atop their heads. In Cetona there were women who could balance basketfuls of goods on their heads while simultaneously carrying buckets of water and sometimes even a child. Costanza was one such woman.

Fresh fruit abounded around us as kids, from the ubiquitous pomegranates in fall, blood-red and juicy and puzzling to take apart, to the cherries in summer, and my favorite pear tree, at the bottom of the steps leading to our fields, where I spent my afternoons feasting until all the pears were gone. Mom jarred tons of tomatoes in summer, which we packed in our cellar for the winter, and in fall she learned to pick olives that we took to the local olive mill.

We lived simply. We had no TV, no phone, heat only when it got uncomfortably cold, and often in summer we had no water, which was not quaint or romantic as some American writers have made it out to be. Sometimes we used solar shower bags that friends brought us from the States.

Yet, to me life seemed complete enough.

Growing up with American parents who had a vast cultural world was, in retrospect, a complement to my life in Cetona, and I was aware even as a young girl that they gave me a special perspective, a leg up. The things I learned from them, their readings and topics of conversation at the dinner table and their friends at dinner parties gave me the ability or hubris in school to argue with teachers and classmates about God and art and politics. I was mostly proud of having foreign parents—I having shed my foreignness but still learning from theirs—except for the rare public embarrassment like my father stalling the car in the piazza while waving here and there.

Dad, who people called Signor Davide, just waved and smiled at everyone, even people he didn't know, and now that I am older I can better imagine the grace he must have felt in this tiny town where he had moved his family and where he considered himself a lucky guest. They waved back, sometimes a bit nonplussed, and I remember that now with admiration. My parents were well liked, perhaps because of that friendliness and humility, or perhaps because they were working people, artists with little money and lots of imagination. Besides, Mom taught piano to half the children in town, and my parents were the only resident foreigners with children at that time. Children are always a bonding glue.

Overall my parents had an affectionate respect for the people of Cetona, and for many years they were content here and satisfied with their endeavors. Of course, Dad lived much like a hermit, working on his violins, reading, and playing music. He was a man who lived in his head.

— *Ma te il babbo ce l'hai?* children sometimes asked me at school. Do you have a daddy?

— *Certo! Il mio babbo è il liutaio!* I'd say, a bit proud, a bit hurt. Of course! My father is the violinmaker.

It's true that people could go months without seeing my father in piazza, and sometimes they didn't know what a *liutaio* was. Yet, his persona and his work were a source of respect and curiosity in town, and his brilliance, courage, and creativity were a source of confidence and surety for me.

— *Mi dispiace ancora che non so' mai venuto a vederlo fa' un violino.* I still regret never coming to see him make a violin, Bennato said to me the other night when we happened on the subject of my father at the Bar Cavour.

But, at home, the courageous and arduous learning and eventual mastery of the craft did not always move speedily or smoothly. There were particular passages in the making of an instrument that were filled with tension—and that filled us with dread—for a misstep almost surely brought financial loss and ensuing anger. Gluing was one of those passages, and varnishing was another: One was rife with occasions for irreversible mistakes, and the other entailed placing the delicate instruments in hot, sunny places, with possibilities of cracking and bubbling, and starting anew.

Shipping an instrument and ensuring its safe delivery were equally tricky, one that I had forgotten until I saw Franco of the *ferramenta* the other day. He and his wife, Fernanda, run the hardware store in the piazza now. I went in to ask Franco to help me stabilize Anna Maria's easel, and he figured out who I was.

— *Il tu' babbo era il liutaio di Borgo! Io lavoravo alla dogana di Arezzo!* he said with a big smile. Your dad was the violinmaker down at Borgo!

Before retiring, Franco worked for many years at the Italian customs office in Arezzo, from which Dad shipped his instruments. Franco recalled the handmade wooden boxes that Dad made and used for shipping—crates engineered to protect the instruments from falls, falling objects and, perhaps worst of all, the hands of careless customs agents. What impressed Franco about these crates was my father's meticulous design and execution.

— *C'erano tutte 'ste viti, tutte alla stessa distanza esatta, e poi dentro era tutto così perfetto. Me le ricorderò sempre!* Franco said smiling with admiration. There were all these screws, all precisely at the same distance, and inside everything was so perfect. I will never forget them!

I remember the boxes too, and I remember Dad coming back from shipping an instrument one day and expressing relief at working, finally, with someone competent. He had a gladness about him that warmed us all. It must have been Franco.

Franco and I share a laugh and I am moved by this memory of my father's meticulousness.

Besides, I say, speaking of precision, you should see my Dad's chopped vegetables!

It threatened rain again today, after raining for the past several days, and I bundled up and set out for a run, seeking the respite and ease this landscape provides me without fail. It is familiar like a favorite glove I used to wear, and simply exhilarating.

When I left, the top of Monte Cetona was covered in mist and dark clouds, as it often is in late fall and through the winter, but, as I moved away from the mountain, the sky opened to a painter's sketch of angry dark purple slashes layered over with happy fast-moving white clouds clearing the occasional patch of bright blue and sunlight.

The fields this time of year are like a seamstress's most delicate handiwork, with carefully stitched rows of trees with leaves the color of terracotta sown between palettes of greens, interspersed with brown patches and rusty ditches. The white of gravel roads takes off here and there like pieces of soft unraveling twine. The occasional tree bursts fire red, each leaf in relief against the green. I pass trees laden with kakis bright as orange Halloween globes hanging from the branches.

Below them brown fields lying fallow since the corn harvest weave seamlessly into expanses of bright green grass, strange remnants of summer or premature promises of spring. Pine trees, dark and tall, line a dirt road going up a hill to a house; on an adjacent hill, rows and rows of vines are turning deep red, ready to lose their leaves for the winter. A sliver of land suddenly catches a ray of sun and shines moss green like an emerald. Olive trees shimmer silvery, broad and expansive next to rows of narrow black cypress trees saluting on the crest of a hill.

A gust of wind brings a flurry of brown leaves to the ground. Soon the trees will be bare.

Voices rise sudden and happy from a field where men have begun picking olives. Through the silvery branches I see the nets, red, on the ground, laced across the grass; olives fall purple here and there and gather together where the land slopes. Someone talks and laughs.

I see chickens in the grass below, near a makeshift shed, and I walk down the hill to see if I can pet them. They run away quickly, frightened. One is black and she reminds me of Bella. I think of her and my other chickens, and Joe, too; images run through my head and suddenly I feel deeply sad and alone. I turn back, climb up the hill back onto the road, and breathe through it.

The road is muddy. I pass the stream by the old mill. The water pools there and gets quite deep. My Bravo would flood there sometimes when Maria and I would go for a ride. I'd always insist that if we rode through fast enough we could make it to the other side, but invariably we got stuck, and we'd push the motorbike out of the water and up the hill, our shoes and pants soaked, until it would start again and off we went. There is a bridge there now, and a beautiful house that was once a ruin.

Along the road I notice patches of some kind of tall prickly grasses we picked in middle school to dry and paint for an art project, maybe to give to our mothers. I remember the joy of painting them and taking them home, though inevitably they would get relegated to the fields as trash. I pass ditches full of tiny wildflowers, dots of color in the late fall palette, and, along the stream, I pass the little stone house that I used to enter with trepidation. When I was little it was abandoned and falling into disrepair; its roof was partly caved in, its windows were broken and its door left ajar. Heavy vines grew in all its crevices, and inside you could make out falling beams and empty bottles. Sometimes I had only the courage to peek through the windows, but sometimes I had guts enough to open the door and take a few steps inside until some noise or a scurrying snake spooked me and sent me running.

Now it has been restored, like a magical cabin in the woods, and it is whimsical and charming. The creatures that I thought lived there, nocturnal monsters and goblins, are long gone, replaced by the occasional renter, and when I run by there I wish I were one of them.

I run along the road, barely more than a path. When we were children, at Carnevale we'd dress up as princesses and gypsies, pirates and maidens, with long skirts and our mother's beads and rings, and occasionally the store-bought costume, and like odd creatures dropped in the fields like Dorothy and Tin Man we'd walk these paths to knock at old *poderi* to ask for treats—what's called *cucco ciccio* in Italy—mostly a couple of eggs and sometimes, if we were lucky, some *strufoli* covered with honey.

I pass the edge of a brown field and a patch of secluded trees. It is known to me—too known, in fact—and I recoil at the memory of a farmer who once lived around here, who worked for a family friend.

He was short and stocky, balding, with olive skin and green eyes and a gravelly voice. He must have been in his fifties or early sixties. He smoked unfiltered cigarettes and his thick fingers and fingernails were stained yellow. He and his wife had a daughter who lived on a hill across the way; she had several children—in fact, was seemingly always pregnant—and sometimes I would play there. Pigs ran around outside in the mud and everything seemed squalid and desolate and ungiving. The children were always dirty, and the mother, too, her fingernails caked with dirt and her clothes stained. I remember not liking being there—feeling sad there—not because of the poverty, but because of a lack of gaiety and hope.

But I did like going on the tractor with this farmer. In fall he tilled the land for seeding corn or wheat or sunflowers, and I liked to ride with him. I'd hop on the seat with my little jeans and tennis shoes, and we'd leave his employer's house, where my mother visited, and ride down the steep hill, then turn left and head out into the country, down a narrow dirt road and onto the fields. I would sit on the seat next to him and keep him company as he worked the field back and forth in rows, until all of it was turned over in chunks, dark and moist. I loved the smell of the earth—my heart already irretrievably lost to this land. When he was finished with one field we would get back onto the road and head to the next, until each field was done. Every now and then he would stop and light a cigarette, but he never spoke much.

One winter day when I was eight or so, I went with him to till. It was a cold, gray day, still, and the landscape brown and misty. I had on my brown sweater, my favorite sweater, and little jeans. I was skinny, with soft brown hair pulled back in a ponytail. It was late afternoon and we had reached the farthest field from the house. At the far end it was bordered by tall trees and shrubs that protected it from view. When he got to that end of the field, he stopped the tractor and put it in idle, then he turned to me, and putting his arm around my shoulders, he pulled me to him. He stuck his hand down my jeans and pushed his thick fingers into my underpants and inside of me, and stuck his tongue in my throat. I smelled his tobacco and dirt and sweat.

It lasted the minutes or seconds it took me to react to the feeling of knowing that something was deeply wrong—that it shouldn't have been this way. I gasped for breath and pushed his face away and jumped off the tractor down into the furrows of the dark brown soil and ran and ran and ran. Everything fell away in terror except my feet running, faster and faster, digging and tripping and rushing through the plowed soil along the bushes all the way to the dirt road and to safety.

When I got to the house where my mom and her friend played Scrabble, I ran in and caught my breath, but I never told what had happened. Did I figure it would ruin the peace? Was the shame just too much to endure? What is it that keeps us silent in the face of horror we have done nothing to deserve? Whatever the case, I blocked it from my mind, until more than fifteen years later, when I was home one summer from college and Tullia and I went to buy cigarettes at the *tabaccheria*. I saw him again, coming out of the store, and he brushed against me, and it all came back. And I finally told.

On this day my mind seeks refuge from memory in the gravel and the puddles on the ground, though it lingers long enough to remember his fat hands and square, thick fingernails, and the light color of his eyes like the sea. I wonder if he molested others, maybe his daughters and granddaughters. They never do it just once.

Over the hill I take in the livid clouds weighing down the sky. The landscape looks like it's painted a foreboding shade of green, but as I round a curve it opens to a slice of hill in full sunlight, like someone thrust a beam of light on it from a theater catwalk just to cheer me up. I stop to grasp this second of humor, the beauty of life, a moment shady and a moment bright.

The ground is muddy and ridged by the back and forth of large tires. A tall blue tractor approaches pulling a dump trailer full of cases of olives, headed to the mill. The farmer waves and smiles as he goes by and I am comforted.

I am comforted by the smallest of things, here.

Along the road are sheds where farmers keep their tools and their animals. Near one of them, surrounded by thick grass, a patch of pearlescent white momentarily deceives me, then I realize they are ducks, foraging in an open field, and I stop to call to them and talk to them. I talk to animals and people alike, wherever I am, and for an instant in this loss of self I am experiencing here I recognize something of my inner truth that bridges the oceans. Who we are is not a matter of geography or interpretation; we simply *are* something, right?

I realize that manifesting that is different here, and I need to give myself space to become anew, to find who I was, or who I am, here, in this place.

Finoglio, the steepest street into town, greets me for the final stretch. I turn and walk backwards so I can look out onto the landscape as I rise. My breathing is labored, the air filling my lungs, brisk though not cold. I make a mental note to pick nettles before it is too late, before it gets too cold, so I can make risotto. Make sure dogs have not peed on them, Romina said.

I breathe in the smell of firewood burning everywhere. We used to hate it growing up, the smell of firewood clinging to our clothes. We smelled like it all winter long, and we felt marked, diminished perhaps, by the smell of the country.

Now it smells true like truth, as clean and honest here as the dirt itself.

After fifth grade, my classmates and I moved up to Cetona's *scuola media*, the middle school, nestled in the *paese vecchio* in a cold stone building that encompassed town hall, the library, and the museum. The school has since moved, but the library is still there and I like to go there to write and research, not for the silence—which, between the unrestrained banter of the women who run it, and the loud questions of those who stop in seeking to pay a ticket or to look for the mayor, is hard to come by—but to get out of the house and see some friendly faces.

While I was there recently, Ilio, Anna Maria's husband, stopped in, looking for the municipal police. His breath was labored and his thick grey curly hair was unkempt and wild, and he sat down to complain to the librarian that he got a ticket while sitting in his car in front of their house. While his story dragged on and he waited for the municipal police to show up, I wandered around the building to use the bathroom and snoop around the old classrooms, still cavernous and cold as hell. Finally, I found one that used to be ours, and while opening the shutters to let the light in, I imagined us all sitting there, laughing and carrying on in our disorderly, smelly classroom. Leonardo, Mirco, my dear Agata, Ausilia, and Natalia ...

Ausilia was the most endearing girl in our class. I used to love going to her house, which was a working farm on the outskirts of town but in walking distance of the piazza. Her family kept animals, and Ausilia often fed them, before school and after. She was shy in class and would easily get flustered under pressure, blushing terribly, which earned her the nickname of *lampadina*—lightbulb.

When I first arrived on this stay I stopped in to say hello to her. I found her folding a pile of tank tops on the counter of her *merceria*, where she sells everything from baby clothes to lingerie and socks. We had not seen each other in decades, but after taking me in for a second she recognized me and smiled broadly. I thought that was you, she said laughing. She came to the other side of the counter and we hugged. Ausilia looks much like she always has—light brown hair pulled back from her face, tall, sharp cheekbones, and a full smile of white, healthy teeth. We have in common our reading glasses now, which she wears on her forehead, and a deep voice, which I had forgotten.

Over the past few months I have stopped to chat with her often, and we have reminisced about our days at the *scuola media*. She gave me news of classmates I have lost track of and others I have seen: Ilia, who still lives in Patarnione—she is married to one of the owners of the supermarket and she is a successful accountant; and Carla Mugnai, a girl with wild, brilliant green eyes who, I discovered, owns a road maintenance company and is getting ready to do work on the road that leads up to the cross on Monte Cetona. This makes me proud somehow, and a bit envious too.

At the scuola media I spent most of my study time with kids in town, up the street. Mirco was one of them, an only child with a small, serious mouth who lived in a stern, silent house across from the Collegiata. His father worked for one of Cetona's big *fattori,* and his mother, a short, rigorous woman, sewed and embroidered gifts for weddings, baptisms, and such. We studied together a lot, at their kitchen table, and while we studied his mother sat nearby, by the window, listening to our every word and looking down impassive at her work, painting with her needle intricate landscapes with flowers, trees, birds, and bees, all strangely lifeless.

Our study-mate was Leonardo, now a baker in town, a happy boy from a Northern family, a bit shy but always sporting at least a half-smile of slightly crooked teeth, framed by red cheeks and curly reddish hair. At his house the atmosphere was no less serious, but when we studied there, every so often I could at least convince them to step out of bounds and do something playful like ringing old ladies' doorbells—or something equally silly and innocent. For a few minutes we'd run up and down the streets laughing and sweating, and Mirco's shyness would fade away and he'd giggle mouth agape and eyes smiling, and we could just be kids at play.

At the *scuola media* we were an undisciplined, smelly bunch, always laughing and moving the chairs around and creating chaos and disorder, full of teasing and mocking, some kind, some less. Often at the center of it all were the kids from Piazze, Cetona's little *frazione*, about ten kilometers away across the countryside, who came by bus and who I remember with great affection.

A *frazione* is an administrative creation that came about during Fascism to incorporate into larger nearby towns those hamlets that were too small to justify their own municipality. The *frazione* may or may not have any relationship or liking with the town to which it is affiliated, and in fact there might be a bit of resentment or antagonism between the two, and such is the case between Cetona and Piazze. Back then, the Cetonesi thought the Piazzaioli were *cignali*, or rednecks, and Piazzaioli, always with a bit of a chip on the shoulder, thought of Cetonesi as the unfriendly uppity townfolk. From my perspective, it looks like relations have improved: The joint marching band, which dates back more than a century and is more mixed and professional than ever, seems to be a bond, and Cetona's new mayor is from Piazze— and a woman, to boot! The unprecedented election of a Piazzaiola put everyone on a more equal footing, though she finds an occasion here and there in her new role to take jabs at the Cetonesi's expense.

Then as now, Piazze is strung along the intersection on the way to San Casciano or Fabro. It includes a bar, a tiny grocery store, a church, a couple of small but surprisingly successful restaurants, a bank branch and post office, a small public park where the old people and children can be seen hanging out as one drives through, and a lot of hardworking people with little time to hang out in piazza, which they do not have anyway (Piazze got its name from clearings that were used to make coal).

In any case, among the Piazzaioli back then in our class—and sources of much of its chaos—were the Podellacqua brothers. Antonello, the youngest, had tight curly brown hair, a winsome smile, and a smart, mischievous personality that sparked constant and playful disorder. His older brother, Maurizio, had straight black hair cut like a friar and a rosy face dominated by big pool-like black eyes. Maurizio was always repeating a grade, and by the time he joined our sixth-grade class he was probably fifteen.

Thinking back now, for them—and for most kids whose families were farmers—school was temporary respite from home and work, and in fact they looked like the wind had blown them in straight from the fields and dropped them at a desk by pure chance. Their books were dogeared and stained and their book bags sat strewn on the floor and stepped on. Their hands were worn and chapped from working outside, and when they brought their homework it was always crumpled and sometimes stained, though the fact that they had done it at all was in itself a feat. When we had to have something signed by a guardian—a permission slip or a report card—theirs and those of other farming children were often signed by a tremulous X, testament to post-war life in the Tuscan countryside. And often this made them the butt of the class's jokes.

— *Ma che ci hai, l'acqua in casa?* Matteo, the future contractor, teased them when their pant cuffs were short, above the ankle, let down by their mother as far as they would go. Do you have high water in your house?

They'd laugh and laugh and shrug him off, proud but maybe a bit hurt.

Luciano was another boy from Piazze, with thick hair the color of straw and narrow brown eyes like slits that easily betrayed his hurt. Luciano was always teased and abused by the Podellacqua brothers: they stole his notebooks, they hid his books or his lunch, and they teased him mercilessly for wearing farm clothes.

— *Mira, mira, ci ha il concio sulle scarpe!* Look, look, he has manure on his shoes, Antonello would say, pointing to Luciano's shoes and enlisting the complicity of Giorgio Buttacavoli, another kid from Piazze, elbowing him in the side. They would explode in laughter and hold their bellies.

Giorgio, a long-faced, skinny kid with big eyes the color of melted cocoa, had skin of Middle-Eastern darkness, which he inherited from his father who, appropriately, was nicknamed Saddat. Giorgio was kind but a natural-born rabble-rouser, and as much as he tried to stop himself, he couldn't resist being pulled into the fray, particularly when it came to teasing Luciano, who every day before coming to school got up to feed his family's animals and milk the cows. He almost never had his homework, and he was always tired, but he took notes and tried to listen to the teachers. He was quiet and polite, and when Maurizio teased him he looked down at his desk, drawing in his breath, his smooth cheeks turning crimson.

When it was time for *merenda*, our snack, Luciano pulled out his *panino*, two thick slices of old Tuscan bread, roughly cut, with virtually nothing between them, maybe a thin piece of prosciutto, a scrap, more fat than meat. Wrapped in wax paper, he put it on his desk guardedly, almost sheltering it with his shoulders, preparing for the onslaught.

— *Dai, via ...,* he'd beg, grimacing, trying to thwart what had not yet started. C'mon, already ...

— *Ma ch'a' porto, il pane co' la sugna?* Maurizio would ask him loudly in Piazzaiolo, laughing from across the room. What did you bring, bread with fat drippings?

But then again, they had brought nothing.

— *Dai, dammelo un pochino, via, dammelo!* Antonello begged him. C'mon, give me some, give me some, c'mon!

And the teasing went on and on.

The girls made no effort to mask their disdain for boys in the *scuola media*, particularly Mariachiara, Andrea's sister. A year older than us, she joined our class our last year of middle school when she flunked her grade. By then she was one of my best friends outside of school, at least on and off, and at one point she became my *compagna di banco,* my desk mate.

Mariachiara was petite, with fleeting dark eyes and a rounded face. She had a fickle, non-caring attitude—her armor against the world—and a restless nervous energy. She bit her fingernails and played with her hair, black and shoulder-length, incessantly, a way, perhaps, of detracting from the shyness and frailty that she hid under disdain and sometimes cutting aloofness. Underneath it all, she just wanted to be loved. She was fifteen by then—but seemingly much older—flirtatious and coquettish, and as is customary in Cetona, she had a crush on an older guy, a vain soccer player who was known in our small pond for his athletic prowess and good looks. Middle school was a pain in the ass to Mariachiara, and she recoiled with disgust from any affiliation with her peers, particularly young boys, and boys from Piazze.

— *Dai, lasciami fa', cretino, imbecille,* she cut sharply if Maurizio even looked her way. Leave me alone, you cretin, you imbecile.

With that she moved her chair away, as if being in the same space would contaminate her.

I loved Mariachiara because she said outrageous, irreverent, silly things that made me laugh, and since she was not big on study-ing—*non ci ho voglia,* or I don't feel like it, was her favorite saying—we spent much of our time in class laughing, giggling, and gossiping. She liked to play with the teachers, taunt them, make fun of them, pretend she had not understood, or she had forgotten. She could be insolent, too, and she instigated trouble a fair amount, on purpose. On a class trip to Amalfi, which our art teacher chaperoned—a young guy who liked girls and might as well have been one of the kids for how much authority he commanded—at night we snuck out of our rooms and went roaming through town, Mariachiara leading the way.

At the *scuola media* we had new teachers, one for math, one for Italian, history, Latin, and geography, one for chemistry and physics, one for French, and the priest, Don Prospero, with whom I got into stubborn arguments about God, whose existence, not surprisingly, he could not prove to my satisfaction. Mariachiara was even more insolent with the priest, openly defying such concepts as resurrection and the virgin birth, which became glaringly absurd once we began to understand the mechanics of making children.

— *Eh si! La Vergine Maria l'ha preso e bello grosso!* she said once to the priest. The Virgin Mary, she got one all right, a big one, too!

And we would all laugh and laugh like we were at the circus.

Several of our teachers were assigned from other towns, as far away as Florence, and they taught us with tolerance and tedium. Pallecchi, our math teacher, was one of them, and our playboy art teacher, whom, Agata commented recently, would have been better suited as the owner of a porn shop, or a *sexy-shop*, as they are called in Italy. They were out of their hometown, annoyed, and tired. Admittedly, we were not an easy or ambitious bunch.

The teachers who taught our main subjects—Italian, history, and geography—were Franco and Giorgio, both locals. Giorgio's father owned a store in piazza, in the building where the family still lives. His parents sent him away to university to become a professor. Later he served as mayor, too, following in the footsteps of his grandfather, who was mayor in 1911. Franco, meanwhile, was the heartthrob of the *scuola media*. He was a sexy guy, tall, lanky, sort of a rebel, with a dark beard and soulful brown eyes, and the girls—Mariachiara mostly—liked to go smell his coat in the teachers' lounge.

Both Franco and Giorgio had things they cared about and wanted us to learn, and I still enjoy the occasional word with both of them—Franco, when I see him bounding through the piazza on his way to buy his several newspapers, and Giorgio and his wife, Giovanna, who walk through the piazza daily at the same time, their arms identically intertwined behind their backs and their step equally paced.

Both Franco and Giorgio were staunch leftists, back then and now, and this seemed to make them more tolerant as teachers and inclined to understanding us. Every now and then Giorgio lost his patience, though, with kids who were present only physically (and sometimes not even that), like Bufalo, a skinny, funny boy with big blue eyes, silver-rimmed glasses, and a laugh that rose through him like a slowly erupting volcano. He joined our class in eighth grade, like Mariachiara, after he flunked. The experience of being held back, however, did not spark academic recovery in him, and he spent most of the day at his desk taking apart and putting back together a series of ballpoint pens like he was working on a mechanical assembly line. He did this over and over, all day long.

— *Ecco!* Giorgio erupted when he got pissed off, throwing up his hands, his face turning red behind his glasses.

— *Guardate! Questo qui dorme, e questo, questo ha riaperto l'officina!* Look everyone, this one is sleeping, he said, pointing to a kid who was always asleep, and this one is back working in his shop!

It is surprising we learned anything. Finally, at 1 p.m. the school bell rang and our smelly, chaotic class emptied out to the town, accompanied by yelling and the violent scraping of chairs against the floors—a last daily injury to our teachers. Off we ran, chasing each other down Via Roma, to freedom. At that age, all we wanted was to get out.

In summer we almost never ran into the kids from Piazze, and over the course of three months lots could change. Maurizio failed again and vanished from our lives, as did other kids whose families needed them on the farm. Giorgio, Antonello, and Luciano finished with us and that was the end of schooling for them. When we parted ways—they to jobs and I to the *liceo* in Montepulciano—they each gave me a picture of themselves taken in an instant photo booth at the Chiusi train station, which I kept all these years.

On this visit I was happy to get news about them: Giorgio di Saddat is a hairdresser, which makes me smile; Antonello manages a company that builds kitchens, and Luciano is a truck driver. I was sorry to not see them, except for Maurizio, who I crossed the other day while I was walking into the piazza with my head in the clouds.

— *Scusa, ma te se' la Sibilla?* he asked, stopping me, his eyes still like black pools.

You probably don't remember me, he said, looking down. I was the black sheep of the *scuola media*.

I was moved that he stopped me and, of course, I remembered him.

I remember everyone, running deep inside my veins.

Perhaps my best friend at the *scuola media* was Natalia.

Natalia had shoulder-length chestnut brown hair that cascaded softly around a well-drawn face, a full mouth, high cheekbones and pretty teeth. She had big dark brown eyes that widened when she was surprised or entertained, and when she laughed she covered her mouth fully with the palm of her hand, leaned her head backward and closed her eyes tightly.

Natalia was tall and shapely, and like many girls around Cetona—and unlike me—she blossomed precociously. Boys and grown men alike began staring at her early on. Natalia shrugged it off in a simple way, a bit wisely and a bit naively at the same time. She was shy and a bit self-conscious: if something hurt her feelings, a shadow fell quickly over her beautiful eyes and she looked away, without speaking. She was easily embarrassed—*mi vergogno* was her default phrase, something between being sincerely shy and being coy—a trait that made her vulnerable and endearing.

Natalia and I became desk mates at the beginning of sixth grade. I loved Natalia because she was funny to me, kind to others, and indulgent. Once she got to know you, she was spontaneous and trusting, and we laughed about the silliest of things. Perhaps because I was a good student, she looked up to me, and her affection lifted me and gave me comfort. We had girlhood in common, and unaffected acceptance. She looked at the world purely and kindly, and I found wonder in her.

Natalia came from the glorious land halfway between Cetona and Piazze, an area called Piandisette. The name—*pian de' sette,* or valley of the seven—came from Roman times, marking a seven-mile point from an ancient and well-traveled Roman road. It was considered, back then, the true *campagna,* remote and reminiscent of a life that people in Cetona wanted to leave behind. It was like a distant world, a past they wanted to shed, historically and, sometimes, individually, too. When I became friends with Natalia, some of the houses at Piandisette were vacant already, abandoned by farmers who were tired of houses full of poetry but no heat or running water and too far from town for the municipality to care. So, they left and sold. By the mid-eighties, the Tuscan countryside was dotted with abandoned old farmhouses falling into ruin and selling for pennies, and by the early nineties they all were bought, with carts and tools and everything inside. What Americans or other foreigners did not buy, Italians bought, and they transformed the *poderi* into *agriturismi,* overly gussied up to accommodate the onslaught brought by Hollywood's and America's discovery of Tuscany.

In a strange irony, by neglect of the Tuscans, Tuscany was pillaged—yet again. Back then, though, Natalia's family hung on, barely, and for me as a child her world contained a foreign but unmistakable solidity and goodness.

Sometimes after school I'd go home with Natalia to do homework and play, though, in truth, play was recognized but vaguely in her family lexicon. The bus left us off on the side of the road in a cloud of dust, and we walked the mile or so up the road to her house as the sound of the bus receded. When you were dropped off, that was that; that is where you stayed till the following day, and it felt like millions of miles away.

Natalia's farmhouse was an old *casa colonica* of stone and tufa, of a kind that barely exist anymore. It had steep brick steps going up the front and a large *aia*, a graveled area in front of the house where the chickens scratched and the tractor was parked, where the dog and cats lay, and where Natalia's grandmother sat out in the sun to warm herself on a rough wooden bench.

A well supplied water to the house, and fetching water was one of Natalia's many chores, though when I visited to do homework, her family freed her a bit from her regular taxing routine of house and farm. There were not many trees around Natalia's house, so when it was sunny the light glared, bright and white, but once you stepped inside, cool darkness drew you into the kitchen, a huge room in which all life of the home unfolded, especially in fall and winter.

Natalia lived with her parents, her grandparents, and her brother, Nico, who was ten years older. Her mother, Iolanda, was beautiful, with a full languid mouth and soft curls framing her face lazily like she had just gotten out of bed, her generous cleavage always tempting from her pretty top or dress. Iolanda dressed nicely for her work in town, cleaning and taking care of the properties of the wealthy when they were not in town.

Natalia's father was much older than her mother, with gray hair and a tired face; he was stern and quiet, and I don't remember him ever talking to me except to say hello in a somber tone. On account of that, people gossiped about Iolanda and her being beautiful. Later, when Natalia took distinctly after her mother, they gossiped about her, too, but they were nothing but good people. Iolanda was loyal to her employers and she worked long hours, coming home in the evening after dark, at dinner time. It struck me that she looked out of place in her own house, in the dark country kitchen lit by one single cold light bulb and the glare of the fireplace, where her husband's mother shuffled about slowly in soft black shoes, feeding the *stufa* and making dinner in her dark kerchief low on her face and the layered dark clothes of widowhood.

Natalia and I sat at the large dark kitchen table doing our homework, quietly, and her grandmother spoke little, every now and then asking Natalia to get up and do something—get firewood, or set the table. Natalia sighed and looked at me apologetically, sometimes blowing her cheeks up and letting the air out heavily as she got up.

— *Uffa* ..., she'd mutter under her breath, a favorite and untranslatable Italian expression that conveys disappointment or annoyance.

Natalia's grandfather, meanwhile, sat on a bench in the hearth of the fireplace, a memorable and now rare structure so large that it accommodated a bench on each side of the fire and several chairs out front. One could sit there far enough to not get burned but close enough to enjoy the warmth and to poke the fire and turn the pieces of roast grilling on an iron grate over red coals pulled aside out of the blaze. In cold winter evenings Natalia's grandfather sat in there, his dark shirt buttoned to his neck, and his cap on his head, his eyes unblinking. Sometimes he roasted chestnuts, and sometimes he made polenta in a huge blackened metal pail hanging above the flames. I remember watching the shadows dance on his dark face.

At Natalia's we ate what there was—*quello che c'è,* they say—and during the school months it was mostly bread, potatoes grilled on the fire, and chunks of *arrosto*, pig and chicken, sometimes rabbit and pheasant. There was always some *prosciutto* or *salsicccia*, or other meats the family cured from their own animals. Her *nonna* made pasta, mostly tagliatelle, thick and rough, and Natalia made *sugo* with chicken livers. We ate quietly at the dimly lit table, Natalia and her mother going out of their way to make sure I was comfortable and fed. Tuscans treat their guests with high regard, and the humbler they are, the more they go out of their way. Still to this day, people do not invite each other over casually.

— *Non fa' i complimenti, eh!* Iolanda would say. It's an expression that means, don't turn down good food out of false reserve or shyness.

After dinner we headed to bed, and that was a great adventure for me. The bedrooms at Natalia's were huge, cavernous, and freezing, closed off from the kitchen. The *prete*, the bed-warming contraption I had seen at Bruno and Adelina's, was our savior, and, fortunately, there was one in every bedroom of the house. If you looked in on the rooms, it looked like there was a huge bloated corpse in the middle of each bed.

At bedtime, Natalia's grandmother would come take the coals and the *prete* out of the bed, and after washing our faces and teeth in a basin, Natalia and I would take off our clothes as quickly as possible and jump into the bed screaming and shivering. The heavy sheets were nearly burning and we pulled them up to the top of our heads.

There, lying in the dark, the rest of the house silent, we talked and giggled until the heat lulled us to sleep.

In the morning, in the freezing cold, we took a sponge bath from a basin of warm water before pulling our clothes back on. In the kitchen, warm from the heat of the *stufa* that was never left to die out, Natalia's grandmother served us milk with malt coffee and stale bread toasted on the *stufa*. While we ate, her grandfather cooked an egg—if there was an egg—in olive oil in a tiny perfectly sized aluminum pan, and he ate it at the table with bread and the fat drippings from the previous night's dinner.

And off to school we went.

Once, when Natalia and I were thirteen or fourteen, we decided to try to smoke. We *wanted* to smoke. It was a rite of passage, a necessity. We saved up change here and there for about a week, and when we had enough money to buy a pack of cigarettes, Natalia volunteered to buy them. If the *tabaccaio* asked—which no one did—she would say they were for her grandfather.

On the established date, Natalia stayed in town and we walked far out into the country to a secluded field where no one could see us. And there we sat and smoked the whole pack of cigarettes, lighting one from the other, until we both were sick and nearly passed out. We lay in the grass till we had to go back in time for Natalia to catch her ride home. After that we got in all sorts of trouble, but all playful. I remember those as some of the most carefree times of my life—elevated, as we were, barely above the play of dolls but not yet hijacked by boys and love.

Eventually, Natalia quit coming to school, or we became separated in different classes, I don't remember, and we lost track of each other. Over the years, though, I never forgot her and the other day I borrowed a car from Mauro and went looking for her house. I was embarrassed to, seemingly, get lost, in Piandisette. It was all nebulous and I could not identify the house. Today, when Natalia picked me up in the piazza and took me there—we had not seen each other in two decades—I understood why.

After her father died, she explained, the family split the house between Iolanda and her father's brothers. The brothers sold their half, which included the upstairs, and the new owners remodeled it in such a way that made it unrecognizable to me, including removing the outdoor stairwell. The house is now stucco'ed and looks nothing like before.

Natalia, on the other hand, is still beautiful, or more beautiful perhaps, her looks matured by a bumpy life, yet tempered and rounded by her good spirit and kindness. Her brown eyes conserve her innate tolerance and patience, unjaded, though, for sure, there is grief there, too. Perhaps it is in the eyes of all of us by now.

It moved me to see her, to reach back in time with the same shared tenderness for a lost chapter of our lives. The survival of this—us—is nothing but a gift without expectation, like finding an old unwrapped present at the back of a drawer from a beautiful Christmas long ago.

Perhaps it's simply that we revisit our childhood memories with increased fondness, knowing that none like this will ever come again.

Walking around her mom's house—Natalia lives elsewhere with her family—we searched in each other's eyes wanting to know what had happened over time. We caught up on children and failed relationships, and we ventured into the surrounding fields.

She pointed to a place where we used to hide to smoke her grandfather's Nazionali. We laughed, then retreated to more important territory. In the quickly falling dusk she pointed across the trees to the farm, now also completely renovated, where, when we were children, Natalia's neighbor Gosto lived.

— *Ti ricordi di Gosto?* she asked. Do you remember?

Yes, I said, but I asked her to tell me again.

We were in seventh grade when Natalia went home from school one day and the mail carrier, a woman, came calling for her.

— *M'accompagni giù da Gosto che gli devo porta' una lettera?* she asked Natalia. Would you walk down to Gosto's house with me? I have a letter for him.

Sure, said Natalia. Gosto was an old, kind man who lived down the road. She had known him since she was born. She had played in his house and run the occasional errand for him. So, off she went.

When they got there, the front door was ajar with the key in the door, as always, but the house was eerily quiet and something felt wrong.

Natalia called for Gosto.

— *Gosto!! Gosto!!* she yelled.

When she got no answer, she ran up the steps and, on the way, she noticed some blood. To a country girl like herself, well, that was normal.

— *Avrà ammazzato una gallina oggi ...,* she thought to herself. Gosto must have killed a chicken today.

She remembers that because it made so much sense. What else could it be?

But when she got to the top of the stairs and she put her head around the corner to look into Gosto's kitchen, she saw him lying on the ground in a pool of blood, his head beaten in. Pools of blood and brain matter caked the floor and the walls, everywhere.

Her eyes fell and ran.

Natalia rushed down the steps and ran to her house like a panicked wild horse, and when she got there she was in shock and couldn't speak. She wouldn't tell her mother what she had seen. Her mom decided to go up to Gosto's to see what had happened, but in the meantime the mail carrier had called the police and they wouldn't let Iolanda see.

Over the following days the police interrogated Natalia relentlessly. They came to the house and turned it upside down looking for a murder weapon—a piece of wood or a metal bar. They wouldn't believe that the night of the murder no one in Natalia's house, a hundred or so meters away, had heard or seen anything.

Eventually they gave up, and it remains one of two murders— both unsolved—that Cetona has ever seen.

When I asked about it in town, they told me the little that is known: Shortly preceding Gosto's murder, an industrialist by the name of Orsini had been kidnapped in the area, near San Casciano. Kidnappings were a common and major event then, a political tactic, a revolt of sorts. I remember rich people being on guard everywhere. Orsini was never found, dead or alive, but police concluded that people from Sardegna who lived in Val d'Orcia had killed him and fed him to a herd of Sardinian pigs, which, much as depicted in *Hannibal*, are known for having a voracious appetite for blood and leaving no trace behind. They surmised that old Gosto liked to roam the countryside around old farmhouses and perhaps he had seen something he was not supposed to see.

And that is still all we know.

Standing there in Piandisette, in the darkness of the woods, Natalia shook her head as if to shake off the chill of the memory. I hugged her and we walked out in the twilight.

Now, out in Piandisette all the *poderi* are restored and polished and the countryside is magnificent. The hills, soft like furs of rabbits, fold into each other in harmony, their crests and seams punctuated by rows of lone cypresses and solitary farmhouses. As I do often in my feasts of beauty, I ran through there today, and on my way back I came to a road I had never taken, ending at an old farmhouse.

An elderly lady was walking up the road slowly, wearing farm clothes and carrying a basket of grass and a sickle. Hearing my footsteps, she stopped and turned around to look, without haste or concern.

I say *buona sera, Signora,* and ask her where the road leads.

— *A casa mia!* she says smiling, pointing with the sickle. To my house!

She puts down her basket and we start talking about other routes to get where I want to go, and while she explains and gestures, I stare at her eyes. They are big and deep blue-gray like rounds of sparkling polished slate. They look warm and familiar, like I've seen them on someone else.

In Cetona, when older people don't know you they don't ask what is your name, but they say, *Di chi sei?* Whose are you? Who do you belong to? I want to ask her the same thing. *Di chi è Lei?*

Instead I ask if I know her. She doesn't tell me her name, but rather she tells me the names of her children, Massimo and Maurizio Fieramosca. I know immediately why I recognize her eyes—exactly like those of her son Massimo, a childhood friend. I laugh and I tell her.

— *Ho fatto le scuole con Massimo!!* I say. I went to school with Massimo, at the *scuola media!*

In truth, I remember him not being in school much, and his mom, laughing with indulgence, tells me why.

— *Che birbo!* she says. What a rascal.

Massimo, in fact, didn't want to go to school, and he dropped out early—I can't remember in what grade. He so hated school that when the bus came he'd run off in the fields, the bus driver chasing along. But it turns out he didn't want to farm either. His parents would take him to the fields and put him in charge of the sheep, but Massimo would climb on a tree and play or fall aleep and the sheep would stray and run away. After giving up on that, they took him to pick olives. There, in their olive groves, he'd climb on the trees and dangle himself from the limbs and the afternoon would be gone and he had picked nothing.

Finally, after battling with this for a year or so, he agreed to go to work and he learned to be a *muratore*, a construction worker and a mason, which he still is, with his brother Maurizio.

— *'N' l'ha' visto 'nco'?* she asks in good Cetonese. Have you not seen him yet?

I shake my head. I look up the hill and I see dogs sleeping on the gravel in the yard. It is peaceful and lovely, and safe, like everything is here. The countryside around us is quiet, and her basket of grass rests on the ground with the scythe tucked inside.

I ask her to say hello to Massimo for me.

She gives me a hug and I am moved at having met her, at our conversation in the lane and the fact that, never having met her, I saw in her eyes the shimmer, the beauty of something I knew from long ago. Only here could that happen to me; only here could eyes transcend time and place and return me whole.

Before I walk on I ask what her name is.

— *Diamante,* she says, smiling. She was named after her grandmother, who died right before her birth. Diamond.

167

The image of Monte Cetona and its cross set against the sky have forever accompanied my life, wherever I have been and at whatever distance from Cetona. I have traced its profile in my mind and in my sleep through the years, indelible.

With its broad footing and imposing contour, Monte Cetona is to the landscape of Cetona and the entire Val di Chiana what a distinguished nose is to a face. Its presence is so essential that the entire landscape revolves around it and cannot be imagined without it. In fact, its position and visibility have long made it into a beacon, a friendly North Star, for travelers and natives alike.

I like to imagine Monte Cetona as a mammoth muscular animal lying on the ground sleeping. His curvaceous spine, which rose from surrounding waters (an ocean?) millions of years ago, reminds me of the soft forms of a sleeping gorilla, perhaps, or a gigantic stubby-haired dog, something DreamWorks would create. And while the mount sleeps, still and quiet, every part of the surrounding world, from Cortona to Montepulciano, from Orvieto to Abbadia, enjoys a different view of his ever-changing morphology and vegetation.

From a distance—from the autostrada heading to Florence, say—with the montagna's profile assertively set on the horizon, it looks like Cetona sits nestled in a crook of its lower slopes, or somewhere in the lower right-hand corner of what appears to be a rather mono-dimensional face. Then, from Cetona itself, it feels more like the town is sitting in the mountain's lap, a bit distended and angled away. You look up and you see the mountain's face, and the cross, plainly looking at you.

But as soon as you leave Cetona and make your way toward Piazze, the perspective on the mountain's face and its summit, ridges, slopes and curves, varies dramatically. As you head toward Piazze and San Casciano, suddenly the mountain is beside you, like you can caress him with the outstretched back of your hand. Then, suddenly you travel into his belly, and by the time you reach San Casciano, moving toward Celle sul Rigo, it's like you've moved suddenly far away from the mountain's face and to a grayer, dustier underbelly where the fur is worn and wispy.

Then, as you travel from Radicofani back toward Sarteano and Cetona on the other side of the mountain you return to Monte Cetona's lush side, a tapestry of green all year round, so rich and deep that in summer when you look at him you can feel the trees with your eyes, almost individually. At times like those I think of our sleeping dog as Monty, and I want to run my fingers through his fur and scratch between his trees, full and bumpy. I notice he has gotten a bad fur trim where someone has chopped a whole dense square of trees. But Monty's fur, Aldo Della Vigna tells me, needs to be trimmed often and rather aggressively so it can reseed and grow back.

Every day, Monte Cetona is a bit different. When the sky is clear with traveling puffy white clouds, the sun casts shadows on Monty that make him look polka-dotted. Those are good days. When the sun is setting and the rays caress him sideways from above Sarteano and Chianciano, his shoulders and crags dress in chiaroscuro and his bulkiest crowns show off like flexed muscles. When it's rainy, there is always a cap over the mountain, sometimes for several days, keeping the cross mysteriously hidden.

— *Se la montagna ha il cappello, vai a casa e prendi l'ombrello!* they say. If the mountain has a hat, go home and get an umbrella!

But in beautiful weather Monte Cetona is a show of openness and splendor, like a creature stretching out and boasting on the landscape. And on those days, when I walk up steep roads that move directly up through the mountain's folds toward the cross, I feel like I could somehow make it to the top and stare right into Monty's eye.

*He* is a presence—a spirit. He is alive.

During wartime, dating back centuries and up through World War II, the mountain was a coveted defensive post from which hundreds of miles of landscape could be monitored. In our lifetime, meanwhile, it has been a long-sought lighthouse for natives, particularly after long absences. On every return I have sought Monte Cetona's profile rising along the *autostrada* long before reaching Cetona from any direction, and every day to this day my heart quickens at the sight of its curvy slopes on the horizon, like seeing a long-lost lover whose absence I have mourned.

Conversely, when leaving, la *montagna* has stayed in my rear-view mirror for kilometers and kilometers, after which it suddenly vanishes at a swerve in the road, fading through my tears. It is the first place I look in the mornings, if I can, and the last at night.

And the cross on its summit is equally spectacular and strangely divine.

Fifty feet tall and twenty feet wide, it's made of black steel tubes and bars intersected in a clean symmetrical pattern that leads the eye upward and outward toward the gods. From afar the cross occasionally catches the light, but on summer days when the sky is so light as to be almost white, the cross is barely perceptible from a distance, like a speck in the sky.

Up close, though, it demands one's attention, and it's mesmerizing.

Today I left my car at the hamlet of Fontevetriana—what used to be a flourishing town and during World War II a prominent post for partisans fighting the Fascists and the Germans—and hiked the last kilometer or so to the top. After a long, steep walk, the gravel road turns into a rough-cut stone path and finally into a thin trail through the woods, full of brilliant green moss soft like a carpet.

After a final climb, steeper and surrounded by dense woods, a ledge of rocks leads to the last few steps up to the cross, and suddenly its presence looms physically through the trees as if a plane were flying over. I look up and there it is, towering right over my shoulder, the top of it cresting in the sky above the trees. I sprint up the rocks to the top and find myself standing right underneath it, and tears fill my face.

I have been here before, many times, a couple of times as a kid, and then a couple of times with Tullia during my years in college or shortly thereafter. The last time, Tullia and I climbed through the metal bars and up the tiny stairwell all the way to the top of the cross. We have photos of us at the top, smiling, breathless and happy.

Now the cross has been locked and can't be climbed. Nonetheless, I am awed by its solemn majesty, perhaps because I am so grateful to be here, and perhaps because things that are eternal and beautiful move me more now that I am cognizant of my own mortality.

I listen to the silence and I hear the sound of the wind and the din of the infinity below. I feel like I can see the whole world, and yet hear nothing of it. I feel shaken and relieved, elated beyond measure and taken aback even by my own love.

— *Si vede il Vaticano da su, eh!* You can see the Vatican's cupola from there! Dino says proudly when I come back down to the piazza.

Dino is a short, dark-mooded man I think of as Amato's sidekick because they are always together, sitting as they are now on the bench in the piazza or by Amato's truck. I am intrigued by the history of the cross, and. encouraged by Dino, I set out to find out something about it, or even better, about someone who might have helped build it.

As usual, Armando's shop seems like a good place to start.

— *Saranno tutti morti ... Mica c'è più nessuno.* There's nobody left. They're all dead, says Amato, pacing around the store, vocalizing a short list of names, his green jacket tight to his chest.

He's silent a minute, looks at the others, then pulls a hand from a pocket and starts ticking off names starting at his thumb.

— *Quello che lavorava per il Carloni ... lui è morto di sicuro,* he says. The man who worked for Carloni—I don't know who he's talking about—is dead for sure. He mentions someone else. Dead, too.

— *Ma 'n' ci lavorò Alfredo della Molla, di Chiusi?* asks Armando. Didn't Alfredo della Molla, from Chiusi, work on it? I don't know who that is, either.

— *Macché!* says Alcide, dismissing that outright, looking at Armando like he's never heard anything so stupid.

— *Va' a chiappa' Alfredo della Molla. O che c'entra?* says Amato, rolling his brown eyes. You go looking for Alfredo della Molla. What does he have to do with it?

Armando shrugs and shuts up, discouraged.

— *Il fabbro ... lui era vecchio, pace all'anima sua. Sarà in paradiso...*, Amato says, ignoring the chatter and continuing his tally. The blacksmith, he says, he was old. Peace to his soul, he must be in heaven by now.

— *Eh, se ha costruito la croce sarà sì in paradiso!* Dino chimes in. If he built the cross, for sure he is in heaven!

Finally, after much banter back and forth under my prodding, someone remembers Fabrizio's dad, Sergio, who they believe built the cement platform for the cross.

Happily, I thank them and go looking for Sergio, down at his *campo*, on the edge of town, toward Chiusi. His *orto* is full of lush artichoke plants like giant octopuses. As I approach I see his parked car and then his familiar chock of white hair sprouting in the greenery. He is cutting grass and he is wearing pants and a sweater and his usual cap. In addition, he has on a woman's house dress in a floral pattern, perhaps his wife's, cut to serve as a large apron—tied around his neck with string. He is covered in little flowers and it makes me smile.

I tell Fabrizio on the phone and he laughs. He says his mom used to argue with his dad all the time because he tied his pants with metal wire.

All said, they were right about Sergio.

Standing in his *orto*—and proud that I found him there—he tells me that he mixed nearly four tons of concrete in a clearing on a downslope a third of a mile from the top of the mountain, the closest accessible place by truck to the cross. He transported the wet concrete over and up with a small cart, rushing to meet the deadline. It took a whole month in the spring of 1967 to pour the massive base.

Sergio shakes his head, still amazed at the feat.

The cross itself was made in Milan, I am told, in steel segments about two meters each, transported to Cetona on the autostrada. After the base was ready, the segments were hauled to the top of the mountain using a huge old red American military jeep left over from the war. Once there, Pino the electrician and two of his workers—Pino had done a lot of high-voltage cable work and was considered the fittest for the job—bolted the first segment to the base. Then, using harnesses and climbing gear, they fastened one piece atop the other till they reached the top.

Then they added the wings, as Pino calls them. He shows me small black and white Polaroids that he brought me of the finished cross and his eyes tear up.

Finally, it was inaugurated in October 1967. The lighting and the benediction by the pope took place the following June. The church, the local priest, Don Mauro, and the authorities had a party and the whole town was invited. Vatican Radio came to broadcast live.

When they lit the cross, they told the people of the town that the pope had brought the electricity from Rome, Sergio told me laughing. In truth, electricity was provided by a truck with a generator hooked up as closely as possible to the cross. For the occasion, Pino and his workers attached wooden boards with tiny lights the whole length and width of the cross and it was magnificent.

— *Era bella davvero,* Sergio says thinking back and looking up at the mountain proudly.

It was beautiful, it really was.

He falls silent, lost in memory, and I fall in it with him, waking a second later to ask about his olive oil, which Fabrizio is always boasting about. In fact, Sergio's greatest pride may be making his own oil, and while we talk about the cross and this and that, he takes me for a walk through his olive grove, shimmering in the light like tinsel.

I can't get enough of the trees, with their majestic trunks and silvery leaves, though, as I have said, when I was little you couldn't get me near an olive tree. Now, I would be honored, and, indeed, I feel lucky to be standing here among them. In summer, when I have usually returned to Cetona, the stature of the olive tree is muted by the glory of the wheat, the yellow of the sunflowers, and the whimsy of the poppies. Now, I enjoy paying renewed honor to the olive tree, its silvery shimmer as intuitive to Cetona's skin and imagery as is the marsh in Charleston, or the tiled rooftops in Rome, dotting the hills with its thin sage-colored leaves and the ancient gnarled trunks that have distinguished this landscape for centuries.

These days, as I run through this countryside, every branch of every olive tree around me is weighed down by the dark purple and bright green fruit, star of the fields and of the daily conversation.

— *L'olive l'ha' colte? Come so'?* people ask. Have you picked your olives? What are they like? How many did you get?

People fret over the time of the month, the weather, whether the olives are plump or thin. Whether they should wait for the *tramontana*, the wind that comes from the north, to give them a final drying out, or whether letting them stay on the trees will give them *la mosca*, which turns into a white worm and eats them from inside out. Maria herself is all in a tizzy about picking or not picking the few olives she has, of which she is immeasurably proud.

Yesterday I stopped by the Fattoria del Biancheto, the local olive mill, and hung out for a while with the owner, Fanny.

— *Vedrai che casino verso le sei,* she says. Wait for 6 o'clock to see the ruckus here.

People come near or after sunset bearing their precious cargo in cases piled high in tractor beds, wagons, trucks, or, those with just a few trees, in baskets. And here at Fanny's they are able to watch their olives go through the milling process until the beautiful liquid the color of fresh spring grass comes out of spigots and pours into whatever containers they have brought. No one's olives are mixed with others: Unless they have too few to run through alone, everyone gets what is essentially an individual yield from one's individual trees.

— *Vengono, stanno qui, guardano. È come un figliolo. È come l'oro,* says Fanny. The clients come here and they stay and they watch their oil being made like watching a child being born.

It's their gold.

Fanny is in her late forties, tall and full-bodied like an oversized boy, with deep, beautiful brown eyes that remind me of a cow's gentleness and a feathered haircut that reminds me of my teenage years. She wins the world with her gregarious nature and her people skills, and she is notoriously *simpatica* to all.

A native, she started the mill twenty-five years ago out of passion for oil. She saw in the industry something like the boom in the wine industry. It didn't come exactly as she expected, but it came in the end, and now her world is flourishing. Her family, which in my youth owned the area's largest agricultural supply and equipment business, in nearby Chiusi, has 12,000 olive trees of its own that produce oil that Fanny sells to buyers around the world. In addition, the mill buys and sells oil from olive growers who produce more than they want or can market, or who pay for their milling with oil.

Fanny is now an oil sommelier and master, she organizes tastings, takes seminars and attends conferences around the world, and she has won several awards for her oil. When she is not at the mill, she is using her people-savvy and simple, unpretentious ways to market and place her product with clients all over the world, from individual buyers to stores like Eataly in New York City. She throws a famous party every year before the opening of the mill, and people who do not receive invitations are nobodies (I was grateful to get one!).

Having grown up on the land, Fanny treats her work with reverence. The mill is impeccably clean, leaving the fragrant smell of fresh oil to reign alone, sweet and distinct. Her staff directs the traffic outside, under the soft panorama of Monte Cetona, and helps unload the olives and load them into the sorting machine. There, in a kaleidoscopically variegated waterfall of purple, green, and black, they go through the process of being washed, delicately separated from leaves and other debris, then transferred to a machine that mills them into a fat paste that is constantly moved by a giant cork screw.

Snaking through a pipe into the next room, the paste is put through a centrifuge that separates oil, water, and pit. The water flows into one large container; the pit is spit out outside into the bed of a tractor; and the oil, lush, glistening, and brilliant green like a sliced kiwi, gushes into a container for a final filtering, and finally comes out of a sparkling steel tube. Here the olive farmers await anxiously with their containers and, no matter how many times they have done it, a look of pride and miraculous wonder.

Olive picking is one of the toughest jobs in agriculture, time-consuming and tedious—even with the new machines that flip the olives off the branches with a tiny helicopter-like propeller—and, if it's cold, exhausting. When I was growing up, our family owned a number of trees. Aldo made us beautiful woven baskets and wooden ladders for the job, which I avoided like the plague. Plus, the trees have to be followed, trimmed in a special way, and fertilized. But in the end, the pride is immense.

— *Quello è estra-vergine, eh!!* says an old man pointing at his oil and looking at me. That is extra-virgin!

He's standing with his wife, both with extra-large grins on their faces. They packed up more than one hundred kilos of oil (a kilo of oil translates to a little more than a liter).

At this time of year, the big talk among Cetonesi is always the yield of oil to quintal of olives, this year nine kilos, ten for the luckier ones. Some are watching mere trickles drip into their bottles, and they show their disappointment.

One year when the yield was nothing short of terrible, an old man in Cetona came to collect his oil and he sat looking inconsolably at the lone bottle sitting under the spout, receiving a mere dribble of oil. The story has become lore.

— *Se lo sapevo venivo co' 'na fetta di pane abbrustito!* he said. If I had known, I would have just come with a slice of toasted bread!

I adore the humor of Cetona as much as the seriousness with which the land is treated and considered, and I am lured to it in reverence as I am to the people who devote their lives to it.

The other day on my run I saw a farmer standing on the edge of a corn field, a piece of equipment marooned in the field behind him. I stopped to chat and he told me he was waiting for a mechanic to come so he could harvest. The corn behind him was dry and browned and ready, finally, but the man shook his head without joy. He told me it costs him 100 euros to seed, fertilize, grow, and harvest a hectare of corn—about two and a half acres—and he recoups barely 90 euros per hectare.

It's hard to ask a farmer why he does what he does. What else would he do?

— *Si fa per fa'*, the man said shrugging. We do it for the sake of it.

That sake is love. Everyone here says farming is the death of man these days, thankless and fruitless. Yet, with this countryside and these fields I struggle to believe that that can be true, so in order to better understand I went to visit with my old friend Attilio Del Buono.

Attilio buys and sells agricultural commodities for a living and he has his thumb firmly plugged in the local farming scene, into which he was born. Five years older than me, he has gentle brown eyes, a handsome, kind smile, and a mellow way. He is soft-spoken and taciturn, though in business I hear he's savvy and shrewd.

His company deals in corn for animals, wheat for humans (soft and hard, *grano duro e tenero,* for pasta and bread), orzo, sunflower seeds for oil and animals, lentils and a few other grains. He buys locally, mostly, from farmers big and small, and sells to people all over Italy—a sunflower oil producer in Milan, a pasta producer in Naples. His trucks carry his name with Cetona (Siena) written big on their sides.

As usual when you start talking about Italy and its policies, the conversation spirals rapidly downward into clichés until your eyes glaze over. Nothing works, bureaucracy is slow, and people cheat and steal. But sitting in his office, in a building halfway between Cetona and Chiusi, Attilio tells me about an agricultural policy that seems to offer a semblance of protection to farmers and land, though, surely, food policy and pricing are much more nefarious matters, having to do, among other things, with the fact that people expect food to cost nothing, especially in America.

Of course, here as everywhere, land is concentrated in the hands of a few. Attilio estimates that about a quarter of the farmers own or rent more than half the available land—renting land is common practice—while half or more of the local farmers control less than a quarter of the land. Anyone who has land to sell turns to those who already own the most and who can afford to buy—and neighbors and friends are not exempt from petty wrangling. It's an old story, and clearly, the smaller the farmer, the tougher the life.

Italy and the European Union, contrary to their American counterparts, regulate the use of the land: It is considered to be a sacred common good. Farmers must, by law, leave five percent of their land uncultivated, unburdened, uncut even, at all times—for the bees and the butterflies, the snakes and the birds, Attilio explains. The fields I have seen fallow here and there throughout my time here make sense now; it helps protect habitat and ensure the productivity of the land, which benefits the farmer as well.

In addition, to ensure diversity in the economy and the landscape as well as the health of the land, big farmers must have under cultivation three types of crops at all times—corn, wheat, and sunflowers, or wheat, corn and orzo, or tobacco. In up to a quarter of the fields one owns, grains must be strictly rotated with replenishing crops such as *erba medica*—alfalfa—for stretches of up to five years. Though those fields during those years produce nothing but alfalfa straw, which is feed for animals, when the cycle ends the fields are replenished and bursting with fertility, ready, once again, for the intense demands of wheat, corn, or sunflowers. This explains the two hills outside Cetona that have been covered in *erba medica* since my arrival and that have become my favorites, lusciously green like a fresh pea except for when they are flowering, which at dusk gives them a distinct lavender tinge.

While they must live by those regulations, Italian farmers receive from the government a subsidy per hectare of land cultivated, which goes a good way toward seeds, labor, and the maintenance of machinery. The subsidy doesn't sound like much to me—and farmers seem to agree it isn't much. Yet, Attilio shrugs: While he has empathy for farmers who say they cannot make a living—after all, he is a farmer himself—with nearly three thousand acres of land in cultivation, owned by him or rented from others, the scale of his enterprise gives him a wider perspective. He says farmers complain all the time: Either it's too wet or too sunny or too dry.

In truth, though, they should draw their balance sheets every five years to account for the worst year and the best, and those in between.

— *Non c'è agricoltore che s'è arricchito, ma si vive. Sennò, erano già andati falliti,* he says. There is not a farmer who has gotten rich, but they survive. If they didn't, they would have gone belly up.

After my conversation with Attilio I run into Gianmaria Vincenti, a third-generation farmer here. He is the second-largest landowner and farmer in the area, after Attilio. Tall, jovial, with thick, greying curly hair, Gianmaria comes into the Bar Sport at the end of his workday for his *aperitivo,* a single glass of white wine.

I ask him how his work is going. His corn's not ready yet, he says, and the rest is all tilling.

We talk about the summer's wheat harvest, and he notes that international commodity forces have reached their tentacles into the bowels of Cetona's tiny economy and deep into his own pocket. He tells me what buyers are paying per quintal of *grano tenero* for bread and for *grano duro* for pasta—a pittance. It's demand and supply, or trade protections or lack thereof, or the machinations of people sitting somewhere on Wall Street, bullying events one way or the other to their filthy advantage. It didn't used to be that way, back when you sold your wheat to the guy who milled flour in the next town. Now it's a global game over which farmers have no control, and, for the most part, little grasp. He said they don't even know what a crop is worth until they take it to market. He is used to it, but he doesn't like it.

— *Si campa,* he says shrugging. We survive, and, he adds, we maintain the environment.

For sure, it's their work that gives the landscape here its soul—this particular and defining patchwork of gold and green reaching as far as the eye can see. Painters of the landscape, I think to myself: Perhaps they should be compensated just for that.

I am taking an incremental approach to my dream of a year in Cetona, unsure of how things will go, balancing gains on one side and losses on the other. I am still breaking even, but I know I need to stay longer, so I moved my flight by a couple of months. I talked with Aram and he says he understands; in fact, he agrees with me. It looks like the trip he has been planning to California to surf—something he has wanted to do for years—is finally coming together. He has bought a van, which he will live in, and he should be leaving soon.

I have been here almost three months now. How am I doing back in my little town?

In the past few weeks I have had my moments of *smarrimento*, of feeling lost, out of place. My brain is always asking questions. Can I live here again? How am I going to support myself? Who am I here? How does place make me different?

Yet, I walk around smiling, incredulous that I am here—that I gifted myself this. I feel like my very roots are shaking with joy, and they shake every time an old lady hugs me and asks how I am, and every time I see Tullia and she hugs me and I am thrilled that I am holding her.

Everywhere I turn I see a face I know, someone who says *Ciaoooo*, and kisses me on the cheek. Everywhere I turn is landscape I have longed for—faces I have longed for. My eyes and ears are hungry, my spirit hungry, my every sense tingling. I relish every moment I can live today exactly the way I am, for what I have in my heart today. I look down and see my vein pulsing, and I am here. Here.

This morning I got my residence so I can buy a car—though I have no money to buy one, but just in case—and Anna put my name, typed, on the mailbox downstairs so I am officially here. The *postina*, the mail carrier, with beautiful long blond hair and a fluorescent vest that grabs everyone's attention as she walks breezily through the piazza, came looking for me. I was happy to see her, considering recent reports of Italian mail carriers found with months of undelivered mail in their cars.

— *È Lei?* she asked, pointing at my name on a *New Yorker* magazine envelope. Is it you? Yes, I said, it is.

Well, she said, I guessed it after they told me your name was Sibilla. She smiled. Now I know where to find you. She had a pile of mail for me, and I was glad to get my *New Yorker*.

# Winter

**D**arkness comes early now, and after dinner the piazza is deserted, as I remembered. A rare lone figure scurries by, but no one lingers. The few souls who go out at night fast approach the bars, the only place to hang out and socialize in the warmth.

Some people refuse to go to the Bar Cavour because they say it's grungy, and some because they have better things to do at home with their families. Yet, alone as I am here, and curious to remake memories and get to know the story of the town again, I am undaunted and I go seeking Giotto and Felice's crafty sense of humor and funny vernacular and the company of their evening regulars. Among them are Bennato, my old neighbor and childhood friend; Sigfrido, a short, bearded guy who works for Attilio's ag business; and Alano, Amato's younger brother, also a carpenter and an old friend of my brother's who I have known all my life. It's a club of guys I like, and they are threads of my old life.

Alano, the last of three kids, is nicknamed Mastro, a moniker that gives him an aura of professional prestige, though in these times of *crisi* his woodworking activity is languishing and he has nearly no work. Alano has salt-and-pepper hair, brown eyes, a pronounced nose, and a warm smile set in a deeply wrinkled but still-handsome face. Above his lips is a thin moustache, and, below, a love patch. Years of woodworking have shaved off parts of or the entire tips of most of his fingers and some of his nails are misshaped like claws.

Alano has a quiet, peaceful demeanor except for when he gets angry and yells—and in those moments he can wake up the dead—or when he tells a good story and gives in to laughter wholeheartedly. Then, his mouth opens wide and the room shakes. He has a smooth, gravelly voice, but vigilant sneaky eyes, and he watches the landscape, mostly the female landscape, a bit like a cat ready to pounce. I tease him that, when with his eyes he follows a woman cross the piazza, which he does a lot—and the younger she is the more intently he follows—that he looks like a wolf, fangs out and drooling. He flirts with me, but it feels innocuous. We go way back, and that suffices for me, in most cases here.

And then there is Sotero.

— *Vieni a bere?* Sotero yells up at me in the window. Do you want to come for a drink?

I look at my watch and laugh. It's late, past 11 p.m., but I pull on my coat and run down the steps. I step quietly out onto the alley, noticing the sharp cold but also the familiar, exhilarating smell of damp stone and burning firewood I have missed so much. I stop to inhale.

Sotero is waiting for me at the entrance to the alley and he kisses me on the cheeks and takes me underarm. It makes me glad to have this man I barely know. That is the Cetona I love, and whose love is one of a kind.

— *Come stai?* he asks me with care. How are you?

Sotero is wiry, ropey, of medium build. He has silvery white hair and a lingering swarthiness that makes him attractive. He came to live in Cetona while I was in college, and in all these years before this stay I had never met him, which seems impossible given that he knows everyone.

We finally met, at the Bar Cavour, when I first arrived. I was having a glass of wine with Giacomo, the ex-mayor, and Bennato, my childhood neighbor, under the fluorescent lights, and Sotero took notice of me, I suspect because I was the new woman in town (and none get past him unnoticed). He introduced himself and shook my hand—and I knew from that that he was not a Cetonese—then he welcomed me back—and I knew from that that he had already asked about me and he knew my story. He looked at me playfully, with warm brown eyes both sly and steeped in goodness, and I immediately liked his friendly disposition.

Now, on cold winter nights he calls up at my window and together we sit to tell stories, or simply to laugh, which is plenty and enough.

Sotero was born a few years after the end of the war—much earlier than I would have thought—up on Monte Cetona in a *podere* between Fighine and San Casciano. An extended family of twenty-three headed up by Sotero's grandfather, who had six children, and the grandfather's brother, who had nine, lived under one roof, with wives and grandchildren. They were sharecroppers. They had stalls and animals and they worked the land. To make ends meet, Sotero's grandfather and his brother worked as *segantini,* cutting crossties for the railroad, work that during cutting season kept them away for weeks, thus leaving the younger boys in charge.

The family's old farmhouse was decrepit and leaky. The kids slept on the floor on jute sacks filled with corn husks.

— *Il prurito! Il rumore!* says Sotero remembering the itching and the noise of the husks. He laughs with tenderness and his cheeks run red.

In winter, snow fell through the patchy roof onto the bedroom floors and the children peeked through the tiles to see the sheep below. There was no bathroom, and no water but in the wells, and everyone worked and contributed to the house. Eventually, though, strife among the wives of the many children caused the extended family to break up. Plus, they didn't want to live there anymore; they wanted a new life in town—anywhere but in the old farmhouse on the mountain.

When they finally moved out, each of the heads of household got three forks and that was that. Sotero tells this matter-of-factly, but he shrugs, quietly, and in the silence I hear that leaving the farmhouse was more of a loss than he makes it out to be.

Sotero moved to Ponticelli with his parents, and there he lived for many years doing everything from construction to running an agricultural supply business. Then, he skips over years and blurs over decades, and sad things, too. Sometimes he looks down or away, serious.

— *No, quello non te lo racconto,* he says sitting outside the Bar Cavour very late one night, the silence enveloping us. That I will not tell you about. I'll tell you that part when you come back, he says, dangling before me any future departure of mine. He has a warm voice, soothing.

Then he looks around, pulling himself back from giving away too much or showing a hand.

— *Bevi? Bevete?* he asks, getting up to order another glass of wine.

Eventually he got a job in a nearby town as a gardener, a fat public-sector job that required so little work of him that he was ashamed to cash his paycheck. He smiles half in shyness and half in shame while he tells me that no one on his work team wanted to work. If you said, let's go work on this or that, they'd say, leave it, we can do it tomorrow.

— *Non avevo guadagnato il pane della giornata ... Quelli anziani non volevano lavorare, e quelli giovani nemmeno. Domani, ti dicevano, domani! Era una vergogna,* he told me. I hadn't earned my daily bread. The old guys didn't want to work, the young ones either. They would always say, tomorrow, we'll do it tomorrow. It was an embarrassment.

That was the job he eventually retired from, with a generous pension, a fact he does not hide. Few would be as honest or self-aware, certainly, in Italy, about that kind of work situation, but it doesn't take long to figure out that Sotero is both sincere and a hard worker. He has the same proud work ethic that all the older people in Cetona have— the people from the country. He and his wife own a piece of property I pass on my jogs where they keep sheep, chickens, horses, and a dozen dogs, and Sotero is always there doing something. Though he is retired, he is always running somewhere, doing something, mostly for someone else. He is involved in every event here, from parades to blood drives and lunches to honor the elderly. He disparages no task, too menial or too small, and that's not something that can be said even of the most flag-bearing of Cetonesi, and perhaps this makes it less surprising that Sotero went to seminary as a kid.

His father sent both him and his brother, but while he was there Sotero was molested by a priest, a seemingly common experience in seminary here, I hear. When Sotero reported the abuse to the head of the seminary, the man accused him of lying and spreading nasty rumors. Sotero, eleven or twelve at the time, felt a rush of anger, and standing as tall as he could, he shoved the director in the chest, causing him to tumble all the way down the seminary's main stairwell. This earned Sotero expulsion, which was exactly what he had hoped for.

The experience left a bad taste in Sotero's mouth, though he has overcome it enough to help Don Prospero with nearly every church event in town, which he does, and talks about, always enthusiastically—almost with the same enthusiasm he expresses about sex and women in a constant stream of comical, lustful commentary.

I feel like one of the guys when I hang out with Sotero, Alano, and Bennato, and whoever else happens to be around. I have no interest in any of them sexually—they are like brothers—but I love their banter, a word jam session of vernacular jokes and stories to which each contributes from his knowledge, perspective, and inclination. With them I feel free to laugh at even the grossest of jokes and stories, of which there are many, and in a single night I laugh more than I do in a week in a world elsewhere.

The other night there was a soccer game on TV at the bar, though a group of us were not paying attention to the game. We were talking about how we all came about, who our dads were, what we do. Someone I didn't know, Drazen, perhaps, the custodian of a big property in town, a big, strong Moldovan, asked for my story and I told an abbreviated version. I told him about my life, that I had been a journalist and a researcher, that I write and paint.

Bennato beamed and put his arm around me proudly. Bennato, who is also a carpenter, is a gray-haired father of two, jaded by many years of hard work. Yet, he still treats me with the indulgence and tenderness shown to a little sister, and our relationship remains crowned by the fact that we grew up together on Borgo.

— *Ma se' partita da Borgo! Da Borgo!* he said, grinning, reminding me of my roots. You started out from Borgo! From Borgo!

One night, Giacomo, the former mayor, was talking about Cetona's mayoral race, which was looming in the spring and for which there were no known candidates. After a brief discussion we concluded that I would make a good candidate, with all the right qualifications, except I lack the most basic one of all: Italian citizenship. How to procure it?

— *Eh, bisogna trovarti un marito Cetonese! Cetonese!* he concluded. We must find you a Cetonese husband! Not Italian, but specifically Cetonese!

The idea immediately sparked a conversation about what I would require in such a candidate and a tentative compilation of a roster of potential spouses. Suggested names ran the gamut from the reclusive bachelor farmer who lives alone in a dark house on the edge of town, to the kind but ancient widower out in the country. I learned in the process that the candidates one could think of as attractive are taken; some who we thought were acceptable and single are actually still technically married—they stay together for tax reasons; and then there are those who, in exchange for citizenship, would expect much more than I would be willing to give.

Limits notwithstanding, we managed to identify several candidates, including Amerigo from my elementary school, who after a generous amount of red wine leaned his head on my chest (he is not tall) and confessed that when we were in third grade he was in love with me.

— *Ero innamorato, ero innamorato! Ero innamorato di te, poi dell'Ida e della Natalia, che lei mi faceva toccare le pocce.* I was in love, he said! I was in love, with you, Ida, and Natalia, because she let me touch her boobies!

All sorts of other secrets came tumbling out, too, and over the course of the winter, the more evenings I spent with the guys at the Bar Cavour and the more fun the time got and the raunchier the stories.

One night we had a lively conversation about prostitution, which then led to blowjobs. Sotero was there, Sigfrido, Bennato, and me. Giotto was subbing for Felice and listening to every word. It started—I do not know how this train of thought started, exactly—when Sotero said that men like him, of his age, like to get blowjobs from young women in their twenties or even earlier. He then described what was better about this—their enthusiasm, willingness, and endurance. Considering his age, I protested with the predictable arguments about sexual exploitation and generational manipulation that one would expect to hear from women at Yale, or someplace heady like that. I believe in these arguments, but in the milieu of the Bar Cavour my arguments sounded hollow like soap bubbles. I even laughed at myself.

— *Lo fanno per lavoro! Gli piace!!* Sotero protested shaking his head! They do it for work! They like it, he said!

Common sense tells us there is no such thing as a happy prostitute. Yet, recently I read an article written by a woman in the States who, by the time she was in her late twenties, had earned half a million dollars being a high-end escort for wealthy Wall Street types. Now, she's applying to grad schools to pursue the career she really wants.

Good for her, I thought; at least she won't have student loans.

— *Si comprano le cose che vogliono! Che c'è di male?* Sotero said. They can buy the things they want! Nice clothes! What's wrong with that?

Sotero brings up the name of a young woman in Cetona who apparently does it for a living (and she is not the first). He starts listing her customers—all local men—and details of their satisfied reviews. Then, as if the conversation could not deteriorate further—oh, and it gets worse and worse, more than I can tell you here—he tells a story about another local woman and her clients and something involving Nutella ... It's way too much information, as they say, but told in such a funny manner and with such ease that it seems innocent like a family picnic. It embarrasses me, yet I laugh with abandon.

Sigfrido quips something and starts mentioning names. He wants to know who the woman is.

— *È la* ...? he asks, smiling, curious. Is it...?

— *Dai, diccelo, diccelo, su,* Sig says, prodding Sotero to reveal who the woman is. C'mon, tell us! Tell us!

C'mon, they all ask.

— *No, basta,* I scream. I don't want to know!

While this goes on, Bennato studies me affectionately. He is silent on these rather provocative topics, more prone to contribute on matters that draw from his role as a leftist malcontent and agitator— inveighing, for example, against the evils of the Internet, the infinite conspiracies of government, Cetona's traffic police, who target him, and the ravages of progress.

*Il progresso viene sempre col regresso.* Progress always comes with regress.

Sotero's eyes move suspiciously from Bennato to me and back.

— *Ma a dottore non ci avete mai giocato voi due?* he asks after learning that we grew up together. Did you ever play doctor, you two?

We laugh. No, we say shaking our heads. We didn't.

—*Non è possibile!* Sotero says, not giving up. It's not possible!

Bennato and I deny, and really, we didn't.

Finally, Alano gets up and goes to the counter.

— *Bevete? L'ultimo, poi si va a casa,* he says. A last wine, then we go home.

We are always the last ones there. Past one, finally Giotto pushes us out the door and closes.

In piazza it's cool and silent like an empty glass. I go upstairs and I look out the window. There is not a footstep, not a cat. The town is almost unimaginably removed and still, in these hills, a tiny cluster of lights that one would not encounter if not by purpose or absolute mistake.

Self-contained, unto itself, Cetona seems to need nothing else.

Growing up, Saturdays were market days in Cetona, as they still are today.

The piazza fills edge to edge with the trucks and booths of merchants who come from all over the area selling food, flowers, clothes, shoes, agricultural tools, pots, pans and kitchen tools, food, cheeses, and grains. There's the pasta man, and the plant man, and the fish monger, and, naturally, the *porchetta* man, always with the longest lines, dispensing slices of whole roasted pig onto freshly baked rolls until there is nothing left but snout and crumbs.

— *Il sale ce lo vole?* he says, asking if you want the salt, spices and crust that crumble off the pig as he's sliced.

Then he wraps the *panino* in a piece of white wax paper and off you go.

When we were little, and through the decades, the *mercato* filled the piazza with people. Ladies from the town dressed nicely for their shopping, with nice shoes and clothes and makeup, which they still do, and farmers from the *campagna* came into town, leaving their Apes at the edge of the piazza, and coming in to bargain for tools or kitchen implements. Their wives stood in their layered skirts and sweaters, handkerchief on their heads—and in winter heavy dark stockings and heavy country shoes—picking through the goods, eyeing the best deals, and buying fish from the fishmonger, otherwise available in Cetona only on Friday mornings. Men gathered in twos or threes and talked head to head.

Back then, some of the merchants would yell out loudly, hawking their wares.

— *Scarpe! Venite, venite, ci so' le scarpe belle!! Ventimila lire, ventimila lire!!* yelled the shoe man, tall, with a plaintive face, red from the cold or the boredom. Shoes! Shoes! Come see the beautiful shoes!

I never liked the shoe man. As kids we always wanted something, and we'd stare at the shoes dreamily, as kids do, but the shoe man was aggressive. He'd tell you the prices and encourage you to try them on, but if you tried them on and decided not to buy them, he would get irritated and curse you under his breath. His wife was *antipatica,* too. The same shoe man still comes to market, and his wife is still *antipatica,* though he has stopped yelling and I don't look at his shoes.

Since the arrival of shopping centers, the *mercato* has lost a bit of its bustle and flair. Yet, the din of the crowd still fills the air and, now as then, people gather in groups to savor the day and mill about. People who have not seen each other in a while run into each other and exchange a few words. Giacomo and Bennato stand over there, eating a *panino* and smoking a cigarette, and other groups of men do the same. I walk about saying hello here and there, surveying the goods and looking for Tullia, who must be here somewhere.

As I roam I think of how in my teens I loved meeting my mom at the *mercato.* By then I had overcome the rebellious phase against my mother and I liked her. I was no longer embarrassed by her foreignness. She had become accustomed to Cetona and its ways, and indeed she was part of it: She knew my friends and their names, and I would follow her around happily while she shopped here and there, stopping to chat with this person or that.

Money was always an issue in our house; there was never excess or thoughtlessness, and never a moment of abandon. But small things could make me happy for a long time—a new pair of shoes, or a new T-shirt—and Mom understood this. She was good to me, slipping me a coin here or there. Sometimes she'd buy me something small, at the market, or give me money to get a magazine at Ottorino's, an institution in Cetona, where they sold everything one could need.

Opened in 1964 by Ottorino—and referred to as Ottorino's long after Ottorino retired and left the store in the able hands of his son Unico—the store sold the only newspapers and magazines in town. In addition, it sold postcards, books, school supplies, and other items such as socks, and sewing and knitting supplies. Anyone in Cetona who read a daily newspaper—locals as well as tourists and people who own houses here—went in there every day, as did ladies who sewed and embroidered, and all the schoolchildren, who shopped there for notebooks, pens and pencils, colors and textbooks.

And bras.

When I shopped for my first bra, I was about fifteen, skinny and flat-chested like a kitchen table, except for two pronounced bumps that needed cover.

Unico, a tall, skinny man like his father, with a broad smile full of teeth and agile, mischievous eyes, stood behind the counter strewn with bras and smirked. He might even have winked. He was humorous and fun.

— *Più piccolo, Unico.* Smaller, Unico, smaller, please, I pleaded, red in the cheeks.

— *'Billa, non c'è più piccolo. Non esiste. Non li fanno! Tanto vale ci metti i cerotti!* he said, calling me with this affectionate abbreviation of my name and putting his hands together in prayer. There is nothing smaller, he said. They do not make bras smaller than that! You might as well use Band-Aids!

Mortified, I left with my first bra, Unico chuckling at the door. He loved to laugh.

Through the years I bought my school supplies there, and through the years when I came back in summer, I bought my newspapers there every morning, one Italian and one American. Unico and his wife, Nuccia, were always among the first to greet me at my returns, wanting my news and, later, news of my mother and father.

For many years my mom had taught their daughter, Barbara, piano lessons, and they were fond of her.

Anyway, some years back the store closed, and the other day, when I saw Nuccia in the piazza, she invited me to go visit her, in her apartment above the store, where the family has lived forever. I wanted to know what had happened to Unico, and the store.

In recent years, she told me, after running the *cartoleria* for decades, Unico insisted they close shop and retire. He had been exhausted of it and by it, and I can understand why: He was up at dawn every morning, seven days a week, to receive the newspaper delivery and to set the papers out for his customers on their way to work or, on Sundays, on their way to their frothy cappuccini and their favorite spot at the bar. Unico had always been quick on his feet and ready with a smile, a quip, or something funny. He knew everyone by name, preference, and habit. But then he had had enough; he wanted to quit.

Nuccia had hoped that retirement would cure Unico of a latent tiredness, but, to the contrary, it plunged him into a restless and clawing depression from which he could not find exit. He was withdrawn and anti-social. Nuccia, dark, strong, immaculately dressed and intensely loyal to Unico—they walked up and down the piazza arm in arm every night of their lives on the left side of the sidewalk, in front of their store—insisted he go see a doctor. The doctor prescribed an antidepressant and requested that Unico come back a few weeks later. They were seeking a cure, searching for a solution.

Then, one hot August morning the sun rose to find Nuccia making coffee in the corner of her kitchen. Standing at her sink getting ready to put the coffee on the stove, she heard a thud. It startled her, but she figured it was the sandwich sign in front of the tourist office a few doors down falling over in the wind, as it did nearly every day, so she put the coffee on the stove, and put out her cigarette in the ashtray on the counter. In the silence of the kitchen she happened to glance out the window and she noticed a small crowd in front of the Bar Cavour, directly across the piazza from her. They were looking in her direction, right at the sidewalk in front of the *cartoleria*, below her windows. They looked horrified and they were talking.

— *Ma che guardano?* Nuccia wondered. What are they looking at?

Curious, she opened her window to look out, and as she did, she saw Unico's feet on the pavement below. Our dear Unico, distraught, perhaps hopeless, or perhaps just chemically unbalanced, had jumped out the window of his own home and to his death, right in front of the store to which he and his family had devoted a lifetime. Right there in piazza.

Unico's laugh rings in my ears, now, when I see Nuccia walking her dog, alone, back and forth in the piazza. I feel heartbreak for her.

Anyway, back to those days of my first bra, by then Mom had many students in Cetona, and children and families loved my mother, her competence and outer sternness, always a big mask to her frail inner world. She was a beloved teacher, and her time spent in people's homes built bridges and connections. My father, on the other hand, got a bit of a reputation for being stern or aloof, in part because of his obscure job, and in part because of my strict curfews. I took the rules of the house seriously, as I did my school work, about which my father was also severe. But he was generally a jovial, friendly man who loved living here. Though he didn't understand everything that was said to him, he always nodded enthusiastically and smiled. He was interested in people, particularly the regular people whose workmanship he respected, like Aldo, or Bastiano, or Fabio Angiolini, the masons and the blacksmith. He was friendly and *simpatico*.

I remember, when I was at the *liceo*, Silvio Della Vigna referred me to his English teacher as a potential babysitter. She taught English in Cortona at the Istituto Agrario, where he and Fabrizio went to school, and she wanted an English-speaking au pair at their beach house in Castiglione della Pescaia, a popular resort where they spent the summer. Her name was Maria Luisa. She had luminous green eyes and coquettish ways, and she came to Cetona with her cousin to meet me.

In piazza they asked for directions to our house. They knocked on the door and my father answered. He said I was not there—it was Sunday—and that I was out with friends on our *motorini*. Surely, if they went up to the piazza, he told them, they would find me eventually. I can picture him telling them this, a bit like a smartass.

— *Che bel babbo che hai!* Maria Luisa said to me first thing. What a handsome dad you have!

And he was. With his smart, dark eyes, his intellectual intensity and curiosity, his mysterious dreams and unusual job, Dad was interesting and attractive. He drew me birthday cards in ink with my friends and my boyfriends caricatured in them, which I liked to show to everyone, and when my school friends came over to do homework he goofed around like he was in a *Saturday Night Live* skit, making faces and dancing. My friends had never known a father like that, and they giggled and wiggled and I felt like I had something special.

And I did. I loved talking with Dad about everything I learned at school, the books I read, and my thinking about many issues. He delved into complex subjects with me, always like I was an adult, and his analytical mind gave me my true substance, my thinking. I admired his knowledge of many topics, from art and history to architecture and literature, and I sat riveted listening to his stories. He had detailed recall of things and people from long, long ago—from Mies van der Rohe, who he had worked for, to untold numbers of artists and architects he had met—and he was a brilliant imitator of people. Everyone he talked about grew mythical and magical, fabulous and larger than life.

Well into my teens, after we finished eating I'd go sit on his lap and sip from the bottom of his espresso and listen to his epic stories. Often, seeking to emphasize a point, he'd reach for a scrap of paper and his ink pen and he'd draw—anything from molecules and hemorrhoids to church arches and keystones, buildings and portraits of people, and anything else one could imagine that illustrated his point. His drawings, like his penmanship, were skilled, distinguished, and, well, exact.

Then he'd swat me on the behind and tell me to get up.

— C'mon, Birdie, I've got to get back to work! he'd say, forcing me up from his lap and walking back to the silence of his workshop to make violins.

Christmas has passed, and New Year's, too. It was my first New Year's in Cetona in many, many years, and I dressed up in a long midnight blue dress I brought for the occasion. I prepared for and soaked up the magic of being in this space of the planet I had missed for so long. I felt exhilarated to be here, yet missing something across the way, caught, somehow, between laughter and tears all night long, a sail between two masts.

I joined Maria and Lauro in a traditional dinner with Giacomo and Ottavia, Tullia and Duccio, and Il Vecchio Jr. at Stefano and Caterina's house, Graziella and Dino's son and daughter-in-law, above the old Osteria Vecchia. It was a loud tableful, festive and intimate, with platters of food, sparkling wine, and the kids, too, Sofia, Filippo, and Giuseppe, each with their budding personalities, simultaneously determined and sweet.

I feel honored to witness the domestic lives of my friends here, which I have missed our entire adult lives, and this makes even this simplest of things an adventure in learning for me. I notice how Caterina loves to cook and showers her guests with attention, as her mother and mother-in-law have always done. She is revered for it, too, and it makes me envious to not be able to host them in my home, a home I don't have here. It strikes me that none of them save for Maria have ever eaten at my table, and I feel somewhat inconsequential or disemboweled because of that. Do I eat? Cook?

Yes, I do—on the other side of the globe.

Maria, too, likes to cook now, in bouts, which I wouldn't have expected. I didn't grow to see her learn to make pasta or set up her home. Now she dotes on Lauro and spends hours cooking, a bit unsurely, sometimes, but persevering. I like to watch her hands, as I remember them—her mother's hands, sensible but not unpretty—with a plain wedding ring, now, chopping and doing, with competence. I notice her way of washing the dishes carefully, or putting away something in her home, an order revealed, a system. Maria's system. We never got to learn this together as grown women.

When the bells chimed midnight, we walked down to the piazza to set off floating balloons like magical red Chinese lanterns. Standing there in the cold holding plastic cups of Prosecco, we watched them rise in the sky like tremulous flames of good will for the world. My phone rang here and there with wishes from the States, including Aram's. Afterwards I went to a party at Marcello's. Bennato and his wife, Adele, were there, and a long table full of people many of whom I had not seen in years. The room was dim but the candles and the people merry, a gathering of tradition and familiarity.

When I walked in, everyone said hello to me and hugged me. I looked around and took it all in and I felt overwhelmed with emotions of all kinds. I felt profound gratitude, and ancient love, and a tremendous loss—having but not having; being but not being. Belonging but not belonging. I put my hands over my face and I wept as they looked on.

Now, the understated sounds of winter fill my days in my apartment as I paint and write.

I hear the joyous din of children in the elementary school playground. They have their break at mid-morning, their *ricreazione*, and in nice weather they run around outside chasing each other and screeching shrilly in freedom and release. A half hour later they are back inside, sitting at their desks.

The garbage truck comes by sometime late morning. I hear the truck idle as the garbage man gets out and unloads the small can at the end of my alley. It's Il Vecchio, the son of Il Vecchino the elder, and he is sweeping slowly.

I look out on the piazza. There is a lot of movement in the mornings at my end, what with the pharmacy a few doors down, the *giornalaio,* and the florist, on the first floor of my building, right below my bedroom window. Vasilika has been particularly busy lately, with All Saints Day and the holidays to commemorate the deceased. People stream to the cemetery carrying flowers that Vasilika lovingly wraps. It is a surprisingly busy place. A truck pulls up, a floral supplier, and Vasilika comes out to buy. On the bench outside her store are a few ladies, Tatiana the *badante,* and her charge, and two other ladies. They talk and laugh with Vasilika as she unloads armfuls of flowers and carries them in the store.

In the background I hear the hum of the ladies talking in the new social club founded on the floor below me, where now retirees gather to play cards and talk. It's a recent development in town that gives the elderly a place to go and socialize besides the *giardinetti,* a tiny public park in front of the elementary school where in pretty weather they gather like lizards in the sun, the women chatting away and the men nodding off.

The bells of San Michele yank me from a daydream. Not fifty feet across from my window, they chime in the early morning, for the mid-morning mass, at noon, and the afternoon mass. And for funerals. Add that to the bells at the school, which chime every hour and half hour, and I need no implement to keep track of the hour. They are my timekeeper, and a constant, and at times grating, reminder of where I am.

I watch as Franco Bianchi, nicknamed Dinderi, the church custodian and the father of my childhood friend Silvia, walks up the church steps and closes the big doors. Signor Bianchi makes me smile with tenderness. The other day he told me that his mother died recently. A friendly, stout woman with glasses and a big smile, she owned a piece of land down Via Sobborgo, not far from our house, and for years we crossed on the street several times a day as I walked to school and she went to her field. She was widowed young, when her husband was killed during the war along with two other men, by a grenade at the hands of the Germans. He had been hiding from the Nazis up at a farm on the mountain, leaving in town his young wife and son, little Franco. When he was killed, they had been married a scarce handful of years, and she was left all alone for the rest of her life. Dinderi tears up while he tells me this, and I stand with him for a moment, imagining his mom walk down the road as if I had seen her just yesterday.

Mauro drives through on his way to his mid-morning coffee at the Bar Sport. I recognize the red car he loans me sometimes. Antonietta, Tullia's mom, comes out of the *macelleria* pulling her little shopping basket and she stops to chat with another lady. They stand close together, Antonietta confiding something. She laughs and moves on. She waves at her son-in-law Duccio, Tullia's husband, who is sitting at the Bar Cavour reading the paper and smoking a cigarette in a shaft of sun.

Then I see Tullia, too. She has the day off. She is smoking a cigarette, hanging out in front of Sabina's store, talking with someone and gesticulating, and the sun is catching her thick black hair curling around her ears. She looks up at me and grins and I feel incredulous that my eyes are upon her. I love her so, and I smile at the fact that she is ignoring her husband and her mom, just over there, and taking a moment for herself. I ask her about this later and she laughs. She says that she and Duccio see each other every morning at the bar on their way to work and they ignore each other.

— *Il caffè lo voglio prende' in pace, scusate.* Forgive me, she says laughing, I want to have my coffee in peace!

One must carve out some solitude here.

Before the stores close at 1 p.m., I run across the piazza to one store or the other to get a few things. I pay an inordinate amount of attention to my hair and pull on something decent. I continue to look at myself from the outside, like I am an experiment here.

I would like that to be different: I would like to be normal, the way I used to be.

At the end of the *scuola media* kids in Italy who intend to continue their education fan out to different high schools based on their interests: *liceo artistico* for art, *scientifico* for the sciences, *classico* for the classics, *linguistico* for languages, *ragioneria* for accounting, and so forth (the system has changed slightly, but is more or less the same). Because it would be too expensive to have that number of high schools in each town—and not enough students to attend them—the schools are located in towns that are approximately central from all directions: Montepulciano is a hub, for example, and Città della Pieve; Perugia and Siena are others.

In the morning, all of us or, rather, those of us who went to high school, took off for schools in different towns: Ottavia to the *istituto magistrale* in Montepulciano, to become a teacher (which she never became); Silvio and Fabrizio to study agriculture in Cortona; Maria for the *liceo scientifico* in Città della Pieve, and me, for the *scientifico* in Montepulciano, in the opposite direction.

I remember walking up Borgo every morning, in every shade of weather, and waiting for the bus in the glow of the lights of the Bar Cavour, with the *omini*—the little men—coming in and out getting their coffees and going to work. We rode a public bus, not a school bus, together with people from all walks of life, going about their business and work, many of them in Chianciano, a thermal bath resort. Among them often was a woman who, when I was little, intrigued me yet frightened me. Sultry-looking, with dark disheveled curls, she looked to me like she had just got out of bed, or she had not yet been to bed. Her blouse was always half open, and her soft breasts spilled out underneath her knee-length overcoat with a fur collar. She was nicknamed la Littorina—*littorina* was the term used for one of the first generation of railcars—because she worked in hotels here and there in the area and she was always on the bus going to and from jobs, a bit like a railcar.

Sometimes while she waited for the bus her thigh-high stockings would creep down her legs, and after tiring of pulling them back up several times, she would duck in a doorway next to the Bar Cavour and yank them off and stuff them in her purse. She would step back out smoothing her coat and her skirt, and I could picture her soft thighs underneath, which filled me with curiosity yet also with sadness and dread.

When the bus arrived, she got on and sat alone, toward the front, and rode the bus with us through Sarteano, then she usually got off, together with others, in Chianciano. We continued on through Sant'Albino before reaching our final stop, just before 8 a.m., in time for us to walk to our school, at the top of the town, in Montepulciano's *fortezza,* for the beginning of classes.

Except in winter, when it was so cold your fingers would freeze in class, it was a beautiful setting, surrounded by meter-thick walls and a beautiful garden that in spring blossomed with flowers and birdsong. From the top of the castle we could see miles and miles of the glorious Tuscan countryside through which my classmates and I traveled each day.

Each morning opened with the roll call, the *appello*: Batelli, a bright son of a doctor from Chianciano; Battisti, a bright, friendly kid from tiny Castiglione d'Orcia; Becherini, dark, with a lazy eye, who slept through most of school except when something enraged him politically; Ciatti, short, a funny musician from Sinalunga; Conciarelli, a kind and nerdy girl, from Montepulciano; Cozzi-Lepri, nice, amenable, daughter of people who owned hotels in Chianciano; Cresti, nicknamed Coscio, perhaps for his hefty thighs, from Trequanda; Delgrasso, from the country, I don't remember where; Ellebori, a beautiful girl, from Chianciano; Franci, tall with tight long curls and a bubbly personality, from Sinalunga; Fix, me, and so forth, until we got to Volpi, from Castiglione d'Orcia, soft-spoken and smart.

Once it was determined that we were all there—and if someone was not we took note, particularly if the absences repeated themselves—our day began, a mixture of banter and chaos and a mostly rigorous exploration of academics that lasted five years. We all took the same classes, together, five hours a day, six days a week: five years of Italian literature and literary criticism, five of Latin and Latin translation, from Cicero to Cesar to Catullus; five of history. Three of philosophy—from Socrates through Russell, Heidegger, Sartre, Beauvoir, Camus, and Schopenhauer, five of foreign language and literature, including reading and translating prose and poetry, five of math, five of various sciences, through advanced chemistry, five of art, religion, and PE. It was all followed, at the very end of our fifth year, by the dreaded *esame di maturità*, similar to the French *baccalauréat*.

Our class brought together people of all economic makeup and cultural standing—children of doctors and lawyers and farmers and store keepers, famous parents, poor parents, and everything in between. There were kids with academic talent and ambition, and some with little of either. We were twenty or so people randomly brought together who spent every hour of every school day together for five years.

On the first day at the new *liceo* I was wearing a checkered blue and red shirt with nerdy sleeves, blue jeans, and tennis shoes. I was skinny and flat-chested and had not yet taken but the slightest interest in boys. I was excited about my new school and my new notebooks and checking out my new classmates. I was a kid, little more than a girl, really, and I felt deeply aware of this when I met my desk mate, Francesca, who, that promising fall day, had on a tight striped cotton knit sweater and tight jeans that showed off a thin and fully developed figure.

Francesca had flawless skin and long straight brown hair and her lips were painted red as were the nails of her slender fingers and her pretty toes, displayed through delicate high-heeled sandals. She had a narrow, straight nose and large dark eyes, immaculately made up. She looked five years older than me, or more, and this fascinated me. It was all a new world to me, outside of Cetona for the first time, on my own.

And I met Sabrina, too, with her creamy porcelain skin, thick, wavy shoulder-length black hair, and large, soulful brown eyes that easily betrayed her inner world. She came from Castiglione d'Orcia, an old castle that rises like a perch overlooking the eternal landscape of the Val d'Orcia, from a humble and rather strict working-class family. Her parents were hard-working and they lived in a post-war apartment building at the edge of town.

From the very first week at the *liceo* Sabrina and I developed what felt like an instinctual bond. Surely it was in part our academic affinity, but there was, no doubt, a yet-undiscerned likeness of soul. Though we were only fifteen, we were already the way we would become: serious and ambitious about our studies, and intellectually minded. But, we also loved to laugh and make jokes, and we found humor and hilarity in the world and people around us. Perhaps that was it—we shared a delicate and safe balance between discipline and fun, and in our new school that tacit communality grounded us.

And certainly no one in the world could possibly have had as much fun as we did in school together, and so innocently. I picture Sabrina's laugh and her beautiful smile of perfect white teeth. When she laughed she often brought her hand to her mouth, with her nails bit to the quick, something that early on communicated her nervousness about living.

Our class melted quickly into a close-knit group, mostly, though certainly we broke down in groups that preferred each other because of our communalities. I liked the kids who were interesting and smart but fun in some way; I liked to poke fun in class and to get in trouble, too, and I was an equal-opportunity classmate, for the most part. Of course, there were better students and worse students, better-looking and worse-looking kids, some smarter, some less. But there were no jocks and no nerds and no bullies to fragment our class. There were no star football players or prom queens that dated each other and made everyone else look puny (though Francesca came close), and in fact there was no football, no prom, no yearbook, no varsity club, and no popularity contests. We didn't leave high school feeling branded like we were losers for life, or winners for life, either. We were just a group of kids who had to spend so much time together each day, and for so many years, that the differences lost their sharp edges and most often morphed into affection, acceptance, and familiarity. We knew each other's idiosyncrasies, likes and dislikes; we knew if we had troubled family lives, and what our parents did. We knew if we were poor or rich, and if we were grieving or living joyfully.

Sabrina and I shared a desk, in the first row, for most of the following five years of school. Together, and before each other's eyes, we grew from innocent girls to grown women dealing with sex, our bodies and self-image, our aspirations and way of being in the world, mutating daily into the people we would eventually become—or were we already who we would be?—with our joy, our unique color, and our wounds.

Sabrina and I confided in each other everything we came into believing—our political ideas, our views on money and society, prejudice, religion, the church, and people, our moral values and judgments as they sprouted like a budding plant in spring. We were nothing less than exploding mentally, and ethically, too. Sitting closely in our chairs, we read ahead through the *Divine Comedy,* sharpening our moral values and opinions, weighing what we thought of who he dispatched where for what sinful trespass. We shared enthusiastically in our disdain for the *ignavi*—those who in times of moral crisis shrirk taking a stance—but when it came to Paolo and Francesca, the castigated lovers, we were not so sure. After all, by then Sabrina and I were learning about falling in love, and feelings changed so quickly: How could we be held accountable?

Every few weeks I took the bus back home with Sabrina and we studied together. Her mom waited for us with lunch, which came late, past 2 p.m. Then, sitting in the silent dining room, used mostly for family gatherings or festive occasions, we studied through the afternoon and into the night. We ate dinner with her parents, under the fluorescent light of the quiet kitchen, and in the morning Sabrina and I took the bus back to Montepulciano and school. Sometimes she came to my house too, which delighted her because my father, contrary to hers, was comical and he loved to entertain her with his foreign ways. I remember a picture of them with a bright red wool scarf draped over both of their heads. Sabrina looks freaked out and amused.

Our teachers at the *liceo* were colorful and interesting, competent, for the most part, and savvy. Loredana Vinciarelli was our rock. Flat-footed, with broad hips and a strong frame, Signora Vinciarelli had black eyes, a waxy complexion and a business-like demeanor. She dressed conservatively, always with nice but plain skirts, and she paced the room lecturing in her subjects, Italian literature and Latin, with long regular steps, cigarette smoke billowing steadily from her nose. She taught us every day for the whole duration of the *liceo*, tirelessly drilling Italian literature and Latin declensions into our heads. She knew us all in our ambitions, skills, and lacunas, and, when things got bad, she was our greatest fan, compassionate and motherly.

When the principal, Salvatore Nocilla, a short man from Sicily, fumed and threatened to kick us all out of school for some thing or the other, like hiding a teacher's car or disappearing for a day, she stood up for us, making him see the nuances and challenges of growing up.

— *Via, Nocilla, so' ragazzi, su! Lasci fa'!!!* she would say. C'mon, Nocilla, let it go. They are kids!!!

Boscherini, our history and philosophy teacher, was redheaded, with pock-marked skin and a dimpled chin. He was a self-avowed Bolshevik and he taught history with a slant: Simplistically, everything about the United States was bad, and everything about Communism was good. But everyone liked him because he believed in what was called *il sei politico,* or a "political C." He didn't believe in flunking, so if you showed up for class and submitted to the tests with some modicum of effort, he passed you.

Everyone at the *liceo* had to have a verbal examination at least twice a semester in every subject. Teachers liked to call on us sometimes based on our roll call list, and sometimes based on a sadistic hunch that someone was not prepared. But most, Boscherini and Vinciarelli included, accepted volunteers: If you had studied and kept up with the work, volunteering allowed you to take the exam at your leisure and spare your classmates the infamy of being caught unprepared.

But not always were there volunteers.

— Does someone what to talk about Descartes today? What were the main points of his thought? Boscherini would ask, waiting for a volunteer to manifest.

The minutes passed and the silence grew heavier. We fidgeted, looked under our desks, pretended we needed to go to the bathroom, or pretended to be absorbed in reading, heads down.

— What about the French Revolution? What was the main thrust of the revolution?

Sometimes classmates who were unprepared and who would have risked a bad grade had their name been called would beg others to come forward.

— *Dai, ti prego, vacci te,* they would say, whispering. C'mon! Volunteer!

They would gang up and negotiate and bribe. If you volunteer in history today, I will volunteer tomorrow in math.

But sometimes teachers had to force or cajole those who never wanted to be tested. There was one student in our class senior year named Bernardini. Her family had come to the area for work, maybe, I don't recall, but she had not been with us the whole time. And she never wanted to be tested.

— *Vieni tu, Bernardini? Ci vuoi provare tu?* Boscherini would ask her. Do you want to try, Bernardini?

We were addressed by last name, mostly, depending on the teacher and how much we were liked.

— *No, non me la sento,* she would say, every single time. I don't feel up to it. I don't feel up to it.

Boscherini would scan the classroom sardonically and move on to another name. Finally, one day Boscherini asked Bernardini once again, *Vuoi provare tu?* Do you want to try?

She said her usual *non me la sento*—I don't feel up to it—and Boscherini sat, wrestling professorial impatience with political principle and plain human outrage.

— *Ma un giorno che dovrai partorire, cosa dirai, non me la sento? Ogni tanto nella vita dobbiamo fare anche cose che non ci sentiamo.* Sometimes in life we have to do things that we do not feel up to. One day when you will have to give birth, what will you say, I don't feel up to it?

Santiccioli, a funny, curly-headed kid from Chiusi with big glasses, was another of Boscherini's targets. Santiccioli was never prepared.

— *M'è morta la nonna,* he would say with impudence. My grandmother died.

After he had used that excuse five or six times—did we really think teachers were so stupid?—Boscherini looked at him and said, *Santiccioli, ma tu quante nonne hai?* Santiccioli, how many grandmothers do you have?

One day Boscherini called on him to be tested in history.

— *Guardi, professore, ieri a Chiusi c'è stato un blackout e non ho potuto studiare. Non c'era la luce!* Santiccioli said, mustering all the earnestness he was capable of. There was a blackout in Chiusi yesterday and I couldn't study! There was no electricity!

The class erupted in laughter, sabotaging all of Santiccioli's efforts to appear serious.

On most days, Boscherini ended his class with the usual sign-off for which he became famous through generations of students at Montepulciano's *liceo.*

— *Eh beh, per oggi ci fermiamo qui.* Well, then, for today we stop here.

On the day Boscherini retired, the students of his senior class erected a large sign at the end of the road to the school that said, *Eh beh, per oggi ci fermiamo qui.* Well, then, for today we stop here. I was sad to learn that Boscherini died a few years ago.

The terror of our *liceo* was a teacher by the name of Salvatore Bonanno, who taught math and physics. He was a manic and formal man from Sicily who dressed in impeccably pressed gray suits, his thinning gray hair slicked back, a ring on his pinky. He spoke with an unintelligible Sicilian accent and his reputation for meanness and sadism preceded him through the generations.

At the blackboard he made the most proficient of students pale and sweaty. Those of us who struggled with math—the great majority under him—had nearly no chance, even after weeks of serious study. I had a tutor for calculus, Gabriella, Lavinia's daughter, the cousin of Agata and Giulia, and afternoons with her gave me a glimmer of hope of being able to solve a problem when I went before Bonanno at the blackboard.

Yet, nearly every time, I got stuck. My classmates, ever supportive, would whisper to me with urgency—as if Bonanno were deaf—and I would stand there flustered until he would send me back to my desk, defeated and frustrated.

He called me *Ficchese*, because he was unable to pronounce a clean x.

— *Vai a sederti, Ficchese,* he'd say. Fix, go sit down. He was the only teacher who called me by my last name.

Back then we had monthly written exams in the main subjects: a four-hour problem-solving math test; a three-hour Latin translation of Cicero or Caesar or whoever struck Vinciarelli's fancy; and a four-hour humanities essay about philosophy, literature, or social or ethical questions. The math and Latin tests were unforgiving, and often we came to each other's aid with flying paper airplanes and ingeniously doctored Marlboro packs full of cryptic text. I know Americans call this cheating and bristle at its very mention, but we considered it helping one another. After all, a copied test never changed anyone's life for the better; no one passed the *liceo* because of cheating, and no one was fooled by the occasional brilliant test. The system was simply too consistently rigorous and the teachers knew us too well to fool anyone.

I never copied, not once—an ethic learned from my American side—but not for lack of offers from my classmates, who always, sometime into the test, made sure I had the solved math problems written out on a piece of paper folded neatly under my desk.

— *Tre* (pronounced like trey without the y), *Ficchese, tre,* Bonanno would say, calling out my name and holding up three fingers as he handed out the graded test, mine often with the problem unsolved.

Meanwhile, at the *liceo,* budding and bursting we developed our thoughts about the world and where we stood in it: capitalism versus socialism, individualism versus the social good. Individualism was and is still viewed by most Italians—and certainly leftist Italians—as a selfish value embodied mostly by greedy America, contrasted with a European proclivity towards social responsibility. The topic always brought my two beings head to head, one learned by osmosis from my parents, and one learned by osmosis in my town, and it pushed me into conflicted arguments. We had impassioned discussions about ethics, power, money—my sense of compassion incensed, yet my ego bruised when we discussed slavery or the Vietnam War.

— *Voi Americani ...,* sometimes my classmates would say, looking at me. You Americans.

*Me? What do I have to do with this? I live here! I am like you!* I screamed inside. Plus, was slavery not European at heart, and colonialism, too?

Having grown up in a town deeply conscious of its agrarian roots, in a country decimated by war and conquered by foreigners more times than can be said, my sense of justice rests firmly with the downtrodden, the minority, the poor, the afflicted, and the vanquished—wherever they reside. This is by natural inclination—on the rebellious leftist side, skeptical of American motives.

Yet, having American parents caused me always to seek out even a thread of reason to confirm the myth of American exceptionalism—the stubbornly ingrained idea that America stands for something different and offers something better than anything else could possibly be. That America is the best country in the world. All that flag-waving and oath-saying makes one feel like there's something to it. Of course, though, while feeling torn, by my teens I felt allegiance to Italy and Europe, not to America.

Hence, to this day my temper flares every time someone uses those two words with me. *Voi Americani.* It is simply not so black and white, on either side.

Back at the *liceo*, seeking to add our voice and outrage to the unfolding world events, which in the early eighties were many and heavy, we walked the streets striking and protesting. We walked out when the Soviet Union invaded Afghanistan, when Ronald Reagan— Reagan was gleefully hated—invaded Grenada, and then, of course, on occasion of the Iran-Contra scandal. We joined strikes when Aldo Moro was assassinated and when unions and workers walked off their jobs.

— *Evviva i lavoratori! Abbasso gli USA!* we'd chant, standing in large crowds in front of the school holding signs and refusing to go to class. Hurray to the workers! Down with the U.S.!

Our years at the *liceo* were passionate, forward-thinking, and romantically idealistic. Sometimes we played hooky down at San Biagio, the beautiful white church at the base of Montepulciano, to which Francesca liked to entice me, succeeding occasionally. We played soccer on the green grass, smoked cigarettes and ate *panini*, then waited for the bus to take us back home, hoping that Nocilla, the principal, hadn't called to inquire where we were.

Assigned to our *liceo* from southern Italy, Nocilla was a short, plump man with a heavy southern accent and no sense of humor. He thought his students a loud mess of lazy bums, with a few exceptions. *Signorina Ficchese,* he called me. I was a good student, ran track, was head of our student council, and he liked me. When I went for college interviews he said he hoped to finally send a single one of his worthless students to a prestigious university, although, of course, he had sent many to prestigious Italian universities.

By the time we were in our fifth year, our class as a whole, the *Quinta B*, was a regular visitor to his office, summoned for smoking in the hallways or playing hooky or hiding the car or the umbrella of

Don Pipo, the Catholic priest who taught religion, at the time still a state-sanctioned class. Of course, by the end of the *liceo* we had made up our minds about the Catholic Church and its history—none of them favorably—and either we got into ferocious arguments with Don Pipo, or, when he walked in, we walked out, *en masse*. We simply did not respect him. Plus, or perhaps most important, Don Pipo was a fat, sweaty, lascivious man who liked to look at the legs of the girls in class. To taunt him, sometimes we wore short skirts and sat in the first row, on purpose, to watch him blush and squirm and sweat. Unable to focus, he'd repeat himself over and over while dabbing his forehead with his handkerchief. The whole class rolled in laughter until the bell rang, thankfully, and off we went, back to our respective towns, exploding like fireworks into the landscape.

And there, in our towns, we all had a full other life.

Mine was full of books and passionate ideas. Noam Chomsky electrified me, speaking to my irreverence and sense of justice, and then Sartre, and Marx, and de Beauvoir. I underlined entire pages earnestly, with the passion that comes from finding one's opinions voiced but by someone much smarter and more eloquent. I also read everything by Oriana Fallaci, and by the middle of the *liceo* I had settled more or less on the aspiration of being a journalist.

And throughout those years I enjoyed the good company of many friends of my parents who filled my life with magic, glamour, and love.

In winter, like now, when it was rainy and gray, I visited with Zia and Zio. Zio was often gone, playing and teaching. He traveled the European musical circles with flair, in beautifully tailored tuxedos and suits, and, it was said, an entourage of lovers. When he was not performing, he was teaching students around Italy and elsewhere, or judging international piano competitions. I loved seeing him when he returned on weekends. He had a winning, flirtatious smile and a generous, contagious laugh that soared through the rooms. When he told stories, which were always full of lore and mystery, his eyes flashed about and his voice undulated up and down with the accompaniment of his large, perfectly manicured hands. Everything about Zio was large and open—his presence, his storytelling, his demands, and his gifts. He often came to our house to cook—zabaglione, and, once, some kind of animal's testicles, which he served in a gravy on rice. He laughed his ass off while I ate them not knowing what they were!

Zia had not had children, and she didn't much like them. When I was a child she had a severe, stern way with me; she upbraided me harshly at the dinner table and treated me much like a nuisance. In my late teens, though, she came to love me and she took me under her wing. She was fascinating and bright. She had written more than one manuscript and had compiled and published volumes of landscape and nature photography that she had spent days shooting in the countryside around Castiglion del Lago and Umbertide. Her own life was worthy of a book, if only I knew enough to tell.

We bonded particularly over French, which she helped me master. We spent hours every week sitting in her kitchen talking in French about the lives and work of writers and philosophers, poring over prose, reading, and perfecting my pronunciation. Zia spoke French fluently from her days in Paris, where she had escaped in her youth from America and where she had met and fallen in love with Zio. She was a passionate reader and a fount of knowledge about all sorts of literary matters, and she shared it all with me, generously. While we talked she smoked tirelessly, letting the smoke of her Dunhills curl out of her lips and up through her nostrils and back out again. She had a clear, broad forehead and a pretty, elegant nose, and her nostrils flared when she laughed. I remember her long, coarse black hair and her thick gold wedding band and practical hands. She traveled seamlessly from English to Italian and French, punctuating it all with peals of throaty laughter that climaxed in squeals of childlike ecstasy.

— But, Sibby..., she'd say. But Sibby! *Mais chérie!*

And then, in winter and summer and in all seasons in between, I had Greta and Pietro, who spun threads of gold around my childhood.

We were having dinner one night at the Pietreto, Cetona's hotel, still commuting to Cremona after buying our house, when they pulled up in an old white convertible Beetle. Greta had red hair held back by a red paisley handkerchief and she wore bright red lipstick. I remember her laughing and her eyebrows arching like Greta Garbo—or the kindest Walt Disney witch.

Pietro, from southern Italy, was tan, with a distinguished Roman nose. He wore tortoise shell-rimmed glasses and his classical features were framed by salt and pepper hair cropped short. He smoked cigars and had a deep laugh and was, well, nothing short of *bellissimo*. They were gorgeous and in love, and as a little girl I could not stop staring at them, there, in this rather cold and empty dining room where voices reverberated.

After we met them, we learned that Greta was Austrian. She and her young sisters had been raised by their mother alone after their father was killed in the war. She had come to Italy in her early twenties to study, and it was there, in Rome, that she met Pietro, on a busy street in the *centro*. Pietro was a prominent forensic doctor twenty or so years her elder, in his forties then, and, awestruck, he had pursued her, following her and flirting with her until she gave in and stopped.

Pietro and Greta had also recently bought a house in Cetona, an abandoned *podere* poised peacefully on a hill a few kilometers outside of town, and it was being restored to be their summer home. Eventually Greta spent the summers there and Pietro commuted to Rome on the train, arriving Friday afternoon and leaving early Monday morning. In winter, though, they both stayed in Rome, living a refined life of glamour. Pietro's brother, Ettore, was a famous movie director, and they ran in the jet-setting crowd with the likes of Marcello Mastroianni, Sophia Loren, Monica Vitti, Alberto Sordi, and Vittorio Gassman. In fact, I later learned that it was the movie crowd that had brought them to Cetona, and eventually they brought many others to Cetona, too. They loved each other immensely: Pupa, he called her; Pupo, she called him.

Greta and Pietro gilded my childhood memories. Theirs was a house of harmony and wonder, spellbinding to me. It was not only that the house itself was beautiful in a warm, giving kind of way, which made it dear to me, or that Greta had exceptional taste and everything was lovingly done and positioned, down to the wooden ox cart that she had preserved on the lawn, and the salvaged animal troughs that held magazines and books in their living room. More important, perhaps, was that Greta imbued everything with a special kind of flair and celebration. She gathered children to make extravagant gingerbread houses, and we made *sciroppo di sambuco* from Queen Anne's lace. There were egg hunts with painted eggs and celebrations for all occasions. At Christmas Greta made her holiday tree out of a bare dead tree she found in the woods and decorated it with delicate white candles and Austrian wooden ornaments that looked like shavings shaped into magical snowflakes. Everything she touched was full of love.

Pietro, for his part, was fun and fun-loving, and he loved me. When I was in my early teens, in summer sometimes I'd walk to their house and we'd sit outside under the pine trees, talking about school, or I'd help Greta do something in the kitchen. Best of all, Pietro and I sat on the swing hanging from a big old branch and together sang an old Patti Pravo song, "Pazza Idea."

*Pazza idea*
*Di far l'amore con te,*
*Mentre lui ...*

Once when I was in my early teens—I was tender-hearted then, always holding one cat or another—Greta and Pietro stopped by the house and said they were going shopping. Could they take me with them? Sure, Dad said.

We got in the car, in Pietro's big Citroen DS, the same model as Ida's dad's, and drove to Chiusi. After walking around and doing a little window-shopping, we stopped in front of a shoe store. My eyes fixed on a pair of red wooden clogs, red like freshly dipped candied apples, with leather stiching up the front. Pietro followed my eyes and dragged me inside, insisting I try them on. I did, shyly, and within minutes we walked out of the store carrying my new red clogs. I felt immense kindness wrapped in those clogs: I had been given something I could never have hoped to have, and I hung onto those clogs for many years. I still think of them with the same pang of nostalgia I harbor for my olive-green *cartella* with the smiley face.

Through my teens, in winter, when Mom and Greta played Scrabble and chatted in German in the warm sitting room of their house, I ventured up to the top floor under the eaves to listen to old records by the Beatles. For sure it was there that I first saw the *Sgt. Pepper's Lonely Hearts Club Band* cover that intrigued me and first listened to that album. And, if the weather was nice, I ventured out into new unknown fields around their house or down secret meandering paths that led to abandoned houses or houses that were occupied only in summer. On the way back to Greta's I'd stop to pick cattails and other interesting weeds, or I'd linger at a pool that gathered from a nearby stream and sit on the rocks to watch the tadpoles.

I loved visiting there. I felt lucky and safe.

The other side of my life, all-pervasive and ever-present, was made of my friends, and I had merely to go outside to have one or more of them at my fingertips.

— *Se non mi vedi in piazza vienmi a chiama', eh!* my girlfriends and I would say to each other. If you don't see me in piazza come call for me!

I was allowed to go out in the late afternoons for an hour or so after homework, and on weekends, and I did, every moment I could, especially if there was tension at home. The embrace of the piazza gave me stability and refuge. So, after lunch on Saturday and Sundays, and, when I was older, after dinner, too, the conversation at home would go something like this:

— *Io esco!* I would say. I'm going out!

— Where are you going? my parents would ask.

— *In piazza!*

— To do what?

— To hang out with my friends! I'd say, as if they had asked the stupidest question in the world.

— That damned piazza, my father would say.

And off I went, no matter the weather or my father's lack of understanding. It was my—the—daily Cetona pilgrimage.

I adored my friends and their company and our places, music, and stories. Every moment I could spend with them, whether it was Mariachiara at that time, or Giulia later, or Silvio and Romina, or Fabrizio and Vincenzo and Massimiliano, Tullia and Raffaella, or Maria or Ottavia or Ida, I stole my moments away and found them. It's not that I depended on them—I have always been most importantly independent. It's just that I loved them! They were my tribe, my clan, and, in some ways, stronger than family.

— And what do you *do* in the piazza?? my father would ask, incredulous at the simplicity of this.

He was right. There was nothing to do in the piazza, nothing institutional or that could be defined as an activity. Yet, as children in little towns come to learn, it contained the whole world most completely, and we found things to do, not all edifying or exciting, but mostly benign and certainly full of companionship. It all sufficed, and indeed, it was rather perfect.

My father, solitary and from another world, couldn't understand the attraction of walking from one end of the piazza to the other over and over, arm in arm with Maria, perhaps, or Ida, gossiping or talking about our new love, or eating a slice of pizza. Or the joy of driving around on our *motorini* to see who might be at the *campo sportivo*, the soccer fields, or the tennis courts. Or sitting under our famous *tiglio*, the linden tree—its shade secretive and welcoming, and, in summer, its smell luxurious and intoxicating—sharing our secrets and laughing.

And even less so, sitting at the fountain—our famous *fontana*. Ahhh, the immense, boundless, complete happiness!! When my father lost patience with me and what he perceived as my useless social life, he'd yell and inveigh against the fountain whose edifying value eschewed him.

— *La fontana! La fontana!!* he'd scream. What do you do sitting at that fucking fountain all day long?

Hexagonal, two-tiered, of white marble, the fountain was our meeting and gathering point. It was a beacon, a place to check in, and the place where, if we sought company, we could always find someone. When we left our houses after lunch or after dinner to meet friends in the piazza, we parked our motorbikes by the fountain and there we gathered and sat and hugged and rubbed each other and held each other's hands. The gathering quickened with urgency if we had something to report—a new love interest, say, or an argument at home, or a piece of curious news. We sat and we talked and watched the world go by, sharing confidences, learning about each other.

Being. Becoming.

In addition, the *fontana* offered the best vantage point to check out the goings-on in the piazza and to stay informed. Anyone walking through the piazza had to go by there, and anyone who drove through the piazza had to drive by there. Whether they were walking or driving, when they came into our sight our heads would move as one to that person or that car and suddenly they became the undiluted subject of our attention and—if Vincenzo was in charge of the conversation—gossip.

Our friend Vincenzo, cunning and funny, was king of the fountain for a while, though in truth you could have three or four different clicks sitting at the fountain at the same time, one on each side. Certainly, though, the angle facing the entrance to the piazza was the most coveted for strategic advantage.

— *Mi', o questo?* Vincenzo would say, directing our attention to some poor soul walking our way. Look, what's up with this guy?

Vincenzo had a handsome face slightly reminiscent of a pugilist, with a squat nose and a strong, broad jaw. He was the son of the woman who ran the *lavanderia,* the dry cleaner, who specialized in gossip as well as making sure everyone in town had flawless clothes, including her son, who was always impeccably coiffed and dressed. Vincenzo took after his mother, always speculating on people's actions—why someone did this or that and what would happen now—and coloring it with bursts of humorous commentary. After he finished his long pontifications, he'd look around the piazza until he saw someone who inspired him to, well, comment more.

— *Mi', chesto è un ucello davvero!*

*Mi'* is the abbreviation of *mira,* the imperative of *mirare,* which is to look. It a single-word expression whose frequency of use and multitudes of meaning are particular to Cetona and its surroundings. You say *Mi'!* with a smile and a happy tone when you unexpectedly see an old friend, or you can sai *Mi'* with an unhappy voice and expression when, for example, your cat has puked on your best chair.

— *Mi' che lavoro!*—they say in Cetona. Look at this mess.

When it comes to the term *ucello,* well, there is no translation. Dork is the closest term I can summon. It can be a person who is dressed oddly, according to standard—say a person with hairy legs who wears black socks with sandals. Or a person who wears pointy white shoes from the seventies with a nice black suit. Or a person with a certain mannerism that kids in their late teens find to be funny or odd, which could be nearly everyone. It's all about prejudgment, and it really has to fit the particular occasion, but, there at the fountain, as soon as Vincenzo identified one such person, immediately we trained our attention and stared—a practice that in Cetona is refined into a true art, together with gossiping.

The Cetonesi take pride in something called *non avere peli sulla lingua,* which literally means to not have hairs on your tongue. It means being honest and saying what's on your mind. Often—and this was particularly true when we were adolescents but carries well into adulthood—this results in people being plainly mean or rude: calling people names, making rude comments, saying hurtful things, all with a sense of pride and entitlement.

— *Ma te perché non capisci un cazzo*, someone would easily say to someone else. Because you don't understand dick!

Anyway, the hours at the fountain were filled with talk and sharing of time, much hugging, storytelling, the occasional argument and tear. Togetherness was really the point of it all.

At one point we had a social club—*il cleb*, it was pronounced—in the empty floor of a house on Via Roma, under Agata's house. Two brothers, whose family owned the building—the oldest of whom was nicknamed Caronte (Charon), as was his father—came up with the idea, and perhaps fittingly, the club was a cavernous dungeon of many rooms nearly dug out in the tufa walls. We had a stereo there, in a nook in the wall, and it gave us a place to hang out that was not the bar. Just us, friends, to talk, play cards, listen to music, and have the occasional party.

For Mariachiara's birthday one year a group of us pooled our money together—I earned a meager allowance doing the dishes and helping around the house—and we hitchhiked to Chiusi to buy her the single "Baker Street." We had a party at the club, and I remember the tremulous anticipation of giving her the record. Standing there in front of the stereo, she unwrapped the record and took it out of the sleeve, and just as her surprise translated into joy and rose onto her face, the record slipped through her fingers and fell to the floor, shattering. I still remember watching the record fall and crack on the tufa, and, of course, we were devastated. "Baker Street" and countless other songs, from "I'm not in Love" to "Baby, Please Don't Go." I thought those songs sprouted from us, right there in Cetona, from our jukebox or the fountain itself.

When Mariachiara and I were best friends we sometimes went to the back room of the Bar Cavour to smoke and play cards, and sometimes we went to her house, a small villa in the countryside a few minutes outside of town. Her parents, Piero and Severa, ran a grocery store and butchery with Giacomo's parents, so in the afternoon they were never home. Mariachiara and I listened to music, talked about this and that, and giggled about boys and much else.

Sometimes Andrea would stop in after soccer practice to shower and change, and, on his way to help out at the store, he'd check on us and make us *merenda*. He was handsome and caring, and he had playful brown eyes, and at some point the image of him with his wet hair and slight inaccessibility lodged itself in me like a seed, though at the time I did not yet know.

By then I had become good friends with Giulia, too, whose parents owned the hardware store. Giulia had thick, dark brown hair, kind brown eyes, generous hips, and full soft breasts that already as a young teenager gave people pause. This, and the fact that she—and many of us— fell into relationships early, gave her a semblance of maturity and toughness and earned her the wrath of Cetona's *male-lingue*, or evil tongues. So simple, it is, to intertwine breasts with morality and appearance with substance. Unrecognized underneath it all was a young girl with a childlike tenderness and a kindness that I cherish to this day. Giulia and I were bonded by our love for animals, a touch of latent melancholy, and a tendency to be hurt by the stupidest and least caring of people to whom we should have paid no mind. I'd go to her apartment in the *case nuove* and we'd pass her white cats from arm to arm as if in so doing we could save everything, our hearts and the world.

Besides the fountain and the vastness of the pizza, the plots of our lives played out in Cetona's third bar, the Bar Sport, which Elide's retirement set on a storied path.

For a short period while we were kids, Diego ran it, the handsome husband of Rossana, the sister of my friend Ida. At the time, Diego was a soccer player for the Cetona team. Dark-skinned, with sexy brown eyes the warmth of a hazelnut and shoulder-length tousled hair, he was—and still is—a laid back, live-and-let-live kind of person, without pronounced agendas or ambitions. I don't think he liked the bar business much: He wanted to sit and chat and smoke cigarettes and watch the soccer game on TV. If we asked him for candy, or a gelato, which we were wont to do, he looked at us like we had just asked him to scale a mountain—particularly with us younger kids, whose expenditures were not worth getting up for.

— *Non mi rompete i coglioni*, he'd say to us. Don't break my balls. Don't bother me!

After that, Tullia's family moved to Cetona, and her parents, Antonietta and Lillo, took over the bar and ran it during the best of our youth, through my *liceo* years and all my returns home from college.

— *Che tempi belli!!* Antonietta says talking about the bar. What beautiful times!!!

Antonietta is short, with short gray hair and little bristly whiskers on her chin now. A smile lights up her face the minute you mention the bar, though Lillo, her husband, starts shaking his head at the memory.

Antonietta says people, even some they don't know, still tell them they miss the days when they ran the bar.

— *Io nemmeno so chi so'!* she says peering at me through her square glasses. I don't even know who they are!

Antonietta, Cetonese born and bred, met Lillo when he came to Cetona to play soccer. After they got married, Antonietta followed him back to Rome where he had a business in truck transport and insurance. They had four children there, including Tullia, but life in the city was stressful and after so many years Lillo decided to retire and move to Cetona, kids and all.

Shortly after, they bought the bar, and it was there, in the back room that Elide had created, that the lives of most of us between the ages of sixteen and thirty unfolded.

Protected and barely penetrated by adults—there was the occasional cigarette-dropping scare—it was the place to be and be seen, the place to go seek company and companionship, to listen to music, talk, confess our darkest secrets, eat gelato, hang out and make out, particularly in winter when there was nothing else to do. Sometimes the back room got so full of kids and so loud that Lillo would rush in and yank out the plug of the jukebox just to get us to cool off a bit and go outside.

— *Aooooo, ma ci annate fori a prenne un po' d'aria invece de sta' sempre quaddentro?* he would say in his Roman dialect, shooshing us out. Would you go outside and get some air instead of staying inside here all the time?

The Bar Sport continued to attract a mix of the intelligentsia of the town and most of the foreigners and weekenders who congregated there at the outdoor tables, shaded by the bar's vast umbrellas and awnings, to drink cappuccino, read the paper, and pontificate. In summer its tables filled from morning past midnight, people spilling over with gaiety and good company.

Though Lillo got aggravated at us when we went back and forth and in and out between the bar and the fountain, running and giggling—and later, strutting—and bothering the stodgier, older customers, he was a tolerant barman who kept an affectionate and fatherly eye on us.

— *Aoooo, Americani', a facce Tarzan, aooo!!* Lillo would yell after me, calling me the little American one and asking me to roar like Tarzan.

Alas, after many years Lillo and Antonietta retired, and our bar entered a phase of ebbs and flows between periods of absolutely forgettable malaise and periods of unmentionable desolation, run by people with bad personalities and even worse business sense, something that through the years irked those of us who believe that ownership of the Bar Sport comes with a duty toward the social fabric of the town—and indeed it does.

A short period of glory came in the early nineties under Cesare, the son of Cetona's late traffic officer, a well-mannered entrepreneurial guy who went to hotelier school and knows good wine and the art of service. He spruced up the bar and crowds came, aided by a bullish market and housing booms around the world. But Cesare moved on, too, eventually.

A few years back, a partnership of businessmen, among them my childhood friend Matteo, now a big contractor in town, bought the whole Bar Sport building and restored it all. They made the top floors into an expensive B&B, with posh rooms designed to give Cetona a hotel *come si deve*—as one should, Matteo says with a hint of civic pride—and they remodeled the bar and the space below into a first-class restaurant. Then they recruited Nilo to run it all—and one cannot visit in Cetona for more than an hour without knowing Nilo.

Nilo has owned or managed a business in town for the past forty years. Tall, with a dark moustache, dark hair combed back, and rectangular dark-rimmed glasses that make his eyes look smaller than they are, he looks a bit like a sociable owl.

Cetonese born and bred, and proud of it, he talks Cetonese fast and in a low monotone except when he's agitated; then he sputters and curses and raises his voice, like most Cetonesi do. His diction is full of colorful old sayings and funny vernacular wisdom, both cutting and loving, and he likes to recall names and stories from decades ago. He takes great pride in the longevity and roots of his relations around town, and he knows the date of birth of everyone in Cetona, dead or alive.

— *La Marga?* I ask, quizzing him on people's birthdates, laughing.

— *È del '23,* he answers, which literally means she belongs to the year 1923.

— *Giuliano?*

— *Del '33.*

— *Ottorino?*

— *Del '18.*

— *Giubbino?*

*— Del '42.*

And on and on he could go.

Nilo began his career running the Bar Cavour from the late seventies to the early nineties. Then, he took over the old Osteria Vecchia from Dino and Graziella and ran that for twenty years. The nineties and beginning 2000s brought a booming economy and people traveled from afar to eat at Nilo's. The restaurant was always bustling and crowded, whether populated by Italians and Cetonesi in winter or fall, or by visitors and travelers in spring and summer, or by a steady mix of the two. The regulars abounded always—myself included on every trip home—as well as a number of fairly prominent customers, including the president of Italy, other politicians, sometimes a queen, news people, and some business tycoons who own houses in the area.

Because of the oft-prominent clientele, whose presence imbues Nilo with a visible frisson of glee, he most often wears nice dress pants and a sharp button-down shirt under his chef's apron. Today it's pale lavender.

*— Io di persone belle e importanti ce n'ho portate a Cetona! Venivano a mangiare da me in tanti, venivano,* he says, recalling the glorious days of the Osteria Vecchia. I brought beautiful people here! They came specifically to eat at my restaurant!

And they still do, now, at his new place. Decorated by an interior designer of international renown, the restaurant is an elegant if a bit staid pale-yellow Upper-East-Side-style establishment that doesn't have a lot of Cetonese character, like the old Osteria did. But, the food is still good, and Nilo and his son, Cristiano, are lovely hosts, running both the restaurant and the Bar Sport with in mind the choosier customers among visitors and the Cetonesi alike.

On the bar side, they upped the prices, removed candy and such from the shelves, removed the pool table and struck down card games. This alienated some of the blue-collar clientele and pushed them all the more enthusiastically into the Bar Cavour's hands. Much to Felice's glee, now there are people who absolutely refuse to go to the

Bar Sport, though in Cetona everything goes in ebbs and flows, and most likely that will change.

In any case, by dint of his business and his business savvy, Nilo holds a cardinal thread in the fabric of Cetona's social and economic life—and in mine, too, which he has come to occupy with familiarity and affection.

— *Ciao, bella,* he says when he sees me. He pinches me, hugs me, cuddles me, looks me in the eyes and knows.

— *Perché se' triste?* he asks. Why are you sad?

Whether I smile or I look away, he perceives my truth and he offers me an ancient knowledge that, well, makes for home. *T'ho visto cresce'!* he likes to say to me. I watched you grow up.

Sometimes when I'm lonely or bored of being in the library or my apartment I come here to write, in the Bar Sport. Nilo likes to keep tabs on me, which does not displease me and, in fact, makes me feel cared for.

— *Dove se' stata 'sti giorni che non t'ho visto?* he asks. Where have you been the past few days? I haven't seen you. What were you doing?

Plus, he and his family feed me well.

Cristiano appears in the door that connects the bar and the restaurant. Tall, with black hair, he is dapper in his waiter's outfit. I ask him if I can eat something, at a table on the bar side, where I can work. Cristiano nods. He is of few words.

Twenty minutes later he brings me a gorgeous plate of pasta—not in a pasta plate, mind you, but on a large flat plate. The pasta is almost spilling over the edges. Sliced zucchini sautéed with tomato, basil and garlic. The sauce clings perfectly to the pasta, *al dente,* with just the right amount of oil, and there is a mound of *parmigiano* on top. It is perfect.

Nilo comes up to the table and chuckles. He puts his hands together in prayer.

— *Ma ora mangi un piatto di pasta così?!* he asks incredulously. You're going to eat a plate of pasta like that?

He takes in my face, smiles, and pinches my cheek. *Bella,* he says.

Through his business and personality—and a special series of Cetonese traits including a sharp ear for good gossip—Nilo gathers information and prides himself for knowing things others might not. He is a database of local information, the kind of material that creates historic and communal memory. He loves to pick up on private conversations, to banter with everyone, local and not, and to tell stories about long-gone personalities. He is trying hard now to bring the locals back into his place, but he equally courts the personalities, such as the former queen of Belgium, who is a regular client at the B&B upstairs and whom he looks at obsequiously and pleasingly, as he does with all people of means and importance.

While I eat, Nilo's regulars file up from the floor below and into the bar. They are men, mostly bachelors, who eat lunch there every day—the Carabinieri, a few local workers who live alone, and Nanni, from Patarnione. Nilo treats them like family: They eat a *primo*, a *secondo*, wine, and water all for a bargain flat price. Then, they get their espresso at the bar and head back to work. Nilo has always had a few of them, for as long as I can remember. A man nicknamed Righetto ate there every day for sixteen years, from the day his wife died in 1991 to when he died in 2007 (Nilo can tell you the exact dates).

As the regulars walk out onto the piazza, a couple comes in and sits down at a table. Lunchtime has passed but they say they are hungry. Nilo walks back into the restaurant and comes back a few minutes later with two panini with prosciutto and serves them. He brings them beer.

— *Tutto bene, signori?* he asks. Everything ok?

He must say those words a few hundred times a day, but he never seems to tire of it.

Nilo likes to sit with me and ask me what I think about what's going on in Cetona. Mostly, though, he wants to lament what he sees going on. He asks me if I remember Aldo Giuliacci, who was mayor when we moved here. And Giulio Bussolotti, a businessman. Yes, I say, I remember them well.

— When I was young those were my role models, he says. Who are the role models in Cetona now?

I struggle to think of any, though I am sure there would be some.

Nilo thinks drinking has become a huge problem in Cetona, particularly among young kids. When we were young it was not like this, I say. No one drank at all.

— Look how things have changed! And no one cares! Nilo says, raising his voice.

— *Nemmeno il prete!* Not even the priest!

*Il prete.*

Don Prospero has been the priest here on and off for close to forty years, though when he was assigned to Cetona he served as underling to a revered older priest, knowledgeable and spiritual. He was young when he taught us at school, and perhaps his most notable trait was that he was handsome, and, indeed, when we were kids he had a reputation for being a womanizer. He looks much the same now—balding and bespectacled, with a round, distrustful face and nearly always a frown. A bit of a malcontent, when you talk to him he looks at you like you could not possibly be telling the truth. Where one could expect faith to manifest in a priest's face as humility and empathy, in Don Prospero it manifests in an outward self-assurance and arrogance. At least that is my impression, but, on the other hand, I don't know him anymore, and he has never known me.

Nilo has a theory that Don Prospero, who many think is more of a businessman than a spiritual man, likes local kids to drink at Le ACLI so he keeps the bar crowded and the church coffers filled, no matter the impact on the moral tenure of the town. Felice, of the Bar Cavour, adds to this the fact that the church does not pay taxes on the bar's revenues, which puts the other bars at a distinct disadvantage. I don't know if any of this is true, but it certainly makes sense.

— *Gli torna comodo!* Nilo says. It's convenient. The priest doesn't care if it's bad for the town and for the kids!

Nilo frets and paces. He looks out the windows of the bar and sighs at the empty piazza.

— *Non c'è nessuno! Nessuno! Guarda!* he says. There is no one in Cetona. Look! He says this several times a day.

Meanwhile, though, today the Bar Sport is thriving. The crowd is usual, more bourgeois and coiffed than the crowd at the Bar Cavour, and punctual among them are what I have dubbed 'the bar ladies,' five or six Cetona women, and sometimes their husbands, who are here at a table every day around 5 p.m.

Angela, the mother of my friend Guido, comes in, takes off her coat, and sits. She is always nicely dressed, with a scarf and ironed corduroys and high-heeled boots. So is Stefania's mom, and particularly Signora Amelia, who lives in Rome but whose family is Cetonese. Ash-blond, bejeweled, in earth-toned elegant skirts and blouses, she captures the attention of the table with dramatic stories told while looking her table-mates in the eyes and gesticulating appropriately.

Guido's dad comes in, dapper and cheerful, and whistling. He gets the paper, sits, and starts reading while whistling. Alvaro and Franca come in, the parents of my friend Giulia, and join the table. They say hello to each other as if they had not seen each other in a week, and they find as much to talk about as if they had not seen each other in a month.

Giovanna, the wife of my old teacher Giorgio, tall and blonde, comes over to rub my back and ask what I am working on. We talk about books for a few minutes, then she joins the others. I hear them talking about the weather, then a telenovela. Health comes up—someone in town is very sick, a little old lady up in town—and death. Local deaths.

They pride themselves on knowing the minute details of people's lives, and they are competitive.

— *No,* says Amelia raising her hand and disagreeing with Giovanna about the date of someone's death.

— *Lui è morto nell' 86, perché nell'85 è morta la Giancarla e me lo ricordo come fosse ieri* ... He died in '86 because Giancarla died in '85 and I remember that as if it were yesterday. That year, she goes on to say, it snowed. Do you remember? Her eyebrows arch knowingly. We had to drive with snow chains and Giubbino wrecked on the Costa dei Capperoni ... Remember, she asks.

Then they all quiet down and lean in. Amelia whispers something I don't hear, and they burst out laughing.

Sitting outside—and much part of the Bar Sport's regular crowd—are some new residents of Cetona, or new since I ceased being one, and since I arrived our paths have crossed easily and often, bringing me the acquaintance, among others, of Bianca and Riccardo, a worldly couple whose presence here is both interesting and ubiquitous.

Bianca, tall, thin, with short dark hair and warm dark eyes, comes from a family of diplomats. She lived in the Middle East, where she was born, Africa, and the United States, and she is well educated and sophisticated. Her main professional interest has been art, which earlier in her life led her to work for several prestigious art dealers, until she married. She is sociable and intense, and she greets and befriends everyone new to town, in part because she speaks English or whatever language comes in handy at the moment, and in part because she has the kind of expansive personality that likes to be in the mix of things.

Riccardo, her husband, the son of a northern Italian business magnate, grew up between northern Italy, home to part of his family, and Tuscany, home to the rest. At the university Riccardo studied agricultural sciences, and he is passionate and knowledgeable about all sorts of things related to the earth, including viticulture, forestry, earth chemistry, and such. Riccardo is strongly built, with a round face and short salt-and-pepper hair. His eyes are green and intelligent, friendly when in good humor, dark when not, a bit like his personality, and a tenderness lies beneath. He is witty and jovial, except for when he argues politics—particularly American imperialism—and when he bickers with Bianca, which, in good Italian fashion, occurs rather frequently and loudly.

Riccardo and Bianca know many people from many walks of life, and I appreciate their wit and varied interests and the fact that they speak English, to which I retreat when Italian does not suit my expression. Much to my distress now, the language in which I thought and felt everything for so many years is no longer the language of my political expression, or of my work—perhaps not even of my deepest truths—so I appreciate being able to slip in and out of it as it suits me. Plus, Bianca has an underlying tenderness and sincere kindness that bond me to her somehow.

Around Bianca and Riccardo rotate in ever-growing circles other faces new to me: a few agreeable couples from Rome and northern Italy, retirees, with houses in town or just outside; a few new Americans who have bought houses in the area, including a couple from somewhere in Florida, and another couple from LA; Brigida, a retired northern European philosophy professor who resides in Cetona part-time; and Ludovico, a retired business captain from an old aristocratic Tuscan family, who owns a big palazzo right behind the piazza.

Elderly now, and always elegantly dressed in pants of warm hues and the softest of cashmere sweaters or linen shirts, Ludovico has the soft, limp handshake of a man who has directed the work of others, and he sits smoking cigars and bemoaning the old days when he had much more land and people who worked for him. Ah, the past.

— I had secretaries and people who worked for me, and all the *poderi* had *contadini* with people who worked for them and kept things clean. There were keepers, and overseers, and workers, he says, puffing on his cigar. Now it's all gone. I have to do it all myself!

I laugh. Aristocracy always entertains me.

Then there is Camille, a snobby and moody French artist who speaks wearily of the French saying they are snobs and moody, and Anaïs, a strong-boned, attractive Frenchwoman from Normandy whose family owns La Vista, one of the most commanding buildings, if not the most commanding, on the face of Monte Cetona, with magnificent views of the Val di Chiana. When she undertook the restoration of La Vista, the biggest job in town, Anaïs sought contractors out of town because the locals, she said, were slow and expensive. This ruffled feathers, but she holds her head high with her detractors and stares out into the piazza proudly with her beautiful, friendly face, smiling unconcerned.

I like strong women like Anaïs. The other evening we sat at the bar having an *aperitivo* and the talk came to the men in Cetona—or perhaps I should say the scarsity of eligible men, which makes for a humorous running commentary among the women of the town.

— Even if we had an inkling, a twitch of desire or craziness, we would be hard-pressed to find a single guy here to bed! she says with her accented, melodious Italian.

She points out to the piazza and we laugh watching the men go by.

I am glad to have made new acquaintances here, and when I sit with them at the tables of the bar I savor the diverse backgrounds, and textured stories, French and English and Italian crisscrossing cacophonously through mixed political views and well-traveled insights.

Meanwhile, though, the world of the Cetonesi turns around us unmoved, like Venus and Earth circling side by side, a bit as it's always been, and I feel grateful yet torn and a bit awkward to be straddling somewhere in the middle.

A rhyme comes to mind, something my friends called me when I was little: *Sibilla, Sibilla, mezza serpe e mezza anguilla.* Half snake, half eel. Half and half.

By the time we were in high school—Maria in Città della Pieve, Mariachiara in Chiusi, me in Montepulciano—our social umbrella encompassed people ranging from our age to people ten or so years older. We were all *ragazzi*—something that loosely describes boys and girls from their teens to their late twenties. We hung out with friends of my brother's age and much older than him, and even if we didn't hang out, we were all always aware of each other's movements and whereabouts. People spun together fluidly in orbits centered around this person or that according to his charisma and our likings of the time. And, of course, they were all boys.

There was the group that gravitated around Vincenzo, Fabrizio, and Massimiliano—Fabrizio, who was working with horses by then, and Massimiliano, the well-mannered son of the woman who owned the jewelry store—stoners, good-natured and funny. There was the group that hung with Bennato and Mario, my beloved neighbors, and Marcello, too, a wiry, raucous blond soccer player. They were what I think of in American terms as small-town blue-collar guys. Andrea hung out with that group too, though he liked to float freely and moodily amidst it all, mostly hanging out with the older soccer players.

Then there was the clan that hung with Teo, Ida's brother, and Pierpaolo, too, sometimes together but not always, popular and the best-looking guys in town.

Pierpaolo was beautiful in a Vogue kind of way, unreachable and charismatic, with a smart, irreverent personality that made him twice as attractive. He had dark curly hair, a slightly aquiline nose, and tight, intelligent brown eyes with a particular light in them, playful and warm, that pulled you in. He was a *sessantottino*, of the group that participated in or sympathized with the revolutionary fervor of the late 1960s—there was a large number of them in Cetona, not surprisingly—and Pierpaolo's rebellious politics gave him an aura of romanticism. That and a signature beard, which my father memorialized in a caricature on my seventeenth birthday card.

For many years Pierpaolo and I traveled in overlapping galaxies, but when I was at the *liceo* he became a leader of our group, partly because of his age, but partly because he had spunk, initiative, and charisma. Free of most inhibitions, sure of himself, he made fun or interesting things happen, like opening a wine bar, or spurring us to get out—to go somewhere.

Teodoro was as popular as Pierpaolo. Tall and skinny, with sexy full lips and a strong nose, Teo had playful amber eyes flecked with green and gold. In them sparkled the bravado of those who know they are good-looking. He wore his brown hair tousled and to his shoulders, for the most part, and he slicked it back with his handsome hands, except for when he did something shocking and dyed it blond or green or shaved it all off, which reinforced his image as *matto*, or crazy, which in some ways he relished and tested. He loved to be crazy.

Teo had enough audacity and personality to earn him constant attention, and, together with the fact that his father doted on him with the best of cars and a constant supply of cash that Teo shared generously with his friends, this made him impossible to resist. Besides— and this gave him star status—Teo was a talented soccer player, a true wizard of footwork: *Uhhs* and *ahhhs* hushed through the stands of the *campo sportivo* when he had the ball. Life danced on the tips of his fingers, like the soccer ball danced at his feet, and for many years he seemed to hold it all.

Anyway, around these personalities and their beings, central and somewhat heroic in our minds, we floated—Maria, Giulia, Ottavia, Mariachiara, Ida, and me—moving through the circles with our own proclivities and characteristics: Maria the most guarded and private, princess-like; Giulia the dreamer, the kindest and most malleable; Ida the funny and invulnerable one, righteous; Ottavia soft-spoken and shy, undefined; Mariachiara a ball of insecure, nervous energy, cute, funny, yet cutting as a knife; and finally, me, idealistic and opinionated, ebullient and accepting, full of possibility, with my magic stone in my pocket, yet rife with vulnerability. At my core, perhaps, was a nascent premonition of something unclear out there for me, and not sure where.

In this galaxy we lived, with our ups and downs, comforts and dreams, and hurt, too. Our social life was often agitated by shifting allegiances, cattiness, periods of not talking to this person or that, attempts to freeze people out, or being frozen out. In retrospect—and this bonds us all to this day—we were all linked, if subconsciously and erratically, by the clashes of our budding identities and yet a universal need to be loved. In a town like Cetona it was not easy to be true to oneself and yet not alienate those one had to coexist with every day. As a result, ours was a dance of compromise and periodic adjustments: We liked each other one week or month and didn't the next, though in one way or the other we all loved each other always, and, for sure, still do.

My letters to Maria from that time reference arguments with Mariachiara and long spans of not speaking to each other—over what I do not know. And yet, over dinner recently Mariachiara and I revisited our intense bond. She reminded me that once she and I walked into the club and tore down all the Styrofoam partitions that the guys had put up to isolate the dampness of the tufa. We were angry because they had kicked us out—for being impertinent, I think—and I know instinctively that we were right. They were assholes.

One winter when we were in our teens it snowed a lot, more than a meter, and the mountain and the surrounding countryside were covered in deep, beautiful white snow. It was unusual to get so much snow here, and to celebrate, twenty or so of us—Silvio Della Vigna, Bennato, Vincenzo, Mario, Massimiliano, Maria, Giulia, Giorgio, and I don't remember who else—headed up to Monte Cetona on foot to play in the snow. I bundled up in my coat and I wore my new winter boots, which I had been so grateful to get as a present. As we set out I remember feeling happiness: I loved my friends; I wanted to *be* my friends, one with them.

After we got to our destination—a clearing somewhere above Belverde—we started to play in the snow, chasing each other and throwing snowballs. Progressively the play got rougher, and slowly the lines were drawn between those who would inflict and those who would receive. They—who, exactly, I don't remember, but I could easily guess—threw me on the ground and began packing the snow in my coat, my sweater, my pants, my boots. Everywhere. In a few minutes I was drenched and freezing and my hands were numb. The fun had vanished and there was nothing but me and them on the mountain, on opposite sides of something. I hated them; I hated them for crossing a line, the same way I still do.

An angst of bewilderment set in—a sense of being different because you would never do that to someone else—and then also the urgent sense that this was important, and of course, it *was* important. That sense of violation and outrage in the face of injustice or meanness stuck with me. I set out down the mountain and back to Cetona by myself, in tears, soaking wet, with bleeding blisters and bruised feelings, and I remember a sense of misery clinging to me for weeks.

The closeness of relationships in Cetona—*la confidenza*, as it's called—brought us greater richness, but also made us more vulnerable to hurt. Maria and I, and Giulia, too, wrote to each other about our bruised feelings—I, having been teased during my awkward fourteen- or fifteen-year-old phase for being flat-chested, or not having a boyfriend. And when the meanness brought us head to head and caused us to splinter, we'd sit on opposite sides of the fountain, at least for a few days.

Then, most everything passed and someone would proffer peace and a round of the piazza.

— *Andiamo a fare un giro?*

And off we'd go.

Around us the town revolved, with its universe of familiar adults walking the piazza and populating the bars and the fountain and our communal memory with their presence, personality, and attention.

There were parents, of course, and neighbors, and relatives, and, beyond them were the comforting characters the town remembers through the generations for the hilarity or tragedy of their lives, or perhaps a singular idiosyncrasy or trait, maybe a way of speaking, or the odd penchant for walking around town in a brown sweater.

The many of them—*i personaggi*—leave behind a story to remember and always much affection. Pichio comes to mind, a farmer-for-hire as tall as a broom stick who walked the town with a signature cap on his head, singing or whistling at all times. At night, when he walked home after the bars closed, he'd always sing a tune, and if he hadn't finished the song when he got there, he'd finish it with his head against his own door, which he was known to do.

Of course, everyone in Cetona remembers Pietraccio, or *bad Pietro*, an odd guy who looked a bit like a crazy Jack Nicholson and who roamed the town like he was lost and lonely, talking to himself. Throughout our childhood Pietraccio collected tin foil and other recyclable materials that he sold to someone. He was ubiquitous. Dark eyes furtive and darting, he'd search through trash cans on street corners and bags that people left on their doorsteps for him, and when people walked by he'd look up and say hello, then he'd sit and exchange a few words with his booming voice, surrounded by his packets and bags. Pietraccio died some years back, while I was gone. I saw his picture at the cemetery just the other day, and the image of him sorting through tin foil in a doorway on a shady alley filled me with nostalgia.

There were a few women characters, too—in addition to Marga, Elide, and la Littorina. La Mema comes to mind, the mother of Cetona's celebrated ceramist, Pippo. She was a staunch anti-Fascist who happily picked a fight with anyone who had the temerity to profess allegiance to that despicable party. Stern, bespectacled, and with hair pulled in a tight bun, she'd walk straight up to Fascists and out them, asking them how they possibly dared! After the war, she courageously traveled the countryside by bicycle to help organize farmers and workers into unions so they could improve their livelihoods. She had undying passion for the downtrodden and the wrongly accused. When the Rosenbergs were tried and convicted of spying, Mema assembled a group of women in town to make a solidarity quilt and mailed it to them—and I would like to know what happened to it. She was a fighter, a real partisan, and a Communist. I would have been lucky to know Mema now, though I conserve of her a pale memory.

Just mentioning Fascists and Partisans brings to mind the old Mucciarelli sisters, stony, hard-featured ladies who were reviled in town for supporting Fascism. One of them was married to one of Cetona's wretched overseers, which did nothing to help the fact that she was already a much-hated teacher. People who had studied under Mucciarelli were envious of us who had had Marga, if one can imagine that.

Her sister, Carmela, was a prickly spinster who drove an old Bianchina and was the target of a vicious and relentless campaign by kids—and others—to make her life miserable, just for the sake of it. Once, in a famous episode people like to tell, Caio, our old neighbor, was leaning on the fountain, as he was wont to do, when she came out of her house and walked to her car, parked by the fountain. Caio called out to her.

— *Carmela, quant'è che 'n' pipi?* he said loudly. How long since you last fucked?

Kids routinely painted lewd messages on her car, and once they even removed her seats and hid them. Every time this happened she went to see Maresciallo Colasanti, the head of the Carabinieri, a tall gentleman of great formality. The mere sight of him walking down the hill from his office in Via Roma, distinguished in his creased black uniform full of stripes and medals, was enough to turn heads in piazza, and indeed, the Maresciallo's compunction and virtuous lifestyle caused people to feel a healthy sense of intimidation. When you passed him on the street he nodded almost imperceptibly and said *buon giorno* without the least hint of a smile, though not arrogantly either. In summer, when the Carabinieri left their office windows open, his powerful voice carried out into the breeze and down the hill, and sometimes even sitting at a table outside the Bar Sport we knew the Maresciallo was in. And angry.

Occasionally the Maresciallo could be heard yelling, and this always peaked the curiosity of Diletta, a lady who lived across the street from the Carabinieri's office, next to Maria's old house, and was a character of sorts herself. When she heard the Maresciallo scream, she would run to Signora Colasanti, her friend, and ask her what had happened. Because the police station and the Colasanti home were internally connected—to give the Maresciallo discreet access to this office at whatever time of day or night—she assumed that Signora Colasanti was in the know.

— *Perché urlava il Maresciallo?* Diletta would ask Signora Colasanti. Why was the Maresciallo yelling? Something must have happened!

Signora Colasanti never had an answer, or if she did she wouldn't say, which sent Diletta onto her own investigations, the results of which she quickly spread around town.

And so, back to old Carmela, as the story goes, when she went to see Maresciallo Colasanti to complain about the kids' pranks or vulgarities, the Maresciallo listened with characteristic poise, trying to calm the difficult woman and keep the peace. Once, though, when she stormed in quoting a particularly obscene message she had found, which included graphic mentions of female body parts, even the Maresciallo struggled to keep his composure.

He looked at her knowingly, struggling against a smile.

— *Eh, ma signora, questi ragazzi giovani ... Lei mette appetito!!!!* Signora, these young boys ... you stimulate their sexual appetite!

By sixteen or seventeen our spotlight shifted quite naturally onto love, and there were many, many loves in Cetona, epic and tremulous and memorable, and we experienced them and plotted them and shared all about them up and down the piazza, pacing and fretting, pursuing and being pursued, and figuring out what it all meant.

It was—or so it seems now—a constant and chaotic falling in and out of love, a shuffling of conquests, abandonments, and reconquests, and because the town was so small, the loves were quite entangled and entangling, threading across friendships and families. It all got me thinking about the concept of a love chart: A. dated B., then B. and A. split and A. started seeing C. Meanwhile B. started seeing D. ... E. loved P. but then she went to A. ... and M. was with N. for a long time, then N. left M. for D., and on and on and on.

It was just life in a place where there was little to do and where we populated each other's lives strongly and intimately. It was our coming of age, a manifestation of affections and attractions in a tiny town suspended in time and space where no code applied other than our own.

In this world blossomed my first true love, for Lucio.

Lucio was twenty-one, five years older than me, and he was a soccer player on Cetona's team. I can close my eyes and revisit his walk across the piazza, in jeans and boots, or hunting camos, a sauntering, really, a bit bowlegged. He was seeing Ottavia at the time, though she and I were not friends as we are now, and I guess I didn't concern myself too much about it.

I was sixteen, with shoulder-length light-brown hair, a hopeful face, tender, a year into the *liceo*. I remember that Lucio had been involved in some Teutonic shift-like love story with a woman from San Casciano who had broken his heart, and at the bars and at the fountain the whole town talked about it, it seemed. That heroic suffering, as if he had been to war, in addition to his soccer prowess, made him romantic and mythical.

I saw Lucio mostly in piazza, or at his father's store, the butcher, where he worked pending other employment. He had finished studying to be an accountant, at *ragioneria* in Chiusi, and he was pondering his next step. I'd go into the store with my mom and he would be there, wearing his white smock smeared with blood against which his blue eyes, a sparkling pure Turkish blue, seemed even starker and more beautiful.

Usually, the tangy smell of blood and flesh in the store nause-
ated me, and when Lucio was not there I waited outside, on the street.
When he was there, though, the nausea miraculously vanished and I
gathered the courage to venture inside to stand in the stink of death
beside my mom and stare at him, exploring his brown curly hair and
his blue eyes and his boyish smile, flirtatious yet shy. He was gentlemanly and kind, and my mom really liked him, which helped.

One Sunday morning while we all milled about the fountain I
remember him standing in a group of hunters near the big linden tree,
in the sunlight. They were back from the hunt, smoking and compar-
ing prey. They held the birds dangling by their feet, showing them
off. The iridescent plumage glistened in the sunlight, stark and beautiful, and from that beauty you would have thought the birds were alive
and ready to take flight except for the limp bodies and slack heads,
joy stolen from them. There was something forbidding about the men
standing there talking about hunting and holding the dead birds—
something foreign and separate like looking at a painting.

From the fountain I stood watching Lucio like he was a mirage—
nothing had happened between us yet—and suddenly, prodded by an
older man in the group who had noticed me looking, he turned and
looked at me, and his blue eyes pierced me like fire, calling blood
to my cheeks. In this indelible frame in my memory I continue to
feel the glistening plumage of the birds, the pearlescent greens, and
Lucio's blue eyes, and the distinct feeling that, in that very second, I
had relinquished part of me to a force mysterious and uncontrollable
and sublime.

Slowly—it happened like a bout of influenza brought on by con-
tagion—he evolved in my mind into something otherworldly, and suddenly I was in love. At sea, without anchor or oars.

At the time, Mariachiara, Andrea's sister, that mischievous trou-
blemaker, was infatuated with another player on the soccer team, and
she resolved that she would lend her efforts to try to make something
happen between me and Lucio. By then, Lucio had been called to serve
in the military, a few months off, and one night he and thirty or so

guys had a big traditional celebratory sendoff dinner in the basement at his parents' house, up *in paese*. Every guy in town—every beautiful soccer player!—was there, anyone who mattered in our little enclave in the world.

After dinner Mariachiara and I walked uptown to spy on them. We were peeking through a crack in the doors leading underneath the house, whispering and giggling as we usually did, when Mariachiara suddenly shoved me with all her strength and forced the double doors to open suddenly inward. I barged scarlet-faced into the middle of the room and all the guys burst out laughing, including Lucio and his father, who, naturally, already had picked up on everything. Out tumbled my secret, and if Lucio had not previously known that I was infatuated with him, he certainly found it out then.

And, so, our relationship was born, not from knowing but from mystery.

— *Cretina, imbecille, stupida!* I cursed Mariachiara all the way back to the piazza. You stupid cretin.

We still laugh about it.

After that, all I remember is the earnestness of his blue eyes and the tenderness of his body one night under a blanket of stars in a corner of grass at the far end of the soccer fields overlooking Cetona and its lights arranged in the dark like a Christmas scene. I assented, and in that one moment, in that one night, the center of my world shifted from dolls and play and an independent discovery of the world to the awe and wonder of love, embodied in a man, and a definition of the world that was no longer so independent.

If you are wondering about our age difference, in Cetona that is not an issue—it was not then and would not be now. No one thought anything of that. There was just love and innocence, and those blue eyes like the sea, and the walk of a cowboy, the run of a soccer player.

A few months later Lucio had to leave. Back then, military service, *il militare* as it's called, lasted one year. You were sent to barracks here or there throughout Italy—some people as far as Sicily or

Milano—and the farther you were sent the more tears you spilled. People did what they could to avoid it: They appealed to friends in high places, feigned mental illness and nervous breakdowns, shot themselves in the hand or foot, had friends break their arm, burned their fingers or hit them with hammers—not for fear that something terrible would happen to them in fighting a war, but because of a dread of leaving home, mostly. Of course, there was also a general disdain for the institution of the military and the concept of war, which Italians have experienced too much of. Mostly, they hated the interruption in their lives. They hated leaving home, mothers, and girlfriends.

Lucio drew Pesaro as his destination, on the east coast of Italy, and took it stoically and with dignity—the way he did everything. When the day came, Nicola, the son of Maresciallo Colasanti, and Attilio Del Buono, who were classmates of Lucio's at *ragioneria*, drove him to the train station in Chiusi, and I went with them.

It was dark and foggy. Winter—January maybe. We got in the car in the piazza; Lucio was carrying a duffel bag and had already said goodbye to his parents. He was somber. We drove slowly and in silence, listening to the Lucio Battisti love songs that had escorted our relationship through the months. "Il Pacco Rosa." "Aver Paura di Innamorarsi Troppo."

> *Aver paura di confessare tutto*
> *Per il pudore d'innamorarsi troppo*
> *Finger che anch'io le altre donne vedo*
> *È un leggero dolor temere di mostrarsi*
> *interamente nudo ...*

Cloistered by fog and the smell of departing trains, we stood on the platform in the station, waiting. Lucio held me and kissed me and said goodbye. He said he loved me. His blue eyes were shadowed with sadness that turned them to slate. When the train stopped, he pushed his bag on and followed. He waved, and we all waved back, and the train chugged off into the fog and the dark and the cold, to a place foreign to us all across the country.

We exchanged letters for a few months, perhaps past his first leave, which I awaited anxiously. But there was no solidity in me. The experience of loving a man had changed my entire perspective on the world and myself, but it had not made it clearer, and by the time he came back a few months later—at sixteen a year was interminable—I had begun seeing someone else, and he was hurt. I hurt him.

Over the years I have come to chastise myself for having been callous in relationships, for leaving, constantly leaving, starting with Lucio, and one night this winter, one of many we spent walking around the piazza arm in arm, I told Lucio how I felt. That I am aggrieved and sorry.

— *Mi dispiace,* I said.

Lucio lives in Rome now, with his wife and son, but he comes to Cetona on weekends to see his mom, who is widowed and lives at *casa famiglia.* He is an accountant for a large real estate company and he has a demanding job. He works long hours and he is weary and tired, but his blue eyes are still disarming and he has the same tenderness about him. The same kindness of soul he had when he held me that night decades ago.

We have run into each other on and off through the years on my visits, a few times spending many hours talking, but this time we have renewed a friendship. When he's in town he waits for me in the piazza late at night. He looks up at my window and I go down to visit with him, and we walk back and forth, back and forth.

We come to the mouth of my alley.

— *Non avevo coscienza. Mi dispiace,* I say, about to cry. I had no conscience. I am sorry.

No conscience: Is that true? A bit thoughtless perhaps, at least, or unaware of my power to break someone's heart—I have always been unaware of that—or unaware of why I couldn't trust things lasting. Already then.

— *Eri giovane. Lascia andare,* Lucio says smiling, his eyes deep into mine. You were young. Let it go.

He pulls me to him and hugs me. I feel him breathe me in.

— *Ti ho sempre voluto bene,* he says. I have always loved you, kept you in my heart.

Lucio is still a hunter, an outdoorsman. Sometimes at night he takes me riding in the countryside to trace running routes I have forgotten. We get out to look at fields and we spot animals here and there running in the glare of his headlights. I tease him for shooting them and ask him what kind of man would do that. He takes a step back and tells me to fuck off. He shows me things and roads and places with the expertise I always knew he had but was not old enough to understand then, or to value. We laugh and avoid each other's eyes. He smells clean, like grass, with a hint of cologne.

At the mouth of the alley I feel him against me. We hang on a second too long. It's so easy.

Yet, I shake my head and remember my vows. To not betray. To not harm. To not fall back into what was—into what I cannot undo and yet I cannot get back. The love is, indeed, still there; yet, everything is different.

I pull away. I kiss him on the cheeks, breathing him in, and I walk up the alley, happy that this man is still in my heart and grieving the day that I lost him.

While I am standing in the window Fortunata walks by and waves up at me smiling, her blue eyes shining like crystals in her rosy cheeks.

— *Vieni giù? Si fa 'na crostata?* she yells up to me, brushing her dark hair out of her face. Do you want to come over? Let's make a *crostata*!!

Fortunata is the mother of my friend Romina, who is married to Silvio, Ave's son, though they are separated now. Her father-in-law, the tough Dolco, sold us our house, and I have known her since then. When I was growing up she'd come and sit with Beppa, our neighbor, and watch over the chickens. She has seen me grow up, as they say here, and she comforts me like a mother.

I bundle up and walk down to the house where she has lived for decades, a post-war building at the entrance to town. She has a new kitchen, aqua green, and it's sunny and light, even in winter. The view of the countryside—the road leading to Piazze ending at the horizon—is magnificent.

While we bake, Fortunata mentions something about her late husband, Benigno, and I realize that, all familiarity aside, I know nearly nothing about her other than the obvious few facts. What did she dream when she was a girl? Who was she?

— *Volevo fa' la levatrice! Ennò?* I wanted to be a midwife. Isn't that the truth, she says dreamily.

I prod her on to tell me more.

— *Ma che ti racconto?* she says, brushing me off and downplaying her life, like Ave and all the women around here do. What is there to tell?

But to me the lives of all people in Cetona I love—and even some I don't—are a fascinating world full of mystery and history, one that I want to know and explore, and so I insist, and she relents, finally, sliding back in memory to 1940, when she was born—premature—in a tiny hamlet called Le Macchie.

It was a chaotic time in Italy, with the Fascists in power and war looming. Le Macchie, in the middle of nowhere on the road between Chiusi and Castiglion del Lago, was bereft of medical personnel, entirely powerless to help. Yet, she says looking up at the heavens, tiny baby Fortunata pulled through to see the beginning of the war.

Her father was what they called a *sensale*, a person who negotiated deals and found and matched sellers and buyers for animals and such things. If you wanted to sell a cow he'd find you a buyer; if you wanted to buy an olive grove, he'd find you one for sale. Her mother worked at a local cannery, canning tomatoes mostly. When Fortunata was about a year old, her father was called to war, and he left. Shortly after, her mother discovered that she was pregnant, and months later twins were born and quickly lost, both.

*Come se non bastasse*, as they say in Italy—as if that were not enough—not long after, in the middle of the war, young Fortunata caught diphtheria, the great wartime killer of children. She was hospitalized and thought to die. They watched her wheeze and writhe, and nearly everyone gave up on her.

But she didn't die. God was not ready to take me, she says, bringing her hands in prayer, blue eyes to the skies in deep faith.

Eventually peace returned, and with it her father, who channeled his energies into tightening the reins on Fortunata. By then, she was on her way to becoming a lovely girl, friendly, shapely and fun-loving, as she is today. She went to school on a bike and spent summers with the local seamstress, learning how to sew and embroider. She sewed her own clothes, and she remembers each of the dresses she made, one prettier than the other. One in particular comes to mind, golden like a buttercup, the memory of which still makes her feel coquettish and pretty.

She studied stenography and dactylography and she helped around the house, but when it came to her dream of becoming a midwife, her father quashed it sternly: She was to stay home, in the little crossroads that was Le Macchie.

Then, when she was nineteen, the boyfriend of a friend, a guy by the name of Giancarlo, cajoled her onto his motorbike and brought her to Cetona to meet a guy he knew. Cetona was only a few kilometers away but, as things were then in the countryside, it might as well have been on the moon, so Fortunata was nervous and impatient. I can imagine her riding side-saddle as they did at the time.

When they got to Cetona, Giancarlo introduced her to his friend Benigno, who, in this country town, stood out for being an educated man: He had attended seminary—he had aspired to be a priest, though, as I understand it, his earthly desires interfered—and was a school teacher, well respected and from a good family. His father, Arduino, who sold us our house, was a butcher and a landowner, a hardworking, thrifty, and wealthy man. Benigno took a liking to Fortunata and courted her—in spite of her father's jealous supervision—and in 1961 he married her in a sumptuous wedding the likes of which the town had never seen.

Like Ave and most women before her, Fortunata moved in with her in-laws, in their house in Piazza Parè, above the butchery. The marriage was a big move for her, and not what she had expected: While she lacked for nothing, she also became the full-time caretaker of her in-laws, her husband, and soon a daughter. She worked in the butcher shop and, in addition, helped her father-in-law in his business, sometimes going to buy and pay for animals, and sometimes butchering them as well.

— *Ho fatto tutto, tutto, tutto per tutti,* says Fortunata putting her face in her hands. I did everything for everyone, from washing to cooking and tending to their needs.

She served lunch in shifts, her father-in-law at noon because he was grumpy and hungry, her mother-in-law at 12:45 p.m. because she wasn't hungry yet, her husband at 1 p.m. when he came home from school, and their daughter, Romina, when she came home from school at 2:10 p.m.

Eventually, some decades later, the family sold the butchery and the building in which it resided and moved into the house where Fortunata lives now—again, all under one roof. There they stayed until Arduino and his wife passed away, and, unexpectedly, Benigno, too. Now Fortunata continues to do and cook for others—her daughter's children, her brother, and whoever else needs her, any time of day or night.

— I had my dreams, and I made a lot of sacrifices, but I did it all willingly. Perhaps this was my role, says Fortunata, looking up at the sky for an answer but accepting that she does not have one.

Fortunata has always been full of laughter and pleasure, and she still is, with a touch of mischief mixed in. She suffers from a lot of arthritic pain, and since my return here I have encouraged her to smoke pot, an idea that, pious and old-fashioned as she is, causes her to laugh hysterically. She is not scandalized, though; she is realistic about nature and life and she sees plenty of humor in both.

Indeed, as we are about to put the *crostata* in the oven, we start gossiping. We happen on the name of a man in town who died some years back.

— *Ma lo sai com'è morto?* she asks. Do you know how he died?

I don't, I say. Her eyes twinkle.

— *Aveva un'amante e erano a letto in un albergo a Chiusi. Facevano l'amore e lui si sentì male e gli morì sopra!* she says. He had a lover, and they were in bed together in a hotel in Chiusi, making love, when he fell ill and died on top of her!

She squeezes my arm and bursts out laughing. She tells me that the woman left the hotel and called the police from a pay phone. No one ever figured out who she was, she says, her eyes dancing with mischief.

— He died on top of her?! I ask incredulously.

— *Non lo so di preciso se gli era sotto o gli era sopra, ma comunque!* I don't know exactly if he was on top or underneath, she says laughing, but that's what happened!

We finish baking and I get ready to leave, still laughing. Fortunata wraps the *crostata* in tin foil and insists I take it with me. She hugs me and kisses me all over my face and I melt at this love, filling me.

— *Ti voglio bene come una figlia,* she says, holding my face. I love you like a daughter!

# Crostata

A *crostata* is an open-faced dessert that is neither a pie nor a cake; more like a tart, I would say. It is called by different names and made in different ways throughout Italy, but when made with jam or custard crème, it is a quintessentially Tuscan thing. I find that *crostata* is often dry and dull: not this one. Fortunata's is buttery, delicious, and perfectly baked. She uses a glass tart dish so she can check the doneness of the bottom. Keep an eye on the cooking time.

Ingredients

> 1 2/3 cups flour, sifted
>
> 7 T. butter at room temperature
>
> ½ cup sugar
>
> 2 eggs (1 whole plus 1 yolk)
>
> 1-2 t. grated lemon rind (avoid the bitter white part)
>
> A pinch of salt
>
> 1 t. sifted powdered yeast (Fortunata uses Pane Degli Angeli, and does not measure it but with the tip of a spoon)
>
> 2 cups plum or quince jam (both handmade in most households here) or another kind of jam that is not too sweet – it's best if it's a bit tart
>
> ½ cup walnuts (halves and smaller)

Directions

Put the flour through a fine-mesh sieve and make a well out of it on a wooden board. Put the sugar in the middle and break the eggs into it. With a fork, start mixing, dragging the flour into the well as you go. When it is about half mixed and the eggs are largely incorporated, add the butter, salt, lemon, and yeast and start working the dough with your hands, using your finger tips to incorporate and break down the butter. Incorporate all the flour on the board, and if needed wipe any dough off your fingers with a bit of extra flour. Roll the dough into a ball (Fortunata bats it across the board from hand to hand several times) and let it rest in a dish in a cool place (fridge or the windowsill if it is cold enough!) for about 20 minutes.

In the meantime, butter and flour a 10-inch tart pan or glass dish and heat your oven to 320 F.

When the dough has rested, roll it out to about ½-inch thickness or less and cut it the size of the pan, keeping the excess. Press the dough into the dish with your fingertips, building a little height along the inside of the dish (not all the way to the top, just enough to contain the jam). When the dough is evenly distributed in the dish, make holes in it with a fork, then pour your jam onto the dough, spreading it evenly with the back of a spoon or a spatula. The jam should be about half-inch thick —more or less 2 cups. Roll out the remainder of the dough and cut strips about ¾ inch wide. Drape the strips carefully on top of the jam, making a lattice (Fortunata also puts strips along the edge of the whole *crostata* to make it look prettier). Place walnut pieces between the lattice strips and bake the *crostata* on the rack in the bottom third of the oven for 35-40 minutes. The *crostata* should be golden and the bottom not burned. Remove and let cool entirely before serving.

## Mantovana

One day Fortunata and I made a *mantovana*, another quintessentially Tuscan desert (though it has historical connections to Mantua, from which it gets its name) that can be served with fruit or a mascarpone cream for a dinner dessert, or with coffee or tea for breakfast. Again, keep an eye on the cooking time and do not overbake.

Ingredients

1 ½ cups sugar

1 large egg plus 4 yolks

2/3 cup butter, melted and cooled

1 ½ cups flour, sifted

Grated rind of 1 lemon

1 tsp. powdered yeast (Pane Degli Angeli), sifted into the flour

1 cup raw pine nuts

½ cup raw almond slivers

Powdered sugar

Directions

Heat your oven to 350 F. and butter and flour a 9-inch round cake pan with higher edges.

With an electric mixer beat the sugar and eggs until the batter is pale in color and doubled in volume, a good 5 minutes. Add the grated lemon, then the melted butter and the flour in batches, alternating a few tablespoons of the flour with a few of the butter, until all is added. Continue beating until all is well incorporated and fluffy, about 10-12 minutes total.

Mix about a quarter of the pine nuts into the batter, then pour the batter in the pan, making sure it is evenly distributed and smoothing with the back of a spatula.

Sprinkle the almonds and remaining pine nuts on top of the batter so they almost form a layer and press them softly into the batter with the back of a spoon.

Bake in the middle of the oven for 25-30 minutes, until golden and the edges pull away from the sides of the pan (do not open the oven door while cooking, Fortunata warns). Test doneness with a toothpick, but do not overbake! Let cool completely and sprinkle with powdered sugar before serving. The cake should be golden outside, and intensely yellow and soft and moist inside!

Around lunchtime the beat of Cetona begins to slow, and the piazza, flooded by midday light, empties and rests. I hear the store shutters pull down and the cars start and pull away, people retreating home as if called by a town-wide gong. It won't be long before the clanking of silverware and the hum of the *telegiornale* spill out into the alleyways through the shutters pulled ajar.

This is a routine I find both orderly and reassuring. I watch as Maria Letizia closes her clothing store, which is opposite my window, and walks to her silver Mercedes followed by her elderly mother, who is always with her, a few inches behind. She is old and frail now—she has aged even since I have been here—and she takes tiny shuffling steps, a bit hunched. Maria Letizia, who is my age, tall and strong, waits for her, gently taking hold of her arm, and holds open the car door while her mother slowly lowers herself into the seat. I find myself smiling at this most patient of gestures.

Meanwhile, the people who had been sitting at the Bar Cavour talking and having their *aperitivo* slowly get up and walk away, in small groups, toward home or a restaurant. Felice, tray in hand, comes out and tidies the abandoned tables, rearranges the chairs, wipes here and there. Arianna, his sister-in-law, leaves her morning shift to go home to make lunch. Giotto will take her place.

Several people walk through the piazza and into Nilo's restaurant, including his regular widowers and bachelors, and now only the lonely linger.

Amato has been sitting outside Armando's store with Armando and Alcide, and Nanni, too, talking, looking out onto the piazza, checking out the women who walk by—there are not many of them. Alcide's wine shop is directly across the piazza from Armando's store, and Alcide oscillates between his store and Armando's to chat, depending on whether he has customers, which he can clearly see from Armando's bench.

When Armando and Alcide close their stores and head home, Amato heads to his mother-in-law's house for lunch, a routine he developed after he was widowed a couple of years back. He told me this the other day, and I am grateful for this small act of sharing that is becoming a bit of a friendship. Amato is shy, a tad weary and straight-laced, yet he has a boyish smile and his eyes are warm, if tinged with a lingering sadness. He told me the other night that he wishes he had had more courage, that he lived with too much prudence. And now, he says, his voice hanging in the air, his hand pointing to the piazza ... Now he spends his days with his buddies talking, or hunting, or down at his *campo*, with his vegetables and chickens.

He gets up slowly, something aching perhaps, and heads to lunch.

An African immigrant—popularly referred to as a *vu cumprà*—is walking through the piazza chasing people down, waving a set of kitchen towels wrapped in plastic. *Vu cumprà* is a derogatory term used to refer to African immigrants who peddle their wares on the street, based, I suspect, on the immigrants' imperfect pronunciation of the Italian *vuoi comprare*, which means do you want to buy. The changing times have curbed use of the term. Now they are called *extracomunitari*, or sometimes *venditori ambulanti*—traveling sales-men—or, most frequently, *uno di questi neri che vendono la roba per strada*. One of these black people who sell stuff on the street. The language may have changed, but the times have barely softened the feelings they and other immigrants incite, in spite of the random outward show of hospitality.

When I was growing up, it was extraordinary to see a black person in Italy, African or African American. In Cetona it was the rarest of events, even up to the late nineties; when I got married I had black guests and I heard a couple of veiled whispers. Now Africans are everywhere, particularly in big cities but even in towns like Cetona. From Nigeria and Congo, Morocco, Senegal, Sierra Leone and Mali, they walk around with big bags of stuff slung over their shoulders: socks, kitchen towels, cigarette lighters, and toys. They come into the bar and pull out socks and kitchen towels, and people ignore them like they are transparent, like no one, absolutely no one, just came up to your table and asked you for help.

I have done the same, though mostly I like to talk with them, to ask where they come from. They are gregarious and friendly, though I feel a bit invaded when they ring my doorbell.

The one in the piazza today is smiling and bounding through with big steps, hoping—I can tell—for brisk sales. I fear for his disappointment. I wonder what kinds of passages and travails bring them here, what kind of misfortune, with more and more people coming to seek refuge and asylum from tyranny and war. And how do they get to Cetona, I wonder, these African ambulatory salesmen?

I feel for people who have come here from such a long way, with so much despair at their backs, the specificity of their individual tribulations muddled in the uninformed and prejudiced public discourse about immigration, often without regard for the difference between refugee status, or asylum, or simple voluntary immigration. Even when people are welcoming, they will still talk about them behind their backs—how much they work or don't, how much they spend. It is always something.

Cetona has its fair share of Eastern European immigrant workers now, and some new African residents, too. It's a new development since I was last here, and while there are pockets of goodwill and the occasional event bridging cultures, the presence of migrants and refugees continues to test the town. The other day Ave was standing in the piazza talking with me and a young woman from Romania walked by, pulling a little girl by the hand. The girl, three or so, was wearing a frilly dress, nice shoes, a coat, and hat. She appeared to not be lacking for anything.

— *Vedi?* Ave said, pointing after her with her chin. *Questa è venuta qui dalla Romania, ha trovato uno, ci ha fatto 'sta bambina, e ora la manteniamo noi.* You see her? She came from Romania, had a baby with someone here, and now we support her.

— *Basta! Ne abbiamo abbastanza qui a Cetona,* she said. Basta, we have had enough!

Ave is echoing a common sentiment, fueled by the fact—or is it rumor?—that the Italian government, which is broke, shells out automatic unemployment benefits to people from European Union countries who come here seeking residence and don't have jobs, whether they sought one or no, and whether or not they had one back in their home country. If they have nice clothes or a car it sparks anger.

— *Ma che ci vengono a fa' qui se hanno tutto da dove vengono?* she asks, putting her hands together in prayer. Why do they come here if they have everything they need whence they come?

Rossana, the sister of my childhood friend Ida, was robbed in her house by three Albanians. The other night we were standing talking in front of Bar Cavour when she saw a Moroccan woman new to town.

— *Non se ne può più di 'sta gente. Siamo invasi!* she says, widening her arms dramatically. We can't stand it anymore! We are invaded!

This reminded her of what happened to her and she told me, with the drama and flashing brown eyes I remember: She was sleeping in her bed on the third floor of her building, down in the new housing, when something woke her up. She had the sang-froid to pretend to sleep, and she watched as three men stood in her bedroom and dug through her drawers and picked through her jewelry.

Three men in her bedroom, shining a light from a cell phone! Her heartbeat was in her throat and she could barely breathe, but she managed to control herself until they walked out and down the stairs. Then she ran to her porch and she screamed for her life—and her car, for which they had taken the keys.

— *Ma te pensa,* she says. Imagine that.

Whatever one thinks about the racial situation, whose complexity cannot be easily summed up, it is shocking indeed. I had never heard the word robbery in the history of Cetona.

Rossana's neighbor two floors down was robbed five times by immigrants. The elderly man went to court to testify on Rossana's behalf.

— *Bisogna caricalli nelle barche e falli rovescia' nel mezzo del mare!* the man told the judge. We should load them onto boats and turn them upside down in the middle of the sea.

— You are not allowed to say that! the judge said.

— Oh yes, I am! the man answered.

He told the judge that the last time the thieves robbed his house they took his car too. He had parked his old car behind his new one to prevent them from stealing the new one; yet, the thieves moved the old car, took the new one, and moved the old one back into its place.

— *Ho detto dieci bestemmie per scalino fino alla porta di casa!* he said. I said ten curses against the Virgin Mary every step I took, all the way up to my apartment, he told the judge.

It seems, for the most part, that most of the immigrants who have settled in Cetona—from Romania and Albania—are hard workers, in construction and gardening. Yet, people don't trust them. They say they have different mores—shifty, ruthless, and accustomed to thievery and lying—and they are changing the culture with their language and their ways.

One of the first weeks I was here, I was at the Bar Cavour one night late, hanging out with Alano, Bennato, and a few others, maybe Sotero. Among them was Piotr, from Moldova. He had a friend with him, Alexei, and they were both glassy-eyed. Piotr started telling war stories about the former USSR's satellite countries and the things the men do at the request of Mother Russia. He said he fought for the Russians and killed many people.

— Do you know what it's like to go into a village and kill people, women and children? he asked in his heavy accented Italian. He wiped his face with his hand and stared far off out the door into the piazza.

In the morning I see him crossing the piazza going to work. He takes care of an important garden in town. It must be Eden to him, and I cannot hold it against him for seeking that, his Eden. And I don't hold it against the African immigrant now bounding through the piazza, either.

While I watch him go, Armando pulls his door shut and he walks through the piazza to his car and home. Sabina's dad, Mimmo, twig-like with sweet blue eyes, always a cap on his head, comes out of Sabina's store and walks slowly toward home, recently emptied by the passing of his wife of decades. A few minutes later Sabina, too, closes her store, and under the bright sunlight she hurries after her father, to help make him lunch. Mixo stays outside, stretched out in the lunchtime sun. Marzia, Mercede's daughter, drives through with her blue Volvo station wagon, then Bennato with his little electric-blue car, going home for lunch.

Isabella is the only person left, seemingly in the whole town, smoking alone in the shade in front of Le ACLI, with at her feet her inseparable little dog, Ernesto, white, the size of a small pig, named after Che Guevara.

Isabella moves me and inspires me. Born in Rome, where she grew up, Isabella has spent her whole existence—she is a handful of years younger than me—wrestling her life away from the clutches of a congenital heart defect. She monitors, cures, rests, takes meds, panics, takes more meds, rests, cures, and monitors more. It is a miracle that she is alive. Isabella, though, is not a complainer, and, in fact, she has developed an explosive sense of humor and a witty, scorching honesty, which coupled with her in-your-face Roman accent and her short hair streaked in flaming red or sometimes purple, make her one of my favorite girls in town. The fact that she drinks—which fuels her spirited stories and quick-fire repartees, based mostly on keen observations of people—brings us together easily in the evening for a glass of wine when no one else is around. Plus, she is kind. She spreads hugs and kisses as she walks through the piazza slowly, Ernesto in tow, a bundle of sweetness and charm. Yet, she manages people here with intelligence and wit, putting them quickly back in their place when they are out of bounds, in words or action. And that, in Cetona, can come in handy.

As the bells mark 1:30 p.m., she puts out her cigarette and begins walking on her way uptown to lunch with her parents, Ernesto shadowing behind. She looks up at me with a smile and waves, and it makes me happy.

Then everything stops. I sit on the sill and gather the silence in my hands.

When we were not at the fountain or clustered around the juke-box at the Bar Sport, we spent our days driving around on our motor-bikes or in the cars of the older guys to the places that all of us in our group associate with our youth—to San Casciano for a walk, or to Città della Pieve for a gelato.

In spring, if the weather was nice, we went for a *giro* in Chianciano. A *giro* is an outing or a jaunt, relaxed and, most often, aimless. Sometimes we hitchhiked, which was fun when we got a ride together, but not so much when we got split up, which reminds me of an unhappy episode of jumping out of a car because the driver pulled out his penis. Once we got to Chianciano, we had gelato and win-dow-shopped, staring into the stores and taking in the pictures of the made-up women and the smells of expensive perfume wafting through the doors.

In summer our days were filled with glorious languor, with noth-ing to do but live—the way summers should be when you're young. We sat at the fountain a lot, talking, watching people go by, and eating gelato and *pizza a taglio*. We drove through the countryside on our *motorini,* Maria and I, and Giulia, too, and we sat in cars to talk and listen to music—mostly Italian song-writers like Lucio Dalla, Lucio Battisti, and Ron.

And sometimes, we invaded people's fields and farms to steal fruit, or preferably to have it offered to us.

— *I fichi so' pronti!* our friend Giorgio Fiori, the son of the vet, would say one inevitable day each August. The figs are ready!

— *Si va? Annamo!* he'd say. Let's go!

Ten or twelve of us would jump on our motorbikes and drive down the kilometer or so to his parents' stately stone house on the outskirts of town, where we'd climb on the beautiful fig tree in the manicured garden. Without fail, the figs were sweet, juicy, and giving, and with Dr. Fiori looking on, we ate them all.

On weekend afternoons, and sometimes after dinner too, we dressed in our coolest clothes and drove our *motorini* or caught a ride to Chiusi to go dancing at Il Punto, or the Bussola, near Chianciano, dark discos with psychedelic lights and low velvet seats closed off by heavy red velvet curtains. With unbearable anticipation we'd queue to get in, and once inside we rushed to join the crowd gathered from surrounding towns to dance to the hits of the time, "Staying Alive," "Ring My Bell," "Enough Is Enough," "Give Me the Night," "Born to Be Alive," and Amii Stewart's "Knock on Wood." Elated and effervescent, we danced till dark, till dinner time, or sometimes till the early morning hours, until someone with a car would give us a ride home. Leaving me in the silent darkness of Borgo, I'd tiptoe my way to the door and up the steps to my room.

Around that time my world became eclipsed by Andrea, the dark-haired, dark-eyed soccer player into whose universe I happened because he was Mariachiara's brother and because in Cetona we all hung out together. From that familiarity something was born, and I came to drape my dreams on him before my dreams were even known to me.

When we first started seeing each other—how or why I do not know—Andrea was getting over a break-up. She had left him, and he was heartbroken. Perhaps because of that, he was cynical, critical, and not at all fun to be around. I knew him to be kind and sweet; I had seen it in him. Yet, his gloom stifled and obscured me. I reread diaries and letters from that time and I cannot retrieve a thread of anything warm or bright the way youthful love should be. And, in fact, I recall writing dark pages in rose-edged diaries full of uncontainable disappointment and resentment for yielding myself to such agony and capitulation of self. Which leads to the question, what makes us fall in love when we are young, and is it even love?

Parking was the thing then, and together with girlfriends of other guys—Mariachiara, or Giulia—we waited around the piazza or the bar to hop in their cars and go drive around the countryside. It was winter then, and I remember his boots and dark gray leather jacket. He'd play pool to his satisfaction—he was skillful, hence that could take hours—then, with a nearly undetectable nod of the chin, he would let me know it was time to go. And off I went, unsure why I was going yet incapable of not going, my heart sinking in my thin chest, my sense of self vanquished and silenced. In some childlike romantic fantasy, not going meant having nothing, and that was worse.

Soon thereafter—a matter of months that in memory feel like years—Andrea broke it off. He said I had done something unforgivable: I had kissed a gorgeous soccer player named Stefano who was in summer retreat in Cetona with the Roma team. His eyes were warm like toasted hazelnuts and his tousled hair golden like caramel. He had a smile that was both innocent and luring and fully aware of its effect, which I will never forget. And he was kind in his ways too.

These soccer retreats, prompted once a year or so by dint of Cetona having a professional-sized soccer field, brought to town a couple dozen self-assured, mostly beautiful, unfamiliar young men whose presence sent a shiver through our little town. After their twice-daily practices, the players, showered, wet hair slicked back, gorgeous faces gleaming in the sun—and they really were always strangely beautiful—strolled through the piazza in their baby-blue uniforms, going to lunch or dinner or taking their evening time off.

They were present just long enough to draw the attention of the girls and women in town, dulled and saddened by their lackluster and limited choices. Quickly eyes would meet, some chemistry would bubble, and something would spark. Every summer produced a few flings, and though most were tenuous and short-lived, they were always memorable. The local guys fumed at this—and the players themselves were not supposed to do this—so these were hidden trysts, brief interludes, kisses stolen behind buildings.

And so it was for me, and others. Mariachiara took to liking a tall, lanky blond player named Alessandro, and they developed a summer tryst full of forbiddenness and play. Stefano and I, meanwhile, started talking somewhere, I don't remember where. He liked me—he really liked me—and smiled at me, and he left me a note somewhere that made my heart flutter. We met to talk here and there, and then one day we kissed, up at the old fountains under Valentino's house. It was sweet and tender, which seemed improbable to me because he was from Rome and a beautiful soccer player and I was a flat-chested girl from Cetona with an asshole boyfriend who cared nothing about me. And I had come to believe that I didn't deserve this prince, even for a single day.

Immediately the kiss became known—probably some lady peeking through a window—and Andrea, sitting smugly in his car, told me I had done something inexcusable. He said it with disdain, his eyes dark and cutting, and I felt wronged and outraged because in truth I had merely betrayed a love already misplaced. Worse yet was that I quickly learned that it was all a pretext, of the most dishonest kind: Andrea had begun to see Maria, secretly. Everyone knew, though, I later learned, and no one told me. It seemed like a matter accepted, a smooth passage that somehow made sense to the inner logic of the town, like I perhaps did not.

Our relationship had been nothing.

When I found out I was crushed and there was no place to hide. The size of Cetona affords no room to flee and the group dynamic carries you inexorably back to the center like a damn bad storm. In this case, even after we broke up and they were officially a couple, they were everywhere I was—at the fountain, at the bar, in the piazza, holding hands, kissing, like daggers to my eyes. And sadly, I was often with them. We'd go places to eat gelato or walk around, in Andrea's new white VW Golf, with Maria in the front seat, strutting like a princess in her new clothes, and me in the back hiding my tears, feeling doubly betrayed, by friend and lover.

The soundtrack of that time was Barbra Streisand's "Woman in Love" and "What Kind of Fool." Why I rode with them still baffles me. I should have stayed home to read a book and told them to fuck off. Yet, to this day Barbra's voice takes me back like a punch to that first cutting realization that love—the love of another—cannot be had or controlled. It is a gift, and nothing can quite soothe from that lesson, not the first time and not the last.

Maria, on her part, had wrapped herself in a blanket of incorrigibility, while I nursed my injury in impotence and immolation, unworthy, in fact, of apology or consideration had she chosen to offer either. But teenagers can be so self-righteous, and so self-injuring, too. I did not confront her nor question her, perhaps too concerned to lose them both, or perhaps because it wasn't worth standing up for. They sailed off into the chronicles of Cetona's great loves—well, for a notable moment, at least.

Meanwhile, on a foggy morning in late September Mariachiara and I skipped school and took a train to Rome, breathlessly, giddily, to visit our beautiful soccer players. We kissed them again, our Roman princes, and for a moment we forgot Cetona and everyone in it.

In summer our ranks swelled with kids from Milano and Rome whose families owned houses up the secluded old alleys of town, or in villas out in the country, and whose presence brightened and renewed us. The town seemed somehow electrified.

Alessandra and Adriana, the twins from Rome came, and Vetralla, and Marcello, who looked like Marcello Mastroianni but with green eyes, and Marco from Milano, and Carola, and Barbara, daughter of a famous movie producer, and Silvia from Milano, whose parents have since retired and live up the alley from me. There was Pipino, from Rome, and Guido from Arezzo, and the heartthrobs of the summers, Stefano (another Stefano) and Giancarlo, from Rome, at whose houses we had lavish parties and picnics. They all came in and out of our lives carrying with them a breath of fresh air and, in the case of Stefano and Giancarlo, large doses of heartbreak. Girls would wait for them into the wee hours just to get a few minutes with them, and then they would vanish again, holding the tender strings to their hearts.

Seasonally Cetona filled with interesting adults, too, friends of my parents—some Italian, some foreign, who lived there part-time—who brought into my life kaleidoscopic stories and who, by their mere diversity, cast onto my world a glow of exoticism and wonder.

One couple, Sir Jack and Lady Nikka, I remember with joy and regret, wishing I had known them better as an adult. They were from England via New Zealand and many years in Africa, and they owned a lovely house on the road to Sarteano, splendidly appointed. Jack was a government lawyer for the crown—including service as attorney general in Zanzibar, whose constitution he was to draft. He had served heroically in the Royal Navy, during the war—the ship he was commanding, in the Tyrrhenian Sea, was hit by a bomb and split in two—and later he became a high-level labor barrister, with all the formality and uprightness that one would expect of an old British guy who served the Queen. And, indeed, he was knighted by her some years later for his service to his country. Among Jack's most noted achievements, to me, was that he prosecuted and convicted, in Nairobi, one of the greatest big-game poachers Africa had ever seen. Of course, when I was little Jack's stature made me speechless in his presence, but my parents loved him for his natural New Zealand friendliness, his down-to-earth approach to people, and his witty sayings, and they remained dear friends until they both passed—or fell off their perch, as Jack would have said.

By the time we met Jack and Nikka, Nikka's brother, Ian, a British colonel, had owned property in Cetona for decades. He had served in Italy during the British occupation and he had returned after the war, purchasing most fortuitously some of Cetona's most prominent properties. Among them was the Parco Terrosi, the marigold-colored building and surrounding park that rise above the piazza and that now belong to fashion mogul Valentino. Eventually he sold that property and others, but what interested me in all this as a young girl was that Colonel Ian had in his employment—or under his wing—a couple by the name of Decimo and Anna, from Rome, and they had two little girls I came to love, Flavia and Arabella.

Decimo had an interesting story himself: Ian had met him in Rome after the war, in a hospital where Decimo was dying, of tuberculosis, and, in fact, he likely would not have lived had Ian not ordered that he be operated immediately and a lung removed. After his recovery, Decimo, smooth-talking and swarthy, went on to have a brief career in acting, with small roles in *Gioventù Bruciata* and *La Sfida;* ownership of a renowned gallery in Rome, in Via Margutta; and, finally, ownership of a hotel at the Vallone, a stunning ochre villa on the way to Sarteano with an imposing view of the valley below. Opened at the apogee of Cetona's star-studded phase, the hotel became a mecca for actors and VIPs from Rome who either followed Decimo to Cetona or ended up there by word of mouth, one following the other.

Anyway, back when we met them, in Ian's employment were two Malaysian men who served as cooks and entertainers. Ian had met them in Malaysia, where he had also served during the war and where he owned property, and eventually brought them back with him to England and, eventually, to Italy. Flavia, Arabella, and I spent many afternoons playing together on Ian's property, and our parents shared sumptuous dinner parties cooked by the Malaysian chefs. Sometimes I was invited to Decimo and Anna's beach house, too, somewhere south of Rome, and the girls and I played on the beach and hung out with Decimo's friends, men with dreamy eyes who smoked long, thin cigarettes and told dirty stories punctuated by winks and innuendo. Like so many others, Decimo is gone now, and Ian, too.

Summers in Cetona brought Emma Bini, the fashion designer, and Philippe, the actor, and their vogueish children from Paris, and Angela Bianchini, a famous Jewish journalist, and, finally, Patrizia and her husband, Felice, a handsome, brilliant Neapolitan geologist and engineer whose advocacy for nuclear energy made him a lightning rod for petroleum companies and eventually landed him in jail for a series of fabricated scandals. He was pardoned by the president of Italy and he went on to serve in the European Parliament, among others. He was a good friend and a fascinating conversationalist who my father cherished.

In summer Laurent came, a Hungarian Jewish philosophy professor at Rutgers, and Gert, the painter, returned, too, with his coterie of friends and his bohemian lifestyle. He smoked cigars and played poker, and he, Laurent, and Dad had vivacious, sometimes heated, conversations about art and ideas that lasted long into the night. We all loved having Gert around, and all the friends we shared with him, too—Cetona's longtime doctor, a handful of young leftist entrepreneurs, a leftist intellectual who had been a partisan in the war, a few famous journalists, and Anna and Aldo, the owners of the Rocca.

Some were dinner party acquaintances brought together by eclectic interests; others were real friends who stuck around a lifetime. All, in any case, swirled magic into my life, in spite of my father's rather monastic lifestyle and Cetona's otherwise limiting social palette. When everyone was in town. they all gathered festively in this house or that, talking about art and politics and chain-smoking over food and wine into the wee hours of the morning. I wish, now, that I could been an adult to join them.

Then, when summer ended, they all left, back to Rome and Milan and Paris, New York and Switzerland, leaving us alone with our silence, our little-town ennui, the trickling fountain, the Bar Sport, the quiet alleys, and the piazza. Houses were darkened and winter rhythms resumed. We made due with the billiards and the music, and, on weekend nights, a trip to La Bussola to dance, or the occasional visit to the *vasche* of San Casciano.

Natural springs pooling hot sulfurous water in large stone baths, the *vasche* were long used in antiquity by local women to wash clothes and linens. In more recent decades after the advent of the washing machine, however, well-positioned as they were in secluded fields outside of town, the *vasche* came to serve more fun-loving purposes, and in every season, even in winter with snow on the ground, we piled in three or four cars and drove to San Casciano to strip off our clothes and step into the murky hot waters to soak, sometimes till dawn. Shrouded by the foggy vapors and the darkness, people smoked joints or drank beer, but mostly we just sat there chatting, enjoying the warmth, talking about this and that.

As a teenager I remember feeling shy about it all—endlessly teased for being flat-chested, perhaps—and I submerged myself with water to my neck. When we got out, our skin tingling from the heat, we dried off with our clothes—no one ever thought of bringing a towel—piled back into the cars, cigarettes burning, music blaring, and headed back to Cetona.

Today I took a drive to San Casciano to revisit the old *vasche*, and I was surprised to discover that a set of manicured stone steps leads a short distance from the baths all the way up into the middle of the town, narrowing as they ascend through the houses. At the top of the steps is a curious plaque that says *Rampichino da Pienza*.

*Rampicare*, or, more correctly, *arrampicare*, means to climb, and when I inquired as to the plaque's origin, I learned that it was placed there to commemorate a most misguided drunk, from Pienza, who, after soaking in the *vasche* and having a number of drinks, decided to scale the stone steps with his car. People with houses on the alley watched from their windows—shaking their heads and laughing, no doubt—as his car clanked up the steps, bouncing up and down, until finally it got stuck between two houses. The town pulled the man's car out and put the plaque up as remembrance, ingeniously nicknaming him Rampichino da Pienza.

One season moved to another—this might have been a year later or more—and the rebel Pierpaolo moved to the center of my heart, bathing it in warm, suffused light.

By then Pierpaolo had long broken up with Emma, shaved off his beard, and, by dint of intelligence and charisma, made friends with wealthy people who had summer houses in Cetona. He had come to love nice things—gold bracelets and cologne, cigars and Berlucchi champagne, and his red motorcycle and well-tailored clothes—and he had embraced a patina of irreverent elegance. Charming, dazzling even, he stood out, and he came to attract a large group of sycophants and some detractors as well.

I fell in among his followers, his lovers, not out of sycophancy but out of respect for his intelligence and affection and, eventually, love, which he nourished in me with the self-assurance of a grown man yet the tenderness of a brother.

His presence in our social umbrella afforded us younger kids exposure to a different, more mature perspective on such things as politics, society, and, yes, sex. As a lover—I must have been seventeen or eighteen by then—he wanted me to embody my feelings and become fully of myself. He wanted to teach me how to make love, and to talk about it, which from this distance makes me smile with tenderness and recoil with shyness all at the same time. Through those touches, those explorations, I expanded myself into a bittersweet and nullifying abandonment of self and yet a scorching discovery of self through another person.

For me it was all terrifying and effacing yet electrifying and affirming. I was vulnerable and unsure of myself, yet I also felt a fount of specialness and fearlessness inside of me. Of course, it was not until much later that I understood what any of it meant, really, but he opened the consciousness of a young girl to the potential of being, finally, a woman—a grownup woman he would appreciate and I would want to be.

In the annals of love, mine with Pierpaolo was a fleeting *storia*—a romantic story, a love of a few months. Too afraid of losing myself in him, impossibly older and out of reach, I moved on. And perhaps, truth be told, Andrea, the dark soccer player, still held a corner of my heart. And yet I am certain to this day that between Pierpaolo and me was a specific and true love and tenderness. I occupied a special place in his well-traveled heart, and he in mine, and so it would be for many years. A remnant of that reaches into my day when I see him in the piazza now, going about his business, sometimes with his wife, and he says hello.

*Ciao Sibi.* It always makes me miss him, still. *Sibi.*

The soundtracks for my time with Pierpaolo—that time in the group's life—were Ron with his album *Una Città Per Cantare* and iconic Lucio Dalla with his album *Lucio Dalla,* love-drenched.

*Là dove il mare luccica*
*E grida forte il vento*
*C'è una vecchia terrazza*
*Vicino al golfo di Sorrento*
*Un uomo abbraccia una ragazza*
*Dopo che aveva pianto*
*Poi si schiarisce la voce*
*Ed incomincia il canto ...*

Pierpaolo went on to have many lovers, many older than me and older than him, even, strewn about in towns here and there, his romances mysterious and some overlapping. He never shared his secrets.

Then, not long after, he began a relationship with Mariachiara, who had had a stubborn crush on him for years and who had pursued him maddingly. Eventually, while I was in college, they married and had a little girl, and another of Cetona's big loves came full circle.

The bells chime 2:00 p.m. and a trickle of life returns to the piazza.

The usual post-prandial group gathers on the church's steps, right in front of my window, to enjoy a warm day in winter. Franco,

Lionetta's husband, a dark-haired construction worker in dusty clothes, is sitting in the sunshine holding his head as he does every day at this hour. Don Prospero, sitting next to him, frowns against the sunlight and they don't say much.

A few minutes later Feriero pulls up in his Ape and joins them.

Understated and polite, Feriero makes up—*is*—the landscape of everyday life here. He is a ubiquitous presence and known to all. You look out the window and you just expect to see his tall frame unfold one leg at a time from his old green Ape and walk over to the Bar Cavour. His work pants are relaxed on his waist, his gait is slow and a bit tired, and his gaze is to the ground. His hair, white and distinguished, is a bit messy, and he exudes peace.

He does this, this visiting in the piazza, every day, rain or shine, winter or summer, short of 7 a.m. when he goes for coffee with the guys; at 2 p.m. when he sits for a moment with the guys to chat; and sometimes late in the afternoon, after his work or workings around town are done, when he sits at the Bar Cavour or on the bench under my window, to rest. Otherwise Feriero is not one to hang out in the piazza much. He is out doing this or that, taking care of someone's field, or doing something for someone.

When I was growing up, Feriero worked for town hall, doing everything from digging graves to driving the school bus, a multi-faceted position that has been held by many of Cetona's best-known citizens. As a school bus driver, Feriero picked up and delivered children all over Cetona's broad, hilly countryside. Ever-attentive—he is someone who notices and knows things—Feriero watched most of us grow up, and he knew all of our names, even kids like me who walked to school.

Later, as the gravedigger and custodian of the cemetery, Feriero buried many of the town's residents. For many years after that, he drove Cetona's garbage truck, a bright blue truck that he threaded through the alleyways of the town. Through the course of his many jobs that connect intimately with his fellow citizens, Feriero became Cetona in a way. He *is* Cetona. Plus, everybody loves Feriero: He has the sort of kindness, the sort of inner honesty, that cleanses you. His whole face lights up in happiness, and a cloud comes over him in sadness.

Every year that I have returned Feriero has greeted me, hugged me, and asked about my family. I think of him with great affection. I like visiting with him down at the Della Vigna tractor shed where he takes care of their *orto*.

When I first arrived, I found him there plucking away at the leftovers of the fall crops, planting garlic.

— *Allora se' tornata dall'America? Ma resti per sempre, m'hanno detto?* he asked. So, you're back from America? Are you staying, forever?

We walked through the rows of rapini, the tomatoes lingering on the brown, dried vines, the peppers, and broccoli, and cauliflower, and he insisted on packing a box of vegetables for me. He picked here and there while telling me that his mom was sick, at *casa famiglia*, and that he had lost his brother not long before. His warm brown eyes darkened with sadness.

As I watch him now from the window, Feriero casually unbuckles his worn leather belt, unbuttons his pants, tucks his shirt in, and buttons and buckles everything back up, unhurried and undaunted—a gesture that is entirely his and that no one pays any mind to at all. While he buckles up, a few others approach and stand around them, among them one of the municipal police officers. They start a discussion and Don Prospero's voice rises above the rest.

The card-playing crowd pulls up a few at a time, Alano in his van and with his man-purse under his arm, lighting a cigarette as he goes. Sotero arrives a few seconds later in his white Jeep and walks in, head down, with short, fast steps, and then Mario, too, a witty, friendly mechanic they call Bruciabenzina (one who burns gas). From my window I hear a soft murmur of voices and the clanking of coffee cups against the counter, the ring distinct in the sleepiness of the sunny piazza.

Silvanino arrives in his extremely noisy dark blue Ape and gets out quickly. His black dog jumps down behind him and makes for the bar. I smile watching Silvanino. He is short and friendly, a house painter, with a mess of curly dark hair and bulging eyes who looks like he just crawled out of an early Renaissance painting and got in a waiting pickup truck, or, as it were, an Ape. He has a *campo* down by the old *lavatoi*, my old playground, at the bottom of the hill below Borgo, where he grows vegetables and keeps all sorts of mechanical refuse, including a hot pink Fiat 500 that is bogged in the ground and grown over with vines.

On my runs I often see him driving down there, or up. There used to be a steep, rocky path leading down, but nature and municipal neglect have combined to wear the path into a plunging mud descent, or ascent, depending on which direction you have to travel. Yet, it seems to matter little to Silvanino, who rides the perilous incline with his Ape or his pick-up truck as if he were driving a chariot in the Coliseum, his small black dog jumping around in the back howling and barking. He is a funny, wild man.

As I sit on the sill watching the piazza in its post-prandial routine, I see Felice outside the Bar Cavour, bussing a table. He has just arrived for his afternoon shift and he is joking around and laughing with some guys sitting outside. Giotto leaves for his afternoon break and crosses the piazza dragging his right leg a touch.

Diego walks around from his mother's house, where he goes every day to have lunch and check on her. He comes around the corner and walks to the Bar Cavour. As he goes, I follow him with my eyes, admiring his light blue button-down shirt, carefully pressed. He is smoking and walking, looking forward, his knees trembling just a touch, and he disappears in the bar.

When I was growing up, Diego, I've mentioned—going back to Cetona's big, big loves—was married to Rossana, the big sister of my childhood friend Ida (she had the home birth that forever stuck in my imagination). He was a soccer player, and he briefly ran the Bar Sport. Eventually, while I was gone, many years later, Diego and Rossana separated, and my old love Pierpaolo and my friend Mariachiara separated, too.

Lo and behold, Diego and Mariachiara got together, though the timing and causality of all this vary according to who's telling the story. In any case, it's been more than ten years now, I think, and whatever scandal there might have been—and one can safely assume there was one here—has been set aside, by most people at least. Diego and Mariachiara are now a stable and happy couple whose love I have come to appreciate in my rediscovery of Cetona's daily life.

And, indeed, at the stroke of 2:10 p.m. Mariachiara pulls up in her little blue car and walks toward Le ACLI in a hurry, looking for Diego. She walks into Le ACLI and comes back out empty-handed. She rounds the corner towards the Bar Cavour, walking quickly, and there she finds him. They walk out into the sunshine together and they sit, in love.

I like watching Mariachiara. It fills me with sweet memories of our youth and many, many laughs. She seems to be a bit shy with me now, which I would like us to overcome somehow, if I can ever catch her. Today she is wearing her black work outfit—black jeans, a black top, a black sweater—and is heading into a busy afternoon as one of the most sought-after physical therapists in the area. She only has a few more moments before she has to go, swamped as she is between an old man who needs a massage, or someone out in the country with a neck problem. Everyone needs her. She also has a twenty-something daughter, with Pierpaolo, who has a young child, and on top of that, she contributes, with Andrea, to taking care of their father, who is losing his memory.

As I watch her I feel like a voyeur, but I cannot get enough of looking at the people who I have loved for a lifetime and whose lives I have so missed—and I mean by this that I have missed the passing of their lives and their lives with me. Now, I seek and find the old habits. In the flip of a hand or a laugh, I locate the children that we were, already sketched out so long ago, and I revisit the last memories I lived with her—her distress over loving Pierpaolo, the song of her laughter in class or after school at her house while she ironed. And then seeing her with her daughter on my returns from college.

Diego has aged well. His hair has grayed and he walks like he is in pain, his knees injured by years of soccer. But he still has mocha skin and those beautiful, sexy chestnut eyes that smile in a way that disarms you. He sits, smoking, chatting away with Mariachiara. I was not here when they fell in love, but they look happy, sitting in the sun together. He looks like he is good to her and, as a woman, that comforts me. I think back to our nervous fragility as girls, afraid to trust; how we'd ignore someone coming towards us, afraid of the disappointment of manifesting gladness for fear that the other would not feel the same.

I secretly hope that Mariachiara has the knowledge that she is loved now, because I can tell from my window that she is. But then again, that knowledge is so delicate even for me.

A group of young guys are laughing and joking in front of Le ACLI, then they get on their scooters and leave. Bennato goes by in his blue car on his way back to work. Diamante's boys, Massimo and Maurizio, pull up in their work truck and get out. Massimo is mumbling loudly about something and I smile. Since I ran into his mom, Diamante, we have seen each other and caught up, and the other night he was complaining about a client for whom he did some tiling work back in the fall.

The client, a man from out of town, had yet to pay him for his work, Massimo said, peppering his story with a particularly colorful round of curses against the Madonna, which I remember him being famous for. Finally, Massimo called the client: If your payment is not in my bank account by Monday morning, he said, I am coming to your house and I am taking every fucking tile off that bathroom wall, one by one.

Did he pay, I asked laughing.

— *Ha pagato, ha pagato, Madonna somara!* he said, nodding fervently. He paid up, he sure did.

The piazza is quiet for a moment, then Mauro Cardetti drives by, going for his *caffè* at the Bar Sport. Mariachiara drives off to work, then I hear the thunderous rise of voices at Le ACLI. Someone must have played a good card.

At some point after Andrea and Maria got together, and Mariachiara and Pierpaolo, too, Teo filled my heart, unforgettably.

There are few women of my age in Cetona and surroundings who don't think of Teo as a great love of theirs—if they were lucky. It may not have been, in reality, a *great* love: It may have been merely a week of passion, or a kiss, or a ride on his wasp-yellow BMW motorcycle.

But when it came to Teodoro, a thread of something—anything—was enough to weave yarns of imaginary romance that would fill one's heart for years. He was a beautiful guy, not perfect but more beautiful because of it. Skinny and tall, he walked chest forward, a bit bow-legged, cigarette in hand, shirt collar turned up. He had a sexy gaze and he looked the world in the eyes, straight on, with his greenish eyes flecked with gold, daring and pissy. And this pissed people off about Teo yet made him supremely attractive to everyone. In a mostly conventional population, Teo stuck out for his bravado and confidence and his way of living that said, I don't give a fuck what you think, though he did, deep inside, and in a town like Cetona that can be a tough battle for the sensitive of heart.

And Teo was that too—sensitive—in spite of the swagger and the ease with which he seemed to live. A life junky, so to speak. He flew about like a butterfly sniffing out the best pollen, the brightest colors, the most vibrant energy, wherever they may be, and he had an electrifying presence that made him the kind of guy that everyone seeks, whose light everyone wanted to bask in.

He came and went on motorcycles and cars always at great speed—he loved speed—and he approached the tortuous curves of the roads around Cetona with the same attitude he approached women: that he didn't give a fuck. He thought that with enough skill and charm he would master them, and tame them, and make them his. And he did. We were all his lovers and friends, the whole town, it seems, his sycophants and geishas, following him around here and there, wherever he wanted to go—and for him nothing was too far or out of reach.

As for me and him, we kissed in phone booths and parked in country lanes at night and made love and smoked cigarettes and listened to great music—Dire Straits, America, and Italy's Pino Daniele. Over the years the fondness never waned in spite of great distance and even marriages. When I returned through the years, we went up to la Rocca and drank beers dangling our feet over the wall of the Cittadella looking down on the lights of the piazza like it was a Christmas manger. Sometimes we kissed and sometimes we cried, and sometimes we pissed each other off and didn't speak for a year. I don't remember that Teo and I ever had an official relationship that opened and closed, and in fact we had a love that lasted a lifetime, fed by the communality of being a bit different and never quite at peace with anything we had.

And perhaps that is what he liked most—giving and taking what he wanted, no strings attached.

And then, with a slight nod of the head he would hop on his motorcycle, the sound rich and sexy, and off he went, at the speed of light, a tender thread of love pulled across our hills.

And then among my loves were some I never understood.

On this stay I spent a little time trying to shed light on them, and this led me, sometime this winter, to go through the Michelangelis in the Torrita phonebook and call all eight of them, one by one.

All were disconnected except for the last, and it happened to be the one I wanted: the mother of the Michelangeli brothers, Athos and Alessandro.

— *Ma Lei i miei figli come li conosce?* Signora Michelangeli asks after I introduce myself. How do you know my sons?

From the *liceo*, signora, I say. I remind her of Francesca and Athos.

— *Ahh*, she says.

Back to that first day when I met Francesca, at the *liceo*, with her tight sweater, high-heeled sandals, and flawless makeup, word spread over the course of the following few days that she dated Athos Michelangeli, who, with his identical twin brother, Alessandro, was a senior, four years ahead of us.

Athos and Alessandro were the princes of the upperclassmen, and legendary. They were known and revered in Montepulciano for their handsome looks—dark, not tall, not short either, with full lips and dark broody eyes, and a despondent and aloof attitude. The attitude was as much part of their persona as were their lifestyle and wealth. Their family was in the fashion business and, because of that, they ran in circles that were at once mysterious and alluring. They had an entourage of loyal and equally handsome friends, they drove a sexy chocolate brown diesel Mercedes-Benz 200 W123, wore lush leather jackets and beautiful clothes, smoked Marlboro reds and lots of pot, and listened to Lou Reed, Led Zeppelin, and the Rolling Stones. They were cool, unreachable, and untouchable. Plus, they reigned over the little pop-up shop that sold our school snacks and sandwiches, which meant they held power over our hunger and money.

By dint of that relationship with Athos, and on top of her own good looks, Francesca had a certain aura.

— *Ahhh*, says Signora Michelangeli holding back further comment, reading me off some phone numbers.

During the *liceo* Francesca and I shared neither routines nor aspirations. Yet, none of that lessened my affection for her, or hers for me. I liked her stories, the vulnerability behind her regal beauty, her naiveté, and her laughter, which often hid fear. In the later years of the *liceo* we shared a desk, on and off, and I listened to her stories of parties and travels with the Michelangeli twins. I helped her with homework and we smoked together in the hallways during breaks.

By then we had much more in common than we had had when we first met, chiefly, love, sex, and heartbreak. Sometimes after school I went home with her to Chianciano and my mom would pick me up on her way back home after her lessons. Francesca's mom would make us lunch, in their post-war highrise building in the new part of Chianciano, then we'd go into Francesca's room and listen to music and call Radio Spot to play our favorite songs.

Francesca and Athos had been seeing each other for three or more years at that point—we were eighteen by then—and often Athos and Alessandro came to pick Francesca up from school. By then the brothers were working for their father, and they'd take Francesca away for a weekend in some hip place or the other, or to Puglia, where their family had some production factories. It was always mysterious, fun, and glamorous, it seemed, though foreign like a telenovela.

Then, one day Alessandro asked Francesca to get us together, me and him. He said he liked me and wanted to spend time with me. He was curious.

— È *molto carina*, he told Francesca, asking her to call me. She is very pretty, he said.

I was secretly thrilled but puzzled at the same time: I was from Cetona, the backwoods, as it were; plus, I was studious and I didn't smoke pot. I didn't quite see our worlds meshing. I didn't see it going anywhere, and I didn't understand what he could want from me.

In any case, intrigued, I guess, or flattered, I called Francesca back. My parents had just gotten a phone, and I remember twirling the cord around my finger, looking out the French doors of the kitchen through my reflection and onto Cetona's countryside while I said it would be ok. It would be nice.

*Carina.* I smiled.

Alessandro must have picked me up from Francesca's house and taken me to Montepulciano, where we hung out at someone's house. We spent several afternoons together around town, at San Biagio, in Piazza Grande, and here and there, talking, and of him with me I remember a joyful and wondrous look, like the world could give nothing but good. The made-up aura, the pretense acquired and worn at the *liceo*, didn't fit. He was neither haughty nor arrogant. Rather, he was tender and kind and a bit unsure of himself. There was something tentative about him, almost chivalrous. I remember manicured hands and soft lips kissing me.

Then, one last time I saw him I remember lying in a bed with him, a narrow bed with white sheets. We had slept together, and he had his arm around me. I remember it as if I were watching myself from the outside in a moment that makes absolutely no sense, and yet not fighting it either. The room was small and dark, somewhere uptown in Montepulciano, and it was dark outside, and I couldn't capture within myself why I was there. Yet, somehow I felt like I had understood something important about choice, and about life, too: that just because I had been invited, it didn't mean I had to go.

It was all an experiment, mostly between me and myself, between expectations and self-definition. Maybe I just wanted to know that the hip boy with the Mercedes liked me, though I don't remember feeling like I knew anyway—or believed it. Or even cared.

Afterwards he left the room so I could get dressed, and that struck me as thoughtful and kind. He *was* thoughtful and kind, tender even, and that stuck with me. Other than that, I don't remember anything about it. It is an intimate episode in an unexplainable vacuum. And I never saw him again.

After his mom gave me his number, I left a message for him and he called me back. My heart skipped. We talked on the phone for a while and he said he wanted to see me, and yesterday he texted saying he was on his way to Cetona. In case I was looking out for him, he said, he was driving a silver Mercedes. I laughed. What else would he be driving?

I thought of our class streaming out of the gate of the *liceo* and he and Athos waiting there at the curb in their old chocolate brown Mercedes with its throaty rumble, "Stairway to Heaven" playing on the stereo and the smoke of a joint threading out the window.

I looked in the mirror and felt ok with my cowboy boots and cut jeans, but nervous nonetheless. I saw him park and I pulled on a shawl. When I walked down from my apartment it was raining and he was standing under the Bar Cavour's awning in a sharpely tailored suit, surrounded by Cetona's old men commenting on the rain.

From beneath the awning they watched us meet and embrace, and it felt unduely romantic. Though his hair is cut close to the scalp and he has lost most of it, I recognized him immediately from his expensive clothes and the face I remembered so clearly. We hugged in the piazza, under the rain. He paused to take me in, to look me in the eyes, and he kissed me on the cheeks, tenderly, as if he didn't want to hurt me.

— *Sono emozionato,* he said. I'm nervous, or emotional. I cupped my hand to his cheek and smiled.

I am too, I said.

We walked through the piazza arm in arm and ducked into the back room of the Bar Sport where we talked for two hours that passed in five minutes. I told him of my life, far away, and he told me of his, surprisingly regular given the aura of his youth and the designs one might have attached to that. He owns a small, high-end men's fashion line. It's his company, not his father's, he pointed out proudly. He built it on his own, and he works and travels constantly to visit suppliers and tailors here and there, to support his family and the taxes that Italy demands now in its new tax righteousness. He has been married for more than twenty years to the same woman, which surprised me and pleased me, and he has two children, now grown. He told me he owns an *oliveto,* an olive grove, and that's where he spends his free time, relieving his stress, pruning his trees.

While he talked I looked at him, tracing him back through my memory. He wears small silver-rimmed glasses now, but he looks the same in every other way—his kind smile and full lips; the brown eyes, a bit weary now; the surprise and youthful wonder in his expressions; his manicured hands, exactly as I remembered them.

The same little children in different bodies, and so we are.

I pulled out an old picture he once gave me of himself so I would remember him. In the picture he has unruly dark hair and he's wearing a black leather jacket and he's rolling a joint. He is barely more than a kid, twenty, maybe, and he is without a care.

— *Questo è a San Biagio.* That's at San Biagio, he said holding the Polaroid.

He had played hooky down at the church, with his brother. He remembered the day, exactly.

I ask him how it happened that we slept together, this incongruity I am trying to make sense of. His face turns tender.

— *Non lo so,* he says smiling. I don't know.

He told me he had thought about it often over the years. On the drive to Cetona he had even called his twin to tell him he was coming to see me and they had talked about it.

— *So solo che eri così carina. Mi piacevi tanto, poi. E poi sei sparita.* You were so lovely, he said. And I liked you so much. But then you disappeared.

I never understood why you just disappeared, he said.

I had never really known any of that. The boy with the chocolate Mercedes had really liked me after all. And I had never known. Or maybe, if I gave myself the power, I didn't care.

Sitting there in the bar, thirty years older both of us, our lives half gone, I felt a sudden surge of tenderness for this singular and un-understood piece of my life into which I had never had insight of myself. Just a sliver of our lives in flux, budding, then fleeting. A girl in search of self; a boy in search of love. Or both in search of love and self. I felt profound joy for seeing him again, this young boy inside the now serious businessman, in his suit, almost surprised by himself.

I wanted to hold his hands and his face and steal that feeling away with me, that morsel of our youth, of life flown; to take it away to a secret place to protect it from time, from forgetfulness and ruin and life, and death, too.

We walked through the piazza slowly, arm in arm, back to his car, then we hugged goodbye for a long time. I watched him drive away in his sleek silver Mercedes, in the rain, the red of the brake lights flashing bright on the pavement, then edging right and disappearing out of the piazza.

The other night I hung out with Alano and Sotero and Bennato and a few others talking and telling stories until very late. When we parted, the piazza was deserted and still, and Alano walked me up the alley. We had had a particularly fun evening laughing together, and he was flirtatious and I was tipsy. When I went to kiss him goodbye on the cheeks he surprised me by kissing me on the mouth, and we kissed. His tongue was warm against the cold, and I felt dizzy with the happiness of being in Cetona. What made me kiss him was laughter, but perhaps also sadness. Missing. The other side.

He hugged me and pressed against me and tried to get me to let him come up.

— *Dai,* he said. C'mon. Let me come up. *Dai, su.*

Aram pierced my heart, his good-looking face, the way I fell in love with him. The way I *am* in love with him, still. My Slim. We have not seen each other in months; communication is virtual, and time is passing.

Yet, I love him still, entirely. His love shores me.

There, pressed against the wall in the Cetona alley I thought of his thin hips, his handsome hands, our love-making, unparalleled. How much he knows about things I care about—the things we care about together—and how smart he is. How special he is. His soul, the kindest I know.

I thought of *ahimsa*, the non-harming principles that led me to vegetarianism. I thought of betrayal and the destructive role it played in my life, and my aspirations for wholeness—the work I did to let go of the chaos. It suddenly all surged forth, and I felt the past caress me like a petal.

Quickly I detached.

— I don't want to do this, I said, retrieving myself. I have a person I love and to whom I am loyal. *Non voglio avere una storia.* I don't want a tryst.

Plus, I added, you have a relationship with Morena, I said, speaking of his girlfriend of many years. Does that not matter to you?

His girlfriend is stout, with short hair, big black eyes, and a Roman nose. She walks through the piazza stolidly, head down, in long skirts, on her way to and from a store she runs off the piazza. Since I arrived she has become friendlier towards me, and we sometimes find ourselves at the same large table at the bar, sharing a drink and a story.

But whether I like her or not—or he loves her or not—makes no difference. I don't really care, I tell him: I don't want to have any relationship that causes harm to anybody, to me or the person I love.

Plus, I don't want to be at the center of some scandalous nonsense in this town at this most important time of mine. I need a clear mind and an unfettered conscience. And I want to be whole.

In the silence of the night I walked up the alley, alone and at peace.

Today my thoughts were marred by clouds of heavy doubt about my writing and my painting as well as the looming pesky questions about my future. I do not know how to support myself here—because I do not have a permit to work—and this continues to undermine my efforts and my tranquility.

To shake it off I put on Bettye LaVette's *Interpretations* and ran toward Sarteano.

About ten kilometers above us, this neighboring hill town has a fabulous municipal Olympic-size swimming pool, an international camping clientele, far more sprawl, and, for some reason I do not understand, a less insular, more evolved population—and not because of the swimming pool, but perhaps.

But what lures me most in that direction is the stretch of countryside between Cetona and Sarteano, an expanse of finely drawn terraces of jade-colored grasses and olive trees that opens wider and wider and grows more and more intricate the farther up you climb. It is simply mesmerizing. The road itself consists of a continuous series of uphill hairpin curves, up and up, that leave Cetona farther and farther down in the valley, with, in between, an ever-more verdant and gorgeous breadth of land.

Sarteano has also long been home to many friends of mine, and indeed there were months in my teens when I and many others spent more awake time in Sarteano than in Cetona. Many friendships were born there: Tiberio, and his brother, Eugenio; my friend Iacopo, who had been my classmate at the *liceo*; Mauro, a sweet guy nicknamed Porchetta; Gianna, and Paola, and Luca, and all sorts of colorful, friendly kids with nicknames of Il Bianco, Fruscio, il Gatto, Gogo, Filippotto, Borsellino, Plise, and Foca. Together, we hung out in Sarteano's *giardini*—the public park—and in its wide piazza, and its many places for ice cream. I relished escaping Cetona's monotony sometimes and making new friends; besides, there was something more open and vivacious about the Sarteanesi, less traditional, less bound.

The guys from Sarteano also spent a lot of time in Cetona, particularly when the pub became a cool place to hang out—*il pub*, pronounced *paab* in Italian. Located underneath the Bar Sport, where part of Nilo's restaurant is now, it had a kitchen, a front room with a long bar counter, a pizza oven and some tables, a large dining room in the back, and outdoor tables, shaded and intimate. When I became of going-out age it was run by Rossana and Teodoro's girlfriend, from Milano. Later, on my summer returns from college it was owned by my friends Baldo, from Trento, and Fiorenza, from Rome. Baldo was a fun, lovable guy with spiky blond hair and blue eyes and a distinct northern accent. They were a gregarious couple, *simpaticissimi*, funny, full of good spirit and hospitality, and on warm summer nights when we lingered outside, never quite ready to call it a night, we always found ways to extend the good time.

— *Si fa una spaghettata?* Baldo would yell out. Should we cook some spaghetti?

We would play music—British and American music that I knew only through my Italian friends, from Pink Floyd to Led Zeppelin and America and Neil Young and more—and we would eat till the wee hours, capping it off by watching the sunrise at the *vasche* in San Casciano, music playing softly into the hills.

*No dark sarcasm in the classroom ... Teacher, leave the kids alone ... We don't need no education ...*

By the time I was nineteen, drugs were pervasive. Everyone, or it seemed to me nearly everyone, smoked pot except for me. One night a whole gang of guys from Sarteano came to the pub and we sat at two tables. There was some kind of conversation about police raids, and someone mentioned that the pub could be next. As if on cue, the doors of the pub flung open and in came a dozen Italian state policemen in dark blue uniforms and big black boots. A couple were dressed in black fatigues, and they looked like they had come looking for something specific.

— No one leaves till we say so, they said, locking the doors.

But a second had passed when I felt something slip between my legs. When I reached down I found a large block of hash wrapped in cellophane. I looked at my friend Iacopo, and then Tiberio, too, and whoever else was at the table, and everyone looked back blankly, ignoring me. I understood what they were asking. I slipped the hash in my pants, and after waiting what I thought was a safe amount of time, I got my bag and walked up to an officer who seemed in charge. I explained that I was a student at the *liceo* and that I had a strict curfew. The officer looked me up and down and opened the door for me.

I escaped. I hid the hash in my motorbike and went home. I heard the following day that the police had strip-searched everyone in the pub but hadn't found anything, and I felt righteous and heroic for having helped my friends, whose liberty I valued.

Relations with Sarteano had a dark side, too, though, a long history of acerbic, medieval-style rivalry fed by a certain bullishness on the part of the Sarteanesi. They had an aggressive fighting streak, and up through our adolescence groups of guys from each of the towns would fight over girlfriends and other matters exactly as if they were stuck in the darkest of the Dark Ages. This used to happen particularly when we were older, eighteen or so, when on weekend evenings we went dancing at La Bussola. The guys would line up against opposing walls, staring at each other, and something would spark: who threw a cigarette butt my way, or who looked at me cross. Or someone would walk straight up to someone's face and punch him, accusing him of something lame like looking at him wrong.

— *M'ha guardato male. Che cazzo vole?* He looked at me wrong. What the fuck does he want?

That would get them going, maybe starting with two, then more would join the fray, and finally it would be a huge pile of guys punching on each other while we girls ran off and finally home.

Eventually it all passed, though, and in summer we'd pack up towels and *panini* and go spend the day at Sarteano's pool, with its cool waters, open grassy fields, and well-stocked café where they sold everything from candy to pizza and gelato. We took the bus in the late morning—after assessing the cap on the mountain—or rode up with our *motorini*, picked our spot in the sun, and spent the day tanning, swimming, and sitting at the edge of the pool, feet dangling in the water, people-watching and flirting with cute boys, which were plentiful in Sarteano. There was nothing but sun and endless, boundless time, and more than one summer love blossomed at that pool, the boys commenting on the girls, and the girls on the boys, wet, sweaty, and young.

In the evening we headed back down the hills and around the hairpin curves leading onto Cetona from above. If it was summer we drove into the afterglow of the setting sun, the rays reaching like tentacles behind Monte Cetona's western slopes, and if it was winter, we delved into the cold and fog that filled the valleys and the countryside in between, the temperature dropping as we went.

There was a sense of completeness to life then, a sense of order, even. Homework was done and there was nothing to do but live, enjoy, and look forward.

Nothing but the simple evanescent serenity of growing up.

And yet, at seventeen or eighteen I developed a prescience, a feeling, almost unconsciously, that I was not destined to remain in Cetona.

My father, I realize now, always addressed my life as if Cetona were a temporary thing, a passage—perhaps because of his experience of growing up in a place he wanted to leave as soon as possible. It was inferred almost that I would be moving on somehow, somewhere, to some other place, perhaps better suited or worthy of me. Was it that that they were American? Was it that, an American view that planted the seed?

I don't know how it happens that our paths take shape; nonetheless, surely I perceived this, and I now know that others did too.

I felt a lot of melancholy at this time, not only for feeling controlled by boys and love, but also because, in fact, Cetona did feel small and entrapping. Judgment and presumption permeated the town and felt defining and hindering at that age. People frequently were mean to each other, full of self-righteous denouncements and verdicts, applying mores simply and without empathy. This offended my free spirit and sense of fairness. I remember speaking out to defend people against *le malelingue* and trying to cast aside judgment, but it was not easy.

It wasn't always, or even often, an accommodating place to be.

My greatest refuge during those times was Allegra's clothing store, Mr. Up, now Mercede's fruit and vegetable store, a tiny box at the edge of the piazza as I climbed the end of Borgo.

Allegra is more than ten years older than me, and I felt at home with and bonded by her older, wiser ways, her real-life experiences and what she liked to do. Tall, thin as a wisp, with long layered black hair that framed a pale, round face with large, dancing black eyes, Allegra was a fount of creativity; she could draw and she could sew, but mostly she knitted the most beautiful sweaters in the world. She interwove leather strips and beads with wool and other materials, and her creations were always a source of magic and wonder for me and the many clients she acquired nationally and internationally. She also was witty, funny, and caring, extremely generous with her time and, later, when I was in college, her clothes.

Mr. Up was my refuge, warm and cozy, with good company and conversation. Allegra and I sat smoking and, in winter, shivering, talking about every topic in the world, from politics to philosophy. With her delicate bird-like voice, and mine ever-deeper, we'd make up funny stories, and try on clothes, and rearrange her shop window, and laugh. Often Tosca joined us, when she was not at university in Pisa, and we regaled each other with our astute observations about life, events, books, movies, the characters in novels, and yes, people in Cetona and their lives and idiosyncrasies, which, however basic and mundane, were always fodder for a full range of opinions and emotions that needed to be expressed in heated conversation, ranging from surprise and indignation to hilarity and simple befuddlement.

— *Ma questa la sapete?* Tosca would begin, mischievously. Have you heard this one?

Who had slept with whom was always the favorite topic, and the juicier the details and the darker the intrigue, the better—if a woman slept with her sister's boyfriend, for example, which happened, or cousins sleeping with each other's husbands, which also happened. And it's not like in Cetona you wouldn't find out! Indeed, in Cetona all is known to someone, and while I was not particularly good at gathering the juicy bits—I found the activity of snooping somewhat objectionable—Tosca was a master of it and I was not above listening and laughing.

Often all this talk snaked its way sneakily back to a woman we nicknamed Madame Bovary, who had bewitched and seduced a number of men related by blood or other semi-familial connections during secretive encounters in far-flung places while wearing short skirts and no underwear. *Senza mutande!* No underwear, people asked incredulously. She had woven a dangerous plot studded with explosive secrets—a scandal waiting to happen!—and as she stood on the precipice of moral downfall, there, from Mr. Up's window we watched, awaiting her future evildoings to become the tastiest subject of our sweet conjecture.

When spring came, we threw open Mr. Up's door and hung out in the doorway, looking and watching the goings-on of the piazza. By the time I was eighteen I was suffering a bit of malaise, needing a larger world. I read a lot and wrote, I set journalism as my lofty professional goal, and I imagined myself out there doing something great. Allegra encouraged me, and finally when I started thinking about university, she incited me to leave my nest and spread my wings.

Meanwhile, during those years of tumultuous romances Sabrina continued to be my greatest confidante outside of Cetona.

In the stolen moments at school while teachers changed classes, but sometimes even during class itself, we passed written notes under the desk to share the burning secrets of our teenage loves, each in our own towns, she with a blond soccer player from Castiglione, me with another, dark-haired, from Cetona. We described them to each other in minute detail, and we confided the evolution of this electric feeling called love. I wrote in my daily scheduler, Peanuts-themed, the name of the loved one circled over the list of homework, translations by Cicero or whoever it was. Already in those notes fermented what would play out as a common agonizing relationship with boys and love, which, it turns out, never changed during the course of our lives. Sabrina and I have lived love unsurely, like an uncomfortable bargain, and, looking back, that seems to have been foretold even when we were classmates.

I wish now we had told all the boys to fuck off; but then again, they were achingly sweet.

After our graduation from the *liceo* Sabri went off to the University of Siena to study finance and banking, a choice her parents made more than herself. They could not indulge her ambition to be a doctor, which she always regretted abandoning. She was no banker at heart. Through the years Sabrina and I wrote each other letters, and on my trips home we visited more or less consistently. I was in her wedding, in Castiglione, and she came to mine, in Cetona, dressed in an azure off-the-shoulder dress in which she looked radiant. Then, on one visit some time later she was breast-feeding her newly born son, Edoardo, and, some years later, a daughter, Caterina. Children seemed to have given her purpose, though not completeness.

Then, somehow, we had not seen each other in close to ten years, all through our forties.

On the train to see her this week, I look at the landscape passing before me: the ramshackle sheds near the patchwork of *orti*, ingeniously rigged against code; boards of scrap wood assembled into chicken coops; and chairs and tables set up for the farmer to rest and *stare a veglia*—to hang out and have a glass of wine. I try to follow places with my eyes—a mysterious shed, a beautiful building next to the tritest of edifices—places I will never visit, home to someone I will never know. Places that contain the happiness alike Cetona's, a little place like that.

When the train stops at a station, I long for the voices of the food and beverage vendors who in decades past crowded the trains on the platforms to sell drinks and *panini* with mortadella.

— *Panini! Aranciata! Birra! Coca-Cola! Panini!!* they yelled as the train pulled in and came to a stop.

As frantic travelers got on and off, famished passengers on the train reached their hands out the windows holding money and yelling out their orders. Quickly, the vendors reached up with the goods and within seconds the exchange was made. Now those food and beverage vendors with their delicious sandwiches and their competent voices that carried through the crowds are long gone, replaced by sad, silent, steely machines carrying old sandwiches whose provenance I do not care to know.

When I got to the train station in Siena Sabrina was there to greet me. As the train slowed and came to a stop, I picked her out in the crowd through the window. She was wearing a wig of highlighted light-brown hair cut at the nape of her neck to mask the effects of the chemotherapy she had been undergoing to treat her breast cancer. Her face was taut and her big brown eyes weary. I knew from looking at her through the window that the illness had exhausted her already. Her life recently has been a relentless gauntlet of treatments that seem to break her rather than fix her.

Standing there in the crowded station we hugged and Sabrina smoothed her wig with her hand, almost unconsciously. I noticed she has stopped biting her nails and it made me smile.

Over the following three days we walked the streets of Siena together and talked. About the death of her parents over the years, which had angered her and left her untethered too soon in life. About our divorces and heartbreak, and about our boyfriends and respective griefs and disappointments, and there have been many. About her work, as a successful bank manager outside of Florence, which leaves her flat. She wanted to be something different, all along.

She was angry about being sick, furious at her cancer, and she was scared. Her fear stood right there before me, all over her face and her eyes that darted here and there and her fingers twitchy and uneasy. I wanted so much to say something that would matter —that she would beat it, that she would make it. All the American pragmatic, optimistic things one hears said. Could I really reassure her of anything at all? Everything felt like a grotesque platitude. I hugged her instead and moved to easier ground in memories, the only certainty we had.

We talked about our impressions of who we had been, and who we had become. Was I happy, she asked? Yes, in many ways yes, I was; but, then, how could I explain the grief I felt, in some measure, always? And Aram far away, this man who I loved more than I had ever loved before, and, yet, who I had endangered to come here ... How to understand that?

And yet, she did. She understood me.

We had changed through the years, but then also stayed the same — our self-images still challenged, our attachments to love still heartbreakingly fragile, our expectations so high. Our selves broken at birth, it seems, like there were some cells missing. We met broken already, like we could never find someone else like us on the other side, and perhaps for the first time we came to recognize that knowledge in each other's eyes and to find some kind of solidarity in it. I saw in her what I feel in me, the same thing I knew at the *liceo*—a fear of never being all that we are, and never being fully loved for all that we are.

And then this sense of eternal grief for something missing. Something ineluctable and unfixable. Life, its immensity too big to grasp.

We let the silence fall on those questions, peacefully. We laughed a lot, too, about old boyfriends.

— You didn't like his thing, she said laughing about an old lover of mine.

She corrected my versions of events. She recalled my every love, and my every tear. She polished my memory of myself, and in fact, she remembered me much better than I did.

We wandered into stores together and tried on clothes together for the first time in our lives. We stepped into churches I had never seen. We visited the Duomo, which neither of us had done in years, and marveled at the beauty beyond imagination that had surrounded us our entire lives and that yet we had never looked at together. We made dinner at her house with her boyfriend and her children, who are young teens and who I had not seen since they were babies. I watched her be a mom, indulgent as I would have expected, and endlessly kind. And I watched her cook.

While she rested in the afternoon, overwhelmed by the fatigue of treatments, I made myself tea in her kitchen and I sat quietly looking at her things — her pots and pans, her wine glasses, her dishes, everything so orderly. I examined how she organized her life, and the pillows on her couch. I revisited our old copy of the *Divina Commedia*, full of our scribbles from the *liceo*. It brought me melancholy, yet it calmed me that she had it. I liked seeing it all. Her life seemed so much more organized than mine and it comforted me. I bathed in her bathtub, which she prepared for me, and used the soap she put out for me. I looked at her makeup and smelled her bottles of perfume, Chanel Number 5 among them, with its scent of roses. Dipping my soul in an intimacy I had forgotten, I used her lotion and I felt cared for.

Mostly, I lived in the warmth of a slice of her that I had not known.

Sabrina lives in a beautiful house on the outer circle of Siena Nord—a bit like my house in Cetona, one side toward town, one side toward the countryside. We stood together on her terrace and looked out at the landscape of golds and greens extending to the horizon, and I thought how lucky she was to be there in that landscape.

And yet, sick.

Upstairs, as we got ready for the night, standing in an atrium outside her bedroom under the soft light of a chandelier, Sabrina took off her wig and turned to look at herself in a large mirror.

I breathed in deeply and looked at her.

Her eyes, dark scared pools, glowed large in the mirror. I walked up to her and touched her porcelain face and ran my hand over her bald head. It was soft and vulnerable and bare in a way I had not experienced anything. She surrendered to my hand trustingly and looked me in the eyes. I felt tears on my face, but she did not question them.

She wanted me to see her, and I saw her, and she knew where my tears came from. Love, my love for her, and my fear for her, too.

I felt overcome by the starkness of the imagery, her strength and survival, yet her frailty and fear, life and the shadow of death mixed into one. In the mirror it all merged—who we were when we sat side by side at our desk at the *liceo,* with all our promise and life ahead, and who we are becoming, faced with our death.

Sabrina glanced back at herself in the mirror, her eyes glowing in her thin face, and she looked luminous and pure and eternal. I was filled with gladness, for being here with her and for being alive.

The following day, on my train ride home in the late afternoon the landscape turned dark and dotted with lights. I watched my reflection in the window next to my fellow passengers, each quiet, absorbed in his or her private thoughts, and I tried to capture the image of my face from years ago. It ran away, elusive.

At a stop, a woman got on with her husband and a baby just a few months old. After she took off her coat and scarf and settled in her seat, the husband handed the woman the baby. Unbuttoning her top, she took out her full white breast and began breast-feeding her child. No covers, no scarf, no anything. The baby's head was like Sabrina's, and she took the breast calmly, fully, in the hum of the train.

An elderly woman sitting across from the mother and the baby watched them and cooed.

— *Ecco. Tutto a posto,* she said, smiling, as the baby began to feed. There, all set. All is good.

And I hope it will be. I certainly hope it will.

Sometime during the course of the *liceo* my father began mentioning the idea of me going to the States for college. How did this happen, I ask myself. How did this idea, whose wisdom—whose fit for me—I have so often questioned, come to be?

What would have happened had I gone to the University of Milan instead? What would have been wrong with that?

Certainly, the impulse came from my father. His life—my parents' lives—had always implicitly represented a larger world, and perhaps even a return to America. Plus, I wouldn't have had the knowledge, or the heart, to trigger the impulse. I didn't *have* the impulse.

To my father, on the other hand, it made sense: My English was rudimentary; Italian university—and Italy as a whole—was chaotic and unaccountable; and, as he saw it, there was a big world out there waiting for me. Of course, my father's perspective would have been colored by his own experience of wanting to leave his hometown as soon as possible, and in his case, preferably never to return. I don't think my father really understood or related to my attachment to Cetona, to Italy, intellectually or emotionally. He didn't expect me to become one with the town, to be like the people of Cetona, which I thought I was, and which, probably, from his perspective, was merely a passing phase that I would quickly outgrow.

By the time I was midway through the *liceo* he had begun ranting about the company I kept and the lack of ambition or intellectual worth of friends and boyfriends. Boyfriends specifically were on his shoot-down list—a regular, sarcastic, cruel tearing down. He didn't take them seriously, like they were cartoon figurines that could never be permanent presences in my future life. Besides, his cultural references did not apply to where I was, where he had brought me, and the language did not apply either. As much as he loved being in Italy, for him it was a half-life, a parenthesis, perhaps.

For me, though, it was the whole deal.

I realize that life in Cetona bred relationships for me—for all of us, perhaps—that likely would not have otherwise sprung in a larger, more diverse world. The spatial limitations of small towns make strange bedfellows; affective affinity surges to cover up for lack of other commonalities and builds a foundation of familiarity and knowledge stronger and more enduring than selective choice—or so it seemed. And I wanted nothing more than to be part of what I was already part of—that familiarity and knowledge. I had been brought here and given this, and now this was me: the music, the love, the fountain, the hills, Maria, Beppa, Ave ... the everything that being part of Cetona made me. It was just the way it was.

But that doesn't mean I would have stayed, anyway.

— *Eri diversa. Sei sempre stata diversa,* Andrea told me recently. You were different. You had always been different.

*Sibilla, mezza serpe e mezza anguilla.*

Perhaps it was inevitable simply because of my parents— because dangling somewhere in the background voice of my life at home was always another identify and, indeed, another intended destiny, that born of American parents and their makeup, expectations and judgments, and their destiny, too. Throughout my life I always viewed them and their culture as a small part of the whole, surrounded entirely as it was by Cetona, but perhaps that small part bled and breathed impermanence and otherness into me like a toxic fume I inhaled unbeknownst to me, and I was never going to stay. People— lovers who could love me only so much because they knew this—said that: You were never going to stay.

Perhaps it was just bait I took to win my father's approval, or meet his standard, which, after all, was the highest I knew, and with my best interest at heart. The problem was that it was an American standard, born of an American life, and it was not my life. But no one thought of adjusting the standard to me.

Whatever the case, let's agree that my realities coalesced to make this idea a fait accompli—I don't remember any debate—and Dad presented me with a list of the ten or so colleges to which I would apply, drawn mostly from the Ivy League. Because there are no guidance counselors in Italy and I would be the only kid to go through this process, my father made my application process his personal charge: He requested the forms, corresponded in his meticulous calligraphy with the schools about deadlines and requirements, and made sure I had enough time to take the SATs not once but twice.

Each week Dad gave me a list of deadlines to meet: essays, teacher recommendations, grade reports, etc. At the *liceo* it was a big deal—my professors had never experienced this—though, in a vacuum, the process was relatively peaceful. There was no competitiveness among friends, and no great pride to it, either. My friends in Cetona, with rare exception, thought Yale was a lock company. And no one, absolutely no one, would be on this path with me.

To be fair, my father aimed high on my behalf, and I think his was an act of love. Nonetheless, all choices were made through his lens, not mine. There was no linguistic consideration, and no consideration of place, of the fact that I would be moving from a miniscule town in Tuscany to New Haven, Connecticut, or Providence, Rhode Island, or Boston. Would I fit? Were they the right places for me?

I can conclude that he had high confidence in me and my abilities, and I am flattered. He was right: I could endure and succeed. But the voyage held many treacherous unknowns, such as my emotional ability to adapt, my cultural and linguistic ability to succeed, and perhaps more importantly, the odds, external and internal, that the match would nurture me to thrive for all I had in me.

To thrive in a universe from which I had been removed and that was no longer mine.

Indeed, since early childhood I had read very little in English and I recoiled from speaking the language much. I understood it, basically, but did not work in it or study in it. By the time I applied to college, I had read *Silas Marner, The Adventures of Huckleberry Finn, Catcher in the Rye,* and one or two Shakespeare plays, which were less decipherable to me than Latin. I spent a month in the care of the Hargraves, dear friends of the family in Rochester, NY, attending a remedial high school summer English class, from which I got kicked out for smoking, then Dad ordered me the SAT prep book and put me on a study regimen (colleges refused to let me take the TOEFL because I was American). I was a straight-A student, save for math, and once I had accepted that this was going to happen, I cooperated.

The closest place for me to take the SATs was an American school in Florence. On the scheduled date I took the train, got off in some suburb famous for the killing of multiple couples by the so-called *Mostro di Firenze*, walked the short way to the prestigious school on the hill, and took the test amid children of expats all of whom were attending American schools. It was the first test I had ever taken in the English language, an unprecedented testing experience from which I retain my first taste of fierce institutional competitiveness and the word *spoonerism*. Absolutely nothing more. Oh, yes, while waiting for the train home, a beautiful lesbian woman accosted me and tried to kiss me. It was an interesting day, all told.

For my applications I wrote compelling if grammatically imperfect essays about my studies and my life, and eventually I came to the States for college interviews. It was the beginning of my experience with the American college gauntlet, the process by which one's ego and sense of privilege become increasingly stroked and refined to feed an ever-expensive educational market and, inevitably, to compound America's ever-growing educational and income disparities. In retrospect, had I understood the makings and code of American college admissions and economics I would have boycotted it all on moral and philosophical grounds.

My interviewers at Yale, Williams, and others stuck to basic and forgettable questions about academics. At Wesleyan, the pinnacle, the academic dean engaged me in an exciting and wide-ranging conversation about capitalism and American individualism in contrast to socialism and my Italian upbringing. And then came Princeton, the low point. The interviewer, an elderly prim woman—how did someone match her to me so thoughtlessly?—asked me to tell her about life at the *liceo*. She wasn't interested in who I was, what I thought or aspired to, or even what we were learning: She just wanted to know *what it was like*, what the grading system was like, and, most important but not in so many words, whether we cheated. Fully aware of Princeton's notorious honor code, to illustrate the camaraderie and cultural atmosphere of the *liceo* I chose to gleefully narrate stories of our class sharing Latin translations on the insides of packs of Marlboros folded like paper airplanes that soared through the smoke-filled air of our classroom. I think I even told her about Don Pipo and us boycotting his class.

I sensed a mathematical nature in the exchange—a weighing and checking off of boxes—and this made me want to shock her. I wanted to ruffle her supercilious ways, to outrage her vapid, condescending concept of intellectual and moral worth. The more the woman paled, the more I talked, and the more she took notes, never for a second considering the cultural context of my stories or trying to broaden the conversation into something greater about my ethics or my education. The gate-keeper to the ivory tower could have turned it around, but she was not interested in any meaningful truth—certainly not my truth.

While making room for legacies and other hypocrites with prestigious last names and large bank accounts, Princeton threw me in its sanctimonious ethical garbage can, without reason.

It was a blessing. In retrospect, I wish they all had.

When the following fall came to Cetona—the fall before my last year of *liceo*—it found us, Andrea and I, parked in the piazza under the great protective branches of the *tiglio*. The windshield was covered with tiny white flowers and the air was filled with the tree's intoxicating sweet scent we all knew so well.

We were talking and listening to music when we heard a rap on the window. It was late, one or two in the morning. Maria stood by the car. From her face I could tell she was upset and she demanded that Andrea get out. Had she known earlier? Had she seen us from her window, or had she heard Andrea's car?

We thought we were hidden, invisible perhaps, in our own world of secluded and robbed happiness. We had been seeing each other secretly for a while by then. I don't remember how it happened, or why ... Andrea had been with Maria for two or three years by then. In the landscape of Cetona's shifting relationships, theirs had acquired a patina of durability. They were the good-looking couple who seemed to represent an assured future happiness, and certainly there was an expectation of them marrying. They were *fidanzati in casa*, which means their parents knew and approved of their relationship, and they went to each other's houses for lunches and dinners. Andrea chauffeured her everywhere and was at her beck and call. Maria was the princess, and he a bit of the unwilling prince.

Little is as it seems.

Sitting at the bar, I ask Andrea how it happened and why. Did I not care about Maria? Plus, why would I even have wanted him back? What brought us back together?

Andrea's eyes these days remind me in their sternness of Sean Connery, dark and brooding. He is regimented and serious, and he inhabits his world rather squarely. His business building custom-made cabinetry and doing other woodworking—he just built the Collegiata's new altar, a splendid piece and an honor—is thriving in spite of the generally listless economy. He is hard-working, self-made, above-board, which in this country is rare; plus, he is doing well, and, as he sees it, everyone should be able to do the same. His perspective—and everyone's here—is firmly rooted in the politics and dysfunctions of Italy, which soak everything with cynicism and to which I can relate now only peripherally. Our worlds are, in fact, at this point, entirely different, and in recent years we have not shared much.

Nonetheless, Andrea is warm and kind to me, sometimes flirtatious when I see him. We remain bonded by an easy, old affection, and, of course, the past is still ours to roam. It is our glue, and it brings tenderness to his eyes.

What drew us back together?

Someone—the mysterious voices of the town—said I had resolved to get him back, out of revenge.

That does not fit me, not then, not now. I have never been the plotting kind, or even strategic. It sounds like something someone in Cetona might say.

I do, instead, vaguely remember a violent fight at La Bussola, late night, involving a guy I was seeing in Sarteano, a toxic matter I had entangled myself in—another mystery, a case of wanting to make things better, of saving someone. Andrea was there and he gave me a ride back to Cetona. In a way, he protected me, kindly—the way I had imagined him to be. The way I had thought he was years earlier. The way I *knew he was*. Through that act of concern we slowly rekindled a friendship, and then a closeness, and, after all those years and all that heartbreak, he redeemed himself to me.

Or maybe he had just stayed inside of me all along, that seed gestating, never gone.

In any case, there we were under the tree, in love this time, and we had been caught.

The following morning was a Sunday, I remember, and I walked up Borgo tentatively, knowing I had to face the judgment of the town— and, my own, of course—and oh, it was waiting for me. It was sunny and people were milling about the fountain and outside the Bar Sport, and wherever I turned no one spoke to me. The news of the betrayal of Maria had spread as if carried by a sleep fairy with her dust, and by morning people were ready to cast their sentence, beginning at Mercede's store. I remember the violence of this, and the outrage in me, so much injustice wrapped in my lap to hold. Mercede herself stood outside surrounded by a group of women, including Maria's mom. They turned away, from me and from Andrea.

That afternoon Maria walked into the bar and threw at his chest (did she miss his face?) all the jewelry he had given her over their time together. Dozens of gold chains and bracelets lay strewn over him cascading like many yellow ribbons onto his legs and the floor. Then she walked out, seething.

— *Che stupida!* she says, bursting out in laughter when I remind her of this. How stupid of me! I could have sold all that gold now!

We laugh about this together like kids, again, and I feel grateful for the balm of time. Over the years Maria and I have talked much and with good humor about this unfortunate chapter, and we have retrieved in our drama good reason for self-deprecation and humor. We have also found some kind of wisdom in it: In the end, things went the way they should have, for her and for me.

I tell her I am sorry, again. You don't need to say it again, she says, rolling her eyes. We are sitting outside the bar, steps from where she threw that gold. She takes my hand and reminds me that, after all, she had done the same to me, and, I would add, rather unapologetically.

In self-denial I want to protest that we were younger when she took Andrea from me. That the stakes were lower. But were they? Did my hurt count less? Not really.

Back to those days, though, and to Andrea and me, in the years since we had had our first relationship he had grown back into a funny, sunny, and sweet person. People in Cetona say I brought out the sun in him, and maybe that's true. I always say that we draw different hues from each other, like color from color. Or maybe it was the fact that I adored him. He was reliable, honest, and generous, and I felt safe. Not to mention that I was enamored of his every part—the dark tousled hair that kissed his shoulders, his smile, playful and tender, his sculpted body, his prowess as a soccer player, his seriousness about his work, his love for his mother, and his funny sense of humor about people and situations. And the way he walked out of the showers after soccer practice, hair wet and slicked back, back taut and damp, and always legs a bit askew, like the goalie he was.

And, finally, and perhaps most important since my youthful wound, he treated me kindly. He hugged me and kissed me everywhere we went like he had won the best prize at the town fair. He loved me, finally, and the fact that we had many detractors—in addition to my father, who, disdaining him, simply ignored him—bonded us perhaps more.

We had six or seven months together before I had to go.

By then I had applied to the colleges of my choice and was eventually accepted. We had a phone, finally, and I had called from our kitchen to get the admissions results. Of course, I told you about Princeton, but when I called Yale, my father, eavesdropping, inferred the good news and did a celebratory jig in the living room, much more heartfelt than mine. Nonetheless, I was proud, and Andrea was, too.

Every evening, after I had finished studying, he picked me up in the piazza to go to his house, silent out in the countryside, where we lay with our arms around each other, talking—about what, and did we care?—and smoking cigarettes, accepting and embracing the today with ease and simplicity. At night we took long rides in his car in the dark in the countryside with the headlights turned off, which scared me yet thrilled me. We sat at the fountain with those who would have us, and I went to his soccer practices and games. The months flew by in stolen happiness.

They were the happiest months of my life, Andrea has said many times over the course of our lives. I would take all the misery in the world in exchange for the happiness of our time together, he told me in letters after I left.

And he did. We did.

As for Maria and me, we didn't talk for a long time, a couple of years, which I did not bemoan. In truth, our friendship had slackened during her relationship with Andrea. She had isolated herself in the steadiness, and, in the meantime, I had spread my wings. But most important, in getting together with Andrea she had hurt me, and the wound had festered. I had never borne her rancor, but when the tables finally turned, in some way I felt like it was OK and I knew that eventually it would pass.

Sometime during college I wrote her a letter, which has gone missing, saying that I was sorry. It went unanswered, and from Cetona I heard that she had nothing to say to me. A year or so later I wrote her again:

"... I hug you anyway, thinking that perhaps the memories of our conversations, of our laughs together, of our reciprocal and common despairs will one day give us ground on which to build new things. *... E un giorno, sedute alla fontana, in uno dei miei tanti viaggi a Cetona, forse torneremo a parlare, ci abbracceremo, mi racconterai degli anni in cui non ti ho vista ... e forse un giorno capiremo che c'è qualcosa di più fondamentale del dolore. C'è la felicità. Ti voglio bene, S.* ... And one day, sitting at the fountain, in one of my many trips back to Cetona we will go back to speaking, we will hug, and you will tell me of the years we didn't see each other ... And one day we will understand that between us there is something more fundamental than pain. There is happiness. I love you, S."

Happily, that would turn out to be true.

I rented a car for two days to take advantage of a ray of sun in a three-month deluge and I went for a ride to Radicofani, Trevinano, and Contignano one day, and then Monticchiello, Pienza, and Montepulciano the next.

In some ways, it was the route to the *liceo*, and I thought back to our old blue and white bus careening through the landscape with Cresti at the helm, the bus driver on my route. Tall, lanky, and bald, Cresti was funny when in the right mood, but steely when someone messed with the peace of his bus, on which we students were customers among other customers. While negotiating the demanding curves up and down the hills, he monitored us, partly with the help of the rearview mirror, and partly with the aid of his sidekick, a short humorless man by the nickname of Fruscio who checked our tickets and kept things clean. He tolerated no bullying, fighting, or messing around, particularly from the troublemakers, mostly boys but a few bully girls too, mostly from Sarteano, one of whom was notorious for picking fights.

Cresti liked me, though, and when he learned that my mom worked in Montepulciano and that we crossed her every day on the drive back to Cetona after school, he began to look out for her white Renault 4. He'd yell for me as he saw her approaching and he'd slow the bus and honk, and I'd run to the window and stick out my arm to wave. Mom would do the same, and then she was gone, around a curve, off to work till evening.

The voyage was a slog then, but now, it seems, from everywhere it bears a gift, a surprise. I saw the piazza of Pienza without a single person in it and I savored the silence of the deserted streets. Driving, I almost went off the road a few times staring out the window at the winter countryside, aching tender in the low light, like coverlets of green velvet thrown over the hills, soft, splendid, and perfect in every way. My dad used to do that—almost driving off the road—distracted by the sight of a house or a hill, head turned in wonder to the countryside the whole way, a habit I found alarming and that now I understand.

Toward Contignano the land gets harsh, with slopes slashed by sharply cut gorges casting deep shadows as if the sun had suddenly gone out within them, only to return uphill to warm fields of the most brilliant of greens and old farmhouses, ancient and still. I followed country roads I had never traveled and saw *borghi* I had never seen, and old forsaken houses with shutters perfect between turquoise and aqua, and abandoned haystacks and pigsties decaying where I could imagine living a different life if I could invent a new one, or a past one if I could remake it. I saw fields I had photographed before in different seasons years ago.

It was late afternoon when I drove back from Monticchiello. The sun was setting already and the light was tender and eternal, made of all the past I remember and the future I care to dream. The sky was one with the fields and the hills, and I realized that it owns me, this landscape owns me.

It marks me, like the touch of a lover, forever enduring.

Nicola, Maresciallo Colasanti's son, drove me to take my *esame di maturità*. We had developed a close friendship through the years, from my days dating Lucio, and we spent a lot of time together, at the pool in Sarteano, and dancing, too, always in our large coterie of friends.

Nicola looked a lot like his dad, and had the same upright composure, but, contrary to his father, he had an easy and contagious laugh that inhabited him without restraint. When he surrendered to it, tears streamed down his face and he threw his head back and shut his eyes in a way that still makes me smile. He had full, well-drawn lips and his central incisors overlapped a bit, and when he laughed he sometimes covered his mouth, which was a signal of utter delight. He liked to talk about things on the edge—sex, oddities, strange gossip— and relished the act of venturing into the forbidden. He had a mischievous side, childlike, and we laughed and laughed.

Yet, when he got pissed off—politics, mostly—his face got crazy, his almond-shaped eyes grew big, and his anger caused him to walk off like he was about to emit smoke from his ears.

— *Se non me ne vo t'ammazzo!* he liked to say. If I don't leave I will kill you!

By then Nicola had graduated from *ragioneria* and he was working as an accountant. Anyway, I loved him dearly and I was happy when he offered to take me to my exam (I think having your parents take you was uncool).

— *Sei pronta?* he asked as I got into his car at the end of the piazza in the early morning.

He looked at me anxiously. I had nothing, no notebooks or books. Not a pencil. At that point what I knew was in my head, and I knew it was there.

The *esame di maturità* worked like this: Every year in late spring a national committee randomly drew and announced the academic subjects in which all graduating students would be examined, three oral and two written, different in each type of school. We greeted the selections with elation or horror depending on our disposition toward the subjects and proficiency: Math was harsh, as was chemistry or Latin, or at the *liceo classico*, Greek.

For the oral exams, in addition to the subjects chosen by the government, each student prepared an additional subject of his or her choice—say, history, or physics—that was either a back-up or a plus.

We had a month or so at the end of school to prepare, on our own, and on the assigned date one by one we went before a committee of teachers unknown to us, assembled randomly from around the country in order to eliminate favoritism. Teachers from Sicily came to Tuscany, and those from Tuscany went to Liguria, and so forth. The only friendly face in the room was a home teacher, an advocate of our choice, and we selected Signora Vinciarelli.

That year at the *liceo scientifico* we drew Italian and math for our written tests, which were day-long affairs, and philosophy and Italian lit for our oral exam. I added French lit to mine. The Italian written test offered a choice of three essay questions that sounded something like this: *The political situation in Italy has been marked by the election of the 100th government in fifty years and the merger of municipalities and regions, with complicated consequences for our political system. Drawing from your study of history, literature, philosophy and science, and particularly our study of Plato, Machiavelli, and Hobbes, Fascism and the history of Europe between the World Wars, please expand on the implications for democracy, exploring predictions for the future both locally and nationally.* I am exaggerating a bit but not wildly.

The oral exam, meanwhile, was meant to be a spry intellectual conversation between the committee and the examinee, an opportunity to blend our subjects and skip and jump more or less fluidly between fields of knowledge. The teachers sat around a long conference table at which a chair was reserved for the examinee, in a room that was open to the public. After an initial awkward hello and introduction, things moved and evolved depending on how prepared we were. In some cases the exam went badly right out of the gate—with deafening silence. A teacher would try to ignite something with a tentative question: What would you like to talk about? Sometimes that worked, and sometimes not.

My exam was seamless, fortunately. I started somewhere and one thread led to another all the way to the end. I remember little of what I talked about—D'Annunzio and Fascism, I remember, and Sartre and Camus. I felt like a butterfly floating in the air between ideas, and fortunately my French sang that day, thanks much to my sweet Zia's expert coaching. But I had worked my ass off; I had spent months preparing, studying in the quiet of the new park they had then built in Cetona and upstairs in the attic of our house.

When I finished, the teachers at the table rose to shake my hand and congratulated me. Vinciarelli was beaming, as was Nicola, who sat through my exam in a chair set against the perimeter of the room.

— *Bravissima*, he said, hugging me proudly.

And that was that, the end of the *liceo* and five years of our lives. There was no ceremony or fanfare, no parades or awards, no robes or gifts: just a sheet of paper in the hallway of the *liceo* with grades posted in black ink. All of us in our class graduated, some of us at the top of the heap, others lost somewhere in the middle, and we moved on to the next chapter of our lives, some to work, some to university in Milan or Bologna, Siena or Florence.

And me, the farthest of all.

Those were happy days that felt charmed and promising, though in retrospect it is hard for me to understand how I compartmentalized all this, wrapping up my exam and getting ready to leave. As if I were catching a subway uptown, or a train to Florence.

What was I thinking? Perhaps I thought I would come back to work and live. How else could it have been? I didn't know how to live anywhere else. Or perhaps I was not thinking, because I couldn't grasp what it meant. I couldn't fathom it. I remember being excited, like I had been chosen, like I was going on a special adventure, perhaps simply because of the meaning that it all seemed to hold for my father.

Birdie, you will have the best of both worlds! he used to say.

After my exam, at the beginning of August Andrea and I took off for a week in Bolzano, near the Austrian border. We met up with Pierpaolo and Mariachiara, who were by then a couple. Up north, the streets and the villages were clean and crisp—everything was so orderly and *northern*—and our hotel was luxurious. We slept in a bed with plump pillows and thick linens the plushness of which I had never seen, and we ate fresh blueberries from the market and delicious food, which Pierpaolo and I loved but Mariachiara and Andrea hated.

As always happened when you put me and Mariachiara together, we giggled and laughed uncontrollably at the least opportune of times, and I think once we were even asked to leave a restaurant, or maybe Pierpaolo himself asked us to leave because he was so embarrassed. In any case, we had a good time, and in spite of the fact that my father was furious about me going—perhaps he thought I would elope—I remember being at peace, having earned a moment with Andrea away from Cetona before my departure.

The refrain among us at the time were verses from Lucio Dalla's song "Anna e Marco," which mentioned the distance from here to America, prophetically:

*... Ma dimmi tu dove sarà*
*dov'è la strada per le stelle*
*mentre ballano si guardano e si scambiano la pelle*
*E cominciano a volare*
*con tre salti sono fuori dal locale*
*con un aria da commedia americana*
*sta finendo anche questa settimana*
*Ma l'America è lontana*
*dall'altra parte della luna,*
*che li guarda e anche se ride*
*a vederla mette quasi paura.*

We drove the long way back from Bolzano on the *autostrada* through the mountains, in the rain, Andrea's hand at the wheel, broad and strong, his mind clear and safe, which I trusted in the most treacherous of conditions at the highest of speeds.

And then I left.

I still try, after thirty years, to make sense of this event, and this is part of what brings me back here. Did I realize how this departure would alter my life?

— *Sì, e no. Ma eri convinta,* says Andrea, back in the bar. Yes and no, in a way, but you were convinced of what you were doing.

You had a goal in mind, he said; you had thought about it. It was what you wanted.

I don't remember it this way, not entirely. All these years my memory has made my father the maker of my fate, the man who willed me to go, who wove the path for my exit—especially in more recent years as I have become so keenly aware of just how vast the impact of leaving Cetona has been on me.

I still believe that is the case. I would never in my heart of hearts have wanted any of this. I had no idea, and no one told me.

I *do* remember a place in me, a part of me that had tired of my small town, and before that, a part that did not really belong, that felt extraneous. I felt independent, and idealistic, and I was bored. I liked the idea of the girl from Cetona heading out into the unknown world, like Ulysses, and people were proud of me—they cheered for me.

And yet. I could have gone to Paris, or to Switzerland instead. I had considered it, in fact, and talked about it with Maria. I had hatched a dream, at one point, of going to interpreter's school in Geneva so I could write in different languages. I would work in Italy, we decided, and Maria and I would be close forever. Forever. It would have been a good thing for me.

What happened to that dream, and to *her*, that girl deep inside me that didn't speak? Perhaps her identity and place in the world were already silently torn and confused between flags and languages and here and there, and already in such a state of veiled unbelonging, that her voice was lost in the hum.

Seeking answers, I go meet Signora Vinciarelli at a restaurant at the top of Montepulciano, by our old school. I am comforted by the sight of this old teacher of mine—her gentle eyes like chocolate drops, her dark hair cut like a page-boy, her stance in the world stable and broad-footed. We are happy to see each other, and I am comforted by the fact that we share enough memory of each other to care to meet.

She asks me about my book.

— È la storia di come Cetona m'ha rovinato la vita, I say, laughing. It's the story of how Cetona ruined my life.

— You mean the story of your internal divide, she asks, with a knowing look.

I nod. I feel like leaning my head on her shoulder and sobbing.

Over food and good red wine we talk about our lives, her daughter and grandchildren, and the loss of her husband to cancer. Then we talk about the liceo, my classmates, Yale, and the decisions that haunt me. Where I belong, and why I left. What home is.

I ask her who I was then, when I was her student. I have forgotten what moved me, and I need to remember.

— You always wanted the truth, about everything, and you saw yourself equal to adults, she told me, reaching back through the years but without hesitation. You were strong, you wanted to participate in the world, and you had important things to do. You believed in things.

— Eri diversa. You were different.

Yes, perhaps I was different, I know that now, but, of course, that didn't mean I had to go across the ocean to be different or to do good things (which maybe my father thought). And it didn't mean that awaiting me across the ocean was some kind of promised land simply because I had been born there—birthplace being the only supporting string of this connection. And for sure it didn't mean I understood anything about the groundlessness of any such idea or illusion.

I understood nothing of how that single turn of events would cleave me and leave me forever like a door hanging from one hinge.

How did I manage to underestimate the pain that lay before me, I ask Andrea, sitting in the bar.

— *È come prendere uno schiaffo,* he says with a cynical laugh. It's like getting slapped. In the heat of the fight, he says, you don't know how much it will sting, how much it will hurt. You don't even understand what it means.

I just didn't understand.

I ask him what we did the few days before I left. Did I go out to say goodbye to people? I ask him how I was, how I was behaving. Was I happy? Was I sad?

A mixture, he says. You were both. You said goodbye to everyone, and you cried.

— *E te? E te come stavi?* I ask. And you, how were you doing?

Andrea looks out onto the piazza and takes a long drag from his cigarette. He stretches his legs out before him and holds in the smoke. His thigh muscles bulge firmly under his work pants. His hands are the same, nails bit short, workman's hands, wide and strong. He exhales and laughs, sort of.

— I had already taken my blow. From the moment you said you were applying for colleges there, I already knew. *Lo schiaffo l'avevo già preso.*

That morning in August, after leaving my parents and my house in the haze of Cetona's pink dawn, we rode silently to Fiumicino.

Andrea left us off with my luggage and went to park. While we waited for him, Tullia fidgeted with my hair and caressed my arms nervously, then together they walked with me through ticketing and to the security line, until they could come no further.

Surrounded by the bustle of the airport, Tullia and I hugged, and then Andrea. He enveloped me with his arms and held me, like the whole world was tethered there in our arms and it would end when we let go.

Then he detached, turned, and walked away. As I advanced through security I turned to watch him move through the crowd. With my eyes I followed his black hair, his T-shirt, cerulean blue, taut across his shoulders, until he and Tullia disappeared.

He never turned back. I knew he wouldn't.

I cried from gate to gate, without pause, in a state of emotional dismemberment, a sense that my heart might well collapse onto itself. Every now and then a stewardess came by to ask if she could help, but there was nothing anyone could do. I did not eat, and I did not drink, and some nine hours later I landed in New York.

A road taken. Another undone.

That afternoon, a stunning Cetona summer day with the crickets pulsing in the fields of newly harvested wheat, Andrea took a note I had left for him with Tullia and went fishing with Diego, down at the Astrone.

— *Non ho neanche pescato. Ho pianto. Mi so' messo lì e ho pianto,* he says, sitting outside the bar. I didn't even fish; I sat there and cried and cried.

Tears well up in my eyes.

Revisiting this grief, his and mine, feels as fresh as touching a flame.

— *Mi dispiace,* I say. I am sorry.

It feels so feeble now, after so long, yet there is nothing I would like to convey with more sincerity.

— *Non ho nessun rimpianto. È stata una storia bellissima per me.* It was a beautiful love story, he says, looking at me with absolute clarity. I don't regret any of it.

He smiles tenderly, his dark eyes playful thinking of something far away, and looks up at the sky.

— For years and years, he says, every time I heard an airplane I looked up and thought of you.

My mother had sent some remote relative money to buy me a set of sheets, a blanket, and some towels. That is what I had with me when I arrived at Yale the following day: my two small suitcases and my towels and sheets in a paper bag that I carried like a cake.

The area around Phelps Gate was a pandemonium of parked cars and students and parents and families unloading furniture, stereos and TVs. I looked at a map and found my building, Lawrence Hall. I walked into our suite as one of my suitemates, Jackie, was unpacking, with her family. She had brought a truckload of stuff, it seemed—clothes, furniture, a couch, lamps, stereo, TV, things for the shared space of the suite.

They turned to look at me as I walked in with my two suitcases, alone and nothing more, my soul slipped into a plastic bag and zipped up tight.

You must be Sybil, they said. I nodded. I don't think I was smiling.

Jackie's father looked me over.

— My oh my, Miss Independence, he said in a heavy southern accent, extending his hand.

I have never understood what that meant, really. Was it a compliment, or a diss? Or a comment on the sadness of the fact that, coming from so far away, I had no one with me?

Preparing for college had been a long road, though I don't remember it wearily perhaps because my father and my teachers had made it seem heroic and ambitious. Plus, I was interested in many things and I wanted a good education: Even I knew what it meant to go to Yale, and the challenge boosted my ego. As Andrea said, at least part of me had agreed. The idea of going off to a demanding place far away and full of learning filled me with infinite fear yet romance, a sense of excruciating ending and exhilarating beginning, and, in a way, it was both. Loss and gain, sacrifice and bravery. A feeling of launch and a sense of death. Who would I be? I wanted to define myself outside of the town and the family. I was going to see who I would become, in the country that, whether I wanted it or not, had always hung backdrop to my life.

*Americanina.* Little American one.

I went for the right reasons, I think. But, in retrospect, how could I have known how defining, in an unexpected way, it would turn out to be?

It's taken me years to understand that, as much as the world out there pulls me—and pulled me then—I am pulled yet more by home, the hills where I became and where I found my identity and sense of wellbeing in the world. And surely there had been no other home for me than Cetona.

Yet, suddenly I found myself awash in a life-or-death effort to survive this upending change—to forget, get over, overcome, make meaning out of, make peace with, make the most of. And make do. Making do in another place.

My freshman year at Yale was searing, nothing short of annihilating for a part of me. It was an exile, partially self-imposed perhaps, but nonetheless an exile to a foreign land seven thousand kilometers away. Thousands of miles away. Measuring, in the silence of my soul, the indomitable distance, I felt an excruciating physical uprooting, a laceration of my heart. I was heartsick and displaced in the barest and most profound of ways.

I looked out onto the world—New Haven—like an alien fallen from a magical foreign land onto a barren, ugly landscape the likes of which I had never seen. The buildings were gray, and there was no horizon to be seen. Plus, the noise, the traffic, and the smell of fast food pierced me. I realize now that all the beauty and harmony that had nourished me my entire life made me into an overly sensitive and defenseless prey to dullness and ugliness in landscape and dwelling.

To defend myself I clung to the image of land I left behind, tracing the profile of Monte Cetona in my head every night before sleep. I sought consolation in whatever small precious things I had brought from the world I left behind—letters or pictures or postcards—and I hung them like amulets all over the walls of the nest that I built with leftovers of furnishings that my roommates kindly donated to me. It was a collage of love, really, and I crowned it all with a spectacular aerial photo of Cetona that my parents sent me and I had carefully framed. I made my nest best I could, with all my points of reference and memories, and I pushed on, with determination, because I felt that not doing so would be faulty and wrong of me.

Everything was overwhelming to me, conceptually and practically: from the fact of being in New Haven, with its flat, sterile skyline, to the academic demands, which were daunting and which I took on doggedly because I didn't know what would happen to me if I didn't. And then there the simple fact of having to function in English. It took me an enormous effort to learn great amounts of complex information and to write in English. No one understood this because I seemed to speak conversational English just fine, if a bit awkwardly. No one knew the void that stood between me and the books and the blank pieces of paper and the missing vocabulary and the long difficult paragraphs of material I had to learn. I had never been taught this.

And—perhaps the most profound thing about being foreign—I lacked the cultural references to derive meaning, from conversations or readings. I didn't understand jokes. I didn't know who Bob Hope was, or David Letterman, or the Three Stooges. I was well read and I knew recent political history, but people in America didn't understand that in other countries you study other history—another version of the world. Mameli's Hymn was my national anthem. I have never known the words to a single prayer in English, or to the Star-Spangled Banner, or the Pledge of Allegiance. I still don't.

For me, everything was to be learned, investigated, understood and made sense of. It was my own interior Far West, in linguistic disguise.

Curious, and striving intellectually, I loaded myself up with demanding courses and I studied endlessly, shutting the door rather impolitely when my roommates had people over and played loud music. My suitemates tolerated me, and I them, but it would take some time for me to be open to friendship with them—and, even then, in limited doses because I felt no kinship with them. We had no common ground.

Everyone at Yale sought out a lifeline to the crowd they felt most similar to them; I saw only difference—and to be fair, nearly no one on the campus had had the life I had. Many—most perhaps—had gone to prestigious prep schools in refined environments populated by kids just like themselves. Even kids who had grown up abroad had gone to American schools. Many were a few years younger than me and had lived wealthy and sheltered lives of privileged sameness. Very few had gone to school with kids whose families lived off the land—and none had grown up in Tuscany!—and perhaps in some Cetonese way I looked uncompassionately at our differences. I had never met entitled ease, yet I was suddenly surrounded by it. I felt myself Cetonese, and only and singularly that, and perhaps that made me the biggest and proudest snob of all.

With minor exceptions, I found people to be U.S.-centric and ignorant about the state of the world, which offended me. I didn't understand the social cliques that they carried from high school to college: frat boys, nerds, jocks, the girls who follow the jocks, and whatever else—labels that conferred some kind of worth my scales didn't register.

In time I acquired my own identity on campus, my Euro look, mostly in black, with long flowing skirts that Allegra sent me, and stylish dusters too, one midnight blue and one white, and beautiful sweaters. I smoked Marlboro reds, was embattled by the world, and was serious.

— Smile! people would say, people I didn't even know, as we ran across campus from class to class. I scoffed back, in anger.

I made friends with other foreigners, and in my rare social time I gravitated toward seniors, older than me, and people who also experienced difference in some way, either by race or by nationality. I met Sophia, a sophomore who was half-American and half-Greek, and had grown up in Greece. She was bilingual and with a similar duality in her life. She understood my homesickness and we bonded over politics and culture. She called me *koukla* and hugged me.

Not long after, I met Robynne, with an exotic Jamaican accent, soft caramel skin, and beautiful eyes the color of hazelnuts, a mix of her father's dark Indian eyes and her mother's, green from the islands. Her father was a doctor and her mother a dancer, and they lived in the Bahamas. Robynne was pre-med, studious and smart, and because of our common foreignness we related to each other in ways no one else there could. We had likeminded views of the world and her presence in my life was immediately consoling.

Slowly I also began to accept the friendship of a small group of people in my residential college—Kevin, the son of a magazine publisher from New York City, and Paul, a basketball player from New Mexico, son of a brilliant scientist at the Los Alamos labs. People liked me—my Italianisms, my strange ways of saying things, my argumentative politics and outrage at the world, my snobbery at football and American things I did not understand. My suitemates were kind to me, too, all said, and I was not to them in equal measure, but it was not out of unkindness. I was hemmed in by sadness, and inconsolable. I didn't know how to be, and my pain, my homesickness, eradicated every soft feeling I could have for my new surroundings.

I look back at pictures from that time and I feel tenderness. My scrapbook seems to capture a decent year, and perhaps it really was, in the end. I wanted to be loving and joyous, as I remember myself then. The moments escape me though. It was so tough, packed with fear, sadness, and anxiety, and, in fact, when I revisit that year in my memory, I would say I should never have come to the States for college. In fact, I doubt I should ever have returned to the States again.

Of course, even pondering that is like trying to imagine a future in a past already drawn and colored in. I would not be me, who I am today. Yet, I mourn the lives I could have had and whose construction might have been less destructive.

At Yale I went from writing beautiful Italian to not knowing how to write almost at all. I went from being an eloquent speaker with a deep knowledge and sense of a language to a bumbling idiot. I went from being loved and known to all to being absolutely unknown and utterly alone. And I went from feeding on a sharply tuned sense of place to roaming a foreign land like an alienated ghost in a state of perpetual missing. A gritty northeastern city took the place of my divine landscape, and my community of humble mountain people was replaced by a happy-go-lucky and boasting crowd that derived great joy from bring privileged.

And I went from safety to a complete lack thereof.

But, some will argue, isn't that what college is supposed to be about—to break us down so we can be rebuilt, anew? It may be, I counter, but who came up with that?

It's an American rite of passage—so contrary to any Italian passage—to be sent, in our youth, as far from home as possible, as if only in distance and deprivation could growth and strength be found, and worth, too. As if our spirits could be tempered—and ambition fulfilled—only by the trial of distance and dishabituation, no matter the grief. Perhaps this stems from a warped interpretation of scripture, or perhaps from some puritan sense of worth, or an American compulsion toward frontier. The abundance of land tempts the imagination and comes to embody the very sense of possibility and fulfillment.

There are aspects I appreciate about that. Nonetheless, losing home, particularly at a young age, reminds me of the unearthing of a young tree, like a willful denial of the most basic biological calling— that toward home.

In that shift of life I lost the footing of the pregnant winter earth, the fresh rush of water by the creek, the intimate compass of the horizon from my bedroom window, the voices of my street, the bending winds of my rides, and the blooming color of the seasons. The treasures of the woods were lost, the colors of the leaves washed away, and, too, the delicate smells of the *ginestra*. And the birds that lived near me, and the comfort of friends.

I lost what comes from staying.

And when we lose that, we are left without shoring, rootless and sad.

Yale was a maddening academic turbine.

In retrospect, counseling and support structure were spotty and insufficient, certainly for me. I had little advice except for my father's, which, though well intentioned and reasoned, was coming from decades earlier and thousands of miles away. I had a freshman counselor, a senior who was kind and compassionate, but the lens through which she viewed the college experience was vastly different from my starting point.

Again, in retrospect, I had no plan and my decisions were not strategic. I didn't know how to pick classes out of a book of hundreds—and so many of them interesting—that needed to fit together like a perfect jigsaw puzzle, both purposeful and bold. We were supposed to navigate the wide waters of academic abundance and to breathe in the intellectual wealth that inevitably would seep into you just by being at Yale, and yet, the academic requirements were dizzying. You had to be courageous yet cautious, adventurous yet wise. There was an academic wildflower field to dance in and pick from, but my bouquet ended up being laborious to hold and somewhat random. I took some interesting classes and learned many things I knew nothing about—it would have been impossible not to—but the program was spotty in quality and direction.

Peter Matthiessen's writing seminars were about true teaching, and my classes in French lit, too, and literature in general. Russian history, too. Islamic history was dreadful, as was most political science, my major, and Directed Studies freshman year. I loved Homer—I have read *The Odyssey* and *The Iliad* many times in my lifetime—but never have those two books been as boring as they were at Yale, so devoid of romance and Ulysses made into some kind of American anti-hero. Not to mention Shakespeare, whose language I could not understand.

In that new world, everything—even the things of which I felt most assured—came into question. I didn't know what I was capable of or good at, or how to channel my talent, in a new language. I wanted to be a journalist, maybe a foreign correspondent, but beyond that I had no idea what to choose or how to spend my time. And there was simply too much pressure, from myself and the environment.

And then there was work—hours and hours of work in the dining hall to pay for part of my education, a fact that still irks me. I am not one to shirk work, but it gives me pause now that a corporate university with astonishing tax-exempt endowments brings students of lower income from halfway around the world to work in the dining hall, or the library, or whatever the work is, while trying to overcome linguistic and cultural barriers and succeed academically. It seems to me that Yale has enough money to spare students the manacle of shifts washing the dishes of wealthier classmates.

Yet, what was not on scholarship was on loan, and what was not on loan was work in the dining hall—and all so, in the end, I could be indentured anyway.

My experience has caused me much reflection on the meaning of college and what we become through it: how our lives, at every step of the way, go from wide and unscripted to increasingly narrow and densely stacked, and certainly the college years are foundational in that narrowing and scripting and stacking.

I have come to believe that the quality of the education one receives at any college is the product of many finicky and unpredictable variables, some tangible and some not. There is no formula for thriving or for succeeding, Ivy League or not. I have posited through the years that we should go to college when we are thirty—when we are intimate with our interests and proclivities, our aptitudes and makeup, our inclinations and the incantations of our mind. Where we find titillation and magic. When we can help others—teachers—help us become better.

I know now, for example, that I should have gotten a double degree in Italian and history, or French and Italian, or French and history, things that built on my life experience, my interests and my aptitudes, already shown. I should have studied translation, and etymology. I should have studied art, but I didn't know I loved art yet.

Every now and then, in reading or in pondering the things I have come to understand about my makeup and my cares—painting, and birds, elephants and words, justice and non-harming—I visit in my imagination professions and vocations I had never thought about. Historian of slavery and movements of people. Cartographer. Ornithologist. Etymologist. Things that move me. The words alone carry me to lands of dream that connect seamlessly to my soul, and I understand why they make sense. *Now* I do. *Now* I have a long list of things I would love to do with my life. But at twenty how do we know?

Of the unlimited possibility of our being, most of us only really ever glimpse but the slightest trace, and often on a darkly lit path.

I plugged onward, trying to make sense of it all, buoyed by a constant flow of consoling and often humorous letters from my friends in Cetona—Allegra, Tosca, Ida, Tullia, and then Zia, and a flood of letters from Andrea. My letters to them must have been sad beyond belief because they all answered, as if in unison, telling me to stay strong and not give up. What would you do in Cetona if you were here, they asked. Grit your teeth! We are thinking of you, but you would be wasted here!

— *Non pensare nemmeno di tornare a Cetona!* Tosca wrote. Don't even think of coming back to Cetona! You have to stay.

Tosca wrote me funny letters full of irony and wit and cunning observations about the town, including Madame Bovary whom she would not let rest. In similar vein, Ida, with her breezy, humor-filled voice, wrote me exuberant letters full of delightful gossip—who was doing what, who had been seen where and doing what, and who said what about this or that.

Then, she'd caution breezily, do not regret this tiny town of ours! Remember how you used to say that our brains were atrophying here?

— *Una noia qui! Non succede niente!* There is nothing going on, nothing!!

Tullia, meanwhile, then and for many years after, kept me abreast of the substantive matters—the heartbeat of Cetona's relationships. Emma began seeing Andrea's cousin, a builder, and they got married, and then Romina and Silvio, Giulia and Mario, and Bennato and Adele, too, and, yes, Pierpaolo and Mariachiara, and Teodoro, and Lucio, and scores of others. Letters and calls, over the months, told me of every event I missed, as if we had all been there around the fountain chatting.

Allegra, on her part, sitting at the old wooden desk in her clothing store at the end of the piazza, engineered to not let a day go by without me hearing from her, the postal system allowing. Sitting and chain-smoking as she did when she was determined, she sent me something nearly every day, whether a postcard or a drawing or a long letter, or a package. She sent funny observations about the people who walked by in front of her store, the new fashions she was selling, books she was reading, her moods, men who were pursuing her, and eventually about how much she was looking forward to selling her store, which was losing money.

Meanwhile, Andrea pushed forward, among people who, for many months after my departure, continued to judge and exclude him. He wrote me sad letters, full of love and missing—the word *amore* written over and over in each one—though never selfishly and always with pride and encouragement for me and my endeavors, trying to understand my new world and support it, so far and unimaginable— even to myself.

Though I look back at my first few years in the States with a bit of self-mockery, I feel also a great deal of compassion. I cannot blame myself for how I felt. In fact, to some degree I still feel the same way, though now under the deafening cover of time.

Three months into my freshman year, I got a letter from my father that read, in part, *There are so many people in this world who would give everything to have the possibilities offered them that you have. … I think you are spending too much time licking your wounds and asking everyone else to lick them too. Snap out of it. Remember, Yale did not accept you as a student just for what they have to offer you, but also for what they felt you had to offer them.*

When I got that letter—whose words still sting as much today as they did that day—I sat down on Elm Street, in front of Yale Station, and right there on the street I cried the bitterest of tears. It was like my father was physically shaking me by the arms from thousands of miles away. I felt sad and sorry, shamed for feeling the way I did. I felt bad for feeling bad, revolted by my own weakness and tenderness, yet not knowing how else to feel. I had been in America three months.

I hated my father for writing that letter, penned from his most uncompassionate and cutting cloth. Rather than trusting in me and seeking support for me, he blamed me and delegitimized how I felt, as if it were the mere cry of a silly, plaintive child.

Through the lashes of his harshness I recognize now the courageous, determined person who, in fact, I was, something that, through time and subsequent experience, I colored over, revised, and forgot. And yet, yet I know that he beat me. He shamed me into silencing my greatest truth, and in doing so, changed the course of my life forever.

Letters after that indicate that I forced myself back to my optimistic self, the girl who from a distance had embraced the world of endless opportunity offered by Yale. With the exception of Zia, who always encouraged me to write my true feelings no matter the consequence, the recipients of my letters, my parents in particular, were elated that I was no longer hanging my head and telling them about it. Consciences were appeased and, with my help, the perception of my reality was transformed to suit their needs and expectations.

The truth is that I did what I had to do to pull through, to make it through, to live up to the illusion of adjustment I had made for myself with the colors added by others—for the shift I did not yet comprehend: I piled a huge truck-full of sand over my heart and I made myself forget, for what turned out to be many, many years,

I developed amnesia for my own pain, and, in so doing, I survived.

In response to a letter from me, my dear Zia wrote:

*You have gone right to the heart of the matter when you say that you must forget certain things until you can remember without hurting. It doesn't come easily, but if you can force yourself to accept the hurting somewhat before you think you can, then you do not risk losing the important things you left behind. On the contrary, your awareness of the painful cost of remembering and cherishing them in your heart of hearts will enhance their value and enrich you as a person, able to accumulate the experiences of things past (I hope one day you'll get to Proust) and assimilate it with things present. And one day your past will move you and merge with your present, and you will be whole.*

I am still waiting for the *remembering without hurting.*

On quiet days I like to sit here and there around town and talk to those who go by, savoring their routine inside the new one I am minting and this particular feeling I have missed about being here.

*Sitting here.*

Eufemia is walking on the side of the road, leaving the *giardinetti*, where the elderly sit to sun and gossip and watch the traffic go by. It is unseasonably warm, and she is wearing her long brown skirt and a yellowish-brownish top I often see her wearing.

I call out, *Ciao, Eufemia!* She turns and smiles.

— *Bellona!* she says, stopping.

She crosses over to chat. Eufemia is the mother of two women who grew up in my brother's circle. She is past eighty, but to me she looks much younger and I can see the vestige of a lush and playful beauty in her. Her curly blond hair is full and a bit wild, and she has bright green eyes and a lovely smile.

Throughout my life I have always viewed Eufemia as a bit temperamental, perhaps even a bit mean. When I was little I'd see her in front of her house on Via Risorgimento with other ladies, and she'd never say hello, even when I was a kid. In fact, she was known for telling you off if she was in the right mood.

On this visit, though, she has been courteous and welcoming, from the very first day she saw me, and we've become friends. I see her pacing the streets rain or shine—she says she can't stand being home with her husband of many years—and when I see her my face lights up.

— *Bellona, sei bellissima*, she says, hugging me, and I hug her back, fully.

She makes me feel loved, and I wonder if Cetona didn't make her mean back then.

The other day we had a good laugh. She told me that when she was growing up, back when the piazza and the roads were still unpaved, the mothers of the girls in town would sit guard at the *giardinetti* to make sure the girls would not venture out of sight to meet boys or men. While they sat there, the women gossiped and said bad things about the girls, particularly the prettiest ones—and I get the sense that Eufemia was among them.

I remarked to Eufemia that the piazza is paved now, but little else seems to have changed. I remember the gossipers of our youth, old ladies and men, too, sitting in judgment here or there around the piazza, commenting on our clothes and the company we kept.

— *Hai ragione, coco!* Eufemia said, heading down the road to her house. You're right about that, honey! Nothing has changed!

Sitting on the wall at the edge of the piazza I watch as Graziella and Dino, now long retired from the old Osteria Vecchia, cross together after lunch on their way to their *campo*, where they grow their vegetables and keep their chickens. When they return in the fading afternoon they walk slowly, Graziella slightly behind Dino, lingering, tired, perhaps, her head tall, stopping to chat here and there, waving to this person or that.

At every return of mine, we have always said hello and hugged and chatted about their health and the health of my parents, and the old memories of the Osteria. Now, I like to sit with Graziella, when I see her sitting somewhere, lazily watching the traffic go by, and comment with her about this and that. Her voice soothes me, and her dark eyes, too, like wells of life.

One day, some time back, when I finally felt that I had earned the old trust back—*la confidenza*—I asked Graziella if I could spend some time with her and cook something, like she used to at the Osteria.

— *A voglia!* she said smiling, looking me in the eye. Sure!

I was elated when she agreed, and best of all, I could tell that Graziella herself was pleased. She has been sick recently; plus, she takes a particular love to win over, and I am happy to have done so.

And so we did, one cold day this winter, in her house, in her little kitchen overlooking the old Osteria's courtyard. Of course, I had to go prodding in her life, but when I asked her about herself she revealed more of the currency of old and ungiving suffering that is the underbelly of Cetona.

— *Ho fatto la vita da somara,* she said, summing it up.

I lived the life of a donkey: They load you up, she said, and when you can't carry it all, they beat you with a piece of wood. They beat you and they tell you to get up.

Born just before the war, Graziella grew up in a family of farmers. Her parents worked *a mezzadria,* and of course their life was poor, but it was bitterly so during and after the war, when Graziella was a child. She went to school until third grade, at which point she became necessary to the economy of the household. While her mother worked in the fields, Graziella took care of the chores of the house and tended the pigs. She was a child, indeed, yet there was no childhood for her. There was land, and work.

In her late teens, she and Dino—they had been childhood friends—got engaged and married. In some ways marriage was hope, of something, and as was custom, it allowed her to leave. But she didn't travel far: She moved in with her in-laws, like Ave and every other woman of that generation in Cetona, and nothing much changed in her life. They farmed and ate off the land.

Then one day her father-in-law heard that the man who at the time ran the Osteria in town wanted to sell. He asked if Graziella and Dino would be interested in running it. At first the task worried Graziella: She managed in the kitchen—she had learned how to cook mostly since getting married—but she was no restaurant chef.

Yet, they agreed to take it on. With the help of the owner of the building, who had a vested interest in seeing the restaurant succeed, Graziella learned to make dishes she had never made, and to make enough for crowds. She practiced, worked, and perfected, with the grit she learned in the place of innocence.

Slowly, people began to come, and then they came back, again and again, until the Osteria Vecchia earned a good reputation and a regular, loyal clientele. Fortuitously, this coincided with the arrival of movie stars and journalists, and the Osteria became the place to be. And after so much misery, Graziella found relief.

— *La vita era dura, Sibilla. Ma finalmente* ... Life was hard back then. But, finally ...

Graziella and Dino loved to dance. They'd dress up and go to parties in farmhouses around the countryside where a musician played the accordion. They'd waltz late into the night, folded into the comfort of the hills. Graziella's dark eyes brighten and she laughs at the memory.

And then ... Her eyes shift and darken.

As the town tells it, it was the occasion of the *festa dell'unità*, the summer festival of the Communist Party, up at the soccer fields. It was a convivial time when people dressed up and got out and celebrated their shared history. Families and friends ate together, and children played about breathless and carefree.

On that warm night, all of Cetona sat eating at the long communal tables and dancing to the music of the accordion rising up and over the hills—the sound that rings in my ears as the score of every summer festival of our youth. Graziella and Dino stayed behind to work at the Osteria, but their little boy, Stefano, six or so, went on to the festival with older friends and cousins. While couples twirled in the rapture of the music, merry and untroubled, little Stefano, playing beside a merry-go-round a few feet away, had the misfortune of standing in a puddle—from a rainstorm earlier in the afternoon—when he leaned against a metal bar that held live wires carrying electricity to the event.

Sudden darkness engulfed the town. The music faded, people stopped dancing and eating, and the sodden ground drained the little boy's life away.

Quickly, someone carried him down the hill and to the Osteria, and there he died, in his mother's arms.

— *Da quel giorno per me è cambiato tutto.* Everything changed that day, Graziella said. My life has been full of torment. *Disgrazia.*

After that, the Osteria Vecchia gave Graziella and Dino something to pour their love into. They filled people's plates and gave them comfort in food and laughter. Dad's epic stories float through my ears, and Zio's voice and laughter, lingering on till the afternoon, till we left the table as the piazza turned to shade.

We shake our heads, lost in memory.

— *Quelli erano tempi belli. Li ricordo come te,* she said, looking in my eyes. Those were beautiful times. I remember them as you do.

After selling the restaurant, Graziella and Dino retired to their little house adjacent to the Osteria and the house of their second son, born a few years after the loss of the first, and his family. Watching her cook now, I picture Graziella emerging from behind the old blackened burners with her singsong voice.

— *Va bene, signori?* she'd ask, coming into the courtyard, smiling.

In their warm kitchen, we sat down to a feast of stuffed artichokes, mushroom crostini, and a beautiful *zuppa di pane,* or bread soup. Dino brought the wine from the cellar and we toasted to old times.

# Zuppa Di Pane

(Serves 4 with a salad, or crostini and a salad)

Ingredients

> 2 large bunches of green Swiss chard
>
> 1 medium red onion
>
> 3-4 celery stems
>
> 1 large or 2 medium tomatoes
>
> ½ kilo cooked cannellini beans
>
> 1 cup olive oil
>
> 4 cups water
>
> 1 handful of course salt
>
> 1 large spoonful of vegetable broth powder or crystals (commonly used here to season sauces)
>
> Half of a good-sized loaf of old Tuscan bread (see note on bread, below)

Directions

*Zuppa di pane* is a hearty peasant food that allows a cook to use vegetables from the garden, even in winter, and leftover, stale bread. It can be served hot in winter and at room temperature in summer.

Chop the chard, leaves and stems, in pieces about an inch in size. It is nice for the consistency of the soup to have some choppiness and irregularity. Dice the onion, celery and tomato, and put all the veggies in a big pot together with the cannellini, olive oil, and water.

Place over a medium flame until it comes to a boil, then lower the heat and cover, cooking for about two hours, until the coarser parts of the chard are cooked. The soup should have equal parts solids and broth. In other words, the broth should be abundant. Check the broth for salt.

Slice the bread coursely, about ¾-inch thick. Place a layer of bread in a big round bowl (or a dish you would like to use to serve the soup in). Ladle the hot soup atop the bread, making sure every part of the bread is soaked by the broth and generously covered with vegetables. Repeat the layering until your serving dish is full. Make sure there is abundant broth in the bowl as the bread will soak up most of it. Cover and let sit in a warm place at least half hour, until ready to serve. Ladle into dishes and drizzle each serving with olive oil and parmesan.

About the bread: The bread should be the densest you can find, with a hearty crust but mostly a thick, dense crumb. Do not use sourdough or any airy, soft breads. It is best if it does not even have yeast (as old, homemade unsalted Tuscan bread was made decades ago). Let the bread harden for a few days before using.

*You have a new world to discover, and you seem well on your way, in enthusiasm, inquisitiveness, and initiative, to implement your discoveries,* Zia wrote me sometime in spring.

In some ways, buoyed by time and exhausted by grief, I was on my way to adaptation, forced or not.

At some point Andrea and I had acknowledged that it was time to let go. I remember reaching a place when I knew it was time to call us changed, or to call me changed. Perhaps it was simply that, in my realism, I had given up. I was living a different reality and I couldn't conceive of someone waiting for me while I found my direction. Perhaps the *Americanina* in me already knew: It would never work. My new and foreign world was vast and unknowable, and I was tired of the grief. I needed to build anew.

Andrea was hurt—and gossip about my life at Yale and his in Cetona didn't help matters, on either side of the ocean—but after some time he resumed writing to share feelings and stories. He encouraged me in my studies, as he later did with the studies and work of his daughter, though I know the grief was longer-lasting than he showed.

And by the end of the school year I had let my true amicable self come out to play long enough to make some friends, and I became close with Paul.

Recruited to Yale to play basketball, he was six feet eight inches tall, with candid cerulean eyes and a joyful, winning smile. He was like a boy in a huge body and he loved to laugh. We took a liking to each other; he would come and study and visit in my room and listen to my stories and look at my pictures, which were always a source of fascination. He loved my Italian mannerisms and we made each other laugh. He was such a breath of fresh air, uncontained and different from anything I had known.

Paul, too, was unsure about Yale; he felt out of place and missed his girlfriend back home, and more than once he threatened to go back to New Mexico and never return. We had this homesickness and lack of surety in common. Only one person that we knew of, a blond kid from Wisconsin named Dan, had dropped out of our class to go back home—he couldn't endure the homesickness—and we didn't want the same to happen to Paul. Or me. God, I thought, what would happen to me if someone else left? Would that mean that I could gain permission to leave, too? That I could return to my nest and find another way, without shame of failure? That I could be forgiven for this weakness, this rejection of Yale for a deeper calling of my heart?

I spent that summer working in New Orleans, home to one of my roommates, where I could get enough work to cover my financial aid requirements and to buy a ticket home. It was a grinding summer: In the early morning I worked an office job at a car leasing office; at 11 a.m. I went to a waitressing job at the Pontchartrain Hotel; and in the late afternoon I went cocktail waitressing at a Mafia-owned dance club, a job that lasted into the night. I shuffled from one job to the other to near exhaustion. It was a nitty-gritty summer, with one goal: making money.

In August I left for four weeks in Cetona of which I remember little except my arrival from the autostrada and the view of Monte Cetona on the horizon that I had longed for every night for a year. The piazza greeted me with its sunny openness and it was, for me, as emotional as being released from a lifetime in prison. I was finally home again.

While I was at Yale, made to feel like I was on some exclusive epic academic voyage of extraordinary importance or valor, my friends were also building their lives: Sabrina was off in Siena studying banking and economics, Luca Batelli was in Milano studying engineering, Giulia was studying nursing, Tullia was becoming a teacher, and Ida was becoming a dentist. My other friends in Cetona were doing their thing too, starting a business or learning a trade.

Andrea meanwhile, had started working for a woodworking company and he had bought a big red Volvo, perhaps, people said, because he knew it was my favorite car. During my month home that summer he taught me how to drive stick shift, at Il Piano, expertly, in the dark, with the moon overhead. The stars enveloped Cetona, as I had not seen them in a year, and the crickets pulsed away in the silence, like I remembered them. Our relationship was briefly rekindled, but we knew the outcome.

I returned to New Haven one late night at the end of August. In the shuttle on the parkway from JFK to New Haven, with the shadows of the streetlights dashing over me, I prepared to transfer myself anew into this other world, and the lingering memory of that recurring passage backwards in space and time always makes the end of August deeply melancholic for me, as my soul continues to pay observance to that particular death of part of me.

Yet, on an emotional autopilot of sorts, I programmed my mind for whatever I needed to do to overcome the passage once more, and in a shift of time and space, amidst the grunge and grit in front of my residential college, with New Haven's sirens screaming and the traffic clattering, the taxi dropped me off and I heaved my big duffel bag over my shoulders and up the steps.

The memory of those returns to New Haven causes my heart to plummet as much as the love I bask in here causes it to soar.

It is—as if by miracle—the same love I knew back then, and which today, fed by the small gestures and encounters of the day and the familiarity of a lifetime, I experience untarnished, most times, by distance or time.

I love looking out onto the piazza and seeing familiar faces, or, even at a distance, familiar shapes and steps, someone I recognize by his hat, or her gait, or the shape of the legs, sometimes even under an umbrella in the rain. It's a knowledge that reaches back to an instinctive place, something tactile, embedded in the depth of my senses. I am relieved to find it still there, within me, as I am comforted by the greetings of dozens during the course of my day.

It is the filigreed web of ancient knowledge and love and trust that crystallizes only once in one place in one's lifetime—home—and for me it starts in the morning in my alley.

Enzo's mother waves at me from her window in a particularly enthusiastic way; I hope she's feeling better, though she didn't open her window and one is never sure. In the piazza I say hello to Tullia while she's going to work; I run into Mario and Elio, my old neighbors from Borgo, and we stop to talk about their chickens. Silvia's dad, off to his morning walk, waves and smiles, and promises to have me over for dinner. At the grocery store, while I run into Antonietta and she asks me about my painting, I recognize Pierpaolo's voice coming from an aisle and I turn and he waves. I run into Maria, going home to make lunch, and we hug. We haven't seen much of each other recently and we recommit to change that.

On my way back into the piazza I stop to talk to Ottavia's mom about her health. She has Parkinson's but she likes to go walking in the woods, looking for mushrooms and berries. I tell her to be careful and she promises to give me some of her delicious artichokes under olive oil this summer if I am still here. She hugs me goodbye. I cross Andrea in his white van and he honks and waves. I stop in at Armando's for something, an apple perhaps. Amato, who saw me running yesterday, lectures me about walking late in the afternoon at dusk. Dino, Amato's friend, scolds me too, with an affection that surprises me.

— *Ti mettono sotto se non metti qualcosa,* he says, with a nod. You'd better wear something fluorescent at night or they'll pull you under, and he's right.

In the afternoon, on my way to my run I pass Diego in his old green Land Rover, on his way to feed his dogs, though he might be going to look for truffles, an activity that engages him of late, I've been told. He smiles at me and waves. A few moments later I cross Silvio Della Vigna who's driving to his fields to check something, and he honks and pulls over to say hi. I run into Fortunata who hugs me and pinches my cheeks.

— *Quando si fa un'altra crostata?* she asks. When are we going to make another *crostata*?

I take a long run in the sun through the countryside and I wave at people I pass—Ilvo, who lives up on the mountain, with his Ape, and Maurizio, who owns a tannery and sells furs, regrettably. I stop to talk with Simonetta, a woman ten or so years older than me, I would guess, with a deep laugh and a mane of long curly graying hair wrapped in a disorderly bun. She lives down below Diamante's house and her dogs bark ferociously when I go by. She has chickens, too, and I like to chase them through the fence to see if I can pet them. Hearing the commotion, Simonetta comes out and she hugs me. She tells me she remembers me from when I was a kid; I feel at a disadvantage, but we seem to like each other. I want to know more about her; I need to make time for so much more.

As I approach Cetona on my way back, it's fast turning dark. Coal-like clouds cover the cross of Monte Cetona, but in a tiny bit of clearing, picking up the light from the sun setting behind the mountain, are tiny puffy gray clouds with a bright pink lining. They surprise me and, smiling, I dare hope for a bright sunny day tomorrow, on winter's tail. I think of Aram, who always notices and shares beauty like that—the unexpected pink in the dark, the miracles of nature, the silver lining. I miss him.

On the final stretch before reaching the piazza, I wave at my old school pal Leonardo as I go past his store, then I wave at Ausilia as I go past hers. At the entrance to the piazza I see Vito. He's from Sarteano originally and we've known each other since we were teenagers, since my days hanging out there. In the years I've been gone, he married a Cetona girl, Fiora, and took a job for town hall doing road maintenance and whatever else is needed around town. He is tall and dark and flirtatious, and we are fond of each other, some kind of puppy love. We exchange a strangely long hug, which we do nearly every time we see each other, and he squeezes me as I run off.

I run to the bakery for my whole-grain bread, then to tell Armando and his gang I am back safely—for today!—and I take stock, in my heart, of their quiet affection. As I head toward home, I see Aldo Della Vigna sitting on the church steps and I stop to say hello. Since my return here, Aldo has become a reassuring confidant, unexpectedly, though I have known him all my life as a big brother of sorts.

Aldo is short but nicely proportioned, with a handsome face, and he has his father's stance, legs apart, arms crossed or in his pockets. He has small, beady eyes and a rounded nose, and he looks a bit like a mischievous boy turned man. He hugs me to him and pulls on me and pulls off a piece of my bread and eats it, then he kisses me on the cheek.

I notice he got a haircut, and his hair, thick and graying, is short to the scalp, which draws my attention to his maimed ear, missing the upper half, remnant of a horseback-riding accident in Cuba years ago. Pulled by the power of the horse, an animal new to him and suddenly angry, Aldo was knocked into the scabrous trunk of a tree with his head and left his ear there. I remember when they came back—the telling of the story, the sexiness of the lore of the accident.

— *Ma che cazzo guardi?* he asks, looking at me. What the fuck are you looking at?

He looks almost serious, but I know him well enough to see the hint of a smile, purposefully disguised. He pulls me to him and hugs me. He rubs the bump on my nose with the back of his fingers and kisses me on the cheek. He calls me *la mia indianina*—my little Indian one—because of my nose. Sometimes he calls me Geronimo, which makes me laugh.

In a town of strong, vocal personalities, Aldo is not expansive or emotional, not often at least. He has his father's stoicism, but he listens and he warms me. He reads my eyes, and I would cradle him and let him hold me if it were not forbidden and I didn't love his wife.

I say goodbye and run upstairs to practice yoga. My mat is laid out on the carpet of my studio. I pull the shades against the bustle outside and the curious woman in the windows of the *palazzo* across from me. As I stand to pull the curtains I watch Vasilika walk from her van carrying a huge bouquet of flowers toward the church. As if sensing my presence, she notices me in the window and looks up to wave.

I let the love seep through me and offer thanks.

Afterwards I realize I have forgotten to buy garlic. I run to my window and see that Armando is still open. Amato is standing in the doorway. I fetch a euro and run down the steps, across the piazza, and grab my garlic while Armando is serving another customer. I leave the money on the counter and wave.

When I run back out, Aldo and a bunch of guys are standing in front of the Bar Cavour. I wave and Aldo throws me a kiss. I would be happy to see him twenty times in a day, a hundred, even.

Giacomo, the ex-mayor, is pacing with a few guys, talking politics. I walk over and he hugs me.

— *Ciao bellona*, he says. Hi, beautiful.

Giacomo is tall, olive-skinned, with thick black hair pushed back from his face. He is graying a bit at the temples, with chiseled, handsome features, an elegant long nose, dark, warm eyes, and a dimple in his chin. He looks a bit like Humphrey Bogart mixed with Gregory Peck, and he has a classic elegance about him, something from another time. He is articulate, smart, and well read. Most notably, perhaps, Giacomo was thirty-one, a rising star in Italy's new Democratic Party (the ex-communists), when he was elected, making him one of the youngest mayors in Italy. He has been out of office for several years now, and he is transitioning between being a member of the council of the province of Siena and being a banker.

We go way back, Giacomo and I. He was the first boy I tongue-kissed—at fourteen, at the soccer fields. He was fifteen. We were standing steps from the little booth where they collected the ticket money for the games, and it was a mid-summer afternoon. I didn't like kissing; I didn't understand the point. I was unmoved. I guess I was not ready.

Nonetheless, we were or played boyfriend and girlfriend briefly thereafter, until I left him on the pretense that he had been seen at the soccer field with Giulia—a total lie. He reminds me of this one night at the bar, still a wee bit hurt. I do remember his big brown eyes looking at me back then and wondering if I even cared. In our teenage years we moved on, always with kid-like affection. I remember him loving Peter Tosh and Bob Marley and playing the same songs in the jukebox at the Bar Sport over and over again, so much so that to this day I cannot hear any song by either of them without thinking of Giacomo.

In any case, through the years Giacomo and I have always liked each other and kept tabs on each other, and we flirt, for fun. Of course, he is Ottavia's boyfriend, and, now, I would never violate that.

The other day was market day and I was shopping for vegetables, a bit uneasily, wanting to buy a lot but not needing much, when I saw him come out of his *palazzo*, a doorway right next to the Bar Cavour. He was going for his Saturday morning *aperitivo*. When he heard me calling him, there at the *mercato*, he turned and he smiled, like he does. We are happy to see each other, like childhood again, and it fills my heart. I am grateful for the timeless love—the kindness and the forgiveness across time and distance.

We kiss on the cheek.

— *Dove vai?* I ask. Where are you going?

He smiles and looks me over lovingly with his big brown eyes.

— To buy the newspaper, he says —*e poi a comprare le mutande.* Then to buy some underpants.

I pause, then I laugh.

— *Perché, te ancora non le porti?* Why, he asks, taking a drag of his cigarette, do you still not wear any? He puts on a smart-ass look and I ignore the question.

I ask him where he goes to buy his underpants and he tells me at Ausilia's.

— *Vieni con me?* he asks, prodding me with a sidewise nod. Are you coming with me?

We walk arm in arm to the *giornalaio* for the paper, then out of the piazza and down the hill to Ausilia's shop. It is cool and breezy, but the sky is opening up to patches of terse azure blue and the sun is shining on us. It is a beautiful Cetona day, and we reach Ausilia's in five minutes.

In her tiny store Ausilia sells everything from bedding to pajamas to intimate-wear. There is merchandise everywhere, and the shelves are packed with tiny boxes with pictures of semi-nude models wearing briefs and lacey panties. I look around while Giacomo starts shopping for underpants. He asks Ausilia to show him briefs of his size, which she knows by heart, and they talk about elastic measurements and tightness—evidently a conversation they have had before.

Ausilia pulls out some striped briefs, dark and light blue, unfolds them, looks them over, then shakes her head knowingly and pushes them aside. She takes several more boxes off the shelf and pulls out the briefs. Some have cherries on the elastic band, some have apples. I note that the cherries are particularly sexy, and Giacomo and I banter back and forth, laughing.

After a while I feel like I am obstructing the shopping experience, so I turn to look at some tank-tops I like. A young woman walks in with her daughter and gets in line behind another woman, older and, I can tell, curious. The shop is tiny, and while Ausilia and I talk about bra size everyone looks and listens, and I remember my mom commenting about the lack of privacy in shopping in Cetona. I see her point now and I laugh, while Giacomo, having exhausted the time he wants to spend on this, settles on something he likes.

— *Quelle che prendo sempre, via.* I'll get the ones I always buy, he says, shaking his head and moving his hands about impatiently.

Ausilia wraps and bags two pairs of briefs for Giacomo and, after exchanging hugs and goodbyes, we walk back to the piazza arm in arm, in the sunshine, chatting *del più e del meno*—of the more and less—and it makes for a moment, a fragment, of the pure perfection that makes my bliss in Cetona.

When I go home I find a bag hanging on the front door with two heads of lettuce, maybe from Ave or Feriero. Upstairs my apartment greets me and I feel safe. I go to the window to sit on the sill and look out. The sky is turning black. I measure the piazza with my eyes and I smile at the rhythm of life here, filling. *Known.*

Part of that is looking down a hill that reminds you of something you did twenty-five years ago right in that spot with someone who is still dear, like stealing cherries with friends, or parking. Or the farmer who I talk to in the country, on my run, and he asks, *Di chi sei?* Whose are you?

Or Tullia's mom leaning out from her balcony and yelling after me, *Li voi du' ova? So' del contadino! Vieni!* Do you want two eggs? They are from the farmer. Come get them! She cares, and that shows me love.

Those things, those considerations, those threads of place and welcome always make me wonder what it would be like to live all of one's life in one place. Of course, part of me—the American part?—cringes at the mere thought: I am a person of the world. I love the diversity, the languages, the skin colors, the landscapes, the music.

Yet—and yet ... if I had not left for college ... I envy the nest. It's not only about being loved; it's also intellectual. Perhaps because I have been away, or perhaps because that's the way I am, I am intrigued by the relationships one can have in a small community, the intimacy of the tribe. You can sit on a bench here, or walk into a store, and immediately step out of yourself and into the lives of others. Those lives bring me happiness and strength, and most often a laugh. I would like to sit down and talk to everyone, to learn everything about them, old and new. I want to talk more with them, and write about them, and paint them, not as specimens but as people I love, whose lives intrigue me. I want to know more.

Some part of me swoops into a dream and reminds me to ask Angiolina how much she wants for her store downstairs. It's for rent. I think of a painting studio, a place to hang my things.

Yes, this could be my home again.

Back at Yale, I waded through my coursework, full of hefty writing requirements and heavy reading lists into which I delved eagerly. I took French, Chinese, and Russian literature, and also some American, with the good fortune of having David Duchovny as my TA, compassionate and thoughtful in addition to good-looking.

I enjoyed my academic work, for the most part, and conceived of ambitious analytical papers and projects that tested the best of my thinking and the worst of my continuing writing challenges. Throughout, Robynne and I sat up into the wee hours solving the world's problems and telling stories of our lives. She loved to hear about Cetona; she made sense of the characters and our interlocking relationships and meandering love lives. What happened after that, she would ask? In a way, she and Sophia saved me—and Paul, too.

Indeed, we both returned, and sometime sophomore year we fell in love and into a steady relationship, full of fun and tenderness. He was genuine and lovely, and our lovemaking exceptional, and our laughter and exchange of ideas awakening and electric, though under the social pressures and stereotypes of Yale we were also a bit mismatched. Paul was an athlete, an all-American, happy-go-lucky guy, amiable, popular and loved on campus and off—particularly later, after he became captain of the basketball team. I, on the other hand, was what right-wing Yalies called a Euro-faggy-pinko-commie: I smoked, read Chomsky, dressed in black and inveighed against the United States. Our differences tested us socially, but made for a productive relationship, my cultural difference and ardor for intellectual banter making Paul more serious-minded while his ease and mildness smoothed some of my sharpest corners. We adored each other, simply.

In summers, I continued to travel to work in different places around the country to fulfil my scholarship obligations and, of course, returning home to Cetona remained my most inspiring goal, no matter the cost. My second summer I spent in Texas. Gary, the man who had managed the hotel where I worked the summer before in New Orleans, had moved to manage the restaurants at a golf resort outside Dallas. Come on, I'll give you a job, he said. I worked on the golf course driving a drink cart and I slept in a waterbed in an apartment with a woman I had never met.

The soundtrack of that summer was Rickie Lee Jones, her album *Chuck E's In Love*. Paul had become my anchor, a true friend and lover—most assuredly the most complete and adult love I had ever experienced—and I missed him, back in Los Alamos with his parents. I spent the summer reading *War and Peace* and *Anna Karenina*, and making sense of Texas, which, instinctively, I didn't like much, with its sprawl and the endless apartment complexes without urbanistic or emotional heart. Or the people I occasionally met who called me *a nigger lover*—not for the last time in my life—and who thought that the U.S. was the only civilized and livable country in the world. I was relieved to leave and never to go back again.

Back in New Haven, I lived in the tower in Ezra Stiles on the floor with Robynne, Monica, a girl of German descent from Connecticut, who was pre-med, and two African American women who also had boyfriends who happened to be basketball players and who would congregate in my room, with Paul, to hang out and chat. We sat around studying and talking about racial politics and American stereotypes, and all sorts of cultural matters of which I knew nothing.

Robynne and I, best friends by then, talked in my room, or hers, about love, sex, or about politics, and she gave me a solid primer on being black in America. Of course, it was a topic that was foreign to me, yet somehow strangely and uncomfortably connected to my life through my southern grandparents, my father's parents, who had a black maid who used a different bathroom from the rest of the family. Stuff from someone else's lifetime and country, as far as I was concerned. Robynne helped me make sense of it all, and I began to see the world through her eyes. I watched what people said and did in a new way. She explained what it really meant when people said, *I don't notice color.* Or, *I like black people.* It changed my social awareness and initiated my understanding of America, with race at its very core.

That summer I went to Chicago to stay with Suzy and Shahan, dear friends of my parents since the 1960s. Armenian—Suzy via Lebanon and Shahan via Syria—they are erudite, knowledgeable, and deeply curious. Shahan's father, an architect, designed and built most of the most prominent buildings in Damascus, which are likely no longer standing now. I loved Suzy and Shahan's languages, backgrounds, and stories, and Suzy's cooking, her marmalades and homemade yoghurt.

That summer Suzy loaned me her car and helped me through what turned out to be another work-packed two months spent babysitting and, at night, cocktail-waitressing in a huge bar-dance club in Evanston. I loved that job; my colleagues were fun, the customers were lively and urbane, and the tips were great. My best customer was a long-haul truck driver who was unattached, a simple man of few words who came in on his days in town, once or twice a week, and drank rum and Coke. Every time he ordered a rum and Coke he gave me $100. One bill.

The first time I protested. It's too much, I argued; it's undignified, ridiculous.

— You're going to an expensive school and you need the money, and I don't have any habits or responsibilities, he said. Keep it!

I was grateful, and I did.

Our cocktail waitress uniform at this bar was fun and provocative, made of a white tuxedo shirt, a teensy black skirt, fishnet stockings, cummerbund, and black high heels. More fun, though, were the nights when we were asked to wear bikinis, or gypsy clothes, or dress-as-you-like. Suzy had closets full of exotic clothes and scarves, fabrics and jewelry from all over the world, and she'd open her closets and delight in putting together the most colorful, fun, and often mildly outrageous outfits.

— *Achchik*, she would say, calling me her pet Lebanese name, you have to make money! You are young! You must show off! You must show off!!

And I did, and it was a good summer.

By senior year I had stopped fighting the American side of my world, more or less, or so I thought. While I still associated everything to Cetona or something there, I stopped crying and thinking about it twenty-four hours a day, and that was a milestone. Between my relationship with Paul, Robynne's friendship, and my rigorous academic work, I adjusted, rolled from roughly cut stone to rough round pebble, settled on my road in America. I was happy, engrossed by my studies and my learning, and Yale was, in fact, exciting.

Finally, in May, Paul and I and our classmates walked in the graduation procession with Paul Newman and got our degrees, proudly. Pictures show us victorious and carefree, sweet and tender, and very much in love. My parents came from Italy, and Maria, too—we had made peace by then, on one of my returns home—and we look happy.

Then, feeling on top of the world, we parted, Paul to play ball in Ireland, and me back to Cetona and then to New York, to attend journalism school at Columbia.

I look back at the decisions, all of them—to stay in the States, to part with Paul, to not return to Italy to live—with confusion and regret and guilt; yet, as often is the case, many factors coalesced into their making. By then I was disdainful of most Italian journalism, a party line of multiple colors, untrustworthy half fact and half fiction, quotes undocumented and unreliable. If I was going to practice journalism, it was going to be rigorous, American-style, the likes of Woodward and Bernstein. The freedom of the press—I believed in that and thought it essential. Plus, by then I owed thousands in student loans, and I had no connections or means to get a job in Italy, or I didn't believe I did. If my dream was, eventually, to be a foreign correspondent in Italy, lacking any other experience, my only way to get there was through journalism school in America.

All in all, there was no impetus for me to return home—maybe because no one thought I would ever stay. It seemed like it wasn't even a card in my deck, so I made the best decision I could with what I had, and I embraced it.

Yet, I look back at these partings—Paul and me, but others also, these enormous loves, lived with everything I had to give—and I struggle to make sense of them now, the seeming ease with which we left each other and placed enormous distance between us with a sense of predetermined inevitability that was simply not worth opposing. Anchorless, we—or was it just me?—just moved on, through these life-changing mileposts and chapters and feelings, like we thought life was going to bring us more such loves to pick and choose from, which in some ways it did and in some ways it didn't.

But, of course, nothing about it was easy.

That summer in Cetona was sublime, lush and sunny and festive, colored by feverish youth and beauty, and youthful hubris. I returned home proud and reaffirmed, and I plunged my feet in with relish, thirsting to take of every happiness for having been away, for having lost so much, as if what I had left immediately behind and the time I had spent away didn't really matter. That I could ignore that. That I could be in Cetona again as if nothing had changed.

I fooled myself somehow that I could separate all the discipline and rigor, the intellectual demands of my studies at Yale and the immense responsibilities of jobs and money, and all the determination it took to hold all that together, and the years I had been away, from the other me—the one that predated all that, with the innocence, freedom, and love—and live like the two didn't know each other.

I sought to ignore my immediate past—four years in college—and looming future—a fast-approaching return to the States—and live only in the present: being in Cetona *now,* quenching my desire to retrieve and rebuild with abandon what I thought I had lost.

I was supposed to sever it all, to separate and be new. But I couldn't. I wasn't. I could not be. Ever.

By then the pub in Cetona had been taken over by Baldo and Fiorenza, who I told you about, he from Trento, she from Rome. The pub was full of people and music, and Baldo, the indomitable reveler, ever reluctant to go to bed, proffered spaghetti at midnight and endless good reasons to stay up through the pink and heart-wrenching sunrises over the countryside that I had so missed and I so miss now. Wherever his adventurous streak would take us we would go. I was always willing; nothing could make up for what I had missed.

Sometimes we piled into his white Fiat station wagon and went to dip naked in those old sulfurous warm waters in which I was no longer shy or shallowed, and sometimes we went for coffee in Rome. We got on the *autostrada* and drove as fast as we could, listening to Terence Trent D'Arby. Then we'd get coffee at the *autogrill,* get off the *autostrada,* pay the toll, get back on, and get off at Chiusi. Once, the guy at the toll booth signaled to a police officer sitting in a car nearby to tell him that Baldo had gotten from Rome to Chiusi in the preposterous time of thirty or so minutes (I was not with him fortunately), and he was given a ticket.

My parents adored Baldo and Fiorenza—they lived just up the street from us and I have a picture of the day they got married—and they often had them for dinner with a mix of their friends for the most foreign of meals my parents liked to make—burgers and sweet corn, or Chinese.

That summer Eugenio also came.

Eugenio was the son of our family friends Mariano and Marisa. We have known each other since we were young children; our parents were friends and shared social circles. They had dinner parties together at each other's houses, and occasionally at the houses of others, together. They'd leave me at Marisa's house for the night with Tiberio and Eugenio, a couple of years older than me, and they'd gang up on me and fart and play stupid jokes.

Eugenio had strawberry blond tightly curled hair and an open face both earnest and mischievous. You got what you saw. He had a dimpled chin and a smile like the sun, almost always on the brink of laughter entirely contagious and boisterous, like he had just told himself a secret joke and he couldn't wait to share it. His brown eyes were quick and astute, clear windows into a soul at once incorrigible and disarming, sly yet terrifically vulnerable.

When we were growing up, Eugenio worked construction, and he worked hard, too. He was handsome, trim and fit, and he made friends with everyone, and he has stayed like that through his life—ropy, innocent, and full of love. While I was gone, he had been the boyfriend of my friend Ida, an intense adolescent love, but she had written me years earlier and said it was all over. She had moved on to other people, Andrea, among them, and then a guy from Città della Pieve.

One weekend that luscious summer—my parents were at the beach—Eugenio and I had drinks at the pub until late, and one night we kissed. He came to sleep at the house, and we made love in my parents' bed, his fingers woven in mine, his face above me, and warmth everywhere, his brown eyes sweet, so sweet and so known, so true.

The sun rose above Città della Pieve with him curled against me, the windows opening to the coverlets of countryside that I had left and that I so longed for. It was the completion of a return, devilish and innocent, with someone so known and so dear. We awoke in the morning and something had been built overnight on a simple platform of familiarity and tenderness, a body into one, something secret and precious. It was like finding a lover in a brother and a brother in a lover, if that idea were not forbidden. It was love of many kinds, with the strongest of bonds of childhood and adulthood.

We spent five or six weeks together, fingers intertwined. I grew to know the feeling of his taut skin on mine, the hardness of his callouses against my fingers, and the tender presence of his company. We hung out mostly at the pub, laughing, talking, drinking Ceres beer, which I had never tasted, driving around in his white Fiat 500, or at the farm that he owned with his brother. The farm was off the grid and drew water from a well. There were no lights and no heat. At night we drove there through Il Piano, in the dark, and we made love surrounded by the sparkling light of the candles that Eugenio placed everywhere in advance of my arrival. There was a competence and a strength about him, and a gaiety, too. Yet he was so docile, like he could not get enough love.

His bedroom was in the attic, and we crawled up a rickety wooden ladder in the dark to get to his bed, playing, screaming laughter into silence. Nothing at all mattered, suspended as we were in the poetry of forbidden-ness and secrecy and the fact that we had fallen in love in the most unexpected of ways. He loved me and made love to me in a savage, all-encompassing way. He would have married me, kept me, been with me, possibly forever, and he was so lovely, in every way.

In the heat of the dusk, or the pitch black of the night, or sometimes the cool of the sunrise, we pulled our clothes back on and climbed back down the ladder, elated, in the middle of the countryside.

For me every moment with him was a jewel stolen from some fate-rigged plot dictating how my life was supposed to go. It was precious and irreplaceable, but, ultimately, hopeless—like everything else. Like Andrea. Like Paul.

Passages.

The soundtrack to my time with Eugenio was Ivano Fossati's song "La Costruzione di Un Amore," a story about building and losing love, like a sandcastle on a beach. It was his favorite song then:

> *La costruzione di un amore*
> *spezza le vene delle mani*
> *mescola il sangue col sudore*
> *se te ne rimane*
> *La costruzione di un amore*
> *non ripaga del dolore*
> *È come un altare di sabbia*
> *in riva al mare ...*

Inevitably, summer ended, marked by another trip to the airport and another departure.

That time Eugenio, Baldo, and Fiorenza picked me up at our house. We said goodbye to my parents and Baldo drove the car down the hill, southward toward Il Piano, the same route as always. He was smoking, and silent, grieving, perhaps. It had been a beautiful summer.

The sun was rising over Città della Pieve bright red in the morning haze like a giant Chinese lantern suspended in the sky. We rode quietly for a few minutes, then Baldo told me to close my eyes.

Eugenio, in the back with me, covered my eyes with his hands, smiling excitedly. Though we were sad, there was a lightness to it, perhaps from routine, perhaps from acceptance. I closed my eyes tightly and let them guide me to what they wanted to show me.

— *Guarda! Guarda!* Baldo suddenly said. What's this on the road? Look, look!

I opened my eyes to find before me a road painted with huge colorful letters, graffiti-like, human-size. For a couple of kilometers of road, perhaps more, and on the walls of the bridge under the *autostrada,* too, they read, *Ciao, Sibilla! Good luck, we love you, come back soon, we love you,* surrounded by hearts and flowers.

They had stayed up all night painting this farewell message for me, and more than ten years later some of the writing and drawings still bled through, like a fading Paleolithic painting, a scrawl in history, a fighting testament to a presence here, a love, a life, and another goodbye.

After so much love, and so much joy, at the airport they hugged me and left me, and off I went.

If the young girl from Cetona thought New Haven was harsh, New York would outdo it.

I lived in Columbia University housing, one of those imposing stone buildings off Broadway, in a room on a hall with seven or eight other people including, on one side, a woman from Bangladesh who wore colorful robes in every hue and, on the other, a cheerful guy from Nigeria. He was a criminal justice student at John Jay, and once a week he went to a market downtown and returned with bags of vegetables and whole dead animals that he cooked on a burner in his room. In the dark and dungy hallway mingled smells of Indian and African cooking and spices that titillated my taste buds, but, alas, our communal kitchen was filthy, the fridge was abominable, and there were roaches the size of mice.

Outside was New York City, miasmic and loud and in which I feared I would drown like a wrapper pulled down a drain after a storm. It was a cesspool of AIDS, homelessness, crime, and racial hatred. There were people living in cardboard boxes on the sidewalk underneath my windows with signs that read, "Dying of AIDS, Please Help." A white woman—a jogger, a Yale graduate—was gang-raped and left for dead in Central Park, and a group of black youth—the wrong people, it turns out—were swiftly arrested and convicted. Coming on the heels of the Howard Beach killing, of a black young man lynched by a white mob, this set the city on fire. There were subway shootings, a synagogue was set on fire, and racial tension was overflowing.

New York City was the learning lab and newsroom for students in the J-School. Every morning we were sent out to cover a real story, from an Associated Press New York list, and we returned at the end of the day to hand in our piece. We covered mayoral press conferences, crime, and borough politics—of which I understood nothing—and trials. A big New York City lawyer was on trial for sexually abusing, with his wife, their adopted child. It was one horrifying and dramatic story after another, and the learning curve was unimaginable.

It was intellectually exciting, yet wholly emotionally alienating for me. What a lonely city. Sometimes I'd get on the subway in the thick of the people crowding against me with their smells and their vacant eyes looking away, and their fears—the palpable fear and distrust—with the pressure of the days and the solitude of the city and the horrors of the society pummeling me, and tears would just flow down my cheeks. It was so damn hard. One day a kind woman, a stranger, hugged me in the speeding train. She detected my sadness and she just smiled at me so kindly—she was Hispanic and I don't even think she spoke English—and I wept against her shoulder, this kind woman who dared to confront and take in my heart.

I missed the physical contact I was used to all my life—a hug, or a holding of hands, the kind of interaction among human beings that can redeem the value of a day or a life and save us.

By then my parents' marriage was unraveling, so far away, and I felt powerless and hopeless. They were fighting and drinking and fighting, and I was anxious and pained. Sometimes I would walk the streets of the Upper West Side searching for answers or simple relief, and once, like a lost child, I wandered into St. John the Divine, with its beautiful gargoyles and tremendous height, and I sat in a pew and I prayed. I cried and I prayed. I asked God to please watch over my family. To help me. To make things all right. I had never done that.

Learning to write in newspaper style was enormously challenging for me, pushing against my natural propensity for complexity and expansive sentences that meandered through those complex thoughts. Though I had the mind for the work, my stories were always too long or, if they were short enough, they felt simplistic and were past deadline.

I didn't understand how things worked sometimes—city councils, or the courts, or how laws were passed in the United States. Plus, I looked at events differently: What struck people as a good story seemed irrelevant to me, in my cultural context, or what I found interesting, others found pedestrian. And, I continued to lack knowledge and cultural references, which made for some comical if humbling moments.

One semester we were required to take a class on ethics in journalism. It was a popular class held in a huge auditorium, and the teacher, Fred Friendly, a famous TV journalist whose importance eluded me, walked the aisles with a microphone posing ethical questions inspired by the news of the day.

One day he stopped in front of my seat and, after asking my name, he said, Ms. Fix, if you found out that Joe Montana had AIDS, would you report it?

As it happened, the San Francisco 49ers had won the Super Bowl that weekend—with records and acrobatics whose importance I didn't understand—but it was not an event that interested me for more reasons than I can list here. I had seen one football game in my life and nothing could have been less interesting to me. Not to mention that the newspapers, with which we were supposed to keep up (I got up at 5 a.m. every day to read them), were brimming with world events of huge import, including Iran-Contra, the fall of the Soviet Union, the Palestinian-Israeli conflict, occupations of Afghanistan, and the aforementioned local riots and killings.

I told Friendly that I would ponder the question if I knew who Joe Montana was, and Friendly and the class erupted in unrestrained and mocking laughter. Disbelief shook the aisles.

— She doesn't know who Joe Montana is!!! they whispered.

I sat back, mocked. Of course, the question was an interesting one, but the ethical substance of it —the whole point—was immediately lost and I felt humiliated and frustrated.

It was a humbling evolution, like trying to pour a churning ocean through a funnel.

The people in our class were interesting, though, from all walks of life and nationalities, and we were bonded by an interest in the world and a commitment to better it through our work as journalists, a belief that at Columbia was imbued with a particular American loftiness and idealism. I made a few lasting friendships that helped me through the stress of having no money and feeling, still, in some ways, like a tree without roots. And I poured myself into my projects with wonder and excitement. A story about Santeria sent me into the bowels of the mysterious West African culture in Harlem and in the Bronx, secretive and forbidden, and my master's thesis, about the demise of Little Italy, pulled me into the closely-knit, clannish recesses of the Italian-American culture, which I was surprised to learn was eons removed from the Italy I came from. They spoke dialects I couldn't understand and thought Italian food something it isn't.

I also worked on a magazine profile about my idol, Oriana Fallaci, the woman whose Italian journalism I did love. When I learned she lived in New York and I chose her as my subject, I wrote her letters, in English and Italian, telling her about me and asking for an interview. Yet, each time her secretary replied, turning me down. I couldn't understand: I had read her every word, felt her every feeling. How could she?

I spent patient hours sitting on her doorstep on the Upper East Side waiting to see if I could catch a glimpse of her, perhaps to speak with her on her way in or out. But I never saw her.

At some point in late fall or early winter I got a playful postcard from Eugenio, my tender summer love, sent from somewhere in South

America, with the picture of a tribesman on a bike. On the back it said, "Maybe this is how I will arrive! See you soon."

He showed up about a month later, with a duffel bag and his mischievous smile.

I don't remember if I had agreed to it, or had even taken the idea seriously, but if I had it had been a mistake. As much as I still wish I could change this, I was completely unprepared and I didn't know how to deal with it: I was vanquished by the demands of school, being broke, having a kitchen full of roaches, worrying about my family, and trying to hold my life together, which at one point I was barely doing. Mere daily survival required every bit of my discipline and control, and I was incapable of incorporating Cetona into it—not the sentiment of it, or the consequences. Plus, I loved Paul, still, and I didn't know how to straddle the gap, at least not gracefully.

Suddenly, in this chaotic, demanding city the tenderness of the previous summer became ruthlessly bracketed in parentheses and it could not be continued or replicated. They were two worlds within me that I did not know how to marry.

In revisiting this, in some ideal way I wish I had just hugged him and asked him to take me back to Cetona to help me figure out how to have a life there. Instead, a shift in place and time severed the love and friendship built in another reality far away. He stayed several days, maybe a week, which I begrudged him, then I asked him to leave. I remember the primal hurt in his eyes, raw, piercing, and unimaginable.

Afterward, on several of my visits home he did not speak to me. Over the years, he got back together with my childhood friend Ida, who had been his teenage love, and on one visit home I met their little girl. While here in Cetona this time, on this voyage of revisiting and re-knowing, I wanted to talk with Eugenio. I wanted to apologize, finally, and explain. But I never got the opportunity, and afraid to upset lives with the turmoil of a memory, I recoiled from creating one.

At one point, I ran into them at the bar. Eugenio spoke to me with coolness, buffered by Ida's presence. She and I talked briefly about a mutual friend with whom they'd had a falling out. Trying to understand what happened, I asked why.

— Life here has moved on while you were away. We are not the same anymore, she said, a bit cutting.

*Qui la vita è andata avanti.*

This stole my breath away, both the triteness of it and the truth of it. I realized that perhaps I have kept everything shielded and frozen in the depth of my heart. Perhaps I want to fix things that can no longer be fixed, and to mourn things that everyone else has finished mourning, and to understand things that perhaps no longer matter.

And no one, no one cares about any of it anymore other than me.

# Spring

**I**n Italian there is a term for surviving or overcoming winter—*svernare*—and that time has come, finally.

The past few months have been rainy and a bit dreary, and Cetona seems to retreat onto itself: quick crossings of the piazza, less chatter, the men clustered under the awnings of the stores, the shoosh of the car tires on the rainy pavement, a lot of card playing and drinking inside—and painting, for me.

Contrary to Fabrizio's warnings, I loved it no less. The rediscovery of winter's rhythms was organic to my being, natural and reaffirming. I drank of the solitude and retreat of winter, its silence. It helped lubricate my creativity and my growth, its den warming my questions.

But with the coming of March the piazza beckons once again, its reawakening calling me to the open windows, luring me to run down the steps and across its wide pavement, as it did in the easier, simpler times of our youth. Irresistible, tantalizing like a stripping lover, Cetona expands anew, unfurling its arms and opening its hands. I walk on its palms and listen to its sounds.

Children carouse on their bicycles, the elderly sit with ease in a shaft of sun, the tables at the Bar Cavour fill with people lingering in the warmth of the afternoon, and the salutations echo longer across the piazza in happy voices, open and giving.

And beyond the town, Cetona's magnificent countryside has changed into a lush dress of the most exquisite sparkling green.

On my run this morning, overdressed already, I shed my sweatshirt, hat, and gloves at the Della Vignas' shed. I left them tucked between the metal bars of their gate for Silvio or Feriero to find and keep for me, and this made me smile.

I was glad to feel the sun on my pale skin and I inhaled the water and earth coming alive, and the scent of new leaves and buds. I thought the winter had been verdant, and it was, the mild temperatures having ensured an abundant sprouting of the wheat, which brightened most fields even on the most wretched of winter days. But now every tone of green is heightened as if someone had turned up the volume of the color, and the most exhilarating greens—like a praying mantis or the feathers of a green grosbeak—blanket the soft slopes and ridges of Monte Cetona like a soft, fresh carpet.

I saw my first pale pink cyclamens and my first violets this winter, which almost brought tears to my eyes, reminding me of when I used to traipse through the woods and gather fragile bunches of them to take to my mom. Now paths and fields are filled with buttercups and the occasional precocious poppy, all too soon. Vineyards are sprouting tender leaves, pear trees are full of white blossoms, and lilacs are in bloom—lilacs, rose and white, the most heavenly of flowers.

And everywhere, farmers are tilling and planting, cleaning and cutting, and new plantings and seedlings dot the *orti*, full of hope and promise.

Back in town, the swallows have arrived. From my open windows I see them flitting about in mid-air at breakneck speed. They dart and dash and soar and circle, then finally they come to rest in nests under the cornices just above my windows. If I turn and look up, I see their heads peeking out from the top of the nests; I see their beady black eyes framed by a bit of white. Then suddenly something calls them—someone perhaps, a friend or a partner?—and they wiggle back out and take off again to circle the tower of San Michele and survey the piazza below. I smile and envy them, their ease and poetry and freedom, their privilege of looking at the world from above.

If only we could be so free.

The scent of spring gives me the same fever it did as kid in school, when open windows called to us and our minds, empty-headed, wandered away from the books open before us. On warm spring days Signora Marga kept the windows open, and from my desk I could see the trees in bloom, ubiquitous, the inebriating smell of grass and warmth carrying me away, leaving me there in body only. And at the *liceo*, when keeping the windows closed and forcing us inside only worsened our restlessness and vapidity, Signora Vinciarelli took us for lessons in the garden of the *fortezza*, hoping a bit of freedom outside would help us concentrate on Leopardi or whoever happened to be the subject of the day. Sometimes it helped; sometimes, toward summer, it made school all the more unbearable. Full of existential longing, we would skip school and go to San Biagio to lie in the grass and look at the sky dreamily.

Growing up, spring always made my heart leap, light, and festive, and mingling.

And finally, I am here to see it again. I revel in this simple, effortless state of being at peace with the world, like waking in a fragrant cocoon.

My cocoon.

In my celebration of the countryside and the new season, I go visit with Costanza, Bennato's mom, our old neighbors on Borgo.

— *Venghi giù che si sta a veglia?* she asked me the other day, in her old Cetonese. Are you coming down to visit a bit?

Because of the way Costanza's house is situated on Borgo, its western wall is shaded and cool through the morning, but in the afternoon, as the sun nears the top of Monte Cetona and prepares to round its final slope, it floods with apricot-hued light. In summer, magenta roses cover it and turn ablaze together with long braids of deep yellow corn cobs hung out to dry. The light and heat enter Costanza and Bastiano's cellar below, drying their florid garlic and onions gathered in the doorway in long silvery braids facing the mountain.

I love to sit outside in the comfort of that small corner of earth, but today we had agreed to go to her field, down at the Piano, so after I call her from her doorstep and she greets me with her high-pitched *Arrivoooooo!!* we walk down past my old house to her shed.

I tuck in next to her in the cab of the Ape and I feel like a child going for a ride in a magic vehicle filled with innocence and surprise. Her dog Ombra hops in and settles between our feet. Costanza is proud of her Ape and loves it. Though Bastiano also had an Ape, she insisted on getting her own so she could be more independent, and she drives her Ape like she does everything, with competence and resolution, sure of the place she earned in this life.

Like old times, Costanza wears her *campo* clothes—her field-wear—and her country boots and heavy stockings. Her arms and legs are taut and muscular as they were when I was little, and her jaw and cheekbones are strong and decisive, giving her a smiling and youthful look. She has good genes and she has aged well, in spite of the work she has done all her life. She doesn't wear the kerchief anymore that used to frame her face in little flowers or polka dots, and her hair is brown, short and tinged with gray.

We go down Via Sobborgo and travel a few minutes through the flat fields of the Piano. After a while Costanza veers left and we descend a deep ravine. We cross a creek, which she maneuvers expertly, and we reach her *campo*.

Consisting of a series of carefully delineated small fields and a couple of makeshift sheds, it sits basking in the light of the Piano like a perfectly set picnic, surrounded by otherwise ramshackle containers to collect rainwater, piles of old materials and scrap lumber to cover stuff up with. All around is a beautiful view of the mountain and Cetona in the distance.

The winter crops are coming to a close, so while we chat about my mom and dad and the illness that carried Bastiano away some time ago, Costanza, ever industrious, picks a few things here and there for me and for her, and she puts them in a plastic bag and tucks them in the back of the Ape. Then she cuts grass for her rabbits and gathers some greens for her chickens and puts them in baskets.

I love watching Costanza. She handles everything with a steadiness and an ease that awe me, from cutting wood with a *pennato*—a blunt and scary tool from the Flintstone farming days—to working a scythe, which she does like it's weightless, innocent even. The other day when I ran by Borgo she was making a hammer, trimming the handle with one tool and hammering the metal with another.

Costanza shows me the two plots of newly plowed earth—earth she plows by hand—where she will plant potatoes, garlic, onions, green beans, tomatoes, zucchini, eggplant, and peppers. She will till, weed and water all summer long and pick the vegetables at sunset in her aloneness in the fields.

— *Mi costa più di quello che ci cavo, ma tanto che fo, 'n' fo l'orto?* she says shrugging. It costs me more than I get out of it, but what am I going to do, not have an *orto*?

Unthinkable, as unthinkable as vines without grapes or the pope without vestments.

Every year my mom bought thick braids of garlic and onions from Costanza and Bastiano, ritual-like. I remember Marisa going down in the cellar to get them, bringing them up proudly, this purchase that pleased my mom, the garlic and the onions healthy and generous, and Bastiano and Costanza flattered and rewarded for their hard work.

*Signor Davide,* Bastiano called Dad before finally letting go of the *signore*, which irked and embarrassed my father.

Earlier this year I went to visit with Costanza and she showed me old pictures of her and Bastiano. They were introduced by a cousin of hers. She lived up on the mountain in a frigid old *podere,* while

Bastiano lived in the house by the creek, now newly restored, that I run by all the time. Costanza showed me a picture of their wedding in 1962, when she was twenty-five. She wore a sensible white suit, as I would have imagined, and sensible black shoes. They were shoes she could wear for other occasions—shoes that she could have taken off running in through the fields. One didn't waste shoes then, or now, and she wouldn't. I saw her from my window the other day walking across the piazza all dressed up. She had on a blouse, a fitted but simple gray skirt, and a pair of dark shoes with a bit of a heel but sensible, like she could use them every day except she would not want to dirty them because she has no tolerance for waste.

— *Si sciupano,* she would say. They will get ruined.

She had a purse over her shoulder. I don't remember ever seeing Costanza dressed up, though I'm sure I have, at my own wedding.

Now that she is widowed she lives with a meager pension, a combination of whatever she and Bastiano could pay into the state from their lives as farmers and Bastiano as a moonlighting construction worker. She tells me how much she receives a month, and I struggle to imagine living on it, even with owning her house on Borgo.

Sitting in the setting sun cresting the top of the mountain, we chat quietly, unhurriedly. About people we know, and the fates of the people who have gone before us. Her days now without Bastiano, and about me and what I am doing here. Loss hangs over us, time, and change. But joy too. The things that are left. Life that continues.

I had talked to Costanza on the phone before I came. I called to check on her and say hello sometime after Bastiano's death. I just wanted to hear her voice.

— *Venghi??* she had asked excitedly. Are you coming?

I had not yet hatched my plan. I was not sure.

— *Non lo so, Costanza. Solo se riesco a vendere delle cose,* I answered. Only if I can sell some stuff.

She had laughed on the phone, and she still laughs thinking back to that, the hilarity of someone making a decision of that enormity on the casualness of selling one's belongings. Or maybe it was the happenstance of it all.

When I finally did come and went to say hi, she hugged me all over, grabbing my boobs and rubbing my hair and my face, like she always does.

— *Vedi che se' venuta?! Lo sapevo che venivi, sa'!* she said. See, you came! I knew you would come back!

Now, sitting here she smiles at me. She doesn't quite understand what I am doing here, or how I am surviving, though she knows I am writing and painting, which are abstract things to her. Am I staying?

The details really don't matter to her, and that relieves me. She looks at my face and she takes it in her hands and rubs it, tears in her eyes. She lets me bask in her love. She knows, instinctively, that I am on some kind of search. A healing. That I am profoundly happy to be here, and it makes her happy to have me here, even though it's unclear how it's going to go.

I don't have answers.

— *Che gli fa? In qualche modo si farà*, she says hugging me. What does it matter? Somehow, we will manage.

We tuck back in her Ape, barely big enough to hold all of our feelings, and we head back across the stream and into the end of the day.

For many years after my graduation from Columbia, as I tried to piece together my adult life, I contemplated and sought comfort in the idea of working in Italy as a journalist. Full of idealism and optimism, I dreamed of starting an American-style newspaper to cover Cetona and surrounding towns. I wanted to live here as a professional, and do what I wanted to do, on the same land with my heart. To forge one person out of two.

Yet, obstacles seemed to be everywhere. Right out of school I had no track record, obviously, and no credibility. Besides, I had no money to ponder the possibility of what might make me happiest. I didn't have the wherewithal or the contacts, or I just didn't know how to do it.

In retrospect I realize that from the moment Yale became part of my life, my choices were narrowed, ironically—by financial duress. I was hemmed in. I had to get a job, quickly, and that would have to be in the U.S. Once that choice was made, I surrendered to a cycle I would never learn to break. Burdened by lack of money, and by then also by the fear of taking my career off track, partly unable or unwilling to stop the momentum of whatever life I was in the midst of building, I stayed in the States, steadily divided—indeed, further divided—between two inner worlds in a relationship of dis-ease.

I was not *serpe* and I was not *anguilla,* as they used to call me in Cetona. I couldn't go back, yet I moved forward reluctantly and with sadness. And going forward moved me forever farther from going back.

Within a month of my graduation from Columbia, I began receiving letters in ever-growing font sizes warning of the dire consequences of defaulting on my student loans, a debt of close to $50,000. What to do? After having lived In Italy some twenty years, I had no idea how to go about working in this dysfunctional country whose journalism I disparaged. I would have liked to work for an American paper in Italy, but I was newer than green and I had no support or connections. Perhaps I didn't have enough faith.

After a brief stay in Cetona, in a panic I returned to New York to look for a job. While I looked, I stayed with friends who kindly extended me shelter. I found a letter I wrote to God around that time asking for help with my financial situation and helping me not be a burden to others. He didn't answer with a check, but within a month or so I did get an offer from the *Times-Union* in Jacksonville, Florida, and I moved there for my first job, covering Atlantic Beach.

On the way to Jacksonville I stopped by my aunt's house in Lynchburg to visit and to pick up the last of my grandparents' fleet of cars, which, since their passing, had been thoroughly exploited by my cousins who lived there. I was thrilled to get this last morsel of family inheritance, but the car, an old cream-colored convertible Le Baron, was worn out and it broke down somewhere in remote West Virginia. A violent vibration nearly catapulted me off the road.

— Your main axle snapped in half, the mechanic said. You are lucky to be alive.

I was grateful. A day and $1,500 later, I was back on the road.

How did I find an apartment? Where did I stay? I don't remember, but a few days later I put a deposit on my first apartment, on the second floor of a two-story building off A1A, the Jacksonville Beach strip, a few blocks from the beach and two blocks from work. There were community tennis courts nearby, a small park, and the neighborhood seemed safe. Rent was $365 a month; it was clean and it was all I could afford. I was twenty-six, enthusiastic and optimistic. And there began my steep lesson on real life in America.

Next door to me lived an elderly couple who invited me to dinner and to Thanksgiving and gave me a chair and other things they no longer used. The wife sat out on the porch with me to talk, and when their children came to visit they showed me off as their promising Yale-graduate neighbor. Downstairs lived a young couple who I befriended but who shortly thereafter started calling me a *nigger lover* when I revealed that I actually thought the black race equal to the white. My landlord, a nice-looking, clean-cut southern guy, was a born-again Christian who came around to proselytize and invite me to church with his wife and children, and later to invite me to bed with him. For me it was all a discovery of America's oddity, an anthropological study of sorts that reminded me a lot of De Tocqueville's *Democracy in America*.

I furnished my apartment with ingenuity and resourcefulness, and, of course, my impetus to nest. I built myself a large, sturdy desk with lumber from Lowes, and a bookshelf, with two-by-fours and cinderblocks. Paul came to visit at one point—we still loved each other, in spite of distance and time, and somehow his Irish team was playing

Jacksonville University—and we went to a yard sale and bought a small dark teak dining room table, four chairs, a burgundy linen table cloth, a set of rose-colored linen dinner napkins, and a small set of china for four. I was elated by my purchases: I kept all of those things for many years—I still have two or three of the napkins—and I smile to think of how much I used, and treasured, those first "adult" belongings. Together with a bed, on the floor, those few things made my apartment complete for the next year or so.

A couple of months later the old Le Baron died, a failed transmission. It was snowing, the first snow the South had seen in a decade or more. I walked to the auto mile, a couple of blocks from my apartment, and up the steps to the trailer that was the dealership's office. I explained that I was recently out of grad school and I had a newspaper job, right there, at the beach, and that I was on foot.

A young skinny salesman with a moustache and a rumpled shirt ran my credit, which was barely existent, and complimented me for my educational pedigree. I am sure you are going to go far, he said.

Then, he got up from his chair and said, I have just the car for you! He invited me to walk outside the trailer with him and he pointed into a sea of cars.

— Do you see that blue car? he asked, pointing out into the rows stretching before us, dozens thick.

I looked into the sea. Which one, I asked.

— The electric blue one ... Do you see it? Blue like a neon sign! he said.

I nodded, sighing.

— Well, that is your car!

I protested, but he said that was the only choice I could afford, and in that moment I understood that my situation would not easily change. Nonetheless, I drove away grateful to have my new electric-blue car, which took me wherever I needed to go for the following six years.

By then, knowingly or not, I had embarked on some kind of version of what might be called the American dream, making myself and finding my way, and the adventure fit the personality traits of mine that still to this day flourish better in America than elsewhere: my fierce independence, my entrepreneurship, my enthusiasm, and my want to get out there and determine my path. I was proving myself to me, with the support of my fans behind me.

I started my job covering the beaches of Neptune, Jacksonville, Atlantic, and Ponte Vedra, and after getting my toes wet I took to reporting like a hunting dog. I cultivated my sources and learned the area, and quickly I rose to cover interesting and complex stories, everything from city hall and business to culture and the cops. After a year I was moved to the Nassau County-Fernandina Beach bureau as the sole writer there. I lived in downtown Fernandina, on the second floor of a white house with floor-to-ceiling windows and immense wrap-around porches, just blocks away from Main Street. I loved the oak trees and this pretty town where I felt at home because of its size and the warmth of the people.

My beat was excellent, a mix of the bizarre and the heartwarming, Nassau County being the backward, redneck manifestation of the two, and Fernandina being the rebellious and irreverent part, a free-spirited, independent-minded place with crazy politics, some artsy folks, and a good number of outlandish characters. Considering how small the community was, I never lacked for a good story, be it Bible reading in schools or a fight for the right to drive on the beach.

Between the big stories came many smaller, but no less colorful: A woman who didn't realize had had shot herself and walked around for a week with a bullet lodged in her head; a woman who shot her neighbor because her chickens were trespassing in her yard; and a funeral home that by mistake mixed the personal belongings of a deceased together with his innards, which ended up being left on the top of the family car and eaten by the family cat. There was voter registration fraud and constant political infighting, but the crowning story came when Nassau County's top sheriff's deputy, a handsome, flirtatious guy, got caught trafficking the drugs that the department aggressively seized from people's cars along the county's busy and well-patrolled stretch of I-95.

The beat was a trove of jewels—I loved reporting—and I loved living in Fernandina, with its smallness, its architecture, and the intimacy of the community. I made lots of friends, built a professional life, and, in some ways, I reproduced a little nest for myself, and it became me.

But the rule I had learned from the ambitious along my way taught me that as a young reporter you should never stay in one place for more than three years. You learn, you build your résumé, and you move on. Perhaps, again, it's an American thing—to move all the time. Americans use place like Kleenex—seeking opportunity, a new chance, a new beginning, a new identity, as if you could rip off a mask and be someone else, or worse, not take the time to recognize who you are. Ah, the liberation of starting anew.

In the process they get farther and farther from who they were. Who do people become in the process? If we are always moving, are we not always visitors, then, a bunch of strangers in motion whose communality is just a temporary use of a place, like molecules traveling in space?

As we lose childhood and memory and the bonds that connect us—traditions, continuity of feelings and knowledge—cultivation of place gets chiseled away. And perhaps that's what Americans miss and envy and go searching for on vacation: places that are old, with people who have lived there forever.

Like Cetona.

My search for what I have lost always leads me back to the cemetery, a place poetic and beautiful where everything, or everyone, can be found again, and sense of it made, in some way.

There, I retrieve people's whereabouts, like herding souls, and, for sure, in recent years I have lost track of many. I have missed so many deaths, and so many funerals, that I have lost count.

So, I come here to see, to learn. To rescue.

In the golden light of the setting sun, the high walls of Cetona's cemetery rise up against the sky like a dark fortress, its ancient cypresses standing like soldiers to guard the sacred and silent. In summer, early morning or late afternoon are the most common times to go to the cemetery, and the town's widows—and the occasional widower—can be seen like pilgrims, alone or in twos, on the quiet meandering road flanked by fields, taking the familiar walk to visit at their husband's grave, flowers in hand. In winter it's best to go in early afternoon, when it's warmer, and the walk is brisk and hurried against the wind and the cold.

Tall wrought-iron gates open onto the cemetery and a broad graveled path lined by cypress trees leads to the far wall of the burial grounds and the private crypts and the chapel. Flanking the path and going all the way to the side and back walls of the cemetery are regularly spaced rows of graves, similar-looking except for small variations in tombstone design or material.

A handful of larger or more glamorous tombstones rise here and there. One bears the name of the Bacosi family, and one of Lionello Balestrieri, Cetona's illustrious painter. And there are a dozen or so elegant family chapels—the Grassini family, an important one, and the Sgarronis, too, the landowners. Mostly, though, everything is simple and modest though not equally tended to. You can tell at a mere glance who is visited often and who not at all, who is remembered daily and with loyalty. Some carry on their chest a heavy vase of dead flowers. Others are still waiting for tombstones, though they look like they have been there some time.

— *La terra si deve assesta' sennò dopo ci vengono le crepe,* Feriero explains as we walk through the shaded paths. The earth has to settle or it will crack later.

Some time back I asked Feriero if he'd come with me to the cemetery. I wanted to walk through with Feriero himself and pick his brain about things. He worked here and dug some of the graves himself. He knows everything about this place I treasure.

With the exception of that sophomoric period in youth when we'd climb the gates at night and chase each other around the cemetery making ghost noises half in play and half in terror, I have always found Cetona's cemetery to be a place of peace and solace.

A place where things can end in poetry.

Women nicely dressed for the visit to their deceased move quietly about, putting flowers on the graves of their lost ones but sometimes also taking care of the grave of someone else, perhaps the husband of a friend who is sick or lives far away. Carrying a watering can, they step softly from the water fountain to the graves and back until the plants are watered and the weeds removed. When they are satisfied with their work, with a muted sign of the cross and a slight curtsy they turn and walk back through the gates and into town, their mourning observed and their loss slightly comforted. Some widows— Maria's mom, Elia, is one—go to the cemetery every day, to piddle, to rearrange, to say hello.

A sacred silence reigns here. If you talk loudly your voice will echo back and forth between the thick stone walls, and those there to mourn or take flowers will look at you disapprovingly. They also look at you curiously if you seem to be walking about aimlessly without someone to honor and remember. On a recent visit of mine, a young guy who works for town hall called the Carabinieri on me because he didn't know me and I appeared to be wandering. There has been a spate of copper thefts at cemeteries; perhaps he thought I was a thief.

— *Che imbecille*. What an imbecile, Graziella said, when I told her. The Carabinieri agreed, though they didn't quite say so.

Cetona's cemetery is like a history book of sorts, recorded in the faces staring out from the plastic-covered photos, some sepia-colored and ancient, the dates of their deaths dating back to the early 1700s. I go there to visit with friends we have lost, and to witness who else in town might have died in my absence. Over the years my friends, particularly Tullia, have been prompt at calling to give me news of the death of our important friends; yet, I have missed the deaths of scores of people who no one could possibly think of telling me about.

Now, Feriero walks through like he's discussing guests in his living room at home, sacred to him, one can see, but also familiar.

We move from grave to grave quietly studying the pictures and the names. I am chagrinned as I see the faces of an old farmer, and a garbage collector, and a former teacher of mine. I am surprised by some of the faces—someone too young, or someone too nice. I see faces that were intimately familiar, yet I knew nothing about the person. I see foreign names I have never heard—perhaps people who died in Cetona during wartime.

If you are looking for a particular grave, or the grave of a recently deceased, you need merely ask someone: If you spend enough time in Cetona, you earn the insider's privilege of knowing where everyone is buried. Give Feriero a name and he will take you right to them.

He walks through the rows, stopping every now and then to pull up his pants by the belt and point.

— *Ma chesto te lo ricordi?* he asks. Do you remember him?

No, I say, not really. And then he starts: He was the brother of the man who married the woman with the store up by the church, they used to live up by Poggio alla Vecchia, they had a son named Franco ... and he goes on and on. I laugh, utterly confused. Every now and then he throws in a precious kernel of information—how the person died, what he did.

He shows me a few graves with funny epitaphs.

— *Lo sapevi che il becchino ...*

Feriero starts to tell me that, in times past, the gravedigger not only dug graves—which now is done by backhoe, I discovered—but he lived at the cemetery, cut the stones, and engraved them, often with words he himself wrote. Sometimes he waxed imaginatively poetic;

on other occasions, he was of few words. *Muratore* (construction worker). *Padre. Mamma.*

Of course, space for the dead is scarce in Cetona's cemetery—and there's no new land to be had. Therefore, at regular and frequent intervals the town digs up the remains of those who were buried in the ground and moves them to ossuaries that line the inside walls of the cemetery like hundreds of matchboxes. In recent years the town added a new wing of ossuaries, much like most Italian towns have added new suburbs, and about halfway down the length of the main grounds are steps leading down to the new section.

Yet, Feriero tells me, Cetona lags behind the increasingly frequent deaths of the oldest and most populous segment of the population. Hence, the town has sped up the pace at which remains are dug up and moved. It's supposed to be a methodical system (after no less than fifteen years in the ground), chronological (the most recent deaths last), and closely tracked, but there seem to be glitches and occasional randomness. On a visit some years back, I found the grave-digger shoveling freshly turned soil back into a grave he had just dug up to move the bones. I stopped to watch and asked him what he was doing.

— *Ho scavato per tirallo su ma n'è pronto!! N'è pronto, e mi tocca rimettelo giù!* I dug to take him out, but he's not ready yet! He's not ready! he said, gesturing with both hands toward the hole in the ground.

I did not ask for details.

Recently, though, Feriero says as he stops to cross himself in front of his mother's grave, they dug up a huge section of old graves and moved them. When they do that they inform all the families of the dead and people come to watch as they clean out the remains and move them to the boxes in the wall. They won't do it again for a decade or so.

I show my disappointment.

— *Perché, volevi vede'?* he asks. You wanted to watch?

He is not mocking me or judging me, which I momentarily fear. He knows I am curious about such things here. I shrug and nod.

The most recently deceased are now in a fresh plot near the entrance, which should accommodate many years-worth of bodies. There have been more than ten deaths since I arrived. Feriero's mother was the first; Amato's nephew, only thirty-eight, is the latest. At the last grave Feriero pauses and makes a sign of the cross.

As we turn to leave, dusk slips over us. The candles of the ossuaries come alive like tiny stars, and the cemetery sparkles in a dance of reveling souls.

After I left for college, my parents' marriage, eaten by a brew of life's usual corrosives—financial strain, professional frustrations, estrangement, and a good splash of alcohol—began to decay at a steady pace. Every phone call things sounded more precarious; every visit home for the summer things were more explosive.

I look back at the video of my childhood and I see there was a time when they were happy, many years, in fact. Decades. What happens to people that frays that connection and everything built upon it? What happens to love—where does it go to die? Certainly, it died.

They called from the kitchen, with Caio and Arzelia sleeping next door, and Costanza and Bastiano up the street, and the fountain trickling, and the rest of my town above—all of them innocent of my undoing. They said that Dad was leaving for the States. They said they expected to get divorced and to sell the house.

I was in my apartment in Florida. It was Christmas, and I was poor and homesick.

— No, not the house, I remember saying. I begged. Please. I was crying.

We have no choice, my father said. Of course, in hindsight I would have answered that yes, he did have a choice. We always all have a choice. You're a grown man: You have a choice to not leave. You have a choice to leave and not take the house. My home.

But standing there holding that phone with my father at the other end already having resolved how it would play out, there was little for me to say. After hanging up, I lay underneath the Christmas tree—my first tree of my own—on the carpet of my nearly bare living room, and I stared up through the branches at the tiny white lights sparkling through my tears.

After shouldering the initial shock, I tried briefly and frantically to see if I could avert the loss of the house: to find someone who could buy it and let my brother and I buy it back, or who would pay off the mortgage and loan my parents money so the house could be rented and kept. But no one could or would help me. There was no will to change the course of things—to keep the family together or to handle the fate of our house more thoughtfully. Perhaps it was already decided in advance, one of those American things—splitting after the kids grow up.

I, meanwhile, was a lowly reporter at the beginning of my career some seven thousand kilometers away, incompetent in the face of such a momentous event. And like so many situations from which I was regretfully absent, I felt powerless.

When you are absent, I have learned, you do not count for much.

The house was sold to Arturo Magli's mother. By then, Arturo had been for a few years the boyfriend of Allegra, my loyal friend with the clothing store. He was an artist, a painter, with a long nose and a jovial face. A relationship blossomed between them, and by the time my parents divorced, they had been together several years. The house could not have been bought by better people.

When I returned home that summer, my parents had gone and I no longer had a house.

It was late afternoon, early August or late July, when I walked down Borgo. I approached the house cautiously, weary of the flame awaiting me, monitoring the tsunami that was brimming in my chest.

I knocked on the familiar brown wooden door—that particular solid sound I knew so well—and Allegra and Arturo greeted me. They hugged me somberly and I walked inside.

Everywhere I looked hurt like daggers. I couldn't talk.

Allegra knew exactly what I needed. She hugged me and said, we'll be out on the terrace. *My* terrace.

I sat for a moment on the cool terracotta steps of the entryway, taking in the dining room table where I had done my homework for so many years. The light from the terrace with the glorious view onto Monte Cetona filtered in softly through the French doors in the living room, and I could hear Allegra and Arturo talking softly outside, there where I had played with pots and pans and where my mother planted marigolds along the walls.

After sitting a while, I forced my legs up the spiral staircase, through my parents' bedroom and up another flight to mine. I opened the shutters and one of them moaned like it always had, as if to greet me after a long voyage. Unfurling before me was the specific view of Città della Pieve that had graced my every day—my unique view onto the world—and below, in the foreground, was the stretch of road to Piazze where my teenage mind had drifted for years in moments of distraction, seeking Andrea's car. In the silence, I heard the familiar sounds of Borgo: an Ape turning around, Costanza's voice up the street, the fountain trickling in the summer, not winterlike. I noticed my armoire and my desk too, still there.

I leaned against the wall and slid down to the floor and sat there. I felt the levees tremble and give, and I let it come forth, that vicious storm that I had kept watch over for years, boiling and brimming. I let it surge and take me under, churning up the details of my life. The childhood runs up the steps. The red clogs. The alarm ringing in the morning. Dad making me lunch. Winter days studying at the kitchen table. The curfews. The sound of Beethoven from below. Making cookies. The sun filtering through the living room. The smell of horse glue heating on the stove. The pear tree at the bottom of the steps. My white sweater with sparkles. Dad yelling. Making paper dolls. My cat.

Peaceful family meals. My black *motorino*. My mother calling for me, Birdie, Birdie. Writing letters to Maria on that floor. The stationery with the little pink roses. The rumbling of Andrea's car. I saw myself running up the street with my olive-green smiley-face book bag on my back, in my little jeans and my magic stone in my pocket.

And then the arguments and the fighting and the packing and departures. The leaving. The grief.

Under the surge, I felt the cocoon break open like a shattered shell, this reel of images and moments unraveling and spilling out and washing up into this sea foam of life, spewing and crashing and vomiting all over me, sitting on this terracotta floor, broken by this merciless grief, sobbing and wailing.

It was sunset when it calmed. I watched the reflections of the sun in the windows of Città della Pieve, brilliant and ablaze, as I had every day of my life since I was a child. I watched the tiny cars catch the light and wondered where people were going. Opposite, I saw the reflection of my face in the panes of glass, no longer a child but feeling never more like one, and with nothing, absolutely nothing, to set it straight. To make it right.

It was the end of childhood for me. The final loss of home. I was twenty-six.

The following day I came back to see Aldo and Beppa, by then elderly, who seemed to have lost as much in my parents' departure as I had. They cried with me, and Aldo, tears falling, his blue eyes swimming, told me about the death of our cat Ying, who they had adopted when my mom finally left, the last in the household. Together we cried for the cat we had both lost, and the past and my family and my house, and everything. Everything.

I remember not a single other thing about that summer in Cetona, my first homeless summer. I don't remember what I did, who I saw, where I went, anything at all, except for this tremendous sense of loss and lack of mooring. I remember only that Mercede, of the vegetable store, approached me in the piazza to say hello, and somehow

I knew that something cruel and unintelligent would come from her mouth.

— *Eh, ma il tu' babbo ci aveva un'altra, io me l'immaginavo,* she said to me. Your dad had another woman, I imagined that all along.

I could have spit on her, that ignorant smug expression. I have never quite forgiven her for that slight, which reminds me that not a single person in Cetona wrote me a letter to say they were sorry for what was happening in my family. Perhaps it was too personal, or perhaps it was just what happened to the *stranieri*—the foreigners. They just left, and no one knew what to say.

But I, for many, many years after that, I continued to feel more or less the same way, my visits to Borgo triggering bottomless wells of pain and anger. I was devastated and inconsolable for having lost my home.

Now, on my walks through town I look down from the Steccato and it feels only slightly better. I recognize bouts of anger, particularly when a seeming infinite number of foreigners comes through the piazza and I learn that they all own homes here and I don't.

House envy, Aldo Della Vigna says making fun of me, and he is right.

I look down onto the red-tiled roof now, and through my bedroom window, and I can picture myself walking out of the house in winter, closing the door softly behind me, my breath steaming in the air, my heart still free of the weight of the future and sure of my return.

I revisit my walks to the piazza to visit with Maria or a boyfriend. I imagine my clothes, and I smell the smell of the street, and I can hear the sounds of winter or summer, Costanza sitting on her porch knitting, her voice carrying up the hill. I see Andrea dropping me off in his VW Golf, just past the house, kissing me goodnight softly on the lips. I tiptoe down the hill and unlock the door and I go up the spiral staircase barefoot, holding my breath. I can hear my parents breathing in their bed not far from me.

Worse, perhaps, I can imagine myself there now, cooking, having a dinner party, sitting writing, or talking on the terrace with Maria, soaking up the particular view of Monte Cetona that belonged to me. Had I had it, it dawns on me with heartbreak, that house would have shored me and given me the foothold to return, the surety to stay.

My regret is magnified by the fact that since the mid-nineties, the house—which has sold again, now to a journalist from Milano— has been renting for thousands of euros a week. Swept in the opulence brought by Tuscany's ever-growing popularity, the house gained a slick pool and the annexation of Aldo and Beppa's property next door. What used to be Aldo's shed, where he hung his ladders and tools and where Beppa kept her rabbits and chickens, has been made into a guest house, and Aldo's *orto* has been made into a patchwork of lush flowers and walkways. The house is covered in lovely flowering vines with purple blossoms, and the shutters are pale sage green. Tourists—I think to myself only half-jokingly—usurp my rights and sleep in my bed. They post pictures of my house on Facebook, boasting about their vacation. Strangers I have met on LinkedIn have been in my house.

I have been meaning to call Livia, the new owner, to ask her to see the house. Maria and I have talked about it several times: Do I really want to see it? Maria looks at me, concerned.

I had decided that I wanted to, but then today, when I was coming back from my run, I walked by and the front door was wide open. A car was parked out front, but there was no one in sight and I peeked in. I saw the living room and the front room, the dining room. There is a lot of art on the walls, some off-white cabinets in the kitchen, I could see, and Dad's cabinets in the bathroom are gone.

Something tore at me, like a wound reopened. Where did your piano go? And where are your violins? What happened to my olive-green book-bag with the orange smiley face? Where did everything go?

Shy of being caught looking in, I ran off.

In the silence of the early afternoon Caino appears down from the alley and sits on the bench under my window with his usual group. Their voices echo and I hear that with him are Cecio and Mario the *fontaniere*, both longtime and prominent presences in the life of the town.

I can detect in the up and down of the voices a tinge of curiosity: Something is happening, for sure, and I go to the window to see.

A full-size tourist bus has entered the piazza and, a moment later, with a great to-do, dozens of children descend. Together, the men on the bench assess what's to come and pontificate about how the bus will turn around now, and where it will park, and what the kids will do.

— *Gli faranno fa' merenda ora!* Caino says, going back and forth with Cecio, (the singular of ceci beans), most known to me as the husband of Evangelina who used to own the shoe store. They will have them eat a snack.

— *Ma no! Li porteranno su al museo!* says Cecio. No, they will take them up to the museum!

— *Ma sta' zitto, a quest'ora il museo è chiuso!* Oh, shut up! At this hour, the museum is closed! says Mario, looking at Cecio.

Mario crosses his arms and makes the Italian *tze* sound—tip of tongue clicking against front teeth—which, compounded with a certain look, wordlessly and outright dismisses even the most important thing said by someone else. It conveys a cross between disdain and absolute dismissal.

Mario, so called *il fontaniere* because he was the caretaker of the fountains and Cetona's water and drainage systems, is tall and dark, and with his beige jacket and large, black square glasses he reminds me of a big owl. Like Nilo.

Caino, on the other hand, is short and a bit stocky, with a prominent red nose, a ruddy complexion, sly, beady brown eyes, and an earthshaking, scratchy laugh. Except for the hottest of days, he always wears a worker's cap on his head. Today it's green and it matches his sweater.

Caino is a fixture in the piazza, like many retired elderly men in town. He is there on the bench under my window nearly every time I look out or walk through the piazza, except for when he is down at his *orto* or walking around town or to the cemetery with Mario, who seems to be his closest friend.

— *Ciao Sibilla, come va?* he says with a big smile, waving at me as I come down the alley into the piazza. His greeting warms me and makes me feel at home.

When I first arrived, back in October, I was standing one afternoon looking at the light in the piazza, that tender and still clarity that comes right before the sun sets and the last light lulls most kindly above the elementary school, when Caino came up to me.

— *Buona sera,* I said.

He looked at me intently for a minute, trying to place me and understand what I was staring at. I told him I was looking at the light.

— *Ma te ti ricordi di me?* he said. Do you remember me?

Of course, I said, of course! You are Caino, Lara and Fiora's father.

— *E te se' la Sibilla, la ragazza di Borgo,* he said. And yes, you are Sibilla, the girl from Borgo.

*La ragazza di Borgo.* I smile, realizing I was the only girl to grow up there among a bunch of boys.

Then he hugged me and shook my hand.

Caino, jovial and good-natured, talks with everyone who passes by, and I love to sit with him to chat, adding to the leaves that make up the book of Cetona's story.

Caino grew up in the 1930s in the countryside around Cetona. His mother died, of pleurisy, when he was four. She had been cutting wood up on the mountain, and in crossing a cold and swollen creek on her way home she got wet and caught a cold. There being no doctors or antibiotics at the time, she died. The couple had eight children, of which Caino was the second-to-last.

His father farmed on properties here and there, and Caino followed suit, quickly learning to work and take care of people's land, hoeing, chopping wood—doing whatever he could to earn food.

— 'N' c'era niente. 'N' ci s'aveva niente, Caino told me as we sat on the bench in the piazza. There was nothing; we had nothing.

I picture nothing, and I believe it.

His eyes scan the piazza, lost in memory.

At mealtime his father would get a small half loaf of bread and slice it in eight—he shows me the slicing with his hands—and that was all there was for the family until the following day.

By the time Caino was seven, a short little boy with ruffled hair, he had found work as a shepherd, watching after someone's animals up on the *montagna*. He had no shoes, and in winter, when ice and snow blanketed the ground, he warmed his feet in the piles of warm cow dung that dotted the fields.

He had no underwear or socks.

— *Mica mi vergogno a dittelo.* I am not ashamed to tell you that, he says, looking straight in my eyes.

Caino went from farm to farm as he was needed, working for people some good and some bad. Once, while working at one farm, he slipped and fell on a step. The farmer who oversaw him slapped him across the face and sent him away. When he returned home that night, after walking miles, his father told him to turn back around and go find another job. He left, that same night, without sleeping, and wandered until he came to another farm, far from home, where they gave him work. That lasted until they no longer needed him, then they sent him away too. Again.

Occasionally he worked for someone kind who bought him a shirt or a pair of pants. That said, he didn't get his first new pair of shoes until he got married, some fifteen years later. Fifty years ago.

When Caino was twelve his father died too, and life got worse—
if that's possible. He was sent off to an orphanage in Siena, run by
nuns. They were not honest nuns, however, and in fact they sold on
the black market all the goods they got from the government to feed
the children. Caino, outspoken, stubborn, and honest from his earliest days—and as he still is—confronted the nuns and incited the other
children to revolt. It was wartime by then, and they were starving;
there was no bread, no salt, no sugar. Meanwhile, just outside of the
orphanage's gates, and in plain view of the children, German soldiers
butchered animals stolen from farmers in the countryside and cooked
them right there, before their very eyes. Famished, Caino watched
from the windows and went to bed holding his crying belly.

As soon as he was old enough to leave, Caino went back home, to
fend for himself, alone more than ever before. Eventually, he learned
construction and went to work for a contractor in Cetona. He made
a living, married his wife, and raised a family, all with dignity and
respect. And here he maintains his life, jovially.

At eighty-three, Caino is retired now. He and his wife live on a
small pension; it's not much, but then, he says shrugging, he owns his
house, he grows his vegetables, and he raises chickens. He is industrious. He goes through fields of harvested corn to pick up scratch for
his animals. He cuts grass for them here and there, where he finds it.

— *Me la cavo. Mi do da fa'.* I manage. I hustle, he says, smiling
humble and content.

After an orphanage and starving and warming his feet in cow
dung, there is no sense that he expects anything; no sense that life
wronged him. Not a bit.

Caino never spent a single day in a school and was never taught
to read or write. He is one of Cetona's forty-one analphabets sixty-five
and older, according to some 2011 census statistic. (I was intrigued to
discover that in Cetona there are two hundred and fifteen people with
university degrees, out of a population of 2,700 or so, and seven hundred and forty-one with high school degrees.) Yet, as a construction

worker he learned to negotiate the drawings of engineers and architects and he applied his knowledge with common sense and honesty.

Contessa Iris Origo, a woman who gained fame internationally for the work she and her husband did on behalf of farmers in the Val d'Orcia before, during, and after World War II, and who has been much written about, was his client. He worked on her famous house, La Foce, reporting to her privately when the contractor cut corners or overbilled her. He made a friend of her.

When he worked for her, Caino tells me laughing, he didn't even have a driver's license. He got his license twenty years ago, finally. Because he doesn't know how to read or write, they tested him verbally and he passed the first time, he says chin jutting in the air.

Taking the test with him was a woman who was a school teacher, and she flunked.

— Sapeva scrive' e legge', e non è passata! Non una volta! Tre volte!! She could read and write and she flunked—not once, but three times!

He screams on the bench, laughter filling his face, forcing his eyes shut. I am filled with affection for him, and respect, and I hug him.

When I first saw him back in October he had an urgency in his eyes.

— Ha' sentito? he asked me immediately, searching my face. Have you heard?

I could sense he wanted to tell me something, and I had heard just enough town gossip already to know, standing right there in the tender light of the piazza, what it would be—a story as ancient as man, yet never less painful: that his son-in-law Antonio had left his daughter Lara for another woman and moved in with her in a house just down the street from his own. I know all this because they all live up and down the alley from me.

I have known Antonio since I was a kid. He and Lara lived on Borgo for a while, and he wore tight jeans and undershirts, or, during the winter, tight sweaters that showed off his biceps and pectoral muscles. He was a looker and a flirt, with closely set, dark, searching eyes, a strong nose, and tight curly hair.

He and Lara had married young and had a baby, and after dinner Antonio would go up to the piazza and Lara would stay home with the baby, growing agitated if Antonio was late coming home. I babysat sometimes while Lara ran errands or cleaned the house—I was twelve or so—pushing the baby up and down Borgo in her stroller until darkness fell and she fell asleep. Sometimes in the evenings I went to their house to watch TV, and Lara told me about how she and Antonio had fallen in love and how she had gotten pregnant. Her black eyes sparkled at the thought of this prince-like, life-saving love she had always longed for, like most girls in Cetona always have.

Through the years it seemed to me that Antonio worked all the time, returning late in the evening, at dark. He got out of his truck slowly, like his muscles ached, and he was dirty and his dark face showed the exhaustion in his brows, how they furrowed closely, almost desperately, over his dark eyes. There was a suffering about him.

And yet, Caino inveighed, *lo puo' crede'?* Can you believe that?

Antonio lives just a few doors up from me now, and every night when he comes back from work he sweeps our alley, which, because of a cosmic twist of currents, on windy days collects all the paper trash from the piazza. Cigarette wrappers, paper napkins from Bar Cavour, abandoned pages of newspapers, wrappings from the market—market days are the worst—lay strewn from one end of the alley to the other, clustering particularly in front of Antonio's gate.

And every night that Antonio comes home to find a trashed alley, he sweeps—no matter the hour or how tired he is. I hear the soft sound of sweeping, broom against stone, slow and methodical. It's an act of conscientiousness and order that endears him to me, that reveals something important about him.

Over the past many months Antonio and I have talked and said hello on the street many times. I pass him on the road while I am running and he is driving to jobs here and there out in the country. Polite and friendly, he always stops to chat, and one night, when he had just gotten back from a job in Rome, he invited me to his house to have a limoncello. He is still ropey, with thick brows and a sweet want in his dark eyes. He showed me his new house, tiny and masterfully restored, and told me about his companion, Adriana, a friendly Albanian woman with a sturdy, straightforward face, with whom he is happy.

Adriana introduced herself to me some time back—she had heard about me from Antonio—and one day she gave me a bouquet of flowers from their lush, lovingly cultivated garden, for me to take to a party because the florist had closed for lunch and left me emptyhanded. She cut the flowers lovingly and wrapped them in newspaper and handed them to me with a hug.

A devil to one, an angel to another.

Now, Caino and Antonio skirt each other in the piazza, one on one side, one on the other, and I feel for them both. Occasionally they run into each other in the narrow alley under my window, and they argue, the details and rancor fresh as if it all had happened yesterday.

In the pastel light, Caino searched my eyes for an answer—a justice, perhaps—that no one can grant, a truth impossible to discern and certainly not mine to judge. Then he walked off, head high, hands in his pockets.

The fallout of life can be hard to take in Cetona, and there's not enough countryside to hide in.

Three years after arriving in Jacksonville I began applying for new jobs across the country and I was called to Charleston, South Carolina, for an interview.

Ever seeking harmony in my landscape, I loved the cobblestone streets, the ocean, the old houses that reminded me of Italy, the architecture sensible and braided in history. Nearly immediately I felt that, if I could not be in Italy—and I couldn't because I didn't know how to find work there—there was no place in the States that could possibly feel more like home to me. In addition, what I knew about the history of South Carolina and the South, particularly about slavery, civil rights, and education (or lack thereof in the case of the latter two), appealed to my sense of outrage and justice, to that primal spirit that had led me to journalism to start. I thought I could be of use there, that there was more important work for me to do, and, in fact, I had exciting beats in Charleston. I covered the kooky community of North Charleston, with its shady backroom politics and insane public figures; the integration of women at The Citadel, South Carolina's military college, with, at the time, its fake generals and staunch obstructionism; and I spent a lot of time writing about the dismal state of education in the state. I was doing meaningful work, I thought, and people in the community were appreciative, something one feels and knows in a small city.

And while I cultivated my work, Charleston fed my native hunger for beauty and harmony of environment. I loved the city, its elegantly proportioned buildings full of the flavor of the past, its lifestyle that accommodates pedestrians, its stores and cobblestone streets, its springs in bloom, the ever-molting skin of the marsh, and the mildness of winters. I loved its rivers and the sea, and the seamless way in which they merge around the peninsula.

Perhaps it is a city that lulls you, or perhaps I found in it something ancient—a rhythm, a pace, a take on life—that would help me miss Italy less.

Of course, I continued to dream of Monte Cetona in all seasons and times of day, and Maria, Ottavia, Tullia, Zia, Greta, Fabrizio, and many others wrote and called, more or less regularly. I kept my fingers dipped in their love while nurturing a feeble dream of return.

And I did try. I tried to get work in Italy, in spurts. Occasionally I asked someone for help to see if I could find a reporting job, something that would use my language skills, my knowledge of Italy, my duality or dualism. But my efforts remained thwarted; I didn't know how to do it. The competition for news jobs in Italy was fierce, and young as I was, I didn't understand what I had to offer or how to cultivate it. I had no mentors to help, with one exception, a powerful Italian businessman who just wanted to sleep with me.

It was just too hard—and it would become harder to scale the divide through time. With pets and new loves and new homes, my feet slipped trying to straddle the watery gorges between two places, nearly tantamount to not living in either, or at all.

So, I coupled my life in Charleston with my yearly returns to Italy, every moment of my vacation, four weeks, then later five, and six—as many as I could afford and get away with, paid or unpaid. I scraped by all year long to make it work, to spend as much time as possible there.

Twice or more the paper sent me to cover the Spoleto Festival in Italy, in Spoleto, and there I made lifelong friends, the Sabatini family, owners of La Macchia hotel, to which I returned for a visit just weeks ago. When I pitched the idea of covering the festival In Italy the first time and they approved it, I felt like I was in a dream: I earned not only my first job as a correspondent, but the opportunity to use my language and my knowledge, something I had wanted to do all my life. I could be *there*, in my totality.

For a while the duality—the straddling—worked, at least in fits and spurts. But, I recognize, it was a patchy mask onto my inner face. Inevitably, when I could not be there, when I missed it so bad it made me cry, the snake would come back to bite, taking in its fiery mouth the delicate shell of my identity, crushing my dreams and cleaving my innermost sense of self and place.

I strained, always, to roll away softly, somewhere across the ocean.

This morning in the hours before daybreak I heard the rumbling of trucks and the noise I associate with the market—vendors erecting stands and unloading lots of stuff.

When I opened my shutters a few hours later, I found the piazza brimming with color from every possible type of blooming plant and flower. It was the annual flower market and festival, and it filled the

385

piazza from end to end and side to side with every hue in a spectacular display of nature's bounty, pinks competing with purples, and yellows with reds. It was spring in a box, wrapped and complete—and I had never seen it before!

Standing at my window looking out, perhaps even more enticing to me than the beauty of the flowers was the stubborn crow of a rooster coming somewhere from the vendors' tents. Cup of tea in hand, I peered from my window until I identified the source of the magical sound: a big cage sitting on the ground in a patch of shade somewhere in front of Giorgio and Giovanna's house, amidst a cornucopia of flowering plants.

I pulled on some yoga pants, washed my face, and minutes later I was at the cage, asking the vendor to please let me hold the rooster—a robust, forceful-looking white bird.

— *Per favore?* I begged.

The man, tall and burly, with eyes the color of a clear summer sky, looked me up and down, humored, it seemed, perhaps a bit skeptical. It didn't even cross my mind to explain or introduce myself; it seemed my love for birds should be self-evident, earning me an inarguable birthright to hold this rooster whose likeness and beauty I so adored.

The man walked over to the big cage, pulled the top up with one hand and, with the other, made a gesture giving me permission to pick up the rooster. I smiled. After positioning my hands strongly around his girth to pin down his wings, I lifted the rooster up and rested him against my chest. I embraced him, holding him firmly yet gently.

The man observed. The bird resisted me stiffly for a few seconds, but when I began caressing his ears and waddles he began to close his eyes. Slowly he rested his face against mine, cheek to cheek the way J.C. used to, my beloved black rooster, and I felt his tension relent. My heart danced.

A crowd gathered around us to look and coo.

— *Mi' la Sibilla col gallo!* someone said incredulous. Look at Sibilla with the rooster! I guess they didn't think I had it in me. They don't know about my birds, maybe. But children took pictures and I earned the owner's respect. We smiled at each other, and after I put the rooster back in his cage, we shook hands and I thanked him.

A few minutes after I left the rooster, I was standing with Maria and Ottavia watching the comings and goings of the crowd when a man named Carlo walked up to me and handed me a shoebox with holes poked in the top.

— *Visto che ti piacciono tanto i volatili ...,* he said, smiling. Since you love winged animals so much ... He tastefully sidestepped the word *uccelli*, which means birds but also dicks.

Inside the box was a young blackbird his daughter had found on a nearby street, fallen from a nest. The baby bird looked up at me with tiny black eyes, and I looked back knowing I had been handed a disappointment in the making.

We spent the following several hours busying ourselves like eager Girl Scouts trying to provide for the bird. We went to Tullia's mother for a bird cage—they have cages full of parakeets on their porch—and we dug up long brown worms from the soil around Ottavia's newly planted vegetable garden. We sought advice from passersby in the piazza, and finally we took the bird to my place and set him up by the window with water and worms.

I watched him peck incompetently at the water and walk around the small cage unsteadily. When he put a foot in the water, I thought to myself that he was not equipped to be there alone and I was not fit to be his mother. Indeed, in spite of our valiant efforts, the poor fledgling died later that night. I found him keeled over, twiggy legs up in the air. I mourned him: I studied his toes, and the turn of his head, and I caressed his tiny grey feathers with my fingertips.

Perhaps he ate too many worms; perhaps he didn't drink enough; perhaps he was cold. Perhaps, as someone said, a baby bird simply cannot live without its mother. I accepted the defeat knowing I had tried, though it made me feel no better, and I gave him to Antonio and Adriana to bury in their garden.

Over the following days of the festival I returned often to the rooster's cage. The man grew talkative and friendly, and even brought a few more birds, including a couple of hens. He seemed glad to let me visit. I opened the big cage by myself and hugged the birds and rubbed my fingers under their wings. I thought of my birds far away, and I was happy to feel, for a moment, a bridge in me that spans the ocean.

Perhaps I could get some chickens here and paint them again? I continue to toy with the idea, while the months pass by and I am not sure which way to go.

Easter came soon thereafter, filling Cetona with people. On Friday night an expectant crowd gathered in front of San Michele to wait for the beginning of the Holy Friday procession. Voices rose from inside—magical chanting—and the flicker of candles filtered through the edges of the big wooden doors, closed to the darkened piazza. Mystery filled the air.

I hadn't seen the procession in years and I was brimming with excitement.

— *Sbrigati che sennò te la perdi!* Giacomo yelled after me as I ran up the alley to get my camera. Hurry or you will miss it!

Suddenly everything went quiet: The church doors opened and out came the leader of the procession, robed, hooded and ominous, followed by a company of similarly hooded men. They descended the church steps and at a slow, haunting cadence they began their mournful march through town, a tradition Cetona has carried out for as long as the town has existed.

With its torches and robes, the procession has a sinister feel, accentuated by the portentous beat of the drums that mark the pace. Lights in the piazza are dimmed, as they are in the streets of the old town, all the way to the Rocca. Two Jesuses on the cross are carried by groups of men, and, in between, a statue of the Virgin Mary, carried by masked people under a canopy. Behind it all follow the people of Cetona, two by two, whispering prayers in unison.

Don Prospero leads the prayer. I hear his voice rising and echoing against the stone buildings.

— *Perdono, signore, perdono per i nostri peccati,* he says over and over as he walks. Forgiveness, Lord, forgiveness for our sins.

And the people repeat, *perdono per i nostri peccati.*

The procession snakes through the piazza, up Via Roma and through the upper alleys of town, then down the Costa de' Capperoni, and back into the piazza and into the church, dark and cavernous, like a mouth eating them all. I see Sotero guiding the hooded people and he waves at me, smiling. The crowd outside disperses and the piazza returns to light. Standing there I wonder if my parents ever came to the procession, all religious affiliation aside. I doubt it, now, and I shake off the strangeness of that.

On Saturday was the blessing of the eggs and the animals. It was cool and a bit rainy, and I was painting, upstairs, windows closed. But as I watched, out of the corner of my eye, women in groups or in couples ascend the steps of San Michele carrying baskets and bags of eggs, I reminded myself of why I am here and what it's costing me. I put down the brush, pulled off my smock, and ran to the fridge to gather a few eggs that Tullia's mom had given me the day before. I put them in a pretty basket I found in the kitchen and ran down the steps, across the street, and into the darkness of the church.

On the steps of the altar were dozens of baskets and bowls covered with pretty fabric napkins, and ladies sat in the pews quietly waiting. I looked around the shade of the church and breathed in deeply, feeling awkward and self-conscious.

The words whispered to me. *Act from your heart.*

I retrieved in me the purity that led me to this church with these eggs, and slowly, trying to calm my breath, I walked to the altar and placed my basket among the others. I walked back to a pew and sat, savoring the perfection and stillness of my presence, of my belonging. I looked up at the altar and gave thanks for being, and for being here.

I had never spent much time in this church over the years, and I sat gratefully in the coolness and the suffused light. I looked at the ladies waiting, and the baskets, and I smiled remembering that Zia liked to bring her eggs to be blessed. Long ago, people brought their animals too, chickens and goats. I wished for my chickens, and an animal kingdom free of suffering.

Don Prospero went back and forth in the shadows behind the altar in his black robe, then finally came out with his aspergillum. He circled around the steps reciting prayers and blessing the eggs. Smoke bellowed around the altar and the steps were suddenly wet. I followed the drops of water with my eyes to see some fall on the eggs I brought. The whole scene was worth painting, if only I could paint it, the smoke rising around the altar, the darkness of it, and yet the hope implicit in the blessing of these eggs wrapped in linens so simply and beautifully.

Then, Don Prospero retreated behind the altar and the women got up to gather their baskets and leave. Fortunata was among them, and when she saw me she came over to hug me. She pinched my cheeks.

— *Piccina, come stai?* she asked, attentively, peering into me with her blue eyes. How are you, little one?

I love her for that. I smile because I am happy to see her, yet I always feel like I'm on the verge of crying because I fear the end of the story. I fear that I will leave again and this will not be mine to keep.

Then, another group of women trickled in, putting more baskets on the altar. Among them is Maria, bearing eggs to be blessed for her mom and her mother-in-law. I watched her put the eggs on the altar, then she saw me and came to sit with me. She hugged me quietly as Don Prospero came out again to repeat his blessing.

My run today took me by the convent of San Francesco, so called I Frati, and up to Belverde. I love to run up there in the silence and the dense folds of the mountain, lush and cool.

Belverde is famous for its caves, a loose cluster of corridors and lookouts that meander through rock formations once inhabited and used as burial sites by our remote ancestors. Saint Francis of Assisi is known to have prayed there, and in his honor a church and convent were built nearby, up on the hill, in the 1300s.

Both Belverde and I Frati are now home to communities founded by Padre Eligio, a Franciscan priest who in the seventies began opening rehabilitation centers for addicts, mostly in convents and other historic and abandoned locations affiliated with San Francis throughout Italy. Here, the clients of the communities work, till the land, and live in fraternal but Spartan seclusion. The properties are stunning both for their natural beauty and the meticulousness of the work the clients do to maintain them.

On this day, the gardens and *orti* of Belverde look orderly and cared for, full of new plantings for summer, as do the flower beds at the convent.

— *Vuole visitare?* a young guy in work clothes asks me as I stop to take in a view of the gardens. Do you want to visit?

— *No, grazie*, I say smiling, shaking my head.

I know it well, I say, exhaling slowly. I got married here.

— *Ah, bene!* he says, waving.

It was the finale of the Spoleto Festival in Charleston and there was a sunset concert at Middleton Place. There would be fireworks and picnics, and beautiful music. Gershwin. Would you like to come, Whitney asked. I have two guys I want you to meet.

I went, and I met Peter. He had just moved to Charleston from New York, and he was an entrepreneur, in finance. Peter was smart, good-looking, generous, educated, and funny. He was a military academy graduate—honorable and lofty—and a graduate of the Fletcher School. He had been a Ranger and a Green Beret, had served in Latin

America, had done work in Afghanistan, and he spoke Arabic and Farsi. I was smitten with the combination of intellect, manliness, and nobility of purpose, and, in spite of that unlikely palette, also kindness.

Within weeks he enchanted me. He romanced me to the songs of Sade, up in lofts above King Street, and he bought me clothes in New York. He took me out to dinner, he wrote me articulate and romantic love letters, and called when he was away. Two months after we met, on his way back to the U.S. after visiting his parents in Greece, he came to visit me in Cetona, and he was the first foreign boyfriend I had ever thought of introducing there. Through his knowledge of Greek, French and Arabic, he cobbled together words to converse with anyone and he put everyone at ease. He was interested in my friends, and everyone in Cetona loved him.

Finally, I met his parents and he met mine, and five months after meeting we moved in together into a charming brick tenement house of historic note on Anson Street. Later we lived in elegant houses on Montagu and Gibbes streets, and finally in a stately home in the French Quarter, which we restored and made beautiful.

I liked my life with Peter. Mostly, I realize now, the security that Peter gave me shored me, comforted me, for the first time in my life, and with it I was lucky to get all the traits one could wish for in a partner: He was charismatic, smart, a great conversationalist, and interesting. He was loyal and honorable. People gravitated to him—they thought he had money, that he was going places—and they liked to be seen with him. Plus, he picked up the check a lot, most generously.

Peter loved music—from Wagner and Handel to the Crash Test Dummies, Grateful Dead, James Taylor, Burt Bacharach, and Frank Sinatra. He was a constant surprise, romantic and eclectic. We danced together in our living room, were invited to many parties, and hosted many dinner parties ourselves. For many years I was a veritable Martha Stewart—which makes me laugh now that I cook barely more than a plate of pasta—and finally I could breathe about buying something for myself.

On New Year's Day a couple of years later, a dreary day in Charleston, Peter took me for a walk on the Battery and asked me to marry him. Though I felt honored and special, I remember the event with a sense of normalcy—of reassurance perhaps, without surprise. We thought we were perfectly matched—in part, for me, because he held the promise of bridging my halves—and everyone else thought so, too.

We decided immediately that we would marry in Cetona. I would not have considered marrying anywhere else—not without my Italian friends, my other half—and Peter liked the romance and the mystique of the idea. Less than two months later we were on a flight to Rome to arrange our wedding. We met with Savina, the florist at the time, we visited venues for the reception and the rehearsal dinner, and we went to Cortona for a tasting at Tonino's, the prospective caterer. It was snowing when we got there, and we sat down for what turned out to be a dozen-course meal, paired with wines, that ended only when Peter assured them they would be hired.

Peter loved everything about my home, my friends, my love for it, and my desire to return here—in fact, he almost bought me a house here, later—though neither of us understood at that time how much it quietly undercut our relationship. I wanted the happy story, and Peter could provide it: He could enable me to bridge my worlds and make it right, I thought.

The night before the wedding we had our rehearsal dinner at I Frati, one of the earliest convents founded by Saint Francis, in 1212. When I was growing up, both I Frati and the church at Belverde were abandoned and near ruin. Wooden boards were erected to keep people from entering the convent, though we often trespassed to play there like secret musketeers, the forbidden mystery and sacredness of the place scaring us yet luring us. After being purchased by Padre Eligio, both properties were lovingly restored and remain equally lovingly maintained.

Our rehearsal dinner took place in a magnificent room with soaring arches. After drinks in the gardens, we sat for platter after platter of spectacular food served at our sumptuously set tables, with candelabra, silver and crystal. Peter had on a stone-colored suit with a white shirt and a hopeful tie. His mother sang to me, and the room was filled with love and good feelings.

We were married the following day in an early evening cere-mony in the tiny church up at Belverde. The church, shaded by tall pine trees, adorned with a few surviving frescos and furnished with simple bench-like pews, is magically perched at the top of a row of steep, uneven stone steps leading to a small, simple, wooden door. My gown, ivory-colored with organza peeking out at the hem, made me feel like a princess. I wore patent leather shoes the color of pearls and a romantic shawl of intricate lace to cover my shoulders. Peter wore a custom-cut black Armani tuxedo suit with a luxurious shirt a perfect white; he was tan, his hair was short to the scalp, and he looked like something out of a Gatsby party.

People flew in from all over—the States, France, and Greece—and crowded together with my friends from Cetona and friends of the family, Italian and other, in the pews of the tiny church. Ave was there, and Costanza, and Silvio and Aldo, Romina and Ottavia and Tullia and Nicola and Sabrina, and Maria. Robynne was there from DC, and Monica from Providence, and Enzo from New York. There were people from the West Coast and Charleston. Everyone was elegantly dressed and in a happy mood, even my parents, who had not seen each other since their divorce.

My father, handsome in a crisp charcoal suit, walked me down the aisle. As we stepped into the church, I paused in the threshold to look at the faces assembled there, and it took my breath away to see my people, my favorite, dearest people, all here in my most special place in the world.

For once in my entire life, everyone was there, and it made me happy as I had never been. Complete, for a single moment.

Don Mauro performed a humorous ceremony in Italian, and, when it ended, the guests helped ring the bells of the church and the sound echoed through the valley to Cetona below. Moments later the caravan of cars from the wedding snaked through the countryside on its way to our reception at Spineto, an abbey founded by a Benedictine monk at the beginning of the past millennium and lovingly restored by a thoughtful, special couple, Marilisa and Franco.

Comprising 2,500 acres of lush property and more than a dozen farmhouses, Spineto is a regal property, historically and in beauty, and there most of our guests, including our parents and relatives, lodged for several nights in gorgeous rooms and suites with meandering corridors and secret staircases, tastefully appointed and lovingly furnished.

It was enchanting. All of it was.

When people gathered for the reception, the abbey looked dazzling in the evening light, soft like apricot fuzz, and the grass surrounding the stone buildings shone like new moss. Maria was wearing a dark blue dress and we took pictures together in the sunset, her long curly hair glowing red, my white veil sparkling. Pictures show me glowing and happy, like a girl in a princess's dress, which I felt like I was.

We had cocktails and appetizers in a shaded area along the outer walls of the abbey, servers bustling about with champagne and trays of delicacies. Then, we sat for dinner at generous round tables set with luminous white china and crystal and candles and positioned at the front of the abbey, among the white marble and green grass. The food was delicious and beautiful, and the wine stellar and abundant.

And that night, at those tables, in the hills above Cetona in the sweet summer air, for the very first time the different strands of my life came together in one place—Cetona, Yale, Charleston, the blood friends of childhood, and the friends of my adulthood; the people who had reared me, old lovers and new, from both of my worlds.

Costanza was there, and the Della Vignas, and Sabrina, and Fabio Angiolini who worked on our house, and Annie and Elio, and Greta and Pietro. Friends from California and New York. Robynne put faces to names she had heard over the decade—she met Andrea and other friends of mine— and Maria put faces to names she had heard from Charleston and college. People made new friends and tried to speak new languages; Peter's family hung out with mine, the Greeks with the Americans, the Italians with the Greeks.

Andrea, there with his new wife and their child, Chiara, looked sharp in an Italian-cut dark blue suit he had bought for the occasion, as everyone else in Cetona had. He wore a crisp white shirt, worn open at the collar without a tie, his tangle of gold chains familiar on his chest, and his dark hair skirted his shoulders. I felt comforted to see him there, yet strangely like I was parting with something tender and dear. His daughter was four or five then, and she wore a shapely azure dress, and at the end of the night I draped my veil around her head and shoulders and she danced, twirling around and around with my veil enveloping her like a magical white thread of light.

My father and mother, seated at different tables, caught up with old friends. My brother sang with the band, and we danced. Our wedding cake was as big as a four-foot round table, a tiered mille-feuilles adorned with wispy white daisies. The reception lingered into the night, almost too beautiful to end, and when Peter went to bed, up in our wedding suite, carefully chosen by Marilisa for its beauty, I stayed behind with straggling guests to smoke a cigarette.

I didn't want to go to bed. I just wanted to stay in that moment, right there, forever.

Before the wedding Andrea had volunteered to help in any way he could. Since our breakup a decade or so earlier, we had preserved a comfortable, loving friendship that we had nurtured every year at my return. He was—and remains—someone I love and feel comfortable turning to in a moment of need, and he is kind to give. I had asked if he could help bring some chairs from Spineto to the church and back, and he had agreed.

The day after the wedding—we were leaving the following day for our honeymoon in Greece and all the guests were dispersing—Peter and I made rounds to settle up bills and thank people. At Belverde we ran into Andrea who was there by himself, in the quiet shadows of the cypress trees, loading up the chairs, taking them out of the church and putting them in the van. He had on cargo pants and a white T-shirt and he looked much as I remembered him the day I left in the August dawn.

We stopped to talk. Peter thanked Andrea in his stilted Italian and they shook hands and hugged. Andrea seemed proud and honored in some way; he liked Peter.

Then, when I said goodbye to Andrea I started crying. Tears convulsed me, in a way that has confounded me over the years.

I thought, for some time, that I was simply moved by everything that had happened—the wedding, the people, seeing my friends. I was also touched in a profound way by the kindness shown to me by so many people, including Andrea. I was moved by the presence of this person I had so loved—with whom I had shared one of the most beautiful and painful experiences of my life—and to whom I was grateful.

But, I have come to understand, mine was a cry of mourning. I cried because, for one single moment, for a beautiful day, I had had everything, or most of everything, that mattered to me—Peter, Cetona, Andrea, and everyone in the world who was dear to me—right there in one place. And for that one single moment since I had left Cetona for college, my heart was whole.

And I knew it wouldn't last—that I simply could no longer have it all.

I sobbed on Andrea's shoulder with Peter looking on. Andrea hugged me and smiled. He cradled my face in his palms and wiped my tears with his thumbs across my cheeks, his hands so familiar to me, wide and strong.

— *Dai* ... he said. It's nothing. It will be ok.

But it never was. It never really would be.

Neither marriage nor time weakened the strings that tied me to Cetona, which continued to pull me softly across the stage of my life.

Cetona was and remained, even after my parents' divorce, the stem of my identity and my affections, and in fact, my family's dissolution strengthened my bond by making Cetona the only fixed pillar in an otherwise unreliable universe of tenuous new meaning.

Even after I was married, it remained the sun around which I revolved.

Of course, my dearest friendships were still there, and I cultivated them assiduously. Maria and Ottavia and Tullia and I, and Silvio Della Vigna, too, and Teo, we called each other routinely, and all year I planned my trip back and saved to ensure that nothing—not my marriage, not anyone—could threaten my yearly time in Cetona. It was natural, this love, an internal life-force of sorts, but it was not necessarily good for my life in the States, professional or emotional. I was simply not committing to another life away from this town.

And when summer came, like a pilgrim to Mecca, I returned, sometimes with Peter, sometimes without.

I cradled in my heart, in my imagination, the approach through the Alps, from the north; seeing England, floating in the sea; descending slowly south through Italy, the pink of the sun rising over the Alps, and slowly making our way south. I had given up on the idea of seeing Cetona from the plane, but I savored searching the countryside for a sign of the most familiar, the approach to Rome, the pine trees on the coast, and finally the sea.

After landing, my rush to get to Cetona began: I would gather my luggage, dash through customs, run to the rental car desk, put my luggage in my car, run to the bathroom there by the circular ramp that leads out of the building, and drive to Cetona, stopping only once to buy water and pee. Listening to Italian music and the chit-chattering on the radio, I raced on the *autostrada* until I made out Monte Cetona rising on the horizon, passed through the toll booth with the familiar little man, and drove the curvy road leading to Cetona.

Finally, in a daze of joy and excitement I arrived in the sunny piazza, drenched in summer light—not once did I return to rain—and there I searched for a parking space and a lifeline, lest I faint in fear and happiness and every emotion in between. Maria or Tullia most often provided me welcome, waiting for me, tending me a hand, mine shaking, my heart fluttering, but sometimes it was enough to walk into the bar to run into someone who would greet me and hug me and make tangible the fact that I was home.

Within minutes I put flesh on the ghosts of the past, always churning in my mind, and was reassured that I existed, that I was who I knew. And that love was eternal, again.

Over the following days and weeks I ran in the landscape I so missed, as I do now, and I sat at the fountain and the bar visiting with old friends, breathlessly. We caught up on our lives, told stories, dusted off our love, and fed our bonds. I visited with the ladies in the piazza and the store owners, and the friends of my family, and reacquainted myself, noticing the changes, assessing the differences.

Mostly, though, I sought out that which had not changed, confirming and feeding the ties of the past, their resilience a triumph over distance and time. And in them I found proof that no matter where else I might live, Cetona was still my home. That confirmation comforted me like nothing else could, renewing my identity and my place in the world.

Indeed, from there my place in the world sprung like a bud on a tree in spring.

And over the course of many years, from being a young woman in college to being a grown adult with a career, marriage, and wrinkles, the fact of standing there in that piazza and breathing in that confirmation made all of it worth it.

Me and Cetona, together again.

Occasionally over the years, as I reconfirmed my bonds and sense of place along Cetona's dusty paths, I made my way to the doorsteps of old loves, long past, to which, though, some thread of my heart remained snagged. It would take nothing but a few hours of talk to rekindle a seed of life in what was otherwise a treasured memory.

I made space for this in my heart, and justified it, childlike, though in another world, in another place, it would not have been justifiable.

And so, one summer a few years later, one beautiful August evening, the last I would be spending here on that visit, I went to say goodbye to an old lover. I was happy; I felt it as a chance to catch up with a lifelong friend who I had missed and whose love had stayed tenderly in my memory.

He expected me. I pulled up and he hugged me, and the happiness of seeing each other was mutual and clear and immediate. He had on a crisp light blue shirt and well-cut jeans. His hair had taken on a bit of gray, and I explored his hands, still manicured and elegant, cuffed by a gold bracelet, and his eyes, brown and playful. He looked, as always, handsome and sure of himself.

I had not seen him in a long time, many years, since he had been in a difficult marriage about which I knew through the grapevine, and since my own wedding. He had opened a bottle of good wine, and, sitting outside on a terrace looking out onto the darkening countryside, we talked about my life, and his, our dreams and disappointments. He told me about his failed relationship, and I told him about my marriage. His eyes showed regret and hurt, and I felt sorry for his sadness, and for mine, too, torn as I felt from here, the ghosts of my heart no less vivid than they had been ten years earlier.

Was I thinking of the past as I sat there? Was the past the present? There was no difference to me. It was a continuum, calling, sweet and yearning, in which time and distance played no part. In my head I heard the song, called "Cara," that had always reminded me of him over the years.

*Conosco un posto nel mio cuore*
*Dove tira sempre il vento*
*Per i tuoi pochi anni e per i miei che sono cento*
*Non c'è niente da capire, basta sedersi ed ascoltare*
*Perché ho scritto una canzone per ogni pentimento*

*E debbo stare attento a non cadere nel vino*

*O finir dentro ai tuoi occhi, se mi vieni più vicino*

Time flew and we opened another bottle of wine. We started talking about our old relationship, many years earlier, and the tenderness that had inhabited it, though he had been a man and I little more than a kid, unsure of everything, including and perhaps mostly myself.

Now there I was, a woman, matured, beautiful, and confident, and he the man I remembered, now also weathered and matured, and still beautiful, both closer to who I wished we had been when we had known each other before. There, in the soft dusk blanketing Cetona, we studied each other and revealed our lives with a new openness, under the kind give of wounds and regrets, and memory, and love. And the sweetness of it all lulled us back and invited us in, and finally he pulled me to him and kissed me.

I floated back through his smile, pulling me through the years, through the images like slides of my life stacked there and immovable, undying, and I landed in his playful eyes, where perhaps I had always left something.

*Why could I not have stayed and lived here?*

My marriage crossed my mind, but it was as if it were a separate reality, like two parallel panes of glass gliding millimeters from each other, distinct and unrelated.

The song rang in my ears:

*Tu corri dietro al vento e sembri una farfalla*
*E con quanto sentimento ti blocchi e guardi la mia spalla*
*Se hai paura a andar lontano, puoi volarmi nella mano*
*Ma so già cosa pensi, tu vorresti partire*
*Come se andare lontano fosse uguale a morire*
*E non c'è niente di strano ma non posso venire*
*La notte sta morendo*
*Ed è cretino cercare di fermare le lacrime ridendo*

*Ma per uno come me, l'ho gia detto*
*Che voleva prenderti per mano e volare sopra un tetto*
*Lontano si ferma un treno*
*Ma che bella mattina, il cielo è sereno*
*Buonanotte, anima mia*
*Adesso spengo la luce e così sia...*

He led me by hand to his bed, and, twenty or so years after our relationship had unfolded, we made love again. He cautioned against it—that later, in the distance, tomorrow, it would sting. But no amount of caution would or could keep me from running to the river of nostalgia and remembrance and dipping in, jumping, in fact, as if swimming in this warm pool here with this ex-lover would make up for what was lost. As if that one act of love could soothe the inside of my heart and wash away the scars of all the longing and homesickness I had endured and make up for all the love felt and discounted and abandoned.

As if holding that warm familiar body whose simple passion transcended years passed, and ascertaining that indeed our bond still existed, could fortify me enough to endure more heartbreak when I went away again, torn again from my place.

As if this could put my pieces back together like a sewn-up doll.

Through my body I wanted to will the past into the present and heal me. I wanted to undo the responsibility that had been stacked onto me, I wanted to slide back through time and be who I was before, loved, whole, before everything was lost, as if this act of intimacy with one man from Cetona could express and exorcise all my love for the whole town. For all the people and ex-lovers and friends. For my lost home. For the landscape, and the smells, and the sounds.

For my lost identity, and my broken shell—maybe even the shell broken from coming here to start.

I took him in me as if I could take Cetona into me and make it mine, make this love infinite, faultless, and endless, and nothing,

nothing at all, mattered to me at that moment more than knowing I was here, here, here, in this bed, in this town, in my place.

Here.

— *Ti volevo bene sul serio...,* he said as we lay talking. I really did love you.

— *... ma l'avevo sempre saputo che te ne saresti andata.*

But I always knew you would go. You would not stay.

The following morning I called him from the airport to say goodbye. I invested every coin I had to hear his voice, to know this had not been for nothing, that it mattered. And it did matter, maybe. But would I have come back? Could he ever have envisioned me coming back again and staying?

Yes, maybe, but I didn't have the faith, and as a result no one else did either.

That night I was back in the United States, a universe apart and a world forever changed. On his side of the ocean he returned to his normal life. And on my side, how could I do the same?

From there the unraveling was clear, and it wouldn't take long. In seeking wholeness I continued to break things apart, mine and those of others, a trail of destruction, and I just couldn't sew them back.

And this time it was for good.

As I recall that act of reckless love, I find myself here, renewing the love once more, yet, once again, endangering something else.

This week I went to Milano for a couple of days. The weather was mild and comforting, and my friends Elio and Sandra took me to the Navigli and Brera, which I enjoyed immensely. The crowds were awakening and the art stimulating.

When I returned Saturday I went to Armando's shop to get a few things. I was picking out my spinach and such when Armando reveals he has a package for me, or he thinks it's for me, at least. I look and I recognize my friend Maryellen's handwriting. I had asked her to ship the box to me if I was not back by April.

— How did this come to you? I ask Armando.

The DSL guy was in a hurry, delivered something, had this package, and asked if they knew the person whose name was on the label. They debated among themselves, Amato scratched his head and hemmed and hawed, then Graziella and Dino gathered around the box and offered their input. Finally, they agreed: We don't know her by that name, they said, but we think that's her. You can leave the package.

I love it.

I take the box upstairs and in it I find clothes and shoes and a few miscellaneous belongings I had forgotten existed. At the time I packed them I thought I might need them, but I am not sure I do now. I look at the things and drop them back into the box and I fall onto the bed with the light flowing through from the piazza.

I look into my closet with its doors flung open and my heart feels heavy. The green dress that reminds me of Aram because he likes it, and the white pants he does not like. A top I never wear. I don't even have a tenth of my clothes here, but, then again, I don't remember what I did with my clothes. What happened to the bright red strapless dress? Did I sell it, or did I pack it thoughtlessly in storage? And what about the lavender one, backless and beautiful, with flowers, and the golden yellow one that tied in a crisscross down the back ... Do I still own it? What about the chocolate shawl I love?

I had never dared to hope to be here this long; I wasn't sure that I would make it—seven months now—so I didn't bring much. But, also, I gave away and sold so much, for nothing—a laundry line the whole width of my front yard strung with clothes for sale for $10 or less to raise money for my trip. Things that in the moment of my extraordinary decision seemed ripe for sacrifice. What I didn't sell went to the battered women's shelter. Somehow right now that enthusiastic magnanimity does not fill me with joy. I have nothing to wear.

I lie back on my bed holding my green dress. I smell my perfume on it, and my body. Once, years ago, Aram and I had broken up and he came looking for me, and I had on that dress. We made up, and now I feel the want in that dress, lingering.

I reach back through the closets of my memory to the dresses I loved the most. The elegant leather jumpers of my childhood paraded on a catwalk before me, perfectly sized, with zippers down the front, gifted to me by my Auntie Phil. A Bronfman, of Seagram's fame, she was my father's partner in architecture at one point. They were close friends, and sometimes after work Dad would go shopping with her, escorting her to stores where the salespeople would bring her tea and coffee and treat her like a queen. I always remember Auntie Phil in overalls, though, blue and white stripes, her signature tiny glasses and hair cut to the scalp. She was a talented, passionate photographer, and she took the very first baby pictures of me, frowning, in the hospital, and, later, most of the pictures that gave me a sense of my childhood before Italy—of the little girl with the magic stone in my pocket. She gave my mom Chanel suits, of tweeds of brilliant colors, with the signature gold chains sewn in at the hem, that my mom eventually passed on to me, and that I no longer have.

I breathe through that, and my mind reaches for the folds of the Chanel dress that Peter gave me. Black, with little golden clasps traveling the whole front of the dress, and cuffs with Chanel buttons. The fabric was lush but cool, and the cut was divinely elegant, narrowing at the waist and flaring out just so, down to slightly below the knee. Peter found it at Saks one day. It was on a sales rack in the luxury clothing corner of the store, overseen by a bespectacled woman named Amelia who had excellent taste and knew how to help those with real money, which we were not. It was reduced down to five thousand-some-dollars from seven or eight, I can't remember.

Peter insisted I try it on. Amelia helped me—she had begun to assist us when Peter wanted me to buy an evening gown, which I had never owned, and then a proper winter coat, and cocktail dresses. And, finally, this. She brought me a pair of Gucci pumps to try with the dress and when I walked out of the dressing room to look at myself in the big mirror I understood the power and magic of haute couture, perhaps for the first time. I breathed in the cool expensive air that smelled slightly of perfume and I took in how beautiful I was and could be. The dress fit me as if Coco herself had stood there and cut it for me, and my anguished flat-chested days at Cetona's cruel fountain fell from me like bad dreams. Peter bought the dress for me, with a beaming grin on his face, like the best thing in the world had just happened to him rather than me. He was so kind to me.

Amelia bagged it for me and hugged me and I stood holding the garment bag like a foreign object. Eventually, though, I wore it, and it became my dress for all solemn occasions—weddings and funerals, and the baptisms of children of South Carolina senators who eventually fell from grace. And, ultimately, my own divorce.

When Peter saw it on me on our court day in the brightly lit hallway of the courthouse fronting Broad Street, he pursed his lips, a slight smile poorly veiling sadness. Nice dress, he said.

I sobbed on the stand giving testimony to my own ruin until the judge agreed that this could not be fixed and she banged the gavel.

It seems like a different lifetime now, but the grief still tears like I am caught on a rusty nail.

I shake off the weight of those memories and walk downstairs and through the piazza to the bar. A small crowd gathers at the counter to feast on the vast assortment of hors d'oeuvres that Nilo puts out, what he calls *regalini*, or small presents.

— *Cinque Campari e cinque regalini!* he yells out at his servers, who quickly assemble plates spilling over with treats. They get more elaborate by the day—crostini with *pomodoro*, dips and mozzarella balls and endless servings of cubed *mortadella* and cheese.

Today Nilo is in a bored mood. He is pacing, then he turns to Federica, the bartender.

— *Dammi una palla di gelato, va'.* Give me a scoop of ice cream (literally, in Italian, a ball).

— *Una palla come?* she asks with her masklike expression. What kind of ball?

— *Come le mie. Media e moscia.* Like mine, medium and limp.

I laugh and walk outside, to a table where Andrea is sitting alone. He is done working for the day and he leafing through the newspaper, drinking chamomile tea.

— *Com'è?* he asks. How's it going?

I'd like to tell him about my romantic ruminations about my clothes and the things I miss, and Aram, at risk, and the things I wish I had, and my regrets about Peter and my marriage, but it's foreign and vague-sounding to someone practical like Andrea. It feels vague and confused even to me; plus, it's too private now. I realize that I would be extending too much of myself. I feel the weight of the days and years not narrated that now make it impossible to open one's life again truthfully. My world is foreign—again, but in reverse—and it seems too hard to try.

I ask how he is. He scowls and inveighs for a moment against Italy and politics: corruption, the *raccomandati*—the people who have jobs through friends in high places—and the jobs created by the party, the left. Everyone is corrupt and dishonest, sick with a brand of dishonesty whose craftiness is peculiarly Italian and whose reach is unimaginable.

He may be right, and probably is, but in this slice of life he sounds faithless. I'd like to ask why—our laughs and sweetness pull me back—but it would feel intrusive. I don't know his secrets, or his disappointments, or the remnants of his dreams.

Yet, I can't reach back through time to know him again. It would take a trust and a commitment now lost to me, and I must accept that. Perhaps if I lived here again ... well, everything would be different.

While I listen to him I think of suggesting he practice yoga, to recapture some serenity, but he would scoff. His back hurts, and his knees.

— *L'unica cosa che non mi fa male è il pisello,* he says, touching his crotch in a celebrated Italian gesture of superstition and comfort. The only thing that doesn't hurt is my dick.

Thank God for that, I say, kissing him goodbye on the cheek.

On my run today, as I went up by Poggio alla Vecchia, a little enclave up on the mountain, and down by Diamante's house, I was buoyed by a surprising sound of music reverberating around the curves and up and down the hills. A joyous mazurka, then a tarantella—the music of Cetona's farmers.

At first, I couldn't identify the source. A house, I wondered, though it seemed improbable given the hour of the day. Plus, people don't play music in their houses here, not much. Then I realized that the sound was moving and likely coming from a vehicle. The idea filled me with joy, and I ran along my route like a kid, hoping to find it.

Finally, there it was, the big red van speeding around a curve and down a hill, a mazurka trailing behind. I tried to catch up, but I couldn't. I thought for sure that I had lost it when, a mile or so later, the music reverberated even louder, and as I rounded a curve past the Fieramoscas' house, there it was the big red van, parked, music blasting!

Laughing to myself I approached the van and a man rolled down the window and smiled, flashing some gold fillings. Balding, with a gold ring on his pinkie, he looked like some kind of a salesman, and, indeed, when he turned down the volume he explained that he sells live birds, chicks, and baby turkeys to farmers in the area. He drives around the countryside using the music as his calling card. He is from Terni, in Umbria, and he has been doing it for thirty years.

His name is Eolo, the Greek god of the winds. Aelous.

I laughed.

— I have been following you! I love your name, and the music! I told him.

His eyes lit up and he smiled back. We chatted for a few minutes and he gave me his card, then I thanked him and ran off. As I went, he turned up the volume and the music filled the countryside again, drawing my thoughts to the summer festivals of the Communist Party up at the *campo sportivo*, with their waltzes and tangos, and the stories of people dancing in the countryside after the war ended.

I stopped and looked out on the countryside, imagining the sounds of shells and the rumbling of military trucks bringing war to this land.

World War II came to Cetona as it did to small towns throughout Italy, moving through as the German and then the British-American fronts advanced through the country. Throughout Tuscany, towns like Cetona with strong agrarian roots and, because of that, strong leftist inclinations, had already become caldrons of anti-Fascist and anti-German sentiment. People wanted peace and out with the Fascists, who were bullying the country, killing and persecuting.

By 1943—and this is a fact few people in the States seem to know—Italian forces had fallen under German control, and many Italians who were against the Germans were taken as prisoners of war. Italy was essentially an occupied country. The Fascist military forces of the so-called New Republic began drafting people to serve under German authority against their will and against their own country. Local farmers and workers refused to enlist, and, under the threat of death, many went into hiding. They took to Monte Cetona and the hills to fight as *partigiani*.

It was a civil war of sorts, countryman against countryman.

Plotting in tense secrecy, the partisans of Cetona and surrounding towns built tenacious grassroots networks to oppose the Fascists and the Germans and to aid the allies as soon as they arrived on the peninsula and moved north. Ever-vigilant of spies among them—fellow citizens and neighbors who were Fascists or Fascist sympathizers—and ever cautious of the ubiquitous and often plain-clothed Fascist police, they met in secret in the countryside to strategize how to find arms and to plan whatever disruptions they could to Fascist and German forces. Often, they hid for many months up on Monte Cetona, which, because of its dense vegetation and its position on the landscape, offered Cetona—and several other towns nestled on its flanks, such as Sarteano, Radicofani and Fontevetriana—a natural buffer and partisans a good hiding place.

I grew up hearing about the partisans, who are heroes in Cetona.

Nello Lorenzoni, known as Il Verdacchio, a short man with red hair and a bulbous nose, used to come to our school to tell us partisan stories. Invited by Marga, our elementary school teacher, he told somber tales about his time hidden up on the mountain, and of guns and bombs that helped turn the direction of the war locally. He told of the occasional spy they uncovered among them, snitches for the Germans or the Fascists, and how they took them to hidden places to shoot them. A man by the name of Il Polacco was one such spy, and in Cetona a road, an intersection, and an old farmhouse are named after him, to memorialize the betrayal.

Pippo, Cetona's ceramist, who takes great pride in the study and history of his town, gave me an interesting book about the partisan movement and the liberation of Cetona and Monte Cetona. Titled *Brigata Simar*, it tells about the campaign of sabotage and resistance that a local brigade of partisans led against the Fascists and the Germans here, leaving their homes courageously in the dark of night and heading up to the frigid mountain in wind and snow.

Among them was Renato Fabietti, who went on to become a prominent intellectual and writer and a dear friend in my parents' larger social circle. He joined the partisans one night in winter of '44, as little more than a kid, and set out for the mountain with Chichio, one of Cetona's favorite characters, a man Fabietti describes as no taller than a broom handle. They gathered with others in *poderi* here and there, secretively, at night, and then dispersed in the woods to hide. There, sometimes helped by farmers, sometimes just out in the cold on their own, they hid, tracked the movements of the Fascists and the Germans, and amassed arms to fight. People say that there are still hidden troves of guns up *in montagna*, left there by the partisans, but their location has remained a secret, now gone with the dead.

Every now and then the partisans managed to surprise a German convoy and derail it, stealing the trucks and detaining the

German soldiers in makeshift concentration camps. Sometimes they sabotaged Germans stealing wheat and other goods from farmers or local granaries, and they put the Germans in jail and gave the stolen food to the local people, who, by then, were starving. On one occasion, they helped rescue some American parachutists whose plane had gone down on Monte Cetona, near Palazzone. The parachutists had ejected from the plane; alas, one had crashed into a tree and been injured beyond repair. His body was taken by cart and mule and buried in San Casciano.

The facts that Nello told us when he came to talk to us in school have gone from my mind—we were children and the war was unimaginable to us—but I remember getting a sense that the partisans, overshadowed by the romance of the American and English liberation, had been given inadequate recognition for their contribution, and this troubled him, understandably. He wanted us to grasp the importance of this.

Then, when he was finished with his stories, he led us in singing the famous song, "O Partigiano," which we all grew up knowing by heart:

> *Una mattina mi son svegliato*
> *O bella ciao, bella ciao, bella ciao ciao ciao*
> *Una mattina mi son svegliato*
> *E ho trovato l'invasor ...*
> *O partigiano portami via*
> *O bella ciao, bella ciao, bella ciao ciao ciao*
> *O partigiano porta mi via*
> *Che mi sento di morir ...*

Nello, unfortunately, died some years back, as have most veterans, and finding people who remember the war with any clarity is nearly impossible.

I was lucky that Agata's parents, Lidiano and Bruna, into their eighties now, told me their war memories over tea and cookies one rainy day. It was like old times, when Bruna made tea for Agata and me in that same kitchen, now repainted and restored.

Lidiano is a vivid storyteller, and although he is in his late eighties and he walks slowly with a cane, he is an avid reader and he has a sharp mind and a good wit. Bruna, short, with coiffed hair and beady brown eyes, interrupts him while he's talking, which aggravates him.

— *Bruna, sta' zitta!* he says. Shut up, Bruna!

During the war, Bruna and her family lived in an old sprawling farmhouse a few yards from the road that leads to Chiusi. Perhaps because of its size, or perhaps because of its location, the house was used initially as command compound by the Germans, and later by the British, and then, during the Allied liberation, by the Red Cross. Quite a storied place.

As Bruna tells it—and she will tell you that she remembers it all as if it were yesterday—during the German occupation the family was sent to live in the cellars and the stalls while the command slept comfortably in the main house. From there, entrenched and unwavering in their orders, the German commandos dispatched the young men of Cetona, or those they could find, to do whatever was necessary to disrupt the Allied and partisan advances—anything from digging trenches to blowing up roads to blowing up bridges. They blew up sections of Via Risorgimento, and the bridge over the Astrone too, which Lidiano and Bruna said was a beautiful arched stone structure the likes of which was never rebuilt.

Lidiano was one of six children in a family of longstanding Communist allegiance. They lived up in Cetona's highest parts, at the Steccato. Their father was a shoemaker, and their mother worked for Terrosi, the landowner. They were poor. Lidiano was too young to fight at the time, and two of his older brothers had already been taken by the Fascists to fight for the Germans. Yet—and he says this with a proud smile—he considered himself a partisan by birth and he did what he could to help the older guys, roaming around town looking for the action.

Cetona did not see heavy fighting or bombings, luckily, yet every now and then someone got killed, or a house got bombed by German troops posted uphill, in Sarteano, from where they monitored the valley below. And sometimes Fascists and partisans came into direct conflict right there in town.

One day, Lidiano told me, a dozen or so German soldiers in retreat were cresting the top of Borgo, at the southern entrance to the piazza, and a group of *partigiani* took a shot at them with their machine guns. They missed, and the Germans were unhurt, but the shots left a large number of bullet holes in the metal gate of the house that sits at the top of the hill, there for all to see. When we were little we'd go stare at the bullet holes; we'd heard stories about them, constantly embellished by details of partisan heroism or German violence. The one I remember the best was that the seven brothers had been lined up by the Germans there and shot in the head, and their mother had been made to watch. Fortunately, that did not happen— not that I was able to confirm. The gate has since been replaced and there is no sign of the bullet holes.

But, Lidiano told me, when those German soldiers who had been fired upon crossed the piazza and moved out into the countryside via the road to the cemetery, they killed seven random men they gathered up here and there—out of revenge, people said. They shot them about their bodies with machine guns and finished them off with a pistol shot to the head, disfiguring them. Among them were Nello's brothers. They each left behind young children and wives.

Renato, the jovial white-haired man who wears the ascots and hangs out at Armando's, lived with his family in a farmhouse uphill from the cemetery. His father had been taken prisoner by the Germans, and Renato, just a boy then, lived with his mother, his aunt, and his older cousin, who looked after him.

One beautiful summer day—there were flowers in bloom, Renato recalls—they were all outside when a group of Fascists and Germans moved through their farmhouse on motorcycles with sidecars. As they drove through, they killed the family's animals, several ducks and a turkey, with their bare hands. The turkey had had babies, he said, and the little birds were scurrying about happily behind their mother, in the green grass. The soldiers swooped the big mother turkey right off her feet and snapped her head off.

Renato's aunt yelled after them.

— *Eh, finirà anche per voi,* she said, using an Italian expression that means the good life will come to an end for you too.

Some of the men—Italians, Fascists—heard her and turned back. They surrounded her and Renato's mother and pointed their machine guns at them. Renato stood there, his life suspended before him. He had no one but them.

Finally, one man pushed his fellow soldiers' guns down with his hand and they retreated, taking the turkey and the ducks to a neighboring house where an elderly woman lived alone. The house was wide open and the soldiers went in, making themselves at home. They took out pots and pans and salt and oil, boiled the animals, and ate them right there on her kitchen table.

The woman was inside but they left her alone, or so she said.

— *Tanto io so' vecchia. Se ammazzavano anche me era uguale,* she said after they went. I'm old; if they had killed me, too, it would have been the same.

On the heels of the retreating Germans came the British and the Americans, mixed with French and Moroccans. They arrived on foot and in trucks from the direction of Piazze. People went to the edge of town to see them come, this long human chain snaking its way through the countryside and up the hill of Finoglio. They brought food and candy, though I also heard of violence and rapes in the countryside.

When they came through Cetona, British and American soldiers camped out where the Germans had before them, here and there, in people's farmhouses. They took a bedroom in Renato's house too and gave him chocolate and coffee. They settled at the Rocca and at the *campo della fiera,* later called the *campo sportivo,* the soccer fields, an elevated grassy opening that through the 1800s and most of the 1900s had been used for livestock fairs, and later for military exercises and encampments.

The British army encompassed soldiers from all over the colonies—Indians and Pakistanis, South Africans and Malaysians—and they performed military exercises in the piazza. The turbans of Indian soldiers, worn atop their British uniforms, dotted the piazza with every shade of red and orange and yellow, brightening the drab wartime landscape and Lidiano's memory.

Meanwhile, out in the countryside huge caravans of trucks snaked forcefully through Cetona's fields and hills, and then, squadrons of American warplanes came flying through the skies, slow and low.

— *Madonnina, dal gran rumore s'assordiva,* Lidiano said, shaking his head. Dear Lord, the noise was so loud as to deafen you.

All told, the war left many dead in Cetona, more than two hundred, according to the memorial plaque in the piazza, and many *infelici,* as they say here—meaning invalid. Yet, slowly the normalcy of peacetime returned.

In the darkness of night, people gathered in the farmhouses to celebrate peace, to dance the waltzes and mazurkas that for years were Cetona's only music. Music filled the land and the stomachs, eased the hearts and healed the wounds of the suffering. I picture the lanterns sparkling and I hear the laughter and the sweet lament of a lone accordion echoing through the rooms and the stalls and the valleys beyond, a thread to recovery and hope.

Slowly, people went back to work, if they had work, Lidiano in a manganese mine in Camporsevoli, some seven or eight miles away. He went on foot every morning and returned on foot every night—an inconceivable walk that began at dark and ended at dark. After the war, Lidiano joined the military, in northern Italy, and with the money he earned he was able to buy his first watch and his first bicycle.

After the war there were no cars in Cetona—only mules—and silence, unforgettable darkness and silence. Papalino, a man who was also the grave-digger, swept the whole town, quietly. I ask where people threw their trash then, and Lidiano laughs. There was no trash, he says. No one threw anything away. We used everything, every scrap of anything.

There was no water in the houses, and no bathrooms. People got water from the fountains in town and heated it in the sun, or, if there was firewood, on their stoves.

— We had nothing but each other, Lidiano's sister Lavinia told me.

When I was growing up, and through my teenage years, Lavinia owned a grocery store in piazza. She seemed crotchety, at least with me, perhaps because my mother did not patronize her store, and I found her so *antipatica* that I would do anything to avoid her—this in spite of the fact that she was aunt to both my friends Agata and Giulia.

But the years have gone by now. Lavinia is in her mid-eighties, bird-like and recently widowed, and I feel a twinge of tenderness when I watch her from my window as she walks to get coffee or to the *giardinetti* to sit with her friends.

One day shortly after I first arrived she recognized me and gave me a big hug, which surprised me and moved me. I asked if I could come visit, and now the slate has been wiped clean.

While we sit in her dimly lit kitchen, in the same post-war building where I spent so much time with Ida's family, she smooths the plasticized tablecloth and offers me coffee.

— *Ti fo il caffè. Lo prendi?* she says, looking at me with her cat-like eyes, brown speckled with green. I thank her and tell her I don't drink coffee much.

— *L'acqua? Il tè?* Water? Tea?

I shake my head.

— *Ma vaffanculo,* she says jokingly, sort of. Go fuck yourself.

We talk about the war until she realizes that it is time for her to walk up to the *giardinetti* to meet her friends. If she does not show up at the regular time, people will come looking for her and ring her bell, which annoys her.

I offer to leave, but she says no, wait. Stay. *Si va su insieme,* simple words that convey Cetona to me, the precious and lost art— in my life—of walking together arm in arm and sharing something, even silence.

Lavinia gets up to dress and get ready.

— *Mica c'è da vergognarsi,* she says. There is nothing to be ashamed about.

No, I say, smiling.

She goes in the bedroom and takes off her pants, wondering aloud what she's going to wear. For a moment I feel embarrassed to see an elderly woman naked, someone I have not seen for so long, or don't even know that well, but then I am moved by the intimacy, plain and honest and asking nothing. I look up and Lavinia is putting on dark blue pants and I see her leg as it goes into the pants. Her skin is dark and healthy and her muscle tone is strong, and I smile thinking that she will be strong to her last day. I think back to when she had the store. Maybe she wasn't crotchety after all; maybe she was just a strong woman with a lot of worry.

I watch her pull on a clean bra and a tank top, then she walks by me to go to the bathroom.

— Look at the beautiful old lady, she says, with a bit of self-mock- ery. *Ma la gallina vecchia fa buon brodo!* The old hen makes good broth. I smile. I want to stop her and caress her, for being the blood of the blood of so many people I love and for sharing of herself with me, but that would be awkward and inexplicable.

In the bathroom she washes her face and arms, rubbing the water up and down her arms. From the bathroom she tells me that she washes every morning. She is afraid to fall ill suddenly and the emergency responders will find her dirty and gossip about her, she says. I laugh, but she is serious, and perhaps right.

After washing she takes care to dress properly, choosing her things. While she dresses she tells me about Gabriella, who is married to Pierpaolo's brother, Massimo, and is the head of the *casa famiglia*, and then she suddenly wonders aloud if she can wear a top she wore yesterday, and I agree with her. No one will notice, she says.

After she gathers her things—her purse, her glasses, her rosary beads, and her Bible—we walk down the steps and out onto the street. We walk up the hill arm in arm and in front of the church I thank her for her stories and her time with me.

She hugs me.

— *Viemmi a trova' presto,* she says. Come see me before long.

One of my favorite retreats on this stay has become Il Merlo, Cetona's other restaurant, nestled in a magical arched space in the guard tower at the top of Via Sobborgo.

It is owned by Daniele and Elisa and their extended families: Elisa is the chef; Daniele is host, server, and sommelier; Elisa's father, Stefano, works in the dining room; and both of their mothers, Marcella and Ottavia, work in the kitchen.

Il Merlo warms my heart with the splendor of its space, distinguished by majestic tall arches dating back centuries, its delicious, creative food, its wine selection, the cleanliness of its glasses, the joviality and kindness of the family, and a nearly bottomless supply of good stories and jokes, mostly from Daniele but some from Stefano, too.

Tall and thin, with a dark beard, a Roman nose and a long narrow face framing smart dark eyes, Daniele looks like a Caravaggio cardplayer—and Elisa, with hair nearly buzzed and her own distinguished nose, does too. But what makes Daniele particularly noteworthy is a restless bubbling nervous energy that, coupled with a superb wit, makes him one of the funniest men in Cetona. His humor, take on the world, and perfect recall and delivery of jokes can stir me from my most melancholic or solitary of moods. I like to sit at the tiny bar writing in my journal, feeling private yet comforted, and listen to him freebase stories while delivering trays of food and bottles of wine to the tables full of expectant customers. He is particularly witty about the town where he was born—in the fumes of the slaughterhouse—and the peculiar people who inhabit it, his fellow Cetonesi.

So, I stop in once a week or so to say hi, have a glass of wine, and break my routine.

A couple of weeks ago over a glass of wine I told Daniele that I had been up to town hall to see a painting by Lionello Balestrieri, a painter born in Cetona in the late 1800s. He earned acclaim in Europe as a romantic painter of crowds and moods and tortured musicians before moving onto an art nouveau-futuristic phase. His is a household name in Cetona—one of a handful—and is revered, understandably. A foundation is dedicated to the preservation of his works and things related to his life, and people talk about him with the pride reserved for a son who left home and made something of himself.

Over the course of the years I had heard Balestrieri's name many times. I had noticed his gravestone at the cemetery, large and imposing compared to most; I had heard my father, an art appassionato and connoisseur, mention his name; and I knew that our family friend Angela owned what had been Balestrieri's home where he retired here at the end of his life.

Never before now, however, had I taken an interest in his work or, I am sad to admit, known much about him, so I was pleased when in the library the other day a Balestrieri catalogue came my way and I decided to ask to see a self-portrait listed as being property of the town. I showed the picture of the painting to Concetta, the director of the museum, who, with her can-do attitude, grabbed a key from a drawer and walked me down the old halls of the *scuola media* to a door. She unlocked it, flipped on the light, and left me.

As I told Daniele, after my eyes adjusted to the dim light, I looked around the room and saw only one small painting hanging on

419

a wall. I moved across the room to look at it, and it was indeed the self-portrait in question. I took it off the hook and was thrilled to be able to see it, but I was troubled to find it cheaply framed, hanging crookedly in this dismal empty classroom, and, worst of all, with dirty glass directly touching the canvas.

It's Cetona's most famous citizen's self-portrait!

Daniele shakes his head, then he starts laughing.

— *Questa è l'antiscienza della scienza, alla Cetonese!* he says, a big sarcastic smile overtaking his face. It's the anti-science of science, Cetonese style!

I look at him puzzled.

— See, he says, half-jokingly, they figured that by putting the glass against the canvas they would have two paintings: the original painting, and the glass with the paint stuck to it!

He cradles his face in his hands and we laugh.

While I sit in the golden light of the room, I watch the people, locals and travelers, who come in and out through the elegant glass doors and sit underneath the warm brick arches to share a meal, a laugh, and a story.

Last night Elide's daughter and grand-daughter, Emanuela and Alessia, were there having dinner. When they got up to pay, we started talking about celebrities who have lived in or visited Cetona in the past decades, of which there have been many.

Spanning music and journalism, industry, the arts and cinema, they include everyone from Fiat's Agnelli family, which has owned houses here for decades—and when Signora Agnelli comes through the piazza people nearly bow; Valentino, who owns the Parco Terrosi; a number of prominent politicians and historians, among them Rosario Villari, who wrote the most famous and widely read high school text-books about Italian history; and former prime ministers and presidents. In addition, in the seventies, eighties, and nineties, many, many famous Italian actors and movie directors found perch in Cetona—from Ettore Scola to Vittorio Gassman, Mario Monicelli, Ruggero

Maccari, father of my friend Barbara, Monica Vitti, Giuliano Gemma, Ottavia Piccolo, famous Italian comic actor Nino Manfredi, and more recently, Gabriele Salvatores, director of the movie *Mediterraneo.*

Story goes that Nino Manfredi, who has since died, pulled into the piazza in a convertible during the Holy Friday procession one year, back in the seventies. He had some other famous people in the car and it drew the attention of the crowd. While the priest continued unperturbed to lead the procession and recite his important-sounding Latin prayers, Manfredi and friends parked the car and went to the bar, and everyone in the procession abandoned rank to follow Manfredi to get a closer look.

— *Il prete rimase lì come un coglione!* laughs Alessia. The priest was left hanging there like a testicle!

One summer, Gassman, who, by then, was at the height of his career and had won acting awards all over Europe, came to town driving a sexy green convertible and took people for rides, including Elide. The car was very low to the ground, and Elide, a smartass, mocked the car.

— *O citto, ma che mi fai sede' per terra?* Hey kid, whatta you doing, making me sit on the floor?

This left Gassman humored, and off he sped with Elide into the countryside.

And then came heartthrob Ronn Moss—Ridge on *The Bold and Beautiful.* He came as a guest at Valentino's place, and on a Saturday morning he went strolling through the market, drawing stares and moans from all the women in town, young and old, sophisticated and not.

At one point on the show Ridge's character had been shot, and people across the globe had mourned him. In the piazza, a rather large woman from the countryside approached him tremulously. She grabbed him by the arm and hugged him.

— *Mostro! Quant'ho pianto quando t'hanno sparo!* You monster, she said in country Cetonese. I cried so much when they done shot you!

We laugh talking about Cetona's humor and personalities, then Daniele starts talking about Alighiero Bencivenni, who had been on my mind just yesterday when I took an epic run through Piandisette and up to Poggio alla Vecchia, a secluded cluster of houses on the mountain.

The countryside was crisp and smelled sweetly of grass and roses and broom grass, *ginestra*, and mimosa, a flower made of tiny bright yellow puffs with a heavenly smell that leaves me puzzled by the infinite joy of small things.

In Piandisette the view of the hills and the fields toward Piazze struck me as particularly achingly beautiful. In my view, this stretch of landscape epitomizes the balanced terracing and palette of greens that make up the perfection of the Tuscan countryside, unparalleled in the world. It so gladdened me that in ecstasy I stopped by the side of the road to dance to Barry White's "You're the First, the Last, My Everything," which came on my iPhone at this perfect moment. A great American song for my very American girl-elation. Cars went by and honked and I waved at them smiling, then I took up the hill with greed, eating them.

Alas, on my way back, which is much harder on this run, up the steep gravel roads through Monte Cetona I developed an ugly blister. I could barely walk. I chose the easiest route back, through Poggio alla Vecchia, and I stopped by Alighiero Bencivenni's mother's house to see if she had a Band-Aid.

— *Signora! Signora!* I yelled out.

She came to the door wiping her hands on her apron, her hair in a kerchief. She said she had been making cookies and she apologized her having dirty hands.

She looked me over.

— *Ma te 'n' sei la Sibilla? Ma te andavi nel pulmino con Alighiero! Ti ricordo bene!* Aren't you Sibilla? You used to ride the bus with Alighiero! I remember you well!

She greeted me enthusiastically and, as fate would have it, she had plenty of bandages on hand.

— *Ma Alighiero 'n l'ha' visto?* she asked with her big smile. Haven't you seen Alighiero?

Alighiero is one of my favorite people in Cetona, the walking image of *simpatia*. We are about the same age—he might be a couple of years older than me—and we grew up knowing each other, in school and outside.

Alighiero's family has lived in Poggio alla Vecchia for generations. They raise calves, chickens, and pigs, and every time I run by there Alighiero's children and others, too, want to show me the animals, which, now that I am vegetarian, troubles me. The entire and single purpose of animals here is to satisfy the needs of man, and anything else is not worth listening to or pondering.

One time I saw a calf there, tied to a wall by a chain so short the animal couldn't move. When Alighiero's dad opened the stall door and showed him to me, I asked him why he kept the calf so constrained.

— *Eh, se lo lascio libero non dà più retta e diventa cattivo. Così invece mi dà retta!* he said, explaining that the calf, a male, would not listen to him if he left him outside or gave him more freedom. He gets mean, he said.

I did not attempt to convince him otherwise. I don't know how to argue this here. Arguments that elsewhere would buoy me leave me speechless here.

In any case, I am fond of Alighiero. He is kind and simple as God made him, as they say here, and he has a funny and clever sense of humor. Plus, he is a good and doting father.

When his son was a little kid, Daniele said, Alighiero would ask him, *Che ci hai tra le gambe?* What's between your legs?

— *La bestia!!* the little boy would answer. The beast!!!

Though Alighiero is not particularly tall or at all overweight, everything about him is a tiny bit oversized, particularly his nose, his ears, and his hands. His fingers, for which he is famous, resemble small sausages, and, in fact, when his arms are hanging down, his hands hang by his side like large Buddha hands of sorts. Daniele's eyebrows shoot up and he laughs just thinking about this.

This winter Alighiero injured himself at work, cutting several of his fingers rather severely. For weeks he walked around town helplessly with his elbows bent and his huge bandaged hands upwards in front of him (hence the abundance of bandages at his mother's house). I would see him in the piazza and ask him how he was. Poor guy, he'd shake his big hands impatiently, itching to go back to work, and my eyes were immediately drawn to his fingers. He'd look down at them dejected.

— *Ma quella degli undici piselli la sai?* Daniele asks me, standing there at the counter of Il Merlo. Do you know the story of the eleven penises?

No, I say laughing, foreseeing.

Story goes that Alighiero was manning the grill at a cookout for some guests at one of the Della Vignas' farmhouses. People hung out by the fire, and there was talking and drinking. A girl who was a bit tipsy stared at Alighiero intensely from afar. Finally, she walked over to the grill to talk with him and she started caressing his fingers.

— *Che belli. Non avevo mai incontrato un uomo con undici piselli!* How beautiful they are, she cooed dreamily. I had never met a man with eleven penises!

I crack up. Imagine, Daniele says: He can please eleven women at one time.

— Yes, Elisa chimes in happily, but they would all have to be very skinny!

It is no surprise that, in Cetona's shadow, over the course of the years I failed to build loyalty for another place. With a foot in whatever my present life was, in the back of my mind I always kept an eye fixed on the irrepressible hope that one day I would come back here to live, to be. And for that hope, that possibility, I would risk anything and everything.

After my divorce, though, the stars lined up to keep me put for a while, to stop me from moving deliriously between two disjointed worlds of tormenting emotional chaos. Life—I like to think of it as a group of benevolent, robed Greek gods—conspired to hold me on one side of the ocean, stateside, and to keep Cetona at bay.

Or, perhaps, it was my subconscious at work, protecting me from myself. Like cutting off an arm to save the body.

After several years working for a law firm on the litigation of an education adequacy lawsuit against the state of South Carolina, an outgrowth of the education reporting I had done for the newspaper, I worked for *Garden & Gun* magazine for some time, and freelanced, but I felt a calling to chart a meaningful, edifying next step. The search—what felt like time in a putrid, panicky swamp—led me back to an idea I had had years earlier, of creating a school curriculum using the study and cultivation of food to teach children everything from math to biology, history to anthropology to economics, and important things about spirituality and the environment.

I was lucky, through a dear friend, to find an angel donor who funded a pilot of my program in Asheville, North Carolina, which I called Terra Summer. It was radical and stirring; parents and children were moved and impacted, and perhaps equally important, the program kept me tethered to North Carolina for four summers. In the evenings I'd sit out on my balcony and smell the cool mountain air that reminded me of Cetona on late summer nights, perhaps because of a combination of altitude, terrain, and vegetation. I felt a sweet sting of nostalgia, but I knew that I was in the right place doing the right thing.

In the meantime, in Charleston, I moved to a poetic, romantic, status-less, falling-down cottage in the country surrounded by oak trees and marsh. Its soulfulness and simplicity spoke to my origins no matter the possums that fell through the ceiling and the raccoons that nested everywhere. Red fox came at night, and all sorts of birds, and I sat watching, on the dock on a tidal creek meandering through Charleston's ever-changing marsh. It was the most beautiful place I had ever lived in America, in a landscape that renewed me.

It was there that Joe, my ginger tabby, then a tiny kitten with big green eyes, found me and became my inseparable friend. It was there, during those same years, that I learned and built my yoga practice, became vegetarian, committed to nonviolence, and promised to not break things up anymore, in my life or that of others. To create beauty and peace only.

As dear as any part of that time, I got my chickens, a flock of twenty-seven baby birds shipped and dropped off at the post office at dawn in a cardboard box about a foot by a foot from which came endearing *peep-peep* sounds. We picked them up expectantly, Aram and I, and brought them to the house and raised them to be big birds, at least most of them: J.C., my regal black rooster, who over time ended up being one-legged and one-eyed; Fred and Frank, charming twin Barred Rock roosters who chased each other and fought incessantly; Benny, a white Italian Leghorn Fascist rooster who bossed all the hens into straight rows, until he became overbearing and we gave him away; and the many hens, one more personable and colorful than the other: Maria, Pesky, Ellie, Rays, Assunta, Bianca, Beppa, Queenie, Bella, Victoria, Little Girl, Fergie, Sarah, Abbey, C.S. Lewis, Rossa, Fingers, Rami, Wings, and La Parisienne.

The chicks, with their cool fingers, warm waddles, and their individual ways of inhabiting the world, some with chutzpah, some with watchfulness, opened me to a new universe of tenderness and beauty and expanded my boundaries of love and familiarity to places I could not have imagined. And they tied me to Charleston, where they breathed and smiled with me.

Finally, the gods led me to painting, which transformed me and filled me with wonder and joy, and to Aram himself, who understood and participated compassionately in my search for stillness and for-giveness. He handed me parts of the puzzle and helped me find oth-ers. He countered with warmth and support my acerbic inner critic, nurtured by the most mordant of teachers. In Aram's world, there is always something kind to be found, to be said—the pink lining in the dark cloud. His insight and evenhandedness, and mostly his goodness, calmed me and kept me. He loved me, in bed and out; we listened to good music, swam in the creek, and ate fully and joyfully.

All told, I stayed away from Cetona seven years—seven years of growth, evolution, even happiness. In some ways, I shed layers of grief and grew to inhabit my full self most fully, even to my own surprise. I returned to be the girl in the picture with the peace sign and the flying sand—the little girl with the magic stone in my pocket.

To be who I was before it all.

Yet, it was always there, Cetona, waiting, breathing within me. The home that would be mine again.

And then I dreamt the orange trees, and, as I knew it would happen—as we all knew—I could not resist the call.

At seven months now, I still love meandering through the rhythm of Cetona with my senses—the pace I have not measured, the color I have not seen, for so long but in memory.

On this Sunday in late spring I renew this love, watching the town move into slower motion like stretching itself out into the warm underbelly of the blooming countryside. People linger in sunny cor-ners and talk a bit longer. The piazza is dotted with people in twos or threes clustering to exchange a few words. Amato and his gang lean against Amato's truck; Alcide is there, and Mario, and Amedeo. Amato's shirt collar is open and he's taking in the sun. His face looks flushed and youthful and his white hair sparkles. Feriero drives up in his Ape and joins them.

I hear singing coming from the church. A few latecomers run up the steps and into its darkness. Some people pull up at Vasilika's to pick up flowers; they come out of their store and arrange them carefully in their car, heading to the cemetery. Giovanna walks by going to get her newspaper.

Church lets out. I see Maddalena, Andrea's mother-in-law, the queen of the ladies, tall and flawlessly dressed. Ave comes out, and Fortunata, and dozens of other ladies. There are many more people than usual. Tullia comes out, too, which surprises me, then I see Sofia: I realize they are preparing for Confirmation. Young girls are dressed in their Sunday outfits and it reminds me of us, too, dressing up as teenagers to come in piazza to show off, to parade. It would fill me with anticipation that I relished, perhaps because so seldom did I have something new to show off: my tiered skirt like an ice-cream sandwich of strawberry, chocolate, and vanilla, or the sweaters Allegra knitted for me.

By noon the Bar Cavour has the monopoly on the sunny side of the piazza. The tables are fanned out and they are full of people basking, reading the paper, drinking cappuccini or Campari. Bar Sport is also full with its regulars, its favorites. Nilo and Federica are shuffling about here and there cleaning tables and delivering drinks. Soon people fan out here and there, heading to Nilo's for lunch, or Il Merlo. It's a Sunday tradition, and both will be packed with people sitting and eating for hours.

I see Giulia crossing the piazza with Mario, her husband. The sun sparkles in her glossy black hair, and I wave. She is my childhood friend whose parents owned the hardware store in the piazza (and she is Lidiano and Lavinia's niece). While I was away she studied nursing, then went to work at *casa famiglia*, taking care of Cetona's elderly and infirm. It's work that suits her, generous and comforting as she is, escorting people through the last passage of their lives. She has pronounced dead dozens of Cetona's elderly and sick, including Maria's grandfather and her own uncle Mimmi, whom she dressed for his funeral in a gray suit with black shoes.

Her work is piercingly personal, yet oddly public. Now that she is on the administrative staff, people run into her in the piazza and ask whether there is a spot for their parent or their infirm grandfather in *casa famiglia*'s limited space.

— *Non ti scorda' del mi' nonno, eh!* they yell at her. Don't forget my grandfather!

She walks through the piazza speedily, trying to protect the thin barrier of privacy away from her work, and I feel admiration for her.

Now, the benches around the piazza are filled with ladies chatting and watching the children go around and around the piazza. Cigarette smoke and a hint of perfume drift through the air. I hear the purr of the ladies talking below, a louder voice and a softer voice taking turns weighing in. Ave, maybe Loredana too, and maybe Angiolina.

When I go downstairs now I will walk by and say hello. I will stop to chat for a minute, affectionately, and they will smile. Someone will ask me how much longer I am staying—*mica parti, no?*—then they will hug me and watch me until I disappear. As I walk away they will say something about me, nice or not depending on their goodwill towards me, then the next person will walk by, or someone will remember something they heard today at the grocery store, and a thread will lead to another, as conversations in Cetona go.

— *Ha' sentito? Quelli del Lombrico hanno comprato la terra là al Piano,* says one lady. Did you hear? Those of Lombrico—a long-standing family nickname—bought land down at Il Piano.

— *Ma che hanno comprato che non ci hanno una lira! Macché!* counters another. They are so broke they couldn't possibly have bought anything, she says, dotting it all with the *tze* sound.

— *Me l'ha detto la sorella della su' cognata ... Lei lo saprà!* His sister-in-law's sister told me, says the first. She must know!

— *Ma lei che ne sa? E poi lei n'è Albanese?* What does she know? asks the third. Plus, isn't she Albanian?

— *Comunque la terra l'hanno comprata, questo lo so per certo.* Well, interjects the first, they bought the land and that I know it for sure.

— *Gli avrà prestato i soldi il su' fratello!* Maybe his brother loaned him the money, speculates the third.

— *Se gli ha prestato i soldi il su' fratello è perché l'ha rubati, che anche lui ne sa più del gatto.* If he did it's because he stole it, says the second. He knows more than the devil, that one.

— *Ma il su' fratello n'è quello che faceva l'amore con la ragazza divorziata, quella delle Piazze?* Isn't his brother the one who was going out with the divorced girl from Piazze, asks the first.

— *Sì, anche quella ... quante ce ne sarebbe da di'! Mmmm, 'n mi fa' parla'!* Ooooh, there could be so much to tell about her, says the second, rolling her eyes. Don't even get me started!

— *Ma perché, n'avevi sentito che andava con un altro lei? Ma mi sa che è rimasta in istato interessante!* Why, asks the third, haven't you heard that she is going out with someone else now? But I think she's pregnant.

— *Macché incinta che i figli non li può ave', o così ho sentito ... Macché!!!* There is no way she is pregnant! She can't have children, says the second lady dismissively, with her *tze* sound. Or so I have heard, she adds.

— *Qualcuno l'ha vista in farmacia!* Well, someone saw her at the drug store, adds the third.

— *In farmacia ci può esse' andata perché è stitica! Che c'entra!* What does that have to do with it? She could have gone to the drug store because she is constipated! interjects the second.

And so the conversation goes, around and around. It's the ingenious art of *ricamare*, or embroidering, but in matters of conversation it means to add on to a story: you take the sketch of what you know, or hear, then add the necessary threads and colors of conjecture and opinion—at best based on personal observation, at worst on mere hearsay—and all of a sudden a thread of apparent truth is woven into a newly fashioned picture, an embroidered piece of fabric that has a texture and a life of its own. Like a magic flying carpet.

The image of the gossiping ladies makes me smile. As I walk through the piazza I feel immune to it, today at least, protected by the goodwill I feel around me.

— *Resta, resta con noi!* they say. Stay here, stay with us!

The other day I saw Nella, Pietraccio's sister, the man who used to collect tin foil. She hugged me tenderly and asked me how things are going.

— *Perché non prendi marito e stai qui con noi?* she asked, looking at me earnestly. Why don't you take a husband here and stay with us?

— *Dovrei trovarne uno che mi piace,* I said. I would have to find one I like.

— *Eh, già! Ti deve anda'. Quello è un piatto che ti trovi sempre davanti.* Of course, she says with a wisdom that makes me laugh: That's a dish you have to face every day; you'd better like it.

Of course, that is a decision among many to consider, which I fear I will have to consider sooner rather than later.

The sun greeted me as I left the house for my run today. I walked through the piazza, ran down Via Sobborgo, down by the *lavatoi,* by le Gore, up to Patarnione, to Bargnano, over to Il Piano, and up towards Vagliara. The countryside was effervescent with color, clean and exhilarating.

Yet, my heart felt like a boulder.

*Dear Sybil,* Aram wrote to me this week. *I came across some pictures you posted of the country around Cetona—one was called 'Amazing Landscape Cetona' and the other 'God's most amazing place'—and they brought tears to my eyes. Actually, what brought tears to my eyes was the way you titled them and the connection I could feel—your connection to your home and your exuberance and love. I have a sense that you aren't coming back, and I just want to say that I want you to choose what really makes you happy, what your heart really needs. I want you to know that if you do choose to stay, it's ok. I'll love you and will be happy for you in the deepest way. You may or may not feel like you know what's next, but I had that feeling and I had to share it with you.*

*With deepest love,*
*Aram*

His words flashed before me. *I want you to know that if you do choose to stay, it's ok.*

At the top of a hill overlooking the Astrone and the *autostrada* I stopped to catch my breath and I couldn't. I leaned over and rested my elbows on my knees and I felt fear choke me.

How long will he wait for a return?

I realize that, in leaving for this experience, I planted the seed of the unknown, and now that unknown has generated the need for a decision. Meanwhile, decisions on the other side of the ocean are being made. I think I had always planned on going back—in part because I fear I don't know how to live here anymore—but now suddenly that may not matter anymore because the perception is that I may not. And knowing me, I understand how he would have thought that. Feared that, perhaps.

Suddenly, again, my relationship with Cetona is recasting ours, as we speak. You, who made my return possible. You, whose love helped me understand all this and whose words are so full of love.

I think of how we met. We were in a bar in Charleston, my favorite, Rue de Jean, and it was Bastille Day. We were drinking and flirting in a large group when the bill came and we raced to the bar to pay. He ended up paying, so I slipped a $50-bill into the inside of his pants. I tried for the pockets, but he swatted me away—and he returned it to me, slipping it into mine. I returned it, and then he to me, our hands venturing playfully deeper into the other's pants. I felt his briefs, and more.

After that, and for months and years after that, we longed for each other through the day, and at last, at the end of the day, we would meet in my bed, in my cabin in the woods, and make love, filling, thirsting, consuming, aching, filling love, his brown eyes locked in mine, him in me.

There were no boundaries, nothing that could not be mine, or his. One. We were one.

Peter comes to my mind, what an elegant dancer he was, of us dancing to the Gypsy Kings in our living room. Of how I finally left him, unable to stay put, unable to choose and to commit. I think of all the years before, my inability to be still, my split loyalties.

And here I am again, my soul divided. It makes me sick to my stomach, all this love, and all this loss.

All—everything—has been in the vortex of this place, my ginger-bread town in the hills. What a fulcrum, what a pillar of strength it has been for me; yet, what a source of constant destruction in my heart. What will be the price today?

On the way back to town I run into a woman from Cetona walking her dog, out in the country, a woman I have known from childhood. She recognizes me and greets me.

— *Ah, Sibilla, ma ti ricordi ancora Cetona?* Ah, you still remember Cetona?

Her question is so absurd that I feel like slapping her in the face, but I smile through my tears.

Yes, I do. I do still remember Cetona.

For May Day the piazza fills with marching bands and rows of tractors from gargantuan to tiny in a boisterous celebration. Cetona, with its long agrarian and leftist tradition, revels in the festivities and the mood is contagiously joyous. Everyone is out, and people cluster on the sidewalks waving flags under the bright sky.

Amidst the tractors I see from my window a small brown donkey hitched to a wooden cart and festively decorated. When I run down, I find out he belongs to Sotero and I go take a picture. People and children circle to look at the donkey, then, on cue, the tractors start up in a rumble of motors. With the donkey leading, they exit the piazza in a slow orderly row followed by the marching bands and a long procession of workers and farmers, and together they will snake through town and out into the countryside and back.

While we wait for the parade to return to the piazza I talk with Caino and Amato and other men standing around watching. They look proud, honored by this day, this event, that connects to something in their shared past. The land, work, maybe even poverty. They nod to themselves something unspoken that I respect and envy.

After the parade returns to the piazza and the tractors take their places anew—children are disappointed that Sotero's cart broke down and the donkey went home—a few political types get on a podium to speak. One encourages the crowd to reject individualism, which reminds me of discussions back at the *liceo,* and I want to raise my hand and protest, but instead I head out for my run, up into Monte Cetona's luscious and fragrant folds full of spring that feed me and take away my every grief.

On the way back, I stop for lunch at Bianca and Riccardo's. They live in a beautiful and beautifully positioned farmhouse off the road toward Chiusi, with a direct view of both Monte Cetona and the valley toward Città della Pieve. They restored the house in a clean, minimalistic way, painting the old wooden beams white and installing untraditional, large grille-less metal windows that afford an unfettered view of the landscape. In their well-appointed kitchen they teach cooking classes on the side, mostly to Americans, and they throw lunches and dinners for a dozen with the ease it would take me to make a peanut butter-and-jelly sandwich, a gift they inherited from their families of great cooks, diplomats, and hosts. They have exquisite taste and everything is lovely; there are flowers, and nice linens and crystal, and always plentiful good wine.

When I arrive, Riccardo kisses me on the cheeks and greets me cheerily, and I am relieved by the bright and endearing green I see in his eyes when he's in a good mood. They have commissioned a painting from me and I wrote a website for their cooking classes. I have grown fond of them—their wit and worldliness—and I appreciate their hospitality.

There is a crowd of people sitting at a beautiful long table outside in the sunshine with platters of delicious food that could have sprung from a magazine. Everyone is in an unusually jovial and agreeable mood, and we sit eating and drinking. Five or six conversations move through the table—it reminds me of my past times with my parents, here—and I am happy to sit next to people I have never met, from Rome.

A friendly man named Tiberio, with closely cropped white hair and a strong southern accent, tells me he used to be in charge of security for the Rome airports. My eyebrows shoot up and I ask him to tell me some good stories, and he begins with the Alitalia baggage handlers who were arrested for stealing from travelers' luggage—clothes, jewelry, money—in airports across Italy. It had been going on for years when they were caught after a long, tangled investigation and finally a videoed sting operation. Tiberio describes the twisted web of people involved, and the bribes, the gifts to lovers and wives, people's belongings, clothes, jewelry, and souvenirs strewn recklessly across the country, and we *ohh* and *ahh* in shock yet not shocked at all. It's been a few years now since it happened, but it reoccurs cyclically and I am inclined to believe that this quintessentially Italian story will repeat itself again.

We skirt the topic of politics, and I am glad to not discuss the United States, and I study the woman across from me, who has jet black hair and a somewhat familiar face. After a few curious looks and probing questions, we discover that we took ballet together when we were little girls —I loved ballet!—and this bonds us immediately across the table and the decades.

I have a particularly dear memory of an image of me in my white tutu, with my hair pulled back in a tight bun, feeling special and airy. The day before our final recital at a large theater in Chianciano I fell from my bike going down the steepest part of Via Sobborgo and cut my knee rather badly. Dad was furious, or maybe just frustrated. The cut imperiled my performance at the recital; lessons had been taxing on the family budget, and ballet didn't necessarily come easy to me. Dad didn't know how to fix that, any of that. I remember sobbing more for disappointing him than for the cut, the scar of which I still carry visibly on my knee. I did dance in the recital, feeling tremulous like a bird, but my ballet career was short-lived.

After lunch I compliment Riccardo on his particularly good *spaghetti all'aglione* and I walk back to the piazza through the countryside, a sweet balm of color and fragrance. I stop to chat with a woman with crisp blue eyes sitting in a field in the late afternoon sun cleaning a basketful of chicory. She has on a flowered housedress and her sparkling white hair catches the sun, and I feel like sitting with her forever, there in that field, getting to know everything about her.

As I walk further into town I see Feriero sitting out on the steps of his building with his family. No doubt, they are talking about the day, the tractors, the past.

We wave and I hear him scream, *Prendi il caffe con noi?* Come have coffee with us! I nod and run down, and we sit for a while talking about this and that. When I head back up the road I run into Nuccia's sister, Grazia—Nuccia who used to own the *cartoleria* with her husband, Unico. I had been thinking I had not seen Nuccia in a few days; I usually see her several times a day and at least once walking her dog.

Grazia tells me that Nuccia has had a stroke and she has been in the hospital for more than two weeks. I am taken aback; I had no idea, which is almost hard to believe. Will she walk? Can she speak? How did I not notice she was not walking her dog?

Back in my apartment the bells chime midnight. I go to the window to close my shutters and I lean out. I look up at the sky and breathe in. I look down to the far end. The piazza is empty; Nilo is closing. The festivity is over. There is no sound.

Yet, I see three people at the end of the piazza, walking, turning around quietly. I recognize Antonello, Bozzini, and Moreno—Antonello the tallest, Bozzini the burliest, and Moreno the thinnest and calmest. They are pacing the piazza, up and down, turning around at the fountain. *Fare un giro di piazza.* They have done this for years, at the same time every night, moonlight or rain.

I watch them, admiring their regularity, their incorruptible pace and conversation and camaraderie. I notice the step, slow and synchronized—not by design but by practice—of these friends in this barely lit piazza in this quiet corner of the earth, telling each other their thoughts, concerns, ideas, though probably not their secrets. Those they don't need to say.

I realize with regret that I have forgotten this habit, too, of sharing so much. I have forgotten how it was that Maria and Mariachiara and Giulia and I, just like them, talked about so much every day, day after day, sitting at the fountain, or pacing the piazza. We knew each other's eyes; we got to know what every crease of a smile meant, or frown, every joy, worry, or fear, like the air we breathed or the leaves falling in autumn.

Wading in that kind of all-enveloping intimacy does not come easy anymore. Life in an American city does not favor closeness, which now must be carefully arranged and scheduled. How not to look away, how not to let so much shine through? I have come to run from it, even when I know that Maria knows my eyes, and Ottavia, too, and it comforts me and I yearn for it. I want the veil to fall and the soul to explode outward naked and bare. Is it adulthood that makes us unlearn that nakedness?

Or maybe, I realize, I have spent too much time in a world where we don't talk, not really. Where people ask you how you are doing and they expect nothing less than an enthusiastic answer. We close in like snails carrying our truth like a house.

From my window the lights of the Rocca rise up into the silent black sky and I feel full of love and regret and loneliness.

Moreno, Bozzini, and Antonello are under my window now and I wish them goodnight.

They look up.

— *Buona notte, Sibi,* they whisper back.

I pull the shutters closed on a beautiful night, and on my solitude.

During the years I was away mending my heart, Cetona's countryside bloomed from spring to summer, rain cascaded through the piazza in fall, and snow fell in winter. Silvio and Aldo harvested wheat and reseeded anew. Festivals came and went. Some stores closed and others took their place. Some people married and had babies, and some took lovers and left their families, which in Cetona is tantamount to a small earthquake. Some people lost their minds, and they were never to be found. The young *tiglio* grew a bit, some new houses were built, and the piazza was paved into a desert of white stone.

The men in piazza watched it all, and some grew older to tell. I heard all this by phone or letter, but I was here for little of it, the fabric of my intimacy eroding under the creeping forgetfulness of time and distance, which I could not stop.

A little bit of death every day, for sure.

And, in fact, perhaps worse, some people died—many, in fact, over the years, and their loss from afar filled me with sadness, worse than if I had been here to see it and to cry with others. Now, as I walk these hills their ghosts call out to me, daily, a siren song of regret for not being here, for not loving more. For leaving.

Nicola died, the son of our Maresciallo and our dear friend.

I revisit his face in the many moments in which he populated my life with joy and distinction. When we saw Lucio off at the Chiusi train station as he left for military duty, and, later, my *esame di maturità*. The time we made our carnival costumes together; our afternoons at the fountain and at the bar; and the evenings dancing under the psychedelic lights of La Capannina to a song he loved, Frankie Valli's "Can't Take My Eyes Off You."

When I left for college he was excited for me, and every time I returned in summer we sat and told stories. The last time I saw him we had a political discussion about something, one of many things that angered him about the United States. Maybe it was the war in Afghanistan, or Iraq, and he walked off irately, red in the face. He had been particularly obstinate about politics that summer—or perhaps he was angry about something else—and he got angry even when I agreed with him, which was most of the time. I regret that now.

Nicola's illness began with stomach pains he neglected. Go see a doctor, Sabina said, please go. As many Italians are wont to do in the face of illness, he preferred to not know if it was something bad. By the time he was diagnosed, his cancer had spread beyond repair. His final few weeks were spent on morphine, in the hospital, where he wanted no one to visit.

He was forty-seven when he died.

The funeral took place on a beautiful afternoon in May. Attilio Del Buono, who owns the ag business, wrote something for the occasion, and Don Prospero read it. Friends carried the casket down the road, followed by Nicola's shocked mother, sister, wife, and young son, with Don Prospero's purple vestments fluttering in the breeze. He was buried in a light blue gym suit like the one I had last seen him in, the one he played tennis in and that looked so nice on him.

Greta, the queen of my childhood memories and castles of gold, died, too.

The last time I saw her we had drinks at the house, in Bargnano. We sat on a bench in the garden on a late summer afternoon, under the big pine trees that surround their house. By then I had left the newspaper, and like a child returning from a heroic adventure, I told Greta and Pietro about my work for the law firm, fighting on behalf of better education for the poor in rural and black counties in South Carolina.

Good Communists that they were, they congratulated me like proud parents. I was like a kid to them coming home to show my conquests. We talked politics a bit, racism, America, Bush. I teased them about the fate of the old USSR, and Pietro and I—Pietro was never above sparring at ideology's expense—had some good laughs.

Greta looked healthy; she looked fine. My dropping into their lives for a moment—as was the case for the lives of everyone I saw on my visits—gave me little more than the glowing reflection of memory mixed with the happiness of the moment.

A sliver of reality.

We parted under the shade of the pine trees, with an old song humming in my ear.

The following summer Greta had a heart attack. She had felt a stifling weight on her chest for a few days, but she postponed going to a doctor, and I suspect she smoked through her concern. When she called for an ambulance they took her to the wrong hospital, then airlifted her to Siena. Apparently, they managed to stop the heart attack in progress, but the following day she had another one and died.

Remnants of dry roses crowd her ossuary now, and I add more when I visit.

Andrea, Greta's nephew, came to town recently and he invited me to walk through the house. It sits dead, like Greta—with her—preserved by Pietro like a mausoleum. In an old bowl on a coffee table we found pictures of us, little. We walked up to the alcove at the top of the house, my favorite old spot, where Greta let me go alone to listen to old records on the ancient stereo. The *Sgt. Pepper's Lonely Hearts Club Band* album sat stacked with hundreds of others like not a day had gone by, as if Greta were downstairs making me hot chocolate, or dying eggs for an egg hunt.

Now, on my runs past their house I walk up their driveway to find a void. The shutters are pulled closed, the ox cart is gone, and the lawn is quiet.

But through the silence I hear the song of children at play somewhere in my heart.

My dear Zia died too, one year I was away.

After I left for college, and almost to the end of her life, Zia corresponded tirelessly with me, writing me at least twice a month in her squiggly handwriting.

*I am sorry that you have to decipher my handwriting,* she wrote me once, *but I cannot type letters: It takes away from the intimacy of our exchange.* And she was right, oh, so right, my dear Zia.

During the best of times, and the worst, Zia was a thoughtful listener and a compassionate confidante about the most difficult matters, including, in college, my painful and critical homesickness, and later my divorce. I have drawers full of her letters, each loving and solicitous and detailed, each beginning with Sybil LUV. Her letters told a great deal about her life—not always openly—which, beneath the veneer of Zio's glamorous profession, or perhaps exactly because of it, held a great deal of loneliness.

On my visits home in summer we visited for hours over copious and cheap wine. She sat in the corner of the kitchen overlooking the glorious countryside toward Piazze, smoking and inquiring like a tender older sister about every aspect of my life, my every care and worry: what I was reading, what I thought of events, what was troubling me or reassuring me. She listened, advised, and counseled.

Over the years we also talked about her—her writing, her photography—and, after Zio's death, about their relationship, his lovers, and their life together, difficult yet heroic—as all of those relationships seemed to me after so many years.

When I drove off at the end of our summer afternoons together, back to my life in the States, Zia would walk outside to see me off. She stood at the corner of the house, by the door into the kitchen, aged and thinner, wearing her Cheshire cat smile and a summer dress buttoned down the front—a summer dress that looked a little more worn each year, and later with heavy stockings and house shoes—and waved goodbye.

There I picture her the last time I saw her, in a silk dress the azure of a deep summer sky.

Over the years the house had become a bit neglected. Zia had fallen many times; she had back problems and leg problems, a good deal of sadness, loneliness, and some financial weariness to add to it. Then, during the few years I did not return, her health declined. We talked on the phone every now and then—I remember her phone number to this day—until she fell once more, broke yet another bone, and she could no longer take care of herself. Screaming and bitching—she was proud and stubborn—she was moved into the *casa famiglia*, and there, I think, her life began to end. Without her independence and her dignity, she lost her will to live.

The familiar letters stopped coming, and I, at a distance, lost track of the decline. Finally, the months passed and this dearest person died, a pauper, alone except for the threadbare care of a niece of Zio's, and Iolanda, Natalia's mom. And neither was there when she died.

Zia was cremated and there was no funeral service to commemorate her. Ave vaguely remembers a mass when Don Prospero mentioned the death of a woman whose name she didn't recognize. She remembers wondering who the deceased was, with no family there to mourn, no one to cry. After living some thirty years in Cetona, she just vanished, without a trace. Her ashes were put in the earth in a corner of Zio's cemetery plot and, like in life, she sits for perpetuity in Zio's company and shadow.

The last time I saw the house it had not yet sold and it sat nearly abandoned. A door had been left ajar and I went in. I walked through the living room, where Zio's piano had been, and upstairs, through their bedroom, with the beautiful fireplace, and the library, once brimming with books, and the rooms where Adelina used to chase me in the piles of corn. It looked like someone had just emptied the house of every possession and forgotten to lock up: Everything was gone, every painting, piece of furniture, dish, knick-knack, everything—stripped bare.

Then, when I turned the corner leading from the kitchen out to the shaded courtyard where we shared so many memorable meals together, I saw hanging on the wall the one single object that had been left behind, overlooked perhaps: a small ceramic plate with a scalloped edge, hand-painted with a dainty yellow bird.

I thought of my paintings of birds, which Zia had never seen, and my nickname, Birdie. My love and understanding of birds.

I was afraid to take it, thinking it might be wrong of me, but after some back and forth I unhooked it from the wall, cradled it in my hands, and took it with me.

This week, when I scaled the fence and walked through the property, picturing Zia waving goodbye in her azure dress, I felt sure that I did the right thing. I know that she left it there for me to find.

And every time I run by her house now, perched over the sunny fields looking out toward Piazze, I hear her calling after me and I wave.

I am trying to live here as if I could really live here longterm, make a living, and be normal. Normal. It's a word whose very essence eludes me constantly—the idea of enjoying my happiness here without too many questions.

Yet, in the cracks of that ephemeral quest I find my joy.

Last night, when I went to bed, I noticed a line of chalk drawings marking the pavement of the piazza from end to end, in preparation—I was told—for an event called *l'infiorata*.

Loosely translated as the flowering, or the coming of the flowers, it's an event inspired by some kind of religious tradition involving the celebration of a miracle and somehow tied to the occasion of the Holy Communion. But its most remarkable manifestation to me is the coloring of these drawings on the pavement of the piazza using nothing but the petals of flowers. Down on hands and knees, and using petals of every hue picked around the countryside over the past week, people color yards and yards of drawings spanning the length of the piazza in a display of kaleidoscopic splendor.

I had never had a chance to see this, so I waited expectantly for morning, hoping for good weather and still skies.

Near seven I pushed open the shutters of my bedroom and looked out onto the town, still and quiet. The sun was rising behind the church and the sky was pink and soft. Beneath my window and through the piazza, clusters of people worked wordlessly on a pastiche of designs in progress, twenty or so meters wide and about one hundred meters in length, from one end of the piazza to the other. Patches of color marked the ground like spilled paint.

Breathlessly, I made a cup of tea, pulled on some yoga pants and a top, washed my face and ran down the steps with my camera and into a sea of petals. The colors—pinks of every shade, reds and whites, and the bright yellow of the broom flower, which just blossomed in the past few weeks—brought tears to my eyes. I could not have chosen a happier place or a more perfect time to be.

I had never tasted this exact happiness.

Pippo and his wife, Antonina, head up the team that draws, while Celso, a soft-spoken gentleman I had never met, and a few others, coordinate the volunteers who fashion the petals into forms and figures. It's mostly the same people who organize everything, minus Sotero, perhaps.

— *Buon giorno, buon giorno,* they whispered, greeting me.

Pippo is the town's ceramist—you have heard me mention him before, and his mom, La Mema. Born in the same house at the top of town where he still lives, just below the Rocca—he likes to say he is the only Cetonese who still lives in the house where he was born—he started dabbling in clay while playing in the creek below my old house, the one with the suspicious red worms.

Pippo didn't want to go to school to study anything other than the art of pottery, so his parents sent him to a ceramics school in Chiusi, led by a priest. At the end of four years he apprenticed with a ceramist in Chianciano and eventually he developed his own style, classical and simple, for which he became known: plain white glazed pottery with clean colored drawings—lines, squiggles, birds. Simple, artful, and classy.

Eventually in the early 1970s he opened his own store in piazza from which his ceramics, aided by his colorful personality and gregarious nature, flooded the world. Sitting in the cool space of their shop—an ancient space that tunnels down into the earth's bowels through archways and secret passageways going back to the Etruscans—Pippo, Antonina, and eventually their son, Franco, made sets of dishes and pots and bowls for visitors from near and a afar, including restaurants in the States. My mom has her set, and every American friend who came to visit us got theirs. My own kitchen has stacks of Pippo's bowls and plates, which I adore.

Besides being a ceramist, Pippo is involved in nearly every event in town, including the *infiorata*. He calls himself a man in love with all things from the past, and all things of Cetona, including photos and stories, though he is also, in true Cetonese style, a vocal critic of his own town.

— *Ma a me chi me lo fa fa' di fa' questo?* he asked rhetorically this morning as he walked by and greeted me, running his fingers through his thick white hair. Who makes me do this?

His weariness suggested a need for more volunteers, so I quickly put my camera down and asked if I could help. I am glad to have this chance: I realize with regret that I have never helped anyone here; I have done nothing for my town. Over the years, I wove dreams of having a newspaper here that would cover the area and help inform the people, but, along with many of my dreams here, that never came to pass.

Now, in this event I seek a small frame of that lost dream.

Moving around the piazza, Celso eagerly directed me to a bag of yellow petals and instructed me to start filling in here and there—he pointed to spots and inferred colors—and, from there, he asked me to color nearly a full drawing, and then another. After that, Antonina needed help decorating the fountain, which we filled with bursts of color in smart patterns she devised, and on and on until we were out of petals and the drawings were complete.

A man with a watering pump came along behind us to wet the drawings so the petals would stay fresh and not blow away. The sun rose quickly above us, and by the time it was mid-morning we had finished and cleaned up and were ready for the crowds.

Thrilled at having helped, I went to shower and change, fulfilled in a childlike way and wishing it would never end.

As I returned, the church emptied out. The procession, led by Don Prospero and the children who had their Holy Communion, walked all over the petals we had so carefully placed and scattered them along. In the middle of the procession were people carrying a canopy ferrying some important church officials in pompous ceremonial robes. They walked over the flowers, which made me cringe a bit, and people on the sidewalks cursed them under their breath, not for the flowers but because of being church bureaucracy.

By lunchtime the flowers were nearly blown away and the piazza emptied, looking disheveled like a room after a very fun party. Later, during the course of the day, several people thanked me for working on the *infiorata* and I felt humbled.

— *Adesso la Sibilla l'abbiamo rifatta Cetonese. Ormai ce la teniamo qui! Ha fatto anche l'infiorata!* said Alessio, Nuccia's son-in-law. We've made Sibilla Cetonese again. *Ormai* we are keeping her here!

Even Don Prospero, who had not spoken a word to me in my whole time here, smiled and thanked me for participating. Celso thanked me, too, and confided that the town needs younger people to carry out the event in future years, if it is to survive.

I would help if I could, I tell him. If I stay, I say ...

It's nearly summer, and in the precious hour before dinner life in the piazza blossoms.

Children are running around in groups and people are milling about, *a veglia*, catching up, talking. Workers done for the day and a few farmers back from the fields grab a glass of wine at the bar before heading home for dinner, or they sit on the benches to look, to assess the day together. Couples are walking up and down the piazza arm in arm.

The light in the west, above the elementary school, mellows to dusty pastels, rose and violet streaking from Sarteano, and a softness descends on the piazza.

I look from my window and I take this snippet of world in my hands as it comes together in some kind of habitual, natural evolution. It is just a random day in Cetona, one like many others, but to me it is utterly magical. I relish the tender, golden light, the ease of movement, and the harmony of it all.

Emanuele and Giuseppe are playing soccer with a group of other kids, kicking the ball here and there not too seriously, trying to avoid the *guardia* and the throngs of older women and younger children walking and running by.

I see Brunetti walk by, an elderly and famous Italian writer whose work is incomprehensible to me and who has lived in Cetona for many years. Once, decades ago, when I was home from college, he took a liking to me and gave me a bunch of red roses. I am not sure if he bought them for me and waited to give them to me or if it was just happpenstance, but I remember his mischievous smile when he handed them to me, a twinkle in his eye under his signature beret that makes him look like he walked out of an alley in a little town in France.

*Grazie*, I said, nonplussed and moved at the same time. We've never spoken since.

He is old now, and he walks carefully but determined. I follow him with my eyes as he approaches Sabina's store, his arm hooked to his caretaker's. Suddenly he releases her arm, pulls out a Styrofoam cup from his coat pocket, and edges into the corner of the wall. He is clearly busy unbuttoning his fly and then peeing in the cup.

When he is finished, he fumbles with his free hand some more, then turns, gives the cup to the caretaker and walks away. The caretaker empties the cup into Sabina's plants and walks away.

I laugh out loud and dial Sabina.

— *Ha pisciato nella pianta?? Ma guarda, accidenti a lui ...*, she screeched. He pissed in the plants??

She promises to seek revenge tomorrow, though she is so sweet she never will.

The doors of San Michele are open. I see Don Prospero in his black robe standing in the penumbra, waiting for his flock. He retreats, and a few minutes later the bells ring. The women slowly trickle into the church from various directions through the piazza. I see Fortunata. She looks up toward my window and waves. A few kids dump their bikes on the ground in front of the church and run in.

A number of caretakers, much like Brunetti's, are walking their charges slowly around the piazza, and the sight fills me with a mixture of tenderness and sobriety, aloneness and comfort.

Clusters of elderly people are sitting on the benches around the piazza, now in the shade—Bruna and Lidiano, and Caino too. Lillo, Tullia's dad, who used to own the Bar Sport, is approaching his spot at Bar Cavour, slowly, leaning on his cane, one short step at a time. Lillo is eighty-six now, and his face is shrunken, his eyes sunken. Often from my kitchen window I see him walking up my alley to their house, pulling himself by the railing.

When he sees me in the piazza he smiles.

— *America Jones*, he says, laughing, echoing his old *America',
ah facce Tarzan!* that he used to yell after me when I was a kid. He
says it every time I walk by, and sitting in his usual triumvirate, with
Giuliano Raschi and Guido's father, they laugh every time as if it were
the first.

On my way to have an *aperitivo* I step into the *giornalaio* to
charge my phone. Stefano is in an expansive mood and when I walk in
he's singing in English. He has the radio on and we dance for a minute,
but the joy suddenly leaves him and he turns the radio off. He tells me
that you can't play a radio in a store in Italy without paying a special
tax. The financial police—the dreaded *guardie di finanza,* which cross
the piazza every so often, sometimes undercover, followed discreetly
by nearly everyone's eyes—raid stores and bars to check.

He shakes his head. Who has money for music these days?

— *Si sta a malapena a galla* ... We barely tread water, he says.

When I was in Milano, this reminds me, I had lunch at a charming café, where, upon asking for the restroom, I was directed down
a staircase and through two rooms that, one could tell, had been
recently renovated. The rooms were painted a lush lacquer red, the
ceiling had plaster molding, and there were elegant alcoves for candles
or some kind of lighting. In one of the rooms chairs were arranged in
rows, to accommodate patrons listening to music, perhaps, and the
whole space struck me as romantic and perfect for dancing. I imagined
people wrapped in the hot embrace of a tango, the lights dimmed, the
music yearning and tantalizing.

And then, just as the image drifted away, I noticed the signs
on every wall: *Vietato ballare!! Vietato ballare!* Dancing forbidden!
Dancing forbidden!

When I went back upstairs and asked the waiter to explain
this oddity, he told me that the restaurant paid a tax to be able to
host bands, but dancing was not included in the price. That required
another tax, which the owner was not willing to pay.

Now, if people get up and dance while listening to music the owner is subject to a fine.

You can't make this stuff up. It's like the taxes you have to pay to get your dog cremated, or your loved one cremated. By weight.

As I leave the store, aromas of food waft through the piazza, the kitchens of the restaurants bubbling, getting ready for the evening. People gather for the *aperitivo* and the card players settle at their tables at the Bar Cavour for their daily games.

I, too, sit among them.

Diego is wearing a white button-down shirt, nicely pressed, and he looks tan and handsome. Lauro, Maria's husband, has just come from work, as have Giacomo and Alano, and they take their seats. Dino, Daniele's dad, is there, and Giacomo's dad, Italo. Two tables of card players.

Osvaldo, a skinny car mechanic with salt and pepper hair who worked for Cardetti for decades, starts the game. He has a defiant face and a fidgety manner, rambunctious and unruly, but he's always polite and friendly to me and I watch him, smiling. Quickly, he starts cursing.

— *Madonna frollosa come una pecora,* he says, launching a series of unpronounceable, untranslatable invectives against the Virgin Mary. *Smettetela di rompermi le palle.* Stop breaking my balls.

Sotero is looking at something in the piazza.

— *Gioca! Gioca!* Osvaldo yells at him impatiently and elbows him.

— *Guardavo la guardia che non è niente male,* Sotero answers. I was checking out the policewoman, who is not shabby.

He smiles to himself and nods. I laugh.

While the games move into their rhythm with hushed cries and bursts of curses, Gastone scoots over with his motorized chair—the aftereffect of contracting polio as a kid, in the early sixties—and positions himself to watch, which he does with aquiline scrutiny while puffing on his little cigar. Quickly, a dozen or so other men gather around in chairs. Among them is Tonfice, il Vecchio, and a nice-looking, quiet man I call Signor Morellini. They sit or stand in a large circle and watch the game, commenting among themselves, every now and then suggesting a move. This gathering—*fare la capannella*—irritates Felice who is mulling about, serving and cleaning off tables. He says the guys steal chairs from other tables and don't even drink anything.

— *Sta male, via. Bestemmiano, le dicono di tutti i colori. Io se fossi un turista 'n' mi ci sedrei lì accanto nemmeno mi pagassero!* It looks bad, he says, his blue eyes incensed. They sit there, they curse ... If I were a tourist, they couldn't pay me to sit next to them.

I reassure him. The tourists probably like it, at least the foreigners, I say. Plus, they don't know what they're saying anyway.

While I sit, Giuseppe, one of Graziella and Dino's grandchildren, walks up to chat and ask how I am. He is ten or so, has big blue eyes, short blond hair, unblemished porcelain skin, and the longest eyelashes I have ever seen. He has a disarming mix of charm and mischief, all wrapped in a precocious sensitivity and sense of humor.

Recently Giuseppe got his report card and it included a mediocre grade in conduct—for being a smart-ass in class.

When presented with this, his mother asked if he could explain it. He shrugged.

— *Potrebbe essere un errore di stampa. Ogni tanto succede nelle pagelle.* It could be a printing error, he said, batting his lashes. It's a well-known fact, he added: Every now and then it happens on report cards.

One evening he came to the table where a group of us were eating at one of Cetona's festivals, and in noting the leftovers on the table, he shook his head, chiding us with his blue eyes.

— *Ma sta male, no ... Che peccato,* he said, fanning his hands out. What a shame.

Today, he looks deep in my eyes and asks how I am. Reassured that I am ok, he hugs me and wanders off to play.

*Aperitivo* time can be crowded, and the municipal police, the hated *guardie*, start monitoring the few parking spaces at both ends of the piazza for abusers of the 30-minute time limit, of which there are many. Many are also those who simply park illegally, pulling their cars up on the curb or on the sidewalk, like Amato, and leaving it there for hours, perhaps too lazy to walk from the parking lots three minutes from the piazza, or perhaps out of unmitigable defiance.

Because of that, ever since the piazza was closed to vehicular traffic, tickets have become a source of great controversy.

Francesco Salviati is the chief of the *guardie*, a tall man with white hair and a kind manner, at least with me, but a rather impassive face when he is trying to do his job. Due to what many say is a notable lack of consistency and common sense in ticketing, Salviati and his team, perhaps like meter maids everywhere, are rather hated in Cetona.

Salviati, the most aggressive enforcer, is the most hated. Berenice comes in a close second, though she and another lady *guardia* are slightly more indulgent, patrolling on foot among the cars and looking here and there to locate or draw the attention of offending owners to invite them to move their cars. Sometimes they even go in the bar and call out for people to move their cars, particularly if the cars are expensive, such as a Mercedes or a BMW, or the car of someone they know and like.

I myself have seen this.

— *Di chi è quella macchina lì fuori?* asked Berenice, walking into the Bar Sport one evening looking pretty and evil at the same time. She is blond and attractive though in an understated kind of way, perhaps because of her uniform.

I looked outside and saw a huge SUV parked obnoxiously right in front of the fountain, in the middle of the street, right by the entrance to the bar.

— *È mia,* said a handsome man sitting comfortably drinking an *aperitivo* with a group of people, absolutely unperturbed.

— *Ah! È lei!* Oh, it's you, said Berenice smiling, addressing the man formally and approaching.

She stood talking with him for a good half hour, laughing and smiling, while his friends finished their drink. Then, they walked to his car at a leisurely pace and drove off.

The other night a beautiful new slick Mercedes sat parked near the fountain for hours—the people, obviously important, were dining at Nilo's—completely ignored by the *guardie*. This irked people, particularly because, the night before, Salviati had stopped in the pouring rain to take pictures of a dozen cars to send the drivers electronic tickets.

Conversely, I have also seen the *guardie*, Salviati included, wait for shoppers like Maria who are running between stores while having left their car nearly in the middle of the road, blinkers flashing, for half hour or more.

The inconsistencies, which I ascribe to faulty human behavior but that here, in the land of conspiracies and collusions, bribes and underhandedness, are interpreted as unabashed favoritism, draw shrill reactions, particularly from people like Bennato, regular residents and drinkers who seem to get tickets all the time.

— *Se mi dice qualcosa le do una schiaffo nel muso*, said Bennato the other night, watching Berenice advance toward his illegally parked car. If she says something to me I'm gonna hit her in the face.

He recently received a series of tickets he considers unfair, though he parks illegally and leaves the car there for hours, against the law. Meanwhile, Andrea is rumored to have something special with the female *guardie* because he crosses the piazza illegally in his van and parks illegally for long stretches at a time without reprimand. I shrug, baffled. It must not be an easy job, I reckon, in a town where people will curse you out at the drop of a hat.

Someone told me that last summer—this must be made up—Salviati ticketed a person for having what appeared to be a large dog sitting in the heat in a locked car. When the owner came back to the car, he took issue with the ticket and started arguing with Salviati.

— *È un peluche!!!* the owner said, exasperated, using the Italian term for stuffed animal. It's a stuffed animal!

— I don't give a fuck what breed of dog it is!! Salviati answered. You can't leave your dog in the car with this heat!!!

This evening Salviati just wants people to move their cars. They get up from their seats slowly. Finally, the bells strike eight. Reluctantly, people part, off to dinner.

The piazza quiets and comes to rest.

When I was down hanging out *a veglia* with Costanza the other day, sitting on her porch, I asked her where Bruno and Adelina live, the couple who worked for Zio and Zia. I saw Bruno some months back getting in his car under my window.

— *Giù alle case nuove*, Costanza said, mentioning the new *ville* and apartment buildings that ring the outskirts of town.

I pondered this awhile, and avoided it too, afraid of something, of being crushed somehow.

But, then, the other day I gave myself courage and decided to search for them in this maze of new construction whose presence alone represents a huge shift in the town, pulling from its historic heart the elderly, people with young children and, generally speaking, people tired of old, cold and rustic.

The shift, which gets people like Pippo cursing against town hall, has, together with the closure of the piazza to vehicular traffic, dispersed the population and eroded the social fabric to the point that in winter—and sometimes in summer, too—there are no locals in town left to talk to.

To me the *case nuove* are an ugly, incongruous maze of abysmal architecture and worse planning, and I don't know my way around at all, though I know many people who live there, including Tullia and Ottavia's mom, and, well, half the town.

Looking for Bruno and Adelina, I meander down the steps and paths, completely lost, until I see someone get out of a car. It happens to be Santino, the house painter. I hadn't seen him in a decade or more.

— *Santino, buona sera, sono la Sibilla,* I say walking up to him.

He puts down his bags and smiles.

— *Sibilla! Come va?* he says, hugging me. We exchange news of family, then I ask him if he knows where Bruno and Adelina live.

— *Bruno, Bruno ...,* he says, talking to himself.

He looks around blankly, then a light bulb goes off and he walks me a way down the street and points to a building down the hill. On the first floor, he says.

He leaves me and I feel suddenly shy—and a bit afraid—of looking in the mirror of life, perhaps. Will they recognize me? Will I bother them? Will it matter?

Bruno is ninety or better now, and Adelina close to it. I have not seen them since I was in college, maybe twenty-five years or more. In all those years I never went to visit them or to say hello, not once. Too caught up with friends, or lovers. I feel shame and regret, heavy, there in my stomach, for having let so much time go by.

I recognize that this may not matter as much to them as it does to me—I think of myself as a fleeting person in their minds, having left so long ago—and it *does* really matter to me. It is about me bringing my affections full circle; to not lose another person here without saying hello, or goodbye.

I walk down the hill, reach the entryway of the building and see their name on the doorbell.

I ring. After a few seconds Bruno comes outside.

— *Chi è?* he asks coming toward me, exploring the space tentatively with his eyes. Who is it?

He stops right in front of me.

I tell him my name.

— *La Sibilla, di Borgo ...*

He scans my face quietly with his blue eyes, the eyes I remember so vividly from childhood, and I watch him reach back through time, locating me somewhere in his foggy mental rolodex. Did I really exist?

He doesn't recognize me at first, and I repeat my name, and I am about to feel the land lessen under my feet when I see a memory brighten his face.

— *La Sibilla ... ma chi, la figlia dell'Irene e Davide?* he asks, searching my face. The daughter of Irene and Davide?

— Yes, I say, yes! like I just won an emotional lottery, being remembered by this old man whose memory is so vivid in me.

Bruno scans my face and kisses me softly on the cheeks. His touch is slow and tentative like that of a near-blind man, and although his mouth smiles slightly with affection, his eyes are robbed of light. I think of him when he was young, the glow of blue in his eyes when he'd greet my father, his toughened bristly cheeks bending to a smile.

Time, toil, fatigue—life—have taken all that away.

While I stand there with Bruno, Adelina approaches the door. Shuffling with difficulty, she comes outside onto the bare terrace. She walks up to me and she looks at me up-close, the way she used to, examining me.

I look at her green eyes, her hair now thin and died a purplish color.

— *Adelina, buona sera, sono la Sibilla,* I say.

I smile and kiss her cheeks and tears pool in my eyes. In a split-second I revisit her curls with sticks in them and the smell of fire and grass, the smells that seared the primordial memories of Cetona into my soul so many years ago. I imagine her in the kitchen and in the fields yelling, *Sibu, la stufa!!!* and I struggle to maintain my composure.

Bruno repeats my name, but she looks at me blankly, and after a minute or so she retreats inside without a scintilla of recognition.

I struggle to move forward with the conversation. I know that Adelina's memory loss has nothing to do with me, and none of it is about me at all, but I feel nonetheless like our past together, so memorable to me in every detail, has become suddenly one-sided and, for that, a bit less true. I can't breathe, like everything has been just a dream—my entire life here, maybe, just an old foggy illusion—and was this really all that important and vital and good? Where did all of those days, those runs along her stockinged legs go, with her worries and her happiness?

As I wipe away the tears, Bruno starts telling me stories, and we linger to talk in the late afternoon light as the sun moves behind Monte Cetona. We talk about Adelina's health, and his, and my parents. Bruno reminisces about this time or the other, their time working for Zio and Zia. Later, when I was in college, Bruno and Adelina went to work for Greta and Pietro, and they loved working there, but at some point they decided to retire and they moved here, to these *case nuove*.

Bruno takes me inside to show me their house. I enter reluctantly like a child afraid of burning herself. It is all so downright heartbreaking, except for the memories, which now are the only thing that keep me standing here.

I ask if they have any old pictures and Bruno says no. They have not one picture. Their house is barely less sparse than it was four decades ago. Adelina sits while we talk, and every now and then she looks at me like I am a curiosity, somehow, but she does not remember who I am. When I say goodbye, she looks at me blankly, and I leave, feeling like a ghost.

For sure, I know, I will never see them again. What I have of them *now*, what I know, is all there is, forever, and this finality makes this last memory bitter. But as I walk back into town, tears surging, I retreat to the comfort of something older, and I find us there, Adelina running with me in the fields, her green eyes and her springy curls surrounded by flowers and laughter.

*Vieni, Sibu! Vieni!!!!*

# Summer

It rained all night throughout Cetona's countryside and I awoke to a crisp and stunning daybreak. Summer is finally here, and Cetona is magnificent.

I have been here long enough to see three of the four seasons unfurl, enough to see nature change its skin and the lives of people change before my eyes. Someone has had a baby, some have died, and life here is moving forward with me in it.

Here.

Brunino is sunning himself on the bench below my window. Dino, Daniele's dad, and a few others, Feriero among them, are already at the Bar Cavour chatting, before 8 a.m. The doors of the church are open to the dark inside, and, outside, a few ladies are waiting for the *farmacia* to open, and a few others to buy flowers from Vasilika.

The hairdresser is washing her windows. A few people are reading the paper at Le ACLI and a few others at the Bar Cavour. I see Pippo as he walks to Le ACLI for his coffee, or perhaps his first glass of wine.

I go for my run. The countryside has taken on its summer dress, full of lace and frill. The ditches and uncultivated fields are blossoming with wildflowers and wild roses and weeds, yellow and periwinkle and purple, the cast-away flowers of muted beauty that smell grassy and dusty and sweet and fill me with longing.

The *orti* are in full bloom, tomatoes ripening on the vines and zucchini flowers sprouting cadmium yellow near the ground. Everywhere are green beans and peppers and lettuces of all types. Someone offers me vegetables nearly every day, for which I am grateful.

Grapevines are packed with new leaves, now grown, and the clusters of grapes are taut and green. Farmers are in the vineyards plowing, trimming here and there, and applying copper. Poppies are in bloom along the rows, and the promise lies in the year ahead, the hope renewed.

Panzanella has returned, to my delight; apricots fill the trees, peaches and *scosciamonache* too, dark purple, elliptically shaped plums that get their name from the thighs of nuns. I run by a field full of plum trees and pick a few. Ave's apricot tree is full of fruit, but she has picked more than she can use for jam and canning.

— *Se le vogliono che le vengano a prende',* she says shrugging. If people want them they can come pick them.

Beyond, out there in the countryside are sunflowers and corn, growing and renewing like miracles of this earth, and the thing I love the most, the fields of wheat, turning by the day and the week from yellow to gold to the color of roasted malt, rich and dark. Work is moving into high gear for people like the Della Vignas. Silvio has started harvesting and his hours will be long for the next few weeks, though the daily rainstorms are making things difficult. Aldo is already complaining.

— *Non ci ho voglia, non ci ho più voglia!* he says, standing in front of the Bar Sport, cupping his hands in prayer. I don't feel like, it, I don't want to do it anymore!

*Avere voglia* or *non avere voglia* are prevalent expressions in the Italian language that indicate desire or wish to do something. Feeling like doing something.

Aldo says his eyesight has changed and his bifocals drive him crazy while trying to harvest with the big combines. He can see the commands, but then he can't see the edges of the fields. On wide open flat fields that's one thing, but harvesting in the steep sloping fields in Val D'Orcia is another.

— *Bisogna sapecci fa',* he says. It is not child's play: It's dangerous work, you've got to know what you're doing.

One summer Silvio was harvesting on a steep hill when the combine tipped over and caught on fire. It rested against some bales of straw that prevented it from flipping over completely and down a deep ravine that would have killed him. And, fortunately. Silvio was not badly injured. When Aldo went to the hospital to see his brother, the arrogant doctor in his white coat was on his way to a coffee. He looked Aldo up and down in his dirty work clothes and said he would not talk to him then and there, that he'd have to make an appointment. Aldo took him by the collar and pinned him to the wall.

He takes a deep breath and makes a hand gesture that explains his moment here, softly thrusting his chin upward. That's who I am, he's saying wordlessly.

He tells me about the bureaucracy of running a business like his: He has a tax ledger for every phase of oil-making—picking, bottling, labeling, selling—and one for every phase of wine-making—harvesting, bottling, labeling, marketing, selling. Crowning it all is something called the *registro dei registri*, the ledger of ledgers, in which he is to document the certification and documentation of all the other ledgers, each properly stamped with ink stamps and revenue stamps, and each with the proper invoices and receipts.

He sighs.

Anyway, I ask teasing him a bit, what makes you so good at harvesting wheat?

— *Noi il lavoro lo facciamo perfetto.* We do perfect work, he says, and there is no fake humility in this.

I ask what that means. We are efficient, punctual, we harvest on time, our machinery is clean and does not break down, and you get the most from your fields, he says. We don't waste. We don't leave wheat behind. You get everything your land produces.

For years, he tells me, they harvested for a field manager who managed a lot of land for a lot of people, and the guy wanted to be paid *bustarelle,* bribes, for hiring one company over another. He wanted a cut of the deal.

Aldo and Silvio refused to pay, but he continued to hire them nonetheless. It would have been impossible to justify not hiring them.

— That is our pride.

I love to watch Aldo's face when he talks about work, his knowledge rooted in a primordial confidence I don't have about anything. I admire it and love it, and I tell him.

— *Si, ma io so' stanco. Non ne posso più.* Yes, that's great, but I am tired. I can't deal with it anymore.

We sit for an *apertivo.* I am happy—honored even—to be with him, to listen to him. It would be hard to quantify how much I miss this person as a symbol of something greater. No one I could tell this to would understand without thinking something bad. It is visceral and old and complicated—something that, I recognize, has led me down perilous paths before.

Above us, in this terse summer sky, are the swallows, immersed in a party, mid-air, dizzying.

Over the past many weeks, by the hundreds they have built or restored their nests under the eaves of the buildings in the piazza, working daily, laboriously, conscientiously, in a dazzling spring of flight. As I sat writing or stood painting or crouched in the window-sill eating my lunch, they filled me with expectation and delight, their dances and ascents and descents mesmerizing in their precision and speed and joy.

They built their cocoons of mud, piece by piece, taking each strand specifically to a chosen spot—how do they know among so many?—every now and then dropping a bit of building material on my sill, welcome and moving.

Over time I have wondered, do they have eggs yet? Have they hatched? Every now and then during the course of the weeks I have leaned out the window twisted like a corkscrew to look up to see what's going on. Nothing. Birds going in and out of their nests. I wish I had a telescope like a corkscrew.

Today, finally, I saw. In one of the two nests right above my bedroom window I saw two tiny black heads peeping out, and one in another. I saw the white under their chins, and their mouths agape, red inside.

— They have hatched, they have hatched! I yelled, leaning out the window.

The mother birds came flying in every so often, every few minutes, with incredible precision, and the little mouths opened to receive. Then the birds took off again in search of more food, coming back moments later, speedily and precisely, to those red mouths in need.

It is their destiny, and their calling, to be here, living among these ancient buildings, in this rhythmical summer glory, their place and purpose clear and joyous.

Around us the bar is packed now, and Nilo is hustling, cleaning tables, moving chairs, inviting people to sit. His staff is in and out carrying trays of drinks.

— *Tutto bene, signori?* Nilo asks, leaning in here and there.

The din of summer renews us and fills us, and all around us it promises to bear fruit.

Bianca and the children are going on a trip to Romania, to the hometown of the children's nanny, Ilana, and Ilana asked if I would take care of her little dog and her house, which is, most improbably, the house in Patarnione that once belonged to Donna, where we spent the first few months in Cetona.

Would I housesit? Of course, I said!!

I have not been in the house in many years, since I visited one summer when Donna and I were both here, and as I unpack my few things I look around with the emotion of return, the years falling away and memory hugging me.

Some things have changed since Donna sold the house: It has a new bathroom downstairs, and the living room and kitchen have been made into one more spacious and sunnier room. But the fireplace from centuries ago is still here, as it was, as is the uneven terracotta floor of warm pale rose.

In the corner of the kitchen sits the old shallow gray stone sink I remember with particular affection. It is unfussed, almost primitive, and cut on a slant to facilitate drainage, and I find unimaginable joy washing a small basket of tomatoes in it for my dinner. I watch the water race downward to the small uneven drain hole, and I can see my mom's hands washing dishes there, her wide platinum wedding band shimmering under the water.

I am here in her place now, alone, and grown—in some ways.

The spiral staircase, made by the same metalsmith who made ours on Borgo, is still there too, and as I go down the stairs I step into my old footprint and I find unbearable tenderness in this. I sit on a step and I take a moment to caress the time gone by from my childhood here, the laundry freezing on the clothes line, the cold we felt here. I'm relieved it is summer now, but the time churns inside of me nonetheless.

The house feels intimate and comforting, as if I had always been here, and relieved by this I go outside with a glass of wine to sit on the terracotta steps to watch the last of the day.

Dusk is approaching; the countryside is soft-hued, and the air is sweet. The sky is a bit baby blue and a bit soft pink, and Monte Cetona sits upfront, nearby, like a solid, big-limbed friend. I find again, exactly the same, that which I have always loved about Patarnione, about this singular place particularly angled to the mountain, which is now darkening to a clear periwinkle. Two tiny lights go on, nestled in its folds. They are always there, those two tiny lights up on the mountain.

Everything is still and so quiet compared to the piazza, and the silence envelopes me gently.

While I sit looking out, Giovanni pulls up in his little blue car. He walks by the house slowly on his way to his dinner alone in the house next door. Now I know what it's like when he pulls up every evening after riding back from the piazza, as he has done every night of his life, to this little quiet corner of the earth that I share now once more with him so improbably.

He already knew I would be here and he stops to chat. I tell him how happy I am to be here with Monte Cetona right there in my face, so very close. He looks up to it, and I think he looks proud, though I think the mountain means something different to him than to me.

Silence falls.

— 'Notte, Giovanni says.

He smiles with his one big wandering eye and with his hands interlaced behind his back he walks to the modern frosted glass door that at some point replaced his mom's old wooden door. He leaves it open to the summer breeze and disappears in the darkness inside, carrying behind the ghost of his mother, Clemenzia, and the din of her voice filling the little square in front of the house.

In the morning I hear an Ape, a tractor every now and then, otherwise nothing. I surveil the fresh air and the mountain set in harmony against the blue sky, and I step back inside. Silence returns. I breathe it in, this apparent nothingness within which is a pulse, an unmistakable pulse of fields and the chirps of a bird and the sound of a gravel road.

From the kitchen window, looking away from the mountain, Cetona sits ancientlike, with the Rocca framed by the pine trees, the layered circles of houses below extending outward, burnt umber, terracotta, and light-colored stone. The view reminds me of all the postcards I received in the States when I first left. It reminds me of the longing, the crushing distance I felt.

The thought of the postcards makes my heart twitch. I can barely look out the window without feeling the grief anew, raw like yesterday.

Are you staying, people ask me now. What about your boyfriend?

— *Ormai non parti più, dai... stai qui!* they say. At this point you're not leaving! C'mon, stay!

*Ormai*, that word. Like you drank three-quarters of a bottle of wine, you might as well finish it up (which I often agree with).

I will never be ready to leave, no matter how long I stay.

I am happy here, simply, without need for elaborate intellectual exercises. Is it the way people age here, or the way they are accessible? Is it Sotero and how he makes me laugh? Or the way people do actually care in some way about each other? The way Mariachiara takes care of her granddaughter. The pride of the farmer. Watching Nilo walk through the piazza, or the way Ottavia opens her door to me. The refreshing lack of artifice. The honesty. The shared time, a common passage of life. That is what binds me.

And the green, the countryside, the infinity of the sky. My sky.

Is that not what happiness is?

And yet, after my painful reacquaintance and finding this love here again, I find myself dissecting it. Is it rose-glassed regression, the childlike warm blanket of a past revisited through the haze of time? No, it's not. It's real love, no less than it was thirty years ago. It just doesn't wipe away.

But is it mine any longer? I am scared to hold it again, to trust in this love. Will it survive my impatience toward Italian bureaucracy? Will it survive the shrugging indifference to morality, the immutability of a society too comfortable to want to disrupt itself, a society that will steal even from its own children? Will it survive the overall chaos of the country (I need to remember that Cetona is but a speck of Italy, and a much more peaceful and cleaner one at that), or the sense of doom—the hammering no, no, no, no—that precedes and accompanies, and ultimately thwarts, any attempts to make anything change or happen here? Will it survive the barking hunting dogs chained in fucking cages smaller than the regular American refrigerator?

Plus, I am a big fan of orderly lines in stores and offices, and even paying taxes, and the common good. I love the common good, and loud rock 'n' roll, and soul music, and American defiance, and blackness. I love black Americans, whose survival and resilience sets me back a few breaths every time I think of American history. And who is the Italian Jimi Hendrix, if one could ever have existed?

I love American courage and the American ability to say fuck it—not in anger but in ingenuity—and the particularly refreshing thing that is the American sense of possibility. Anything *can* be.

And I love an American man, a particularly beautiful American man.

Yet, even while I think this, half of my brain drifts toward a dream. If I could make a living here, independent of the system, and have a relatively normal life, I would stay. I would find a different apartment, up in town, and work and live, or a small place in the country where I could have chickens and paint them. Can I have that? Work. I need for my work to matter. Work matters to me, not only as a means to pay bills, but as a manifestation of self, of self-realization. I value the importance of work—the value of contributing to the well-being of society whether by a garden or a positive energy. I think back to my favorite Emerson saying: *To laugh often and much; to win the respect of intelligent people and the affection of children ...*

Perhaps that is what made me leave Cetona to start, the understanding that that mattered to me, and I was not sure—or my father was not sure—that it mattered to others equally, and now I am not sure how to be that person here—how to carry on with my goals and ambitions in a pond whose parameters are different. I feel like a ghost without a context, without value, neither for what I contribute nor for what I think. I am no one save an affection of the past. I am hearsay, a spirit floating.

And what is happiness across the ocean, on the other hand? I find myself weighing things like putting stacks of drugs on the pans of an old-fashioned scale. On one side, I have comfort of more recent knowledge, but profound regret for loss I cannot undo. Here, I don't have work or a work permit, or citizenship.

And, yet, I think, looking out the window, I have *this*, and the voluminous space it occupies in my heart. And in some ways, that *does* suffice. It lulls me and fills me, like a lover with whom chemistry is perfect, something one cannot argue with or contradict. It simply *is*.

I don't have an answer. I am paralyzed, hanging from a thread that seems spun by my head but is really much greater, reaching into my very cells. Perhaps there is no wholeness for me out there. My father's old adage, you'll have the best of two worlds ... There is no such thing as the best of two worlds. It does not exist.

I simply have neither.

Back in town. I check on the swallows again, for the umpteenth time. I grin in confirming that they are there, and, too, they have grown. In one nest are still two birdies, now competing for space to stick their heads out, and in the other at least one. I have hope that I will see them fly, and I look forward to it.

I mark nine months here. So much elation, and so much still to do, to understand. My need for security beckons; my retirement account is suffering. Yet, I have not been here this long in so long. It took me such courage to get here. Why go again?

When I return to live in my apartment I feel a bit bare and over-sensitive, like I am hitting a corner with my hip all the time.

A cat run over in the road. A mean word spoken about someone. *Le malelingue*, the mean tongues, wagging. The caged and barking hunting dogs everywhere. Cars barreling down the road mindlessly. The trash on the road.

A contrast strikes me between the ennobling, sacred beauty of this land, yet a social callousness that stings, a coarseness that hurts me. I am sensitive to everything that is not perfect here, as if something inside of me were trying to push me away from my own self, to discourage me from belonging again.

I retreat to bad memories, as if they will make my choice easier. That old, filthy man on the tractor who violated me, and the men who showed us their dicks in their cars when we hitchhiked. People just turned a blind eye—to that, and worse.

In high school, when I worked for Signora Marmorini in Castiglion della Pescaia, they had a beach house just two blocks from the water. She'd send me grocery shopping into town with my bike to pick up a ricotta cake or fresh bread, and as I rode I loved the smell of the cakes wafting from the bakery, and, down on the boardwalk by the beach, the aroma of the clams and *telline* sautéing in garlic wafting from the kitchens on the beach. The whole beach smelled of cooking and families and summer vacation. I remember the clink of glasses as tables were set on the terraces on the beach and families gathered in the sun to wait for a table.

Amidst it all, I spent many hours of my free weekend nights cueing to use the pay phone to call Cetona. My friends would gather in the phone booth of the Bar Sport to cheer me up. I missed Cetona, even from there!

— Nothing is happening here, they'd say!

At the beach, on the other hand, the scene was lively, animated, at the time, by the mystique of corrupt politicians in the news and the sordid affairs between the locals and the summer guests, women, mostly, tanning topless and titillating on the hot sands alone, their husbands busy with their jobs in the stifling cities, Arezzo, Florence, and Rome. The husbands came on weekends to join the families, to share Sunday lunches or maybe a few days here or there.

One such husband was the cousin of my boss, a regular at the house, a middle-aged dermatologist from Arezzo. One day, when I was sent home early to start prepping lunch, he came to the house, alone, with some pretext. I had met him before many times; he was a funny guy, or he thought he was funny. He'd check our skin on the beach to tell us how well we would age or whether we'd get cellulite when we got old.

That day when he came to the house I told him no one was there. The silence felt foreboding, and I hoped he would turn around and leave, but he came in anyway. Pulling the door shut behind him, he followed me into the kitchen and quickly pinned me against the wall. He tried to kiss me and pull down my bathing suit, and I remember running from one corner of the room to the other, barefoot, running from his blue eyes all crazy and his face and curly black hair sweaty. I remember feeling my heart beat and knowing that I would never give in to this no matter the cost. I was seventeen or so.

Then I heard the sound of the front door open—it was *la nonna* coming home to help me make lunch, or rather, to make sure I was doing it right—and she saved me, though I never told, and she never knew. I didn't want to lose my job and the money I needed to buy my *motorino*. It was just one of those things that happened, that we just overcame, many of us.

A year or so later, when I was hanging out in Sarteano a lot, there was a girl our age or so with long black hair, bright blue eyes, and a sweet but frightened look. I'd see her every now and then walking through Sarteano's piazza or the park. She was big-boned and awkward and she'd look around with an absent, wandering gaze, naïve yet teasing. It was known that she was different in some way; *è matta*, they'd say, or *mica c'è tutta*, she's not all there—and sometimes kids teased her and ganged up on her. Just watching her made me feel vulnerable and scared, and silently I always feared that bad things would happen to her.

Indeed, one day a group of guys, four, five, six, I don't know exactly how many, took her somewhere, a barn out in the country, I think, and had sex with her. They gang-raped her, for, surely, she could not have consented in any true way. Afterward she was seen wandering around town all messed up, in a disheveled skirt and a pink top, dirty and with semen in her hair, looking lost.

What had happened became known almost immediately. I knew some of the guys rumored to be involved—I think—and indeed, we are still friends. They talked about it and laughed about it, and someone might even have bragged. People laughed and snickered and shook their heads.

— *Per carità*, they said, pitying her but not rising to stand up for her.

I was horrified and sickened, and yet, I too did nothing. I talked with one or two of them and tried to find out who had done what to this odd girl that no one cared about, but everyone just shrugged and averted their eyes.

Let it go, they said. *Lascia sta'*. There was nothing to be done.

Of course, there was, but this kind of thing, of thinking, is ancient and stubborn. Last week, in a conversation at the bar, a person I know posited that a guy from Cetona who a few years ago killed his wife was justified—and indeed, right—because she was going to leave him and this would have ruined him financially. He shot her, in the middle of a street in Città della Pieve, a cold-blooded, premeditated murder, and got seven years in jail. Too long, they said; he was a good guy.

Seriously? The conversation irks me and frustrates me. No place is singular in this, yet I want my town on this hill, on this noble land, to be perfect, and enlightened, and harmonious, and it's not. It's insular, sometimes closed-minded, and often acrimonious and difficult, hostile even. And in some ways, I struggle.

The other night at the Bar Cavour I made the mistake of commenting on the mediocrity of the *pastrignocchi* at Cetona's eponymous festival. *Pastrignocchi* are a kind of *pici*, or something negligibly different, that Cetona has taken to champion as its own.

Of course, every Italian, by mere dint of birth, considers him- or herself an expert food critic and connoisseur, so this got everyone yelling about every festival food in the area, with Sotero leading the charge.

Taking offense—understandably, since he is one of the organizers—he countered that the *pastrignocchi* are the best festival food around, better than the *bico* in Piazze, or the pici in Celle, or the *ciaffagnone* of San Casciano.

— *Il ciaffagnone a San Casciano fa schifo,* someone said. *Ciaffagnone* is a kind of pancake, fried and served with cheese or Nutella. In San Casciano, they say, it is terrible.

— *No, il bico fa schifo,* countered Sotero. No, the *bico* is disgusting.

At this, five other people started arguing about the correct way to make *bico*, something between an unleavened flatbread and a pizza crust, finally ending with a *vaffanculo, ma te che cazzo ne sai?* Fuck off, what the hell do you know?

Whatever might be said—and probably my criticism was not helpful—the *sagra dei pastrignocchi* might even be successful from a food sales perspective, but it offers little to do but eat, and then it ends and the town returns to darkness, unchanged. I sense a lack of esprit, or purpose, and this leads back to a central question that vexes a little, ancient town like Cetona, and that is, how to modify and engineer its very fabric and flavor—its traffic patterns, events, urban design, paint colors—in such a way that contributes to the integrity and soul of the town and keeps the economy vibrant.

And how to get people to agree on it all, to boot!

Impossible, some say.

— *So' i Cetonesi che so' fatti così. Non gli piace niente,* says someone. It's the Cetonesi who are like this. They are persnickety, disdainful, and sometimes even a tad unfriendly.

There's certainly some truth to this, which troubles me and reminds me of something Pippo said recently, in a conversation about Cetona's problems (which always lead inevitably back to the closed piazza and what to do about it).

— *Non gli è stata insegnata l'accoglienza ai Cetonesi. C'è ancora quello che dice 'vaffanculo a te e a chi ti ci porta!'* he said. The

Cetonesi have not been taught hospitality. There are still those who tell outsiders to go fuck themselves and go back where they came from!

Pippo shakes his head, disgruntled about it all—particularly since Cetona could use attracting some tourism to keep it alive—and he's not the only one. In fact, the other day I was talking with a woman who lives in Rome but whose grandparents are from Cetona and who has spent every summer of her life here. When she arrived for the holidays this year, she was unloading her car and an old lady walked by and said exactly that.

— *Accidenti a voi e chi vi ci porta!* I curse you and whoever brought you to Cetona.

I feel privileged that no one has said that to me, at least not to my face.

— *E il matrimonio l'altra settimana?* Pippo asks, mentioning a wedding here recently of the daughter of a famous Italian businessman.

The man, they tell me, has owned a villa here for many years and his presence adds prestige to the town. He donated money for the restoration of the Collegiata and is *simpatico* and respected.

Anyway, the wedding was a shindig: Florists came from Florence and decorated the Collegiata with stunning white flowers and more than a dozen young olive trees. Hundreds of people in the latest and highest fashion came from all over, and it brought business to town, well, if nothing else for Nilo.

Town hall kindly accommodated the event by closing a street uptown for a few hours and by letting vans cross the piazza to shuffle guests back and forth. It was nice; I enjoyed watching it all from my windows.

— *Eppure tutti ci hanno da di'!* Pippo said, with a gesture of disgust. And yet, the Cetonesi have to say something, don't they?

Why are you letting them close the street? they grumbled. Why are you letting them use the piazza? Why didn't they use the local florist? And, why did they not ticket the vans crossing the piazza?

Pippo takes a sip of wine and looks out onto the piazza.

— *Vogliono tutti critica' e di', ma non fanno niente se non gli torna bene.* Everyone wants to criticize. They won't do anything unless it serves their interests.

— You know what the real problem is? someone else interjects. *Che alla gente di Cetona non gl'interessa niente! Niente! L'unico interesse e` il disinteresse!* he says. People in Cetona are not interested in anything! Anything! The only interest is disinterest! If there's a person with a passion, people will rub at it, talk about it, criticize it, wear away at it until the person is an outcast.

I am remined of something Marcello Bennati once said, a generational Cetonese, the guy who used to stick his cats' paws onto walnut halves and push them down into the piazza. He spends a lot of time in China now and is unvarnished in his opinions.

— *So' cani! I Cetonesi so' cani!* Cetonesi are dogs! Dogs!

Maybe. It's a cantankerous medieval mountain breed, stubborn, suspicious, and proud of it, I think half-jokingly.

In truth, though, sometimes I just have to agree. I am troubled by the strident tone of the conversations, aggressive and critical. *You're wrong. You should do this, you should do that, you are wrong to do that, you shouldn't do this.* People speak, often, without knowing even what the other person is thinking, or hearing what they are saying. I can't get enough time to gather my thoughts to say what I mean. They yell and interrupt. I say, I love the cemetery, and the other says, I hate the cemetery, or another says, I don't give a fuck about the cemetery. And, then, suddenly the conversation moves onto something else, the topic left unexplored. Nothing is learned and no new idea produced. By the end of it all I feel silenced, shoved, stuck.

I analyze this. Where has my Cetonese side gone, if I ever had one? I consider the American way, the diplomacy, that has been caging me, wearing me down for years, particularly in the South ... Now here at times I feel like I cannot even explore the complexity of my ideas, and ideas—their richness and ambiguity—are part of how I live in the world. This leads me to existential questions about meaning and identity, what makes us *us*, what gives us any stability in shifting time and space and environment.

The other night at the bar some people started talking about personalities, and after I said something, Isabella said to me, *sì, ma io lo so come sei fatta te! Ti conosco!* I know how you are! I know you! It's a common saying that dates familiarity far back in time, to our birth, as if we were handed a personality immutable and unchanging. Is who I am who I was? Are the two things the same? Yes, perhaps at heart they are; perhaps I am still what they knew, and I am that. I recognize something comforting about having an identity, even if it is partially inaccurate or incomplete. And yet, have we not all changed— one hopes?

I consider that I may have a place that knows not my past, and one that knows not my present, and this hems me in and upsets me.

Then, I sit in a group around Riccardo and Bianca. The whole coterie is around—Ludovico with his aristocratic airs, and Camille the snooty French artist, and the Americans from Florida, and some other people I don't know. Words circle meaninglessly, a joke here and there, no serious thread to follow, discursive, prosaic. I feel like I don't learn anything. Is it just me, and why don't I know how to do this anymore?

Someone starts talking about a woman who owns a property here. I thought they were friends with her, but they start criticizing the food she serves at dinner parties and how her fridge smells. I feel embarrassed for sitting there. My head hurts. Around us children are yelling and parents are yelling at the kids.

Then Riccardo looks at my shoes—flat, red baby-doll shoes that feel to me like they have super powers, though they appear to not be working right now.

— *Le tue scarpe sono orribili,* he says. Your shoes are horrible.

I know he's partially goading me, but he's partially serious.

— *Sono così brutte che sono anti-stupro.* They are so ugly they are insurance against rape.

All sorts of arguments flood my head about rape and the suggestion that rape has anything to do with shoes. I have completely lost my sense of humor on this topic and many others. Plus, leave my fucking shoes alone! Bianca chimes in, annoyed. I am wishing she didn't, but she does and they start arguing.

After a few minutes another man at the table, snooty-nosed and with clothes two sizes too small, from the north via Puglia and not even living in Cetona, starts quizzing me about why I have come back.

He wants to know what I am looking for here, as he puts it.

— *Cosa stai cercando qui?*

I try to rephrase the questions in terms of a personal experience, a return home, the dearest of my life, which needs no challenge, no justification. It's my life, after all.

— *Un tuffo nel passato?* he asks. A dive in the past?

No, not really, I say. I am trying to understand something about me in the present.

I try to explain, but it's complicated and personal. I stammer ... My words fail as his questions pursue, not inspired by kind curiosity but more by personal judgment. What's it to him anyway?

— *Avrai sprecato un anno della tua vita. Non ne verrà niente.* You will have wasted a year of your life, he says, his lips curling. Nothing will come of it.

Tears flood my eyes. Who, and in what miserable universe, says something like that?

Seeking comfort and silence, I get up and go for a walk around the piazza. I walk a few laps alone in a big rectangle, looking down, following the pattern of the pavement's stone striping like a tightrope walker. I feel completely and singularly alone in my feelings and in my inner world.

At the end of the piazza I notice Ave sitting on a bench with a few other ladies. Her arms are crossed over her chest and she is talking breezily. She sees me approach and her brow furrows, but she smiles and waves. Her brown eyes are full of love and acceptance.

— *Sibilla, vieni, ti siedi con noi?* she asks, tilting her head toward the bench. Sibilla, come, do you want to sit with us?

I sit, lean my head on her shoulder, and I cry. She puts her hand on my cheek and holds me.

A medieval festival full of color and sound filled the piazza for several days recently with games, flame-throwers and flag-throwers—another event I had never seen.

People of all ages dressed in sumptuous period costume paraded through town at the beat of sinister-sounding drums, painting the alleys with ochre and blue, red and gold. Split into teams, they reenacted historic battles and flag- and javelin-throwing competitions and races carrying jugs full of water atop wooden boards. I was mesmerized by the beauty of the costumes and the competence of the flag- and flame-throwers, and I took hundreds of pictures. I was also impressed by the organization of it all.

— *Tanto mica dura,* a friend of mine said shaking his head. It won't last anyway. Too much infighting, jealousies, commentary. I hope he's wrong.

After the festivities end, the piazza is left to its solitude, just a few people drawn here and there by the soft weather and the season. Bennato, Lapo, and Silvanino are talking in front of the bar. Every now and then they laugh, then they stand quietly, their cigarettes glowing in the dark.

Cars are parked in no-parking zones and even on sidewalks. The municipal police never come at night, so people take advantage of it. Strangely, Salviati appears out of nowhere, possibly running late at a meeting, and suddenly there is a flutter of people running out of the bars to move the cars.

Salviati raises his voice with a kid who parked on the sidewalk. *Ma che mi prendi per il culo?* he yells. Are you dicking me around? The kid quickly moves his car. After all the cars are reshuffled to different places around town—just long enough for Salviati to leave and the cars moved back to where they were—the piazza returns to calm.

Past midnight, Alano and Isabella call for me under my open window and lure me downstairs for a glass of wine. I don't feel like putting on shoes, so I go down barefoot and I smile running on the clean, smooth stone, freedom tickling my toes. When they see me barefoot, they fling off their shoes, too, and we run around the piazza barefoot, on the cool stone, laughing like children, innocent and ecstatic. I had never run in the piazza (or in any other public space) barefoot in all of my life—in all of my life!—and it is remarkably simple and deeply joyous. I do a headstand in the middle of the deserted piazza, with tears of happiness streaming upward rather than downward, and we laugh and run around more.

The following day a nosy woman approached Isabella.

— *Ma che facevate in piazza te e la Sibilla ieri sera, eh?* the woman asked her. What were you and Sibilla doing in piazza last night?

Isabella furled her brow.

— *Ma te che fai, dormi in finestra per fatti i cazzi dell'altri?* she answered. What do you do, sleep in the fucking window to mind other people's business?

Even when you do things with the best intentions, here someone will find fault. And, in fact, just when I need no more reminders of how much this simple small-town constraint irks me ...

For the *notte di San Lorenzo*, the night of the shooting stars, the Della Vignas hosted an enchanting evening of reveling and dancing on the street in front of their cantina. A four-course meal was served paired with wines from their cellars. Bianca was there, and Tiberio and his wife, Alano and Morena, the Americans from Florida, and several other couples. And the whole town.

The women wore party dresses and the mood was exuberant and happy. A talented musician from the area worked the crowd while singing everything from Neapolitan folk songs and opera arias to rock and the Bee Gees. A crowd filled the street dancing and singing in a fun, light-hearted atmosphere, the young mixing with the old, people who knew each other and not, until midnight came and the party had to stop. It was a magical evening.

Afterwards, walking home through the piazza among a group of people, I realized I had not talked with Morena, Alano's girlfriend, all evening, so I went up to her and asked her how she was doing.

With her hand she made a gesture as if to shoo me away.

— *Guarda, non mi parlare,* she said. Don't talk to me. She turned away from me and continued to walk.

I was taken aback. I stopped and said, what's wrong?

— *Vuoi sapere che c'è?!* she said immediately, as if she had been waiting to be asked. You want to know what's wrong?

— *Te devi lasciare stare la roba mia!!* she screamed, getting in my face. You need to leave my stuff alone!!

By then it was well past midnight. The lights in the piazza were dimmed, but there were still people seated at tables at the Bar Cavour and at the Bar Sport, and a few people lingering in clusters here and there.

— What are you talking about? I asked, stunned.

As you might recall, many months ago, sometime this winter, I turned down the idea of a tryst with Alano. Since then, I rebuffed his flirtations and advances, at one point going the extra mile to avoid him. But months have passed and things had returned to normal. We are just friends.

She huffed and puffed and finally she screamed.

— *L'hai invitato a casa tua, e questo non lo dovevi fare, hai capito?!* You invited him to your house and you shouldn't have done that!! She repeats, *Lascia stare la mia roba!* My stuff.

In the past many weeks, I have had a lot of fun with Alano, mostly with Isabella, too, and the other night they came up to my place for a glass of wine. I wanted them to taste a new batch of kimchee I had made. We played some music, talked about painting, and then they left.

— Isabella was with us. We are all friends, I said, trying to reassure her.

— *A me la figura della cornuta non me la fai fare, capito?* she yelled, unappeased. I'm not going to let you make me look like a *cornuta*, which means, literally, a horned one, one who has been betrayed. Leave my stuff alone, she repeated!!

While she is yelling at me, I think of the great honor I have felt being loyal to Aram over all the past many months—the cleanliness and serenity that have come with that choice. My virgin year, I think, with relief. It has made me so happy to have loved him so entirely.

I should have walked off then, but I didn't. I got upset and raised my voice, telling her that if she is *cornuta* she can thank her boyfriend, not me.

People gathered outside the Bar Cavour to watch. Sabrina the waitress came out as well as Felice. At the other end, Nilo watched and others. Who else was at the Bar Sport? Who knows.

After yelling at me a few more minutes, she started making fun of me dancing. I had done nothing scandalous or wrong. I had just had fun. Shooing her dress in imitation she yelled, *E te così ci vai a fare in America, capito? In America devi andare a fare questo, non a Cetona.* You go do this in America, you understand? She pointed a hand to the end of the piazza, as if showing me the door.

At that, I turned and walked away, up the alley to my apartment. When the piazza calmed, Isabella and Silvanino beckoned from under my window and we sat on the sidewalk talking. They had witnessed it all.

This does not add good energy to my life, I say to them in tears. It makes me want to leave.

They shake their heads. You can't let this.

— *Questa è Cetona, e lo sai. L'hai sempre saputo.* This is Cetona and you know it, you have always known, Isabella says, reminding me of what a great time she had at my house that night.

The following morning I came out onto the piazza feeling naked and bruised. I felt the same feeling I had had before in Cetona, of being in a fish bowl—and I had forgotten how deeply unpleasant it is. You encounter people and they say hello, but you don't know who knows what or what they are thinking, though you know they know something, for sure, and for sure they are talking about it because they think they know it all.

The most upsetting strand of the feeling to me is that they don't know the truth, but they are going to judge and talk regardless. I felt incensed and upset. I tried so hard to avoid any entanglements here; I tried so hard to avoid being at the center of anything like this—exactly like this.

Over the next few days, everyone in town had something to say about the matter, little of which was comforting, and now the episode is weighing on me. I feel like my spirit is not at home. A feeling of foreignness, of not being able to fly here, of being caged, judged, impeded, has descended on me. An ancient feeling. I suddenly wonder whether I ever belonged here.

I suddenly miss the people in America who helped me put my mind to good use and elevate my spirit. To educate me and make me a better human being. I feel that both my mind and my spirit are in peril now, and, in the process, I have endangered precious things. Everything feels in peril.

But is it about Cetona, or is it about injustice in general? I try to separate the two, and I realize I am looking for an ideal, and that is unfair too.

When I see Aldo at the end of the piazza I nearly burst out crying and I tell him about it, though I am sure he already knows.

He is quiet for a moment.

— *Prima o poi doveva succede'. Sei una targa facile. Sei qui da sola, e fatta come sei ... Non gli stai bene in mano...*

It was bound to happen, he says quietly. You're an easy target. You're here by yourself. Plus, the way you are ... You don't fit in their hand—an expression that means they don't know what to make of you. You rankle people. Your free spirit, he says.

I sigh sadly.

— *In caso ti sei dimenticata, vive' a Cetona n'è facile. Anzi.* In case you forgot, living in Cetona is not easy. To the contrary, Aldo says as we pace around the piazza.

I remember that now. It sounds familiar, primordial. Yet, I have lost my ability to handle it.

— So, what is one supposed to do? I ask.

— *Ne' ti puoi fa' 'na corazza, e neanche puoi evita'.* You can't build armor around you, nor can you avoid, because here ... he fans his hands out to the piazza.

— You have to push through, the way you used to. You have to be who you are, but it takes strength. And then you have to find the people on whose shoulders to cry when the wounds come, and I know, they will come ...

He turns and smiles knowingly.

Can I be who I really am and live happily here, free-spirited like light, the girl with the magic stone in my pocket, or does this place cast darkness on me? I feel completely lost.

I shake my head and tears well up in my eyes. Aldo rubs my nose. I wish I could cry on his chest, but who knows what people would think.

Certainly, something bad.

Still reeling from the episode with Morena, and also foretelling a bad ending with Aram that I cannot control, I woke up upset. The negative side of all this is coming to light, and I blame myself for thinking it wouldn't. Had I forgotten this about Cetona? And did I think there would not be consequences?

There have always been consequences to Cetona, for me. Is it me, or is it Cetona?

I have lost my moment in the sun and I feel like retreating where no one will see me. Months back, Ottavia gave me a key to her house, with its spit of grass in secluded privacy, and I can walk there in a minute, just past Le ACLI, to get an hour of sun in peace. I can strip down to my panties and read in the sun, alone, unseen and undisturbed.

While I am there I listen to the sweet banter between a child and her grandmother in an adjacent garden. The grandma babysits the child in the morning, until lunchtime, when the mother comes back from work. A thick, tall hedge separates us and prevents me from seeing them, but I hear them nearly every time I am here and, aided by their conversation, I imagine what they do. While the grandmother goes about her chores, she talks with the little girl who plays in the grass and chases bugs and lizards and asks a lot of questions.

— *Nonna! Questo cos'è?* she asks in her high-pitched voice. Grandma, what is this?

— *Cosa?* What, answers the grandmother, and she walks over to see.

This time it's a curled-up bug, a *troiolina*, which reminds the grandmother of a rhyme from her childhood.

— *Quand'ero piccola come te, me la diceva sempre mia nonna questa filastrocca,* she says to the child. When I was little like you my grandmother recited it all the time.

She recites the rhyme for the little girl, who laughs and repeats it word by word, then goes quiet, back to the bug. The grandmother goes back inside the house to do something and she comes back out a minute later to ask, as she does every day, what the little girl wants for lunch.

— Do you want chicken or a cutlet? she asks. The girl cannot be older than three or four, I would guess, and I smile at the choices, or the fact that she gets choices at all. Today she goes for the cutlet.

— *La pasta come la vuoi, col sugo?* How do you want your pasta, with meat sauce?

The little girl is talking to herself about something, but the question is leading and the grandma already knows the answer.

— *No, in bianco, nonna, in bianco!* she says. No, grandma, *in bianco*, which means with butter and cheese.

I envision the grandmother shrugging and shaking her head.

— *La vole sempre in bianco!* she says to herself, walking back inside. She always wants it *in bianco!*

The grandmother is busy in the kitchen for a few minutes while the little girl rummages about, then the grandmother returns and starts singing a song. She sits down and I imagine that the little girl comes to sit next to her, and they start singing together. I listen to them, smiling, and finally the mother comes home, disrupting everything, and they all go inside to eat lunch.

The garden falls into silence.

I took with me a letter I received at the end of freshman year of college, nearly thirty years ago, from Signora Vinciarelli, our indomitable Italian teacher at the *liceo*, the adult who, at the time, together with Zia, must have known me best of all. She was writing me back in response to a letter in which, I surmise, I shared concerns about how I would feel coming home.

Imagine that.

Her letter reads in part, *Here, everything moves forward as usual, sometimes with greater interest, sometimes with greater monotony. Every now and then I receive a visit from your classmates...they give me some news and we talk about 'the one far away.' ... I am pleased to hear of your continued and intense feelings towards your town, which honor you. You have not been overwhelmed by the cult of America that would overtake us provincials. You have maintained the autonomy of feeling and thought that have always been a credit to you. I confess that I smiled at your statement that San Francisco is the most beautiful place in the world* after *Cetona, but I know your sentiment is sincere and that you will always have a place among the Cetonesi, even the incredibly backward, who were scandalized by the behaviors of the young American girl at the* liceo, *who will be more scandalized by the young woman who returns from Yale, and who will continue to be scandalized when that young girl becomes a grown woman and will return through the years. This is by now (she uses the word* ormai*) part of your existence, an indelible part of your personality. This is who you are. Nonetheless, you should never fear coming home, or coming face to face with your past, no matter what experience you have ahead of you... Do not fear seeing Italy again, and if you do not feel at ease, do not blame yourself. Your doubts, your feelings, are deep sentiments and proof of a beautiful soul, as the romantics would say, who is no longer afraid of showing itself as it takes full consciousness of itself. Maturity, as you know, comes not with a degree, but with life's tests, and you have the fortune and the responsibility of facing tests that are not granted to all. With love, Loredana*

I lie back in the grass, in the silence. The years fly backward through my head as I try to recapture who I was when I received that.

Have I not always known that Cetona could not be different for me now? Did I not always know that my self would abrade here, like Signora Vinciarelli herself knew, yet that I would never be able to get away from its sweet call beckoning me home like a siren?

— *Eri straniera, ma non per nazionalità. Eri te,* Signora Vinciarelli said over lunch. You were foreign, but not because of nationality.

It was just you—the way you are. It's your way of being in the world. The magic stone.

So, it's not Cetona. It's me.

Perhaps, then, that means I don't belong perfectly anywhere. I just need to do my best *somewhere*. The somewhere I love the most; where I feel the happiest.

I am confounded about measuring this now, with so much at stake again, and around lunchtime I attempt to skirt the piazza to go for a walk.

Bianca spots me and flags me down.

— *Scappi?* she yells, waving. Are you running away?

I am glad to see her, comforted by her generous ways, and we stop to talk in the alley by the post office. I burst out crying and she hugs me. In retrospect Bianca was the one new friend I made in a year in Cetona and I am happy for that. I cherish her and her company. With her background split among places and cultures I think she understands something about me. Plus, she is kind to me.

In the alley she invites me to stop by the house for lunch after my run, which I do. Riccardo is in a jovial mood and he hugs me. He makes a delicious *aglio, olio e peperoncino*, mildly hot and comforting. As usual, I tell him the pasta is perfect, and as usual he smiles and says, *lo so*. I know.

In the late afternoon I hug them goodbye, grateful for their company and hospitality, and I walk back toward town, happy to be in the silence of the countryside, with the sound of the crickets and the birds and the swaying of the trees. Mid-August is now past, and the landscape is changing softly. Unburdened now of its wheat, the land is being plowed under to be seeded anew, and everywhere in the fields are tractors working, painting the landscape in large and continuous rows of brown over brown. The only remaining large swatches of green are fields of corn and sunflowers, though the large yellow blooms have begun to rest their heads downward.

As I walk my paths through the countryside, I smile to see that some of the houses that have been closed all year are finally open and inhabited, albeit for this one week of late summer celebration. The shutters are parted, and the windows, newly borne to the light, look like large gaping eyes in faces awakened and somewhat surprised. Swimming pools are uncovered, and from the usually quiet lanes I hear laughter of families and children.

In the piazza, children are screaming and playing, running up and down with their bicycles and their toys. The tables at the bars, both Bar Cavour and Bar Sport, are overflowing with people sitting in ever-growing circles, talking and laughing.

At dinnertime I hear voices of revelers coming from an apartment above the Bar Cavour. The windows are open and I recognize the language to be American English. I realize it's the American women who have been here a few days and who I met sitting at the Bar Cavour. They are from Georgia and Florida, mostly, maybe one from Texas. Yesterday I saw them getting in a van heading out for a day trip, and I wanted to ask if I could go too.

I stand below their window and listen to them talking and laughing, and I see the frescoed ceiling through the windows, the most beautiful apartment on the piazza, I am told.

I want to yell up, can I come up, can I join you? I miss something about the States, and my dad, and my house, and Aram, and my cat, and my friend Maryellen, and while I listen to them I imagine a regular life there, something simple, uncomplicated. Something without all this division, this grief, this trial by distance.

Standing under their windows I cup my face in my hands in true loss. I don't know how to go back—when I am there I miss everything about being here—and yet, yet I am not sure I know how to stay here either. I don't know where I belong.

It's been so long since I've known.

I feel a twinge of abandonment. I push it back. I try to find focus, the beginning of a decision.

One place. What would it be like, to have one place?

It is nearly the end of a beautiful, memorable summer, and as I return to my apartment, in the specific blue of the sky I presage fall and my tenth month here.

Aram has written saying he has decided to move to Los Angeles. He did not invite me, and out of defensiveness I said I wouldn't go anyway. Perhaps he has become convinced that I am not coming back; perhaps we are both too afraid that our dreams preclude each other. Or perhaps our relationship was simply not strong enough to endure this.

And now what? I cannot bear the thought of returning to Charleston and you not being there, your street empty, the specter of your ghost hanging in the air, a scent, my memory of you hanging in the stairwell, the soft click of your door closing, the sound of your guitar playing softly beyond the door. My yelling up to you, and you coming down the stairs. Sitting out on your stoop waiting for you to come back from surfing, and finally seeing you come down the street, the familiar rumble of the old Volvo pulling in the driveway. The times I came to your door and I knew from the stillness that you were not there, that you were not beyond that door. My disappointment, then the sound of the building entryway slamming behind me.

The silence of your absence will crush me.

To forget—and trying to make the most of what I have here—I run to Chiusi to pick up a rental car for a few days.

The run is long and jarring because of the trucks and the traffic, and the ugliness and industrial sprawl at the entrance to Chiusi. Yet, I like running along the fields and the vegetable gardens that line most of the journey. There is a beautiful *orto* up on a hill, lovingly cultivated by a balding man with a long face who runs a stand at the *mercato* Saturdays. It is laden with the last of the late summer crops—tomatoes and zucchini, peppers, melons, green beans, and eggplant. Not long from now the artichoke plants will flourish in long rows, spindly and spiderlike, and next to them will be cabbage plants, with their large rounded leaves, and fennel, spiky and wispy.

In approaching Chiusi I like walking along the railroad tracks and seeing the trains come and go. The Freccia Rossa bursts through on its own track at the speed of light. I take in the particular smell of the rail yard—metal and tar—and I hear the voice on the loudspeaker announcing the arrival of the train from Florence carrying fifteen minutes of delay. *Il treno delle quattordici per Firenze Santa Maria Novella in arrivo al binario sette con quindici minuti di ritardo.*

The voice picks some chord in my heart and makes me melancholic. Departures. Goodbyes. The SATs. Nostalgia. I think of many trips to Florence with Ottavia, Maria, and Tullia over the years, and coming back on the train from Rome during college, alone, searching for the mountain on the horizon.

And, of course, leaving Lucio there that night.

I walk by the gas station where I fill up the tanks of the rental cars before I return them and I wave at the owner, a big burly man who is standing outside putting gas in a car. He smiles and waves. Across the street, the circus is setting up and it makes me recoil to see the animals being unloaded.

Cetona used to have a circus, too. It came to town once a year and set up in the parking lot of the slaughterhouse, Elide's old *macelli.* There were animals and acrobatic acts, and as kids we peeked through the seams in the tents and tried to get in for free. It seemed interesting, mildly, but it was nothing compared to when the *fiera* came to Cetona, much before our time. There was a fire-eater, who, to hear my old teacher Giorgio Doricchi tell it, in addition to exhaling fable-like flames, broke chains strapped around his chest with the mere power of his muscles and withstood the brunt of kids cleaving boulders on his bare chest with a giant mallet. There was a callous-remover, too, with frightening knives and torches, and a storyteller, who sang beautiful stories of love and war. I think we missed the best that any circus could have offered, and eventually it stopped coming. Not enough people, I guess.

By the time I get back to Cetona the sky is cobalt blue and transparent almost, and the cross of San Michele sits starkly against the sky. The bell tower is lit in a peaceful orange glow, and the sunlight lingers in the west achingly, longingly, like it does only a few nights each year. The days that won't let go, like new lovers.

A few people sit in front of Le ACLI. I see Lapo with his big curly hair, and Isabella with Ernesto. Bar Cavour's tables are packed with people laughing and talking. It's warm and pleasant. A few tourists leave Il Merlo after an early dinner and walk through the piazza, pausing to admire the special place that it is. Children ride their bikes around the piazza, racing each other, while their mothers, in good Italian fashion, shout after them, *Fate piano! Non sudate sennò prendete freddo!* Slow down! Don't sweat or you'll catch cold! I see Diego and Mariachiara, lingering. Diego has got a haircut and it looks nice, and for once Mariachiara looks like she's not in a hurry.

Nuccia is being pushed around the piazza by her daughter and her new caretaker from Morocco. After yet another stroke, it seems unfathomable yet unavoidable to think that she will not walk again. In a fraction of a flash, a minute of chaos in her body, she has gone from a sassy woman with manicured nails and a cigarette in her mouth, gossiping about this and that, to a sallow body that she can no longer control. I wonder what will happen to her too.

The last of the sun disappears behind Monte Cetona, and shadows descend across the mountain, quickly, in frames, starting from the bottom, across the first tier of olive groves, the rows of cypresses, then up across the tilled fields and orchards in the middle of the mountain, and slowly up through the thicker woods and groves higher up. It's like the gods spread a huge purple blanket over the mountain, preparing it for the night.

Then, suddenly it's dark. A few large cars go by and drive behind the piazza to the front of Bar Sport. Something is happening at the end of the piazza, but I struggle to see. Then I remember Nilo mentioned it yesterday, the Queen of Belgium is back. A couple of vans drive through the piazza, though they are not supposed to. The lights of the upstairs rooms of the *locanda* come on. The Queen is getting settled, with due regard, and afterwards Nilo and Ami will close the restaurant and go home to sleep.

The evening air is chilly, mixing a remnant of summer languor with a new scent of fall, and it smells nice. Upstairs I look around my studio and I find comfort in looking at all my paintings—paintings of Cetona, which I had never painted before. Now I have many, and I love them.

One day they will hang in my home. When I figure out where that will be.

Today was the procession in commemoration of the Madonna of Belverde, and, more generally, a heartfelt festivity among the church-going people of Cetona. I can't remember when I last participated, if ever, so I decide to go the whole way and hear Don Prospero say mass up in Belverde's church, where I got married.

It's a beautiful day, mingling vague tails of summer with the hint of autumn, and as usual, when I'm surrounded by Cetonesi I'm never disappointed. As I stand leaning against the wall looking around the church and trying to focus on what Don Prospero is saying, I hear Cecio outside talking loudly about this thing and that. His voice is reverberating into the church so loudly that I can barely hear the priest.

— *Tutti i giorni andava giù in campagna e poi prendeva la somara...* he is saying loudly, telling a story about some man and his donkey.

Inside, his wife, Evangelina, is shaking her head with exasperation. She looks over to a woman standing next to me near the doorway.

— *Va' fuori, per favore, e digli un pò di sta' zitto!* she whispers, pointing her arm at the door. Go outside, please, and tell him to shut up!

The woman goes outside and Cecio's voice quiets slightly, though, like a kid, he continues to tell his story, which I regret not hearing. I smile to myself and turn my attention to Don Prospero at the head of the church talking about Belverde's Madonna.

Then he leads the church in prayer and leaves his followers with an admonition.

— *Durante la processione non parliamo delle olive, o dei campi, o s'è venuto bono il vino.* During the procession let's not talk about the olives, or the fields, or how good the wine is this year, he says smirking, knowing his flock.

Let us walk in silence, honoring the Madonna. *In silenzio.*

People spill out from the church onto the gravel road below and Don Prospero organizes us single file so we do not talk about the olives or the wine. The marching band from Piazze is leading the procession, and Don Prospero follows behind with the members of Mondo X carrying the Madonna on their shoulders, reciting prayers.

After traveling a hundred feet or less, people are merging into pairs and leaning in and talking about the olives and the wine, and about someone's funny little dog that is walking between us like a mascot. People are joyous and festive and they are gossiping about this and that. I walk between them elated to be part of it all.

From my place in the procession I see Tullia a few steps ahead. She is here solely because Sofia is playing in the band, and I laugh to myself watching her look distractedly in every direction, her mind who knows where. I *pssst* her, like we're in grade school, and when she turns to look we laugh, and the whole town is just walking through the countryside and carrying on.

My mind travels to a story Pippo told me once about a similarly light-hearted procession, in wartime perhaps, during which the priest, who was also leading the event, grabbed a chicken in the road and hid it under his vestments. Unbeknownst to the priest, the chicken's legs were poking out from his robe.

To alert him to this visible trespass, an acolyte, the custodian of the church, began singing in faux Latin.

— *Coprite cotta mea che si vede le zampealisi,* he sang. Untranslatable Cetonese pig Latin mentioning the words *cover* and *see* and *legs.*

The priest understood the message and he answered back in more faux Latin while discreetly pulling closed his robe.

— *Fatto bene parlarmi in gerguli o villan futtorboli.* More untranslatable Cetonese pig Latin conveying that he got the message.

The people, not knowing what the priest and the acolyte were saying, figuring it was the usual Latin church-speak, answered in chorus.

— *Amen.* And on the procession went.

On another occasion—I love to hear these funny stories because they embody the temperamental personality and genetic irreverence of the Cetonesi—the man leading the procession, Massimo, a colorful fellow who liked a drink, came to a point in the ritual when the participants who were assigned to wear hoods were supposed to stop and take them off.

— *Fermi! Toglietevi i cappucci,* Massimo ordered, stopping the procession. Stop! Take off your hoods! Take them off now!

Perhaps they didn't hear him, or perhaps they weren't paying attention.

— *Toglietevi i cappucci! Forza!!* he said again. Take off your hoods!

Again, everyone ignored him. Finally, he got pissed off, and indifferent to the solemnity of the occasion, he yelled out, using one of Tuscany's most blasphemous curses.

— *Madonna scannata! Ho detto scappucciatevi!* Goddammit, I said, take your fucking hoods off!!!

Finally, that got their attention!

On another occasion, during the procession at Belverde, a hare crossed the road in front of the man who was carrying the cross. The man stopped and flung the cross at the hare over his shoulders. After he retrieved the cross, the priest turned in shock and reprimanded the man, who then threw the cross to the ground and walked off, abandoning the procession together with his closest friends. The same happened when the guy playing the cymbals got into an argument with the priest. He threw the cymbals at the priest and took off.

How wonderful my Cetona can be.

Berenice, the traffic officer, helped me get a room in Cortona, her hometown, and I decide to go for a short trip. My most vivid experience with Cortona had been, thus far, the organization of my wedding reception at Tonino's, and as soon as I pulled into town I saw the restaurant and thought of the day with a mix of regret and celebration.

Within the next several hours of the afternoon, though, I replaced old memories with new by discovering Cortona's immense trove of churches, one more beautiful than the other. I visited ten or so, and at the church of San Niccolò, tiny, with a Signorelli painting, I sat in a pew and considered praying.

In the evening I sat at a table on the *corso* and had a glass of crisp white wine while writing in my journal. I watched the people walk by and pondered the bourgeois taste and way of living that puzzles me about the Italians, so concerned about *la bella figura*—good appearance, or good impression. I studied their look, their matching cashmere sweater sets and perfectly pressed pants, so cautious and compliant and utterly un-individual. It's like a team of fashion police descended on the country and ordered everyone to wear that particular shade of beige for the year, and it's everywhere. Beige. Images of people walking on a street in New York filled my mind. I realize sometimes there is a lot I like about America.

The most beautiful thing about being in Cortona is the view of Monte Cetona from afar, stretched out in the landscape like a drawing in Saint-Exupery's *Le Petit Prince*—like a snake that has eaten a couple of duck eggs! From Cetona the mountain seems to rise suddenly out of nothing, but from Cortona you can see that it belongs to an elongated ridge, a mountainous chain of sorts, that begins and ends a long way from Cetona. Yes, distance does give perspective, at least sometimes.

The landscape around Cortona is not nearly as beautiful as Cetona's, and as I drive back I am happy to see Cetona's fields and Monte Cetona up close.

After returning and putting my stuff down upstairs I come back out and see the Signora framed by the window.

— *Non t'avevo vista più e pensavo che fossi partita! Mi dispiaceva!* she says, opening the window and smiling. I had not seen you and I thought you had left. I was sorry!

It moves me that she would have noticed and cared, and I thank her and reassure her. A few minutes later I run into Valeria's mom, who lives a bit further up the alley, and she says the same thing, and then Giuditta, too.

— *Era andata via?* she asks me. Did you go away?

I realize I had not seen her in a while and I had missed her. It takes time to become re-accustomed to seeing someone daily, even several times a day.

— *No, solo un paio di giorni,* I say. Just a couple of days.

I sense that Giuditta and I would hug if only we didn't think the other would be embarrassed. She smiles. I ask how her work is.

— *Si va avanti,* she says. We move forward.

She is carrying her usual bundles, which remind me of her chickens, and I ask her if she would appreciate table scraps for her chickens, something I have meant to ask her for a while now.

— *Certo!* she says, smiling. Certainly! I can mix them with their bread and cornmeal, she adds.

I am not surprised; Giuditta is thrifty and wise. We discuss a delivery system and she suggests that I hang the leftovers in a bag on my door handle. She will pick them up on her way out. I agree and we smile at each other. I feel like we cemented something important and it makes me feel strangely happy.

Like many things, I should have done this much, much sooner, I think to myself.

In spite of all my happiness here, today I booked my flight back to the States.

To be truthful, it was not an act of volition, or even of reason. I called to check on the status of my flight and the woman on the phone told me I would lose my return ticket unless I used it by that date. You'll have to buy a new ticket, she said.

With the seconds ticking by on the phone, that old fear kicked in—a bite of panic—and I booked. I panicked at the thought of not having a ticket back, like a door closing.

I was not prepared.

— *Perché, Sibilla? So' rimasta male. Pensavo rimanevi...,* Ottavia says, looking at me confused.

I'm stung, she said. I thought you were going to stay.

I look down. I too thought I was. It is hard to explain.

— *Mi dispiace,* says Maria, looking at me sadly. Tears grow in her eyes.

— *Speravo trovassi il modo per restare. Mi sono abituata ad averti qui di nuovo.* I am sorry. I thought at this point you would find a way to stay. I got used to having you here again.

I don't know how to explain that I don't feel equipped here. I don't have any money, I cannot support myself, and I feel slightly illegitimate. Besides, I want to go hug my father, and my cat, left behind.

A relationship may be hanging in the balance: It may already be too late, but I should go find out.

Mostly, I now have grown another side, and I don't know how to live without it.

And yet, as I look out my window I feel the pull now, the nostalgia kicking in, the loss, already, I feel it all viscerally, and I know it could not be different.

I console myself that I will have done what I came to do—to spend a gift of time here. To give myself a year here. I must accept that and be happy with it. My other self shakes her head. *Why be happy with that? What is wrong with you?*

Am I making a mistake?

Forty-some days to go, and so much yet to do, to understand, to love. Just what I came for.

To process the idea of this inexorable countdown I go for a long run. It has rained a lot in the past few days and the countryside is cleansed and fresh and vivid, the greens gleaming, the streams frothing and full. Everywhere are tractors humming and working.

At a turn by Greta's old house I pause because I cannot breathe. In the gush of a stream I double over onto myself and I sob. I don't understand what I am doing. Again, I have rationalized my heart to the extent that I cannot read myself anymore.

I am giving up, and I am returning.

Later I tell Aldo that I have booked my ticket. I can't quite say it. If I had to describe Aldo in his own words I would say, *Non è uno che si sbilancia tanto.* He's not one to unbalance himself, to show a lot of emotion. But he doesn't need to. His eyes skid away.

— *Mi mancherai, Aldo,* I say, looking him in the eyes, trying to hold from looking down. I will miss you. It's been great to spend time with you, I say. My voice cracks.

I will miss you too, he says. He hugs me and rubs the bump on my nose. *Il mio Geronimo.* My little Geronimo.

I ask Aldo if I can harvest grapes with them before I go. I got here too late in October last year. It'll be several weeks away yet, the way the weather has been. The grapes are delicate; there hasn't been enough sun. It will be touch-and-go depending on the weather. I will wait.

I tell Sotero that I booked my flight. He looks serious, sad.

— *Davvero? Ma scherzi?* Really? Are you joking?

No, I say, shaking my head.

We are riding in his car. He has given me a ride from the countryside back in the rain. He pulls over in the piazza and turns to me.

— *Se ti va, prima che parti ... prima che parti facciamo l'amore.* If you want, before you leave we can make love, he says, smiling.

I laugh softly, partially in humor because he is so disarming and funny, and partially in grief, because of all this love lost again. I don't know what to do with that. I don't take the love seriously or the grief, either. Is it true, and sincere? Does it really matter whether I am here or not, anymore? At one point, long ago, I knew. I knew that it did matter. But now ... nothing matters except within me. It's like a callus. I don't know how to believe.

It is habit *ormai*—the saddest habit one can possibly have.

September has come and the trees have taken on a sweet whisper of yellow, portending the beauty that's to come, soon, perhaps even before I leave. Tomatoes are rotting on the browning vines and the fall crops are going in—lettuces, broccoli, winter cabbage, and fennel.

I feel a surge of nostalgia contemplating the return of fall. Already, so soon, we have come full circle. Apples are turning in the orchards, some deep yellow, some red. Everywhere is a hum of tractors working, people tilling in the olive groves, cleaning out fields to be hoed and seeded, and transporting sunflower seeds, finally harvested. The vines are loaded with grapes, taut and black. I walk through a field to pick a bunch and I eat it. It's sweet and delicious. Farmers have begun carrying wood into their houses, and on my jogs I pass packed trailer-tractors full of chopped wood, treacherously negotiating these tight curves.

It's a stunning day, crisp and sunny, and it's market day. The murmur of the crowd reaches up and into my windows. I close my eyes and savor it. I hear voices I know, among them Caino. I see clusters of people talking *fitto*, as they say here—talking close. I would like to swoop down and know what they are saying, not out of malicious curiosity but because they are in the know about this town I love. They are talking about the grapes, or someone.

Yesterday I heard that an old man in an Ape, a farmer, someone I don't know, was robbed by three guys just outside of town. Romanians, they said. They talked him out of his Ape on the pretext of selling him some vegetables. The man told them he was a farmer—that he didn't need vegetables—but they pleaded, and out of kindness the man pulled out his wallet to give them a few euros. The thugs yanked his wallet from his hands and jumped in their car to drive away. When the man held onto their car door, they kicked him off, knocking him to the ground and down an embankment.

People shake their heads. What is the world coming to when something like this happens in Cetona?

I look down and I see Pierpaolo walking across the piazza. He looks down at his phone as he crosses people. I wonder what his life is like, if he is happy. I miss him, and I am sorry I have not had a chance to talk with him, to tell him that.

Memories dance through my head, moments of indelible connection with people. I realize with disappointment that I cannot maintain or revive those with everyone. In spite of all the love I may have in me, it may not have anything to do with me. It is life: marriages, fears, things to be protected, and things I cannot control. And things I have lost a right to be part of.

Or maybe it has everything to do with me: too much burnt soil. Too many scars left behind. Scars everyone wants to forget.

As Ida said, *la vita è andata avanti*. Life has moved on.

Later, in the afternoon, I venture out. The light has dimmed and the shadows are long, and the piazza seems more solitary. Vacationers have gone, for the most part, and Eufemia is wandering. Her husband died suddenly a couple of weeks ago and she seems to wander more now, looking lost. She stops and looks around, her eyes ringed with red, her hair more disheveled. When I see her I hug her and tears fill her eyes. What will become of her?

Lillo and Giuliano are sitting at Bar Cavour in the sun, as they were eleven months ago and six months ago and three months ago, and last week, though it crosses my mind that at some point they won't, perhaps before my next time back. Pippo is laying out some pottery on the sidewalk in front of his shop, in the sun, and Cristiano is setting the tables outside at Nilo's, spreading the sage green tablecloths. Lidiano, Agata's dad, is on his afternoon walk in the sun, slowly, with his cane, and Bruna is sitting on a bench, talking with a friend, a shawl draped on her shoulders.

I feel a need for some kind of emotional food, or reassurance. Maybe forgiveness. I don't know what to hang onto, who to talk to about this churning decision inside, and this leads me to the embrace of the cemetery, where everything ends. Where peace must be found. Perhaps it's a goodbye of sorts, a taking stock till the next time, and as I leave the piazza I stop by Vasilika's and buy twenty beautiful white roses, their petals pearlescent and delicate, fit for a farewell.

On the way to the cemetery, a man is cutting a field of alfalfa and the air is fragrant and fresh. The walls of the cemetery rest ancient and golden on the hill, waiting. I walk through the main gate and go to the section where the most recently deceased now rest.

I look at the names of the people who have died since I have been here—eighteen now— beginning with the most recent, Eufemia's husband. Simple letters on a stone:

Enzo Rossi
Pasquina Puliti

Amato Crociani
Salvatore Balsamo
Adelia Vanni
Ernesto Ceccobao
Francesco Forlano
Loriana Patrizzi
Violanda Venturini
Bruno Baglioni
Ida Ferranti
Elena Setti
Domenico di Matteo
Angiolina Pallottai
Simone Canuti
Biagio Calanna
Aldo Pascucci
Esterina Innocenti.

I walk through the silent paths and through to the family crypts I have never much known, and I find my old teacher Marga's place of rest, next to her husband. I revisit her face and her laughter, and her meanness, too, and I leave a rose, for her and for my childhood with her.

I pass Bufalo's grave, the kid who reassembled pens in class at the *scuola media*, who died young of lung cancer, at forty-five. Unico is next, with my memories of my first bra and his winking smile, and then Raffaella, a once-dear girlfriend who also died early of cancer. They lie just steps away from each other, like they would party together in paradise. I plan to be with them one day, and as I walk on I leave a rose for each.

Steps from them rests Teo, yes, Teo with the yellow motorcycle traveling at the speed of light, pulling the thread of love around the countryside.

He died a few years back while I was gone, in the aftermath of a car accident that left him paralyzed from the waist down. The story is too sad to tell, really, and its cruelty and exactness never strike me as less so, even now. I have to barely close my eyes to recall his smile, arrogant and tender, and the spirit that fled in the wind. It continues to make me wonder about the frailty that breaks some of us, why it is, how it happens, and why no one can do anything about it. It just is.

The other night I saw Teo's nephew, Diego's son, Adriano, cross the piazza. It gives me a shiver to look at him. Though he is stockier and shorter, he has that same shameless playful smile that makes you want to undress and cry, a perfect blend of Teo and Diego. When I first arrived in Cetona on this stay, I saw him standing under a lamppost in the piazza, talking with a friend, and I went over to say hello. I looked at his eyes, brown, flecked with gold, an amber light within them. They hold so much that I know, that is dear and that I miss.

Standing under the lamppost I caressed his beard and I smiled.

You remind me of your uncle, I said. I took him in, his eyes, and said goodnight, like parting with a ghost of a love long lost.

I stop at his grave, with the little picture of his smile still daring against the quiet white marble, and I leave a rose.

I walk along the rows and then down to the old part of the cemetery to see the ossuaries, row upon row of boxes with names, dates of birth and death, and the small oval picture. I walk through slowly, looking at each face, one by one. I leave a rose in a corner here and there. I leave roses for all—Nicola, Greta, Zia, Zio, and more.

I am moved to see how many faces reach out to me from the dormant creases of my mind. They reach out to me in black and white memories that no amount of years can erase. Some of them died decades ago, in the early or mid-1980s, when I was still at the *liceo*. Many died while I was away. I had to move flowers to see the dates of death to make sure, really, that they had died that long ago. They just dropped out of my landscape, my universe, the threads that make up the fabric of a town like this, pulled, gone. I didn't notice but for seeing their faces now, looking back at me.

Yet, one by one I kept them somewhere inside of me, and I feel so glad, so glad to have grown up here with them, so glad to have crossed paths with them.

I find the ossuary of that old farmer, the man on the tractor. The picture is bad and he looks like a floating ghost, but I recognize him nonetheless. I feel some pity, then I take it back.

— *Testa di cazzo,* I say under my breath as I walk on. You asshole.

I recognize a man who I saw in the piazza as a kid, his pocket-watch always neatly tucked into his dapper and dignified black suit, and then Bastiano, and then finally I find Beppa and Aldo, whose graves I had looked for years in vain. I had to go ossuary to ossuary, and there they are.

While I look for a pen in my purse, I rest my notebook onto the marble slab framing Beppa's ossuary and I smile. I think for a moment that it may be disrespectful, then I imagine Beppa saying, *Appoggia pure, appoggia, Sibilla! Tranquilla!!!* Rest it there, Sibilla, no worries!

I laugh to myself and I leave a rose for her, and I wish I had taken many more roses, enough for every grave, for every soul, for those I knew and those I didn't. Those I wish I had held, and whose story I wish I had known.

One for every grief, and one for every joy. And one for every goodbye.

I realize that nowhere, absolutely nowhere in the world will I ever have this bond again, and the awareness of this finiteness and singularity sends me mourning through the streets like a lost, howling dog. Picture *Il Cane*—and this makes me laugh, at least.

Today I stopped at the Steccato to look down at my house, and while heading back toward the piazza I ducked into the Collegiata. I sat in the silence to think, to gather my thoughts, to meditate. To cry.

To pray.

The note of a cello, Villa-Lobos, rose through the church, fragment of a memory of a concert there. My mom had accompanied the cellist and the church filled with a murmur of awe. Cetona's old ladies crowded in the pews and dabbed their cheeks, and my family was there, and the town.

The music stopped.

Please, I begged, please let me understand just one good thing from all that is happening; that I may come to the head of one single thread—a sense of me, a sense of place, something that enlightens me. Where to go. Where I can be one person in one home that is whole. That encompasses everything I am. My entire indentity, simply.

Sitting there I think back to the conversations I have had through the course of my life in the States. They always start the same way.

*Where are you from?* Italy.

*Were you born there?* No, but I grew up there.

*Oh, you don't have an accent.* No, I don't.

*Do you speak Italian?* Yes, I do.

*How long did you live there?* Twenty years.

*Do your parents still live there?* No.

*Do you still have a home there?* No.

*Are your parents Italian?* No.

*Do you go back there?* Yes.

The parsing goes on and on.

*Why do you go back there if your family is not there? Why don't you have an Italian accent? Do you have Italian blood?*

And finally, *Oh, it must have been a fantastic experience growing up there.*

It was not an experience, motherfucker. It was my life. It *is* my life.

Crying in the pew of this church, I curse the moment I was brought here. I wish I could have just grown up normal in Chicago, with my magic stone in my pocket, with one place to be mine. And yet I wish I had never been born anywhere other than here. I wish I had emerged from that altar in front of me, the new altar Andrea built, and Monte Cetona outside.

Help me, please, I asked looking up at the cross. Help me let go of this grief, of this love. Help me un-feel. Help me un-be.

But do I really want to un-feel or un-be? This love is the key to me, to what has made me, to all that I feel and that I am. And how can anyone dare question that? I was the luckiest person alive to grow up here. How can I un-want that?

Out into the sunshine I walk up to Le Monache, down under the arch to the lookout with the view of the countryside and the road to Piazze, and I pick a daisy. I sit on the wall picking off petals.

*He loves me, he loves me not. He loves me, he loves me not. He loves me* ... and I think I know that he does, but it may no longer matter. I have lost him already. In some ways, now I just wish I could let it go and say fuck it, I am staying here. But I can't bring myself to. I am afraid of making a mistake, of losing more, or again.

Now it is night. Serafina's husband is sweeping in front of the bar. A couple of kids are sitting on the church steps, smoking a cigarette. I feel the calendar turning and I wonder how I can possibly leave my gingerbread town in the hills, again, again, again. The feeling fills me with despair and I whisk it away.

I go downstairs to walk around the piazza, now deserted. The air is crisp and fragrant of pines and fields, and as I walk I follow the song of two tawny owls talking from opposite ends of the piazza. *Hooo hooo. Hooo hooo.* Perhaps they are males asserting their territories, one by the elementary school, the other by the tower of the Carabinieri.

They say, here, that the song of an owl portends bad things—death for the ill, in particular—yet the song is sweet and soothing and I prefer to think they are lovers calling.

Back upstairs in my bed I hear them through the shutters and they lull me to sleep, here, in this dearest place of mine.

*Hooo hooo. Hooo hooo. Hooo hooo.*

I ran an errand in Città della Pieve today, and after meandering through the beautiful countryside toward San Casciano, I saw the sign for Salci, a medieval hamlet that I remember from my youth and that reminds me of my father and his passions.

Dad discovered Salci on one of his rovings and he fell in love with it: He envisioned an artists' colony there, a utopian retreat for painters and violinmakers and other artisans, and the spark of that fantasy stayed in my memory and led me to turn off at the sign.

I followed the gravel road, crossing fields of pasturing cows and miles of sloping dark green hills, until I came to the town's entrance, a well-preserved tower with battlements, part of a castle built in the 1400s. Even in these parts such a sight is an odd anachronism and it reminds me a bit of a cartoon I used to watch about a dragon that lived in a castle exactly like it.

A large arched *porta* leads inside the village, where a grassy area, a piazza of sorts, opens between the town's *palazzo ducale*—where the duke used to live—and what used to be stores and formal housing for the courtesans. Gothic windows adorn the second floor and look out toward the countryside. Through another *porta* with a clock tower is a second piazza, this one encircled by humble housing for the people of the town, the back of the *palazzo ducale*, and a 15th-century church with a tall, shapely bell tower.

Rising high up in the hills that, at one time, bordered the Granducato of Tuscany and the Marchesato of Castiglion del Lago—deadly enemy territories—Salci was strategically important and, hence, heavily contested through the centuries by Orvieto and Città della Pieve. In the middle of the 1500s the pope made it into a papal duchy and assigned it a duke, whose family then controlled the town for three centuries, until the unification of Italy. Being a duchy, I learned, Salci had the power to issue coin, call for markets and fairs, and to have its own military and prison, which gave the town power and bustle. Its position near the Via Francigena, which leads to the Vatican, brought it travelers and pilgrims and led the town to become a haven for bandits and traffickers as well as convicts and others seeking to avoid the law.

I can picture markets there, carts with animals, people working, children and the elderly, sitting. At the back of the town, where the last house fades out, is Monte Cetona, stark against the sky.

After the unification of Italy, in 1861, the town was purchased by a private family, and then by another, and, eventually, in more recent history, the town was partitioned: Parts of it were returned to the public under the authority of Città della Pieve—the access to town, for example, and the open squares; parts of it were retained by the previous owners; and the church was retained by the Vatican, together with the house of the priest, right above it.

When Dad had his vision, or dreamed of it, shall we say, there were still a few residents here and there. Now Salci is completely abandoned: It looks like the entire population got up one morning and left, pushed out by ransacking bandits or killed by disease. Flowers pots sit hanging from the walls, empty, and yellowed curtains hang in windows.

As I walked cautiously through the ruins, shored up to prevent the caving in of the ceilings, I imagined what my father's eyes had dreamed: artisans making violins, artists painting in the courtyards, a dance studio, and musicians practicing through the open windows.

But signs to keep out put me on edge.

— *C'è nessuno?* I yelled out. Is anybody here?

After a few minutes a man in dark blue coveralls came out of a building next to the church and watched me as I approached, shielding the sun from his eyes. He was tall and fit and his tousled black hair was combed back from his assertive face, grazing his broad shoulders. He had a dominant nose and greenish brown eyes, closely set.

— *Marcello Marchini,* he said introducing himself and extending a strong hand.

Born 1947, he added—way older than I would have thought. I introduced myself. I told him I am from Cetona and that I wanted to know something about Salci.

He started talking and I could not believe my fortune. He was born in Salci, as were his grandfather, father, and son. His family thrived there when the town was part of a big farming enterprise, owned by the Paganini family, from 1908 to 1964. Together with the hamlet itself, the farming business encompassed dozens of farmhouses and much land.

After we talked awhile in the sunshine, Marcello invited me upstairs. He pointed at the windows and said he was making lunch.

— *Devo mettere l'acqua per la pasta e le salsicce,* he said. I have to put the water on for the pasta and the sausages.

I looked up at the windows, a bit reluctant, wondering what he was doing there cooking sausages in this abandoned place, but I followed him upstairs, into what used to be the priest's house.

In a large living room he pointed to black-and-white pictures of his grandparents, taken in the piazza just outside, and then to others, of his parents and his own son. A wooden stand holding a large book took up a corner of the vast room and he invited me to take a look. It was the colonial accounting ledger from 1931, and on huge handwritten pages it documented every animal and farm implement and piece of food kept by every family every month on every *podere* that was part of the *azienda*—twenty-six families in Salci itself and fifty-two farmhouses in the country. Thousands of items were listed in beautiful calligraphy and in exquisite detail: the fur color of the animals and the weight of the victuals, and how many jars of tomatoes or baskets of fruit. Seasons of abundance, and, too, lean times. In the list was the entire daily history of a community—life itself.

Over the years, like all the farmhouses that had functioned under *mezzadria* around Cetona and elsewhere, these farmhouses, too, became vacant, were sold off, and restored.

What made people leave Salci, I asked Marcello.

The last descendant of the family who has owned the town in most recent times awoke in the early eighties to the idea that he wanted to sell the town to developers. Suddenly he began to declare the houses unfit to live in and started forcing people out. He just wanted everyone out. Some people left quickly and were happy to go, but others resisted and stayed on until the late nineties, including the priest, Don Pietro, who was the last to leave, after forty-eight years there.

Some people didn't know what do to or where to go. One elderly woman, rather than leave for some unknown place, hanged herself right there in front of her kitchen window. Her body swayed in the shadows like the future of the town, and the image lingers in my mind.

Now, since the town emptied out, the owner has been vacillating about selling. In the meantime, everything is crumbling and no one has the money to buy it.

Marcello told me he has a car mechanic shop in Ponticelli, where he lives most of the time. He has been a car mechanic all his life—this would explain his coveralls—and he knows all the car mechanics in the area.

— *Conosco il Cardetti, Osvaldo, ...* he said happily, mentioning our mutual car mechanic friends in Cetona, his hand gesturing across the way.

While looking around the house I asked Marcello how he came to be in this house cooking sausages. He explained that he served his military service in the Carabinieri, and because he distinguished himself as a talented mechanic, he was chosen to work for the Vatican repairing land machinery at Castel Gandolfo, the pope's summer home.

After his military service ended, he kept good connections with the church, and when Salci emptied out and the priest left, he persuaded the Vatican to let him manage and take care of the priest's house.

He showed me the work he has done on it, then he took me down to the church, which in spite of beautiful frescos and altars, is badly vandalized and in disrepair, like the rest of the town.

We went back upstairs to the quiet kitchen.

— *Com'era Salci quand'eri piccolo?* I asked Marcello. What was it like when you were growing up?

— *C'era un tabaccaio...* he said, beginning a list on his fingers.

A tobacco store, a grocery store, a small school, a post office, a doctor and his family, a midwife, and, naturally, the priest and his Perpetua, the woman who took care of the priest. Some forty people in all, he said, counting them out by name.

— *Si stava bene qui,* he said, looking out the window soberly. We were content here.

He shook his head like shaking off a dream.

— *'N' ci s'aveva bisogno di niente.* We needed for nothing.

I know what he means. I can picture it as it was, and my father's vision, too. If only one had the money.

After walking me outside, in the shadow of his castle in the hills Marcello hugged me goodbye and went back upstairs to his sausages, hissing on the grill in his otherwise dead town.

Today Aram moved to California. He shipped his stuff, took some things to my storage unit, and left me his car, with a friend. It's the car I associate with Aram, whose rumblings have for years announced his arrivals, even to Joe.

When he talked to me yesterday his apartment sounded hollow like a shell. I imagined him closing up, the sound of his door shutting, the echo of the thud on the stairwell, the Charleston Yellow Cab waiting outside in the dark.

Half hour before his flight I was walking through some fields down below Massimo Fieramosca's house. Massimo called after me and we chatted about his *orto* and what he's planting for next year. While we talked I thought of how many minutes had passed. I pictured Aram in the deserted Charleston airport, waiting, and the air outside heavy and humid, a gray Air Force flight landing in the hazy morning sky. I pictured his bags, his hair pulled back in a ponytail, his tan, nice-looking hands. His feet in flip-flops, his ankles. His face, sober and maybe a bit worried.

Images—of a reality slipping through my fingers—rushed through my head as I stood on the side of the road, thousands of miles away, on the other side of the earth.

— Safe travels, Slim, I texted. I wish you good luck on this big adventure. I love you.

— Thank you, baby, he wrote back. Thinking of you this morning. I love you too.

— For sure this day is marking something, and I feel my earth shifting, I wrote.

— Similar feelings here, he answered.

As I texted I walk past some beautiful yellow wildflowers, tall and brilliant. I had noticed them blooming over the past week or two. I took a picture and sent it to him.

— I love you, Sybil. Getting on the plane.

— Goodbye, my love.

At the time of his scheduled departure from Charleston I felt him separate from me, something shifting inexorably, irretrievably, a heavy, dark gravestone moving into place, over my head. I walked a mile or so along the road, clutching my phone. I passed Caino in front of his *orto* and I waved but I could not speak.

A few meters later I crumbled on the wall of Le Gore, down at the foot of Borgo, overlooking a shallow creek. It is a wall I used to walk on when I was a kid, forty years ago, pretending to do a balancing act like I was in a circus, laughing, my arms extended into the air, the creek flowing beneath me.

A choice has been made, whether I made it or not.

Back in my apartment I called Maria. She heard my cry on the phone.

— *Arrivo subito*, she said, and she came, within minutes.

She held on to me as I sobbed for what must have felt like an infinity to her. I had not done that with her in so many years, since my divorce. Then, we sat and she held my hand, like we used to hold hands, and we laughed.

Aram took me places I had not been and helped me discover realities of myself I had never known. He pushed me farther into myself and out into the world. With him and through him I saw something new in places and people and color, and mostly myself. I lost my fears and stayed. I stayed with him. I learned to stay after a lifetime of running. I understood that I could be loved, really, and to trust that.

But then ...

Today the sky is less blue; the colors are faded. I am glad to not be in Charleston tonight. I feel like a floating soul again, with no place to go, no one waiting for me.

Unmoored, and alone again.

I let Cetona comfort me, with its laughter, its silence, and its light, and I try to forget the other side.

I come out near sundown to enjoy my favorite hour and to chat with Ottavia and Sabina at Sabina's store. Ottavia doesn't work on Monday afternoons and it's nice to see her out and about, though I can tell from her expression that Italy's recession is worrying her. I hug her and the conversation shifts to me. I recoil from talking about Aram, or Morena, so I leave for a walk around the piazza and gravitate towards Aldo.

He is standing in front of Bar Cavour with his hands in his pocket. He looks worn-out. He tells me he went to check his new vineyard, planted all in Sangiovese, and the grapes are not ripening as they should. The harvest is looming now and Aldo is concerned.

— *Non perdere fiducia,* I say. Don't lose hope. Go talk to the grapes, I proffer. Caress them. Aldo laughs and pinches my cheek.

— Don't forget I want to harvest with you! I say. He promises to let me know when. He is waiting for a few more days of sunshine.

I walk to the Bar Sport and order a glass of wine and chat with Natale, an older man who comes in every evening for his one *aperitivo* at the end of the work day taking care of the Agnelli family properties here. Sometimes when we come to the bar at the same time, and we are each alone, we share the small round table in front of the counter— everyone's favorite table—and he tells me stories of growing up after the war, *in campagna,* up on the mountain.

When I was researching the history of the cross on Monte Cetona I learned that Natale's family has owned extensive property at the top of the mountain dating back some five hundred years. I revere and envy that—I am blown away, really. When I tell him that, he smiles and nods, with modesty.

He says goodbye and I watch him walk away in the dusk, a lovely evening already full of fall.

Ortensia, an abandoned and sweet gray and white cat that has made the bar her home, sits at my feet while I write, watchful of Nilo, who hates her. Tullia hurries by and blows me a kiss with a big smile. She is carrying groceries and is going home to make dinner. She has a busy schedule in the evenings, juggling her daughter's dance and marching band practices. School has started again, and this morning from my windows I heard the children screaming.

Maria drives up from Borgo, back from her second daily visit to her mom, and she pulls over to say hi. I walk over and we hug. She is always in a hurry, taking care of the house, or doing something for Lauro, or mostly her mother, whose care has somehow come to rest entirely on her shoulders. They are duties she carries with grace mostly, yet every now and then I see a crack of exasperation. I look at her tenderly, assessing her level of tiredness, and she does the same with me, measuring my worry, my readiness to go back.

— *Niente?* she asks, tentatively. Any news? I shake my head.

The mere sight of her comforts me; I feel better in her presence, as if she wrapped a blanket around me.

We hug and recommit to dinner later this week. Time has been slipping by and we haven't seen enough of each other over the past many months. Life seems busier here sometimes than in a big metropolis.

A few visitors are wandering through the piazza checking out their dinner options. Il Merlo is closed; they retreat to Nilo's, and Nilo is outside to greet them.

I cherish this time of the day when people go home and the piazza empties. I watch Taddeo De Rosa walk up the alley to his house, back from his job in Rome. Mercede walks out of her store and pulls the door shut. Sara's dog is barking upstairs in her apartment, and Sara will soon join him. Sabina closes her shop. Armando closes, too, and Nanni walks to his car slowly and gets in, heading home to dinner alone in Patarnione.

The neon green sign over the pharmacy turns off. Silence returns, except for the turmoil of my heart.

# Fall

**A**h, the glory of the *vendemmia*!
My memories of the grape harvest date back to the stompings at Zio and Zia's with Bruno and Adelina. Fortunately, many, many bottles of excellent wine have come between me and that memory, including the Della Vignas', so spending a couple of days harvesting grapes on the Della Vigna property was like living a dream.

It made me giddy happy, beyond any reasonable expectation.

Perhaps it's that the grape harvest is so important to life in Cetona and I wanted to be part of that. Perhaps it's simply that I was elated to be in a vineyard just down the road from my old house, in the sunshine. And perhaps it was the great company: Feriero, Amato, Mario, Drazen, Sotero, and, finally, Aldo, ordering us about.

I got there late—everyone else was already situated and cutting away—and when I walked up they cheered me, wanting to know where I was.

— *Ma dov'eri? Dormivi? Da sola?* Where were you? Were you sleeping? Alone?

— *Era l'ora!* Aldo says, with a smartass look. It's about time!

Grapevines grow grapes on two sides of a trellis, among heavy twisting foliage. Often the vines are so intertwined between trellis and foliage that it's difficult to extricate the grapes from one side, which makes picking them a work for pairs—two people, one on each side of the vine, moving together in synchrony, establishing a pace that is both efficient and pleasurable.

I spent most of the *vendemmia* working in tandem with Amato, unraveling mysterious grape threads through the trellises and listening to his stories of growing up on farms around Piazze and Cetona. As I listen I see in him the solemnity and lack of frill that come from growing up on the land not knowing what tomorrow will bring. There is a seriousness, a directness, in his approach to life.

Conversely, I look down the vineyard and hear Sotero, our indefatigable comic, telling one lurid story after another, or talking about a new type of Viagra released in the States, or something along those lines. Yet, there is matter-of-factness in Sotero, too, and I ponder the similarity of their backgrounds, bonded by the land.

Someone starts telling a story about a man whose daughter no one wanted to marry.

— *Aveva un culo grosso come un fienile e era bassa così.* She had an ass like a hay pile and she was this short, says whoever was telling the story, extending his arm in front of him to indicate waist-high.

They all shake their heads, dismissing the image of the poor girl, then Sotero quips, *Mica male, però. Altezza perfetta!* Not bad—perfect height!

I knew it was coming and I laugh loudly. I cannot help it. Feriero smiles and shakes his head.

We work in silence for a while, filling the red baskets that Drazen takes from us heaping and returns to us empty. Aldo moves the tractor forward as Drazen fills the dump trailer, and every now and then he disappears to take the grapes to the *cantina sociale*, the community cellar, on the way to Piazze, where they will be weighed and mixed with the grapes of others to make a cooperative wine. Aldo directs us through the rows, setting aside grapevines he wants us to harvest separately to make his own wine, his delicate Sangiovese.

I enjoy the clipping noise coming from the rows, from my own hands, and the sun on my face, my boots digging into the soft earth and the purple stickiness on my fingers. When the bunches of grapes between us get impossibly tangled, I let Amato's eyes guide me silently. Moving his scissors expertly, his widower's gold wedding ring catching the sunshine, he'll cut the least accessible bunch and leave me the rest, the easiest, which he points to with a nearly imperceptible movement of the chin.

— *O questa la lasci?* he'll sass me if I leave a cluster behind. Are you going to leave that one? It would be a shameful waste, I know, and I strive to earn his respect.

At one point we move our work to a few rows of vineyard fronting Via Sobborgo, down below my old house. A car approaches and stops and the two guys inside say hi.

— *Che paio strano che siete insieme!* Sotero says loudly, laughing. What an odd couple you are. Have you been out shopping for condoms and Viagra together?

They laugh and say, yes, on your prescription card!! And off they go, among general laughter.

Amidst all that, the guys talk with me about my planned departure, which now they all know about, taking turns making predictions about whether I will catch the flight or not. Feriero looks at me with apprehension.

— *Sibi, perché vai?* he asks. Why are you going?

They generally agree that something magical or catastrophic needs to happen for me to not take the flight, or to take the flight and come back quickly, which is what they think should happen. Their logic and speculation touch me. They tip-toe around what awaits me in America—someone mentions a boyfriend and someone else quickly changes topic, protectively—and as they discuss this I feel loved and cared for.

At 1 p.m. Ave serves us lunch, as always delicious—*penne all'aglione*, *peperonata*, a veal roast, grilled zucchini, pears and cheese, and salad. And red wine, naturally. I help Ave drain the pasta and mix it and take everything to the table. She watches carefully; she trusts no one but herself. I hug her and reassure her that her reputation will not be ruined! Being at the table with Ave and Aldo, with Feriero and Amato and Sotero, listening to their banter and their stories, asking me if I want more food, teasing me and joking, makes me feel loved like I never feel anywhere else, and indeed, I know that I am not, that I cannot be loved more than this.

But the unavoidable lingering sadness is the countdown, which Amato does not hesitate to bring up as soon as we return to the grapevines after lunch.

— *Ma se' sicura che parti, davvero? Ma via ...* he says, shaking his head. Are you sure you're leaving? C'mon. Don't go.

It's a glorious morning, with a haze of fog but the sun peeking through. I look out though my half-open shutter and notice the absence of the regular guys. Ah, I remember: Hunting season opens today.

Lucio comes to mind, many years ago, in camouflage, standing near the piazza's *loggie* among hunters on a late Sunday morning. His cologne comes to mind, and his blue eyes, and the birds dangling in their shimmering plumage. I have seen many pheasants this year on my runs, hidden in ditches of long wild grasses. I surprised them and frightened them with my steps on the country roads. Yet, no matter how frightened, they are still reluctant to take flight and they run ahead like funny chickens. Why shoot them?

I head out into the countryside for my run, down my most wild of routes, down roads that are barely cleared from fields. Snakes quickly cross my mind, then I hear intermittent gunshots here and there, a shot traveling through the landscape and then the arch of sound ending abruptly—in the trunk of a tree, I hope.

On a hill overlooking the autostrada I scan the landscape for a sign—to measure what appears to be now a love lost, on one hand, against the love gained here, on the other, knowing already that I will not stay because I do not know how to make it work. As I will not commit to others, others will not commit to me. I cannot work, I have no one to help me, plus, I cannot imagine not seeing Aram again.

I must go.

I breathe heavily though the hills and run into some hunters packing up.

— *Buon giorno! Avete preso niente?* I ask, smiling. Good morning! Did you kill anything?

— *Niente!* they answer, shaking their heads. Nothing!

— *Meno male!* I say, slowing down. Thank goodness! That's good! They laugh and smile after me.

One man, nice-looking and older, with thick hair and dark brown eyes, lights a cigarette and shrugs. I slow to a halt. He tells me he goes hunting because he likes being in nature. He rarely takes a shot. I rejoice.

— *Bravo,* I say and I smile. He smiles and waves and somehow I know he'll never take another shot.

I am far from town now, miles and miles away, yet I feel nothing more than a hunger to continue, to see, to feel. I find myself in Piandisette, below a farm where I always see white cows at pasture, the Tuscan *Chianine*, as they are called, creamy-furred animals with sweet black eyes that were once ubiquitous on this land and now are rarely seen. I saw one the other day being transported in a truck, and I figured she must have come from here, so I decide to stop in and see if I can pet them.

When I walk up to the house—a manicured farmhouse surrounded by flowers, bales of straw piled high, and agricultural implements—a beautiful young woman with long hair the color of chestnuts greets me with a smile.

She says she sees me running all the time.

— *Te sei la Sibilla, no?* she asks. You're Sibilla, right? You know my mom, Gianna.

Of course, I say, we have known each other since we were children. Luana, she says introducing herself and extending her hand. She is tall and strong, with a firm handshake. I tell her that I've been admiring their animals from afar, on my runs, and I ask her if it would be OK for me to see them. I realize it's around lunchtime and I apologize for intruding.

— *A voglia! Vieni, vieni! L'acqua per la pasta bolle, e non c'è che buttarla.* Absolutely! she says, smiling. Come, come! The water is boiling and there is nothing to do but throw the pasta in.

As we walk through the property she tells me that her family has raised *Chianine* since her grandfather started the business more than sixty years ago. Today it's run by her father and her uncle and the whole family lives there on the property. I feet a twitch of envy.

We come to a huge open-air building where two dozen or so male calves and grown bulls are housed, tied to metal railings partitioning the space in pens. She points to the star bull, a massive animal with a sign hanging above his head. Born in 2012. Still a baby. She explains how the animals are rotated through the various pens based on their growth—she points to each one—and finally she points to the one closest to the door.

— *Questo è l'ultimo,* she says. This is the last one.

She is quiet for a minute.

— *Quando arrivano qui so' pronti per il macello.* When they get here they're ready for slaughter.

In the pen is an enormous animal. He is lying down, motionless, and his bottomless resigned black eyes meet with mine. My tears surge forth. I don't mean to, but it happens. Luana looks at me.

— *Eh si …. Purtroppo…,* she says. Yes, unfortunately…

I walk away from the animal, bidding farewell in my heart. We walk through the building and out into the sunshine. Before us, in a rich lime-green field surrounded by the perfect landscape that stretches to Piazze, stand another thirty or so *Chianine*, eating straw from a huge trough. They are all females, Luana explains, kept in perpetuity as long as they can have babies. Several have small babies feeding at their teats.

I take in the beauty of the animals and their dark eyes, their tails swaying peacefully, and I tell Luana I am vegetarian. She nods and she says, in fact—*infatti*—when the cows leave for slaughter she gets choked up, too, even though she has grown up around this business since she was a little girl—or perhaps because she has grown up around it. She doesn't like to eat meat, even chicken, she says. I bristle at the *even chicken*.

— *Anche al nonno gli dispiace,* she says. Even my grandfather gets tears in his eyes, she says, even after all these years.

As we walk back up toward the house in the magnificent field, I comment that one day this business will be hers to manage, to run—hers with a cousin. I envy her the opportunity inherent in this, and I envy her this amazing swath of land, glorious, unlike any in the world. It is *hers* to keep *forever*. But I don't envy her this, living with the eyes of the cows.

Perhaps she will do something different with it. I wish that for her. We hug warmly and I thank her for the tour and her hospitality.

— *Saluta tua mamma,* I say. Say hello to your mom for me, and I run off into the silence of the countryside, freeing and soothing.

Back in the piazza I find the scene I remembered, the guys in camouflage standing around talking. It looks like no one but the animals had luck today. Sotero is there and Amato, and a bunch of others, gesticulating. Some have their dogs with them. I feel grateful that they are empty-handed.

I stand in the window looking at them, wondering what they are saying. Then Sotero looks up and waves at me, a big smile shining in his ruddy face. My phone rings; it's him.

— *Sei bellissima oggi! La Madonna in finestra!* he says. You are beautiful today. The Madonna in the window!

It sounds like the name of a painting and I laugh.

I could stay for Sotero alone, if only I could stay.

In the last remaining weeks, I took a short trip to say goodbye to dear friends here and there, the Sabatini family in Spoleto, at their hotel, La Macchia, and Sabrina, in Siena.

Sabrina is readying herself for another surgery, perhaps a double mastectomy, and another round of chemotherapy. Her hair has begun to grow back—a tight Afro, she laughs. She looks beautiful and healthy, and she thought she was healthy, and yet she is not: The cancer is back, and the medicine is not stopping it. She feels like she has fallen into an abyss—purgatory is her choice description, from our favorite book—and she is not being let out. I tell her that the thoughts that populate her head make a difference and she must be positive to heal. I want to believe in that force, but it doesn't seem to apply. She smiles, but her big brown eyes tell me she is scared.

Over dinner in her green kitchen she tells me that I can live for free in her cottage behind her house. She shows it to me and it is as perfect as any house could be, with a spacious room for painting, a big table for writing, and a lovely view of the Senese countryside. I would need nothing more. I could help her with the kids, she says, teach them English, and help her recover.

She says I can stay forever. Forever—*quanto vuoi*. As long as you want.

She meant it, too. The resilience of her love for me humbles and stuns me. She had missed me, and I hadn't really ever grasped that.

In her soft mellifluous voice she asks about my plans. She takes my hand in hers. We look down at our hands intertwined, her fingers thin and pale, as I remember them from thirty years ago.

— *Quando torni*? she asks. When are you coming back? She shakes her head as she asks and doesn't look at me. Maybe she already knows I will not come back soon enough.

We hug and we promise it won't be long before we see each other again.

— A presto, Sabri.

Of course, I did not hug her enough.

In Spoleto I visited the Sabatinis to say goodbye. I took Claudio a painting of a group of chickens surrounding a flirtatious black rooster. I want to express my gratitude for their hospitality and friendship and to honor Claudio's chickens, which he so loves. Claudio notices I forgot to sign the painting, so he and Carla take me to buy a brush and a tube of paint. Then they drive me to Eggi, a poetic hamlet a jog from Spoleto, where they want to show me a house they recently bought for their retirement. They will move there soon, when the restoration is finished, and their daughters will take over management of the hotel.

In Eggi, Claudio walks me through the house proudly, showing me which space will become what: He has space for a vegetable garden, a convivial dining room, and a room for him, where he can be alone to think, which he needs, he says laughing, with all the women in the family. He makes me smile.

Then he comes to an annex across a walkway, private and lovely.

— *E questa è la stanza della Sibilla...* he says. This is Sibilla's room, for when she comes back.

He looks at me.

— You can come back and stay as long as you want, he says. It's your space, anytime.

I know he means it and it makes me cry, tears slipping down my cheeks slowly. I don't even know what to say because people here love me more than anyone I know on the other side of the ocean. I hold on to this and I say goodbye, promising a return soon.

After my trip to Spoleto I drove to the beach, to Albinia, to put my feet in the Mediterranean, something I had not done in decades. I took the idyllic route through San Casciano, Acquapendente, Sorano, and finally the jewel, Pitigliano, one of the most beautiful towns one can see. My father always loved it too, and it continues to surprise me the way it rises out of the earth, a town built on an island of tufa, soaring miraculously and with so much strength out of the surrounding landscape. I walked the streets of the town and wondered what it would be like to live there. I jotted down the number for an apartment for rent, which I knew I would never call. It must be cold there in winter, and lonely, but surely interesting.

It was a gorgeous summerlike day, allowing for miles and miles of unobstructed views. Through the mountains past Pitigliano, where the land reaches its highest point before beginning its descent to the sea, I glimpsed a clear view of the water, far away, shimmering in the sunlight. On the beach, nearly empty, I took off my shoes and rolled up my pants and walked for a while along the edge of the sea, the enchanting and celebrated Mediterranean, clear and aquamarine. It was warm enough to swim, and I regretted not having a bathing suit. It would have freed me and soothed me to cleanse my fears in the sea and to rest my skin on the hot sand.

I sat and burrowed my feet in the sand. I thought of Aram and I imagined our bodies caressed by the same waters, mine and his, merging somewhere on the rolling planet. Will I ever see him again? Could it be that two people could part like this? I consider what my friends say, that it's important for us to talk face to face, to see each other. For sure you will do that, right, Maria asks me pressingly.

It is hard to imagine that I am going to leave Cetona and travel all that distance to say goodbye, perhaps never to be able to return again.

But you don't know, Maria says. You don't know what will happen. You must go to find out.

True, but again, it's a big risk to take for nothing. If we say goodbye here, at least I have Cetona.

On the beach is a brown man walking along carrying a heavy load of wares, mostly jewelry, artfully balanced on a combination of sticks and plastic boxes hanging from his neck. When he stops in front of me I look at the jewelry and ask him in Italian how his life is here, how he is doing.

— *Bene*, he says smiling peacefully.

I ask him where he is from and he says Bangladesh. He tells me he has two jobs—one in summer walking the coast selling jewelry, the other in winter, in Rome, selling scarves and other seasonal ware. He can be where he wants, he says, and he manages to make a living. I feel happy to hear that this is so for this man from so far off, surely with circumstances worse than mine.

Why not for me?

Wanting to buy something to help him and remember him by, I choose a long necklace of seafoam green glass, and sitting there in the sand I roll it in my hand. It feels solid and cool, and though I will likely never wear it, I like that it comes from this beach on this special day via this peaceful Bangladeshi man.

I contemplate his life, so far from his home, yet so simple, and mostly happy. Where he wants it to be. I wish him luck, and he walks on with his sticks and wares while I get back in my car and drive to Cetona.

Back in my apartment I feel soothed by my day at the beach. I feel nourished by the travels and the roads and the sight of the vast shimmering waters.

Now, it's time to go to bed. I look out and a few people are crowded in front of Le ACLI. Mario is drinking a beer, and Lapo is smoking a cigarette. I recognize his height and the shape of his head. Ernesto, the little white pig, is sitting beside their feet. Brunino takes off in his Ape and his blinker, left on, blinks out into the night, around the piazza and up Via Roma.

Sotero pulls up, back from a dinner of beans and onions that I turned down earlier, and he waves me down for a drink and a laugh about something involving Viagra, I am sure.

— *Vieni? Dai!!* C'mon!

I walk up the alley going the other way, toward Tullia's parents' house. I cross Serafina, Giuditta's sister, and she smiles at me, and it pleases me. Maybe Giuditta has vouched for me.

I pass the house where a Romanian family lives, a cordial couple and their two daughters, pretty and well mannered. They always smile and say hello. I smile at the irony of it all: If I were Romanian I could live here and work, regardless of education, experience, or talents. But I am American, and I grew up here, and I cannot. Could the U.S. become a state of Europe, I muse jokingly, reversing what some call the colonization of Italy by the U.S.? The idea makes me smile. It would make things right in more than one way.

Is marrying an Italian really what I must do to stay? Strange that it has never happened already.

At midnight the piazza sits in silence with the full moon glowing above, my last in Cetona for this time.

Across the ocean it's time for the sun to set over Charleston, and I think of the tradition Aram and I had of driving down to the bridge on Wappoo Road to watch the sunset at the edge of the Stono River, broad and peaceful. We'd put up the hatchback of his old Volvo and tailgate, talking, watching the dark water lap at the road and the sky change from pink to purple, gray and lapis, violet and orange streaking softly across.

It was our ritual, a beautiful coda of peace at the end of the day to regroup, he and I, in the beauty of Charleston, before dinner, sometimes after making love in the late afternoon. We'd take glasses and a bottle of wine, and we'd toast to each other and always kiss after saying cheers. Sometimes Aram would take pictures of me, of us, Polaroids, and I would tack them on my fridge.

Out in the countryside the grapevines are turning crimson like rivulets of blood coursing through the green. The grapes are gone, and now the smell of must hangs everywhere on paths near homes and cellars. The silvery olive trees are full of dark purple fruit, but they say there will be no harvest: There has been too much rain.

The countryside is largely dark brown now, the tilled earth resplendent and redolent, showing its bare beauty unencumbered. The hum of tractors comforts me as I walk the country roads, the earth around me thick and dark and moist in rows and clumps awaiting seed now and the beginning of the cycle, anew.

I pass a farmer up by Donna Morta who has been tilling for several days. I see him standing by his tractor and it looks like he's done.

— *Buon giorno!* I say, waving. *Ha finito di lavorar' la terra?* Are you finished tilling?

He nods and smiles, looking at his fields, rays of sun glistening against the soil and onto his face.

A few months from now it will all be wheat, sprouting light. I think for a moment that I will not be here to see it, and I wince. I think that someone I love might die while I am away, and I don't want that. I want to be here, yet I also want to be somewhere else.

Bettye Lavette plays on my phone, and I cry listening to her cry, along with me, through these fields. I pass Greta's house and I look up. It would have been her birthday soon. I think of her in an ambulance, rushing.

Below the hill leading to her house I see an embankment of precious pale pink cyclamens. I stop, enchanted. The delicate flowers sit in dappled light and look like tiny dots of pink frosting against the woodsy brown earth. They are perfect, and I am blessed for seeing them.

On my way back into town I stop to chat with Vito, my old friend from Sarteano who works for town hall. He and his colleagues are busy repaving and fencing around the stream down by Borgo, where a set of large trash collection bins are parked. The town doesn't collect trash residentially, so people take their trash to the bins. I remark on how ugly the fencing is. Vito assesses me flirtatiously, then straightens his face and explains that the fencing is necessary: If it's not there, he says, more trash goes in the stream than in the containers. I understand what he means; I've seen the trash collectors empty the bins and drive away leaving more trash on the ground than they take away. It's a dump.

While we stand there talking, a man pulls up, someone I've seen around town and who Vito knows, obviously. He sits in his car and watches them work for a minute. Vito turns to him in silence, signaling he's listening.

— *Già che ci siete...,* the man says with a slight smirk, seeing what they are doing. While you're at it—paving, he means—why don't you stop by and fix those gaping holes in the road in front of my house?

He elaborates and Vito seems to know what he's talking about. He looks at him flatly.

— *O meglio,* the man continues, a smile cresting on his face, *lasciatemi l'asfalto che tanto so fa' meglio io che voi.* Or better yet, he says, just leave some asphalt at my house since I know how to do a better job than you do, I can tell that already.

Vito smirks and I howl laughing. Ah, the Cetonesi, what ingrates! The man starts laughing, too, and pulls away. Vito rubs his face with his hands and shakes his head, then he hugs me, like he always does, and I run off, glad for that passing moment of hilarity and affection.

When I come into town, Graziella and Mario the *fontaniere,* the man who reminds me of an owl, are sitting on the wall by the old gas station. I stop to say hello and Graziella gives me a hug. She knows I am leaving. By now most everyone knows I am leaving. They have seen me haul boxes, take out trash.

Three weeks.

— *Ma mica parti. Ma davvero parti?* Mario asks me as I sit on the wall with them. You're not leaving. Are you really leaving?

— *Mi dispiace che parti,* Graziella says. I am sorry you are going.

She looks me in the eye and I inhale. I explain why, what I have to do. I am not sure what I am saying. I have fed myself a line—that I have to go to resolve some things—and it is now choking me.

— *Devi anda' a fa' quello che devi fa', poi torni.* You've got to go do what you have to do, then you'll come back, Graziella says, caressing my face.

— *Ti auguro tante buone cose,* she says. I wish you many good things.

Many good things.

I can't talk about it really, only in short, rational explanatory sentences. If I do not have complete control, I feel my lip quiver and I need to breathe and focus on something other than me. The rationality of my departure slips away for a moment; it eludes me.

I understand nothing of what I am choosing to do, or why, except the acceptance of something that seems predetermined. Again.

If something were waiting for me, I think to myself, this would make sense, but as it is ... And even at that, even if something *is* waiting for me, does it compensate or change anything?

Daylight has shortened dramatically and people are scurrying home now that it's 7:00 p.m., the town folding onto itself in its fall rhythm. The bar ladies part early and I watch them go. The scenes from a year float before me, together with the words we have exchanged during this time. The joy I have derived from getting to know people again washes into me. How lucky I was to grow up here, and how much tenderness I have felt in confirming a shared voyage, our humanity, even at the great distance of time.

I listen to the sounds, the small movements, the bells chiming eight, Mimmo walking home, Don Prospero talking. A ball bounces under my window, Filippo's for sure. I close my eyes and fill in the blanks: Taddeo De Rosa is back from work ... Bianca and Riccardo are at the bar ... Felice's voice rises, and a burst of laughter pierces the evening.

Day 7.

A violent thunderstorm breaks out late in the afternoon and it pours for hours. The piazza is a torrent, a foot or more of water coursing through it angrily, and the country roads are turned into rivulets and streams.

At Armando's store, where I run to seek shelter and company, Amato and the others are looking out, speculating about what all the rain will do to the fields and the coming harvests. If the fields were already seeded—and they agree on this by shaking their heads in unison—the deluge will wash away the seed and there will be no crop in summer. If they were not yet seeded but already plowed, it will do something equally nefarious. They nod.

Looking bleakly out the open door, Amato shakes his head and makes the *tze* sound, conveying damn shame. I understand now the importance of conversations about the weather here: It's boring until it's your livelihood, then it really matters.

I stand in the doorway next to Amato and we look up at my windows, which I neglected to lock. They are busting open then slamming shut, and I am worried that it's raining into the apartment. For sure it is, Amato says plainly, pointing at the noticeable horizontal thrust of the rain. I like listening to him, his wisdom against my stupidity for leaving the windows open. For not living here anymore, and for leaving again.

I don't have an umbrella, so Amato borrows one from Armando and offers to walk me home, across the piazza and up my alley, in this torrent of water in which part of me wishes to lie down and be swept away.

I roll up my jeans and take off my boots and Amato takes me underarm tightly and walks me across this foot-high river. He holds me steadily and I feel charmed walking barefoot through the piazza with this kind, handsome man I have finally gotten to know after so many years. He leaves me at my door and I hug him, wishing to hold onto him longer, to not let go of him, or anyone, ever, like a river of humanity holding onto me in this horrible grief and exhilarating joy of living.

I wish I could tell him how fond of him I have grown—perhaps to love him in some way—but he would feel deeply embarrassed, and I would likely be misunderstood, and so I don't say anything and I watch him walk away under the umbrella, and I regret that.

Later, while it continues to rain outside in the deserted town, I sit in the Bar Cavour with the usual guys, chatting and laughing, drinking a glass of the usual white wine under the dirty fluorescent lights.

— *Bevi? Bevete?* Sotero asks going to the counter. Are you drinking?

He orders five white wines.

My departure is looming over us. Sotero doesn't want to talk about it; no one wants to bring it up. I don't either. We skirt it. We don't need to say anything.

I listen to them talk about work, and something or the other about politics, then someone mentions they saw me running in the rain this morning, before the deluge started.

I nod. It was glorious, though serendipitous, and I explain: I got to the beginning of Borgo right as it began pouring, and by the time I reached the piazza I was soaked. In the middle of the deserted piazza, gathering in me all the gratitude of which I felt capable, I stopped, widened my arms, closed my eyes, and raised my face to the rain to give thanks for having this time, here, in this place, with this water running down my face. I have always loved running in the rain here, with the smells of rain and dirt mixing like lovers over the lush green land, and had I not been concerned about this silly town, I would have knelt in the water to weep and laugh in the river of my tears and the water of the sky.

Later people were gossiping. I laugh in chagrin. I am still taken aback and perplexed about what people in this little place notice, and, then, about the things they find worthwhile conversing about, understanding nothing and yet ascribing people bad motives or *brutta figura.*

In my heart I wish them a mere second of the purest elation I feel when I run here, or any simple joy I feel here, in this countryside. I have that strength—the strength for joy, and for love. But I don't have the strength for meanness.

Sitting there with Sotero, Bennato, and Giacomo, I say that I would love to run naked in the middle of the night, with no one around. The idea, a conceptual construct, fills me with wonder and laughter. I imagine the shiver of freedom that would come with that. Where, after all, would one have to go to do that?

The guys look at me quietly, then they look at each other. They don't say anything, and they don't smirk either, and I feel lucky for that. For a mere second, I feel like they might have finally understood me.

Felice, standing behind the counter, looks at me playfully.

— *Se lo fai, io posso sta' qui, zitto zitto a guarda'? Non ti do mica noia!* If you do it, he says, his eye sparkling with mischief, can I stay here quietly and watch? I won't bother you, I promise!

Day 5.

I awake to a gorgeous morning, with dense gray clouds hanging over Monte Cetona, but in the northwest, above the elementary school, flawlessly blue.

I look out and see Giorgio and Giovanna, my old teacher and his wife, crossing the piazza to their house, walking side by side. I think of the bar ladies; they are on a bus together on the way to France for a four-day guided tour. I imagine them gossiping and laughing on the bus, then I imagine them in the Bar Sport this winter, talking. I realize I won't be here. Everything could change between now and the next time. I feel the fabric pulling, that terrifying feeling of tearing in my fibers.

The other side of my brain reassures me it's all right. I will see Aram, and I have important things to accomplish. Things to do. Joe. Seeing my father, who I miss. NPR. America.

I think of what Graziella said when she hugged me the other day, talking about my departure.

— I wish you wouldn't go, but if you have to, she said, *che Dio ti porti tutta la fortuna di cui hai bisogno.* May God bring you all the good luck you need.

Angiolina is sitting on the bench under my window and I still consider running down to ask how much she wants for her store. I could paint there, I could hang my things. More Americans are buying houses here; they would buy my paintings. I could have a studio here. I could make this work—if only I believed. If only I thought I could survive here. Illegally? How?

I discard the idea. For now, I must go. I don't know how to follow the answer.

I look up toward the blue sky and ponder the route I will take on my run today. I assess the four runs I have left ahead of me: to Belverde once; the long Poggio alla Vecchia-Piandisette route once, although my heart feels weak for that because of the length; the one by I Poggi and Bianca and Riccardo's house once, if it's not too muddy; and my old standby, Donna Morta, the real thing.

I try to fend off the feeling of frenzy that is creeping into me, trying to prepare for my reentry—to what, and where?—yet to cherish with mindfulness every second I have left here. I fend off the impending melancholy, the thought of getting to Charleston alone. I picture it, the airport, the city. I have no home; a friend is lending me her apartment, and I am lucky to have that.

On my run I notice the sparkling green of the grass in the olive fields, grasshopperlike, and the artichoke plants stretching out like giant spiders with long feisty legs. Each gifts me beauty and perfection, in its own way.

After my run, around lunchtime, in the piazza, sun-drenched and deserted, I see Adamo, the gardener. He is standing outside the Bar Cavour having his post-prandial beer before going back to work. He waves at me and I stop to chat. He asks how I am, given the looming departure, and I indicate so-so with my head.

Adamo smiles at me, then tells me he has a friend back home in Sardegna who works up north somewhere. On every visit home, beginning a couple of days before he has to go back up north, he sits on a wall outside his house and sobs like a little boy. I remind him of him, Adamo says, laughing softly, not with mockery but rather with affection and empathy.

I laugh out loud, humored by the image of a rotund dark guy sitting on a wall in Sardegna, turquoise water ahead, weeping.

— *Vedrai, così farò io!* I say, laughing. You'll see! I will do the same!

I walk to Ottavia's to drop off some stuff and she walks with me back to the piazza. I get a gelato from the Bar Sport and we sit on the church steps in the sun like little girls stealing the last of summer's moments, though it's already fall. We chit-chat about this and that, we say hi to this person and that, and then we're silent and that's OK too. Ours is the kind of friendship in which it's all right to be present and absent, serene and preoccupied at the same time. And then we laugh about something and I walk her back to her house. It's time for her to go back to her store, and we hug goodbye.

I go back upstairs to pick through my clothes, packing boxes to send off and boxes to stay, like an insurance policy against fate, an amulet for my safe return. Ottavia will keep them for me; she is protective of them already.

I look around and sit thinking about my life, how simplified it has become, without my belongings, my hair products, a car, any new clothes, or even old clothes, without my books, my furnishings, and no TV. I have not watched TV in a year. I have become stronger for that, for all of that. I feel easier and calmer, and I am grateful to Cetona for that, for returning me to who I was when I left many moons ago, when there was no hot water in winter sometimes, and no water at all in summer. It was not charming, but it was edifying and meaningful and real, and I feel edified by it now.

There is almost nothing left of my having been here. I have to focus intently to grasp the exhilarating fact that I was here a whole year. I have to repeat it to myself that I was here, in Cetona, a whole year, my body in this place, again, as I was once, my eyes graced by this every day for a whole year. Here.

I smile. I was here again.

I decide it's time to let go of some of the last dearest objects, the ones that signal that I am really leaving. Among them is Anna Maria's easel, the *cavalletto di campagna* that she generously pulled up from her cellar when I first arrived, with its shaky legs, like me. I feel my way back to the joy of getting that easel from her and bringing it upstairs and discovering that it would do just fine, and in fact it did.

With melancholy, I pick the easel up in my arms together with a box full of solvents and other painting supplies. I also take with me a painting, a gift for Anna Maria, of an eccentric, curious bird that reminds me of her.

Standing in her white smock, her springy curly hair wild as usual, and her friendly face, she hugs me and thanks me. No, I say, thank you for the easel that allowed me to paint!

— *Ti metto tutto da parte. Torna presto,* she said, hugging me. I will set it all aside for you. Come back soon and you can have it all back.

As I am walking home I see Feriero.

— *Allora parti?* he asks. So, are you leaving?

I nod.

— *Mica piangerai!* he says, looking at me tenderly. You're not going to cry, are you?

I cry every day, I say.

— *Allora resta! Resta qui con noi che ti vogliamo tanto bene qui!!* he says. Then stay! Stay here with us, we who love you so much here!

And I feel it too, like no other place in the world.

Later in the afternoon Sotero comes out from behind Le ACLI in his jeep. He sees me in the window and he pulls over underneath. He looks up at me and he smiles, but with sadness.

— *Ormai ci siamo, eh?* he says. We're there.

My departure, he means—it's time.

*Ormai.*

I nod. Tears well up in my eyes.

— *Ci vediamo stasera allora,* he says. See you tonight.

I come out and walk into Armando's store for a lemon. Amato and Alcide and the gang look me over but are quiet, like there's something hanging in the air.

— *Mi sa che 'sta partenza è come la mia pel militare,* Amato says somberly. This departure looks like mine for the military.

He is sitting in one of Armando's two chairs. He looks at me with his sweet brown eyes. He is smiling, yet he is not.

— *Cioè?* I ask. Which is?

— *Triste,* he says. Sad.

I purse my lips and nod.

His gaze travels from me down to the floor. He is silent for a while and no one speaks. Then he starts telling of his departure for the military, his loneliness and fear. It must have been about the year I was born, an unsettling time in the world.

— *Non ho pianto, ma quasi. Non ero mai uscito da Cetona,* he says. I didn't cry but almost. I had never left Cetona. There were 4,000 people in my barracks. I wasn't used to that.

The story is familiar to me.

— *C'era la gente che si tagliava le vene. Ero triste e spaventato.* There were people who were cutting their veins. I was sad and scared.

I know what you mean, I say. I won't cut my veins, but, for sure, I know how it feels.

Day 3.

It's dawn on Saturday and the vendors are setting up their booths at the market. It's my last *mercato* in Cetona.

From my window I take in the colors and the faces of the vendors. The man from Chiusi; the woman with the best melons. The sun is streaking in shyly from the east and everyone's wares look fresh and bright. The vegetable guys who set up their truck right across from my window—a short balding guy who eats huge panini with *stracchino* and a tall good-looking guy with long salt-and-pepper hair tied in a ponytail—are sprucing up their lettuces and culling through their fruit. I smile looking at them. Every time I buy something from them they say, if you don't like it throw it back at us from your window. I remind myself to do it before I go.

Slowly people are trickling into the piazza from here and there. I see Riccardo under my window buying plants, and I smile because he has such a tender streak, choosing and growing his plants so carefully. A few early shoppers are already heading back home with flowers for the cemetery and bags of goods. Savina has had her coffee and is lighting her cigarette at the corner; Don Prospero is talking on the phone in front of the church. Palmina, Ottavia's mom, is looking at the flowers, carefully, and I think of her Parkinson's and how she will fare after I have gone, and I notice the cyclamens against her face, bursting with flair, red, and the color called *ciclamino* in their honor.

The sun is burning off the haze and it promises to be a pretty day, and it makes me wish my life were settled. Settled, like the sky now. A house in Cetona, my things, work to support myself, my painting, and writing, a regular life. Perhaps someone who loves me who wants to be in the same place I do. Why, why can I not have this?

Guido is walking his dog. I contemplate again the scenario of marrying for citizenship, to be able to work, and if I set my mind to it I bet I could do it. Yet, I continue to pack. I am almost packed. I have taken nearly everything I am leaving behind to Ottavia and Maria. Maria came to get her portrait of Lauro, and I gifted her another painting for her birthday, a glimpse of Vicolo del Sole. Ottavia came to get a painting, too, a townscape of Finoglio, the street where she grew up. She and Maria will pick up a few more things at the end. I am still packing my paintings, deciding what to do with them. I feel pressure, but it helps me to know I am relatively organized and ready.

*Ready.* I will never be ready to leave. I can never be. And what am I ready for?

Before dinner, Sotero has a drink with me at the bar and tries to convince me to let him pay my rent so I can stay.

It's not about that, I tell him, though it partially is.

I know, he says. I just don't want you to leave. You can stay, I will pay your rent.

I say I can't do that, and he says, ok, I will pay your rent and you can have sex with me.

I recognize in this his flirtatiousness but also an undefiled love and a kindness.

Cetona's love. A bit careless, a bit dirty. Humorous. Take it or leave it. *Sibilla, tutti la vogliono ma nessuno la piglia.* But love nonetheless.

Finally, late at night I decide to take Felice his portrait, at the Bar Cavour. I painted it back in the winter, when Cetona was as its dreariest and I craved something warm that would absorb me. I embarked on a series of portraits, which I had never painted before.

The painting of Felice, framed by a rose-colored background, with the collar of his black shirt at his neckline, captures Felice's innate *simpatia*, his full features, and a meaty smile that combines wonder with shyness.

Some time ago, when I told him I had painted him, Felice blushed. His face filled with modesty as if he had been naked. He is not the sort of person who would ever in his entire life imagine someone painting him. Of all people, *him*. Beneath the blush a fleeting shadow of pleasure crept in, brought on perhaps by the realization that a woman would have considered him long enough to paint him. But his shyness overwhelmed it and it flew away.

— *'N' me lo fa' vede' nemmeno che tanto non mi piace! Non mi piaccio per niente io!* Don't even show it to me because I'm not going to like it anyway, Felice said shaking his head matter-of-factly and sounding flustered.

His words echo in my ears. *I don't like myself at all.*

I look over the portrait, smile to myself, and decide it's time. I dance around the living room giving myself courage against impending rejection. After checking from the window that there is no one left at the Bar Cavour, I grab the portrait, run down the stairs and down the alley, and all the way to the bar where Felice stands alone under the fluorescent lights cleaning the coffee machine.

He is wearing his black uniform and dirty red apron, and he's tired. I can tell from his look, wondering what brings me at this hour. He just smiles at me without anger or expectation, but I can tell he is suspicious. A good Cetonese. After a few shy minutes with my hands behind my back, making small talk, I prop the painting on the bar, against a bottle.

— *Ecco il tuo ritratto!* I say, like a kid who has brought a cake. Here is your portrait!

Felice looks at me surprised. I watch him wrap his head around my words, then he stops his work and walks over to the other side of the counter. He takes in the painting, slowly, and I see his expression travel from skepticism to surprise to wonder and, finally, to joy— unquestionable joy.

He puts down his rag and takes the small painting in his big hands, carefully, like picking up a baby. A luminous smile fills his face, and I want to cry.

— *Mi piace moltissimo! Grazie!* I like it immensely, he says, beaming. Thank you.

He looks at it longer, then looks back at me.

— *Mi hai reso molto, molto felice,* he says, surprising me. You made me very, very happy.

And that was worth my entire stay.

Day 2.

Today I awoke to the blanket of fog that is the signature of fall in Cetona.

With distinct awareness of my time and my place I took measure of the four seasons that have unfurled behind me, as I had dreamed, all the way back to the magical first fog I witnessed here a year ago.

I love the way the fog hangs here, shrouding us from the world, and then the way it lifts slowly like a matrimonial veil, revealing the scenery like an unfolding mystery.

Seated in my windowsill I had tea, then I breathed in and got dressed for my second-to-last run.

I took the road to Piazze and a car almost ran me over. In the fog I felt safer running the country roads, so I cut over to Patarnione and up through the hills. The same dogs that have barked every day I have run by them barked their last bark to me and I hushed them, running along.

I took Donna Morta and went all the way to the mountain road to Belverde, the cross sitting above me. I was exhilarated yet fatigued, my heart heavy and crying silently, and my thighs were burning a burn they will not taste again until I return. The countryside is still and dewy and cool. Through passages in the woods all the vegetation is covered by white threads like gossamer, so fine that from a few feet one struggles to make out what they are. But I near and I recognize the tiny, tightly-knit spider webs dotted by the finest droplets of water that make them look like strings of divinely strung miniature pearls.

Yes, I have seen this before, and I am grateful, again.

Roads up on the mountain are lined by piles of cut firewood, fields and fields of cut wood, and I quickly think back to the sound of saws I have been hearing for the past few weeks. I think of Monte Cetona and hope he will not be shorn bare. I look up at the cross and I breathe. Pomegranates are on the trees, with their rose-colored, taught skins and bright green leaves. I think of red juice dripping down our chins when we were little, and my house, and the cherry tree.

It is all just like it was when I arrived, and like it was in my memory, and at every step through the hills I say goodbye to this countryside that has inhabited my days, dreams, and imagination for my entire life, and for this entire year.

Back down from the mountain I run through the countryside to say goodbye to Diamante and Simonetta. Neither is home, but I wave anyway and I run further up, around the curves to Zia's house, vacant as always. I climb over the fence and up the driveway and I walk through the house, untouched in months.

I sit on the front stoop for a moment and I bid farewell to Zia as I remember her long ago, standing there in her turquoise dress waving goodbye. I realize I am in a game with myself, only myself, with no one to weigh in. If only I could talk with Zia now. She, after all, left Boston for Europe and never looked back.

I climb back over the gate and head back toward Cetona, running, recording the countryside in my brain, to my left the fields of alfalfa of the most brilliant of greens, and to my right the freshly turned soil, dark brown and ready for reseeding.

The smell of the earth carries for miles and it makes me stop like a dog catching a scent. I come onto my knees onto the dirt and I rejoice that I've seen these fields in this season twice now in twelve months, and tears of joy and grief streak my face as I pick up a clump of earth—*una zolla*, a word I love and seems so foreign now. I bring it to my nose and wish I could carry it with me in my pocket. I breathe in the scent and release the earth reluctantly through my fingers. I stand up looking around, willing to burn these hills in my memory, but they are already there, like carbon copies I have never forgotten.

After my run I take Ave to lunch at Il Merlo. She had invited me for a last *pranzo* at her house, but I want to steal her away from the burners and make her happy, so I invited her out instead.

Ave is flattered and she dresses up in an elegant linen dress the color of ivory. She points out that she dressed up for me, and she wears beautiful black shoes and her hair is nicely done. She wanted to wear the shoes she bought for my wedding, which she still has, she points out, but these were a better fit for the dress, right, she asks looking at me. I smile at this gesture that sums up so much about Ave—her kindness and her practicality and humility—and I just want to hug her and stay, here, with her.

We sit at a table inside and I invite her to eat everything she wants on the menu, and she does and she even has wine. I can't eat; my stomach is closed and I feel sick. I watch Ave while she eats; she tells me stories in a hushed voice, cognizant of the surroundings, but with spirited eyes. She looks healthy and beautiful, and I hang that image in my heart. I wish for her wellbeing. She's like a mom to me now, after this year together, and I look forward into the future to the day I will hug her again. I will say goodbye to her last, as I head out of town.

I have two nights left in Cetona, and tonight I am invited to Maria and Lauro's, with Ottavia and Giacomo.

Maria looks beautiful in a long burgundy dress, and I dressed up too, though I am shy to be at the center of attention as if it could make this departure any worse. Maria has made a vegetarian feast for me— my favorite radicchio and pecorino salad and a pasta with tomatoes and artichokes. There are crostini, and cheeses, and Ottavia brings pastries for dessert. She bought them in Chiusi especially for me.

In the softly lit kitchen we drink good wine and we listen to Al Stewart and "Enough Is Enough," the ode to our youth. Lauro and Giacomo indulge us lovingly on the other side of the living room as we dance, hug, and cry. I cry for the time gone, never to return, and for the present, so moving and soon to be gone as well.

We take pictures and look back at them with a mix of joy and acceptance, not disappointed in these new versions of ourselves, different yet the same, linked by the same love, graced by it, still, and matured by it. Yet I wish we had not lost so much, too. So much time, habits, grief, happiness, days. Life.

I am moved to look at Maria's face, framed by her unruly curls and now adorned with small glasses; I am moved by our wrinkles, testament to our history, our togetherness, this whole lifetime we have shared, across time and distance. I think of all the forgiveness that has passed between us—for youthful but no less hurtful trespasses, things poorly said, the simple imperfection of being the people we are—and this friendship strong like a gushing river, pushing through undeterred by the hiccups, carrying us to the end.

Now, time provides a tapestry for who we are, something we can read together like a book, a woven cloth. We look at it, and I feel their lives together in me, in my veins, in my flesh. I hold Maria's hand and I feel her heartbeat and mine.

We recommit to see each other tomorrow, and we hug.

On the last day I run errands. I run here and there, and I wave at people as if nothing were happening. I am looking around, pretending. I have decided to not say goodbye to anyone except for Ave and Eufemia and Fortunata, who I plan to hug on the street casually, maybe.

And Aldo. I see him in the piazza, and he hugs me and kisses me lightly on the lips. He looks at me go and turns to walk away and that's it. That's it, till some other time. The next time.

I go to Armando's and I hug him, and Nanni. In the more than forty years I have known Nanni it is the first time I have ever hugged him, this big scary guy with the big red eye, and I hold on a moment longer. He gives me a kiss on the cheek and it soothes me for a moment.

After I walk out, I stop at a table at the bar where Amato is seated, and Graziella and Dino. I cannot not say goodbye. I tell them to take care while I am away. That is all I can say. Amato hugs me awkwardly and kisses me on the cheek. He is sad too, I think, though perhaps surprised by it.

I walk around, taking in my gingerbread town, hoping that if I stare extra hard everything will stay impressed in me longer, like the sense of touching someone's skin. Like the horizon years ago.

As the sun sets I am still running about here and there taking stuff to Ottavia's. She will keep it for me for when I come back. *Per quando torni*, she says smiling, wanting to believe, yet not believing. When you come back.

Finally, the most precious light of the day comes, the dearest golden clarity, and I manage to go down to the piazza to be still in this light, for a moment, one last time. I get a glass of white wine from Giotto.

While he polishes my glass he asks if tomorrow is the fateful day and I nod.

We will miss you, he says, looking at me through his square lenses.

— *Ti fischieranno le orecchie. Ti penseremo tutti i giorni.* We will think of you every day. Your ears will ring.

I hug him goodbye and I walk outside. I take in the piazza in the remaining baby-blue light coming from Sarteano, and the settling color of lilac, golden and still, from the south. I feel crazed—breaking, perhaps—running images through my mind but programmed already for the duty I have chosen ahead and that I don't know how to scuttle.

For a moment I contemplate the idea of staying in bed, not catching the flight and seeing what would happen, and while I think about it I spin among people like a butterfly. Maria, Ottavia, and Tullia come to meet me in the piazza for an *aperitivo*. Isabella comes and we get a glass of wine and we toast and hug. I sit for a moment with Pippo and Giuliano. I hug Lillo and Armando. I want to run to everyone, every person in the piazza, and hug them for their dear lives and mine. I don't have enough time, even if destiny gave me an extra day. I look at Ottavia and I want to cry in her arms, to sob till I can breathe again with ease. I smile instead.

Against my strongest will the last of the golden light disappears, the last light of this last day, and darkness settles upon us. Everyone comes into my mind—Pierpaolo, Teo, Maria, Andrea, Eugenio, Ave, Beppa, Lucio—all the eyes that have held my soul, and while I gather them inside me, everyone leaves and goes home and the piazza empties.

By myself I go to Nilo's for a plate of pasta, my last meal, so to speak—I had decided I could not do a big goodbye feast—and the routine of this comforts me simply. As always, Salvatore pours the wine, Cristiano brings the food, and Nilo comes and hugs me. They are attentive and caring. When I go to pay the bill it's on them, they say, one of many meals they have offered me over this past year. We hug goodbye without saying much, sorrow suspended, and I walk outside to take in my silent and deserted piazza.

As I look out, I realize that my sanity exists only through denial of my grief, and I must ignore some side of me to pull this off, once again. I welcome the chime of midnight, and I set out to walk through town one last time. My footsteps echo in the shadows of the streets, up through town, up through Via Roma and the Steccato, and I think of people in their beds, sleeping.

Then, I move down the steep alleys that take me toward Borgo, now in full darkness. When I get there, I see that the people who are using my house are burning a fire in the fireplace and a warm orange light spills out through the glass door onto the street, like a big red candle flickering in the night.

I sit to rest for a moment in the glow on the pavement that my feet coursed long ago, in front of the door to the home that was mine, and I try to calm my moaning cry inside, realizing fully that I will never be able to let go—never, ever, ever, as long as I live.

I sit and breathe, then I finally get up on my feet and say goodbye to my house and the tug of this ancient pain and I return to my ascent through town in the dark. The safety and familiarity of this pitch-black darkness reassures me as no darkness elsewhere ever could.

Back in the piazza I sit waiting for everyone to leave, and finally, in night's stillness, I set out to pace for my spot. I measure the familiar marble striping and choose the place I think is most centered to be Cetona's heart, like mine. After circling it and gathering my dress and my shawl, I lie down, my back to the ground like a snow angel. I feel the cold under me and I let it pass. I wish that I could be naked and the marble stripped back to the gravel it once was.

Me and this earth spinning in space.

In the silence and emptiness, both miraculous, I look up at the sky and the stars contained within the buildings, then I close my eyes and surrender to the white stone under my flesh, here, in this town, the soil that reared me and affirmed me. In the quiet of my mind I hear my heart beat and the echo of the steps I took here long, long ago, running through these stone streets and these alleys, around the curves of Borgo and down green-pastured hills, before I grasped who I was, or glimpsed who I would become, and the schisms ahead.

When I was still the little girl with the magic stone in my pocket, with one home, unbroken by grief.

In my mind, with my eyes closed, I see her, the little girl, and I chase her, her straight, shoulder-length brown hair swaying from side to side and her green smiley bag bouncing on her back. I try to catch up with her, to slip my feet into her footsteps, like in a long relay with myself, but I realize I can't.

I cannot catch up.

She stops and she looks back. She tries to hand me back the magic stone, but I can't reach her. I can't touch her hand.

She smiles, a bit sadly, and then she's gone.

Andrea offers to drive me to the airport—for old time's sake—and we set a time, below my apartment. I'll find you, he says.

An hour or so earlier, Maria, Ottavia and Tullia and I have agreed to meet to say goodbye in front of the florist. Standing there in the early afternoon sunlight we hug and laugh and cry and let go, and then we do it all over again. I give them stuff to keep for me and they pack it in their cars.

I'll be back soon, I say, trying to lighten things. We'll see each other again soon.

— *Dai, tanto torni presto,* they echo. Anyway, you'll be back soon.

We repeat that over and over again.

Diego and Mariachiara are sitting on the steps of the church in the sunshine. Diego is smiling tenderly, watching us hug and let go and then hug again. We look like children leaving for summer camp. Finally, I let go of Ottavia's hand, and Maria's. Through a smile Ottavia dries her tears, waves, turns, and walks toward home. I turn and go back up the alley. I hear Maria pull away in her car, and Tullia, too.

Upstairs, I stand for a moment quietly in my apartment until the sound of their cars quiets. I go to the bedroom windows and look out, holding on with my eyes. I close the windows one by one, pulling the curtains slowly. Diego and Mariachiara look up and then away. I look around my apartment, now entirely empty of my belongings. I carry my luggage down the steps and out onto the alley.

Holding onto the door knob, I take a deep breath, then I pull the door shut. My knees feel shaky. I put my fingers in the slot of the mailbox and I slip the key in for Anna. The thud of the key dropping feels harsh like a guillotine. I reach my fingers in and I realize that I cannot get it back, though, of course I could, with a single phone call. I leave the typed sticker with my name on the mail box like an amulet.

I turn and look up and I see Enzo's mother looking down at me through the panes of glass. She sees my luggage and she opens the window.

— *Va via, Sibilla?* she asks, looking disconcerted, shaking her head. Are you leaving?

I nod. It's all I have to give.

— *Mi dispiace! Come mi dispiace!* she says looking sad and bringing her hands to her flushed face. I am so sorry!

Me too, I say.

— *Stia bene, Signora. Alla prossima volta,* I say, forcing a smile of encouragement. Be well. For the next time.

I know I may not see her again if I don't return soon, like many others who I know I will never see again. I push back that thought, haunting. We wave and I walk down with my stuff.

Andrea arrives and loads my suitcases in the car. Caino and his gang are on their bench, in the shade. We have already said goodbye, but I wave again.

— *Buon viaggio!* Caino yells out with his gravelly voice. He smiles and waves, and I nod.

I want him to stay well, too. To be here, again.

I look around.

Andrea sits in the car looking at me, measuring me patiently. It's time—*that* time, again—and there's nothing more to do. I get in and Andrea starts the car. I feel like I can smell a car from long ago, a white Golf GT. As he maneuvers in front of the church I wave to the guys in front of Le ACLI. Marcello crosses in our path and he waves. Mariachiara has gone to work. The piazza is still.

Slowly we head out of town, down Via Risorgimento. Eufemia is sitting on her doorstep. I try to wave, but her image flies by and she doesn't see me.

We pass Ave's house and skirt around Cetona and down by Le Gore. I look back and see my house. The year of pictures flies by. We turn on the road to Piazze; I see Feriero's Ape down at the Della Vignas.

Andrea puts on his blinker and veers toward Il Piano, the same way we went thirty years ago but now later in the year, the landscape different. I see my favorite fields of alfalfa, green like a baby pea. The countryside is glistening in the sunshine. Cetona is now at my back, and I turn to look. I have been through this before, this exact same thing. I put my finger in the wound and it burns like salt, that same pain again.

Did I think it would be different? How could it possibly be?

I could stop it, again. I could.

We turn onto the road to Fabro. Andrea shifts, third, fourth, fifth gear, and Monte Cetona is behind me, and then Cetona is gone.

— *Stavolta non mi sembri tanto convinta,* Andrea says after a while. This time you don't seem so convinced.

He looks me over. Maybe this is just a replay, and we want it to be different. Which time, I want to ask, was I ever *convinta*?

He knows I am not—I never was; I don't need to tell him. He actually knows something about me.

He drives on a few more minutes, in silence, to Ponticelli, and right before we reach the entrance to the *autostrada* he slows down. He eyes a place to stop and expertly pulls over in a shady lot, pulling the handbrake.

He turns his body to look at me. I can almost imagine the blue of the T-shirt and the gold chains underneath unraveling over my face.

— *Sibilla, un biglietto è un biglietto, n'è mica un braccio. Se ne rifa un altro. 'N' vole di' mica che devi parti' per forza adesso. O mai.*

A ticket is a ticket, he says. It's not an arm. You can buy another one. It doesn't mean you have to go now. Or ever.

He pauses. You don't *have* to go.

Ever.

I lower my face in my hands, then I look out. I glance at the road ahead, then I look back at my luggage in the back seat. So much has already been done.

*Ormai.*

Andrea sits patiently, the motor idling. I look at him. I exhale.

— *Hai ragione,* I say. You're right. You are absolutely right.

He puts the car in gear and pulls out onto the road.

# Epilogue

When I landed in the late October night I felt disoriented. The heat of Charleston sprung me back years to a place that felt entirely unchanged, stuck in time as if I had never left. Yet, I couldn't recognize the roads, and nothing turned out to be the same.

Aram is happily resettled in California. A visit to LA confirmed our love, for sure, but did not help us put things back together. Too much trust has gone, and too much faith lost. And I have never been able to drive down his street again.

Equally crushing, a few days before I returned, Joe, my orange tabby who I longed so much to embrace again, went missing on the streets of South Miami, where he ran spooked by house workers. He has never been seen again, in spite of searches throughout Florida and beyond. I don't know if he is dead or sleeping on someone's bed: Whatever has happened to him, not a day goes by that my heart does not tighten for him. I am so sorry, for him and for me.

Frankly, since I returned, mine has been a daily balancing act to stay above a sea of grief. In some ways. I think that if I had presaged this ending I would not have come back. I would have allowed myself to stay—to *really* try to stay. I needed permission to invest the courage to try to stay, to win the fear, and I would have granted it.

No, I do not regret my choice to go home. I think back to the dream about the orange trees with Maria and Ottavia and I feel happy that I listened.

I do know the names of the trees now again, and the names of the streets. I can smell the gravel roads I had forgotten, and the clumps of deep brown dirt. And I know now more than ever about this place I call home and its people, its urges, battles, and destiny.

I came to sit in the sun of the church steps, and to walk every street and corner, and I did that. I came to take in the land, the sight like balm to my heart, and I did that. I came to apologize to some, and I did that, or I tried. I came to understand and remember old loves, those immense loves into which I gave so much of my youthful self, and to put my adult face to the feelings I had forgotten and couldn't explain, and I did that.

I came to talk with the elderly I might never see again, to hug Ave, and to run to the cross, and to get to know Amato, and to laugh with Nilo. I came to get to know Maria again and see what her life is about. And I did all of that. I came to see Tullia smile and hear her counsel and meet her daughter, and to look into Ottavia's kind brown eyes. I came to see Sabrina again, before she died—and she did die, together with many others since my return.

I came to be an adult: to listen, to look, to see, to love, again, anew, this place and who I thought I was and could be here. And I did that. And I learned a few empowering things about myself that I had discounted, or forgotten, or never known, and that gladdens me.

I realize, starkly, that Cetona and its people will do what they have always done, which is to go on, like they have through the centuries, past the conquests and the famines and the wars, like they do every day of every week at the same hour, for years and years. God willing, Amato will come into the piazza and park illegally; Armando will open his store; Daniele will open his restaurant; Maria will drive through on the way to her mom's; Tullia will have new students; Eufemia will pace, and Nilo will survey the piazza and feed beautiful food to his clients. Don Prospero will say mass, Aldo will harvest, we hope, and Silvio will seed, Ave will cook, Osvaldo and Sotero and Diego will play cards, and Bozzini will pace. And the sun will rise above Città della Pieve and set behind Monte Cetona, until something calamitous, a death, changes the course, the footwork, slightly and briefly.

Then, new dust will settle, and then blow away, and the town will move on, again. The people of Cetona are mountain people. Survivors.

Cetona will be the same, or mostly, whether I ever return again.

Yet, nothing about me will ever be the same. I have loved this, this beautiful time I have ever given myself, tending to the wound I have carried for so long and retrieving the strength, the beauty, and the shoring that this town gifted me for a lifetime. I was courageous to return to this town in which all my happiness and all my grief are forever entwined.

Of course, my biggest question remains, and that is, where do I belong.

I do not have an answer, and I cannot make the decision. I waited long enough to lose one thing dear to me, or more, but I didn't make a commitment to stay. I didn't take up Sabrina's offer to live in the cottage, or Sotero's offer to pay my rent. I didn't follow the seed of a dream of renting a studio on the piazza to paint and live. Some of it was circumstance, but some of it was ... the other side calling.

So, perhaps, finally I must conclude that I am made of two parts, bonded in the cage of my chest yet divided by an ocean, and never will they be one. I know, I think finally and completely, that wherever I choose to be, I will never be whole again.

Will I learn to rest somewhere? I wish that for myself, and all those like me.

In the meantime, as I look out the window into the darkening American sky, I see a cluster of tall black trees in which, with a mere whisper of my imagination, I find the curves of a familiar mountain and a tiny gleaming cross at the top. And as I lose myself in it, I know that deep in my heart I will never stop seeking return.

# Acknowledgments

I thank all the people in Cetona and in the States who have supported and encouraged me during the making of this story. Together with thanks, I offer my apologies and regret to all those who I hurt in my search for place and wholeness. I think you know who you are.

Thank you to the people stateside who offered me shelter during summers and vacations in college and grad school, away from home, chiefly Mary Ann and Bob Hargrave and Shahan and Suzy Sarrafian. Thank you to Robynne, Monica, Sophia, and Paul for years of friendship, and to everyone who supported me along the way with a loan, a trip, a visit, or a dinner to check up on me. You all helped me survive.

Thank you to everyone who made my return to Cetona possible—Andrea Arcamone, to start—and who smoothed my return to Charleston a year later: Maryellen and Reggie Gibson, you have my gratitude for your love and support, Christine and Tommy McGee, for your deep and selfless generosity, and Donatella Cappelletti Della Porta for your sisterly Italian friendship. And finally, to Aram, whose love and grace made me truest to myself and enabled me to test my dream. You have my unending love and gratitude.

Thank you to my early teachers, Franco Fazzi, Marga, and Signora Vinciarelli, and to the memory of Peter Matthiessen, who inspired me to continue writing.

Infinite love goes to Lucia, Cinzia, and Fabiola, and to all my friends from Italy who have stayed with me a lifetime, some of them (Simone, Ciccio) unnamed in this book. To my Zia, who continues to inspire me from beyond; to Joe, who I lost because of all this; and to my father and mother, whose courage and pursuits gave me the special life I have had.

My special thanks go to Susan Fix, Fairy, Donna Levine, Marsha Guerard, and Abbey Peruzzi for reading and insight; to editor Anne Cole Norman for her thoughtful suggestions; to Harriet McLeod for support of many kinds; to Reggie Gibson for the cover sketch; to Aram for the cover design; and to my friend Dr. Miriam DeAntonio for giving most generously toward this book's publication.

Foremost, I thank Cetona for giving me roots and the inspiration to write this memoir, told through the lens of my memory to the best of my recollection.

The people and stories therein are real, though some names are changed and the timing of some occurrences is modified for narrative flow (but not significantly). I hope to have treated and represented Cetona and every character in an authentic and kind manner, mirroring my affection and respect.

And finally, thank you, Dad, for everything. I am sorry I didn't finish in time. —S.F.

**Sybil Fix**, a painter, award-winning journalist, writer, and translator, is a graduate of Yale University and the Columbia University Graduate School of Journalism. She lives in Charleston, South Carolina, but she is planning her next return to Tuscany any time now. This is her first book. You can find her blog at thenarrativeark.com.